TEACHER'S GUIDE & LESSON PLANNER

WITH CD-ROM

WORD BY WORD

Second Edition

PICTURE DICTIONARY

Steven J. Molinsky • Bill Bliss

Contributing Authors
Sarah Lynn
Diane Terry
Valerie Ashenfelter

PEARSON
Longman

CONTENTS

Word by Word Teacher's Guide & Lesson Planner, second edition
Copyright © 2006 by Prentice Hall Regents
Pearson Education, Inc.
All rights reserved.
No part of this publication may be reproduced, stored in a retrieval system, or transmitted in any form or by any means, electronic, mechanical, photocopying, recording, or otherwise, without the prior permission of the publisher.

Pearson Education, 10 Bank Street, White Plains, NY 10606

Editorial director: Pam Fishman
Vice president, director of design and production: Rhea Banker
Director of electronic production: Aliza Greenblatt
Director of manufacturing: Patrice Fraccio
Senior manufacturing manager: Edith Pullman
Marketing manager: Oliva Fernandez
Text design: Wendy Wolf

Cover design: Tracey Munz Cataldo/Warren Fischbach
Text composition: TSI Graphics
Illustrations: Richard E. Hill

ISBN 0-13-193544-5
Longman on the Web
Longman.com offers online resources for teachers and students.
Access our Companion Websites, our online catalog, and our
local offices around the world.

Visit us at longman.com.

Printed in the United States of America
1 2 3 4 5 6 7 8 9 10 – WEB – 09 08 07 06 05

Welcome to the second edition of the *WORD BY WORD* Picture Dictionary!

Our goal is to make vocabulary learning come alive as a dynamic communicative experience that prepares students for success using English in everyday life, in the community, in school, and at work.

Clear, vibrant illustrations and simple, accessible lesson pages are designed for clarity and ease-of-use with learners at all levels.

More than 4,000 words and 138 topics are presented in a careful, research-based sequence of lessons that integrates students' development of grammar and vocabulary skills.

1 bookcase
2 picture/photograph
3 painting
4 mantel
5 fireplace
6 fireplace screen
7 DVD player
8 television/TV
9 VCR/video cassette recorder
10 wall
11 ceiling
12 drapes
13 window
14 loveseat
15 wall unit
16 speaker
17 stereo system
18 magazine holder
19 (throw) pillow
20 sofa/couch
21 plant
22 coffee table
23 rug
24 lamp
25 lampshade
26 end table
27 floor
28 floor lamp
29 armchair

Model conversations depict contexts and situations in which people use the words in meaningful communication. Students engage in dynamic, interactive practice as they create new conversations based on the models using the words in the lesson.

A. Where are you?
B. I'm in the living room.
A. What are you doing?
B. I'm dusting* the **bookcase**.

* dusting/cleaning

A. You have a very nice living room!
B. Thank you.
A. Your _____ is/are beautiful!
B. Thank you for saying so.

A. Uh-oh! I just spilled coffee on your _____!
B. That's okay. Don't worry about it.

Tell about your living room.
(In my living room there's ....)

Additional conversations help students use the vocabulary in expanded contexts and offer practice with key functional communication skills such as complimenting, apologizing, and asking for information.

Writing and discussion questions in each lesson encourage students to relate the vocabulary and themes to their own lives as they share experiences, thoughts, opinions, and information about themselves, their cultures, and their countries.

Teaching Strategies

This Teacher's Guide offers step-by-step instructions for each *Word by Word* lesson. Here's a quick overview of suggested strategies for presenting and practicing the vocabulary in each lesson:

1▶ Preview the Vocabulary: Activate students' prior knowledge of the vocabulary by brainstorming with students the words in the lesson they already know and writing them on the board, or by having students look at the transparency or the illustration in *Word by Word* and identify the words they are familiar with.

2▶ Present the Vocabulary: Using the transparency or the illustration in the text, point to the picture of each word, say the word, and have the class repeat it chorally and individually. (You can also play the word list on the Audio Program.) Check students' understanding and pronunciation.

3▶ Vocabulary Practice: Have students practice the vocabulary as a class, in pairs, or in small groups. Say or write a word, and have students point to the item or tell the number. Or, point to an item or give the number, and have students say the word.

4▶ Model Conversation Practice: Some lessons have model conversations that use the first word in the vocabulary list. Other models are skeletal dialogs, in which vocabulary words can be inserted.
- a. Preview: Have students look at the model illustration and discuss who they think the speakers are and where the conversation takes place.
- b. The teacher presents the model or plays the audio one or more times and checks students' understanding of the situation and the vocabulary.
- c. Students repeat each line of the conversation chorally or individually.
- d. Students practice the model in pairs.
- e. A pair of students presents a conversation based on the model, but using a different word from the vocabulary list.
- f. In pairs, students practice several conversations based on the model, using different words on the page.
- g. Pairs present their conversations to the class.

5▶ Additional Conversation Practice: Many lessons provide two additional skeletal dialogs for further conversation practice with the vocabulary. Have students practice and present these conversations using any words they wish. Before they practice the additional conversations, you may want to have students listen to the sample additional conversations on the Audio Program.

 **6▶ Spelling Practice:** Have students practice spelling the words as a class, in pairs, or in small groups. Say a word, and have students spell it aloud or write it. Or, using the transparency, point to an item and have students write the word.

7▶ Themes for Discussion, Composition, Journals, and Portfolios: Have students respond to the questions (at the bottom of the page) as a class, in pairs, or in small groups. Or, have students write their responses at home, share their written work with other students, and discuss as a class, in pairs, or in small groups. Students can keep a journal of their written work. These compositions can also serve as examples of student progress in portfolios of their work.

8▶ Expansion Activities: See the next two pages for an overview of the rich variety of resources offered for reinforcing and expanding students' vocabulary learning.

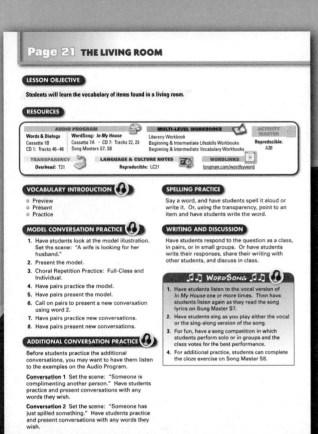

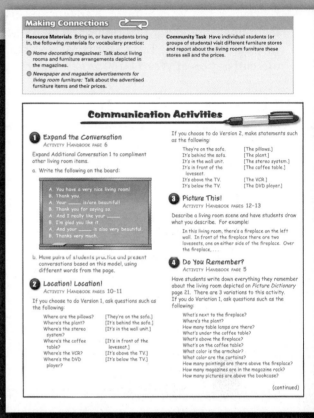

The most complete set of teaching tools imaginable for effective lesson planning, instruction, and assessment!

Teacher's Guide features :

- **Comprehensive resources** for each lesson are conveniently listed for quick and easy lesson planning.

- **Step-by-step teaching instructions** provide all-skills strategies for using the program with students at a wide range of levels and learning styles.

- **"Making Connections" activities** connect students to the world outside the classroom through suggested real-world resource materials and community tasks.

- **Internet WordLinks** expand vocabulary themes through technology as students explore related topics through the *Word by Word* companion website.

- **Over 1,500 communication activities** including games, tasks, brainstorming, discussion, movement, drawing, miming, role-playing and communication activities reinforce students' vocabulary learning in a way that is stimulating, creative, and fun.

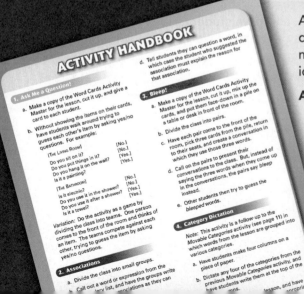

An **Activity Handbook** in the Appendix highlights 65 dynamic student-centered activities designed to promote motivating and communicative vocabulary learning—an ideal reference tool for new and experienced teachers.

Activities include:

Ask Me a Question!	Miming Game
Associations	Mystery Word!
Category Dictation	Picture This!
Concentration	Question the Answer!
Crosswords	Tic Tac Definitions
Daffy Debate!	Word Clues
Guess the Object!	. . . and many more!

The *Word by Word* Lesson Planner is provided in two convenient formats: a book of reproducible masters and a CD-ROM.

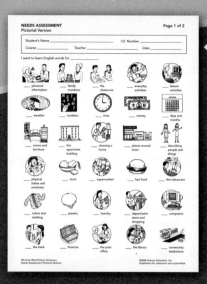

Needs Assessment forms in pictorial and checklist versions help determine students' needs and interests.

Lesson Planner forms enable teachers to plan and time instruction at three different levels, and a **Performance-Based Lesson Assessment** form provides a tool for evaluating and documenting student participation and performance. (The forms on the CD-ROM allow instructors to type in information and then print out customized versions.)

Language & Culture Notes for each lesson are an ideal resource for teachers and reading enrichment for intermediate-level students.

Activity Masters include ready-to-use word cards, activity sheets, games, and other reproducibles suggested in the Teacher's Guide activities.

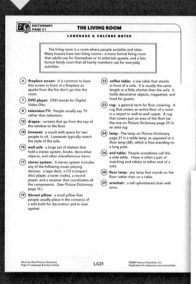

Song Masters for each WordSong in the Audio Program provide lyrics and cloze exercises for motivating vocabulary practice through music.

An **Activity Bank of Unit Worksheets** on the CD-ROM provides valuable supplemental practice through Vocabulary Review activities and Grammar Worksheets for all units in *Word by Word*.

The complete *Word by Word* program includes flexible multi-level workbooks and outstanding instructional support materials!

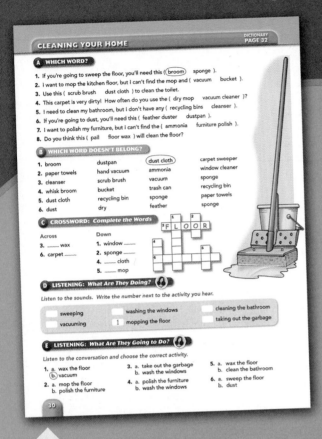

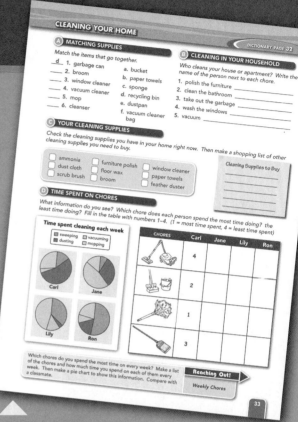

Vocabulary Workbooks at Beginning, Intermediate, and Literacy levels feature motivating vocabulary, grammar, and listening practice (Audio CDs included).

Lifeskills Workbooks at Beginning and Intermediate levels provide standards-based activities, community tasks, and reading comprehension lessons that prepare students for the types of assessment common in standardized tests.

The **Audio Program** offers clear, easy-to-use listen-and-repeat practice with all the vocabulary in *Word by Word*, interactive practice with all the conversations, and entertaining WordSongs that highlight key vocabulary through music.

Picture Supplements include Color Transparencies for every lesson page and Vocabulary Game Cards for introducing and practicing vocabulary.

Bilingual Editions and a Testing Program are also available.

UNIT 1 — Personal Information and Family

TOPICS	DICTIONARY	TEACHER'S GUIDE
Personal Information	1	2–4
Family Members I	2	5–7
Family Members II	3	8–9
Unit 1 Communication Activity Review	1–3	10

AUDIO PROGRAM

Words & Dialogs
Audio Cassette 1A
Audio CD 1:
  Tracks 2–9

WordSong: *What's Your Name?*
Audio Cassette 7A
Audio CD 7 Tracks 16
  (Vocal) & 17 (Sing-along)
Song Masters S1, S2

WORKBOOKS

For Multi-Level Practice
Literacy Workbook
Beginning Lifeskills Workbook
Beginning Vocabulary Workbook
Intermediate Lifeskills Workbook
Intermediate Vocabulary Workbook

WORDLINKS

Internet Resources through the
***Word by Word* Companion Website**
http://www.longman.com/wordbyword

ACTIVITY MASTERS

Reproducibles for Communication Activities
A1–A6

TRANSPARENCIES

Full-Color Overheads for Class Practice
T1–T3

LANGUAGE & CULTURE NOTES

Information for Teachers &
Intermediate / Advanced Students
LC1–LC3

LESSON OBJECTIVE

Students will learn the vocabulary of personal identity.

RESOURCES

AUDIO PROGRAM		
Words & Dialogs	**WordSong: *What's Your Name?***	
Cassette 1A	Cassette 7A • CD 7: Tracks 16, 17	
CD 1: Tracks 2–4	Song Masters S1, S2	

MULTI-LEVEL WORKBOOKS

Literacy Workbook
Beginning & Intermediate Lifeskills Workbooks
Beginning & Intermediate Vocabulary Workbooks

ACTIVITY MASTERS

Reproducibles: A1–A5

TRANSPARENCY
Overhead: T1

LANGUAGE & CULTURE NOTES
Reproducible: LC1

WORDLINKS
longman.com/wordbyword

VOCABULARY INTRODUCTION

Preview

Activate students' prior knowledge of personal information vocabulary by doing either or both of the following:

1. Brainstorm with students the personal information words they already know and write them on the board.

2. Have students look at the transparency or the illustration in the *Picture Dictionary* and identify the words they already know.

Present

Using the transparency or the illustration on *Picture Dictionary* page 1, point to the picture of each word, say the word, and have the class repeat it chorally and individually. (You can also play the word list on the Audio Program.) Check students' understanding and pronunciation of the vocabulary.

Practice

As a class, in pairs, or in small groups, have students practice the vocabulary in either or both of the following ways:

- Say or write a word, and have students point to the item or tell the number.

- Point to an item or give the number, and have students say the word.

MODEL CONVERSATION PRACTICE

1. Preview: Have students look at the model illustration and discuss who they think the speakers are and where the conversation takes place. The scene: "Someone is registering at a college."

2. Present the model or play the audio one or more times. Check students' understanding of the situation and the vocabulary.

3. Have students repeat each line chorally and individually.

4. Have students practice the model in pairs.

5. Call on a pair of students to present a conversation based on the model using word 2:
   A. What's *your first name?*
   B. *Gloria.*

6. Have pairs of students practice several conversations based on the model using different words on the page.

7. Call on pairs to present their conversations to the class.

ADDITIONAL CONVERSATION PRACTICE

Before students practice the additional conversations, you may want to have them listen to the examples on the Audio Program.

Conversation 1 Have students practice and present conversations with any words they wish. (Students should use real information about themselves.) For example:

   A. What's your *zip code*?
   B. *02481.*
   A. Did you say *02481*?
   B. Yes. That's right.

Conversation 2 Review the names of letters of the alphabet. Then have students practice and present conversations, using their last names. For example:

   A. What's your last name?
   B. *Kitano.*
   A. How do you spell that?
   B. *K-i-t-a-n-o.*

SPELLING PRACTICE

Say a word, and have students spell it aloud or write it. Or, using the transparency, point to an item and have students write the word.

WRITING AND DISCUSSION

Call on students to give their names, addresses, and contact information. Or have students interview each other in pairs or in small groups. Have each student choose a person to interview outside of class, writing down that person's name, address, and contact information.

WORDSONG

1. Have students listen to the vocal version of *What's Your Name?* one or more times. Then have students listen again as they read the song lyrics on Song Master S1.

2. Have students sing as you play either the vocal or the sing-along version of the song.

3. For fun, have a song competition in which students perform solo or in groups and the class votes for the best performance.

4. For additional practice, students can complete the cloze exercise on Song Master S2.

Making Connections

Resource Materials Bring in, or have students bring in, the following materials for vocabulary practice:

- *Application forms:* Have students practice filling them out.

- *Envelopes with names and addresses:* Have students identify first name, last name, address, apartment number, city, state, and zip code.

- *The telephone book:* Have students look for names, addresses, telephone numbers, and area codes.

Communication Activities

1 Stand in Order
ACTIVITY HANDBOOK PAGE **14**

a. Review the alphabet.

b. Have students arrange themselves in a line alphabetically according to their first names. They will need to talk with each other, asking and answering questions about what their first names are and how they are spelled.

c. When they are all arranged, have them call out their names. Check to see if they're in correct alphabetical order.

You can also do the same activity with last names.

2 Telephone
ACTIVITY HANDBOOK PAGE **14**

Begin the activity with the following statement: "My address is 22 Center Street."

You can also do the activity with a sentence using any other personal information vocabulary from *Picture Dictionary* page 1.

3 Class Directory
ACTIVITY MASTER **1**

a. Duplicate the Class Directory and give a copy to each student.

b. Have students complete the charts by circulating around the room and asking questions to get the information they need. For example:

> What's your last name?
> How do you spell that?/Can you spell that, please?
> What's your address?
> What city is that?/What city do you live in?
> What's your zip code?
> What's your phone number?
> What's your e-mail address?

Possible expansion: Since each student will now have his or her own class directory, suggest to them that they might like to call on the telephone or write a short note to another student in the class . . . just to say "Hello!"

(continued)

4 Role Play: Application Forms
ACTIVITY MASTER 2

a. Obtain blank application forms from places in the community, such as a bank, hospital, insurance company, or school, or use Activity Master 2.

b. Divide the class into pairs. Have one member of the pair be the interviewer, asking questions of the applicant and filling in the information on the form.

c. Have students in each pair switch roles.

5 Information Gap: Application Forms
ACTIVITY MASTER 2

a. Fill out two application forms with identical information.

b. Delete information from each category on one of the forms. For example: Application A has the information for first name, street number, and zip code. Application B has the information for last name, street name, and city name.

c. Have students work in pairs and ask each other questions in order to complete both application forms.

6 Role Play: Trio Introductions

a. Divide the class into groups of three.

b. Student A asks Student B his or her name, address, and telephone number.

c. Student C writes down the answers, if necessary questioning Student B about spelling.

d. Student C then introduces Student B to the class by reading the information he or she has written down.

7 The Question Game

a. Divide the class into two teams.

b. Write answers to personal information questions on cards. For example:

Tom Watson	10 Grove Street
01945	513-549-3872

c. A student from Team 1 picks a card and reads the answer on the card.

d. A student from Team 2 creates a question for the answer on the card. For example:

Team 1 Student: Tom Watson
Team 2 Student: What's your name?

Team 1 Student: 10 Grove Street
Team 2 Student: What's your address?

8 Get the Rhythm!

a. Model for the class how people say phone numbers in American English. For example, the number 237-9054 is pronounced *two three seven [pause] nine oh five four.*

b. Have students call out their phone numbers using this stress pattern as you write their numbers on the board.

9 The Name Game

The purpose of this activity is to reinforce the importance of knowing whether a name is a male's name or a female's name.

a. Divide the class into two teams.

b. Call out common English names. [As a reference, see the list of men's and women's names on Activity Master 3.]

c. Have team members take turns identifying whether a name is for a male or a female. A student gets one point for each name correctly identified.

10 Names and Nicknames
ACTIVITY MASTERS 3, 4, 5

a. Duplicate Names & Nicknames (Activity Master 3) and give a copy to each student.

b. Give students time to study the list of names. Then see how many they can remember by doing the following:

1. Make a copy of the Name Cards (Activity Master 4) and Nickname Cards (Activity Master 5) and cut them up into cards.

2. Give half the students Name Cards and half the students Nickname Cards.

3. Have students walk around the room trying to find their matching name.

LESSON OBJECTIVE

Students will learn the vocabulary of immediate family members—parents, children, and grandparents. (Extended family members are depicted in the next lesson.)

RESOURCES

AUDIO PROGRAM		MULTI-LEVEL WORKBOOKS
Words & Dialogs Cassette 1A CD 1: Tracks 5–7	**WordSong: *What's Your Name?*** Cassette 7A • CD 7: Tracks 16, 17 Song Masters S1, S2	Literacy Workbook Beginning & Intermediate Lifeskills Workbooks Beginning & Intermediate Vocabulary Workbooks

TRANSPARENCY	**LANGUAGE & CULTURE NOTES**	**WORDLINKS**
Overhead: T2	Reproducible: LC2	longman.com/wordbyword

VOCABULARY INTRODUCTION

Preview

Activate students' prior knowledge of vocabulary for family members by doing either or both of the following:

1. Brainstorm with students the words for family members they already know and write them on the board.

2. Have students look at the transparency or the illustration in the *Picture Dictionary* and identify the words they already know.

Present

Using the transparency or the illustration on *Picture Dictionary* page 2, point to the picture of each word, say the word, and have the class repeat it chorally and individually. (You can also play the word list on the Audio Program.) Check students' understanding and pronunciation of the vocabulary.

Practice

As a class, in pairs, or in small groups, have students practice the vocabulary in either or both of the following ways:

- Say or write a word, and have students point to the item or tell the number.
- Point to an item or give the number, and have students say the word.

MODEL CONVERSATION PRACTICE

There are two model conversations—one for female family members and the other for male family members.

1. Preview the first model. Have students look at the illustration and discuss who they think the speakers are and where the conversation takes place. The scene: "Two people are talking at the office."

2. Present the model or play the audio one or more times. Check students' understanding of the situation and the vocabulary.

3. Have students repeat each line chorally and individually.

4. Have students practice the model in pairs.

5. Call on a pair of students to present a conversation based on the model using word 3:

   A. Who is he?
   B. He's my *father*.
   A. What's his name?
   B. His name is *Donald.*

6. Preview the second model. The scene: "Two people are talking at the office."

7. Present and practice the second model using steps 2–4 above.

8. Call on a pair of students to present a conversation based on the second model using word 4:

   A. Who is she?
   B. She's my *mother*.
   A. What's her name?
   B. Her name is *Rosa.*

9. Have pairs of students practice several conversations based on the models using different words on the page. Tell students they may use any first names they wish in their conversations.

10. Call on pairs to present their conversations to the class.

ADDITIONAL CONVERSATION PRACTICE

Before students practice the additional conversations, you may want to have them listen to the examples on the Audio Program.

Conversation 1 This is a three-way conversation. Have students practice and present conversations in groups of three with any words they wish. For example:

    A. I'd like to introduce my *brother*.
    B. Nice to meet you.
    C. Nice to meet you, too.

Conversation 2 Have students practice and present conversations with any words and names they wish. For example:

    A. What's your *granddaughter's* name?
    B. Her name is *Jennifer*.

    A. What's your *son's* name?
    B. His name is *Robert*.

SPELLING PRACTICE

Say a word, and have students spell it aloud or write it. Or, using the transparency, point to an item and have students write the word.

WRITING AND DISCUSSION

Have students share information about their families and tell about family photos as a class, in pairs, or in small groups. Or have students write their responses and describe their photographs at home or in class, share their written work with other students, and discuss as a class, in pairs, or in small groups.

Making Connections

Resource Materials Bring in, or have students bring in, the following materials for vocabulary practice:

● *Magazine pictures showing family members:* Have students identify family members in the pictures.

● *Family photographs:* Have students talk about the photographs.

Communication Activities

① Family Tree

a. Put on the board the following family tree based on the family depicted on *Picture Dictionary* page 3:

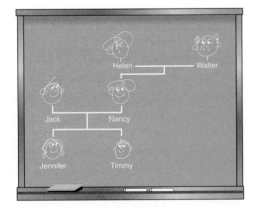

b. Elicit family member words in the following way:

    Nancy is Jack's . . . *wife*.
    Jennifer is Jack's . . . *daughter*.
    Jennifer is Timmy's . . . *sister*.
    Timmy is Jennifer's . . . *brother*.
    And he's Helen's . . . *grandson*.

You can also ask questions such as:

    How is Nancy related to Jack? [Nancy is Jack's wife.]
    How is Jack related to Jennifer? [Jack is Jennifer's father.]

c. Call on students to make similar statements for other students to complete with the correct family member word.

② Family Tree Game

a. Divide the class into two teams.

b. Have members of each team take turns answering questions about the family tree on the board (see Activity 1). You may use one or more of the following question types:

• State a name, and have a student make a family relationship statement. For example:

    Jack: [Jack is Nancy's husband./Jack is Jennifer's father.]
    Timmy: [Timmy is Nancy and Jack's son./ Timmy is Jennifer's brother.]

- Give two names, and have students state the relationship. For example:

    Jennifer and Helen: [Jennifer is Helen's granddaughter.]
    Walter and Nancy: [Walter is Nancy's father.]

- Make a statement about a family relationship and have students name the person. For example:

    This person is Jennifer's brother. [Timmy]
    This person is Nancy's father. [Walter]

- Make true/false statements about the family relationships. If the answer is false, have students correct it. For example:

    Jennifer is Nancy's daughter. [True.]
    Helen is Timmy's mother. [False. She's Timmy's grandmother.]

- Ask yes/no questions about the family relationships. For example:

    Is Helen Walter's wife? [Yes, she is.]
    Is Timmy Nancy's daughter? [No, he isn't.]

Option: Have a student from Team 1 ask a question for a student from Team 2 to answer, and vice versa.

3 My Family Tree

Have students create family trees of their own families and, as a class, in pairs, or in small groups, take turns telling about their families.

Variation: Divide the class into pairs, and have Student A tell about his or her family member while Student B draws a family tree based on the relationships that Student A describes.

4 Family Photo Album

Bring in, or have students bring in, a photo album and tell the class about the photographs. You can also display the photographs on a bulletin board or a desk, have students guess whose photographs they are, and then have students tell about their photographs.

5 Family Portraits

In pairs, have students ask each other about their family members. For example:

    What's your grandfather's name?
    How old is he?
    Where does he live?

When the interviews are complete, have students introduce their partners' families to the class.

6 Whose Family Is It?

a. Have each student write two or three sentences about his or her family. For example:

    My daughter is a tennis champion.
    My husband is a pilot.
    My grandmother is 92 years old.

b. Make a master list of the sentences and distribute copies to students in the class.

c. Have students guess who wrote the statements.

Variation: Have students write their statements on cards. Collect the cards and give one to each student (making sure that students don't get their own cards). Have students circulate, asking questions to find out who wrote the statements. For example:

    Is your daughter a tennis champion?
    Is your husband a pilot?
    How old is your grandmother?

7 Class Discussion: Family Words

As a class, in pairs, or in small groups, have students tell common ways in their language of referring to close family members. For example, in English:

    mother: mom/mommy/mum/mummy/ma
    father: dad/daddy/papa/pa
    grandmother: grandma/grammie/granny/nana
    grandfather: grandpa/gramps/grampie/
    granddad

LESSON OBJECTIVE

Students will learn the vocabulary of extended family members.

RESOURCES

AUDIO PROGRAM		MULTI-LEVEL WORKBOOKS	
Words & Dialogs Cassette 1A CD 1: Tracks 8, 9	**WordSong: *What's Your Name?*** Cassette 7A • CD 7: Tracks 16, 17 Song Masters S1, S2	Literacy Workbook Beginning & Intermediate Lifeskills Workbooks Beginning & Intermediate Vocabulary Workbooks	

TRANSPARENCY	LANGUAGE & CULTURE NOTES	WORDLINKS
Overhead: T3	Reproducible: LC3	longman.com/wordbyword

VOCABULARY INTRODUCTION

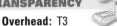

Preview

Activate students' prior knowledge of the vocabulary for extended family members by doing either or both of the following:

1. Brainstorm with students the words for extended family members they already know and write them on the board.

2. Have students look at the transparency or the illustration in the *Picture Dictionary* and identify the words they already know.

Present

Note: This lesson depicts through a family tree the more extended relationships of the family from the previous lesson (now labeled with names). The previous lesson focused on the husband and wife (Jack and Nancy), their children (Jennifer and Timmy), and the wife's parents—the children's grandparents (Helen and Walter). Here in this family tree, we again see the children and the wife's parents, and also the wife's brother (Frank), his wife (Linda), and their son (Alan).

Before presenting the words, have students practice saying the names of the family members in the illustration. Then have students look at the transparency or the illustration on *Picture Dictionary* page 3 as you introduce the people in the family tree while pointing to them:

Jack and Nancy are husband and wife. Helen and Walter are Nancy's mother and father. Jennifer and Timmy are Jack and Nancy's children. Jennifer is their daughter, and Timmy is their son. Frank is Nancy's brother, and Linda is his wife. Alan is Frank and Linda's son.

Since the vocabulary in this lesson is based on interrelationships of family members depicted in the family tree diagram, it is best to present the new words in the context of the sentences below the word list that describe these relationships. First, call on students to repeat each of the eleven new words chorally and individually. (You can also play the word list on the Audio Program.)

1. Have students look at the model illustration and discuss who the characters are. The scene: "Nancy, the mother from the family on page 2, is showing a friend a photograph of her family. She's telling her friend how everybody in the family is related."

2. Present the 1st sentence: "Jack is Alan's uncle." Check students' understanding of the relationship by referring to the family tree diagram.

3. Have students repeat the sentence chorally and individually.

4. Call on students to complete each of the remaining sentences. After each one, check students' understanding of the relationship by referring to the family tree diagram. Then have students repeat the sentence chorally and individually.

ADDITIONAL CONVERSATION PRACTICE

Before students practice the additional conversations, you may want to have them listen to the examples on the Audio Program.

Conversation 1 Have students practice and present conversations with any words and any names they wish. For example:

    A. Who is he?
    B. He's my *nephew*.
    A. What's his name?
    B. His name is *Peter*.

Conversation 2 This is a three-way conversation. Have students practice and present conversations in groups of three, using any words they wish. For example:

    A. Let me introduce my *mother-in-law*.
    B. I'm glad to meet you.
    C. Nice meeting you, too.

Tell students they can use words from both pages 2 and 3 of the *Picture Dictionary* in these conversations.

SPELLING PRACTICE

Say a word, and have students spell it aloud or write it. Or, using the transparency, point to two people in the family tree and have students write the word that describes their relationship to each other.

WRITING AND DISCUSSION

Have students draw their family trees and tell about their relatives as a class, in pairs, or in small groups. Or have students write about their relatives at home or in class, share their written work with other students, and discuss as a class, in pairs, or in small groups.

Making Connections

Resource Materials Bring in, or have students bring in, the following materials for vocabulary practice:

● *Magazine pictures showing family members:* Have students identify family members in the pictures.

● *Family photographs:* Have students talk about the photographs.

Communication Activities

1 Who Are They?

a. Have students look at the family tree diagram on *Picture Dictionary* page 3.

b. Make statements about members of the family and call on students to complete them. For example:

    Jack is Helen's . . . *son-in-law*.
    Alan is Jack's . . . *nephew*.
    Linda is Timmy's . . . *aunt*.
    Frank is Helen's . . . *son*.
    Frank is Jennifer's . . . *uncle*.
    Linda is Nancy's . . . *sister-in-law*.
    Linda is Alan's . . . *mother*.
    Jennifer is Frank's . . . *niece*.

c. Call on students to make similar statements for others to complete.

2 Role Play

a. Divide the class into groups of six to eight.

b. Set the scene: "Two friends meet in a restaurant. One of the friends is having dinner with his or her family. That person introduces all his or her family members to the friend."

c. The groups should decide who the family members are and then present their scenes to the class.

Activities 2–6 on pages 6–7 are also appropriate for this lesson.

Unit 1 Communication Activity Review

1 Information, Please!

a. Choose a page from the telephone directory and make copies for every student in the class. On half the pages, blank out the telephone numbers. On the other half, leave the numbers on the page.

b. Divide the class into pairs. Give one student the pages with the phone numbers and the other student the pages without the numbers.

c. The student with the phone numbers is the Information Operator. The other student calls Information for the phone number of any person on that page. For example:

   A. Can you give me the number of Alan Park, please?
   B. What's the address?
   A. It's 49 Oak Street.
   B. The number is 202-342-6983.
   A. Thank you.

2 Class Discussion: The History of Our Names

As a class, in pairs, or in small groups, have students talk about naming traditions in their countries. For example:

   What are popular first names for males and females?
   What is your family name? Does it come from your father or your mother?
   Does your given name mean something in your language?
   Do you have a middle name?
   Are you named after someone in your family?

3 A Family Member

a. Have students write one or two paragraphs about a special person in their family. Have them consider the following questions:

   What's his/her name?
   Where does he/she live?
   Where is his/her place of birth?
   What's his/her occupation?
   Why is this person special to you?

b. Have students share their writing in pairs.

4 Class Survey

a. Conduct a class survey, with each member of the class responsible for collecting specific information. Examples of questions you might want to have students ask each other are:

   How many brothers/sisters/aunts/uncles/ cousins do you have?
   How old are your children/brothers/sisters?
   How old are your grandparents?
   Is anybody in the class a twin?

b. As a class, in pairs, or in small groups, have students tabulate the data in order to figure out:

   Who has the most brothers/sisters/aunts/ uncles/cousins?
   Who has the oldest children/brothers/ sisters?
   Who has the youngest children/brothers/ sisters?
   How many sets of twins are there in the class?

5 Family Member Concentration
ACTIVITY HANDBOOK PAGE 3
ACTIVITY MASTER 6

Have students shuffle the cards and place them face-down in four rows of 5 each, then attempt to find cards that match.

6 Family Member Match Game
ACTIVITY HANDBOOK PAGE 11
ACTIVITY MASTER 6

Have students find the person whose card matches theirs.

7 Go Online: Identity Theft

Have students conduct online research on identity theft. Have them consider the following questions:

   What is identity theft?
   How can someone steal my identity?
   How can I prevent it?

Students can read information pamphlets on the Federal Trade Commission's website at www.consumer.gov/idtheft/or. They can also do a key word search on a search engine with the key words Identity Theft.

UNIT 2 Common Everyday Activities and Language

AUDIO PROGRAM

Words & Dialogs
Audio Cassette 1A
Audio CD 1:
   Tracks 10–27

WordSong: Another Day
Audio Cassette 7A
Audio CD 7: Tracks 18
   (Vocal) & 19 (Sing-along)
Song Masters S3, S4

WORKBOOKS

For Multi-Level Practice

Literacy Workbook
Beginning Lifeskills Workbook
Beginning Vocabulary Workbook
Intermediate Lifeskills Workbook
Intermediate Vocabulary Workbook

WORDLINKS

Internet Resources through the
Word by Word **Companion Website**

http://www.longman.com/wordbyword

ACTIVITY MASTERS

Reproducibles for Communication Activities
A7–A20

TRANSPARENCIES

Full-Color Overheads for Class Practice
T4–T14

LANGUAGE & CULTURE NOTES

Information for Teachers &
Intermediate /Advanced Students
LC4–LC14

VOCABULARY GAME CARDS

For Vocabulary Practice,
Activities, & Games
Cards 1–66

LESSON OBJECTIVE

Students will learn the vocabulary of a school classroom.

RESOURCES

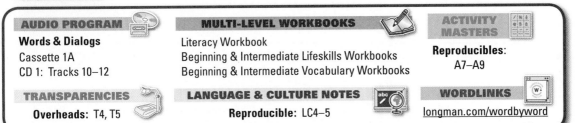

AUDIO PROGRAM

Words & Dialogs
Cassette 1A
CD 1: Tracks 10–12

MULTI-LEVEL WORKBOOKS

Literacy Workbook
Beginning & Intermediate Lifeskills Workbooks
Beginning & Intermediate Vocabulary Workbooks

ACTIVITY MASTERS

Reproducibles:
A7–A9

TRANSPARENCIES

Overheads: T4, T5

LANGUAGE & CULTURE NOTES

Reproducible: LC4–5

WORDLINKS

longman.com/wordbyword

VOCABULARY INTRODUCTION

- Preview
- Present
- Practice

MODEL CONVERSATION PRACTICE

There are two model conversations—one for *next to* and the other for *on*.

1. Have students look at the first model illustration. Set the scene: "The school custodian is talking to the teacher's aide."

2. Present the first model or play the audio one or more times. Check understanding of the preposition *next to*.

3. Choral Repetition Practice: Full-Class and Individual.

4. Have pairs practice the model.

5. Have pairs present the model using words 2 and 3:

    A. Where's the *teacher's aide*?
    B. The *teacher's aide* is next to the *student*.

6. Have students look at the second model illustration. Set the scene: "Two students are talking."

7. Present and practice the second model using steps 2–4 in the left column. Check students' understanding of the preposition *on*.

8. Have pairs present the model using words 20 and 4:

    A. Where's the *pen*?
    B. The *pen* is on the *desk*.

9. Have pairs practice new conversations.

10. Have pairs present new conversations.

ADDITIONAL CONVERSATION PRACTICE

Before students practice the additional conversations, you may want to have them listen to the examples on the Audio Program.

Conversation 1 Have students practice and present conversations with any words they wish.

Conversation 2 Have students practice and present conversations with any words they wish.

SPELLING PRACTICE

Say a word, and have students spell it aloud or write it. Or, using the transparency, point to an item and have students write the word.

WRITING AND DISCUSSION

Have students respond to the question as a class, in pairs, or in small groups. Or have students write their responses, share their writing with other students, and discuss in class.

Resource Materials Bring in, or have students bring in, the following materials for vocabulary practice:

● *School supply catalogs:* Talk about the classroom supplies depicted in the catalogs.

● *Magazine pictures of school classrooms:* Talk about the classrooms.

Community Task Have individual students (or groups of students) visit different classrooms in your school and report about objects they saw in the classrooms.

Communication Activities

1 Clap in Rhythm
ACTIVITY HANDBOOK PAGE 3

Have students name different classroom words to a clapping rhythm.

2 Chain Game: In Our Classroom . . .
ACTIVITY HANDBOOK PAGES 2–3

Begin the chain as follows: "In our classroom there's a globe," and have students continue it. For example:

Teacher: In our classroom there's a globe.
Student 1: In our classroom there's a globe and some chalk.
Student 2: In our classroom there's a globe, some chalk, and some markers.
Etc.

3 Find It!

Note: All the items depicted on *Picture Dictionary* page 5 are also found in the classroom scene on page 4.

a. Divide the class into pairs.

b. One student looks at the classroom scene on *Picture Dictionary* page 4, and the other student asks that person to point to the items from page 5 in the classroom. For example:

Where's the pencil sharpener?
Where's the monitor?
Where's the calculator?

4 True or False?

Point to objects in the classroom and make statements about them. Have students decide whether the statements are true or false. If a statement is false, have students correct it. For example:

This is a globe.   [False. It's a map.]
This is a pen.   [False. It's a pencil.]
This is a monitor.   [True.]

5 Movable Categories
ACTIVITY HANDBOOK PAGE 11
ACTIVITY MASTER 7

Call out the following categories and have students go to the appropriate side of room:

things you look at
things you listen to
things you use to write
furniture
things that use electricity
things that are on the wall
things that go in a student's bag
things you use to study math
things you use to study English

6 Category Dictation
ACTIVITY HANDBOOK PAGE 2

Dictate words that fit into any four of the above categories.

7 Finish the Sentence!
ACTIVITY HANDBOOK PAGE 7

Begin sentences such as the following for students to complete:

Every student sits on a . . . *chair.*
You tell the time by looking at the . . . *clock.*
The person who helps the teacher is the . . . *teacher's aide.*
We keep books in our classroom in the . . . *bookcase.*
You write on the whiteboard with . . . *markers.*
You fill a binder with . . . *notebook paper.*
When you work at a computer, you look at the . . . *monitor.*
The teacher tells the class to read page 5 in the . . . *book/textbook.*
At the computer you type on a . . . *keyboard.*
When your pencil is dull, you use a . . . *pencil sharpener.*

(continued)

8 Do You Remember?
ACTIVITY HANDBOOK PAGE 5

Have students write down everything they remember about the classroom depicted on *Picture Dictionary* page 4.

If you do Variation 1, ask questions such as the following:

> Where's the globe?
> Where's the teacher?
> Where's the keyboard?
> Where's the ruler?
> What's next to the globe?
> What's next to the teacher's desk?

9 Drawing Game
ACTIVITY HANDBOOK PAGE 6
ACTIVITY MASTER 7

Have teams compete to identify classroom items drawn by one of their team members.

10 What's the Question?
ACTIVITY HANDBOOK PAGE 16

Describe various classroom objects, and have students respond by asking: "What's a/an _____?" For example:

> Teacher: It's where you put up announcements or other papers.
> Student: What's a bulletin board?

> Teacher: I need this if I make mistakes in my notebook.
> Student: What's an eraser?

> Teacher: I use this to write on a whiteboard.
> Student: What's a marker?

> Teacher: It's where I put old papers and other things I don't want to keep.
> Student: What's a wastebasket?

> Teacher: I sit on it.
> Student: What's a seat/chair?

> Teacher: It tells time.
> Student: What's a clock?

> Teacher: It helps me solve difficult math problems.
> Student: What's a calculator?

> Teacher: I use this when I need to draw a straight line.
> Student: What's a ruler?

> Teacher: I use this to put something on the bulletin board.
> Student: What's a thumbtack?

11 Tic Tac Definitions
ACTIVITY HANDBOOK PAGE 15
ACTIVITY MASTER 8

Have students fill in the tic tac grid with any nine classroom words they wish. Give definitions such as those in Activity 10, and have students cross out on their grids the words you have defined.

12 What Am I?
ACTIVITY HANDBOOK PAGE 15
ACTIVITY MASTER 7

a. Make a copy of the Classroom Word Cards and cut it up into cards.

b. Pin a card on each student's back so that the student doesn't see what classroom item he or she *is*.

c. The student must discover his or her *identity* by asking yes/no questions. For example:

> Do you write with me?   [No.]
> Do you look at me?   [Yes.]
> Am I on the wall?   [Yes.]
> Am I a screen?   [No.]
> Am I a bulletin board?   [Yes.]

This can be done as a class, in pairs, or in small groups.

13 Classroom Match Game
ACTIVITY HANDBOOK PAGE 11
ACTIVITY MASTER 9

Have students find the person whose card matches theirs.

14 Read, Write, and Draw
ACTIVITY HANDBOOK PAGE 13

Have students write each other letters in which they describe their classroom.

15 Daffy Debate!
ACTIVITY HANDBOOK PAGE 5
ACTIVITY MASTER 7

Have students debate which classroom items are more important to a classroom than others.

16 Inventions
ACTIVITY HANDBOOK PAGE 9

Have students invent a new classroom item and then present their ideas to the class.

LESSON OBJECTIVE

Students will learn classroom directions commonly given by teachers.

RESOURCES

AUDIO PROGRAM

Words & Dialogs
Cassette 1A
CD 1: Track 13

MULTI-LEVEL WORKBOOKS

Literacy Workbook
Beginning & Intermediate Lifeskills Workbooks
Beginning & Intermediate Vocabulary Workbooks

ACTIVITY MASTER

Reproducible:
A10

TRANSPARENCIES

Overheads: T6, T7

LANGUAGE & CULTURE NOTES

Reproducible: LC6–7

WORDLINKS

longman.com/wordbyword

VOCABULARY INTRODUCTION

- Preview
- Present
- Practice

MODEL CONVERSATION PRACTICE

The directions are grouped into twelve action sequences, with five actions in each sequence.

1. Introduce the first action sequence.

   a. Say "Say your name," demonstrate it, and have students in the class say their names.

   b. Say "Repeat your name," demonstrate it, and have everybody repeat their names.

   c. Say "Spell your name," demonstrate it, and call on a few students to spell their names.

   d. Say "Print your name," demonstrate it with your name on the board, and invite a student to the board to follow your direction.

   e. Say "Sign your name," demonstrate it, and invite another student to the board to follow your direction.

   (You can also play the action sequence on the Audio Program.)

   f. Call on individual students to be the teacher and give these five directions to other students. You should also be a student and follow the directions.

2. Introduce the other action sequences in a similar manner: Say each direction, demonstrate it, have students follow your directions, and then call on individual students to give the directions for others (and you) to follow.

SPELLING PRACTICE

Say a phrase, and have students spell it aloud or write it. Or, using the transparency, point to an action and have students write the phrase.

WRITING AND DISCUSSION

Have students take turns being the teacher, giving as many directions to their students as they wish. They may do this with the whole class, in pairs, or in small groups.

Making Connections

Resource Materials Bring in, or have students bring in, the following materials for vocabulary practice:

- *Magazine pictures of school classrooms:* Talk about the classrooms.

Community Task Have individual students (or groups of students) visit different classrooms in your school and report about classroom actions they saw.

Communication Activities

1 Whisk!
ACTIVITY HANDBOOK PAGES 16–17

Name actions from *Picture Dictionary* pages 6–7 and replace the verbs with the word *Whisk*. Students must fill in with an appropriate verb. For example:

Whisk your book.	[Open your book./Close your book.]
Whisk your hand.	[Raise your hand.]
Whisk down.	[Sit down.]
Whisk the shades.	[Lower the shades.]

2 Miming Game: What Am I Doing?
ACTIVITY HANDBOOK PAGE 11
ACTIVITY MASTER 10

Have students take turns pantomiming classroom actions. The class tries to guess what the person is doing. For example:

You're printing your name.
You're signing your name.

3 Miming in Sequence

a. First review the past tense of the verbs on *Picture Dictionary* pages 6–7.

b. Divide the class into pairs.

c. One student pantomimes a series of actions, and the other then says what the person did. For example:

You opened your book, took notes, closed your book, and put it away.

4 What's the Object?
ACTIVITY HANDBOOK PAGE 16

Call out a verb from the vocabulary list and have students add an appropriate direct object. For example:

close . . . *your book*
raise . . . *your hand*
answer . . . *the questions*
correct . . . *your mistakes*
hand in . . . *your homework*

5 Telephone
ACTIVITY HANDBOOK PAGE 14

Begin the activity with the following instructions: "Look in the dictionary, look up a word, pronounce it, read the definition, and copy the word."

6 Listen and Number
ACTIVITY HANDBOOK PAGE 10

In pairs, have one student make up a story using classroom action words and have the other student number the pictures in their order of occurrence in the story.

7 Class Discussion: Schools Then and Now

Have students think about classrooms they had as children or classrooms their parents had as children. As a class or in small groups, discuss the following:

What was the classroom like?
What technology did the teacher use?
What was in the classroom?
How was the classroom different from our classroom today?
What did students do in class? Did they speak to each other or only to the teacher?
Were the classroom rules different?
How is studying different today?
Do you think students learn faster with computers and technology?
Do you think students learned faster with only a teacher and books?
Do you think education is better today than it was when you (or your parents) were children? Why?

LESSON OBJECTIVE

Students will learn common prepositions of location.

RESOURCES

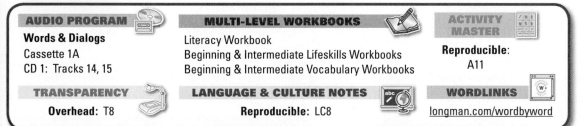

AUDIO PROGRAM

Words & Dialogs
Cassette 1A
CD 1: Tracks 14, 15

MULTI-LEVEL WORKBOOKS

Literacy Workbook
Beginning & Intermediate Lifeskills Workbooks
Beginning & Intermediate Vocabulary Workbooks

ACTIVITY MASTER

Reproducible:
A11

TRANSPARENCY

Overhead: T8

LANGUAGE & CULTURE NOTES

Reproducible: LC8

WORDLINKS

longman.com/wordbyword

MODEL CONVERSATION PRACTICE

There are two model conversations. The first model is for words 1–10—prepositions that require only one object, and the second model is for word 11—a preposition that requires two objects.

1. Have students look at the first model illustration. Set the scene: "The school custodian is talking to a teacher."
2. Present the model.
3. Choral Repetition Practice: Full-Class and Individual.
4. Have pairs practice the model.
5. Have pairs present the model.
6. Call on pairs to present a new conversation using word 2.
7. Have pairs practice new conversations.
8. Have pairs present new conversations.
9. Have students look at the second model illustration. Set the scene: "Two students are talking."
10. Present and practice the second model using steps 2–5 above.

SPELLING PRACTICE

Say a word, and have students spell it aloud or write it. Or, using the transparency, point to an item and have students write the word.

WRITING AND DISCUSSION

As a class, in pairs, or in small groups, have students tell about the location of items in the classroom on *Picture Dictionary* page 4 and the location of items in their own classroom. Or have students write their descriptions, share their writing with other students, and discuss in class.

Making Connections

Resource Materials Bring in, or have students bring in, the following materials for vocabulary practice:

● *Magazine pictures of school classrooms:* Talk about the location of classroom objects.

Community Task Have individual students (or groups of students) visit different classrooms in your school and report about the location of objects they saw in the classrooms.

Communication Activities

1 What's the Question?
ACTIVITY HANDBOOK PAGE 16

Describe the location of objects on *Picture Dictionary* page 8 and have students respond by asking: "Where's the _____?" For example:

Teacher: It's above the bulletin board.
Student: Where's the clock?

Teacher: It's next to the table.
Student: Where's the bookcase?

Teacher: It's under the table.
Student: Where's the wastebasket?

Teacher: It's in the pencil sharpener.
Student: Where's the pencil?

Teacher: It's to the left of the mouse.
Student: Where's the keyboard?

2 Talk in Circles

Have students take turns asking and answering questions about the location of different objects on *Picture Dictionary* page 8. For example:

Student 1: Where's the wastebasket?
Student 2: Under the table.
[to Student 3] Where's the globe?
Student 3: To the left of the dictionary.
[to Student 4] Where's the bookcase?
Etc.

3 Telephone
ACTIVITY HANDBOOK PAGE 14

Begin the activity with the following sentence: "There's a computer on the desk between the bookcase and the chalkboard."

4 Location! Location!
ACTIVITY HANDBOOK PAGE 10 (VERSION 2)

Make statements about the classroom scene on *Picture Dictionary* page 4 such as the following:

It's on the floor next to the desk.
[The wastebasket.]
It's in front of the screen.
[The overhead projector.]
It's on the bookcase next to the pencil sharpener.
[The globe.]
It's on the wall above the whiteboard.
[The loudspeaker.]

It's on the wall above the bookcase.
[The bulletin board.]
It's on the wall to the right of the chalkboard.
[The map.]
It's on the wall to the left of the chalkboard.
[The screen.]
It's on the wall below the clock. [The chalkboard.]
It's on the table to the left of the keyboard.
[The mouse.]

Follow-Up: Make statements about the location of items in your own classroom.

5 Chain Game: In Our Classroom . . .
ACTIVITY HANDBOOK PAGES 2–3

Begin the chain as follows: "In our classroom there's a globe on the bookcase," and have students continue it. For example:

Teacher: In our classroom there's a globe on the bookcase.
Student 1: In our classroom there's a globe on the bookcase and a clock above the door.
Student 2: In our classroom there's a globe on the bookcase, a clock above the door, and a pen on the teacher's desk.
Etc.

6 True or False?
ACTIVITY HANDBOOK PAGE 15

Make statements such as the following about the classroom on *Picture Dictionary* page 4. Have students decide whether they're true or false. If a statement is false, have students correct it. For example:

The eraser is next to the chalk. [True.]
The bulletin board is below the bookcase. [False. It's above the bookcase.]
The P.A. system is above the whiteboard. [True.]
The screen is next to the bulletin board. [False. It's next to the chalkboard.]
The monitor is to the left of the keyboard. [False. It's to the right of the keyboard.]
The globe is on the bookcase. [True.]
The wastebasket is next to the map. [False. It's next to the teacher's desk.]
The printer is on the teacher's desk. [False. It's on the table.]

Follow-Up: Make statements about the location of items in your own classroom.

7 It's a Puzzle!

ACTIVITY HANDBOOK PAGE 9

Cut out pictures of classrooms and create puzzles out of the pictures for students to identify and put together by asking questions. For example:

In my picture, there's a map on the wall.
In my picture, the teacher is in front of her desk.
Do you have a computer in your picture?
Is there a book on the teacher's desk?

8 Picture This!

ACTIVITY HANDBOOK PAGES 12–13
ACTIVITY MASTER 11

Read the following and have students draw what you describe:

There's a chair behind the teacher's desk.
There's a chalkboard on the wall above the chair.
There's a clock above the chalkboard.

There's a map to the left of the chalkboard.
There's a P.A. system above the map.
There's a table under the map.
There's a monitor on the table.
There's a printer to the left of the monitor.
There's a keyboard in front of the monitor.
There's a mouse to the right of the keyboard.
There's a bulletin board to the right of the chalkboard.
There's a screen to the right of the bulletin board.
There's a table below the screen.
There's an overhead projector on the table.
There's a bookcase below the bulletin board.
There's a globe on the bookcase.
There's a dictionary to the left of the globe.
The globe is between the dictionary and a pencil sharpener.
There's a book on the teacher's desk.
There's a pen on the book.
There's a pencil to the left of the book.
There's an eraser to the right of the book.

LESSON OBJECTIVE

Students will learn the vocabulary of everyday personal hygiene and meal activities.

RESOURCES

AUDIO PROGRAM		MULTI-LEVEL WORKBOOKS	VOCABULARY GAME CARDS
Words & Dialogs Cassette 1A CD 1: Tracks 16–18	**WordSong:** *Another Day* Cassette 7A • CD 7: Tracks 18, 19 Song Masters S3, S4	Literacy Workbook Beginning & Intermediate Lifeskills Workbooks Beginning & Intermediate Vocabulary Workbooks	Cards 1–20

ACTIVITY MASTERS	TRANSPARENCY	LANGUAGE & CULTURE NOTES	WORDLINKS
Reproducibles: A12, A13	**Overhead:** T9	**Reproducible:** LC9	longman.com/wordbyw•

VOCABULARY INTRODUCTION

- Preview
- Present
- Practice

MODEL CONVERSATION PRACTICE

1. Have students look at the model illustration. Set the scene: "Somebody is telling things he does every day."

2. Present the model.

3. Choral Repetition Practice: Full-Class and Individual.

4. Have pairs practice the model.

5. Have pairs present the model.

6. Call on pairs to present a new conversation using words 5, 6, and 8.

7. Have pairs practice new conversations using different words on the page. Tell students they may use any three actions from the list in their answers.

8. Have pairs present new conversations.

ADDITIONAL CONVERSATION PRACTICE

Before students practice the additional conversations, you may want to have them listen to the examples on the Audio Program.

Conversation 1 Have students practice and present conversations with any words they wish.

Conversation 2 Have students practice and present conversations with any words they wis

SPELLING PRACTICE

Say a word or phrase, and have students spell it aloud or write it. Or, using the transparency, point to an item and have students write the wo or phrase.

WRITING AND DISCUSSION

Have students make a list of things they do eve day, and then discuss these everyday activities as a class, in pairs, or in small groups. Have ea student interview a few friends outside of class about their everyday activities and then report the results of their interviews back to the class.

Making Connections

Resource Materials Bring in, or have students brin in, the following materials for vocabulary practice:

- *Magazine pictures of everyday activities:* Talk about what people are doing.

- *Advertisements for products showing people doing various everyday activities:* Talk about th actions depicted in the ads.

VOCABULARY GAME CARDS

Have students practice vocabulary, do activities, and play games with Vocabulary Game Cards 1–20. Activities and games are described in the set of cards.

Communication Activities

1 Miming Game

ACTIVITY HANDBOOK PAGE 11
ACTIVITY MASTER 12

Have students take turns pantomiming everyday activity words. The class tries to guess what the person is doing. For example:

You're brushing your teeth.
You're combing your hair.

2 Whisk!

ACTIVITY HANDBOOK PAGES 16–17

Have the class try to guess an everyday activity a student is thinking of by asking questions with the word *whisk*. For example:

Do you *whisk* at mealtime? [No.]
Do you *whisk* in the morning? [Yes.]
Do both men and women *whisk*? [No.]
Do women *whisk*? [No.]
Do you use water when you *whisk*? [Yes, usually.]
 [Answer: shave]

3 Chain Game: I Got Up This Morning and . . .

ACTIVITY HANDBOOK PAGES 2–3

Begin the chain as follows: "I got up this morning and took a shower," and have students continue it. For example:

Teacher: I got up this morning and took a shower.

Student 1: I got up this morning, took a shower, and brushed my teeth.
Student 2: I got up this morning, took a shower, brushed my teeth, and combed my hair.
 Etc.

4 Everyday Activity Associations

ACTIVITY HANDBOOK PAGE 2

Call out everyday activity words and have groups write down as many associations as they can think of. For example:

wash my face: [water/washcloth/soap/towel/ clean]
brush my teeth: [toothpaste/morning/ toothbrush]
make breakfast: [toast/milk/coffee/pancakes]

5 What's the Object?

ACTIVITY HANDBOOK PAGE 16

Call out verbs and have students add appropriate objects. For example:

take . . . *a shower/a bath*
make . . . *breakfast/lunch/dinner/the bed*
get . . . *dressed/undressed*
brush . . . *your hair/your teeth*

(continued)

6 Find the Right Person!

ACTIVITY HANDBOOK PAGES 6–7
ACTIVITY MASTER 13

Practice the following questions before having students do the activity:

> What time do you get up?
> Where do you eat breakfast or lunch?
> Do you make your bed every day?
> When do you take a bath or shower?
> What time do you go to bed?

Have students walk around the classroom interviewing other students. When a student gets a *yes* answer, that student writes in the other person's name and then continues interviewing others until getting a *yes* answer to all the questions.

7 Who Wrote This?

a. Have students write three statements about themselves on a piece of paper without writing their names. For example:

> I get up at 5:15 every morning.
> I take a shower before I go to bed.
> I always make my bed.

b. Collect the statements and read them to the class. Have students guess who wrote each set of statements.

Variation: Collect the papers, redistribute them to the class, and have students walk around asking questions about the information on the paper until they find the person who wrote it.

8 Guess What I Did Yesterday!

a. Divide the class into pairs.

b. Have each student choose any four activities from *Picture Dictionary* page 9 and number them 1–4 in the order in which he or she did them.

c. Partner A asks Partner B questions to find out what Partner A did and in what order. For example:

> A. Did you take a bath yesterday?
> B. No, I didn't.
> A. Did you make breakfast yesterday?
> B. Yes, I did.
> A. Did you take a shower yesterday?
> B. Yes, I did.
> A. Did you take a shower before you made breakfast?
> B. Yes, I did.
>   Etc.

d. Then reverse roles.

9 Movable Categories

ACTIVITY HANDBOOK PAGE 11
ACTIVITY MASTER 12

Call out the following categories and have students go to the appropriate side of the room:

> activities you do in the morning
> activities you do in the evening
> activities you do to your body
> activities you do in the kitchen
> activities you do in the bathroom
> activities you do in the bedroom
> activities you do to stay clean
> activities you do to look more attractive

10 Listen and Number

ACTIVITY HANDBOOK PAGE 10

In pairs, have one student make up a story using everyday activities and have the other student number the pictures in their order of occurrence in the story.

LESSON OBJECTIVE

Students will learn the vocabulary of everyday household and recreational activities.

RESOURCES

AUDIO PROGRAM		MULTI-LEVEL WORKBOOKS	VOCABULARY GAME CARDS
Words & Dialogs	**WordSong:** *Another Day*	Literacy Workbook	Cards 1–32
Cassette 1A	Cassette 7A • CD 7: Tracks 18, 19	Beginning & Intermediate Lifeskills Workbooks	
CD 1: Tracks 19–21	Song Masters S3, S4	Beginning & Intermediate Vocabulary Workbooks	

ACTIVITY MASTERS	TRANSPARENCY	LANGUAGE & CULTURE NOTES	WORDLINKS
Reproducibles: A14, A15	**Overhead:** T10	**Reproducible:** LC10	longman.com/wordbyword

VOCABULARY INTRODUCTION

- Preview
- Present
- Practice

MODEL CONVERSATION PRACTICE

1. Have students look at the model illustration. Set the scene: "Two friends are talking on the telephone."
2. Present the model.
3. Choral Repetition Practice: Full-Class and Individual.
4. Have pairs practice the model.
5. Have pairs present the model.
6. Call on pairs to present a new conversation using word 2.
7. Have pairs practice new conversations.
8. Have pairs present new conversations.

ADDITIONAL CONVERSATION PRACTICE

Before students practice the additional conversations, you may want to have them listen to the examples on the Audio Program.

Conversation 1 Set the scene: "Two friends are talking on the telephone." Have students practice and present conversations with any actions and any names they wish.

Conversation 2 Check understanding of the future with *going to*. Then have students practice and present conversations with any actions they wish.

SPELLING PRACTICE

Say a word or phrase, and have students spell it aloud or write it. Or, using the transparency, point to an item and have students write the word or phrase.

WRITING AND DISCUSSION

Have students respond to the question as a class, in pairs, or in small groups. Or have students write their responses, share their writing with other students, and discuss in class.

VOCABULARY GAME CARDS

Have students practice vocabulary, do activities, and play games with Vocabulary Game Cards 1–32. Activities and games are described in the set of cards.

Making Connections

Resource Materials Bring in, or have students bring in, the following materials for vocabulary practice:

- *Magazine pictures of everyday activities:* Talk about what people are doing.
- *Advertisements for products showing people doing various everyday activities:* Talk about the actions depicted in the ads.

Communication Activities

1 Expand the Conversation
ACTIVITY HANDBOOK PAGE 6

Expand the model conversation to ask about other family members.

a. Write the following on the board:

> A. Hello. What are you doing?
> B. I'm _____ing.
> A. What's/What are _____ doing?
> B. He's/She's/They're _____ing.
> A. And how about _____?
> B. He's/She's/They're _____ing.

b. Have pairs of students practice and present conversations based on this model, using different words from *Picture Dictionary* page 10.

2 Miming Game: What Am I Doing?
ACTIVITY HANDBOOK PAGE 11
ACTIVITY MASTER 14

Have students take turns pantomiming everyday activity words. The class tries to guess what the person is doing. For example:

> You're washing the dishes.
> You're feeding the baby.

3 Whisk!
ACTIVITY HANDBOOK PAGES 16–17

Have the class try to guess an everyday activity a student is thinking of by asking questions with the word *whisk*. For example:

Do you *whisk* every day?	[Yes.]
Do you *whisk* in the kitchen?	[No.]
Do you *whisk* for enjoyment?	[Yes.]
Is *whisking* a household chore?	[Yes.]
Do you *whisk* outside?	[Yes.]

> [Answer: walk the dog]

4 Chain Game: After Breakfast Today! . . .
ACTIVITY HANDBOOK PAGES 2–3

Begin the chain as follows: "After breakfast today, I cleaned the house," and have students continue it. For example:

> Teacher: After breakfast today, I cleaned the house.
> Student 1: After breakfast today, I cleaned the house and did the laundry.
> Student 2: After breakfast today, I cleaned the house, did the laundry, and ironed clothes.
> Etc.

5 Everyday Activity Associations
ACTIVITY HANDBOOK PAGE 2

Call out everyday activity words and have groups write down as many associations as they can think of. For example:

> wash the dishes: [water/detergent/dishes]
> do the laundry: [clothes/washing machine/dryer]
> go to work: [walk/drive/take the bus/take the subway]

6 What's the Object?
ACTIVITY HANDBOOK PAGE 16

Call out verbs and have students add appropriate objects. For example:

> feed . . . *the baby/the dog/the cat/the fish/the kids*
> wash . . . *the dishes/the car/the clothes*
> clean . . . *the house/the apartment/the garage/the basement*

7 Find the Right Person!
ACTIVITY HANDBOOK PAGES 6–7
ACTIVITY MASTER 15

See instructions for Activity 6 on page 22. Example:

> Do you clean the house?
> Do you wash the dishes?
> Do you like to iron?
> Do you study every day?
> Do you do the laundry?
> Do you take the bus?
> Do you walk the dog?

8 Who Wrote This?

See instructions for Activity 7 on page 22.
Example:

> I walk my dog every day after breakfast.
> I vacuum my rugs every Saturday morning.
> I always make my bed.

9 Guess What I Did Yesterday!

See instructions for Activity 8 on page 22.
Example:

A. Did you clean the house yesterday?
B. No, I didn't.
A. Did you do the laundry yesterday?
B. Yes, I did.
A. Did you iron yesterday?
B. Yes, I did.
A. Did you do the laundry before you ironed?
B. Yes, I did.

10 Movable Categories
ACTIVITY HANDBOOK PAGE 11
ACTIVITY MASTER 14

Call out the following categories and have students go to the appropriate side of the room:

activities you do outdoors
activities you do in the house
activities you do in the morning/afternoon/
   evening
activities that involve food
activities children do
activities parents do

11 Listen and Number
ACTIVITY HANDBOOK PAGE 10

In pairs, have one student make up a story using everyday activities and have the other student number the pictures in their order of occurrence in the story.

12 Discussion: Who Does the Household Chores?

As a class, in pairs, or in small groups, have students discuss who does the chores in their households. If you wish, you can make a chart on the board of the different chores each student does.

LESSON OBJECTIVE

Students will learn the vocabulary of leisure recreational activities.

RESOURCES

AUDIO PROGRAM		MULTI-LEVEL WORKBOOKS	VOCABULARY GAME CARDS
Words & Dialogs Cassette 1A CD 1: Tracks 22–24	**WordSong:** *Another Day* Cassette 7A • CD 7: Tracks 18, 19 Song Masters S3, S4	Literacy Workbook Beginning & Intermediate Lifeskills Workbooks Beginning & Intermediate Vocabulary Workbooks	Cards 1–48

ACTIVITY MASTERS	TRANSPARENCY	LANGUAGE & CULTURE NOTES	WORDLINKS
Reproducibles: A16, A17	**Overhead:** T11	**Reproducible:** LC11	longman.com/wordbyw

VOCABULARY INTRODUCTION

- Preview
- Present
- Practice

MODEL CONVERSATION PRACTICE

1. Have students look at the model illustration. Set the scene: "Two friends are talking on the telephone."
2. Present the model.
3. Choral Repetition Practice: Full-Class and Individual.
4. Have pairs practice the model.
5. Have pairs present the model.
6. Call on pairs to present a new conversation using word 2.
7. Have pairs practice new conversations.
8. Have pairs present new conversations.

ADDITIONAL CONVERSATION PRACTICE

Before students practice the additional conversations, you may want to have them listen to the examples on the Audio Program.

Conversation 1 Set the scene: "Two friends are talking on the telephone." Have students practice and present conversations with any words they wish.

Conversation 2 Have students practice and present conversations with any words they wish.

SPELLING PRACTICE

Say a word or phrase, and have students spell it aloud or write it. Or, using the transparency, point to an item and have students write the wc or phrase.

WRITING AND DISCUSSION

Have students respond to the questions as a class, in pairs, or in small groups. Or have students write their responses, share their writ with other students, and discuss in class.

VOCABULARY GAME CARDS

Have students practice vocabulary, do activities, and play games with Vocabulary Game Cards 1–48 Activities and games are described in the set of cards.

Making Connections

Resource Materials Bring in, or have students brin in, the following materials for vocabulary practice:

- *Magazine pictures of leisure activities:* Talk abou what people are doing.
- *Advertisements for products showing people doing various leisure activities:* Talk about the actions depicted in the ads.

Communication Activities

1 Miming Game: What Am I Doing?
ACTIVITY HANDBOOK PAGE 11
ACTIVITY MASTER 16

Have students take turns pantomiming leisure activities. The class tries to guess what the person is doing. For example:

> You're watching TV.
> You're playing basketball.

2 Whisk!
ACTIVITY HANDBOOK PAGES 16–17

Have the class try to guess a leisure activity a student is thinking of by asking questions with the word *whisk*. For example:

Do you *whisk* every day?	[Yes.]
Do you *whisk* outdoors?	[No.]
Do you *whisk* in the morning?	[No.]
Do you *whisk* in the afternoon?	[No.]
Do you *whisk* in the evening?	[Yes.]
Do you *whisk* with friends?	[Yes. Sometimes.]
Do you *whisk* in the kitchen?	[No.]
Do you *whisk* in the living room?	[Yes.]

> [Answer: watch TV]

3 Chain Game: This Weekend
ACTIVITY HANDBOOK PAGES 2–3

Begin the chain as follows: "This weekend I'm going to watch TV," and have students continue it. For example:

> Teacher: This weekend I'm going to watch TV.
> Student 1: This weekend I'm going to watch TV and play cards.
> Student 2: This weekend I'm going to watch TV, play cards, and read a book.
> Etc.

4 Secret Word Associations
ACTIVITY HANDBOOK PAGE 14

Have students choose a leisure activity, brainstorm associations with that activity, and see if the class can guess the activity. For example:

pen/paper/envelope:	[write a letter]
e-mail/Internet/mouse:	[use the computer]
beach/pool/lake:	[swim]

5 Likes and Dislikes

a. Have students make two columns on a piece of paper. Tell them to label one column <u>I like to</u> and the other <u>I don't like to</u>.

b. Dictate leisure activities and have students write them in the appropriate column. For example:

<u>I like to</u>	<u>I don't like to</u>
play cards	practice the piano
watch TV	play basketball

c. In pairs, have students compare their responses and discuss what leisure activities they enjoy most.

6 What's the Object?
ACTIVITY HANDBOOK PAGE 16

Call out verbs and have students add appropriate objects. For example:

> watch . . . *TV/a movie/the news/people*
> play . . . *the guitar/the piano/the violin*
> read . . . *a book/the newspaper/a story*

7 Who Wrote This?

See instructions for Activity 7 on page 22. Example:

> I watch TV every afternoon.
> I don't like to exercise.
> I like to play cards.
> I play the guitar every day.

8 Guess What I Did Yesterday!

See instructions for Activity 8 on page 22. Example:

> A. Did you watch TV yesterday?
> B. No, I didn't.
> A. Did you read the newspaper yesterday?
> B. Yes, I did.
> A. Did you exercise yesterday?
> B. Yes, I did.
> A. Did you read the newspaper before you exercised?
> B. Yes, I did.

(continued)

9 Movable Categories
ACTIVITY HANDBOOK PAGE 11
ACTIVITY MASTER 16

Call out the following categories and have students go to the appropriate side of the room:

activities you do outdoors
activities you do in the house
activities you do in the morning
activities you do in the afternoon
activities you do in the evening
activities you do with friends
activities children do
activities adults do

10 Listen and Number
ACTIVITY HANDBOOK PAGE 10

In pairs, have one student make up a story using leisure activities and have the other student number the pictures in their order of occurrence in the story.

11 Interview: What Do You Do For Fun?
ACTIVITY MASTER 17

a. Duplicate the Leisure Activities Interview and give a copy to each student.

b. Divide the class into pairs and have students interview each other, using these questions as a guide.

c. Have the pairs report back to the class.

12 Daffy Debate!
ACTIVITY HANDBOOK PAGE 5
ACTIVITY MASTER 16

Have students debate which leisure activity is more educational, more relaxing, or healthier than the others.

LESSON OBJECTIVE

Students will learn common everyday expressions.

RESOURCES

AUDIO PROGRAM
Words & Dialogs
Cassette 1A
CD 1: Track 25

MULTI-LEVEL WORKBOOKS
Literacy Workbook
Beginning & Intermediate Lifeskills Workbooks
Beginning & Intermediate Vocabulary Workbooks

ACTIVITY MASTERS
Reproducibles:
A18, A19

TRANSPARENCIES
Overheads: T12, T13

LANGUAGE & CULTURE NOTES
Reproducible: LC12–13

WORDLINKS
longman.com/wordbyword

VOCABULARY INTRODUCTION

Preview

Brainstorm with students and write on the board expressions they know for greeting people, saying good-bye, introducing themselves and others, getting someone's attention, expressing gratitude, saying you don't understand, and calling someone on the telephone.

Present

Using the transparency or the illustrations on *Picture Dictionary* pages 12 and 13, point to each of the characters in the illustrations, say the word or phrase, and have the class repeat it chorally and individually. (You can also play the expressions on the Audio Program.) Check students' understanding and pronunciation of the expressions. Each time set the scene:

- 1: "These people are greeting each other."
- 2: "These people are at a bus stop."
- 3: "These people are walking their dogs in the park."
- 4: "It's evening, and this teacher is greeting his students."
- 5–6: "Two co-workers are greeting each other."
- 7–8: "Two students are talking in the cafeteria."
- 9: "Two co-workers are leaving work at the end of the day."
- 10: "These two people are coming home after a dance."
- 11: "These friends are leaving a restaurant."
- 12–14: "These are two new neighbors."
- 15: "A woman is introducing her husband to a friend."
- 16: "This young man needs to talk to his supervisor."
- 17: "This student wants to ask a question."

- 18–19: "A customer at a supermarket is thanking someone who is helping her."
- 20: "This office worker doesn't understand his supervisor's instructions."
- 21: "He wants her to say the instruction again."
- 22: "This boy is calling his girlfriend."
- 23: "His girlfriend is home."
- 24: "His girlfriend isn't home."

Practice

- Say an expression, and have students point to the character who says it.
- Point to a character, and have students tell what that person is saying.

SPELLING PRACTICE

Say an expression, and have students spell it aloud or write it. Or, using the transparency, point to a character in one of the scenes and have students write the expression.

Making Connections

Resource Materials Bring in, or have students bring in, the following materials for vocabulary practice:

- *Magazine pictures of people greeting one another, saying good-bye, making introductions, and making telephone calls:* Have students tell what they think the people are saying.

Community Task Tell students to pay attention to how people in their community greet one another and say good-bye—on the street, at work, and in public places. Have students report their observations to the class.

Communication Activities

1 Disappearing Dialogs
ACTIVITY HANDBOOK PAGE 5

Write one or more of the following dialogs on the board. For each dialog, gradually erase words and call on students to read the conversation. Continue erasing words until the dialog has *disappeared*.

> A. Hi. How are you?
> B. Fine, thanks. And you?
> A. Fine, thanks. What's new with you?
> B. Not much. And you?
> A. Not too much.

> A. Hello. My name is Ken.
> B. Hi. I'm Susan.
> A. Nice to meet you.
> B. Nice to meet you, too.

> A. I'd like to introduce my wife.
> B. Nice to meet you.
> C. Nice to meet you, too.

> A. Excuse me.
> B. Yes?
> A. May I ask a question?
> B. Sure.
> A. Is Mr. Park going to get here soon?
> B. Yes. Very soon.
> A. Thanks.
> B. You're welcome.

> A. Excuse me.
> B. Yes?
> A. May I ask a question?
> B. Sure.

2 Conversation Match Game
ACTIVITY HANDBOOK PAGE 11
ACTIVITY MASTER 18

Have students find the person whose card matches theirs.

3 Cultural Differences

a. Have students present introductions to the class in their own language. If possible, have students present introductions between men and men, women and women, and men and women.

b. Have the class observe the introductions. Tell students to note the following:

> Do they smile at each other?
> Do they shake hands or bow?
> Do they look directly at each other?
> How close to each other do they stand?

c. Have the class discuss their observations.

4 What's Wrong with the Conversation?
ACTIVITY MASTER 19

a. Divide the class into small groups.

b. Make a copy of Activity Master 19 for each group.

c. Tell students that there is something *wrong* with each of the conversations. Their task is to come up with a better version of each.

LESSON OBJECTIVE

Students will learn the vocabulary of different climate and weather conditions.

RESOURCES

AUDIO PROGRAM
Words & Dialogs
Cassette 1A
CD 1: Tracks 26, 27

MULTI-LEVEL WORKBOOKS
Literacy Workbook
Beginning & Intermediate Lifeskills Workbooks
Beginning & Intermediate Vocabulary Workbooks

VOCABULARY GAME CARDS
Cards 49–66

TRANSPARENCY
Overhead: T14

LANGUAGE & CULTURE NOTES
Reproducible: LC14

WORDLINKS
longman.com/wordbyword

VOCABULARY INTRODUCTION

- Preview
- Present
- Practice

MODEL CONVERSATION PRACTICE

There are three model conversations. Introduce and practice the first model before going on to the second and third. For each model:

1. Have students look at the model illustration. Set the scene:

   Model 1: "A husband and wife are talking."
   Model 2: "A husband and wife are talking."
   Model 3: "Someone is calling her friend who is on vacation."

2. Present the first model with word 1, the second model with word 14, and the third model with words 22 and 20.

3. Choral Repetition Practice: Full-Class and Individual.

4. Have pairs practice the model.

5. Have pairs present the model.

6. Call on pairs to present a new conversation using word 2 for the first model, word 15 for the second model, and words 23 and 21 for the third model.

7. Have pairs practice new conversations.

8. Have pairs present new conversations.

SPELLING PRACTICE

Say a word, and have students spell it aloud or write it. Or, using the transparency, point to an item and have students write the word.

WRITING AND DISCUSSION

Have students respond to the questions as a class, in pairs, or in small groups. Or have students write their responses, share their writing with other students, and discuss in class.

VOCABULARY GAME CARDS

Have students practice vocabulary, do activities, and play games with Vocabulary Game Cards 49–66. Activities and games are described in the set of cards.

Making Connections

Resource Materials Bring in, or have students bring in, the following materials for vocabulary practice:

- *The weather section of the newspaper:* Talk about the weather in different cities around the country and around the world.

- *Taped radio and TV weather forecasts:* Listen for how the forecasters describe the weather.

- *Magazine pictures depicting people and activities in various climatic conditions:* Talk about the weather and the activities.

Communication Activities

1 Tell a Story

Ask each student to choose one of the scenes on *Picture Dictionary* page 14 that depicts a weather word. Have students make up stories based on their scene, describing the situation and telling about what people are doing. As a class, in pairs, or in small groups, have students tell their stories.

Variation: Bring in pictures from magazines depicting different weather conditions and seasons, and have students make up their stories based on these pictures.

2 Read About the Weather

Make copies of weather maps and forecasts from the newspaper. Ask and answer questions about the predictions for different cities and regions of the country.

3 Suggestion Box

a. Write on the board:

Let's _____!
Let's not _____!

b. Tell what the weather is, and have students suggest what to do, or what not to do. For example:

> Teacher: It's sunny!
> Students: Let's go swimming!
> Let's go on a picnic!
> Let's not stay inside!
> Let's not go to English class!

4 Weather Websites

Have each student research a different city in the world on a weather website and report back what they learned.

5 What Did They Say?

Record the weather from the radio or TV, and have students listen and discuss what they hear.

6 Weather Talk!
ACTIVITY HANDBOOK PAGE 17

Have students choose a weather condition and think about it for a few minutes. Call on individual students to speak for one minute about their weather word.

7 Weather Role Play

Give pairs of students a piece of paper and ask them to write down two weather expressions and two unrelated verbs. Collect the papers and distribute them randomly to other pairs. Each pair then creates a dialog using the four words. Have the pairs present their dialogs to the class.

8 It's a Puzzle!
ACTIVITY HANDBOOK PAGE 9

Cut out pictures of weather conditions and create puzzles out of the pictures for students to identify and put together by asking questions. For example:

> My picture has lightning.
> My picture has a dust storm.
> Is it sunny in your picture?

9 How Do You Feel?

As a class, in pairs, or in small groups, have students discuss how certain weather conditions make them feel.

10 Mystery Word Association Game
ACTIVITY HANDBOOK PAGES 11–12

Have students write associations for weather *mystery words* for others to guess. For example:

> hot/dry/skin hurts/eyes hurt   [dust storm]
> electricity/thunder/bright   [lightning]
>   lights/scary

11 Telephone
ACTIVITY HANDBOOK PAGE 14

Begin the activity with the following sentence: "Sleet and freezing rain with temperatures in the low twenties."

12 Who Said It?

a. Give each student a piece of paper and ask them to write answers to the following four questions:

> What kind of weather do you like the most?
> What kind of weather do you like the least?
> What do you do when it's sunny?
> What do you do when it's raining?

b. Collect the papers, read each one, and see if the class can match the answers with the students who wrote them.

Unit 2 Communication Activity Review

1 Bleep!
ACTIVITY HANDBOOK PAGE 2
ACTIVITY MASTERS 7, 10, 16

Have students create conversations based on four word cards that they select.

2 Movable Categories
ACTIVITY HANDBOOK PAGE 11
ACTIVITY MASTERS 12, 14, 16

Place all the word cards in a bag. Have each student select two cards. Call out the following categories and have students go to the appropriate side of the room:

activities people do indoors
activities people do outdoors
activities people do every day
activities most people do only once a week
activities people do in the evening
activities people do in the morning
activities people do in the afternoon
activities that require electricity
learning activities

3 Miming Game
ACTIVITY HANDBOOK PAGE 11
ACTIVITY MASTERS 10, 12, 14, 16

Have students take turns pantomiming the activities. The class tries to guess what the person is doing. For example:

You're opening your book.
You're reading the newspaper.

4 Whisk!
ACTIVITY HANDBOOK PAGES 16–17
ACTIVITY MASTERS 10, 12, 14, 16

Have the class try to guess the card a student is holding by asking questions with the word *whisk*. For example:

Do you *whisk* every day?	[Yes.]
Do you *whisk* in the classroom?	[Yes.]
Do you *whisk* at home?	[Yes.]
Do you *whisk* food?	[No.]
Do you *whisk* with a friend?	[No.]
Do you *whisk* alone?	[Yes.]
Are you quiet when you *whisk*?	[Yes]
Do you like to *whisk*?	[Yes.]

[Answer: read]

5 Write About It!

a. Have students imagine an ideal vacation. Have them consider these questions:

Where are you going?
Who is going with you?
What are you going to do there?
What's the weather going to be?
Why is this your favorite place?

b. Have students share their writing in pairs.

6 Class Surveys: Vacations

a. Conduct a class survey, with each member of the class responsible for collecting specific information. Examples of questions you might want to have students ask each other:

When was the last time you took a vacation?
Where did you go?
What did you do?
How was the weather?
Do you recommend the place you visited?
Why or why not?

b. As a class, in pairs, or in small groups, have students tabulate the data in order to figure out the answers to these questions:

What time of year do most students take their vacations?
What is the most popular place to visit on vacation?
What is the most popular thing to do on vacation?
Which vacation places have the best weather?

7 Small Talk
ACTIVITY HANDBOOK PAGE 14
ACTIVITY MASTER 20

Give each pair of students a Small Talk Card and have them practice and prepare a role play based on that situation. After each role play, have the class discuss:

Where are they?
What are they doing?
What's the weather like?

Topics	Dictionary	Teacher's Guide
Numbers	15	35–37
Time	16	38–40
Money	17	41–43
The Calendar	18	44–46
Time Expressions and Seasons	19	47–48
Unit 3 Communication Activity Review	15–19	49

AUDIO PROGRAM

Words & Dialogs
Audio Cassette 1A
Audio Cassette 1B
Audio CD 1:
  Tracks 28–42

WordSong: *To Be With You*
Audio Cassette 7A
Audio CD 7: Tracks 20
  (Vocal) & 21 (Sing-along)
Song Masters S5, S6

WORKBOOKS

For Multi-Level Practice
Literacy Workbook
Beginning Lifeskills Workbook
Beginning Vocabulary Workbook
Intermediate Lifeskills Workbook
Intermediate Vocabulary Workbook

WORDLINKS

Internet Resources through the
***Word by Word* Companion Website**
http://www.longman.com/wordbyword

ACTIVITY MASTERS

Reproducibles for Communication Activities
A8, A21–A29

TRANSPARENCIES

Full-Color Overheads for Class Practice
T15–T19

LANGUAGE & CULTURE NOTES

**Information for Teachers &
Intermediate / Advanced Students**
LC15–LC19

Page 15 NUMBERS

LESSON OBJECTIVE

Students will learn cardinal and ordinal numbers.

RESOURCES

AUDIO PROGRAM	MULTI-LEVEL WORKBOOKS	ACTIVITY MASTER
Words & Dialogs Cassette 1A CD 1: Tracks 28–31	Literacy Workbook Beginning & Intermediate Lifeskills Workbooks Beginning & Intermediate Vocabulary Workbooks	**Reproducible:** A8
TRANSPARENCY Overhead: T15	**LANGUAGE & CULTURE NOTES** Reproducible: LC15	**WORDLINKS** longman.com/wordbyword

CARDINAL NUMBER INTRODUCTION

Preview

Activate students' prior knowledge of cardinal numbers by writing cardinal numerals consecutively on the board, starting with 1, and having students say the ones they know.

Present

Say each cardinal number consecutively, write the numeral on the board, and have the class repeat it chorally and individually. Check students' understanding and pronunciation of the numbers. (You can also play the word list on the Audio Program.)

Practice

As a class, in pairs, or in small groups, have students practice the cardinal numbers in either or both of the following ways:

- Say a cardinal number, and have students write the numeral.
- Write a numeral or a number in words and have students say it.

MODEL CONVERSATION PRACTICE

The first two model conversations in this lesson practice cardinal numbers. Introduce and practice the first model before going on to the second. For each model:

1. Have students look at the model illustration. Set the scene:
   - Model 1: "A grandmother and grandson are talking."
   - Model 2: "Two people on a date are talking."

2. Present the model using any number you wish.

3. Choral Repetition Practice: Full-Class and Individual.

4. Have pairs practice the model.

5. Have pairs present the model.

6. Call on pairs to present a new conversation using an appropriate number.

7. Have pairs practice new conversations.

8. Have pairs present new conversations.

ORDINAL NUMBER INTRODUCTION

Follow the same steps as you did for cardinal numbers.

- Preview
- Present
- Practice

MODEL CONVERSATION PRACTICE

The third and fourth model conversations in this lesson practice ordinal numbers. Follow the steps above for introducing and practicing the models.

- Model 3: "Two neighbors are talking."
- Model 4: "A cab driver is talking to a New York tourist."

SPELLING PRACTICE

Say a number, and have students spell it aloud or write it. Or, using the transparency, point to a number and have students write the word.

Have students respond to the questions as a class, in pairs, or in small groups. Or have students write their responses, share their writing with other students, and discuss in class.

Making Connections

Resource Materials Bring in, or have students bring in, the following materials for vocabulary practice:

● *Telephone book addresses and telephone numbers:* Practice saying the numbers.

● *Newspaper sports scores:* Tell the scores.

Community Task Have students compile a list of places in the community where they see numbers—for example: on street signs, building signs, buses, trains, clocks.

Communication Activities

1 Stand in Order
ACTIVITY HANDBOOK PAGE **14**

a. Give each student a card with a cardinal number written on it. The numbers shouldn't be in succession. Also, some should be omitted to make the activity more fun.

b. Have students say their numbers aloud and then arrange themselves in a line from the lowest to the highest number.

Variation 1: Do the activity with ordinal numbers.

Variation 2: Have students write the number of their street address and arrange themselves in a line accordingly.

2 Tic Tac Numbers
ACTIVITY MASTER **8**

a. Duplicate the Tic Tac Grid and give a copy to each student. Have students fill in the grid with any nine numbers from 1 to 50. For example:

7	16	4
25	8	37
11	42	9

b. Call out numbers from 1 to 50 in random order and tell students to cross out any number they hear that's on their grids.

c. The first person to cross out three numbers in a straight line—vertically, horizontally, or diagonally—wins the game.

Have the winner call out the numbers to check accuracy.

Variation: Have a student call out the numbers.

3 Number Line-up

a. Divide the class into groups of five students.

b. Give each student a card with a single digit cardinal number on it. One card must have the number zero. A possible set might be the numbers 0, 1, 2, 3, and 4.

c. Call out large and small numbers, and have students arrange themselves into the number. For example:

20	3021
201	43,021
120	30,214
1203	

4 Listening Practice

Dictate similar-sounding numbers and have students write the number they hear. For example:

third/thirty	nineteen/ninety
thirteen/thirty	sixteenth/sixtieth
fourteen/forty	seventeenth/seventieth
fifteen/fifty	eighteenth/eightieth
sixteen/sixty	nineteen/ninetieth
seventeen/seventy	twenty/twentieth
eighteen/eighty	sixty-six/sixth-sixth

(continued)

5 Buzz

a. Choose a cardinal number from 1 to 9 as the *buzz* number (e.g., 5).

b. Have students count consecutively, beginning with the number 1. Any time a number comes up that contains 5 or a multiple of 5, the student says "buzz" instead of that number. For example:

   1, 2, 3, 4, buzz, 6, 7, 8, 9, buzz, 11, 12, 13, 14, buzz . . .

6 Before and After

Call out two cardinal numbers such as 33 and 59. Students must say "33 comes before 59" or "59 comes after 33."

Variation: Do the activity with ordinal numbers. Also, students can take turns calling out numbers.

7 Necessary Numbers

a. Brainstorm with students and write on the board the types of numbers that are important in people's everyday lives. For example:

   telephone number
   street number
   apartment number
   emergency contact telephone number
   police phone number
   fire department number
   ages of family members
   important dates such as birthdays and
      anniversaries
   doctor's telephone number
   local directory assistance
   social security number
   passport or visa number
   credit card number
   car license number

b. Have students make a list of the numbers that apply to them personally.

8 Important Numbers in My Life

Have individual students come to the board and write a number that is important in their lives. The other students then guess why the number is important.

9 Who Sits Where?

a. If students sit in rows in your classroom, draw a blank seating chart on the board. Then ask questions about where people are sitting and write in students' names. For example:

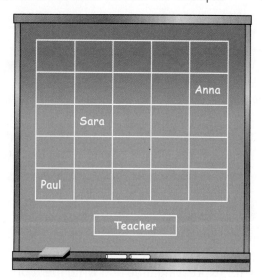

   Who is in the first seat in the first row?
      [Paul]
   Who is in the third seat in the second row?
      [Sara]
   Who is in the fourth seat in the fifth row?
      [Anna]

b. After the chart is completed, you can ask questions such as:

   Where is Paul sitting?
   [He's in the first seat in the first row.]
   Where is Sara sitting?
   [She's in the third seat in the second row.]
   Where is Anna sitting?
   [She's in the fourth seat in the fifth row.]

10 Who Was First?

Have students recall who walked into class first, second, and third, etc.

11 Silly Numbers

Have students make up silly phrases using a number, an adjective, and a noun with the same initial sound. For example:

   two tired teachers
   three thirsty things
   five filthy frogs

Variation: Do this activity as a *chain game* in which each student repeats everything that has come before and then adds his or her own silly phrase.

LESSON OBJECTIVE

Students will learn ways of telling time.

RESOURCES

AUDIO PROGRAM

Words & Dialogs
Cassette 1A
CD 1: Tracks 32–35

MULTI-LEVEL WORKBOOKS

Literacy Workbook
Beginning & Intermediate Lifeskills Workbooks
Beginning & Intermediate Vocabulary Workbooks

ACTIVITY MASTERS

Reproducibles:
A21, A22

TRANSPARENCY
Overhead: T16

LANGUAGE & CULTURE NOTES
Reproducible: LC16

WORDLINKS
longman.com/wordbyword

THE VOCABULARY FOR TELLING TIME

Preview

Brainstorm with students words they already know for expressing time and write them on the board. Then have students look at the illustrations at the top of *Picture Dictionary* page 16 and identify the time expressions they already know.

Present

If you feel your students need the practice, review the cardinal numbers from 1 to 60. (See *Picture Dictionary* page 15.) Then draw a large clock face on the board or make one out of a paper plate with movable hands for displaying the time. Practice telling time by the hour. As you point to the numbers on the clock, say: *It's one o'clock. It's two o'clock.* Have students repeat each time expression chorally and individually. Using the same approach as above, introduce time expressions for the quarter and half hours and minute expressions from *oh one* to *fifty-nine*.

Using the illustrations at the top of *Picture Dictionary* page 16, point to the picture, say the time expression, and have the class repeat it chorally and individually. Check students' understanding and pronunciation of the vocabulary. (You can also play the word list on the Audio Program.)

MODEL CONVERSATION PRACTICE

The first two model conversations are for telling time. Introduce and practice the first model before going on to the second. For each model:

1. Have students look at the model illustration. Set the scene:

Model 1: "Two people at a bus stop are talking."

Model 2: "Two strangers are talking in front of a movie theater."

2. Present the first model with *two o'clock* and the second model with *two fifteen*.

3. Choral Repetition Practice: Full-Class and Individual.

4. Have pairs practice the model.

5. Have pairs present the model.

6. Call on pairs to present a new conversation using an appropriate time expression.

7. Have pairs practice new conversations.

8. Have pairs present new conversations.

A.M., P.M., NOON, AND MIDNIGHT

Preview
(See above.)

Present

Teach *noon* and *midnight*. Explain that from midnight until noon is A.M. Set a clock face and give a few examples. Explain that from noon to midnight is P.M. Set a clock face and give a few examples.

MODEL CONVERSATION PRACTICE

The third and fourth model conversations practice A.M., P.M., *noon,* and *midnight*. Follow the steps above for introducing and practicing the models. Present the third model with *two P.M.* and the fourth model with *noon*.

Model 3: "A man is talking to someone at the ticket counter of a train station."

Model 4: "A passenger is talking to a flight
attendant on an airplane."

SPELLING PRACTICE

● Say a time expression, and have students write
the numbers.
● Say a time expression, and have students write
the words.

WRITING AND DISCUSSION

Have students respond to the questions as
a class, in pairs, or in small groups. Or have
students write their responses, share their writing
with other students, and discuss in class.

Making Connections

Resource Materials Bring in, or have students bring
in, the following materials for vocabulary practice:

○ *Movie listings in the newspaper:* Talk about the
movie schedule.

○ *Television listings in the newspaper:* Talk about
the times students' favorite programs are on TV.

○ *Train, plane, and bus schedules:* Talk about the
arrival and departure times of the trains, planes,
and buses.

○ *A map depicting different time zones:* Compare
the time in different time zones.

Communication Activities

1 Listen and Draw
ACTIVITY MASTER 21

a. Duplicate the Clock Times and give a copy to each
student.

b. Call out times, and have students draw the hands
on their *clocks*.

c. Have pairs check each other's clocks and compare
answers.

2 Find the Right Person!
ACTIVITY HANDBOOK PAGES 6–7
ACTIVITY MASTER 22

Practice the following questions before having
students do the activity:

Do you get up before 6:00 A.M.?
Do you go to bed after midnight?
Do you get up early on Sunday mornings?
Do you watch TV in the morning?
Are you usually late for English class?
Are you always on time for appointments?

When a student gets a *yes* answer to a question, have
that student ask for more information. For example:

A. Do you get up before 6:00 A.M.?
B. Yes, I do.
A. When do you get up?
B. At 5:30.

3 Time Around the World

a. Have students look at *Picture Dictionary* page 172.

b. Practice talking about what time it is in various
places. For example:

A. It's 3:00 p.m. here. What time is it in London?
B. It's 9:00 p.m.
A. It's now 11:00 a.m. Wednesday. What time is it in
Tokyo?
B. It's 1:00 A.M. Thursday.

4 Discussion: Early, Late, or On Time?

a. Write the following events and start times on the
board:

Work	9:00
A job interview	10:30
A lunch date	12:00
A train	8:10
A party	8:00
A wedding	2:00
A concert	8:00
English class	2:00
A date	8:00
A sports game	7:30
A meeting with a teacher	2:30
A doctor's appointment	10:00
A business appointment	11:30

(continued)

b. As a class, in pairs, or in small groups, have students discuss what time a person should arrive for each of these events. Have students give reasons for their answers.

c. Ask students:

What time is too early to arrive?
What time is too late to arrive?

5 Time Expressions

a. Write the following expressions on the board:

to save time	to run out of time
to spend time	to have time to spare
to waste time	to watch the clock
to kill time	to work around the clock
to lose time	to work against the clock
to make up for lost time	

b. Discuss the meanings of these expressions, and ask students to write *true* statements about themselves using each of these expressions.

c. Write the following expressions on the board:

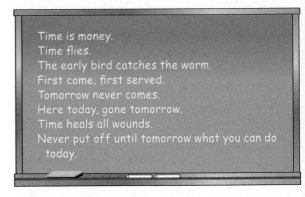

Time is money.
Time flies.
The early bird catches the worm.
First come, first served.
Tomorrow never comes.
Here today, gone tomorrow.
Time heals all wounds.
Never put off until tomorrow what you can do today.

d. As a class, in pairs, or in small groups, discuss what these expressions mean.

e. Have students tell expressions dealing with time in their culture and compare them with the ones above.

LESSON OBJECTIVE

Students will learn various denominations of money and their names.

RESOURCES

AUDIO PROGRAM
Words & Dialogs
Cassette 1A
CD 1: Tracks 36–39

MULTI-LEVEL WORKBOOKS

Literacy Workbook
Beginning & Intermediate Lifeskills Workbooks
Beginning & Intermediate Vocabulary Workbooks

ACTIVITY MASTER
Reproducible:
A23

TRANSPARENCY
Overhead: T17

LANGUAGE & CULTURE NOTES
Reproducible: LC17

WORDLINKS
longman.com/wordbyword

COIN VOCABULARY INTRODUCTION

- Preview
- Present
- Practice

MODEL CONVERSATION PRACTICE

The first two model conversations practice coins. Introduce and practice the first model before going on to the second. For each model:

1. Have students look at the model illustration. Set the scene:

   Model 1: "A young child is talking to her mother."

   Model 2: "Two co-workers are talking at a vending machine."

2. Present the model.

3. Choral Repetition Practice: Full-Class and Individual.

4. Have pairs practice the model.

5. Have pairs present the model.

6. Call on pairs to present a new conversation using an appropriate number.

7. Have pairs practice new conversations.

8. Have pairs present new conversations.

CURRENCY VOCABULARY INTRODUCTION

Follow the same steps as you did for the coins.

- Preview
- Presentation
- Practice

MODEL CONVERSATION PRACTICE

The third and fourth model conversations in this lesson practice currency. Follow the steps above for introducing and practicing the models.

   Model 3: "A husband is talking to his wife as he leaves to go to the supermarket."

   Model 4: "A customer is talking to a cashier in a store."

SPELLING PRACTICE

Say a word, and have students spell it aloud or write it. Or, using the transparency, point to an item and have students write the word.

WRITING AND DISCUSSION

Have students respond to the questions as a class, in pairs, or in small groups. Or have students write their responses, share their writing with other students, and discuss in class.

Resource Materials Bring in, or have students bring in, the following materials for vocabulary practice:

○ *Real currency from the United States and different countries:* Talk about the currency names and values.

○ *Newspaper advertisements for various products with their prices:* Talk about the prices of the items.

○ *The monetary exchange rates printed in the newspaper:* Compare exchange rates for different currencies.

Community Task Have individual students (or groups of students) visit different types of stores and report about the prices of items.

Communication Activities

1 **What's in the Bag?**

Put some real coins in a paper bag. Have one student at a time reach into the bag, pick up a coin, and identify it without looking at it.

Variation: This activity may also be done as a game with teams competing against each other to see how many players identify the coins correctly.

2 **Making Change**

a. Divide the class into small groups.

b. Write several money amounts on the board.

c. Have students break down the amount into change in as many ways as possible. For example:

    $1.25   5 quarters
              12 dimes and 1 nickel
              2 half dollars and 1 quarter
              Etc.

3 **Money Line-up**

a. Divide the class into groups of seven.

b. Give each student a card with a single-digit cardinal number on it, or a decimal point, or the dollar sign ($). One card must have the number zero. A possible set might be:
$, ., 0, 1, 2, 3, 4.

c. Call out large and small money quantities, and have students arrange themselves into the amount. For example:

    $20.43 $120 $30.21
    $201.34 $1203 $302.14

4 **Money Match Game**

ACTIVITY HANDBOOK PAGE 11
ACTIVITY MASTER 23

Have students find their *money match.*

5 **Money Game: What's the Total?**

a. Make some *play* bills and coins and put them into several envelopes. Number the envelopes and put them on your desk.

b. Divide the class into several teams. Tell a member of each team to come up to your desk and take an envelope.

c. The students in each team then take the *money* out of their envelope, add it up, write the number of the envelope and the amount of money on a separate sheet, return the envelope, and pick up another.

d. The first team to add up the money in all the envelopes and have the correct total wins the game.

6 **Tic Tac Change**

a. On the board, make a grid with nine spaces and write an amount of money in each. For example:

$1.49	$5.75	$4.33
$.49	$27.55	$42.86
$21.06	$51.10	$99.99

b. Divide the class into two teams, Team X and Team O.

c. A student from Team X chooses a space and breaks down that amount of money into the *fewest* coins and bills possible. The class decides whether the student is correct. If he or she is correct, an X goes into that space.

d. A student from Team O chooses a space and does the same.

e. The first team to get three correct answers—either diagonally, horizontally, or vertically—wins the game.

7 What Coins Do I Need?

a. Brainstorm with the class things that require the use of coins. Write the list on the board. For example:

vending machines that sell drinks
vending machines that sell snacks
washers and dryers in laundromats
vending machines that sell gum and candy
stamp machines
newspaper vending boxes
public telephones
parking meters

b. Have students do *field research* by finding out what coins are needed for each of these items and then report their findings back to the class.

8 Investigate Money Around the World

a. Ask students what money denominations they know from different countries around the world. Write the names on the board.

b. Have each student chose one denomination to investigate. Students can visit the website www.x-rates.com to find exchange rates of any currency and look at photos of each currency.

9 Money Security

a. Discuss how governments makes money secure so that people cannot copy it and make counterfeit money. Show the class a money bill and ask:

Can I copy this bill and use it in a store? Why not?
What is special about the bill?
How do you know if the bill is real?

b. Have students investigate how the U.S. government makes its money secure. Have them visit the website of the United States Mint (www.moneyfactory.com) or the Federal Reserve Bank (www.phil.frb.org/consumers/money.html) and report back to the class.

LESSON OBJECTIVE

Students will learn how to express years, months, days, and dates.

RESOURCES

AUDIO PROGRAM

Words & Dialogs
Cassette 1B
CD 1: Tracks 40, 41

WordSong: *To Be With You*
Cassette 7A • CD 7: Tracks 21, 22
Song Masters S5, S6

MULTI-LEVEL WORKBOOKS

Literacy Workbook
Beginning & Intermediate Lifeskills Workbooks
Beginning & Intermediate Vocabulary Workbooks

ACTIVITY MASTERS

Reproducibles:
A24, A25

TRANSPARENCY
Overhead: T18

LANGUAGE & CULTURE NOTES
Reproducible: LC18

WORDLINKS
longman.com/wordbyword

VOCABULARY INTRODUCTION

- Preview
- Present
- Practice

MODEL CONVERSATION PRACTICE

There are five model conversations. Introduce and practice the first model before going on to the others. For each model:

1. Have students look at the model illustration. Set the scene:

   Model 1: "This person isn't sure about the year."
   Model 2: "This person isn't sure about the month."
   Model 3: "This person isn't sure about the day of the week."
   Model 4: "This person doesn't know today's date."
   Model 5: "This person is asking about a birthday, anniversary, or appointment."

2. Present the model using an appropriate year, month, day, date, and event.

   Model 1 is about years (students supply the words).
   Model 2 is about months of the year (words 13–24).
   Model 3 is about days of the week (words 6–12).
   Model 4 is about calendar dates (students supply the words).
   Model 5 is about special events (words 26–28).

3. Choral Repetition Practice: Full-Class and Individual.

4. Have pairs practice the model.

5. Have pairs present the model.

6. Call on pairs to present a new conversation using a different word.

7. Have pairs practice new conversations.

8. Have pairs present new conversations.

SPELLING PRACTICE

Say a word, and have students spell it aloud or write it. Or, using the transparency, point to an item and have students write the word. Then say dates and have students write the dates in numbers and words (e.g., 8/15/09 and August 15, 2009).

WRITING AND DISCUSSION

Have students respond to the questions as a class, in pairs, or in small groups. Or have students write their responses, share their writing with other students, and discuss in class.

♫♫ WORDSONG ♫♫

1. Have students listen to the vocal version of *To Be With You* one or more times. Then have students listen again as they read the song lyrics on Song Master S5.

2. Have students sing as you play either the vocal or the sing-along version of the song.

3. For fun, have a song competition in which students perform solo or in groups and the class votes for the best performance.

4. For additional practice, students can complete the cloze exercise on Song Master S6.

Making Connections

Resource Materials Bring in, or have students bring in, the following materials for vocabulary practice:

○ *Calendars from different years:* Talk about days and dates on the calendars.

○ *History book of famous dates:* Identify dates of important events in history.

○ *Astrology predictions:* Talk about predictions for different days.

Communication Activities

1 What's the Day?

Ask questions about days. For example:

What's the day today?
What day was yesterday?
What will the day be tomorrow?
What day is the day after tomorrow?
What day was the day before yesterday?
What day will it be three days from now?

2 What's the Date?

Ask questions about dates. For example:

What's the date today?
What was yesterday's date?
What will the date be tomorrow?
What was the date two days ago?

3 Before, After, and Between

Have students complete phrases such as

September is before _____.
August is after _____.
April is between _____ and _____.
Thursday is after _____.
Sunday is before _____.
Friday is between _____ and _____.

4 What's the Question?
ACTIVITY HANDBOOK PAGE 16

a. Put on the board:

> How many _____s are there in a _____?

b. Give the following answers, and have students come up with the appropriate questions. For example:

7   [How many days are there in a week?]
12   [How many months are there in a year?]
52   [How many weeks are there in a year?]

365   [How many days are there in a year?]
30, 31, or 29   [How many days are there in a month?]
24   [How many hours are there in a day?]

5 Stand in Line
ACTIVITY MASTER 24

Variation 1: Make a copy of the Month Word Cards, cut it up, and distribute the cards randomly to students. Have them line themselves up chronologically starting from January.

Variation 2: Have students arrange themselves in a line according to their birth dates (month and day only). They will need to ask and answer questions in order to line themselves up chronologically from January 1st through December 31st.

6 Months of the Year Run

a. Divide the class into teams of four students each and give each team a marker or piece of chalk.

b. Have the team stand at least five feet from the board. Have one student from each team run up to the board, write the month *January,* and return to the group.

c. The next team member runs to the board and writes the month *February.*

There can only be one member of each team at the board at one time. The first team that writes all the months of the year in correct order and form wins.

Variation 1: Have students do the activity with days of the week.

Variation 2: Have students do the activity with the abbreviated forms of the months or the days of the week.

(continued)

7 Monthly Schedules

ACTIVITY MASTER 25

a. Fill in the Calendar with the correct dates for this month, duplicate it, and give a copy to each student.

b. Tell students to write down for each day of the month what they did and what they will be doing—appointments, plans, activities, or events in their lives.

c. Have students ask and answer questions about their schedule for the month. For example:

A. What will you be doing on _____?
B. I'll be working.

A. Are you busy on _____?
B. Yes. I have a doctor's appointment.

You should also ask about holidays and students' birthdays during the month.

8 My Favorite Day

a. Have pairs of students discuss their favorite day of the year.

What day is your favorite day? (Is it a holiday, a birthday, or another special day?)
What do you do on this day?
Why is it your favorite day?

b. Have students report back to the class about the person they interviewed.

9 Monthly Expressions

a. Write these expressions on the board or on a handout:

March comes in like a lion and goes out like a lamb.
April showers bring May flowers.
The dog days of August.

b. Ask students what they think these mean and if there are any similar or other expressions in their languages about months of the year.

c. Tell students the following common way of remembering the number of days in each month:

Thirty days has September,
April, June, and November.
All the rest have thirty-one,
Except for February, which has twenty-eight.

d. Ask what ways different cultures and languages have for remembering the number of days in a month.

10 Investigate Calendars from Around the World

a. Have students go to www.world-calendar.com. This website allows students to view a holiday calendar of any country.

b. Tell each student to double-click on a country and choose five holidays that they think the class would find interesting. For each of these holidays, have them write the name, the date, and a brief description of the holiday.

c. Have students report their findings to the class.

LESSON OBJECTIVE

Students will learn the vocabulary of times of day, time expressions, and the four seasons.

RESOURCES

AUDIO PROGRAM

Words & Dialogs
Cassette 1B
CD 1: Track 42

WordSong: *To Be With You*
Cassette 7A • CD 7: Tracks 20, 21
Song Masters S5, S6

MULTI-LEVEL WORKBOOKS

Literacy Workbook
Beginning & Intermediate Lifeskills Workbooks
Beginning & Intermediate Vocabulary Workbooks

ACTIVITY MASTERS

Reproducibles:
A26, A27

TRANSPARENCY

Overhead: T19

LANGUAGE & CULTURE NOTES

Reproducible: LC19

WORDLINKS

longman.com/wordbyword

VOCABULARY INTRODUCTION

- Preview
- Present
- Practice

SPELLING PRACTICE

Say a word or phrase, and have students spell it aloud or write it. Or, using the transparency or a calendar, point to an item and have students write the word or phrase.

WRITING AND DISCUSSION

Contrast the simple past tense—used to talk about *yesterday/last week*—with the future *going to*—used to talk about *tomorrow/next week*. Remind the class that the simple present tense is used to talk about daily habits and routines (*I go to the supermarket once a week*).

Have students respond to the questions as a class, in pairs, or in small groups. Or have students write their responses, share their writing with other students, and discuss in class.

Making Connections

Resource Materials Bring in, or have students bring in, the following materials for vocabulary practice:

- *Calendars or personal agendas:* Talk about plans or events on different days.

- *Magazine pictures depicting people and activities in various seasons:* Talk about the seasons and what people are doing.

Communication Activities

1 Category Dictation
ACTIVITY HANDBOOK PAGE 2

Dictate clock times that fit into the categories morning/afternoon/evening/night. For example:

five fifteen A.M.	[morning]
six forty-five P.M.	[evening]
twenty to three P.M.	[afternoon]
a quarter past 12 A.M.	[night]

2 Information Gap: Wendy's Weekend
ACTIVITY MASTER 26

a. Divide the class into pairs.

b. Before doing the activity, write times such as the following on the board, model for students how to express them, and have students practice saying them.

9:00	at nine o'clock
3:30	at three thirty
10:00–1:00	from ten o'clock to one o'clock
3:00–5:30	from three o'clock to five thirty

c. Make copies of the schedules in Activity Master 27. Cut them in half and give one member of the pair Schedule A and the other, Schedule B.

d. Have students ask each other about the missing information and fill in their schedules. For example:

Student A: What did Wendy do last night?
Student B: She had dinner with friends at seven o'clock. She arrived home and watched TV at nine o'clock.

Student B: What's Wendy going to do this morning?
Student A: She's going to clean the apartment and do the laundry from eight thirty to twelve thirty.

e. The pairs continue until both have filled in their schedules.

f. Have students look at their partner's schedule to make sure that they have written the information correctly.

3 Seasonal Activities

Have groups of students make a list of all the activities they can think of that are appropriate for each season. Compare the lists.

4 Find the Right Person!
ACTIVITY HANDBOOK PAGES 6–7
ACTIVITY MASTER 27

Before doing the activity, practice questions in the past, simple present, and future: *going to*. Model the following questions and have students repeat:

Did you clean?	Do you walk?
Did you watch TV?	Do you exercise?
Did you use . . . ?	Do you like . . . ?
Did you get home?	Are you going to see . . . ?
Do you cook?	Are you going to go . . . ?

Unit 3 Communication Activity Review

1 Who Wrote It?

a. Give each student a piece of paper and ask them to write answers to these three questions:

> What is your favorite season? Why?
> What is your favorite time of day? Why?
> What is your favorite day of the week? Why?

b. Collect the papers, read each one, and see if the class can match the answers with the students who wrote them.

2 Information Gap: Bus Schedules
ACTIVITY MASTER 28

a. Divide the class into pairs.

b. Make copies of the schedules in Activity Master 29. Cut them in half and give one member of the pair Schedule A and the other, Schedule B.

c. Have students ask each other questions such as the following and fill in their copy of the schedule accordingly.

> How many buses are there on Tuesday morning? What time do they leave?

> How many buses are there on Friday afternoon? What time do they leave?

d. When students have completely filled in their schedules, have them look at their partner's schedule to make sure that they have written the information correctly.

e. Finally, have them work together to answer the questions at the bottom of their copies of the Activity Master. (Each student has different questions, so they need to work together to complete the information.)

3 Daily Activities
ACTIVITY MASTER 29

a. Divide the class into small groups.

b. Give each group a copy of Activity Master 29.

c. Have students work together to make a list of activities people often do at those times.

d. Have the groups share their list of activities with the class.

4 True or False?
ACTIVITY HANDBOOK PAGE 15

Make statements such as the following, and have students decide whether the statements are true or false. For example:

> March is the third month of the year.
>   [True.]
> October is the ninth month of the year.
>   [False. It's the tenth month of the year.]
> Wednesday is on the weekend.
>   [False. Wednesday is a weekday.]
> This date is correct—December two, two thousand and nine.
>   [False. It should be December second, two thousand and nine.]
> This date is correct—July three, one thousand nine hundred and ninety-nine.
>   [False. It should be July third, nineteen-ninety-nine.]
> 6:30 A.M. is in the evening.
>   [False. It's in the morning.]
> 2:45 P.M. is in the afternoon.
>   [True.]
> In the United States the three winter months are June, July, and August.
>   [False. The three winter months are December, January, and February.]
> Last year was [2009].
> Yesterday was [Monday].
> Next month is [November].

UNIT 4 Home

TOPICS	DICTIONARY	TEACHER'S GUIDE
Types of Housing and Communities	20	51–52
The Living Room	21	53–55
The Dining Room	22	56–58
The Bedroom	23	59–61
The Kitchen	24	62–65
The Baby's Room	25	66–67
The Bathroom	26	68–70
Outside the Home	27	71–72
The Apartment Building	28–29	73–74
Household Problems and Repairs	30–31	75–77
Cleaning Your Home	32	78–79
Home Supplies	33	80–82
Tools and Hardware	34	83–84
Gardening Tools and Actions	35	85–87
Unit 4 Communication Activity Review	20–35	88

AUDIO PROGRAM

Words & Dialogs
Audio Cassette 1B
Audio Cassette 2A
Audio CD 1:
  Tracks 43–66
Audio CD 2:
  Tracks 2–19

WordSong: *In My House*
Audio Cassette 7A
Audio CD 7: Tracks 22
  (Vocal) & 23 (Sing-along)
Song Masters S7, S8

WORKBOOKS

For Multi-Level Practice
Literacy Workbook
Beginning Lifeskills Workbook
Beginning Vocabulary Workbook
Intermediate Lifeskills Workbook
Intermediate Vocabulary Workbook

WORDLINKS

**Internet Resources through the
Word by Word Companion Website**
http://www.longman.com/wordbyword

ACTIVITY MASTERS

Reproducibles for Communication Activities
A8, A30–A51

TRANSPARENCIES

Full-Color Overheads for Class Practice
T20–T35

LANGUAGE & CULTURE NOTES

**Information for Teachers &
Intermediate / Advanced Students**
LC20–LC35

LESSON OBJECTIVE

Students will learn the vocabulary of different types of housing and communities.

RESOURCES

AUDIO PROGRAM

Words & Dialogs
Cassette 1B
CD 1: Tracks 43–45

MULTI-LEVEL WORKBOOKS

Literacy Workbook
Beginning & Intermediate Lifeskills Workbooks
Beginning & Intermediate Vocabulary Workbooks

TRANSPARENCY
Overhead: T20

LANGUAGE & CULTURE NOTES
Reproducible: LC20

WORDLINKS
longman.com/wordbyword

VOCABULARY INTRODUCTION

- Preview
- Present
- Practice

MODEL CONVERSATION PRACTICE

1. Have students look at the model illustration. Set the scene: "Two friends are talking at a health club."
2. Present the model with words 1, 10, and 13.
3. Choral Repetition Practice: Full-Class and Individual.
4. Have pairs practice the model.
5. Have pairs present the model.
6. Call on pairs to present a new conversation using words 2, 11, and 14.
7. Have pairs practice new conversations.
8. Have pairs present new conversations.

ADDITIONAL CONVERSATION PRACTICE

Before students practice the additional conversations, you may want to have them listen to the examples on the Audio Program.

Conversation 1 Set the scene: "Someone is calling for a taxi." Have students practice and present conversations with any words from 1–12 they wish.

Conversation 2 Set the scene: "Someone is calling the Emergency Operator." Have students practice and present conversations with any words from 1–12 they wish.

SPELLING PRACTICE

Say a word, and have students spell it aloud or write it. Or, using the transparency, point to an item and have students write the word.

WRITING AND DISCUSSION

Have students respond to the questions as a class, in pairs, or in small groups. Or have students write their responses, share their writing with other students, and discuss in class.

Making Connections

Resource Materials Bring in, or have students bring in, the following materials for vocabulary practice:

- *Housing magazines:* Talk about the different types of homes depicted in the magazines.

- *The "Home" section of newspapers:* Talk about types of homes and home prices.

Community Task Have individual students (or groups of students) visit different communities and report about the types of homes they saw.

Communication Activities

1 Housing Associations
ACTIVITY HANDBOOK PAGE 2

Call out housing words and have groups write down as many associations as they can think of. For example:

apartment: [elevator/superintendent/rent/ balcony]

dormitory: [college/students/roommate]

2 Secret Word Associations
ACTIVITY HANDBOOK PAGE 14

Have students choose an item from the lesson, brainstorm associations with that word, and see if the class can guess the word. For example:

animals/garden/the country: [farm]
students/university/cafeteria: [dormitory]
river/fishing/small: [houseboat]
tall buildings/traffic/buses: [the city]

3 Housing Talk!
ACTIVITY HANDBOOK PAGE 17

Have each student choose, or assign to each student, a different type of housing or community. Have students think about their word for a few minutes. Call on individual students to speak for one minute about their word.

4 Tell Me a Story

Have each student choose a type of housing or community and make up a story about what it's like to live there. As students tell their stories to the class, have others ask them questions about what it's like to live there.

5 For Rent! For Sale!

a. Cut out newspaper advertisements for rentals or sales of different types of housing—houses, apartments, townhouses, duplexes, etc.

b. As a class, in pairs, or in small groups, have students compare prices in different communities for these different types of housing.

c. If you wish, you can have students create role plays where they make telephone calls about renting or buying these places.

6 Housing Histories

a. Have student make three columns on a piece of paper and write <u>Type of House</u>, <u>Where</u>, and <u>When</u> at the top of each column.

b. In the first column, have students write the type of house they lived in; in the second column, where this house was; and in the third column, when they lived there. For example:

Type of House	Where	When
farm	Mato Groso Do Sol, Brazil	1979–1987
townhouse	São Paulo, Brazil	1987–1996
apartment	Chicago, Illinois	1997–2004
house	Evanston, Illinois	2005–now

7 Be an Observer!

Have students tour their neighborhoods, note the types of housing they find, and then report back to the class.

8 Debate: Which Type of Housing Is Best?

a. Ask for two student volunteers.

b. Have each choose a different type of housing or community and then debate in front of the class why they think it's the best place to live.

c. The other students can then decide who they thought was the most persuasive.

d. Have other volunteers debate other types of housing.

9 Real Estate Role Play

a. Collect pictures of different types of housing.

b. Give half of the students several pictures apiece. These students are *real estate agents*.

c. The other half of the class are people looking for places to live. Each of these people *visits* a real estate agent, who tries to rent or sell the properties for which they have the pictures.

LESSON OBJECTIVE

Students will learn the vocabulary of items found in a living room.

RESOURCES

AUDIO PROGRAM		MULTI-LEVEL WORKBOOKS	ACTIVITY MASTER
Words & Dialogs	**WordSong:** *In My House*	Literacy Workbook	
Cassette 1B	Cassette 7A • CD 7: Tracks 22, 23	Beginning & Intermediate Lifeskills Workbooks	**Reproducible:** A30
CD 1: Tracks 46–48	Song Masters S7, S8	Beginning & Intermediate Vocabulary Workbooks	

TRANSPARENCY	LANGUAGE & CULTURE NOTES	WORDLINKS
Overhead: T21	**Reproducible:** LC21	longman.com/wordbyword

VOCABULARY INTRODUCTION

- Preview
- Present
- Practice

MODEL CONVERSATION PRACTICE

1. Have students look at the model illustration. Set the scene: "A wife is looking for her husband."
2. Present the model.
3. Choral Repetition Practice: Full-Class and Individual.
4. Have pairs practice the model.
5. Have pairs present the model.
6. Call on pairs to present a new conversation using word 2.
7. Have pairs practice new conversations.
8. Have pairs present new conversations.

ADDITIONAL CONVERSATION PRACTICE

Before students practice the additional conversations, you may want to have them listen to the examples on the Audio Program.

Conversation 1 Set the scene: "Someone is complimenting another person." Have students practice and present conversations with any words they wish.

Conversation 2 Set the scene: "Someone has just spilled something." Have students practice and present conversations with any words they wish.

SPELLING PRACTICE

Say a word, and have students spell it aloud or write it. Or, using the transparency, point to an item and have students write the word.

WRITING AND DISCUSSION

Have students respond to the question as a class, in pairs, or in small groups. Or have students write their responses, share their writing with other students, and discuss in class.

♫♫ WordSong ♫♫

1. Have students listen to the vocal version of *In My House* one or more times. Then have students listen again as they read the song lyrics on Song Master S7.
2. Have students sing as you play either the vocal or the sing-along version of the song.
3. For fun, have a song competition in which students perform solo or in groups and the class votes for the best performance.
4. For additional practice, students can complete the cloze exercise on Song Master S8.

Resource Materials Bring in, or have students bring in, the following materials for vocabulary practice:

- *Home decorating magazines:* Talk about living rooms and furniture arrangements depicted in the magazines.

- *Newspaper and magazine advertisements for living room furniture:* Talk about the advertised furniture items and their prices.

Community Task Have individual students (or groups of students) visit different furniture stores and report about the living room furniture these stores sell and the prices.

Communication Activities

Expand the Conversation
ACTIVITY HANDBOOK PAGE 6

Expand Additional Conversation 1 to compliment other living room items.

a. Write the following on the board:

> A. You have a very nice living room!
> B. Thank you.
> A. Your _____ is/are beautiful!
> B. Thank you for saying so.
> A. And I really like your _____.
> B. I'm glad you like it.
> A. And your _____ is also very beautiful.
> B. Thanks very much.

b. Have pairs of students practice and present conversations based on this model, using different words from the page.

Location! Location!
ACTIVITY HANDBOOK PAGES 10–11

If you choose to do Version 1, ask questions such as the following:

Where are the pillows?	[They're on the sofa.]
Where's the plant?	[It's behind the sofa.]
Where's the stereo system?	[It's in the wall unit.]
Where's the coffee table?	[It's in front of the loveseat.]
Where's the VCR?	[It's above the TV.]
Where's the DVD player?	[It's below the TV.]

If you choose to do Version 2, make statements such as the following:

They're on the sofa.	[The pillows.]
It's behind the sofa.	[The plant.]
It's in the wall unit.	[The stereo system.]
It's in front of the loveseat.	[The coffee table.]
It's above the TV.	[The VCR.]
It's below the TV.	[The DVD player.]

Picture This!
ACTIVITY HANDBOOK PAGES 12–13

Describe a living room scene and have students draw what you describe. For example:

> In this living room, there's a fireplace on the left wall. In front of the fireplace there are two loveseats, one on either side of the fireplace. Over the fireplace, . . .

4 Do You Remember?
ACTIVITY HANDBOOK PAGE 5

Have students write down everything they remember about the living room depicted on *Picture Dictionary* page 21. There are 3 variations to this activity. If you do Variation 1, ask questions such as the following:

> What's next to the fireplace?
> Where's the plant?
> How many table lamps are there?
> What's under the coffee table?
> What's above the fireplace?
> What's on the coffee table?
> What color is the armchair?
> What color are the curtains?
> How many paintings are there above the fireplace?
> How many magazines are in the magazine rack?
> How many pictures are above the bookcase?

(continued

5 True or False?
ACTIVITY HANDBOOK PAGE 15

Make statements such as the following about the scene on *Picture Dictionary* page 21. Have students decide whether the statements are true or false. For example:

The plant is behind the sofa.	[True.]
The pictures are in the wall unit.	[False. They're over the bookcase.]
The speaker is under the stereo system.	[False. It's next to the stereo system.]
The DVD player is below the television.	[True.]
The woman is sitting on the loveseat.	[False. She's sitting on the sofa.]
The television is in the corner of the room.	[True.]
The man is sitting on the sofa.	[False. He's sitting in the armchair.]
The magazine rack is next to the armchair.	[False. It's next to the loveseat.]
The floor lamp is next to the sofa.	[False. It's next to the armchair.]
There are two pillows on the loveseat.	[False. There are two pillows on the sofa.]

6 Read, Write, and Draw
ACTIVITY HANDBOOK PAGE 13

Have students write each other letters in which they describe their living rooms.

7 It's a Puzzle!
ACTIVITY HANDBOOK PAGE 9

Cut out pictures of living rooms and create puzzles out of the pictures for students to identify and put together by asking questions. For example:

My picture has a green loveseat next to a fireplace.
I have a wall unit with a television and a DVD player.
Do you have a bookcase in your picture?
There's a coffee table in front of the sofa in my picture.

8 Ask Me a Question!
ACTIVITY HANDBOOK PAGE 2
ACTIVITY MASTER 30

Have students walk around trying to guess each other's living room items by asking yes/no questions. For example:

Do you sit on it?	[No.]
Do you put things on it?	[No.]
Do you hang it on the wall?	[Yes.]
Is it a painting?	[Yes.]

9 What Can You Do in the Living Room?
ACTIVITY HANDBOOK PAGES 15–16

Have students make a list of all the things you can do in the living room. For example:

relax	sit in front of the fireplace
watch TV	take a nap
listen to the radio	play a game
talk with guests	read

10 Mystery Word Conversations
ACTIVITY HANDBOOK PAGE 12

Have groups create mystery conversations about a living room item without naming it. The class tries to guess what the *mystery word* is. For example:

A. Would you please close them? The sun is in my eyes.
B. No problem. Is that better?
A. Now it's so dark we need to turn on the lamp!

[Answer: drapes]

11 Finish the Sentence!
ACTIVITY HANDBOOK PAGE 7

Begin sentences such as the following for students to complete:

You hang pictures on the . . . *wall.*
The table in front of the sofa is the . . . *coffee table.*
It's smaller than a sofa. It's a . . . *loveseat.*
The top part of the fireplace is called the . . . *mantel.*
You can play movies and music on a . . . *DVD player.*
When I watch the news, I turn on the . . . *television.*
I keep my magazines in a . . . *magazine holder.*
On top of my lamp there's a very pretty . . . *lampshade.*
It's usually green and it grows with sun and water. It's a . . . *plant.*
It keeps the fire from coming out of the fireplace. It's a . . . *fireplace screen.*

12 Create an Ideal Living Room

Have students write a description of an ideal living room. In their writing have them explain why this living room is the ideal room for them. Encourage them to draw a floor plan to accompany their description.

LESSON OBJECTIVE

Students will learn the vocabulary of items found in a dining room.

RESOURCES

AUDIO PROGRAM		MULTI-LEVEL WORKBOOKS	ACTIVITY MASTER
Words & Dialogs Cassette 1B CD 1: Tracks 49–51	**WordSong:** *In My House* Cassette 7A • CD 7: Tracks 22, 23 Song Masters S7, S8	Literacy Workbook Beginning & Intermediate Lifeskills Workbooks Beginning & Intermediate Vocabulary Workbooks	**Reproducible:** A31

TRANSPARENCY	LANGUAGE & CULTURE NOTES	WORDLINKS
Overhead: T22	**Reproducible:** LC22	longman.com/wordbyword

VOCABULARY INTRODUCTION

- Preview
- Present
- Practice

MODEL CONVERSATION PRACTICE

1. Have students look at the model illustration. Set the scene: "One friend is complimenting another on her dining room."
2. Present the model.
3. Choral Repetition Practice: Full-Class and Individual.
4. Have pairs practice the model.
5. Have pairs present the model.
6. Call on pairs to present a new conversation using word 2.
7. Have pairs practice new conversations.
8. Have pairs present new conversations.

ADDITIONAL CONVERSATION PRACTICE

Before students practice the additional conversations, you may want to have them listen to the examples on the Audio Program.

Conversation 1 Set the scene: "A salesperson and a shopper are talking in a store." Have students practice and present conversations with any words they wish.

Conversation 2 Set the scene: "Two friends are talking." Check understanding of *yard sale*—a yard or driveway sale of household items people no longer want. Have students practice and present conversations with any words they wish.

SPELLING PRACTICE

Say a word, and have students spell it aloud or write it. Or, using the transparency, point to an item and have students write the word.

WRITING AND DISCUSSION

Have students respond to the question as a class, in pairs, or in small groups. Or have students write their responses, share their writing with other students, and discuss in class.

Making Connections

Resource Materials Bring in, or have students bring in, the following materials for vocabulary practice:

- *Home decorating magazines:* Talk about dining rooms and furniture arrangements depicted in the magazines.

- *Newspaper and magazine advertisements for dining room furniture:* Talk about the advertised furniture items and their prices.

Community Task Have individual students (or groups of students) visit different furniture stores and report about the dining room furniture these stores sell and the prices.

1 Expand the Conversation

ACTIVITY HANDBOOK PAGE 6

Expand the model to ask about other dining room items. Student B may answer any way he or she wishes.

a. Write the following on the board:

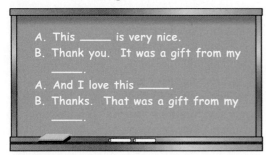

A. This _____ is very nice.
B. Thank you. It was a gift from my _____.

A. And I love this _____.
B. Thanks. That was a gift from my _____.

b. Have pairs of students practice and present conversations based on this model, using different words from the page.

2 Location! Location!

ACTIVITY HANDBOOK PAGES 10–11

If you choose to do Version 1, ask questions such as the following:

Where's the vase?	[It's next to the candlestick.]
Where's the pitcher?	[It's on the buffet.]
Where's the china?	[It's in the china cabinet.]
Where's the butter dish?	[It's between the platter and the salt shaker.]
Where's the coffee pot?	[It's on the tray on the buffet.]
Where's the chandelier?	[It's above the table.]
Where's the sugar bowl?	[It's on the tray on the buffet.]
Where's the fork?	[It's to the left of the plate.]
Where are the spoon and knife?	[They're to the right of the plate.]
Where's the glass?	[It's between the mug and the cup and saucer.]

If you choose to do Version 2, make statements such as the following:

It's next to the platter.	[The butter dish.]
It's over the dining room table.	[The chandelier.]
It's to the left of the mug.	[The bowl.]
It's in the man's hands.	[The salad bowl.]
It's next to the salt shaker.	[The pepper shaker.]
It's inside the china cabinet.	[The china.]
It's under the fork.	[The napkin.]
It's on the tray next to the coffee pot.	[The teapot.]
It's on the tray next to the sugar bowl.	[The creamer.]
They're to the right of the glass.	[The cup and saucer.]

3 Picture This!

ACTIVITY HANDBOOK PAGES 12–13

Describe a dining room scene and have students draw what you describe. For example:

In this dining room, there's a buffet against the right wall. There's a round table and six dining room chairs in the middle of the room. On the table there's . . .

4 Do You Remember?

ACTIVITY HANDBOOK PAGE 5

Have students write down everything they remember about the dining room depicted on *Picture Dictionary* page 22.

If you do Variation 1, ask questions such as the following:

What's on top of the buffet?
How many things are on the dining room table?
How many lights are in the chandelier?
How many plates are in the china cabinet?
What's next to the salt shaker?
What's hanging over the table?
What color is the tablecloth?
What's over the buffet?
What's in the vase?
How many candlesticks are on the table? (continued)

5 True or False?

ACTIVITY HANDBOOK PAGE 15

Make statements such as the following about the scene on *Picture Dictionary* page 22. Have students decide whether the statements are true or false. For example:

The pitcher is on the tray.	[False. It's next to the tray.]
The platter is on the buffet.	[False. It's on the table.]
The napkin is on the plate.	[False. It's to the left of the plate.]
The spoon is to the right of the plate.	[True.]
The man is holding the serving dish.	[False. He's holding the salad bowl.]
The chandelier is over the china cabinet.	[False. It's over the table.]
The cup is on the saucer.	[True.]
The tablecloth is on the table.	[True.]
The painting is over the buffet.	[True.]
The coffee pot is in the china cabinet.	[False. It's on the buffet.]

6 Read, Write, and Draw

ACTIVITY HANDBOOK PAGE 13

Have students write each other letters in which they describe their dining rooms.

7 Miming Game

ACTIVITY HANDBOOK PAGE 11
ACTIVITY MASTER 31

Have students take turns pantomiming the dining room object on the card or what someone might do with the object. The class tries to guess what the object is.

8 It's a Puzzle!

ACTIVITY HANDBOOK PAGE 9

Cut out pictures of dining rooms and create puzzles out of the pictures for students to identify and put together by asking questions. For example:

My picture has a square table with four dining room chairs.
There's a long buffet with a sugar bowl and creamer on it.
Is there a china cabinet in your dining room?

9 What's the Question?

ACTIVITY HANDBOOK PAGE 16

Describe one of the dining room objects on *Picture Dictionary* page 22, and have students respond by asking: "What's a/an _____?" or "What's _____?" For example:

Teacher: You put it on top of the table.
Student: What's a tablecloth?

Teacher: This is what we call a set of dishes.
Student: What's china?

Teacher: You put flowers in it.
Student: What's a vase?

Teacher: You use it to serve water.
Student: What's a pitcher?

Teacher: You drink water from it.
Student: What's a glass?

Teacher: You drink coffee from it.
Student: What's a cup?

Teacher: You use this to clean your mouth and fingers after you eat.
Student: What's a napkin?

Teacher: It is a very beautiful light that hangs over the table.
Student: What's a chandelier?

10 Guess What I'm Thinking Of!

ACTIVITY HANDBOOK PAGE 8

Have students take turns thinking of dining room items for others to guess. For example:

Does it hold food?	[Yes.]
Do you use it to serve food?	[Yes.]
Is it made of wood?	[Yes.]
Is it a salad bowl?	[Yes.]

11 It's Something That . . .

ACTIVITY HANDBOOK PAGE 9
ACTIVITY MASTER 31

Have students give definitions of dining room words to each other beginning with "It's something that . . . " For example:

It's something that you use to serve water.	[A pitcher.]
It's something that you use to cut meat.	[A knife.]
It's something that you use to eat soup.	[A spoon.]
It's something that hangs over the table.	[A chandelier.]
It's something that you put flowers in.	[A vase.]

LESSON OBJECTIVE

Students will learn vocabulary related to items found in a bedroom.

RESOURCES

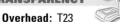

AUDIO PROGRAM	MULTI-LEVEL WORKBOOKS	ACTIVITY MASTER
Words & Dialogs — Cassette 1B, CD 1: Tracks 52–54 **WordSong:** *In My House* — Cassette 7A • CD 7: Tracks 22, 23, Song Masters S7, S8	Literacy Workbook Beginning & Intermediate Lifeskills Workbooks Beginning & Intermediate Vocabulary Workbooks	**Reproducible:** A8

TRANSPARENCY	LANGUAGE & CULTURE NOTES	WORDLINKS
Overhead: T23	**Reproducible:** LC23	longman.com/wordbyword

VOCABULARY INTRODUCTION

- Preview
- Present
- Practice

MODEL CONVERSATION PRACTICE

1. Have students look at the model illustration. Set the scene: "A husband and wife are upset when they see a bug in their bedroom."
2. Present the model.
3. Choral Repetition Practice: Full-Class and Individual.
4. Have pairs practice the model.
5. Have pairs present the model.
6. Call on pairs to present a new conversation using word 2.
7. Have pairs practice new conversations.
8. Have pairs present new conversations.

ADDITIONAL CONVERSATION PRACTICE

Before students practice the additional conversations, you may want to have them listen to the examples on the Audio Program.

Conversation 1 Set the scene: "A shopper is talking to a salesperson in a store." Have students practice and present conversations with any words they wish.

Conversation 2 Set the scene: "Two family members are talking." Note the use of *Oh, no!* to signal something negative. Have students practice and present conversations with any words they wish.

SPELLING PRACTICE

Say a word, and have students spell it aloud or write it. Or, using the transparency, point to an item and have students write the word.

WRITING AND DISCUSSION

Have students respond to the question as a class, in pairs, or in small groups. Or have students write their responses, share their writing with other students, and discuss in class.

Making Connections

Resource Materials Bring in, or have students bring in, the following materials for vocabulary practice:

- *Home decorating magazines:* Talk about bedrooms and furniture arrangements depicted in the magazines.

- *Newspaper and magazine advertisements for bedroom furniture:* Talk about the advertised furniture items and their prices.

Community Task Have individual students (or groups of students) visit different furniture stores and report about the bedroom furniture these stores sell and the prices.

Communication Activities

1 Expand the Conversation
ACTIVITY HANDBOOK PAGE 6

Expand the model with a bug that keeps moving around the bedroom.

a. Write the following on the board:

> A. Ooh! Look at that big bug!
> B. Where?
> A. It's on the _____?
> B. I'll get it.
> A. Quick! Before it gets in/on/under the _____!
> B. Oh, no! Now it's in/on/under the _____!

b. Have pairs of students practice and present conversations based on this model, using different words from the page.

2 Location! Location!
ACTIVITY HANDBOOK PAGES 10–11

If you choose to do Version 1, ask questions such as the following:

Where's the alarm clock?	[It's on the night table.]
Where's the jewelry box?	[It's on the dresser.]
Where's the comforter?	[It's on the bed.]
Where's the mirror?	[It's above the dresser.]
Where's the clock radio?	[It's on the night table.]
Where are the blinds?	[They're on the window.]
Where's the bed frame?	[It's under the box spring and mattress.]
Where's the bed?	[It's next to the window.]
Where are the curtains?	[They're on the window.]

If you choose to do Version 2, make statements such as the following:

It's at the end of the bed on top of the bedspread.	[The comforter.]
It's between the fitted sheet and the blanket.	[The flat sheet.]
It's under the bedspread and on top of the blanket.	[The electric blanket.]
It's on the dresser.	[The jewelry box.]
It's on the wall above the dresser.	[The mirror.]
It's under the box spring.	[The bed frame.]
It's on top of the box spring.	[The mattress.]
It's at the head of the bed.	[The headboard.]
It's next to the bed and under the window.	[The night table.]
It's on the night table behind the clock radio.	[The lamp.]

3 Picture This!
ACTIVITY HANDBOOK PAGES 12–13

Describe a bedroom and have students draw what you describe. For example:

> In this bedroom, there's a bed and a chest of drawers on the left wall. There's a night table to the left of the bed. On the night table there's . . .

4 Read, Write, and Draw
ACTIVITY HANDBOOK PAGE 13

Have students write each other letters in which they describe their bedrooms.

5 Do You Remember?
ACTIVITY HANDBOOK PAGE 5

Have students write down everything they remember about the bedroom depicted on *Picture Dictionary* page 23. If you do Variation 1, ask questions such as the following:

> How many night tables are there?
> Where's the comforter?
> What's the girl holding?
> What's on the dresser?
> How many pillows are there?
> How many blankets are on the bed?
> What color is the carpet?
> What color are the curtains?
> What's over the bed?

6 True or False?

ACTIVITY HANDBOOK PAGE 15

Make statements such as the following about the scene on *Picture Dictionary* page 23. Have students decide whether the statements are true or false. For example:

There's one pillow on the bed. [True.]
The mirror is above the chest. [False. It's above the dresser.]
There's a bedspread on the floor. [False. The bedspread is on the bed.]
There are two windows. [False. There's only one window.]
There are two clocks on the nightstand. [True.]
There are five drawers in the chest. [True.]
The box spring is on top of the mattress. [False. The box spring is under the mattress.]
The jewelry box is on the chest of drawers. [False. It's on the dresser.]

7 It's a Puzzle!

ACTIVITY HANDBOOK PAGE 9

Cut out pictures of bedrooms and create puzzles out of the pictures for students to identify and put together by asking questions. For example:

My picture has a bed with a red bedspread.
Does the bed in your picture have a comforter?
There's a chest of drawers next to the door in this bedroom.

8 What's the Question?

ACTIVITY HANDBOOK PAGE 16

Describe one of the bedroom objects on *Picture Dictionary* page 23, and have students respond by asking: "What's a/an ____?" or "What's ____?" For example:

Teacher: You put these on windows to block out the light.
Student: What are blinds?

Teacher: On very cold nights you plug this in and sleep under it.
Student: What's an electric blanket?

Teacher: It's the bottom sheet.
Student: What's a fitted sheet?

Teacher: It's the top sheet.
Student: What's a flat sheet?

Teacher: It holds clothes and has a mirror over it.
Student: What's a dresser?

Teacher: It wakes you up in the morning.
Student: What's an alarm clock?

Teacher: You can see yourself in this.
Student: What's a mirror?

Teacher: You place this under your head when you sleep at night.
Student: What's a pillow?

Teacher: This gives light to the bedroom.
Student: What's a lamp?

9 Tic Tac Definitions

ACTIVITY HANDBOOK PAGE 15
ACTIVITY MASTER 8

Have students fill in the tic tac grid with any nine bedroom words they wish. Give definitions such as the following, and have students cross out on their grids the words you have defined:

It's a small table next to the bed. [nightstand]
It's a blanket that heats up with electricity. [electric blanket]
It supports the box spring and mattress. [bed frame]
It's a place to keep clothes. [chest]
It's a thick blanket stuffed with polyester or feathers. [comforter]
It covers the floor. [carpet]
It's a piece of fabric that hangs over the lower part of the bed. [dust ruffle]
It's a piece of material that covers a pillow. [pillowcase]
It's the fabric that covers windows. [curtains]
It's a clock that rings at a certain time. [alarm clock]

10 Cooperative Definitions

ACTIVITY HANDBOOK PAGE 4

Have groups write definitions of bedroom words and then pass their definitions to other groups.

11 How to Make a Bed

a. Divide the class into pairs, and have one member of each pair instruct the other on how to make a bed.

b. Call on a few volunteers to give instructions to the class, and have the class decide how good the instructions are.

12 Create an Ideal Bedroom

Have students write a description of an ideal bedroom. In their writing, they should explain why this bedroom is the ideal room for them. Encourage them to draw a floor plan to accompany their writing.

LESSON OBJECTIVE

Students will learn the vocabulary of items found in a kitchen.

RESOURCES

AUDIO PROGRAM

Words & Dialogs
Cassette 1B
CD 1: Tracks 55–57

WordSong: *In My House*
Cassette 7A • CD 7: Tracks 22, 23
Song Masters S7, S8

MULTI-LEVEL WORKBOOKS

Literacy Workbook
Beginning & Intermediate Lifeskills Workbooks
Beginning & Intermediate Vocabulary Workbooks

ACTIVITY MASTERS

Reproducibles:
A8, A32

TRANSPARENCY

Overhead: T24

LANGUAGE & CULTURE NOTES

Reproducible: LC24

WORDLINKS

longman.com/wordbyword

VOCABULARY INTRODUCTION

- Preview
- Present
- Practice

MODEL CONVERSATION PRACTICE

1. Have students look at the model illustration. Set the scene: "A husband and wife are upset about their broken refrigerator."
2. Present the model.
3. Choral Repetition Practice: Full-Class and Individual.
4. Have pairs practice the model.
5. Have pairs present the model.
6. Call on pairs to present a new conversation using word 2.
7. Have pairs practice new conversations.
8. Have pairs present new conversations.

ADDITIONAL CONVERSATION PRACTICE

Before students practice the additional conversations, you may want to have them listen to the examples on the Audio Program.

Conversation 1 Set the scene: "A shopper is talking to a salesperson in a store." Have students practice and present conversations with any words they wish.

Conversation 2 Set the scene: "Two people are talking in a kitchen." Have students practice and present conversations with any words they wish.

SPELLING PRACTICE

Say a word, and have students spell it aloud or write it. Or, using the transparency, point to an item and have students write the word.

WRITING AND DISCUSSION

Have students respond to the question as a class, in pairs, or in small groups. Or have students write their responses, share their writing with other students, and discuss in class.

Making Connections

Resource Materials Bring in, or have students bring in, the following materials for vocabulary practice:

- *Home decorating magazines:* Talk about kitchens and the kitchen items depicted in the magazines.
- *Newspaper and magazine advertisements for kitchen items:* Talk about the advertised kitchen items and their prices.

Community Task Have individual students (or groups of students) visit different stores in the area and report about the kitchen items these stores sell and the prices.

Communication Activities

1 Expand the Conversations
ACTIVITY HANDBOOK PAGE 6

Expand the model with other problems in the kitchen.

a. Write the following on the board:

> A. I think we need a new _____.
> B. I think you're right.
> A. We also need a new _____.
> B. I agree.
> A. And the _____ is getting old.
> B. You're right. We should buy a new one.

b. Have pairs of students practice and present conversations based on this model, using different words from the page.

Also, expand Additional Conversation 2 to ask about other items on sale. Speaker B, the salesperson, may respond any way he or she wishes.

> A. Excuse me. Are your _____s still on sale?
> B. Yes, they are. They're _____ percent off.
> A. And how about your _____? Are they on sale?
> B. _____.

2 True or False?
ACTIVITY HANDBOOK PAGE 15

Make statements such as the following about the scene on *Picture Dictionary* page 24. Have students decide whether the statements are true or false. For example:

> The microwave is above the stove. [True.]
> The canisters are on top of the refrigerator. [False. They're on the counter.]
> The dishwasher detergent is under the sink. [False. It's on the counter.]
> The toaster oven is next to the stove. [True.]
> The oven door is open. [False. The oven door is closed.]
> The toaster is between the tea kettle and the blender. [False. It's between the tea kettle and the coffeemaker.]

> The pot holders are on the wall over the sink. [False. They're on the wall over the stove.]
> The spice rack is on the wall over the electric can opener. [True.]
> The trash compactor is next to the stove. [True.]
> The food processor is on the counter. [False. It's on the table.]

3 Drawing Game
ACTIVITY HANDBOOK PAGE 6
ACTIVITY MASTER 32

Have teams compete to identify kitchen items drawn by one of their team members.

4 Movable Categories
ACTIVITY HANDBOOK PAGE 11
ACTIVITY MASTER 32

Call out the following categories and have students go to the appropriate side of the room:

> things that use electricity to work
> things you can put in the oven
> things that hold liquid
> things that hold food
> things you use to wash dishes
> things that make noise
> things you use for cooking
> things that heat food
> things that you keep on a wall
> things you use to eat food
> things you use to dry hands and dishes
> things that use water

5 Category Dictation
ACTIVITY HANDBOOK PAGE 2

Dictate words that fit into the above categories.

6 What Can You Do in the Kitchen?
ACTIVITY HANDBOOK PAGES 15–16

Have students make a list of all the things you can do in the kitchen. For example:

> cook dinner
> put away the groceries
> make a salad
> wash the dishes
> listen to the radio
> dry the dishes
> drink a cup of coffee
> cut up vegetables

(continued)

7 It's a Puzzle!

ACTIVITY HANDBOOK PAGE 9

Cut out pictures of kitchens and create puzzles out of the pictures for students to identify and put together by asking questions. For example:

My picture has a large refrigerator on the left wall. There's a round kitchen table with four chairs in my picture.
Is there a trash compactor in your kitchen?

8 Tic Tac Definitions

ACTIVITY HANDBOOK PAGE 15
ACTIVITY MASTER 8

Have students fill in the tic tac grid with any nine kitchen words they wish. Give definitions such as the following, and have students cross out on their grids the words you have defined:

People use it to open cans. [can opener]
It's full of recipes. [cookbook]
It freezes food and water. [freezer]
It keeps food cold. [refrigerator]
It holds foods like flour and rice. [canister]
It's the soap people use when they wash dishes by hand. [dishwashing liquid]
It heats up foods in seconds. [microwave]
You use this to boil water on the stove. [tea kettle]
It's the soap you use to wash dishes in the dishwasher. [dishwasher detergent]
It heats with electricity or gas on the top of a stove. [burner]

9 It's Something That . . .

ACTIVITY HANDBOOK PAGE 9
ACTIVITY MASTER 32

Have students give definitions of kitchen words to each other beginning with "It's something that . . ." For example:

It's something that you use to heat food very quickly. [A microwave.]
It's something that keeps foods cold. [A refrigerator.]
It's someting that cleans dishes automatically. [A dishwasher.]
It's something that holds dishes in the kitchen. [A cabinet.]
It's something that holds small jars of spices. [A spice rack.]

10 Guess What I'm Thinking Of!

ACTIVITY HANDBOOK PAGE 8

Have students take turns thinking of kitchen items for others to guess. For example:

Does it heat food?	[Yes.]
Is it very fast?	[No.]
Do people use it to bake foods in?	[Yes.]
Is it an oven?	[Yes.]

11 Question the Answer!

ACTIVITY HANDBOOK PAGE 13
ACTIVITY MASTER 32

Students pick Kitchen Word Cards and think of a question for which that word could be the answer. For example:

Card: cookbook
Student: Where do you find recipes?

Card: dish towel
Student: What do you use to dry dishes?

Card: refrigerator
Student: Where do you keep fresh milk?

Card: freezer
Student: Where do you keep ice?

12 Connections

ACTIVITY HANDBOOK PAGE 4
ACTIVITY MASTER 32

Have students make connections between two kitchen items. For example:

placemat—cutting board
You put dishes on a placemat.
You put things on a cutting board before you cut them.

cabinet—potholder
You can hang a potholder on a cabinet.

refrigerator—burner
A refrigerator keeps food cold.
A burner cooks food.

trash compactor—microwave oven
Both use electricity.
Both are appliances.

Kitchen Crossword

ACTIVITY HANDBOOK PAGES **4–5**

Have students connect kitchen items to create a crossword. For example:

```
        D
D I S H W A S H E R
        S
        H
        R
        A
        C
C O O K B O O K
```

 Ranking

ACTIVITY HANDBOOK PAGE **13**

Have students review the kitchen items on *Picture Dictionary* page 24 and choose:

the ten most essential items for a kitchen
the ten least essential items for a kitchen
the three items they use the most
the items that have been in kitchens for
  100 years
the five most expensive items
the five items that use the most electricity

15 **Read, Write, and Draw**

ACTIVITY HANDBOOK PAGE **13**

Have students write each other letters in which they describe their kitchens.

16 **Create a Dream Kitchen**

Have students write a description of a *dream kitchen*. In their writing, they should explain why this kitchen is the ideal room for them. Encourage them to draw a floor plan to accompany their writing.

17 **Inventions**

ACTIVITY HANDBOOK PAGE **9**

In pairs or small groups, have students invent a new kitchen item. Have them draw a picture of it, name it, and describe what it's used for. Have students present their ideas to the class.

LESSON OBJECTIVE

Students will learn the vocabulary of furniture, baby equipment, and toys found in a baby's room.

RESOURCES

AUDIO PROGRAM		MULTI-LEVEL WORKBOOKS 	ACTIVITY MASTER
Words & Dialogs Cassette 1B CD 1: Tracks 58–60	**WordSong:** *In My House* Cassette 7A • CD 7: Tracks 22, 23 Song Masters S7, S8	Literacy Workbook Beginning & Intermediate Lifeskills Workbooks Beginning & Intermediate Vocabulary Workbooks	**Reproducible:** A33
TRANSPARENCY 	LANGUAGE & CULTURE NOTES		WORDLINKS
Overhead: T25	**Reproducible:** LC25		longman.com/wordbyword

VOCABULARY INTRODUCTION

- Preview
- Present
- Practice

MODEL CONVERSATION PRACTICE

1. Have students look at the model illustration. Set the scene: "Someone has just received a baby gift."
2. Present the model.
3. Choral Repetition Practice: Full-Class and Individual.
4. Have pairs practice the model.
5. Have pairs present the model.
6. Call on pairs to present a new conversation using word 2.
7. Have pairs practice new conversations.
8. Have pairs present new conversations.

ADDITIONAL CONVERSATION PRACTICE

Before students practice the additional conversations, you may want to have them listen to the examples on the Audio Program.

Conversation 1 Set the scene: "Two friends are talking." Have students practice and present conversations with any words they wish.

Conversation 2 Set the scene: "Two friends are talking." Have students practice and present conversations with any words they wish.

SPELLING PRACTICE

Say a word, and have students spell it aloud or write it. Or, using the transparency, point to an item and have students write the word.

WRITING AND DISCUSSION

Have students respond to the questions as a class, in pairs, or in small groups. Or have students write their responses, share their writing with other students, and discuss in class.

Making Connections

Resource Materials Bring in, or have students bring in, the following materials for vocabulary practice:

- *Newspaper and magazine advertisements for baby equipment:* Talk about the items and the prices.
- *Brochures and catalogs of baby equipment:* Talk about the items and the prices.
- *Baby and parenting magazines:* Talk about the baby rooms in the magazines.

Community Task Have individual students (or groups of students) visit different stores where baby room furniture and baby equipment are sold and report about the items and the prices.

Communication Activities

1 Movable Categories
ACTIVITY HANDBOOK PAGE 11
ACTIVITY MASTER 33

Call out the following categories and have students go to the appropriate side of the room:

> things that move
> things the baby sits in
> things the baby plays with
> things to use outside
> things the baby lies on
> things with wheels
> things that are portable
> furniture

2 Category Dictation
ACTIVITY HANDBOOK PAGE 2

Dictate words that fit into the above categories.

3 Do You Remember?
ACTIVITY HANDBOOK PAGE 5

Have students write down everything they remember about the baby's room depicted on *Picture Dictionary* page 25. If you do Variation 1, ask questions such as the following:

> Where's the mobile?
> What's the baby doing?
> What's on the changing table?
> What's under the window?
> What's on top of the chest of drawers?
> Where's the diaper pail?
> What color is the crib?
> Where's the night light?
> Where's the swing?
> Where's the doll?

4 Drawing Game
ACTIVITY HANDBOOK PAGE 6
ACTIVITY MASTER 33

Have teams compete to identify baby room items drawn by one of their team members.

5 Got It!
ACTIVITY HANDBOOK PAGE 7

Have groups of students ask yes/no questions in an attempt to identify baby room items. For example:

Is it a toy?	[No.]
Is it a piece of furniture?	[No.]
Does it help carry the baby?	[Yes.]
Does it have wheels?	[Yes.]
Is it a carriage?	[No.]
Is it a stroller?	[Yes.]

6 What's the Question?
ACTIVITY HANDBOOK PAGE 16

Describe an item from the baby's room on *Picture Dictionary* page 25 and have students respond by asking: "What's a/an _____?" For example:

Teacher: It's something the baby plays with that makes noise.
Student: What's a rattle?
Teacher: You use this to listen to the baby when you aren't in the room.
Student: What's a baby monitor?
Teacher: You use this to rock a very young baby to sleep.
Student: What's a cradle?
Teacher: It's something the baby uses to move around a room before the baby can walk.
Student: What's a walker?
Teacher: It's the container that holds dirty diapers.
Student: What's a diaper pail?

7 Daffy Debate!
ACTIVITY HANDBOOK PAGE 5
ACTIVITY MASTER 33

Have students debate which baby room items are more important than others.

8 Let Me Tell You About My Room

Have students tell about a baby's room from a baby's point of view . . . by pretending they're babies again! They can tell all the things they have in their rooms, what they play with, what they like the most, etc.

9 Ranking
ACTIVITY HANDBOOK PAGE 13

Have students review the baby room items on *Picture Dictionary* page 25 and choose:

> the five most essential items for a baby
> the five least essential items for a baby
> the items that people used to take care of babies 100 years ago
> the items that people used to take care of babies 50 years ago
> the items that students used when they were babies

11 Create an Ideal Baby's Room

Have students write a description of an ideal baby's room. In their writing, they should explain why this room is the ideal room for a baby. Encourage them to draw a floor plan to accompany their writing.

LESSON OBJECTIVE

Students will learn the vocabulary of items found in a bathroom.

RESOURCES

AUDIO PROGRAM

Words & Dialogs
Cassette 1B
CD 1: Tracks 61–63

WordSong: *In My House*
Cassette 7A • CD 7: Tracks 22, 23
Song Masters S7, S8

MULTI-LEVEL WORKBOOKS
Literacy Workbook
Beginning & Intermediate Lifeskills Workbooks
Beginning & Intermediate Vocabulary Workbooks

ACTIVITY MASTERS
Reproducibles:
A8, A34, A35

TRANSPARENCY
Overhead: T26

LANGUAGE & CULTURE NOTES
Reproducible: LC26

WORDLINKS
longman.com/wordbyword

VOCABULARY INTRODUCTION

- Preview
- Present
- Practice

MODEL CONVERSATION PRACTICE

There are three model conversations, each describing the location of an object with a different preposition: *next to, on, in.* Introduce and practice the first model before going on to the second and third. For each model:

1. Have students look at the model illustration. Set the scene: "A husband is talking to his wife. He can't find things in the bathroom."
2. Present the model.
3. Choral Repetition Practice: Full-Class and Individual.
4. Have pairs practice the model.
5. Have pairs present the model.
6. Call on pairs to present a new conversation. For a conversation based on the first model, use words 5 and 2; for a conversation based on the second model, use words 11 and 12; and for a conversation based on the third model, use words 23 and 26.
7. Have pairs practice new conversations.
8. Have pairs present new conversations.

ADDITIONAL CONVERSATION PRACTICE

Before students practice the additional conversations, you may want to have them listen to the examples on the Audio Program.

Conversation 1 Set the scene: "Two family members are talking." Have students practice and present conversations with any words they wish.

Conversation 2 Set the scene: "A parent is upset about the mess a child made in the bathroom." Have students practice and present conversations with any words they wish.

SPELLING PRACTICE

Say a word, and have students spell it aloud or write it. Or, using the transparency, point to an item and have students write the word.

WRITING AND DISCUSSION

Have students describe their bathrooms as a class, in pairs, or in small groups. Or have students write their descriptions (perhaps including a diagram) at home or in class, share their written work with other students, and discuss as a class, in pairs, or in small groups.

Making Connections

Resource Materials Bring in, or have students bring in, the following materials for vocabulary practice:

- *Home decorating magazines:* Talk about the bathrooms depicted in the magazines.
- *Newspaper and magazine advertisements for bathroom products:* Talk about the advertised bathroom items and their prices.

Community Task Have individual students (or groups of students) visit different bathroom fixture stores and report about the items these stores sell and the prices.

Communication Activities

1 Expand the Conversation
ACTIVITY HANDBOOK PAGE 6

Expand Additional Conversation 2 to include other *accidents*.

a. Write the following on the board:

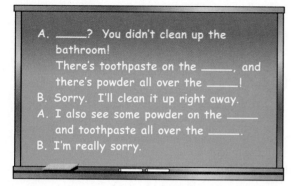

A. _____? You didn't clean up the bathroom!
There's toothpaste on the _____, and there's powder all over the _____!
B. Sorry. I'll clean it up right away.
A. I also see some powder on the _____ and toothpaste all over the _____.
B. I'm really sorry.

b. Have pairs of students practice and present conversations based on this model, using different words from the page.

2 Location! Location!
ACTIVITY HANDBOOK PAGES 10–11

If you choose to do Version 1, ask questions such as the following:

Where's the hand towel?	[It's between the washcloth and the bath towel.]
Where's the toilet paper?	[It's next to the toilet.]
Where's the soap dish?	[It's next to the soap dispenser.]
Where's the hamper?	[It's under the shelf.]
Where's the hair dryer?	[It's on the vanity.]
Where are the toothbrushes?	[They're in the toothbrush holder.]
Where's the medicine cabinet?	[It's over the vanity.]
Where's the electric toothbrush?	[It's on the vanity.]
Where's the sponge?	[It's on the side of the tub.]

If you choose to do Version 2, make statements such as the following:

It's hanging on the side of the bathtub.	[The rubber mat.]
It's between the faucet and the soap dish.	[The soap dispenser.]
It's next to the vanity and under the shelf.	[The hamper.]
It's on the floor next to the tub.	[The bath mat.]
It's on the toothbrush holder.	[The cup.]
It's under the man's feet.	[The scale.]
It's on the toilet.	[The air freshener.]
It's next to the plunger.	[The toilet brush.]
It's on the floor next to the vanity.	[The wastebasket.]

3 Drawing Game
ACTIVITY HANDBOOK PAGE 6
ACTIVITY MASTER 34

Have teams compete to identify bathroom items drawn by one of their team members.

4 It's a Puzzle!
ACTIVITY HANDBOOK PAGE 9

Cut out pictures of bathrooms and create puzzles out of the pictures for students to identify and put together by asking questions. For example:

My picture has a yellow bathtub with a green and white shower curtain.
Where's the vanity in your picture?
Do you have a hamper in your picture?

5 True or False?
ACTIVITY HANDBOOK PAGE 15

Make statements such as the following about the scene on *Picture Dictionary* page 26. Have students decide whether the statements are true or false. For example:

The hamper is open. [True.]
The man is drying his hair. [False. He's standing on the scale.]
The window is open. [False. It's closed.]
The medicine cabinet is open. [True.]
The rubber mat is hanging over the side of the vanity. [False. It's hanging over the side of the tub.]
The hair dryer is on the shelf. [False. It's on the vanity.]
The soap dispenser is next to the faucet. [True.]
The fan is in the wall. [False. It's in the ceiling.]
The mirror is over the hamper. [False. It's over the vanity.]
The toothbrush holder is next o the medicine cabinet. [True.]

(continued)

6 Tic Tac Definitions

ACTIVITY HANDBOOK PAGE 15
ACTIVITY MASTER 8

Have students fill in the tic tac grid with any nine bathroom words they wish. Give definitions such as the following, and have students cross out on their grids the words you have defined:

It's where people keep their medicine. [medicine cabinet]
People use this to clean their teeth. It uses electricity. [electric toothbrush]
After a shower a person stands on this to dry off. [bath mat]
It clears the air in the bathroom. [fan]
People use this to clean the toilet. [toilet brush]
It makes the air smell sweet. [air freshener]
It cleans people's skin. [soap]
It measure's a person's weight. [scale]
You can see yourself in this. [mirror]
You use this to dry your skin. [towel]

7 Picture This!

ACTIVITY HANDBOOK PAGES 12–13

Describe a bathroom and have students draw what you describe. For example:

In this bathroom, there's a bathtub on the left side. Straight ahead is the toilet, and on the right is a vanity. On the vanity, there's . . .

8 Movable Categories

ACTIVITY HANDBOOK PAGE 11
ACTIVITY MASTER 34

Call out the following categories and have students go to the appropriate side of the room:

things you use to clean the body
things that hold other things
bathroom fixtures (i.e., things that are permanently attached and cannot be moved)
things you use when you take a bath or a shower
things for the toilet
things made of cloth
things made of plastic
things that hold water
things that get wet

9 Category Dictation

ACTIVITY HANDBOOK PAGE 2

Dictate words that fit into the above categories.

10 Ask Me a Question!

ACTIVITY HANDBOOK PAGE 2
ACTIVITY MASTER 34

Have students walk around trying to guess each other's bathroom items by asking yes/no questions. For example:

Is it electric?	[No.]
Does it get wet?	[Yes.]
Do you use it in the shower?	[No.]
Do you use it after a shower?	[Yes.]
Is it a towel?	[Yes.]

11 Cooperative Definitions

ACTIVITY HANDBOOK PAGE 4

Have groups write definitions of bathroom words and then pass their definitions to other groups.

12 Question the Answer!

ACTIVITY HANDBOOK PAGE 13
ACTIVITY MASTER 34

Students pick Bathroom Word Cards and think of a question for which that word could be the answer. For example:

Card: toilet brush
Student: What do you use to clean the toilet?

Card: rubber mat
Student: What do you put in the bathtub so you won't fall?

Card: toothbrush
Student: What do you use to clean your teeth?

Card: soap
Student: What do you use to wash your hands?

13 Bathroom Match Game

ACTIVITY HANDBOOK PAGE 11
ACTIVITY MASTER 35

Have students find the person whose card matches theirs.

14 Read, Write, and Draw

ACTIVITY HANDBOOK PAGE 13

Have students write each other letters in which they describe their bathrooms.

15 Create an Ideal Bathroom

Have students write a description of an ideal bathroom. In their writing, have them explain why this bathroom is the ideal room for them. Encourage them to draw a floor plan to accompany their writing.

LESSON OBJECTIVE

Students will learn the vocabulary of objects found on the exterior of a home.

RESOURCES

AUDIO PROGRAM
Words & Dialogs
Cassette 1B
CD 1: Tracks 64–66

MULTI-LEVEL WORKBOOKS
Literacy Workbook
Beginning & Intermediate Lifeskills Workbooks
Beginning & Intermediate Vocabulary Workbooks

TRANSPARENCY
Overhead: T27

LANGUAGE & CULTURE NOTES
Reproducible: LC27

WORDLINKS
longman.com/wordbyword

VOCABULARY INTRODUCTION

- Preview
- Present
- Practice

MODEL CONVERSATION PRACTICE

1. Have students look at the model illustration. Set the scene: "A wife is talking to her husband about their broken lamppost."
2. Present the model.
3. Choral Repetition Practice: Full-Class and Individual.
4. Have pairs practice the model.
5. Have pairs present the model.
6. Call on pairs to present a new conversation using word 2.
7. Have pairs practice new conversations.
8. Have pairs present new conversations.

ADDITIONAL CONVERSATION PRACTICE

Before students practice the additional conversations, you may want to have them listen to the examples on the Audio Program.

Conversation 1 Set the scene: "Someone is calling Harry's Home Repairs." Have students practice and present conversations with any words they wish.

Conversation 2 Set the scene: "Two friends are talking on Monday morning." Have students practice and present conversations with any words they wish.

SPELLING PRACTICE

Say a word, and have students spell it aloud or write it. Or, using the transparency, point to an item and have students write the word.

WRITING AND DISCUSSION

Have students respond to the questions as a class, in pairs, or in small groups. Or have students write their responses, share their writing with other students, and discuss in class.

Making Connections

Resource Materials Bring in, or have students bring in, the following materials for vocabulary practice:

- *Pictures from garden and home magazines and websites:* Talk about the exteriors and the front and backyards of the homes that are depicted.

- *Brochures and catalogs from hardware and home building supply stores:* Talk about the items and the prices.

Community Task Have individual students (or groups of students) visit different neighborhoods and report about the homes they saw.

Communication Activities

1 Expand the Conversation
ACTIVITY HANDBOOK PAGE 6

Expand the model to include other broken items.

a. Write the following on the board:

> A. When are you going to repair the
>   _____?
> B. I'm going to repair it next Saturday.
> A. You also need to repair the _____.
>   It's in very bad condition.
> B. I know. I'll repair it soon.

b. Have pairs of students practice and present
   conversations based on this model, using
   different words from the page.

2 Do You Remember?
ACTIVITY HANDBOOK PAGE 5

Have students write down everything they remember
about the picture of outside the home depicted on
Picture Dictionary page 27.

If you do Variation 1, ask questions such as the
following:

> How many windows are there in the front of the
>   house?
> How many windows are there in the back of the
>   house?
> Is the back door open?
> What's on the patio?
> How many people are in the backyard?
> Is the front door open?
> What's the man doing in the driveway?
> How many front steps are there?
> Where's the satellite dish?

3 What's the Question?
ACTIVITY HANDBOOK PAGE 16

Describe an item from outside the home on *Picture
Dictionary* page 27 and have students respond by
asking: "What's a/an _____?" For example:

> Teacher: This is on the top of a house.
> Student: What's a roof?
>
> Teacher: This is where you can keep your car.
> Student: What's a garage?
>
> Teacher: This cuts grass.
> Student: What's a lawnmower?

4 Picture This!
ACTIVITY HANDBOOK PAGES 12–13

Describe the outside of a house and have students
draw what you describe. For example:

> This house has a door in the center with two windows
> on either side of the door. There's a two-car garage
> on the left side of the house. In the back of the
> house, . . .

5 Finish the Sentence!
ACTIVITY HANDBOOK PAGE 7

Begin sentences such as the following for students to
complete:

> To see if someone is home, you ring the . . . *doorbell*.
> You keep your car in the . . . *garage*.
> To open the door you turn the . . . *door knob*.
> You cut the grass with a . . . *lawnmower*.
> To receive many television channels in your home you
>   can use a . . . . *satellite dish*.
> You look for your mail in the . . . *mailbox*.
> People cook meat outside on a. . . . *barbecue*.
> To protect your regular door from bad weather, you
>   can use a . . . *storm door*.

6 Same and Different Pictures

a. Bring to class several pictures of the outsides of
   houses.

b. Divide the class into pairs.

c. Give each member of the pair a different
   picture and have them discover the differences
   and similarities in their pictures by asking and
   answering questions.

7 What Can You Do in the Yard?
ACTIVITY HANDBOOK PAGES 15–16

Have students make a list of all the things you can do
in the yard. For example:

have a barbecue	read
plant flowers	sunbathe
play with the children	mow the lawn
relax	wash the windows

8 Create an Ideal Yard

Have students write a description of an ideal yard
for their ideal home. In their writing, they should
explain why this yard is their ideal yard. Encourage
them to draw a picture to accompany their writing.

LESSON OBJECTIVE

Students will learn vocabulary related to looking for an apartment, signing a lease, moving in, and the structures and objects that may be found in an apartment building.

RESOURCES

AUDIO PROGRAM

Words & Dialogs
Cassette 1B
CD 2: Tracks 2–4

MULTI-LEVEL WORKBOOKS

Literacy Workbook
Beginning & Intermediate Lifeskills Workbooks
Beginning & Intermediate Vocabulary Workbooks

ACTIVITY MASTERS

Reproducibles:
A8, A36–A39

TRANSPARENCIES
Overheads: T28, T29

LANGUAGE & CULTURE NOTES
Reproducible: LC28–29

WORDLINKS
longman.com/wordbyword

VOCABULARY INTRODUCTION

- Preview
- Present
- Practice

MODEL CONVERSATION PRACTICE

1. Have students look at the model illustration. Set the scene: "Someone who wants to rent an apartment is talking to the landlord of a building."
2. Present the model.
3. Choral Repetition Practice: Full-Class and Individual.
4. Have pairs practice the model.
5. Have pairs present the model.
6. Call on pairs to present a new conversation using word 20.
7. Have pairs practice new conversations.
8. Have pairs present new conversations.

ADDITIONAL CONVERSATION PRACTICE

Before students practice the additional conversations, you may want to have them listen to the examples on the Audio Program.

Conversation 1 Set the scene: "A realtor is showing someone a new apartment." Have students practice and present conversations with any words they wish.

Conversation 2 Set the scene: "Someone is talking to his or her parents on the telephone about a new apartment." Have students practice and present conversations with any words they wish.

SPELLING PRACTICE

Say a word, and have students spell it aloud or write it. Or, using the transparency, point to an item and have students write the word.

WRITING AND DISCUSSION

Have students respond to the question as a class, in pairs, or in small groups. Or have students write their responses, share their writing with other students, and discuss in class.

Making Connections

Resource Materials Bring in, or have students bring in, the following materials for vocabulary practice:

- *Pictures of apartments and apartment buildings from magazines:* Describe the buildings.
- *Brochures from apartment complexes:* Talk about the buildings and the facilities.
- *Classified advertisements for apartments for rent:* Go over abbreviations in the ads and talk about the apartments. Compare apartments and prices.
- *Internet listings for apartments available for rent:* Talk about the apartments and the prices.

Community Task Have individual students (or groups of students) visit different neighborhoods and report about apartment buildings they saw.

Communication Activities

① Chain Game: In My Apartment Building
ACTIVITY HANDBOOK PAGES 2–3

Begin the chain as follows: "In my apartment building there's a superintendent," and have students continue it. For example:

Teacher: In my apartment building there's a superintendent.
Student 1: In my apartment building there's a superintendent and a laundry room.
Student 2: In my apartment building there's a superintendent, a laundry room, and a trash chute.
Etc.

② Tic Tac Definitions
ACTIVITY HANDBOOK PAGE 15
ACTIVITY MASTER 8

Have students fill in the tic tac grid with any nine apartment building words they wish. Give definitions such as the following, and have students cross out on their grids the words you have defined:

This moves up and down and stops at every floor. [elevator]
This is the place where mail is delivered. [mailbox]
This is a bell that rings in the apartment to let the tenants know that someone wants to speak to them on the intercom. [buzzer]
This is a small hole with a magnifying glass that allows the person in the apartment to see the hallway. [peephole]
This is the owner of an apartment building. [landlord]
This is a safety device that signals to the fire department and to building residents that there is a fire. [fire alarm]
This is the person who manages and does repairs in the apartment building. [superintendent]
This is a room with one or more washers and dryers for tenants to use. [laundry room]
This is a small hot tub with a motor that makes the water bubble and swirl around. [whirlpool]
This is the person who lives in an apartment. [tenant]

③ Concentration
ACTIVITY HANDBOOK PAGE 3
ACTIVITY MASTER 36

Have students shuffle the cards and place them face-down in four rows of 6 each, then attempt to find cards that match.

④ Apartment Building Match Game
ACTIVITY HANDBOOK PAGE 11
ACTIVITY MASTER 37

Have students find the person whose card matches theirs.

⑤ Apartment Building Talk!
ACTIVITY HANDBOOK PAGE 17
ACTIVITY MASTER 38

Give students an Apartment Building Word Card, and have them speak to the class for one minute about that item.

⑥ Role Play: Renting an Apartment

Collect several ads for apartment rentals. Divide the class into pairs and give half of the students several of these ads apiece. These students are *rental agents*. The other half of the class are people trying to find apartments to rent. Each of these people visits a rental agent, who tries to rent them one of the apartments for which they have ads.

⑦ Mystery Role Plays

a. Divide the class into small groups.

b. Either suggest one of the situations below, or have each group decide on a situation that they *reenact* for the rest of the class. The other students must figure out the identity of the people speaking and what's happening. Some possibilities:

The doorman is having a discussion with a stranger who wants to enter the building.
A fire alarm is going off.
It's midnight, and someone is knocking on your door.
The elevator is broken, and you have to get to the twelfth floor with several bags of groceries.
You're returning to your apartment with a friend late at night. There are no lights in the parking lot.

⑧ Locate the Conversation!
ACTIVITY MASTER 39

a. Make multiple copies of Activity Master 39 and cut it into cards.

b. In pairs, have students read the conversations and match them to locations in an apartment building.

c. When all the students have matched their cards, have them take turns reading the dialogs aloud for the whole class.

LESSON OBJECTIVE

Students will learn the vocabulary of housing problems and service repairpeople who fix these problems.

RESOURCES

AUDIO PROGRAM

Words & Dialogs
Cassette 1B
CD 2: Tracks 5–7

MULTI-LEVEL WORKBOOKS

Literacy Workbook
Beginning & Intermediate Lifeskills Workbooks
Beginning & Intermediate Vocabulary Workbooks

ACTIVITY MASTERS

Reproducibles:
A40, A41

TRANSPARENCIES
Overheads: T30, T31

LANGUAGE & CULTURE NOTES
Reproducible: LC30–31

WORDLINKS
longman.com/wordbyword

VOCABULARY INTRODUCTION

- Preview
- Present
- Practice

MODEL CONVERSATION PRACTICE

1. Have students look at the model illustration. Set the scene: "A husband and wife are upset. They've having problems in their home."

2. Present the model with Problem 1 and Repairperson A (*plumber*).

3. Choral Repetition Practice: Full-Class and Individual.

4. Have pairs practice the model.

5. Have pairs present the model.

6. Call on pairs to present a new conversation using Problem 5 and Repairperson B (*roofer*).

7. Have pairs practice new conversations.

8. Have pairs present new conversations.

ADDITIONAL CONVERSATION PRACTICE

Before students practice the additional conversations, you may want to have them listen to the examples on the Audio Program.

Conversation 1 Set the scene: "Two friends are talking." Have students practice and present conversations with any words they wish.

Conversation 2 Set the scene: "Two friends are talking." Have students practice and present conversations with any words they wish.

SPELLING PRACTICE

Say a word, and have students spell it aloud or write it. Or, using the transparency, point to an item and have students write the word.

WRITING AND DISCUSSION

Have students respond to the question as a class, in pairs, or in small groups. Or have students write their responses, share their writing with other students, and discuss in class.

Making Connections

Resource Materials Bring in, or have students bring in, the following materials for vocabulary practice:

- *Home repair magazines:* Talk about home repair problems and ways to fix them.

- *The Yellow Pages in the telephone book that list home repairpeople:* Talk about the different types of repairpeople and reasons for calling them.

Communication Activities

1 Expand the Conversation
ACTIVITY HANDBOOK PAGE 6

Expand Additional Conversation 1 so that Speaker B also has problems.

a. Write the following on the board:

> A. I'm having a problem in my apartment/house.
> B. What's the problem?
> A. _____.
> B. You know, I'm also having a problem.
> A. Really, what's the matter?
> B. _____.
> A. That's terrible!

b. Have pairs of students practice and present conversations based on this model, using different words from the page.

2 Telephone
ACTIVITY HANDBOOK PAGE 14

Begin the activity with the following sentence: "The chimneysweep is on the roof, the plumber is in the bathroom, and the exterminator is in the kitchen."

3 What Am I?
ACTIVITY HANDBOOK PAGE 15
ACTIVITY MASTER 40

Pin word cards on students' backs and have them ask yes/no questions to identify which repairperson they *are*. For example:

Do I work outdoors?	[No.]
Do I fix things made of wood?	[No.]
Do I fix electrical things?	[Yes.]
Do I fix appliances?	[Yes.]
Am I an appliance repairperson?	[Yes.]
Do I work outdoors?	[Yes.]
Do I fix things?	[No.]
Do I build things?	[No.]
Do I clean things?	[Yes.]
Am I a chimneysweep?	[Yes.]

4 Associations: What Do They Fix?
ACTIVITY HANDBOOK PAGE 2

Call out the name of a household repairperson and have groups write down everything that repairperson can fix. For example:

plumber: [toilets/kitchen sinks/heating systems/gas heaters/sewers/bathroom sinks/garbage disposals]
carpenter: [stairs/doors/walls/shelves/cabinets/closets/front porches/decks]
appliance repairperson: [dishwashers/washing machines/dryers/refrigerators/trash compactors]

5 General-to-Specific Clue Game
ACTIVITY HANDBOOK PAGE 7

Possible clues:

Clue 1: I fix things.
Clue 2: My services are expensive.
Clue 3: You can call me for emergencies.
Clue 4: I come to your house.
Clue 5: I use wrenches.
Clue 6: I sometimes get my feet wet.
Clue 7: I fix sinks and toilets.

[Answer: a plumber]

6 Finish the Sentence!
ACTIVITY HANDBOOK PAGE 7

Begin sentences such as the following for students to complete:

My bathtub is . . .
The wall in my living room is . . .
My refrigerator is . . .
My doorbell is . . .
My front door is . . .
The air conditioning isn't . . .
Our hot water heater isn't . . .
The paint in my hallway is . . .
My stove isn't . . .
Call an exterminator! Look at all those . . . !

7 Home Repair Match Game
ACTIVITY HANDBOOK PAGE 11
ACTIVITY MASTER 41

Have students find the person whose card matches theirs.

8 **Chain Story**
ACTIVITY HANDBOOK PAGE **3**

Begin the story as follows: "I have a lot of problems in my house!"

9 **Role Play: A Little Problem!**

a. Divide the class into pairs.

b. Have students create role plays in which someone is calling about work done by a repairperson that was not done well.

c. Have students present their role plays to the class.

10 **What's the Story?**

Have each student choose a person depicted on *Picture Dictionary* pages 30 or 31 and tell a story about that person. Possible questions to answer:

What's his/her name?
What's his/her occupation?
Where does he/she work?
What does he/she do at work every day?
Is the work interesting? Why or why not?
What are his/her hours?

11 **Discussion: Household Repairpeople**

As a class, in pairs, or in small groups, have students tell about times they've had repairpeople fix things at their homes.

12 **Finding a Repairperson**

Bring in the Yellow Pages in the telephone directory. Describe different household problems, and have students practice looking up various repairpeople.

13 **Ranking**
ACTIVITY HANDBOOK PAGE **13**

Write the names of household repair occupations on the board, and have students rank all of them according to the following criteria:

Which job gets paid the best?
Which job is the most interesting?
Which job is the most dangerous?
Which job would you most like to have?

14 **Daffy Debate!**
ACTIVITY HANDBOOK PAGE **5**
ACTIVITY MASTER **40**

Have students debate which repairpeople are more important than others.

LESSON OBJECTIVE

Students will learn the vocabulary for actions, equipment, and products used for household cleaning.

RESOURCES

AUDIO PROGRAM
Words & Dialogs
Cassette 1B
CD 2: Tracks 8–10

MULTI-LEVEL WORKBOOKS
Literacy Workbook
Beginning & Intermediate Lifeskills Workbooks
Beginning & Intermediate Vocabulary Workbooks

ACTIVITY MASTERS
Reproducibles:
A42, A43

TRANSPARENCY
Overhead: T32

LANGUAGE & CULTURE NOTES
Reproducible: LC32

WORDLINKS
longman.com/wordbyword

VOCABULARY INTRODUCTION

- Preview
- Present
- Practice

MODEL CONVERSATION PRACTICE

There are two model conversations—the first for actions, words A–I, and the second for household cleaning utensils, words 1–24. Introduce and practice the first model before going on to the second. For each model:

1. Have students look at the model illustration. Set the scene:

   Model 1: "A wife is calling her husband."
   Model 2: "A husband and wife are talking."

2. Present the model.
3. Choral Repetition Practice: Full-Class and Individual.
4. Have pairs practice the model.
5. Have pairs present the model.
6. Call on pairs to present a new conversation using word B for the first model and word 2 for the second model.
7. Have pairs practice new conversations.
8. Have pairs present new conversations.

ADDITIONAL CONVERSATION PRACTICE

Before students practice the additional conversations, you may want to have them listen to the examples on the Audio Program.

Conversation 1 Set the scene: "A customer is talking to a salesperson in a store." Have students practice and present conversations with any words they wish.

Conversation 2 Set the scene: "A customer is talking to a salesperson in a store." Have students practice and present conversations with any words they wish.

SPELLING PRACTICE

Say a word or phrase, and have students spell it aloud or write it. Or, using the transparency, point to an item and have students write the word or phrase.

WRITING AND DISCUSSION

Have students respond to the questions as a class, in pairs, or in small groups. Or have students write their responses, share their writing with other students, and discuss in class.

Making Connections

Resource Materials Bring in, or have students bring in, the following materials for vocabulary practice:

- *Advertisements for household cleaning products:* Talk about the products, their prices, and what they're used for.

- *The items and directions for use:* Talk about how and when to use the products.

Community Task Have students visit different stores that sell household cleaning products and report about the products and the prices.

Communication Activities

1 Clap in Rhythm
ACTIVITY HANDBOOK PAGE 3

Have students name household cleaning items to a clapping rhythm.

2 Letter Game
ACTIVITY HANDBOOK PAGE 9

Say statements such as the following and have teams compete to identify the items:

I'm thinking of a household
  cleaning item that starts with *b*.   [broom]
I'm thinking of a household
  cleaning item that starts with *s*.   [sponge]
I'm thinking of a household
  cleaning item that starts with *f*.   [floor wax]
I'm thinking of a household
  cleaning item that starts with *d*.   [dustpan]
I'm thinking of a household
  cleaning item that starts with *a*.   [ammonia]

3 Drawing Game
ACTIVITY HANDBOOK PAGE 6
ACTIVITY MASTER 42

Have teams compete to identify the items drawn by one of their team members.

4 Concentration
ACTIVITY HANDBOOK PAGE 3
ACTIVITY MASTER 43

Have students shuffle the cards and place them face-down in three rows of 6 each, then attempt to find cards that match.

5 Movable Categories
ACTIVITY HANDBOOK PAGE 11
ACTIVITY MASTER 42

Call out the following categories and have students go to the appropriate side of the room:

things you use with water
things you use to clean the floor
things you use to clean the bathroom
things you use to clean the windows
things you use to polish the furniture
things you use to clean the living room
things you use to clean the kitchen

6 Category Dictation
ACTIVITY HANDBOOK PAGE 2

Dictate words that fit into three of the above categories.

7 Chain Game
ACTIVITY HANDBOOK PAGES 2–3

Begin the chain as follows: "I'm going to clean my house. First I'm going to vacuum all the carpets," and have students continue it. For example:

Teacher: I'm going to clean my house. First I'm going to vacuum all the carpets.
Student 1: I'm going to clean my house. First I'm going to vacuum all the carpets. Then I'm going to dust the furniture.
Student 2: I'm going to clean my house. First I'm going to vacuum all the carpets. Then I'm going to dust the furniture. Then I'm going to polish the furniture.
Etc.

8 True or False?
ACTIVITY HANDBOOK PAGE 15

Make statements such as the following about the scene on *Picture Dictionary* page 32. Have students decide whether the statements are true or false. For example:

In Picture A, the man is sweeping the floor with a carpet sweeper. [False. He's sweeping the floor with a broom.]
In Picture C, the man is mopping with a sponge mop. [False. He's mopping with a wet mop.]
In Picture F, the man is waxing the floor with floor wax. [True.]
In Picture I, the woman is taking out the recycling bin. [False. She's taking out the garbage can.]

9 Miming Game
ACTIVITY HANDBOOK PAGE 11
ACTIVITY MASTER 43 (WORDS ONLY)

Have students take turns pantomiming household cleaning actions. The class tries to guess what the person is doing.

10 Question the Answer!
ACTIVITY HANDBOOK PAGE 13
ACTIVITY MASTER 42

Students pick Household Cleaning Word Cards and think of a question for which that word could be the answer. For example:

Card: scrub brush
Student: What do you use to clean the toilet?
Card: floor wax
Student: What do you use to make the floor shiny?
Card: cleanser
Student: What do you use to clean a sink?

Students will learn the vocabulary of various supplies for the home.

RESOURCES

AUDIO PROGRAM	MULTI-LEVEL WORKBOOKS	ACTIVITY MASTERS
Words & Dialogs Cassette 2A CD 2: Tracks 11–13	Literacy Workbook Beginning & Intermediate Lifeskills Workbooks Beginning & Intermediate Vocabulary Workbooks	**Reproducibles**: A44, A45
TRANSPARENCY	LANGUAGE & CULTURE NOTES	WORDLINKS
Overhead: T33	**Reproducible**: LC33	longman.com/wordbyword

VOCABULARY INTRODUCTION

- Preview
- Present
- Practice

MODEL CONVERSATION PRACTICE

1. Have students look at the model illustration. Set the scene: "A daughter is talking to her father."
2. Present the model.
3. Choral Repetition Practice: Full-Class and Individual.
4. Have pairs practice the model.
5. Have pairs present the model.
6. Call on pairs to present a new conversation using word 2.
7. Have pairs practice new conversations.
8. Have pairs present new conversations.

ADDITIONAL CONVERSATION PRACTICE

Before students practice the additional conversations, you may want to have them listen to the examples on the Audio Program.

Conversation 1 Set the scene: "Two family members are talking." Have students practice and present conversations with any words they wish.

Conversation 2 Set the scene: "Two family members are talking." Have students practice and present conversations with any words they wish.

SPELLING PRACTICE

Say a word, and have students spell it aloud or write it. Or, using the transparency, point to an item and have students write the word.

WRITING AND DISCUSSION

Have students respond to the questions as a class, in pairs, or in small groups. Or have students write their responses, share their writing with other students, and discuss in class.

Making Connections

Resource Materials Bring in, or have students bring in, the following materials for vocabulary practice:

- *Newspaper advertisements for home supplies:* Talk about the items and the prices.
- *Catalogs from hardware stores:* Talk about the items and the prices.
- *The smaller, more portable items themselves:* Go over the directions for using them.

Community Task Have individual students (or groups of students) visit different stores that sell home supplies and report about the items and the prices.

Communication Activities

1 Stand in Order

ACTIVITY HANDBOOK PAGE 14
ACTIVITY MASTER 44

Have students arrange themselves alphabetically according to the Home Supply Word Card they have.

2 Talk in Circles

a. Write on the board:

above	below	in		next to
behind	between	in front of	on	

b. Have students take turns asking and answering questions about the location of different objects on *Picture Dictionary* page 33. For example:

Student 1: Where's the flashlight?
Student 2: Between the plunger and the tape measure. *[to Student 3]* Where's the paint roller?
Student 3: In the paint pan. *[to Student 4]* Where's the duct tape?
Etc.

3 Location! Location!

ACTIVITY HANDBOOK PAGES 10–11

If you choose to do Version 1, ask questions such as the following:

Where's the paint thinner?	[It's next to the paint.]
Where's the sandpaper?	[It's next to the roach killer.]
Where's the extension cord?	[It's on the wall behind the flashlight.]
Where's the fly swatter?	[It's on the door.]
Where's the mousetrap?	[It's under the step ladder.]
Where are the lightbulbs?	[They're next to the batteries.]
Where's the electrical tape?	[It's next to the masking tape.]
Where are the fuses?	[They're in front of the lightbulbs.]
Where's the glue?	[It's behind the work gloves.]
Where's the paintbrush?	[It's on the floor next to the paint pan.]

If you choose to do Version 2, make statements such as the following:

It's on the wall under the electrical tape.	[The duct tape.]
It's next to the flashlight.	[The plunger.]
It's on the wall over the tape measure.	[The extension cord.]
Its on the door next to the fly swatter.	[The yardstick.]
It's next to the oil.	[The glue.]
It's on the floor next to the paint.	[The paint thinner.]
It's between the sandpaper and the bug spray.	[The roach killer.]
It's under the step ladder.	[The mousetrap.]
It's next to the electrical tape.	[The masking tape.]
They're under the masking tape and next to the lightbulbs.	[The batteries.]

4 True or False?

ACTIVITY HANDBOOK PAGE 15

Make statements such as the following about the scene on *Picture Dictionary* page 33. Have students decide whether the statements are true or false. For example:

The man is painting the chair red.	[True.]
He's using a paintbrush to paint the chair.	[False. He's using a spray gun.]
The paint roller has white paint on it.	[False. It's clean.]
The fly swatter is next to the plunger.	[False. It's next to the yardstick.]
The flashlight is above the step ladder.	[True.]
The work gloves are in front of the glue.	[True.]
The yardstick is on the wall.	[False. It's on the door.]
There are five fuses.	[False. There are three.]
There are two cans of paint.	[False. There's only one can of paint.]
The paint thinner is on the table.	[False. It's on the floor.]

(continued)

5 Picture This!
ACTIVITY HANDBOOK PAGES 12–13

Describe a utility room scene and have students draw what you describe. For example:

> There are three shelves in the utility cabinet. On the top shelf, there are three fuses and two lightbulbs. On the second shelf, there's . . .

6 Guess the Object!
ACTIVITY HANDBOOK PAGES 7–8

Tell what different home supply objects are used for and have students guess the item. For example:

> You use it to see in the dark. [A flashlight.]
> You use it to measure the length of something. [A yardstick./ A tape measure.]

7 Miming Game
ACTIVITY HANDBOOK PAGE 11
ACTIVITY MASTER 44

Have students take turns pantomiming the use of home supply items. The class tries to guess what object the person is using.

Note: Some items such as fuses and masking, electrical, and duct tape are not possible to mime definitively and should be pulled from the word cards for this game.

8 Home Supply Match Game
ACTIVITY HANDBOOK PAGE 11
ACTIVITY MASTER 45

Have students find the person whose card matches theirs.

9 Home Supply Associations
ACTIVITY HANDBOOK PAGE 2

Call out home supply words and have groups write down as many associations as they can think of. For example:

insect:	[fly swatter/bug spray/roach killer]
light:	[flashlight/batteries/extension cord/ lightbulbs/fuses]
electricity:	[extension cord/lightbulbs/fuses/ electrical tape]
paint:	[paint roller/paintbrush/paint thinner/wall/ceilings/spray gun]
tape:	[masking tape/electrical tape/ duct tape]

10 Daffy Debate
ACTIVITY HANDBOOK PAGE 5
ACTIVITY MASTER 44

Have students debate which home supply items are more important than others.

11 Inventions
ACTIVITY HANDBOOK PAGE 9

Individually, in pairs, or in small groups, have students invent home supply items. Have them draw a picture of the object, name it, and describe what it's used for. You may wish to have the class vote for the most clever and most original invention.

Page 34 TOOLS AND HARDWARE

LESSON OBJECTIVE

Students will learn the vocabulary of tools typically used by people for home repairs.

RESOURCES

AUDIO PROGRAM
Words & Dialogs
Cassette 2A
CD 2: Tracks 14–16

MULTI-LEVEL WORKBOOKS

Literacy Workbook
Beginning & Intermediate Lifeskills Workbooks
Beginning & Intermediate Vocabulary Workbooks

ACTIVITY MASTER
Reproducible:
A46

TRANSPARENCY
Overhead: T34

LANGUAGE & CULTURE NOTES
Reproducible: LC34

WORDLINKS
longman.com/wordbyword

VOCABULARY INTRODUCTION

- Preview
- Present
- Practice

MODEL CONVERSATION PRACTICE

1. Have students look at the model illustration. Set the scene: "Two neighbors are talking."
2. Present the model.
3. Choral Repetition Practice: Full-Class and Individual.
4. Have pairs practice the model.
5. Have pairs present the model.
6. Call on pairs to present a new conversation using word 2.
7. Have pairs practice new conversations.
8. Have pairs present new conversations.

ADDITIONAL CONVERSATION PRACTICE

Before students practice the additional conversations, you may want to have them listen to the examples on the Audio Program.

Conversation 1 This conversation is for singular tools (1–15, 17–24). Set the scene: "Two family members are talking." Have students practice and present conversations with any words they wish.

Conversation 2 This conversation is for plural tools (16, 25–30). Set the scene: "Two family members are talking." Have students practice and present conversations with any words they wish.

SPELLING PRACTICE

Say a word, and have students spell it aloud or write it. Or, using the transparency, point to an item and have students write the word.

WRITING AND DISCUSSION

Have students respond to the question as a class, in pairs, or in small groups. Or have students write their responses, share their writing with other students, and discuss in class.

Making Connections

Resource Materials Bring in, or have students bring in, the following materials for vocabulary practice.

- *Newspaper advertisements for tools:* Talk about the tools and the prices.
- *Catalogs and brochures from hardware stores:* Talk about the tools and the prices.
- *Children's tool set:* Identify the tools and show how to use them.
- *The tools themselves:* Identify the tools and show how to use them.

Community Task Have individual students (or groups of students) visit different hardware stores and report about the tools these stores sell and the prices.

Communication Activities

1 ## Chain Game: I'm Going to the Hardware Store
ACTIVITY HANDBOOK PAGES 2–3

Begin the chain as follows: "I'm going to the hardware store to buy a hammer," and have students continue it. For example:

> Teacher: I'm going to the hardware store to buy a hammer.
> Student 1: I'm going to the hardware store to buy a hammer and pliers.
> Student 2: I'm going to the hardware store to buy a hammer, pliers, and an ax.
> Etc.

2 ## Telephone
ACTIVITY HANDBOOK PAGE 14

Begin the activity with the following sentence: "I'm looking for the chisel, the wrench, the scraper, the vise, and the screwdriver."

3 ## Talk in Circles

Have students take turns asking and answering questions about the location of tools on *Picture Dictionary* page 34. For example:

> Student 1: Where's the wrench?
> Student 2: Next to the monkey wrench.
> *[to Student 3]* Where are the pliers?
> Student 3: In the mother's hands.
> *[to Student 4]* Where's the hacksaw?
> Etc.

4 ## Location! Location!
ACTIVITY HANDBOOK PAGES 10–11

If you choose to do Version 1, ask questions such as the following:

Where's the handsaw?	[It's above the hacksaw.]
Where's the hand drill?	[It's between the wire stripper and the level.]
Where's the chisel?	[It's between the monkey wrench and the scraper.]
Where's the vise?	[It's on the workbench.]
Where's the mallet?	[It's between the hammer and the ax.]
Where's the screwdriver?	[It's next to the Phillips screwdriver.]
Where's the plane?	[It's in front of the toolbox.]
Where's the hammer?	[It's next to the mallet.]
What's the mother doing?	[She's assembling her son's toy car]

If you choose to do Version 2, make statements such as the following:

It's to the right of the mallet.	[The ax.]
It's to the left of the woman.	[The vise.]
It's in front of the toolbox.	[The plane.]
It's to the right of the wrench.	[The monkey wrench.]

5 ## True or False?
ACTIVITY HANDBOOK PAGE 15

Make statements such as the following about the scene on *Picture Dictionary* page 34. Have students decide whether the statements are true or false. For example:

The toolbox is on the floor.	[False. It's on the workbench.]
The vise is on the wall.	[False. It's on the workbench.]
The level is in the toolbox.	[False. It's on the wall.]
The ax is larger than the mallet.	[True.]

6 ## Movable Categories
ACTIVITY HANDBOOK PAGE 11
ACTIVITY MASTER 46

Call out the following categories and have students go to the appropriate side of the room:

things that cut
things that hold other things in place
things that require a pounding action
things that require a screwing action
things that require a *back and forth* action
things that have moving parts

7 ## Category Dictation
ACTIVITY HANDBOOK PAGE 2

Dictate words that fit into three of the above categories.

8 ## Miming Game
ACTIVITY HANDBOOK PAGE 11
ACTIVITY MASTER 46

Have students take turns pantomiming using tools. The class tries to guess what tool the person is using.

9 ## Drawing Game
ACTIVITY HANDBOOK PAGE 6
ACTIVITY MASTER 46

Have teams compete to identify tools and hardware items drawn by one of their team members.

LESSON OBJECTIVE

Students will learn vocabulary for outdoor gardening actions and associated gardening tools and equipment.

RESOURCES

AUDIO PROGRAM
Words & Dialogs
Cassette 2A
CD 2: Tracks 17–19

MULTI-LEVEL WORKBOOKS
Literacy Workbook
Beginning & Intermediate Lifeskills Workbooks
Beginning & Intermediate Vocabulary Workbooks

ACTIVITY MASTERS
Reproducibles:
A47–A49

TRANSPARENCY
Overhead: T35

LANGUAGE & CULTURE NOTES
Reproducible: LC35

WORDLINKS
longman.com/wordbyword

VOCABULARY INTRODUCTION

- Preview
- Present
- Practice

MODEL CONVERSATION PRACTICE

There are two model conversations—the first for actions, words A–H and the second for gardening tools, words 1–20. Introduce and practice the first model before going on to the second. For each model:

1. Have students look at the model illustration. Set the scene:

   Model 1: "Two neighbors are talking."
   Model 2: "A father and son are talking."

2. Present the model.

3. Choral Repetition Practice: Full-Class and Individual.

4. Have pairs practice the model.

5. Have pairs present the model.

6. Call on pairs to present a new conversation using word B for the first model and word 2 for the second model.

7. Have pairs practice new conversations.

8. Have pairs present new conversations.

ADDITIONAL CONVERSATION PRACTICE

Before students practice the additional conversations, you may want to have them listen to the examples on the Audio Program.

Conversation 1 Set the scene: "Two friends are talking." Have students practice and present conversations with any words they wish.

Conversation 2 Set the scene: "Two neighbors are talking." Have students practice and present conversations with any words they wish.

SPELLING PRACTICE

Say a word or phrase, and have students spell it aloud or write it. Or, using the transparency, point to an item and have students write the word or phrase.

WRITING AND DISCUSSION

Have students respond to the questions as a class, in pairs, or in small groups. Or have students write their responses, share their writing with other students, and discuss in class.

Making Connections

Resource Materials Bring in, or have students bring in, the following materials for vocabulary practice:

- *Newspaper advertisements of garden supplies:* Talk about the items and the prices.

- *Catalogs from garden supply stores:* Talk about the items and the prices and what the tools are used for.

Community Task Have individual students (or groups of students) visit different stores that sell gardening supplies and report about the items these stores sell and the prices.

Communication Activities

1 Drawing Game
ACTIVITY HANDBOOK PAGE 6
ACTIVITY MASTER 47

Have teams compete to identify the items drawn by one of their team members.

2 Concentration
ACTIVITY HANDBOOK PAGE 3
ACTIVITY MASTER 48

Have students shuffle the cards and place them face-down in five rows of 4 each, then attempt to find cards that match.

3 Stand in Order
ACTIVITY HANDBOOK PAGE 14
ACTIVITY MASTER 47

Have students arrange themselves alphabetically according to the Gardening Tools Word Card they have.

4 Guess the Object!
ACTIVITY HANDBOOK PAGES 7–8

Tell what different garden objects are used for and have students guess the item. For example:

You use this to cut the grass.	[A lawnmower.]
You use this to dig a small hole to plant flowers.	[A trowel.]
You use this to water the lawn.	[A sprinkler.]
You use this to gather leaves.	[A rake.]
You use this to dig a large hole.	[A shovel.]
You use this to cut back a hedge or bush.	[Hedge clippers.]
You use this to remove weeds.	[A weeder.]
You place all the dead leaves in this.	[A yard waste bag.]
You use this to make plants grow.	[Fertilizer.]
You use it to stop and start the flow of water on a garden hose.	[A nozzle.]

5 True or False?
ACTIVITY HANDBOOK PAGE 15

Make statements such as the following about the scenes on *Picture Dictionary* page 35. Have students decide whether the statements are true or false. For example:

> The woman in Picture A is mowing the lawn with a shovel. [False. She's mowing the lawn with a lawnmower.]
> The man in Picture B is throwing vegetables on the ground. [False. He's throwing vegetable seeds on the ground.]
> The woman in Picture C is using a sprinkler to plant flowers. [False. She's using a trowel.]
> The person in Picture D is watering the flowers with a watering can. [True.]
> The woman in Picture E is raking the leaves with a nozzle. [False. She's raking the leaves with a rake.]
> The man in Picture F is trimming the hedge with pruning shears. [False. He's trimming the hedge with hedge clippers.]
> The woman in Picture G is pruning the bushes with a hoe. [False. She's pruning the bushes with pruning shears.]
> The man in Picture H is weeding the garden with fertilizer. [False. He's weeding the garden with a weeder.]

6 Miming Game
ACTIVITY HANDBOOK PAGE 11
ACTIVITY MASTER 48 (WORDS ONLY)

Have students take turns pantomiming gardening actions. The class tries to guess what the person is doing. For example:

> You're mowing the lawn.
> You're weeding.

7 Chain Game
ACTIVITY HANDBOOK PAGES 2–3

Begin the chain as follows: "I'm going to work in the yard. First I'm going to mow the lawn," and have students continue it. For example:

Teacher: I'm going to work in the yard. First I'm going to mow the lawn.

Student 1: I'm going to work in the yard. First I'm going to mow the lawn. Then I'm going to prune the bushes.

Student 2: I'm going to work in the yard. First I'm going to mow the lawn. Then I'm going to prune the bushes. Then I'm going to trim the hedges.

Etc.

8 Movable Categories
ACTIVITY HANDBOOK PAGE 11
ACTIVITY MASTER 47

Call out the following categories and have students go to the appropriate side of the room:

things you use to dig
things you use to water plants
things you use to cut plants
things you use to clean up a garden and yard
things you use to grow plants
things with wheels
things that carry other things

9 Category Dictation
ACTIVITY HANDBOOK PAGE 2

Dictate words that fit into three of the above categories.

10 Gardening Match Game
ACTIVITY HANDBOOK PAGE 11
ACTIVITY MASTER 49

Have students find the person whose card matches theirs.

11 Secret Word Associations
ACTIVITY HANDBOOK PAGE 14

Have students choose a gardening item, brainstorm associations with that word, and see if the class can guess the word. For example:

lawnmower / fertilizer / grass seed / rake / hose:	[lawn]
grass / vegetable seeds / water / garden:	[watering can]
rake / leaf blower / yard waste bag:	[leaves]
rake / hoe / vegetable seeds / fertilizer / work gloves:	[garden]

12 Ranking
ACTIVITY HANDBOOK PAGE 13

Have students look at the gardening tools on *Picture Dictionary* page 35 and choose the five items they use the most.

13 Daffy Debate!
ACTIVITY HANDBOOK PAGE 5
ACTIVITY MASTER 47

Have students debate which gardening tools are more important than others.

14 Gardening Tips

In small groups, have students discuss the following questions. After their discussion, have them share what they learned with the class.

Do you like to work in the garden?
What's in your garden?
What are your favorite vegetables to grow?
What are your favorite flowers? Why?

15 Inventions
ACTIVITY HANDBOOK PAGE 9

Individually, in pairs, or in small groups, have students invent a gardening tool. Have them draw a picture of the object, name it, and describe what it's used for. You may wish to have the class vote for the most clever and most original invention.

Unit 4 Communication Activity Review

1 Secret Word Associations
ACTIVITY HANDBOOK PAGE 14

Have students choose a room, brainstorm associations with that room, and see if the class can guess the room. For example:

coffee table/sofa/VCR/ fireplace:	[living room]
crib/changing table/diaper pail/toy chest:	[baby's room]
tablecloth/serving bowl/ table/chairs:	[dining room]
tub/sink/towel/toilet:	[bathroom]

2 Drawing Game
ACTIVITY HANDBOOK PAGE 6
ACTIVITY MASTERS 30, 31, 32, 33, 34, 38

Have teams compete to identify the items drawn by one of their team members.

3 Bleep!
ACTIVITY HANDBOOK PAGE 2
ACTIVITY MASTERS 40, 46

Have students create conversations based on four word cards that they select.

4 Movable Categories
ACTIVITY HANDBOOK PAGE 11
ACTIVITY MASTERS 32, 42, 44

Place all the above word cards in a bag. Have each student select two cards. Call out the following categories and have students go to the appropriate side of the room:

- things that use water
- things that wash
- things that kill insects
- things that use electricity
- things that make noise
- things that heat up
- things that clean the floor
- things related to garbage
- things you use to paint
- things that use batteries

5 Miming Game
ACTIVITY HANDBOOK PAGE 11
ACTIVITY MASTERS 43, 48

Have students take turns pantomiming the words. The class tries to guess what the person is doing.

6 Home Life Concentration
ACTIVITY HANDBOOK PAGE 3
ACTIVITY MASTER 50

Have students shuffle the cards and place them face-down in three rows of 6 each, then attempt to find cards that match.

7 Do It Yourself!

a. Write on the board these home repair projects:

> The front steps are broken.
> The power is out in the living room.
> The toilet is clogged.
> The faucet is leaking.
> You have to build a new deck.
> Your lamppost is broken.
> There are insects all over the house.
> A drainpipe is broken.
> The back door is stuck.
> The paint in the living room is peeling.
> There are mice in the house.
> The hot water heater isn't working.

b. Have pairs of students choose two situations and decide what home supplies and tools they would need to fix the problems.

c. Have each pair share their list with the class.

8 Housing Quiz Game
ACTIVITY MASTER 51

a. Divide the class into four teams.

b. Copy and cut up Activity Master 51 and place cards face-down in a pile.

c. Have the teams take turns picking a card and answering the questions. Give each team a time limit (either 30 seconds or 1 minute) to answer each question.

d. The team with the most correct answers wins.

Topics	Dictionary	Teacher's Guide
Places Around Town I	36–37	90–91
Places Around Town II	38–39	92–94
The City	40–41	95–97
Unit 5 Communication Activity Review	36–41	98

AUDIO PROGRAM

Words & Dialogs	WordSong: *The City*
Audio Cassette 2A	Audio Cassette 7A
Audio CD 2:	Audio CD 7: Tracks 24
Tracks 20–28	(Vocal) & 25 (Sing-along)
	Song Masters S9, S10

WORKBOOKS

For Multi-Level Practice

Literacy Workbook
Beginning Lifeskills Workbook
Beginning Vocabulary Workbook
Intermediate Lifeskills Workbook
Intermediate Vocabulary Workbook

WORDLINKS

**Internet Resources through the
Word by Word Companion Website**

http://www.longman.com/wordbyword

ACTIVITY MASTERS

Reproducibles for Communication Activities
A52–A58

TRANSPARENCIES

Full-Color Overheads for Class Practice
T36–T41

LANGUAGE & CULTURE NOTES

**Information for Teachers &
Intermediate /Advanced Students**
LC36–37—LC40–41

VOCABULARY GAME CARDS

**For Vocabulary Practice,
Activities, & Games**
Cards 67–122

LESSON OBJECTIVE

Students will learn the vocabulary of various retail stores and other places in the community.

RESOURCES

AUDIO PROGRAM		MULTI-LEVEL WORKBOOKS	VOCABULARY GAME CARDS
Words & Dialogs Cassette 2A CD 2: Tracks 20–22	**WordSong:** *The City* Cassette 7A • CD 7: Tracks 24, 25 Song Masters S9, S10	Literacy Workbook Beginning & Intermediate Lifeskills Workbooks Beginning & Intermediate Vocabulary Workbooks	Cards 67–94

ACTIVITY MASTERS	TRANSPARENCIES	LANGUAGE & CULTURE NOTES	WORDLINKS
Reproducibles: A52, A54	**Overheads:** T36, T37	**Reproducible:** LC36–37	longman.com/wordbyword

VOCABULARY INTRODUCTION

- Preview
- Present
- Practice

MODEL CONVERSATION PRACTICE

1. Have students look at the model illustration. Set the scene: "Two friends just met on the street."
2. Present the model.
3. Choral Repetition Practice: Full-Class and Individual.
4. Have pairs practice the model.
5. Have pairs present the model.
6. Call on pairs to present a new conversation using word 2.
7. Have pairs practice new conversations.
8. Have pairs present new conversations.

ADDITIONAL CONVERSATION PRACTICE

Before students practice the additional conversations, you may want to have them listen to the examples on the Audio Program.

Conversation 1 Set the scene: "Two friends just met on the street." Have students practice and present conversations with any words they wish.

Conversation 2 Set the scene: "Two family members are talking." Have students practice and present conversations with any words they wish.

SPELLING PRACTICE

Say a word, and have students spell it aloud or write it. Or, using the transparency, point to an item and have students write the word.

WRITING AND DISCUSSION

Have students respond to the question as a class, in pairs, or in small groups. Or have students write their responses, share their writing with other students, and discuss in class.

♫♫ WORDSONG ♫♫

1. Have students listen to the vocal version of *The City* one or more times. Then have students listen again as they read the song lyrics on Song Master S9.
2. Have students sing as you play either the vocal or the sing-along version of the song.
3. For fun, have a song competition in which students perform solo or in groups and the class votes for the best performance.
4. For additional practice, students can complete the cloze exercise on Song Master S10.

VOCABULARY GAME CARDS

Have students practice vocabulary, do activities, and play games with Vocabulary Game Cards 67–94. Activities and games are described in the set of cards.

Resource Materials Bring in, or have students bring in, the following materials for vocabulary practice:

○ *Magazine and newspaper pictures of different places around town:* Talk about the places and things people do there.

○ *Neighborhood maps showing locations of stores:* Have students talk about the maps and tell which places they know—the names of the places and why they go there.

Community Task Have individual students (or groups of students) walk around an area of your city or town and report about the places they saw.

Communication Activities

See the Communication Activities on pages 93 and 94 for *Places Around Town II*.

LESSON OBJECTIVE

Students will learn the vocabulary of various retail stores and other places in the community.

RESOURCES

AUDIO PROGRAM		MULTI-LEVEL WORKBOOKS 	VOCABULARY GAME CARDS
Words & Dialogs	**WordSong:** *The City*	Literacy Workbook	Cards 67–122
Cassette 2A	Cassette 7A • CD 7: Tracks 24, 25	Beginning & Intermediate Lifeskills Workbooks	
CD 2: Tracks 23–25	Song Masters S9, S10	Beginning & Intermediate Vocabulary Workbooks	

ACTIVITY MASTERS	TRANSPARENCIES	LANGUAGE & CULTURE NOTES 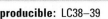	WORDLINKS
Reproducibles: A52–A55	**Overheads:** T38, T39	**Reproducible:** LC38–39	longman.com/wordbyword

VOCABULARY INTRODUCTION

- Preview
- Present
- Practice

MODEL CONVERSATION PRACTICE

1. Have students look at the model illustration. Set the scene: "A husband and wife are talking. They're looking for the hair salon."
2. Present the model.
3. Choral Repetition Practice: Full-Class and Individual.
4. Have pairs practice the model.
5. Have pairs present the model.
6. Call on pairs to present a new conversation using word 2.
7. Have pairs practice new conversations.
8. Have pairs present new conversations.

ADDITIONAL CONVERSATION PRACTICE

Before students practice the additional conversations, you may want to have them listen to the examples on the Audio Program.

Conversation 1 Set the scene: "Two strangers are talking on the street." Have students practice and present conversations with any words they wish.

Conversation 2 Set the scene: "Two strangers are talking on the street." Have students practice and present conversations with any words they wish.

SPELLING PRACTICE

Say a word, and have students spell it aloud or write it. Or, using the transparency, point to an item and have students write the word.

WRITING AND DISCUSSION

Have students respond to the question as a class, in pairs, or in small groups. Or have students write their responses, share their writing with other students, and discuss in class.

VOCABULARY GAME CARDS

Have students practice vocabulary, do activities, and play games with Vocabulary Game Cards 67–122. Activities and games are described in the set of cards.

Making Connections

Resource Materials Bring in, or have students bring in, the following materials for vocabulary practice:

- *Magazine and newspaper pictures of different places around town:* Talk about the places and things people do there.

- *Neighborhood maps showing locations of stores:* Have students talk about the maps and tell which places they know—the names of the places and why they go there.

Community Task Have individual students (or groups of students) walk around an area of your city or town and report about the places they saw.

Communication Activities

The following activities are appropriate for both *Places Around Town I* and *Places Around Town II*. You can do the activities separately for each lesson or together for both lessons.

1 Expand the Conversation

ACTIVITY HANDBOOK PAGE 6

Expand Additional Conversation 1 on *Picture Dictionary* page 37 to have people tell why they're going to those places.

a. Write the following on the board:

A. Hi! How are you today?
B. Fine. Where are you going?
A. To the _____. I'm going there to _____. How about you?
B. I'm going to the _____. I have to _____.
A. Well, take care.
B. You, too.

b. Have pairs of students practice and present conversations based on this model, using different words from *Picture Dictionary* pages 36–39.

2 What's the Place?

ACTIVITY HANDBOOK PAGE 16

Describe a reason for going to places around town, and have students try to guess which place you're talking about. For example:

A man goes there to get a haircut. [A barber shop.]
People go there to buy building tools. [A hardware store.]
People go there to exercise. [A health club.]
People buy necklaces and rings there. [A jewelry store.]
People buy CD's and cassettes there. [A music store.]
People go there when they're sick. [A clinic/ A hospital.]
People buy small gifts and cards there. [A card store.]
When people are away from home, they stay there. [A motel.]

3 Concentration

ACTIVITY HANDBOOK PAGE 3
ACTIVITY MASTERS 52, 53

To do the activities separately for each lesson, have students shuffle the cards on each Activity Master and place them face-down in three rows of 6 each, then attempt to find pairs that match. (If you wish to do the activity for both lessons simultaneously, shuffle both sets and place them face-down in six rows of 6 each.)

4 True or False?

ACTIVITY HANDBOOK PAGE 15

Make statements such as the following about the scenes on *Picture Dictionary* pages 36–37 and/or pages 38–39. Have students decide whether the statements are true or false. For example:

The customer in the bakery is a woman. [True.]
Someone is buying a book in the book store. [True.]
A young boy is buying candy in the candy store. [False. A young girl is buying candy.]
There are three people waiting in the clinic. [True.]
The salesperson in the car dealership is a man. [False. The salesperson is a woman.]
The children in the day-care center are playing ball. [False. They're playing with blocks.]
A young woman is picking up her pictures at the photo shop. [False. A young man is picking up his pictures.]
Two people are sitting on the benches in the mall. [False. One man is sitting on the bench.]
A woman and her children are buying food at the supermarket. [False. A woman and a man are buying food.]
Two children are playing in the toy store. [False. One boy is playing with a ball in the toy store.]

5 Finish the Sentence!

ACTIVITY HANDBOOK PAGE 7

Begin sentences such as the following for students to complete:

You deposit money in a . . . *bank*.
You get your clothes cleaned at a . . . *dry cleaners*.
You can buy chocolate in a . . . *candy store*.
You get medicine at a . . . *drug store*.
You buy tools at a . . . *hardware store*.
You buy watches and rings in a . . . *jewelry store*.
You mail letters and packages at a . . . *post office*.
Children study in a . . . *school*.
You can rent a movie from a . . . *video store*.

(continued)

6 Class Directory

Have everybody in the class supply the names and addresses of places around town they are familiar with and/or recommend. Compile the information and create a class directory.

7 Comparing Places Around Town

As a class or in pairs, have students tell how stores and other places around town in the United States are different from or similar to those in their countries.

8 Tell Me About Your Job

Find out if anyone in the class works at one of the places depicted on *Picture Dictionary* pages 36–39. If so, have that person tell something he or she does there, and have others guess where the person works. For example:

    A. I sell tickets.
    B. Do you work at a movie theater?
    A. No, I don't.
    B. Do you work at a travel agency?
    A. Yes, I do.

Have the person then tell more about his or her job.

9 What Can You Do There?
ACTIVITY HANDBOOK PAGES 15–16

Have the class brainstorm all the things a person can do, see, or buy in a particular place. Write their suggestions on the board.

10 Clues
ACTIVITY HANDBOOK PAGE 3

After one student leaves the room, have the class think of a statement they can make about a place in town. For example:

    I go there every morning to buy the paper.
    I sometimes go there at night to buy milk.
    I go there because I like to buy lottery tickets.
    I go there because it's less crowded than the
      supermarket.

    [Answer: convenience store]

11 Daffy Debate!
ACTIVITY HANDBOOK PAGE 5
ACTIVITY MASTERS 52, 53 (WORDS ONLY)

Have students debate which places around town are more important than others.

12 Mystery Word Conversations
ACTIVITY HANDBOOK PAGE 12

Have groups create mystery conversations about places around town without naming the place. The class tries to guess where the conversation is taking place. For example:

    A. I'm here to see a patient, Manuel Romero.
    B. He's in Room 217 on the second floor.
    A. How do I get there?
    B. Take that elevator over there.

    [Answer: hospital]

13 Places Around Town Match Game
ACTIVITY HANDBOOK PAGE 11
ACTIVITY MASTERS 54, 55

Do each Match Game separately. Have students find the person whose card matches theirs. When all the pairs have been matched, have students say their lines for the whole class. Everybody should then decide where each conversation takes place.

14 Ranking
ACTIVITY HANDBOOK PAGE 13

Have students look at one page at a time of the *Places Around Town*. Have them discuss their answers to the following questions in pairs or small groups:

    Which five places do you visit most often?
    Which places *don't* you visit?
    Which three places would you like to have in your
      neighborhood? Why?
    Which three places would you *not* like to have in your
      neighborhood? Why?

15 Around Town Research

a. Have each student select a place around town he or she would like to learn more about.

b. Then have students write out a list of questions they would like to have answered about that place. For example:

    What do they sell there?
    What hours are they open?
    What are the prices of some of the products?
    Are the prices expensive or reasonable?
    Are the salespeople friendly?

c. Students should then visit that place, research answers to the questions, collect any pertinent information and/or interview as many people as necessary, and then report back to the class.

LESSON OBJECTIVE

Students will learn the vocabulary for a city intersection and surrounding buildings.

RESOURCES

AUDIO PROGRAM		MULTI-LEVEL WORKBOOKS	VOCABULARY GAME CARDS
Words & Dialogs	**WordSong:** *The City*	Literacy Workbook	
Cassette 2A	Cassette 7A • CD 7: Tracks 24, 25	Beginning & Intermediate Lifeskills Workbooks	Cards 67–122
CD 2: Tracks 26–28	Song Masters S9, S10	Beginning & Intermediate Vocabulary Workbooks	

ACTIVITY MASTER 	TRANSPARENCIES	LANGUAGE & CULTURE NOTES	WORDLINKS
Reproducible: A56	**Overheads:** T40, T41	**Reproducible:** LC40–41	longman.com/wordbyword

VOCABULARY INTRODUCTION

- Preview
- Present
- Practice

MODEL CONVERSATION PRACTICE

The location of each of the words can be described as being either *on, in, next to, between, across from, in front of, behind, under,* or *over* another.

1. Have students look at the model illustration. Set the scene: "Two strangers are talking on the street."

2. Present the model with the preposition *next to* using words 1 and 7. Check students' understanding of the situation and the vocabulary.

3. Choral Repetition Practice: Full-Class and Individual.

4. Have pairs practice the model.

5. Call on a pair of students to present a conversation based on the model with the preposition *between* and words 7, 1, and 11 using steps 3–5 above.

6. Call on pairs to present a conversation with the preposition *in front of* and words 2 and 1.

7. Have pairs practice new conversations.

8. Have pairs present new conversations.

ADDITIONAL CONVERSATION PRACTICE

Before students develop their speeches, you may want to have them listen to the example on the Audio Program.

Have students pretend they're running for mayor of their city. As part of their campaign, they're going to deliver a speech in which they promise to take care of all their city's problems. Have students spend time rehearsing their speeches and then deliver them with as much expression and enthusiasm as possible to the citizens of the city (the other students in the class). You might want to have the class vote on the most effective speech, and that person can be declared the *winner* of the election.

> Example:
>
> If I am elected mayor, I'll take care of all the problems in our city. We need to do something about our *streets.* We also need to do something about our *sidewalks.* And look at our *sewers*! We REALLY need to do something about THEM! We need a new mayor who can solve these problems. If I am elected mayor, we'll be proud of our *streets, sidewalks,* and *sewers* again! Vote for me!

SPELLING PRACTICE

Say a word, and have students spell it aloud or write it. Or, using the transparency, point to an item and have students write the word.

WRITING AND DISCUSSION

Have students respond to the question as a class, in pairs, or in small groups. Or have students write their responses, share their writing with other students, and discuss in class.

Have students practice vocabulary, do activities, and play games with Vocabulary Game Cards 67–122. Activities and games are described in the set of cards.

Making Connections

Resource Materials Bring in, or have students bring in, the following materials for vocabulary practice:

○ *Maps of downtown areas:* Identify streets and places.

○ *Magazine and newspaper pictures of city scenes:* Talk about the scenes.

○ *Postcards or printouts of Internet websites showing city scenes:* Describe the scenes.

Community Task Have individual students (or groups of students) visit different areas of your city or town and report about what they saw.

Communication Activities

1 Location! Location!
ACTIVITY HANDBOOK PAGES 10–11

If you choose to do Version 1, ask questions such as the following:

> Where's the garbage truck?
> Where's the subway station?
> Where's the jail?
> Where's the courthouse?
> Where's city hall?
> Where's the bank?
> Where's the parking lot?
> Where's the police station?
> Where's the meter maid?
> Where's the mayor?
> Where's the parking garage?

If you choose to do Version 2, make statements such as the following:

> It's next to the fire station. [The office building.]
> He's on the corner near the drive-through window. [The street vendor.]
> It's in front of the courthouse. [The taxi stand.]
> It's across from the parking lot. [The courthouse.]
> It's on the corner across from the police station. [The newsstand.]
> He's in the middle of the intersection. [The police officer.]
> They're on the corner of every street. [The street signs.]
> It's on the sidewalk in front of the courthouse and city hall. [The fire hydrant.]
> It's next to the fire station. [The parking garage.]
> It's on the sidewalk in front of the police station. [The mailbox.]

2 Movable Categories
ACTIVITY HANDBOOK PAGE 11
ACTIVITY MASTER 56

Call out the following categories and have students go to the appropriate side of the room:

> vehicles
> people
> buildings
> public transportation
> things that are on a sidewalk
> things that are on a street

3 Do You Remember?
ACTIVITY HANDBOOK PAGE 5

Have students write down everything they remember about the city scene depicted on *Picture Dictionary* pages 40–41.

If you do Variation 1, ask questions such as the following:

> What building is next to the police station?
> How many taxis are on the street?
> Where's the newsstand?
> How many buses are on the street?
> How many pedestrians are in the scene?
> How many people are waiting for the bus?
> How many people are waiting for the subway?
> How many street lights are there?
> How many buildings are there?
> What's the meter maid doing?
> Is the police officer speaking with anyone?

4 Picture This!

ACTIVITY HANDBOOK PAGES 12–13

Describe a street scene and have students draw what you describe. For example:

> In this city there's a long street with two tall office buildings on either end. Next to the office building on the left is a bank with a drive-through window. Across from the bank there's . . . .

5 Connections

ACTIVITY HANDBOOK PAGE 4
ACTIVITY MASTER 56

Have students make connections between two city items. For example:

> bus—taxi
> They both carry passengers. The bus is much larger than a taxi.
>
> curb—intersection
> You step over the curb before you cross an intersection.

6 Drawing Game

ACTIVITY HANDBOOK PAGE 6
ACTIVITY MASTER 56

Have teams compete to identify city items drawn by one of their team members.

7 Read, Write, and Draw

ACTIVITY HANDBOOK PAGE 13

Have students write each other letters in which they describe a city scene.

8 Who Are These People?

Have students use their imaginations to tell about each person in the city scene on *Picture Dictionary* pages 40–41. For example:

Who are they?	What are they doing?
Where are they?	Where are they going?

9 General-to-Specific Clue Game

ACTIVITY HANDBOOK PAGE 7

Possible clues:

> Clue 1: I cost money.
> Clue 2: I have a driver.
> Clue 3: I use gas.
> Clue 4: I go along the street.
> Clue 5: I transport many people.
>
> [Answer: a bus]

10 A City Scene

Have students write a description of the city scene on *Picture Dictionary* pages 40–41. They should decide on a name for the city and describe what they see. For example:

> It's a very busy afternoon on Main Street in Yorktown. There's a police officer directing traffic at the intersection of Main Street and Central Avenue. There are a lot of pedestrians on the street. Some are crossing at the crosswalk. Others are walking along the sidewalk. There are many buildings nearby. There's a jail on the corner. Next to the jail, there's a courthouse. (Etc.)

11 City Associations

ACTIVITY HANDBOOK PAGE 2

Call out city words and have groups write down as many associations as they can think of. For example:

bus:	[bus driver/change/seat/bus stop/passenger]
intersection:	[crosswalk/pedestrians/traffic light/traffic]
fire station:	[fire truck/firefighter/fire hydrant/fire alarm box/911]
taxi:	[taxi driver/taxi stand/tip/gasoline/yellow]
jail:	[crime/criminal/courthouse/lawyer/police officer]

12 Secret Word Associations

ACTIVITY HANDBOOK PAGE 14

Have students choose a city item, brainstorm associations with that word, and see if the class can guess the word. For example:

judge/lawyers/trial/law:	[courthouse]
newspapers/magazines/candy/maps:	[newsstand]
trains/tokens/commuters/seats:	[subway]

13 Chain Story

ACTIVITY HANDBOOK PAGE 3

Begin the story as follows: "Officer Lopez directed traffic in front of the courthouse today. It was a difficult day."

Unit 5 Communication Activity Review

1 True or False Definitions
ACTIVITY HANDBOOK PAGE 15

Give true and false definitions of community words and have students decide which are true and which are false. For example:

> A curb is the edge of a sidewalk. [True.]
> A meter maid is a person who cleans houses. [False. A meter maid is a person who checks parking meters.]
> A pedestrian is a person who drives a car. [False. A pedestrian is a person who walks.]
> A street vendor sells food on the street. [True.]
> A mall is a big store. [False. A mall is a big building with many different stores inside it.]
> A library sells books. [False. A book store sells books. A library loans books.]
> Only men go to a hair salon. [False. Both men and women have their hair cut in a hair salon.]
> A card store sells paper and office supplies. [False. A card store sells cards and small gift items.]
> A photo shop is a place where a professional photographer takes pictures. [False. A photo shop is a place where a person gets pictures printed.]

2 Around Town Match Game
ACTIVITY HANDBOOK PAGE 11
ACTIVITY MASTER 57

Have students find the person whose card matches theirs.

3 Mystery Word Conversations
ACTIVITY HANDBOOK PAGE 12

Have groups create mystery conversations about any of the places on *Picture Dictionary* pages 36–41 without naming the place. The class tries to guess where the conversation is taking place. For example:

> A. Where did we leave our car?
> B. Hmm. I can't remember. Did we leave it on the first floor?
> A. I don't think so. I'm pretty sure we left on the second or the third.
>   [Answer: parking garage]

> A. Could you please tell me when we get to the Central Square stop?
> B. Sure. Take a seat nearby so you can hear me when I call it out.
> A. Thanks.
>   [Answer: bus]

4 Secret Word Associations
ACTIVITY HANDBOOK PAGE 14

Have students choose community items, brainstorm associations with those items, and see if the class can guess the words. For example:

lawyers/trials/jury/ judges:	[courthouse]
young children/toys/ playground:	[day-care center]
magazines/newspapers/ maps/candy:	[newspaper stand]
underground/noisy/ fast/transportation/ crowded:	[subway]

5 Community Quiz Game
ACTIVITY MASTER 58

a. Divide the class into four teams.

b. Copy and cut up Activity Master 58 and place cards face-down in a pile.

c. Have teams take turns answering the questions. Give each team a time limit to answer each question (30 seconds or 1 minute).

d. The team with the most correct answers wins.

6 To Do Lists

a. Have students individually write a list of all the things they need to do this week.

b. In pairs, have students trade lists and then write all the places their partners need to go to get everything done. For example:

To Do	Places to Go
pick up clean shirts	cleaners
get milk, cheese, and bread	supermarket or convenience store
get a new cell phone	electronics store
make copies of notes	copy store or library
get a subway pass	subway station

7 Where Did You Go and What Did You Do?

a. Have students list all the places they went during the past week.

b. In pairs, have students discuss where they went and what they did there.

c. At the conclusion of the activity, ask the class: "Who went to the most places this week?"

UNIT 6 Describing

Topics	Dictionary	Teacher's Guide
People and Physical Descriptions	42–43	100–101
Describing People and Things	44–45	102–104
Describing Physical States and Emotions	46–47	105–107
Unit 6 Communication Activity Review	42–47	108

AUDIO PROGRAM

Words & Dialogs	**WordSong:** *Opposites*
Audio Cassette 2A	Audio Cassette 7A
Audio CD 2:	Audio CD 7: Tracks 26
Tracks 29–35	(Vocal), 27 (Response), &
	28 (Sing-along)
	Song Masters S11, S12

WORKBOOKS

For Multi-Level Practice
Literacy Workbook
Beginning Lifeskills Workbook
Beginning Vocabulary Workbook
Intermediate Lifeskills Workbook
Intermediate Vocabulary Workbook

WORDLINKS

Internet Resources through the
***Word by Word* Companion Website**

http://www.longman.com/wordbyword

ACTIVITY MASTERS

Reproducibles for Communication Activities
A8, A59–A62

TRANSPARENCIES

Full-Color Overheads for Class Practice
T42–T47

LANGUAGE & CULTURE NOTES

**Information for Teachers &
Intermediate /Advanced Students**
LC42–43—LC46–47

VOCABULARY GAME CARDS

**For Vocabulary Practice,
Activities, & Games**
Cards 123–154

LESSON OBJECTIVE

Students will learn the vocabulary that describes people's age, physical conditions, and physical characteristics.

RESOURCES

AUDIO PROGRAM
Words & Dialogs
Cassette 2A
CD 2: Tracks 29, 30

MULTI-LEVEL WORKBOOKS
Literacy Workbook
Beginning & Intermediate Lifeskills Workbooks
Beginning & Intermediate Vocabulary Workbooks

TRANSPARENCIES
Overheads: T42, T43

LANGUAGE & CULTURE NOTES
Reproducible: LC42–43

WORDLINKS
longman.com/wordbyword

VOCABULARY INTRODUCTION

- Preview
- Present
- Practice

MODEL CONVERSATION PRACTICE

There are four model conversations. Introduce and practice each before going on to the next. For each model:

1. Have students look at the model illustration. Set the scene:

   Model 1: "Two friends are talking."
   Model 2: "Two friends are talking."
   Model 3: "Someone took this woman's purse. A police officer is asking her some questions."
   Model 4: "A little boy can't find his grandmother at the mall. A mall security guard is asking him some questions."

2. Present the model.

3. Choral Repetition Practice: Full-Class and Individual.

4. Have pairs practice the model.

5. Have pairs present the model.

6. Call on pairs to present a new conversation based on each model.

   Model 1: Students should use other words for height, weight, and hair.
   Model 2: Students should use other words for height and hair.
   Model 3: Students should use other words for height, weight, age, and hair.

   Model 4: Students should use other words for height, weight, age, hair, and other physical characteristics.

7. Have pairs practice new conversations.

8. Have pairs present new conversations.

SPELLING PRACTICE

Say a word, and have students spell it aloud or write it. Or, using the transparency, point to an item and have students write the word.

WRITING AND DISCUSSION

Have students respond to the questions as a class, in pairs, or in small groups. Or have students write their responses, share their writing with other students, and discuss in class.

Making Connections

Resource Materials Bring in, or have students bring in, the following materials for vocabulary practice:

- *Pictures from fashion magazines:* Describe the people in the pictures.

- *Pictures from magazines and newspaper articles:* Describe the people in the pictures.

Communication Activities

1 Telephone
ACTIVITY HANDBOOK PAGE 14

Begin the activity with the following description: "She's a tall thin teenager with short straight black hair and brown eyes."

2 Guess Who I Am!

a. Ask students to write on a piece of paper three or more sentences describing themselves. Students should not write their names on their papers.

b. Collect the students' descriptions, read them to the class, and have students guess who wrote them.

Variation: Put all the descriptions on a handout and make a copy for each student in the class. Have students then guess who everybody is.

3 Do You Remember?
ACTIVITY HANDBOOK PAGE 5

Find a scene with lots of people in it in a magazine or newspaper. For 30 seconds show the class the scene, and have students write down descriptions of each person in the scene.

4 True or False?
ACTIVITY HANDBOOK PAGE 15

Make statements such as the following about words from the lesson. Have students decide whether the statements are true or false. For example:

A toddler is a one-week-old baby. [False. A toddler is a one- or two-year-old who can walk.]
An infant is a very young baby. [True.]
A middle-aged person is between the ages of 20 and 30. [False. A middle-aged person is between the ages of 40 and 60.]
Vision impaired means a person cannot see well. [True.]
Hearing impaired means a person cannot speak well. [False. Hearing impaired means a person cannot hear well.]
Slim means "heavy." [False. Slim means "thin."]
A senior citizen is a person who is 65 years or older. [True.]
Blond hair is yellow. [True.]
A bald person has a lot of hair on his head. [False. A bald person has little or no hair on his head.]
A teenager is a person between the ages of 13 and 19. [True.]

5 Investigate It!

Explain to the class that advertisements try to target their products to a certain age and type of person.

a. Bring to class several magazines.

b. In pairs or small groups, have students look at advertisements in the magazines and decide what kind of person is the target of each advertisement. Have students answer the following questions:

Is this advertisement for men or women?
Is this advertisement for young or old people? What age?
Is this advertisement for people who are heavy or thin?
Is this advertisement for pregnant women?

c. Have students share their ideas with the class. For example:

This advertisement is for senior citizens because the person in the ad is elderly and the product is about retirement.

I think this advertisement is for middle-aged mothers of young children because it shows a picture of a happy baby with a middle-aged woman.

LESSON OBJECTIVE

Students will learn sets of opposite adjectives used to describe people and things.

RESOURCES

AUDIO PROGRAM		MULTI-LEVEL WORKBOOKS	ACTIVITY MASTER
Words & Dialogs Cassette 2A CD 2: Tracks 31–33	**WordSong:** *Opposites* Cassette 7A • CD 7: Tracks 26–28 Song Masters S11, S12	Literacy Workbook Beginning & Intermediate Lifeskills Workbooks Beginning & Intermediate Vocabulary Workbooks	**Reproducible:** A8

TRANSPARENCY	LANGUAGE & CULTURE NOTES	WORDLINKS
Overheads: T44, T45	**Reproducible:** LC44–45	longman.com/wordbyword

VOCABULARY INTRODUCTION

- Preview
- Present
- Practice

MODEL CONVERSATION PRACTICE

1. Have students look at the model illustration. Set the scene: "Two friends are talking. One is asking about the other person's car."
2. Present the model.
3. Choral Repetition Practice: Full-Class and Individual.
4. Have pairs practice the model.
5. Have pairs present the model.
6. Call on pairs to present a new conversation using the question for words 3–4 on *Picture Dictionary* page 45.
7. Have pairs practice new conversations using different paired words and the corresponding questions on page 45.
8. Have pairs present new conversations.

ADDITIONAL CONVERSATION PRACTICE

Before students practice the additional conversations, you may want to have them listen to the examples on the Audio Program.

Conversation 1 Have students practice and present conversations with any words they wish.

Conversation 2 Have students practice and present conversations with any words they wish.

SPELLING PRACTICE

Say a word, and have students spell it aloud or write it. Or, using the transparency, point to an item and have students write the word.

WRITING AND DISCUSSION

Have students respond to the questions as a class, in pairs, or in small groups. Or have students write their responses, share their writing with other students, and discuss in class.

♫♫ WORDSONG ♫♫

1. Have students listen to the vocal version of *Opposites* one or more times. Then have students listen again as they read the song lyrics on Song Master S11.
2. Have students sing as you play the vocal version, the response version, or the sing-along version of the song.
3. For fun, have a song competition in which students perform solo or in groups and the class votes for the best performance.
4. For additional practice, students can complete the cloze exercise on Song Master S12.

Resource Materials Bring in, or have students bring in, the following materials for vocabulary practice:

- *Magazine and newspaper pictures of various people, places, and things:* Describe the people and things in the pictures.
- *Postcards:* Describe the places.

Community Task Have individual students (or groups of students) walk around an area of your city or town and write down one thing they see that can be described by each of the following adjectives: *new, old, large, small, fast, slow, straight, crooked, wide, narrow, high, low, clean, dirty, smooth, rough, loud, quiet, beautiful, ugly, open, closed, expensive, cheap, fancy, plain.* Have students compare their lists.

Communication Activities

1 What's the Opposite?

Divide the class into teams. Call out an adjective and have students raise their hands and tell you the opposite adjective. The team with the most correct answers wins.

Variation: Write the adjectives on flashcards. Students take turns picking the cards and giving the opposite adjective.

2 Adjective Associations
ACTIVITY HANDBOOK PAGE 2

Call out adjectives and have groups write down as many nouns associated with the adjectives as they can think of. For example:

soft:	[a pillow/a baby's skin/a kitten/a blanket/ a rug/skin]
loud:	[a voice/a noise/music/a party/a TV/ an ambulance]
dirty:	[a house/a kitchen/sneakers/glasses/ hands]
open:	[a door/a box/a museum/a store]
sharp:	[a knife/a needle/an edge]

3 Guess Who I Am!

a. Ask students to write on a piece of paper three or more adjectives that describe themselves. Students should not write their names on their papers.

b. Collect the students' descriptions, read them to the class, and have students guess who wrote them.

Variation: Put all the descriptions on a handout and make a copy for each student in the class. Have students then guess who everybody is.

4 Alphabetical Adjectives

a. Have students practice saying the alphabet from A to Z.

b. Write a phrase on the board such as *I know an awful man.*

c. Have students take turns describing the man with adjectives beginning with consecutive letters of the alphabet. For example:

    I know a bald man.
    I know a clean man.
    I know a dirty man.
    I know an energetic man.

Variation: Have students think of combinations of an adjective and a noun, both beginning with the same letter. For example:

    a beautiful bird
    a cheap chicken
    a dirty dish
    an easy exercise

5 Tic Tac Antonyms
ACTIVITY HANDBOOK PAGE 15
ACTIVITY MASTER 8

Have students fill in the tic tac grid with any nine descriptive words they wish. Call out adjectives from *Picture Dictionary* pages 44-45. On their grids, have students cross out the opposites of the adjectives you have named.

(continued)

Here's What I'm Thinking Of!

ACTIVITY HANDBOOK PAGE 8

Have students describe objects they see in the classroom. For example:

A. It's small, shiny, and hard. It can be messy if it opens up.
B. A pencil sharpener.
A. It's smooth, thin, and long. It has a sharp point.
B. A pencil.
A. It's heavy and large. It's dark and shiny.
B. The teacher's desk.

Other students try to guess what the object is.

 True or False?

ACTIVITY HANDBOOK PAGE 15

Make statements such as the following about any scene on a previous page of the *Picture Dictionary* which you would like to review. Have students decide whether the statements are true or false. For example (Page 21—The Living Room):

The curtains are dark. [True.]
The rug is large. [False. It's small.]
The woman's hair is curly. [True.]
The living room is messy. [False. It's neat.]
The man is heavy. [False. He's thin.]
The magazine rack is empty. [False. It's full.]
The window is wide. [True.]

 Compare It!

This activity can be used if your students have already studied comparatives of adjectives.

a. Review the formation of comparatives. Write on the board:

```
_____er than
more _____ than
```

b. Give examples of comparisons. For example:

(Student A) is taller than (Student B).
Our classroom is smaller than (the auditorium).
Our city is more beautiful than (_____).

c. Tell students to open their *Picture Dictionaries* to the list of adjectives on pages 44-45.

d. Give pairs of nouns such as the ones below and call on students to make comparisons using an appropriate adjective from the list (for example: *fire is hotter than ice/a cow is bigger than a dog*).

fire/ice
a hill/a mountain
a dog/a cow
the city/the country
an elephant/a mouse
a bicycle/a car
English/Spanish
sneakers/high heels
the sun/the moon
my neighbors/your neighbors
a child/an adult
my apartment/your apartment
day/night
a Mercedes/a Ford

Variation: Divide the class into groups and have each group come up with 5 noun pairs for the other groups to compare.

9 **Adjective Idioms**

a. Divide the class into small groups.

b. Write on the board:

```
         (adjective)    (noun)
as _____ as _____
```

c. Tell students that a simile is an expression that describes something by comparing it to something else. For example: *as quiet as a mouse, as hard as a rock.*

d. Have each group come up with nouns that could complete the following expressions. After they have given their versions, give them the common English expressions (in brackets below). Compare the groups' responses and discuss how their native languages might express similar comparisons.

as neat as _____ [a pin]
as easy as _____ [pie]
as slow as _____ [molasses, a mule]
as good as _____ [gold]
as light as _____ [a feather]
as smooth as _____ [silk]
as pretty as _____ [a picture]
as fat as _____ [a pig]
as skinny as _____ [a toothpick]
as straight as _____ [an arrow]
as thin as _____ [a rail]
as old as _____ [the hills]
as cold as _____ [ice]
as clean as _____ [a whistle]
as poor as _____ [a church mouse]
as sharp as _____ [a tack]

LESSON OBJECTIVE

Students will learn vocabulary that describes different ways that people feel.

RESOURCES

AUDIO PROGRAM
Words & Dialogs
Cassette 2A
CD 2: Tracks 34, 35

MULTI-LEVEL WORKBOOKS
Literacy Workbook
Beginning & Intermediate Lifeskills Workbooks
Beginning & Intermediate Vocabulary Workbooks

VOCABULARY GAME CARDS
Cards 123–154

ACTIVITY MASTERS
Reproducibles:
A59–A62

TRANSPARENCIES
Overheads: T46, T47

LANGUAGE & CULTURE NOTES
Reproducible: LC46–47

WORDLINKS
longman.com/wordbyword

VOCABULARY INTRODUCTION

- Preview
- Present
- Practice

MODEL CONVERSATION PRACTICE

There are two model conversations. Introduce and practice the first model before going on to the second. For each model:

1. Have students look at the model illustration. Set the scene:
   Model 1: "An office assistant is talking to her boss."
   Model 2: "A husband is concerned about his wife."

2. Present the first model using word 1, and present the second model using word 2.

3. Choral Repetition Practice: Full-Class and Individual.

4. Have pairs practice the model.

5. Have pairs present the model.

6. Call on pairs to present a new conversation using word 3 for the first model and word 4 for the second model.

7. Have pairs practice new conversations.

8. Have pairs present new conversations.

SPELLING PRACTICE

Say a word, and have students spell it aloud or write it. Or, using the transparency, point to an item and have students write the word.

WRITING AND DISCUSSION

Have students respond to the questions as a class, in pairs, or in small groups. Or have students write their responses, share their writing with other students, and discuss in class.

VOCABULARY GAME CARDS

Have students practice vocabulary, do activities, and play games with Vocabulary Game Cards 123–154. Activities and games are described in the set of cards.

Making Connections

Resource Materials Bring in, or have students bring in, the following materials for vocabulary practice:

- *Magazine and newspaper pictures of people expressing various emotions:* Describe the emotions in the pictures.

Communication Activities

1 Why Do They Feel That Way?

a. Write the following on the board:

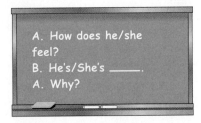

A. How does he/she feel?
B. He's/She's _____.
A. Why?

b. Based on this conversational framework, have students give reasons for the way people are feeling in the illustrations on *Picture Dictionary* pages 46 and 47. For example:

[3] A. How does he feel?
    B. He's exhausted.
    A. Why?
    B. He just ran five miles.

[14] A. How does he feel?
    B. He's disappointed.
    A. Why?
    B. He didn't win first prize.

2 Category Dictation

ACTIVITY HANDBOOK PAGE 2

Dictate words that fit into the following categories:

positive feelings
negative feelings

3 Class Survey: What Do You Do When You're _____?

a. Write on the board:

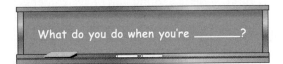

What do you do when you're _____?

b. Have pairs of students use this question to ask each other how they express each of the physical states and emotions on *Picture Dictionary* pages 46 and 47. Possible examples:

When I'm upset, I cry.
When I'm frustrated, I eat candy.

c. Have the pairs report back to the class. This should lead to an interesting discussion of the various ways people react to how they're feeling. (You may wish to tabulate the results on the board.)

4 Emotions Match Game I

ACTIVITY HANDBOOK PAGE 11
ACTIVITY MASTER 59

Have students find the person whose card matches theirs.

5 Emotions Match Game II

ACTIVITY HANDBOOK PAGE 11
ACTIVITY MASTER 60

Have students find the person whose card matches theirs.

6 Pictures That Talk

a. Bring in, or ask students to bring in, several pictures that show different kinds of feelings. The pictures should be clear and as large as possible.

b. Have students study each picture, focusing on details such as facial expressions, gestures, what people are wearing, and what things they're doing.

c. Have students talk about how the picture makes them feel and why they feel that way—in other words, what it is about the picture that brings out these emotions.

This can be done as a class, in pairs, or in small groups.

Variation: Have students make up stories about the pictures.

7 Body Language

a. Discuss with students the fact that we show how we feel not by just words but by our *body language*—our gestures, posture, and facial expressions.

b. Both you and students should demonstrate *non-verbally* emotions from the vocabulary list. Discuss cultural differences and similarities in the way emotions are expressed.

Variation: Both you and students demonstrate body language, and have others guess your physical state or emotion.

8 Mystery Word Conversations

ACTIVITY HANDBOOK PAGE 12

Have groups create mystery conversations about emotions without naming them. The class tries to guess what the emotion is. For example:

A. You don't look so good. What happened?
B: Oh, everything is terrible today. I didn't get the summer job I wanted. I have a cold. And I got a bad grade on my English test.

[Answer: miserable]

9 Emotion Role Plays

ACTIVITY MASTER 61

Make a copy of the Emotion Role Plays, cut it up, and give pairs or groups of students cards to role play. After each role play, have the class identify the emotion expressed.

10 Find the Right Person!

ACTIVITY HANDBOOK PAGES 6–7
ACTIVITY MASTER 62

Have students walk around the classroom asking each other: "Are you happy today?" "Are you annoyed today?" etc. When a student gets a *yes* answer, that student writes in the other person's name and then continues interviewing others until getting a *yes* answer to all the questions.

11 Write a Story

a. Have students write a story telling about a time they felt one of the following emotions:

shocked
exhausted
surprised
proud
embarrassed

b. Have students share their writing with a partner.

12 Guess the Synonym!

Individually, in pairs, or in small groups, see if students can guess the correct emotion synonym for the following idioms:

A. He really *blew his top*!
B. I know. He was really _____. [furious]

A. She's pretty *hot under the collar*!
B. I know. I wonder why she's so _____. [angry/mad]

A. Why are you *down in the dumps* today?
B. I'm feeling very _____. [sad/unhappy]

A. I think they've finally *reached the boiling point*!
B. I know. They're very _____. [angry]

A. She *feels like a million dollars*!
B. You're right. She's really _____. [happy]

A. Why did he *go to pieces*?
B. I'm not sure why he got so _____. [upset]

A. I'm *fit to be tied*!
B. Why are you so _____? [angry]

A. They're *on top of the world*!
B. I know. They're very _____. [happy]

A. I *feel blue* today.
B. Why are you so _____? [sad/unhappy]

A. She's been feeling a little *out of sorts* recently.
B. I know. I think she's getting _____. [sick]

A. I'm *tickled pink*!
B. I know. You're very _____. [happy]

True or False Definitions

ACTIVITY HANDBOOK PAGE 15

Give true and false definitions of *describing* words and have students decide which are true and which are false. For example:

> A tall person is six feet tall. [True.]
> A short person is two meters tall. [False.]
> A book can be thick. [True.]
> A pillow can be sharp. [False.]
> A room can be messy. [True.]
> A car can be rich. [False.]
> A computer can be honest. [False.]
> A building can be tall. [True.]
> Hair can be crooked. [False.]
> A person's eyes can be dark. [True.]

2 **Finish the Sentence!**

ACTIVITY HANDBOOK PAGE 7

Begin sentences such as the following for students to complete:

> A miserable person is someone who . . .
> A heavy person is someone who . . .
> A senior citizen is someone who . . .
> A hearing-impaired person is someone who . . .
> A teenager is someone who . . .
> A toddler is someone who . . .
> A pregnant woman is someone who . . .
> A bald man is someone who . . .
> A jealous person is someone who . . .
> A homesick person is someone who . . .

3 **Category Dictation**

ACTIVITY HANDBOOK PAGE 2

Dictate words from *Picture Dictionary* pages 42–47 that describe the following nouns:

> a person
> a thing
> an animal

4 **Describe It!**

a. Bring to class small objects for students to describe. For example:

> an apple
> car keys
> a book
> a CD
> a cup
> a carrot
> a cell phone
> a pair of scissors
> a pen
> a stapler

b. Divide the class into small groups, and give each group a different object.

c. Have each group list all the adjectives they can think of to describe the object. Set a one minute time limit.

d. Have each group then pass their object to the next group for them to describe.

e. After all the objects have traveled around the classroom, ask the groups for their descriptions. Have the class vote on the best description for each object.

AUDIO PROGRAM

Words & Dialogs
Audio Cassette 2A
Audio Cassette 2B
Audio Cassette 3A
Audio CD 2:
  Tracks 36–65
Audio CD 3:
  Tracks 2–18

WordSong: *Supermarket Sally*
Audio Cassette 7A
Audio CD 7: Tracks 29
  (Vocal) & 30 (Sing-along)
Song Masters S13, S14

WORKBOOKS

For Multi-Level Practice
Literacy Workbook
Beginning Lifeskills Workbook
Beginning Vocabulary Workbook
Intermediate Lifeskills Workbook
Intermediate Vocabulary Workbook

WORDLINKS

Internet Resources through the
***Word by Word* Companion Website**
http://www.longman.com/wordbyword

ACTIVITY MASTERS

Reproducibles for Communication Activities
A8, A63–A82

TRANSPARENCIES

Full-Color Overheads for Class Practice
T48–T64

LANGUAGE & CULTURE NOTES

**Information for Teachers &
Intermediate /Advanced Students**
LC48–LC64

VOCABULARY GAME CARDS

**For Vocabulary Practice,
Activities, & Games**
Cards 155–224

LESSON OBJECTIVE

Student will learn the names of fruits commonly eaten in the United States.

RESOURCES

AUDIO PROGRAM
Words & Dialogs
Cassette 2A
CD 2: Tracks Tracks 36–38

MULTI-LEVEL WORKBOOKS
Literacy Workbook
Beginning & Intermediate Lifeskills Workbooks
Beginning & Intermediate Vocabulary Workbooks

VOCABULARY GAME CARDS
Cards 155–186

ACTIVITY MASTERS
Reproducibles:
A63, A64

TRANSPARENCY
Overhead: T48

LANGUAGE & CULTURE NOTES
Reproducible: LC48

WORDLINKS
longman.com/wordbyword

VOCABULARY INTRODUCTION

- Preview
- Present
- Practice

MODEL CONVERSATION PRACTICE

There are two model conversations—the first for words 1–23 and the second for words 24–32. Introduce and practice the first model before going on to the second. For each model:

1. Have students look at the model illustration. Set the scene:

   Model 1: "A son and father are talking."
   Model 2: "A wife and husband are talking."

2. Present the model.
3. Choral Repetition Practice: Full-Class and Individual.
4. Have pairs practice the model.
5. Have pairs present the model.
6. Call on pairs to present a new conversation using word 2 for the first model and word 25 for the second model.
7. Have pairs practice new conversations.
8. Have pairs present new conversations.

ADDITIONAL CONVERSATION PRACTICE

Before students practice the additional conversations, you may want to have them listen to the examples on the Audio Program.

Conversation 1 Set the scene: "Two family members are talking." Have students practice and present conversations with any words they wish.

Conversation 2 Set the scene: "Two family members are talking." Have students practice and present conversations with any words they wish.

SPELLING PRACTICE

Say a word, and have students spell it aloud or write it. Or, using the transparency, point to an item and have students write the word.

WRITING AND DISCUSSION

Have students respond to the questions as a class, in pairs, or in small groups. Or have students write their responses, share their writing with other students, and discuss in class.

VOCABULARY GAME CARDS

Have students practice vocabulary, do activities, and play games with Vocabulary Game Cards 155–186. Activities and games are described in the set of cards.

Resource Materials Bring in, or have students bring in, the following materials for vocabulary practice:

- *Newspaper advertisements for fruits:* Find out which fruits are on sale this week.

- *Nutrition books and pamphlets:* Find out how many portions of fruit a person should eat each day.

- *The fruits themselves:* Invite the class to taste different fruits.

Community Task Have individual students (or groups of students) visit different supermarkets and investigate the current prices of certain fruits. Have students report their findings to the class.

Communication Activities

1 Expand the Conversation
ACTIVITY HANDBOOK PAGE 6

Expand the model conversation to include more fruits and places.

a. Write the following on the board:

> A. This _____/These _____ (is/are) delicious! Where did you get (it/them)?
> B. At _____.
> A. And I love this _____/these _____s!
> B. I got (it/them) at _____. That's the best place to buy _____s.

b. Have pairs of students practice and present conversations based on this model, using different words from the page.

2 Clap in Rhythm
ACTIVITY HANDBOOK PAGE 3

Have students name different fruits to a clapping rhythm.

3 Concentration
ACTIVITY HANDBOOK PAGE 3
ACTIVITY MASTER 63

Have students shuffle the cards and place them face-down in three rows of 6 each, then attempt to find cards that match.

4 Listen and Number
ACTIVITY HANDBOOK PAGE 10

In pairs, have one student make up a story using fruit words and have the other students number the pictures in their order of occurrence in the story.

5 Letter Game
ACTIVITY HANDBOOK PAGE 9

Say statements such as the following and have teams compete to identify the items:

I'm thinking of a fruit that starts with *a*.	[apple]
I'm thinking of a fruit that starts with *s*.	[strawberry]
I'm thinking of a fruit that starts with *l*.	[lemon]
I'm thinking of a fruit that starts with *c*.	[cherry]
I'm thinking of a fruit that starts with *m*.	[mango]
I'm thinking of a fruit that starts with *p*.	[plum]
I'm thinking of a fruit that starts with *g*.	[grape]
I'm thinking of a fruit that starts with *n*.	[nectarine]
I'm thinking of a fruit that starts with *f*.	[fig]

6 Word Clues
ACTIVITY HANDBOOK PAGE 17
ACTIVITY MASTER 64

Have students take turns giving clues to team members who try to guess the word. For example:

[The word is *apple*.]
Team 1 Player: "red or green"   [Team 1 guesses]
Team 2 Player: "crunchy"   [Team 2 guesses]
Team 1 Player: "from a tree"   [Team 1 guesses]

[The word is *pineapple*.]
Team 1 Player: "juicy"   [Team 1 guesses]
Team 2 Player: "yellow"   [Team 2 guesses]
Team 1 Player: "tropical"   [Team 1 guesses]

(continued)

7 Ranking
ACTIVITY HANDBOOK PAGE 13

Choose several items from *Picture Dictionary* page 48 and write them on the board. Have students rank them from fruits they like the best to fruits they like the least. For example:

strawberries
bananas
plums
nectarines
kiwis
honeydew melons

Variations: Students can also rank these foods by the price of the fruit (*expensive* to *inexpensive*) or the frequency with which they eat them (*often* to *seldom*).

8 Likes and Dislikes

a. Have students make two columns on a piece of paper—one column with the heading <u>I like</u> and the other with the heading <u>I dislike</u>.

b. Dictate words from the lesson, and have students write the items in the appropriate column. For example:

<u>I like</u>	<u>I dislike</u>
tangerines	papaya
nuts	coconut
bananas	figs

c. In pairs or in small groups, have students compare their answers.

9 Movable Categories
ACTIVITY HANDBOOK PAGE 11
ACTIVITY MASTER 64

Call out the following categories and have students go to the appropriate side of the room:

fruits with seeds
fruits with a pit
fruits you eat with the skin
fruits you don't eat with the skin
red fruits
yellow fruits
round fruits
oval fruits

10 What Am I?
ACTIVITY HANDBOOK PAGE 15
ACTIVITY MASTER 64

Pin word cards on students' backs and have them ask yes/no questions to identify which fruit they *are*. For example:

Am I round?	[Yes.]
Am I red?	[No.]
Do I have seeds?	[Yes.]
Do I grow on a tree?	[No.]
Do I grow on a bush?	[No.]
Do I grow on a plant?	[Yes.]
Am I juicy?	[Yes.]
Am I a cantaloupe?	[Yes.]

11 Drawing Game
ACTIVITY HANDBOOK PAGE 6
ACTIVITY MASTER 64

Have teams compete to identify fruit items drawn by one of their team members.

12 Fruit Investigation

a. Have students go to a supermarket or fruit stand and find out the following:

What fruits are sold there?
How much are they?
Which is the cheapest? Which is the most expensive?
How are they sold—by weight? by the item?

b. Have students compare the results of their surveys.

13 The Taste Test

Ask each student to bring in a piece of fruit. Make a fruit salad for the class to share, and as students are eating the salad, have them tell which fruits they like the best.

14 Funny Fruits!

a. Have students associate the name of a fruit with an adjective having the same initial letter. For example:

an *awful* apple
a *bad* banana
a *mixed-up* mango

b. Have students draw pictures of their funny fruits.

LESSON OBJECTIVE

Students will learn the names of vegetables commonly eaten in the United States.

RESOURCES

AUDIO PROGRAM
Words & Dialogs
Cassette 2A
CD 2: Tracks 39–41

MULTI-LEVEL WORKBOOKS
Literacy Workbook
Beginning & Intermediate Lifeskills Workbooks
Beginning & Intermediate Vocabulary Workbooks

VOCABULARY GAME CARDS
Cards 187–224

ACTIVITY MASTERS
Reproducibles:
A65, A66

TRANSPARENCY
Overhead: T49

LANGUAGE & CULTURE NOTES
Reproducible: LC49

WORDLINKS
longman.com/wordbyword

VOCABULARY INTRODUCTION

- Preview
- Present
- Practice

MODEL CONVERSATION PRACTICE

1. Have students look at the model illustration. Set the scene: "A husband and wife are talking. The husband is making a shopping list before he goes to the supermarket."
2. Present the model.
3. Choral Repetition Practice: Full-Class and Individual.
4. Have pairs practice the model.
5. Have pairs present the model.
6. Call on pairs to present a new conversation using words 2 and 17.
7. Have pairs practice new conversations.
8. Have pairs present new conversations.

ADDITIONAL CONVERSATION PRACTICE

Before students practice the additional conversations, you may want to have them listen to the examples on the Audio Program.

Conversation 1 Set the scene: "Two people are talking at the dinner table." Have students practice and present conversations with any words they wish.

Conversation 2 Set the scene: "A parent is talking to a child at the dinner table." Have students practice and present conversations with any words they wish.

SPELLING PRACTICE

Say a word, and have students spell it aloud or write it. Or, using the transparency, point to an item and have students write the word.

WRITING AND DISCUSSION

Have students respond to the questions as a class, in pairs, or in small groups. Or have students write their responses, share their writing with other students, and discuss in class.

VOCABULARY GAME CARDS

Have students practice vocabulary, do activities, and play games with Vocabulary Game Cards 187–224. Activities and games are described in the set of cards.

Making Connections

Resource Materials Bring in, or have students bring in, the following materials for vocabulary practice:

- *Newspaper advertisements for vegetables:* Find out which vegetables are on sale this week.
- *Nutrition books and pamphlets:* Find out how many portions of vegetables a person should eat each day.
- *The vegetables themselves:* Invite the class to taste different vegetables.

Community Task Have individual students (or groups of students) visit different supermarkets and investigate the current prices of certain vegetables. Have students report their findings to the class.

1 Expand the Conversation
ACTIVITY HANDBOOK PAGE 6

Expand the model conversation to include other vegetables.

a. Write the following on the board:

> A. What do we need from the supermarket?
> B. We need _____(s) an _____(s).
> A. Anything else?
> B. Yes, actually. Could you also get some _____(s) and some _____(s)?
> A. So that's _____(s), _____(s), _____(s), and _____(s). Right?
> B. Yes, that's right.

b. Have pairs of students practice and present conversations based on this model, using different words from the page.

2 Clap in Rhythm
ACTIVITY HANDBOOK PAGE 3

Have students name different vegetables to a clapping rhythm.

3 Concentration
ACTIVITY HANDBOOK PAGE 3
ACTIVITY MASTER 65

Have students shuffle the cards and place them face-down in three rows of 4 each, then attempt to find cards that match.

4 Letter Game
ACTIVITY HANDBOOK PAGE 9

Say statements such as the following and have teams compete to identify the items:

I'm thinking of a vegetable that starts with *a*.	[asparagus]
I'm thinking of a vegetable that starts with *p*.	[pea]
I'm thinking of a vegetable that starts with *y*.	[yam]
I'm thinking of a vegetable that starts with *o*.	[onion]
I'm thinking of a vegetable that starts with *g*.	[garlic]
I'm thinking of a vegetable that starts with *b*.	[broccoli]
I'm thinking of a vegetable that starts with *e*.	[eggplant]
I'm thinking of a vegetable that starts with *l*.	[lettuce]
I'm thinking of a vegetable that starts with *c*.	[corn]

5 Listen and Number
ACTIVITY HANDBOOK PAGE 10

In pairs, have one student make up a story using vegetable words and have the other student number the pictures in their order of occurrence in the story.

6 Clues
ACTIVITY HANDBOOK PAGE 3

After one student leaves the room, have the class think of ways to describe a vegetable. For example:

> You eat it raw.
> You buy it by the pound or by the individual vegetable.
> You have to peel it.
> You usually eat it in a salad.
> It's long.
> It's green.
>
> [Answer: a cucumber]

7 Ranking
ACTIVITY HANDBOOK PAGE 13

Choose several items from *Picture Dictionary* page 49 and write them on the board. Have students rank them from vegetables they like the best to vegetables they like the least. For example:

tomatoes
cucumbers
asparagus
potatoes
artichokes
mushrooms

Variations: Students can also rank these foods by the price of the vegetable (*expensive* to *inexpensive*) or the frequency with which they eat them (*often* to *seldom*).

8 Likes and Dislikes

a. Have students make two columns on a piece of paper—one column with the heading I like and the other with the heading I dislike.

b. Dictate words from the lesson, and have students write the items in the appropriate column. For example:

I like	I dislike
red peppers	garlic
lima beans	onions
corn	broccoli

c. In pairs or in small groups, have students compare their answers.

9 Movable Categories

ACTIVITY HANDBOOK PAGE 11
ACTIVITY MASTER 66

Call out the following categories and have students go to the appropriate side of the room:

green vegetables
yellow vegetables
red vegetables
salad vegetables
cooked vegetables
long vegetables

10 What Am I?

ACTIVITY HANDBOOK PAGE 15
ACTIVITY MASTER 66

Pin word cards on students' backs and have them ask yes/no questions to identify which vegetable they are. For example:

Am I green?	[Yes.]
Do you cook me?	[Sometimes.]
Do I taste good?	[Sometimes children don't like you.]
Am I spinach?	[Yes.]

Do you eat me raw?	[Yes, sometimes.]
Am I green?	[No.]
Am I brown?	[Yes.]
Do you eat me often?	[No.]
Am I a mushroom?	[Yes.]

11 Drawing Game

ACTIVITY HANDBOOK PAGE 6
ACTIVITY MASTER 66

Have teams compete to identify vegetables drawn by one of their team members.

12 It's a Puzzle!

ACTIVITY HANDBOOK PAGE 9

Cut out pictures of vegetables and create puzzles out of the pictures for students to identify and put together by asking questions. For example:

My picture has red and yellow vegetables.
I have a picture with a big green salad.
Do you have carrots in your picture?

13 Vegetable Investigation

a. Have students go to a supermarket or vegetable stand and find out the following:

What vegetables are sold there?
How much do they cost?
Which is the cheapest? Which is the most expensive?

b. Have students compare the results of their surveys.

14 The Taste Test

Ask each student to bring in a piece of vegetable. Make a vegetable salad for the class to share, and as students are eating the salad, have them tell which vegetables they like the best.

15 Vegetable Talk!

ACTIVITY HANDBOOK PAGE 17
ACTIVITY MASTER 66

Give each student a Vegetable Word Card, and have them speak to the class for one minute about their word.

16 Our Favorite Vegetable Dishes

Have students choose a favorite food item on *Picture Dictionary* page 49 and describe their favorite way to prepare that food item. For example:

My favorite vegetable dish is salad. I love salad with lettuce, radishes, cucumbers, carrots, tomatoes, and scallions. I eat a salad every day.

LESSON OBJECTIVE

Students will learn the names of different kinds of meat, poultry, and fish and shellfish.

RESOURCES

AUDIO PROGRAM

Words & Dialogs
Cassette 2A
CD 2: Tracks 42–44

MULTI-LEVEL WORKBOOKS

Literacy Workbook
Beginning & Intermediate Lifeskills Workbooks
Beginning & Intermediate Vocabulary Workbooks

TRANSPARENCY

Overhead: T50

LANGUAGE & CULTURE NOTES

Reproducible: LC50

WORDLINKS

longman.com/wordbyword

VOCABULARY INTRODUCTION

- Preview
- Present
- Practice

MODEL CONVERSATION PRACTICE

1. Have students look at the model illustration. Set the scene: "A husband is leaving the house to go to the supermarket."
2. Present the model.
3. Choral Repetition Practice: Full-Class and Individual.
4. Have pairs practice the model.
5. Have pairs present the model.
6. Call on pairs to present a new conversation using word 2.
7. Have pairs practice new conversations.
8. Have pairs present new conversations.

ADDITIONAL CONVERSATION PRACTICE

Before students practice the additional conversations, you may want to have them listen to the examples on the Audio Program.

Conversation 1 Set the scene: "A shopper is talking to a clerk in a supermarket." Have students practice and present conversations with any words they wish.

Conversation 2 Set the scene: "Two family members are shopping at the supermarket." Have students practice and present conversations with any words they wish.

SPELLING PRACTICE

Say a word, and have students spell it aloud or write it. Or, using the transparency, point to an item and have students write the word.

WRITING AND DISCUSSION

Have students respond to the questions as a class, in pairs, or in small groups. Or have students write their responses, share their writing with other students, and discuss in class.

Making Connections

Resource Materials Bring in, or have students bring in, the following materials for vocabulary practice:

- *Newspaper advertisements for supermarket items:* Talk about the kinds of meat and fish available at the supermarkets.

- *Nutrition books and pamphlets:* Compare the nutritional value of various types of meat, fish, and shellfish.

Community Task Have individual students (or groups of students) visit different fish and meat markets and investigate the current prices of certain items. Have students report their findings to the class.

Communication Activities

❶ Expand the Conversation
ACTIVITY HANDBOOK PAGE 6

Expand the model conversation to include other meat, poultry, and seafood items.

a. Write the following on the board:

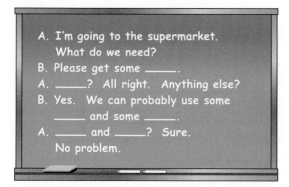

> A. I'm going to the supermarket. What do we need?
> B. Please get some _____.
> A. _____? All right. Anything else?
> B. Yes. We can probably use some _____ and some _____.
> A. _____ and _____? Sure. No problem.

b. Have pairs of students practice and present conversations based on this model, using different words from the page.

❷ Clap in Rhythm
ACTIVITY HANDBOOK PAGE 3

Have students name different meat, poultry, and seafood words to a clapping rhythm.

❸ True or False?
ACTIVITY HANDBOOK PAGE 15

Make statements such as the following about the foods on *Picture Dictionary* page 50. Have students decide whether the statements are true or false. For example:

> Scallops are a kind of fish. [False. Scallops are a kind of shellfish.]
> A turkey is smaller than a duck. [False. A turkey is bigger than a duck.]
> Bacon is a kind of pork. [True.]
> Halibut is a shellfish. [False. Halibut is a fish.]
> Ham is a kind of beef. [False. Ham is a kind of pork.]
> Shrimp is a kind of poultry. [False. Shrimp is a kind of shellfish.]
> Crabs are larger than lobsters. [False. Lobsters are usually larger than crabs.]
> Salmon meat is pink. [True.]
> Steak is a kind of poultry. [False. Steak is a kind of beef.]
> Turkey, duck, chicken, and ham are all poultry. [False. Only turkey, duck, and chicken are poultry.]

❹ Chain Game
ACTIVITY HANDBOOK PAGES 2–3

Begin the chain as follows: "I'm going to the store to buy some steak," and have students continue it. For example:

> Teacher: I'm going to the store to buy some steak.
> Student 1: I'm going to the store to buy some steak and some shrimp.
> Student 2: I'm going to the store to buy some steak, some shrimp, and some duck.
> Etc.

❺ Category Dictation
ACTIVITY HANDBOOK PAGE 2

Dictate words that fit into the following categories:

> meat
> poultry
> fish
> shellfish

❻ Ranking
ACTIVITY HANDBOOK PAGE 13

Choose seven food items from *Picture Dictionary* page 50 and write them on the board. Have students rank them from foods they like the best to foods they like the least. For example:

> steak
> chicken breasts
> shrimp
> lobster
> scallops
> pork chops
> leg of lamb

Variations: Students can also rank these foods by their price (*expensive* to *inexpensive*) or the frequency with which they eat them (*often* to *seldom*).

❼ Favorite Meat and Seafood Dishes

Have students choose a favorite food item from *Picture Dictionary* page 50 and describe their favorite way to prepare that food item. For example:

> My favorite dish is leg of lamb. We cook the leg of lamb over a fire for many hours. I eat the cooked meat with mint sauce. It's delicious.

LESSON OBJECTIVE

Students will learn the names of different kinds of dairy products, juices, and beverages.

RESOURCES

AUDIO PROGRAM

Words & Dialogs
Cassette 2B
CD 2: Tracks 45–47

MULTI-LEVEL WORKBOOKS

Literacy Workbook
Beginning & Intermediate Lifeskills Workbooks
Beginning & Intermediate Vocabulary Workbooks

ACTIVITY MASTER

Reproducible:
A67

TRANSPARENCY

Overhead: T51

LANGUAGE & CULTURE NOTES

Reproducible: LC51

WORDLINKS

longman.com/wordbyword

VOCABULARY INTRODUCTION

- Preview
- Present
- Practice

MODEL CONVERSATION PRACTICE

1. Have students look at the model illustration. Set the scene: "A daughter and father are talking. The daughter is leaving the house to go to the supermarket."
2. Present the model.
3. Choral Repetition Practice: Full-Class and Individual.
4. Have pairs practice the model.
5. Have pairs present the model.
6. Call on pairs to present a new conversation using words 2 and 16.
7. Have pairs practice new conversations.
8. Have pairs present new conversations.

ADDITIONAL CONVERSATION PRACTICE

Before students practice the additional conversations, you may want to have them listen to the examples on the Audio Program.

Conversation 1 Set the scene: "A shopper is talking to a clerk at a supermarket." Have students practice and present conversations with any words they wish.

Conversation 2 Set the scene: "Two family members are shopping at the supermarket." Have students practice and present conversations with any words they wish.

SPELLING PRACTICE

Say a word, and have students spell it aloud or write it. Or, using the transparency, point to an item and have students write the word.

WRITING AND DISCUSSION

Have students respond to the questions as a class, in pairs, or in small groups. Or have students write their responses, share their writing with other students, and discuss in class.

Making Connections

Resource Materials Bring in, or have students bring in, the following materials for vocabulary practice:

- *Newspaper advertisements for supermarket items:* Talk about the kinds of dairy products, juices, and beverages available at the supermarkets.

- *Discount coupons for supermarket items:* Talk about what coupons are available this week for food items.

- *The smaller, more portable supermarket items themselves:* Invite the class to taste different flavored fruit juices.

- *Nutrition books and pamphlets:* Compare the nutritional value of drinks that are 100 percent juice and those that are a fruit punch or are made from a drink mix.

Community Task Have individual students (or groups of students) visit different supermarkets and investigate the current prices on certain items. Have students report their findings to the class.

Communication Activities

1 Expand the Conversation
ACTIVITY HANDBOOK PAGE 6

Expand the model conversation to include other dairy products, juices, and beverages.

a. Write the following on the board:

> A. I'm going to the supermarket to get some _____. Do we need anything else?
> B. Yes. Please get some _____. Oh, and before I forget, we also need some _____ and some _____.
> A. Some _____ and some _____? Sure. Is that it?
> B. Yes, that's everything.

b. Have pairs of students practice and present conversations based on this model, using different words from the page.

2 Clap in Rhythm
ACTIVITY HANDBOOK PAGE 3

Have students name different drinks to a clapping rhythm.

3 True or False?
ACTIVITY HANDBOOK PAGE 15

Make statements such as the following about the foods on *Picture Dictionary* page 51. Have students decide whether the statements are true or false. For example:

> Yogurt is a juice. [False. Yogurt is a dairy product.]
> Decaf has caffeine. [False. Decaf has no caffeine.]
> Tofu comes from eggs. [False. Tofu comes from soy beans.]
> Orange juice is usually in the dairy section of a supermarket. [True.]
> Skim milk has no fat in it. [True.]
> Margarine is made from milk. [False. Margarine is made from vegetable oil.]
> Diet soda has sugar in it. [False. Diet soda has no sugar in it.]
> Cocoa is the same as hot chocolate. [True.]

> Juice paks are small packages of juice that are easy to carry in a lunch box. [True.]
> Cream cheese and cottage cheese are the same. [False. Cream cheese and cottage cheese are different kinds of cheese.]

4 Ask Me a Question!
ACTIVITY HANDBOOK PAGE 2
ACTIVITY MASTER 67

Have students walk around trying to guess each other's food items by asking yes/no questions. For example:

> Do you drink it?   [Yes.]
> Is it a cold drink?   [No.]
> Is it coffee?   [Yes.]
>
> Do you drink it?   [No.]
> Is it made from milk?   [No.]
> Do you eat it with bread?   [Yes.]
> Is it margarine?   [Yes.]

5 Word Clues
ACTIVITY HANDBOOK PAGE 17
ACTIVITY MASTER 67

Have students take turns giving one-word clues to team members who try to guess the word. For example:

> [The word is *milk*.]
> Team 1 Player: "white"   [Team 1 guesses]
> Team 2 Player: "drink"   [Team 2 guesses]
> Team 1 Player: "fresh"   [Team 1 guesses]
>
> [The word is *tomato juice*.]
> Team 1 Player: "natural"   [Team 1 guesses]
> Team 2 Player: "red"   [Team 2 guesses]
> Team 1 Player: "salty"   [Team 1 guesses]

6 Listen and Number
ACTIVITY HANDBOOK PAGE 10

In pairs, have one student make up a story using food item words from *Picture Dictionary* page 51 and have the other student number the pictures in their order of occurrence in the story.

(continued)

7 Ranking
ACTIVITY HANDBOOK PAGE 13

Choose several items from one food category on *Picture Dictionary* page 51 and write them on the board. Have students rank them from foods they like the best to foods they like the least. For example:

coffee
tea
cocoa
herbal tea
instant coffee

Variation: Students can also rank these foods by the frequency with which they eat or drink them (*often* to *seldom*).

8 Likes and Dislikes

a. Have students make two columns on a piece of paper—one column with the heading I like and the other with the heading I dislike.

b. Dictate words from the lesson and have students write the items in the appropriate column. For example:

I like	I dislike
orange juice	coffee
cheese	eggs
grape juice	tofu

c. In pairs or in small groups, have students compare their answers.

9 Survey

a. Give each student or pair of students one of the following questions:

How many glasses of milk do you drink in a week?
How many cups of coffee do you drink in a day?
How many cups of decaffeinated coffee do you drink in a day?
How many sodas do you drink in a week?
How many diet sodas do you drink in a week?
How many cups of tea do you drink in a week?
How any cups of herbal tea do you drink in a week?
How many glasses of orange juice do you drink in a week?
How many eggs do you eat in a week?

b. Have students circulate around the class and survey their classmates.

c. When students are finished, have them tally their results and present them to the class in a bar graph.

d. Discuss the following questions:

Do these results surprise you?
Does this class have healthy drinking habits?

10 Commercials

Divide the class into groups, and have each group create a commercial for one of the food items on *Picture Dictionary* page 51 and then present it to the class.

LESSON OBJECTIVE

Students will learn the names of different kinds of deli foods, frozen foods, and snack foods.

RESOURCES

AUDIO PROGRAM
Words & Dialogs
Cassette 2B
CD 1: Tracks 48–50

MULTI-LEVEL WORKBOOKS
Literacy Workbook
Beginning & Intermediate Lifeskills Workbooks
Beginning & Intermediate Vocabulary Workbooks

ACTIVITY MASTER
Reproducible:
A68

TRANSPARENCY
Overhead T52

LANGUAGE & CULTURE NOTES
Reproducible: LC52

WORDLINKS
longman.com/wordbyword

VOCABULARY INTRODUCTION

- Preview
- Present
- Practice

MODEL CONVERSATION PRACTICE

1. Have students look at the model illustration. Set the scene: "A husband and wife are shopping at the supermarket."
2. Present the model.
3. Choral Repetition Practice: Full-Class and Individual.
4. Have pairs practice the model.
5. Have pairs present the model.
6. Call on pairs to present a new conversation using words 2 and 14.
7. Have pairs practice new conversations.
8. Have pairs present new conversations.

ADDITIONAL CONVERSATION PRACTICE

Before students practice the additional conversations, you may want to have them listen to the examples on the Audio Program.

Conversation 1 Set the scene: "A clerk is talking to a customer at the deli counter of a supermarket." Have students practice and present conversations with any words they wish.

Conversation 2 Set the scene: "A shopper is talking to a clerk in a supermarket." Have students practice and present conversations with any words they wish.

SPELLING PRACTICE

Say a word, and have students spell it aloud or write it. Or, using the transparency, point to an item and have students write the word.

WRITING AND DISCUSSION

Have students respond to the questions as a class, in pairs, or in small groups. Or have students write their responses, share their writing with other students, and discuss in class.

Making Connections

Resource Materials Bring in, or have students bring in, the following materials for vocabulary practice:

- *Newspaper advertisements for supermarket items:* Talk about the kinds of deli, frozen foods, and snack foods on sale at the supermarkets this week.

- *Discount coupons for supermarket items:* Talk about what coupons are available this week for food items.

- *The smaller, more portable supermarket items themselves:* Invite the class to taste different deli and snack foods.

- *Nutrition panels on the back of snack food boxes:* Compare the nutritional value of various snack foods.

Community Task Have individual students (or groups of students) visit different supermarkets and investigate the current prices on certain items. Have students report their findings to the class.

1 Expand the Conversation
ACTIVITY HANDBOOK PAGE 6

Expand the model conversation to include other deli, frozen foods, and snack foods.

a. Write the following on the board:

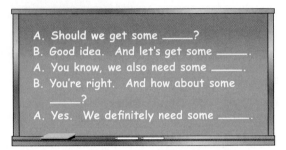

```
A. Should we get some _____?
B. Good idea.  And let's get some _____.
A. You know, we also need some _____.
B. You're right.  And how about some
   _____?
A. Yes.  We definitely need some _____.
```

b. Have pairs of students practice and present conversations based on this model, using different words from the page.

2 True or False?
ACTIVITY HANDBOOK PAGE 15

Make statements such as the following about the foods on *Picture Dictionary* page 52. Have students decide whether the statements are true or false. For example:

Provolone is a kind of meat. [False. Provolone is a kind of cheese.]
Cole slaw is made with cabbage. [True.]
Bologna is a kind of cheese. [False. Bologna is a kind of meat.]
Salami is already cooked and ready to put in a sandwich. [True.]
Popcorn is a frozen food. [False. Popcorn is a snack food.]
Pretzels are a deli food. [False. Pretzels are a snack food.]
Mozzarella is a kind of cheese. [True.]
Roast beef is already cooked beef. [True.]
You can buy ice cream at the deli counter of a supermarket. [False. Ice cream is frozen and is in a supermarket freezer.]

3 Listen and Number
ACTIVITY HANDBOOK PAGE 10

In pairs, have one student make up a story using food words from the lesson and have the other student number the pictures in their order of occurrence in the story.

4 Letter Game
ACTIVITY HANDBOOK PAGE 9

Say statements such as the following and have teams compete to identify the items:

I'm thinking of a deli food that starts with *a*.	[American cheese]
I'm thinking of a deli food that starts with *s*.	[salami]
I'm thinking of a deli food that starts with *p*.	[pasta salad]
I'm thinking of a deli food that starts with *t*.	[turkey]
I'm thinking of a frozen food that starts with *i*.	[ice cream]
I'm thinking of a snack food that starts with *p*.	[potato chips]
I'm thinking of a snack food that starts with *n*.	[nuts]

5 Ranking
ACTIVITY HANDBOOK PAGE 13

Choose several items from a category on *Picture Dictionary* page 52 and write them on the board. Have students rank them from foods they like the best to foods they like the least. For example:

```
cole slaw
macaroni salad
cheddar cheese
mozzarella
salami
```

Variations: Students can also rank these foods by the price of the food (*expensive* to *inexpensive*) or the frequency with which they eat them (*often* to *seldom*).

6 Movable Categories
ACTIVITY HANDBOOK PAGE 11
ACTIVITY MASTER 68

Call out the following categories and have students go to the appropriate side of the room:

meats
salads
frozen foods
foods with vegetables in them
snack foods
drinks
cheeses

7 Likes and Dislikes

a. Have students make two columns on a piece of paper—one column with the heading <u>I like</u> and the other with the heading <u>I dislike</u>.

b. Dictate words from the lesson, and have students write the items in the appropriate column. For example:

<u>I like</u>	<u>I dislike</u>
turkey	corned beef
potato salad	seafood salad
tortilla chips	frozen dinners

c. In pairs or in small groups, have students compare their answers.

8 What Am I?

ACTIVITY HANDBOOK PAGE 15
ACTIVITY MASTER 68

Pin word cards on students' backs and have them ask yes/no questions to identify which food they *are*. For example:

Am I a kind of cheese?	[No.]
Am I a frozen food?	[No.]
Am I a snack food?	[Yes.]
Am I made from vegetables?	[Yes.]
Am I potato chips?	[Yes.]

9 Deli Investigation

a. Have students go to a deli counter at a supermarket and find out the following:

What meat, cheeses, and salads do they sell?
How much are they?
Which is the cheapest? Which is the most expensive?

b. Have students compare the results of their supermarket visits.

10 The Taste Test

a. Have students bring different kinds of snack foods to class.

b. Place the foods around the room each with a paper and pen in front of it.

c. Have students circulate around the room trying the snack foods and writing comments on the papers.

d. Read the comments aloud to the class and summarize class findings.

11 Snack Food Survey

Have students investigate how often their classmates eat certain snack foods.

a. Have students chose one snack food item from the lesson (or any other snack food they know) and ask their classmates: "How often do you eat _____?"

b. Have students circulate around the class to survey their classmates.

c. When students are finished, have them tally their results and present them to the class in a bar graph.

d. Discuss the following questions:

Do these results surprise you?
Does this class have healthy snack food habits?

12 The Best Sandwiches in Town!

a. In small groups, have students design a delicious deli sandwich using some of the foods from this lesson and from previous lessons.

b. Have students present their sandwich creations to the class.

c. Have the class vote on which sandwich sounds the most delicious.

13 Commercials

Divide the class into groups, and have each group create a commercial for one of the food items on *Picture Dictionary* page 52 and then present it to the class.

LESSON OBJECTIVE

Students will learn the names of different kinds of grocery items.

RESOURCES

AUDIO PROGRAM
Words & Dialogs
Cassette 2B
CD 2: Tracks 51–53

MULTI-LEVEL WORKBOOKS
Literacy Workbook
Beginning & Intermediate Lifeskills Workbooks
Beginning & Intermediate Vocabulary Workbooks

ACTIVITY MASTER
Reproducible:
A69

TRANSPARENCY
Overhead T53

LANGUAGE & CULTURE NOTES
Reproducible: LC53

WORDLINKS
longman.com/wordbyword

VOCABULARY INTRODUCTION

- Preview
- Present
- Practice

MODEL CONVERSATION PRACTICE

1. Have students look at the model illustration. Set the scene: "A husband and wife are shopping at the supermarket."
2. Present the model.
3. Choral Repetition Practice: Full-Class and Individual.
4. Have pairs practice the model.
5. Have pairs present the model.
6. Call on pairs to present a new conversation using words 2, 9, 16, and 31.
7. Have pairs practice new conversations.
8. Have pairs present new conversations.

ADDITIONAL CONVERSATION PRACTICE

Before students practice the additional conversations, you may want to have them listen to the examples on the Audio Program.

Conversation 1 Set the scene: "A shopper is talking to a clerk in a supermarket." Have students practice and present conversations with any words they wish.

Conversation 2 Set the scene: "A shopper is talking to a clerk in a supermarket." Have students practice and present conversations with any words they wish.

SPELLING PRACTICE

Say a word, and have students spell it aloud or write it. Or, using the transparency, point to an item and have students write the word.

WRITING AND DISCUSSION

Have students respond to the questions as a class, in pairs, or in small groups. Or have students write their responses, share their writing with other students, and discuss in class.

Making Connections

Resource Materials Bring in, or have students bring in, the following materials for vocabulary practice:

- *Newspaper advertisements for supermarket items:* Compare this week's prices for various grocery items.
- *Nutrition panels on the back of condiment bottles:* Compare the nutritional value of various condiments. Pay special attention to salt and sugar content.

Community Task Have individual students (or groups of students) visit different supermarkets and investigate the current prices of certain items. Have students report their findings to the class.

Communication Activities

1 True or False?

ACTIVITY HANDBOOK PAGE 15

Make statements such as the following about the foods on *Picture Dictionary* page 53. Have students decide whether the statements are true or false. For example:

Ketchup is a baked good. [False. Ketchup is a condiment.]
Flour is a baked good. [False. Flour is a baking product.]
Rolls are a baked good. [True.]
Rice and macaroni are canned goods. [False. Rice and macaroni are packaged goods.]
Salt and pepper are condiments. [True.]
Vinegar is a vegetable. [False. Vinegar is a condiment.]
Salad dressing is a jam. [False. Salad dressing is a condiment.]
Cake is usually sweet. [True.]
Pickles are green. [True.]
Canned goods are in a refrigerator in the supermarket. [False. Canned goods are on supermarket shelves.]

2 Location! Location!

ACTIVITY HANDBOOK PAGES 10–11

If you choose to do Version 1, ask questions such as the following:

Where's the tuna fish? [It's next to the canned fruit.]
Where's the salsa? [It's next to the salad dressing.]
Where are the English muffins? [They're between the bread and the cake.]
Where's the mustard? [It's between the ketchup and relish.]
Where's the spaghetti? [It's in front of the noodles.]
Where's the soy sauce? [It's between the spices and the mayonnaise.]
Where's the mustard? [It's next to the ketchup.]
Where are the rolls? [They're next to the pita bread.]
Where's the sugar? [It's between the flour and the cake mix.]

If you choose to do Version 2, make statements such as the following:

It's to the right of the tuna fish. [The canned fruit.]
It's behind the salsa, next to the olive oil. [The vinegar.]
They're between the bread and the cake. [The English muffins.]
It's between the ketchup and relish. [The mustard.]
It's in front of the canned soup. [The tuna fish.]
It's between the spices and the mayonnaise. [The soy sauce.]
It's between the jam and the peanut butter. [The jelly.]
They're between the pepper and the soy sauce. [The spices.]
It's behind the pita bread. [The cake.]
It's between the flour and the cake mix. [The sugar.]

3 Category Dictation

ACTIVITY HANDBOOK PAGE 2

Dictate words that fit into the following categories:

canned goods
condiments
baked goods

4 General-to-Specific Clue Game

ACTIVITY HANDBOOK PAGE 7

Possible clues:

Clue 1: It tastes good with fresh fruit on top.
Clue 2: It's a packaged good.
Clue 3: People pour milk on it.
Clue 4: People eat it for breakfast.
Clue 5: It's usually brown.
    [Answer: cereal]

Clue 1: It comes in many different colors.
Clue 2: It's sweet.
Clue 3: People eat it for breakfast.
Clue 4: People put it on toast.
Clue 5: People put it on a sandwich with peanut butter.
    [Answer: jelly]

(continued)

5 Likes and Dislikes

a. Have students make two columns on a piece of paper—one column with the heading I like and the other with the heading I dislike.

b. Dictate words from the lesson, and have students write the items in the appropriate column. For example:

I like	I dislike
cake	spices
cookies	mustard
pickles	peanut butter

c. In pairs or in small groups, have students compare their answers.

6 Ranking

ACTIVITY HANDBOOK PAGE 13

Choose several food items from one of the categories on *Picture Dictionary* page 53 and write them on the board. Have students rank them according to the frequency with which they eat them (*often* to *seldom*). For example:

salt
pepper
spices
olive oil
vinegar

Variation: Have students look at all the items on *Picture Dictionary* page 53 and identify the ten items they think are the most important to have in their kitchens.

7 Food Associations

ACTIVITY HANDBOOK PAGE 2

Call out food items from the lesson and have groups write down foods that accompany that food. For example:

cereal:	[fruit/milk]
ketchup:	[hamburger/hot dog/potatoes]
cookies:	[milk]
English muffins:	[butter/margarine/jam/jelly/ cream cheese]

8 Movable Categories

ACTIVITY HANDBOOK PAGE 11
ACTIVITY MASTER 69

Call out the following categories and have students go to the appropriate side of the room:

salty foods
sweet foods
cooked foods
canned goods
jams and jellies
condiments
baked goods
packaged goods
foods that have to be in the refrigerator once they
  are opened

9 Do You Remember?

ACTIVITY HANDBOOK PAGE 5

Show students for 30 seconds one page of a supermarket flyer. Then have students write down all the food items they remember having seen depicted in the flyer.

10 Commercials

Divide the class into groups, and have each group create a commercial for one of the grocery items on *Picture Dictionary* page 53, then present it to the class.

LESSON OBJECTIVE

Students will learn the names of different kinds of household supplies, baby products, and pet foods.

RESOURCES

AUDIO PROGRAM
Words & Dialogs
Cassette 2B
CD 2: Tracks 54–56

MULTI-LEVEL WORKBOOKS
Literacy Workbook
Beginning & Intermediate Lifeskills Workbooks
Beginning & Intermediate Vocabulary Workbooks

ACTIVITY MASTER
Reproducible:
A70

TRANSPARENCY
Overhead T54

LANGUAGE & CULTURE NOTES
Reproducible: LC54

WORDLINKS
longman.com/wordbyword

VOCABULARY INTRODUCTION

- Preview
- Present
- Practice

MODEL CONVERSATION PRACTICE

1. Have students look at the model illustration. Set the scene: "A shopper is talking to a clerk in a supermarket."
2. Present the model.
3. Choral Repetition Practice: Full-Class and Individual.
4. Have pairs practice the model.
5. Have pairs present the model.
6. Call on pairs to present a new conversation using word 2.
7. Have pairs practice new conversations.
8. Have pairs present new conversations.

ADDITIONAL CONVERSATION PRACTICE

Before students practice the additional conversations, you may want to have them listen to the examples on the Audio Program.

Conversation 1 Set the scene: "Two family members are shopping in a supermarket." Have students practice and present conversations with any *non-count* items they wish.

Conversation 2 Set the scene: "Two family members are shopping in a supermarket." Have students practice and present conversations with any *count* items they wish.

SPELLING PRACTICE

Say a word, and have students spell it aloud or write it. Or, using the transparency, point to an item and have students write the word.

WRITING AND DISCUSSION

Have students respond to the question as a class, in pairs, or in small groups. Or have students write their responses, share their writing with other students, and discuss in class.

Making Connections

Resource Materials Bring in, or have students bring in, the following materials for vocabulary practice:

- *Newspaper advertisements for supermarket items:* Compare this week's prices for various supermarket items.

Community Task Have individual students (or groups of students) visit different supermarkets and investigate the current prices of certain items. Have students report their findings to the class.

Communication Activities

① Expand the Conversation
ACTIVITY HANDBOOK PAGE 6

Expand the model conversation to include other household supplies, baby products, and pet food.

a. Write the following on the board:

> A. Excuse me. Where can I find _____?
> B. _____? Look in Aisle _____.
> A. And how about _____?
> B. _____ (is/are) in Aisle _____, next the _____.
> A. Thanks.

b. Have pairs of students practice and present conversations based on this model, using different words from the page.

② Chain Game
ACTIVITY HANDBOOK PAGES 2–3

Begin the chain as follows: "I went to the supermarket and got some plastic wrap," and have students continue it. For example:

> Teacher: I went to the supermarket and got some plastic wrap.
> Student 1: I went to the supermarket and got some plastic wrap and some baby food.
> Student 2: I went to the supermarket and got some plastic wrap, some baby food, and some baby cereal.
> Etc.

③ True or False?
ACTIVITY HANDBOOK PAGE 15

Make statements such as the following about the items on *Picture Dictionary* page 54. Have students decide whether the statements are true or false. For example:

> Diapers are household items. [False. Diapers are baby products.]
> Formula is a special milk product for babies. [True.]
> Wipes are the same as napkins. [False. Wipes are wet, and you use them to clean a baby.]
> You use straws to eat baby food. [False. You use straws for drinks.]

> Liquid soap is a beverage. [False. Liquid soap is a household item.]
> Plastic wrap is a pet food. [False. Plastic wrap is a household item.]
> Baby cereal is a kind of food. [True.]
> People usually wash paper cups and paper plates in the dishwasher. [False.]
> Paper towels, toilet paper, napkins, and tissues are all made of paper. [True.]

④ Location! Location!
ACTIVITY HANDBOOK PAGES 10–11

If you choose to do Version 1, ask questions such as the following:

Where are the straws?	[They're behind the tissues and the paper plates.]
Where's the toilet paper?	[It's in front of the paper towels.]
Where's the aluminum foil?	[It's behind the plastic wrap.]
Where's the soap?	[It's in front of the liquid soap.]
Where's the formula?	[It's between the baby cereal and the diapers.]
Where are the paper cups?	[They're between the napkins and the straws.]
Where are the paper towels?	[They're behind the toilet paper.]
Where are the trash bags?	[They're behind the sandwich bags.]
Where are the tissues?	[They're between the napkins and the paper plates.]
Where's the plastic wrap?	[It's between the aluminum foil and the waxed paper.]

If you choose to do Version 2, make statements such as the following:

It's to the right of the paper plates.	[The toilet paper.]
It's behind the soap.	[The liquid soap.]
They're between the paper cups and the paper towels.	[The straws.]
They're in front of the paper cups.	[The tissues.]

It's between the baby cereal and the diapers. [The formula.]

It's between the aluminum foil and the waxed paper. [The plastic wrap.]

They're next to the paper cups. [The napkins.]

It's next to the cat food. [The dog food.]
It's next to the wipes. [The baby food.]
They're behind the sandwich bags. [The trash bags.]

 5 Category Dictation
ACTIVITY HANDBOOK PAGE 2

Dictate words that fit into the following categories:

paper products
baby products
pet food

 6 General-to-Specific Clue Game
ACTIVITY HANDBOOK PAGE 7

Possible clues:

Clue 1: It's a paper product.
Clue 2: You throw it away after you use it.
Clue 3: People use it at picnics.
Clue 4: It's round.
Clue 5: People put food on it.
  [Answer: paper plate]

Clue 1: It's hard and dry.
Clue 2: It works only when you use it with water.
Clue 3: It's smooth in water.
Clue 4: It smells good.
Clue 5: People use it to wash their hands.
  [Answer: soap]

7 Ranking
ACTIVITY HANDBOOK PAGE 13

Choose several items from a category on *Picture Dictionary* page 54 and write them on the board. Have students rank them according to the frequency with which they use them (*often* to *seldom*). For example:

straws
napkins
tissues
paper towels
paper cups

 8 Movable Categories
ACTIVITY HANDBOOK PAGE 11
ACTIVITY MASTER 70

Call out the following categories and have students go to the appropriate side of the room:

paper products
plastic products
baby products
products to keep food fresh
products for pets
foods
products for cleaning or wiping the body
products you use with water
products you use for eating

 9 Finish the Sentence!
ACTIVITY HANDBOOK PAGE 7

Begin sentences such as the following for students to complete:

You clean your nose with a . . . *tissue.*
You wipe water from the floor with a . . .
  paper towel.
You wash your hands with . . . *soap.*
You put trash into a . . . *trash bag.*
A baby drinks . . . *formula.*
You feed a dog . . . *dog food.*
You feed a cat . . . *cat food.*
You can drink a soda with a . . . *straw.*
You feed a baby . . . *baby cereal/baby food.*
Before a baby knows how to use a toilet, a baby uses
  . . . *diapers.*

10 Do You Remember?
ACTIVITY HANDBOOK PAGE 5

Show students for 30 seconds a page of a supermarket flyer. Then have students write down all the items they remember having seen depicted in the flyer.

 11 Commercials

Divide the class into groups, and have each group create a commercial for one of the household supplies, baby products, or pet food items on *Picture Dictionary* page 53, and then present it to the class.

LESSON OBJECTIVE

Students will learn about supermarkets.

RESOURCES

AUDIO PROGRAM		MULTI-LEVEL WORKBOOKS
Words & Dialogs Cassette 2B CD 2: Tracks 57, 58	**WordSong:** *Supermarket Sally* Cassette 7A • CD 7: Tracks 29, 30 Song Masters S13, S14	Literacy Workbook Beginning & Intermediate Lifeskills Workbooks Beginning & Intermediate Vocabulary Workbooks

TRANSPARENCY	LANGUAGE & CULTURE NOTES	WORDLINKS
Overhead T55	Reproducible: LC55	longman.com/wordbyword

VOCABULARY INTRODUCTION

- Preview
- Present
- Practice

MODEL CONVERSATION PRACTICE

There are two model conversations—the first for words 1–8, 11–19, and 21–25, and the second for words 9, 10, and 20. Introduce and practice the first model before going on to the second. For each model:

1. Have students look at the model illustration. Set the scene: "A husband and wife are talking. They just walked into a very large supermarket."
2. Present the model.
3. Choral Repetition Practice: Full-Class and Individual.
4. Have pairs practice the model.
5. Have pairs present the model.
6. Call on students to present a new conversation using word 2 for the first model and word 10 for the second model.
7. Have pairs practice new conversations.
8. Have pairs present new conversations.

SPELLING PRACTICE

Say a word, and have students spell it aloud or write it. Or, using the transparency, point to an item and have students write the word.

WRITING AND DISCUSSION

Have students respond to the questions as a class, in pairs, or in small groups. Or have students write their responses, share their writing with other students, and discuss in class.

♫♫ WORDSONG ♫♫

1. Have students listen to the vocal version of *Supermarket Sally* one or more times. Then have students listen again as they read the song lyrics on Song Master S13.
2. Have students sing as you play either the vocal or the sing-along version of the song.
3. For fun, have a song competition in which students perform solo or in groups and the class votes for the best performance.
4. For additional practice, students can complete the cloze exercise on Song Master S14.

Resource Materials Bring in, or have students bring in, the following materials for vocabulary practice:

○ *Discount coupons for supermarket items:* Show students how to read coupons. Identify the expiration date, the type of discount, and any restrictions or requirements for redeeming the coupons.

○ *Advertisement fliers for supermarkets:* Have students identify the location of the supermarkets and describe the quality of their merchandise.

Community Task Have individual students (or groups of students) visit different supermarkets and report about the quality of the produce, the range of prices, the length of checkout lines, and the cleanliness of the stores.

Communication Activities

1 Expand the Conversation
ACTIVITY HANDBOOK PAGE 6

Expand the model conversation to include other supermarket items.

a. Write the following on the board:

> A. This is a gigantic supermarket!
> B. It is! Look at all the _____(s)!
> A. I know. And do you see all the _____(s)? Can you believe it?
> B. No. I've never seen so many _____(s)/so much _____ in one supermarket before!

b. Have pairs of students practice and present conversations based on this model, using different words from the page.

2 True or False?
ACTIVITY HANDBOOK PAGE 15

Make statements such as the following about the scene on *Picture Dictionary* page 55. Have students decide whether the statements are true or false. For example:

> There are three customers in line at the express checkout counter. [False. There's only one customer at the express checkout counter.]
> There's one customer at the can-return machine. [True.]
> The manager and the clerk are in the Dairy Section. [False. They're in the Produce Section.]
> The customer paying at the checkout counter has plastic bags. [False. He has paper bags.]

> There's a bagger at the express checkout counter. [False. There isn't a bagger at that counter.]
> The customer at the express checkout counter has a shopping cart. [False. She has a shopping basket.]
> There's candy at the regular checkout counter. [True.]
> There are two customers at the bottle-return machine. [False. No one is at the bottle-return machine.]
> In the supermarket on page 55, two checkout counters are open. [True.]

3 Do You Remember?
ACTIVITY HANDBOOK PAGE 5

Have students write down everything they remember about the supermarket depicted on *Picture Dictionary* page 55.

If you do Variation 1, ask questions such as the following:

> Where is the manager?
> How many customers are in the express checkout?
> How many cashiers are there?
> How many baggers are there?
> How many people are at the can-return machine?
> How many people are at the bottle-return machine?

4 Picture This!
ACTIVITY HANDBOOK PAGES 12–13

Describe a grocery store and have students draw what you describe. For example:

> In this supermarket, the Dairy Section is against the left wall. In the middle there's a large Produce Section. In that section, there are apples, pears, and bananas.

(continued)

A Trip to the Supermarket

The following activities involve students doing supermarket research.

- Give students a list of supermarket items. Have them go to a supermarket and find out in which section the items are located. Have them make a list of other items found in the same section and report back to the class.

- Have students find out how many different places in a supermarket they can find the same food item. For example:

    peas: in the Produce Section
    in the Canned Goods Section
    in the Frozen Foods Section

    pasta: in the Produce Section
    in the Packaged Goods Section
    in the Frozen Food Section (as part
    of a frozen dinner, for example)

- Have students go to a local supermarket and find out what customer services are offered (for example, check cashing, film developing).

 Economical Shopping

Talk with students about ways in which people can save money when they do their food shopping (for example, comparison shopping, using coupons). Then do one or more of the following activities:

- Bring in fliers or newspaper ads from two or three supermarkets and compare prices of sale items.

- Bring in manufacturers' coupons and talk about them.

- In pairs or small groups, have students, using coupons and sale items, plan a dinner for six people. Then have the class compare the content and cost of the meals.

- Have students go to a supermarket and compare prices of different brands of the same product.

LESSON OBJECTIVE

Students will learn the names of different containers and quantities for foods.

RESOURCES

AUDIO PROGRAM	MULTI-LEVEL WORKBOOKS	ACTIVITY MASTERS
Words & Dialogs Cassette 2B CD 2: Tracks 59–61	Literacy Workbook Beginning & Intermediate Lifeskills Workbooks Beginning & Intermediate Vocabulary Workbooks	**Reproducibles:** A8, A71
TRANSPARENCY Overhead: T56	**LANGUAGE & CULTURE NOTES** Reproducible: LC56	**WORDLINKS** longman.com/wordbyword

VOCABULARY INTRODUCTION

- Preview
- Present
- Practice

MODEL CONVERSATION PRACTICE

There are two model conversations—one for singular quantities and the other for plural quantities. Introduce and practice the first model before going on to the second. For each model:

1. Have students look at the model illustration. Set the scene:

    Model 1: "A wife is talking to her husband as he is leaving to do some errands."
    Model 2: "A father is talking to his son as he is leaving to do some errands."

2. Present the model.
3. Choral Repetition Practice: Full-Class and Individual.
4. Have pairs practice the model.
5. Have pairs present the model.
6. Call on pairs to present a new conversation using word 3 for the first model and word 4 for the second model.
7. Have pairs practice new conversations.
8. Have pairs present new conversations.

Key to the items depicted:

1. a *bag* of flour/potato chips/cookies
2. a *bottle* of ketchup/soda/salad dressing
3. a *box* of cereal/cookies/raisins/tissues
4. a *bunch* of bananas/carrots/grapes
5. a *can* of soda/soup/coffee/tuna fish
6. a *carton* of milk/orange juice/eggs
7. a *container* of yogurt/cottage cheese/blueberries
8. a *dozen* eggs
9. a *head* of lettuce/cabbage
10. a *jar* of mayonnaise/salsa/olives/baby food
11. a *loaf* of bread (plural: *loaves*)
12. a *pack* of gum
13. a *package* of rolls/pita bread
14. a *roll* of paper towels/toilet paper/waxed paper
15. a *six-pack* of soda/water
16. a *stick* of butter/margarine
17. a *tube* of toothpaste
18. a *pint* of ice cream/sour cream
19. a *quart* of milk/chocolate milk
20. a *half-gallon* of skim milk/orange juice/ice cream
21. a *gallon* of bottled water
22. a *liter* of soda
23. a *pound* of butter/ground meat

ADDITIONAL CONVERSATION PRACTICE

Before students practice the additional conversations, you may want to have them listen to the examples on the Audio Program.

Conversation 1 Set the scene: "One family member is talking to another." Have students practice and present conversations with any words they wish.

Conversation 2 Set the scene: "A shopper is talking to a clerk in a supermarket." Have students practice and present conversations with any words they wish.

SPELLING PRACTICE

Say a word, and have students spell it aloud or write it. Or, using the transparency, point to an item and have students write the word.

WRITING AND DISCUSSION

Have students respond to the questions as a class, in pairs, or in small groups. Or have students write their responses, share their writing with other students, and discuss in class.

Making Connections

Resource Materials Bring in, or have students bring in, the following materials for vocabulary practice:

○ *Newspaper advertisements for supermarket items:* Identify the different types of containers and packages that are used for the foods featured in the advertisements.

Community Task Have students (or groups of students) visit different supermarkets and investigate how many different kinds of containers or packages are used for one food product. Have students report their findings to the class.

Communication Activities

1 Expand the Conversation
ACTIVITY HANDBOOK PAGE **6**

Expand the model conversation to include other containers and quantities.

a. Write the following on the board:

> A. Please get a _____ __ _____ when you go to the supermarket.
> B. A _____ __ _____? Okay.
> A. And we also need (2/3/4/5) _____s __ _____.
> B. (2/3/4/5) _____s __ _____? Sure. Anything else?
> A. Oh, yes. We need a _____ __ _____ and (2/3/4/5) _____s __ _____.

b. Have pairs of students practice and present conversations based on this model, using different words from the page.

2 Clap in Rhythm
ACTIVITY HANDBOOK PAGE **3**

Have students name different container words to a clapping rhythm.

3 Beanbag Toss

a. Divide the class into two groups. Have each group sit in a circle.

b. Have students toss a beanbag back and forth. As they toss the beanbag, they begin a phrase that the student who catches the bag must finish. For example:

> Student 1: A bag of . . . [*tosses beanbag*]
> Student 2: [*catches beanbag*] A bag of flour. A loaf of . . . [*tosses beanbag*]
> Student 3: [*catches beanbag*] A loaf of bread.
>   Etc.

4 Container Pictures

Bring in pictures of supermarket items. Have students identify the items as you hold up the pictures—for example: *a jar of mayonnaise, two bags of cookies, a head of cabbage.* This activity can also be done in pairs or in small groups.

5 Telephone
ACTIVITY HANDBOOK PAGE **14**

Begin the activity with the following sentence: "I need to get a bag of pretzels, two liters of diet soda, and a quart of chocolate ice cream."

6 Name That Container!

Call out the name of a container or quantity, and have students repeat it, adding an appropriate noun. For example:

> Teacher: jar
> Student: a jar of jam
>
> Teacher: quart
> Student: a quart of milk

Variation: Reverse the procedure. Call out the name of a food item and have students come up with the appropriate container or quantity. For example:

> Teacher: jam
> Student: a jar of jam
>
> Teacher: milk
> Student: a quart of milk

Both of these activities can be done as games with competing teams.

7 Concentration
ACTIVITY HANDBOOK PAGE 3
ACTIVITY MASTER 71

Have students shuffle the cards and place them face-down in four rows of 5 each, then attempt to find cards that match.

8 Container Associations
ACTIVITY HANDBOOK PAGE 2

Call out container phrases and have groups write down as many associations as they can think of. For example:

> a head of: [lettuce/cabbage]
> a bunch of: [grapes/carrots/bananas]
> a box of: [macaroni/crackers/cereal]
> a jar of: [mustard/olives/pickles/mayonnaise]

9 Chain Game
ACTIVITY HANDBOOK PAGES 2–3

Begin the chain as follows: "I went to the supermarket and bought a head of lettuce," and have students continue it. For example:

> Teacher: I went to the supermarket and bought a head of lettuce.
> Student 1: I went to the supermarket and bought a head of lettuce and a pint of ice cream.
> Student 2: I went to the supermarket and bought a head of lettuce, a pint of ice cream, and a pound of apples.
> Etc.

10 Listen and Number
ACTIVITY HANDBOOK PAGE 10

In pairs, have one student make up a story using container words and have the other student number the pictures in their order of occurrence in the story.

11 True or False?
ACTIVITY HANDBOOK PAGE 15

Make statements about the foods and containers on *Picture Dictionary* page 56. Have students decide whether the statements are true or false. For example:

> Soda comes in jars. [False. Soda comes in bottles.]
> Mayonnaise comes in bottles. [False. Mayonnaise comes in jars.]
> Margarine comes in containers and in sticks. [True.]
> Eggs come in cartons. [True.]
> Paper towels come in tubes. [False. Paper towels come in rolls.]
> Potato chips come in six-packs. [False. Potato chips come in bags.]
> Milk comes in six-packs. [False. Milk comes in cartons.]
> Water comes in six-packs. [True.]
> Toothpaste comes in tubes. [True.]
> Tuna fish comes in bunches. [False. Tuna fish comes in cans.]

12 What Did You Buy at the Supermarket?

In pairs or in small groups, have students tell what they bought the last time they went to the supermarket. Make sure they specify a container or quantity for each item.

13 Tic Tac Quantities
ACTIVITY MASTER 8

a. Duplicate the *Tic Tac Grid* and give a copy to each student. Have students fill in the grid with any nine vocabulary words they wish from *Picture Dictionary* page 56. For example:

can	jar	quart
bunch	roll	box
bottle	head	liter

(continued)

b. Call out the name of a supermarket item. If a student has a container or quantity that the item comes in written on the grid, the student should write the name of the item in the appropriate box. For example: *bananas*.

can	jar	quart
bunch bananas	roll	box
bottle	head	liter

c. The first student to write in three items in a straight line—either horizontally, vertically, or diagonally—wins the game.

d. Have the winner call out the words to check for accuracy.

14 What Are We Going to Make?

a. Divide the class into groups.

b. Have each group think of something they want to prepare to eat and then, based on that, make a list of ingredients they would need to buy.

c. A student from each group takes a turn reading that group's *shopping list,* and others guess what it is they're going to make. For example:

> a dozen eggs
> a half-pound of onions
> a quart of milk
> a pound of mushrooms
> a half-pound of cheese
> a loaf of bread
> a stick of butter
> a jar of strawberry jam
>
> [Answer: a mushroom, cheese, and onion omelet with toast and strawberry jam]

15 What Do We Need?

a. Divide the class into several groups.

b. Tell the class what you'd like to make, and have them tell you what you need to buy at the supermarket. For example: "I'd like to make tuna fish sandwiches for my family today."

c. Possible ingredients:

> a loaf of bread
> a can of tuna fish
> a jar of mayonnaise
> a head of lettuce
> a bunch of celery

d. Compare the different groups' suggestions.

16 Same and Different
ACTIVITY HANDBOOK PAGE 13

Write pairs of container and quantity words on the board, and have students think of similarities and differences between the pairs. For example:

jar—bottle

Same:
> Both are plastic or glass.
> Both hold liquids.

Different:
> Jars have wide tops so that a knife or a spoon can fit into them.
> Bottles have narrow tops.
> Bottles usually hold liquids.
> Jars hold liquids or solids.

Other possible items to compare are:

> carton—container
> roll—tube
> liter—quart
> bag—package

LESSON OBJECTIVE

Students will learn the units of measurement for liquids and solids.

RESOURCES

AUDIO PROGRAM
Words & Dialogs
Cassette 2B
CD 2: Tracks 62–65

MULTI-LEVEL WORKBOOKS
Literacy Workbook
Beginning & Intermediate Lifeskills Workbooks
Beginning & Intermediate Vocabulary Workbooks

ACTIVITY MASTER
Reproducible:
A72

TRANSPARENCY
Overhead: T57

LANGUAGE & CULTURE NOTES
Reproducible: LC57

WORDLINKS
longman.com/wordbyword

VOCABULARY INTRODUCTION FOR UNITS OF LIQUID MEASURE

The top portion of the page depicts units of liquid measure.

● Preview
● Present
● Practice

MODEL CONVERSATION PRACTICE

There are two model conversations for liquid measure. Introduce and practice the first model before going on to the second. For each model:

1. Have students look at the model illustration. Set the scene:

   Model 1: "A husband and wife are cooking together."
   Model 2: "Two friends are talking about the fruit punch."

2. Present the model.

   Present the first model with teaspoon (*add one teaspoon of water*).
   Present the second model with cup, pint, and quart (*two cups of apple juice, three pints of orange juice, and a quart of grape juice*).

3. Choral Repetition Practice: Full-Class and Individual.

4. Have pairs practice the model.

5. Have pairs present the model.

6. Call on pairs to present a new conversation using appropriate units of measure.

7. Have pairs practice new conversations.

8. Have pairs present new conversations.

VOCABULARY INTRODUCTION FOR UNITS OF DRY MEASURE

The bottom portion of the page depicts units of dry measure.

● Preview
● Present
● Practice

   Note that teaspoons and tablespoons can also be used for dry measure—for example, "a teaspoon of sugar/a tablespoon of salt."

   Give other examples of dry measure, such as "a pound and a quarter/a pound and a half/two and three-quarters pounds."

MODEL CONVERSATION PRACTICE

There are two model conversations for dry measure. Introduce and practice the first model before going on to the second. For each model:

1. Have students look at the model illustration. Set the scene:

   Model 3: "The clerk at a deli counter is talking to a customer."
   Model 4: "Two friends are talking at a picnic."

2. Present the model.

   Present the third model with *a quarter of a pound*.
   Present the fourth model with several different units of dry measure—for example, *two pounds of ground beef, a pound and a half of beans, two pounds of tomatoes, and six tablespoons of chili powder.*

3. Choral Repetition Practice: Full-Class and Individual.

4. Have pairs practice the model.

5. Have pairs present the model.

6. Call on pairs to present a new conversation using appropriate units of measure.

7. Have pairs practice new conversations.

8. Have pairs present new conversations.

SPELLING PRACTICE

Say a word, and have students spell it aloud or write it. Or, using the transparency, point to an item and have students write the word.

Making Connections

Resource Materials Bring in, or have students bring in, the following materials for vocabulary practice:

● *Cookbooks:* Have students read recipes aloud to practice interpreting the abbreviations for units of measure.

● *Measurement items (teaspoon, tablespoon, cup, quart, gallon, scale, and if possible a liter measurement):* Have students practice dry and liquid measures. Ask: How many teaspoons are in a tablespoon? How many cups are in a pint? How many pints are in a quart? How many quarts are in a gallon? Is a quart smaller or larger than a liter? How many liters are in a gallon?

Communication Activities

1 Question-Answer Game

a. Write on the board:

How many _____s are there in _____

b. Divide the class into two teams.

c. Using the model on the board, have each team come up with a list of ten questions to ask the other team. For example:

> How many ounces are there in a cup?
> How many pints are there in a quart?
> How many ounces are there in half a pound?
> How many cups are there in two pints?

d. The team with the most correct answers wins the game.

2 Measurement Match Game
ACTIVITY HANDBOOK PAGE 11
ACTIVITY MASTER 72

Have students find the person whose card matches theirs.

3 What's the Question?

a. Write on the board:

How many _____s are there in _____?

b. Call out a number, and have students use the model on the board to respond with the appropriate equivalency question. For example:

> Teacher: 8
> Student: How many ounces are there in a cup?
>
> Teacher: 3
> Student: How many teaspoons are there in a tablespoon?

You can also do this activity as a game with competing teams.

4 Telephone
ACTIVITY HANDBOOK PAGE 14

Begin the activity with the following sentence: "The ingredients for rice pudding are two cups of rice, three cups of milk, one egg, and one and a half teaspoons of spice."

5 Let's Cook!

Bring to class the ingredients for a simple recipe and the appropriate utensils. Prepare the recipe and talk about the measurements of the ingredients as you proceed.

6 Tic Tac Measurements

a. Check understanding of *more than, less than,* and *equal to.* For example:

> 5 is *more than* 4.
> 25 is *less than* 29.
> 16 ounces is *equal to* a pound.

b. Put a grid such as the following on the board:

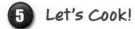

1 pt. 1 cup	1 qt. 4 cups	1 Tbsp. 3 tsp.
3 pts. 1 qt.	1 gal. 3 qts.	8 ozs. 1 lb.
1 cup 8 fl. ozs.	2 cups 1 pt.	2 pts. 32 fl. ozs.

c. Divide the class into two teams: Team X and Team O.

d. The first player from Team X chooses a square on the grid (for example, the middle one) and tells the relationship between the two measurements ("One gallon is more than three quarts" or "Three quarts is less than one gallon").

e. If the student is correct, put an X in that square. If the student is incorrect, the square remains *open.*

f. The teams take turns choosing a square and stating the relationship between the measurements until one team wins by correctly answering three in a row—vertically, horizontally, or diagonally.

7 Mystery Recipes

a. Have groups write down recipes without naming the dish.

b. The groups read their recipes aloud to the class, and the class tries to guess the dish.

8 Units of Measure Associations
ACTIVITY HANDBOOK PAGE 2

Call out a food, and have students write down as many ways to measure that food as they can think of. For example:

chicken: [a quarter of a pound/half a pound/three-quarters of a pound/a pound]
milk: [a teaspoon/a tablespoon/1 fluid ounce/a cup/a pint/a quart/a gallon]
butter: [a teaspoon/a tablespoon/a cup/a quarter of a pound/a half a pound/three-quarters of a pound/a pound/a stick]

LESSON OBJECTIVE

Students will learn the verbs to describe steps in food preparation.

RESOURCES

AUDIO PROGRAM	MULTI-LEVEL WORKBOOKS	ACTIVITY MASTER
Words & Dialogs Cassette 2B CD 3: Tracks 2–4	Literacy Workbook Beginning & Intermediate Lifeskills Workbooks Beginning & Intermediate Vocabulary Workbooks	Reproducible: A73
TRANSPARENCY Overhead: T58	**LANGUAGE & CULTURE NOTES** Reproducible: LC58	**WORDLINKS** longman.com/wordbyword

VOCABULARY INTRODUCTION

- Preview
- Present
- Practice

MODEL CONVERSATION PRACTICE

1. Have students look at the model illustration. Set the scene: "A son is offering help to his mother."
2. Present the model.
3. Choral Repetition Practice: Full-Class and Individual.
4. Have pairs practice the model.
5. Have pairs present the model.
6. Call on pairs to present a new conversation using word 2.
7. Have pairs practice new conversations.
8. Have pairs present new conversations.

Key to the actions depicted:

1. *cut (up)* the carrot
2. *chop (up)* the onion
3. *slice* the bread
4. *grate* the cheese
5. *peel* the orange
6. *break* the egg
7. *beat* the eggs
8. *stir* the soup
9. *pour* the water
10. *add* the salt
11. *combine* the eggs and the milk
12. *mix* the flour and the sugar
13. *put* the cookies in the oven
14. *cook* the rice
15. *bake* the potatoes
16. *boil* the eggs
17. *broil* the fish
18. *steam* the broccoli
19. *fry* the chicken
20. *saute* the mushrooms
21. *simmer* the beans
22. *roast* the turkey
23. *barbecue/grill* the steak
24. *stir-fry* the vegetables
25. *microwave* the frozen meatballs

ADDITIONAL CONVERSATION PRACTICE

Before students practice the additional conversations, you may want to have them listen to the examples on the Audio Program.

Conversation 1 Have students practice and present conversations with words 1–25.

Conversation 2 Have students practice and present conversations with words 14–25.

SPELLING PRACTICE

Say a word, and have students spell it aloud or write it. Or, using the transparency, point to an item and have students write the word.

Have students respond to the question as a class, in pairs, or in small groups. Or have students write their responses, share their writing with other students, and discuss in class.

Making Connections

Resource Materials Bring in, or have students bring in, the following materials for vocabulary practice:

● *Cookbooks:* Have students bring in their favorite recipes.

● *Video of a TV cooking program:* Have the class watch the cooking show and write down any words from *Picture Dictionary* page 58 they hear in the program.

Communication Activities

1 Expand the Conversation
ACTIVITY HANDBOOK PAGE 6

Expand the model conversation to include food preparation steps.

a. Write the following on the board:

```
A. Can I help you?
B. Yes.  Please _____.
A. Can I do anything else?
B. Yes.  You can also _____ and
   _____.
A. Sure.  I'll be happy to.
```

b. Have pairs of students practice and present conversations based on this model, using different words from the page.

2 Concentration
ACTIVITY HANDBOOK PAGE 3
ACTIVITY MASTER 73

Have students shuffle the cards and place them face-down in three rows of 6 each, then attempt to find cards that match.

3 Tell Me What to Do

a. Write the verbs from *Picture Dictionary* page 58 on the board.

b. Call out a food item and have students respond with different ways it can be prepared. For example:

```
Teacher: carrot
Students: peel it
          grate it
          slice it
          chop it
```

```
Teacher: soup
Students: stir it
          pour it
          boil it
```

Note: To make the activity more interesting, use real food items as props.

4 Listen and Number
ACTIVITY HANDBOOK PAGE 10

In pairs, have one student make up a recipe using food preparation words and have the other student number the pictures on *Picture Dictionary* page 58 in their order of occurrence in the recipe.

5 Movable Categories
ACTIVITY HANDBOOK PAGE 11

Give each student a card with a food item written on it. Then call out the following categories and have students go to the appropriate side of the room:

```
foods you slice
foods you boil
foods you chop
foods you broil
foods you grate
foods you fry
foods you peel
foods you steam
foods you stir
foods you beat
foods you barbecue
foods you saute
foods you stir-fry
foods you pour
foods you microwave
foods you bake
foods you simmer
foods you roast
```

(continued)

6 Category Dictation

ACTIVITY HANDBOOK PAGE 2

Dictate any four of the above categories, and have students write each at the top of one of the columns. Dictate food items, and have students write the items in the appropriate column.

7 What Am I Going to Make?

a. Ask each student to bring in a recipe.

b. As a class, in pairs, or in small groups, a student reads his or her recipe instructions and others guess what the recipe is for.

c. If you wish, compile a *Class Recipe Book* of students' recipes.

8 Mixed-Up Recipes!

Write directions for simple recipes on cards and distribute the cards. Have students arrange themselves into a logical recipe. For example:

peel the potatoes

cut up the potatoes

fry the potatoes

put the fried potatoes on paper towels

add salt

serve the potatoes with ketchup

put a tea bag in a cup

boil water

pour the water into the cup

wait three minutes

take the tea bag out of the cup

add milk and sugar

drink

Variation: Have groups of students write their own directions on separate pieces of paper and have other groups put the directions in a logical order.

9 Ridiculous Recipes!

One student begins with the first step of an imaginary recipe. For example: "Put three eggs in a bowl." The next student adds another step to the recipe. For example: "Pour in seven cups of milk." Other students continue adding preparation steps to the *ridiculous recipe.* Either you or a student can write the recipe instructions on the board as students give them.

Variation:

a. One student writes the first instruction on the first line of a piece of paper, folds the paper over so the writing is hidden, and passes the paper to the next student.

b. The second student writes the second instruction, folds the paper, and passes it to a third student, and so forth around the room.

Some very *ridiculous recipes* should result!

LESSON OBJECTIVE

Students will learn the names of a variety of kitchen utensils and cookware.

RESOURCES

AUDIO PROGRAM

Words & Dialogs
Cassette 2B
CD 3: Tracks 5–7

MULTI-LEVEL WORKBOOKS

Literacy Workbook
Beginning & Intermediate Lifeskills Workbooks
Beginning & Intermediate Vocabulary Workbooks

ACTIVITY MASTER

Reproducible:
A74

TRANSPARENCY

Overhead: T59

LANGUAGE & CULTURE NOTES

Reproducible: LC59

WORDLINKS

longman.com/wordbyword

VOCABULARY INTRODUCTION

- Preview
- Present
- Practice

MODEL CONVERSATION PRACTICE

1. Have students look at the model illustration. Set the scene: "Two neighbors are talking."
2. Present the model.
3. Choral Repetition Practice: Full-Class and Individual.
4. Have pairs practice the model.
5. Have pairs present the model.
6. Call on pairs to present a new conversation using word 2.
7. Have pairs practice new conversations.
8. Have pairs present new conversations.

ADDITIONAL CONVERSATION PRACTICE

Before students practice the additional conversations, you may want to have them listen to the examples on the Audio Program.

Conversation 1 Set the scene: "Two family members are in the kitchen." Have students practice and present conversations with any words they wish.

Conversation 2 Set the scene: "This is a commercial for a store named *Kitchen World*." Have students practice and present their commercials, using appropriate props if possible.

SPELLING PRACTICE

Say a word, and have students spell it aloud or write it. Or, using the transparency, point to an item and have students write the word.

WRITING AND DISCUSSION

Have students respond to the questions as a class, in pairs, or in small groups. Or have students write their responses, share their writing with other students, and discuss in class.

Making Connections

Resource Materials Bring in, or have students bring in, the following materials for vocabulary practice:

- *Kitchenware brochures and catalogs:* Talk about the advertised kitchen items and their prices.

- *Newspaper and magazine advertisements for kitchenware:* Talk about the advertised kitchen items and their prices.

- *Small kitchenware utensils from home—for example, a knife, grater, spoon, measuring spoon, pot, pan, cookie sheet:* Have students explain how to use each utensil, using the verbs from *Picture Dictionary* page 58.

Community Task Have individual students (or groups of students) investigate the various types and prices of a particular kitchen item by visiting different kitchen stores in the area or looking on the Internet.

Communication Activities

1 Expand the Conversation!
ACTIVITY HANDBOOK PAGE 6

Expand the model conversation to include other kitchenware items.

a. Write the following on the board:

> A. Could I possibly borrow your _____?
> B. Sure. I'd be happy to lend you my _____.
>
> A. Thanks. And one more thing . . . Could I also borrow your _____ and your _____?
> B. Well, I'm actually going to be using my _____ soon, but you can certainly borrow my _____.
> A. Thanks very much. I appreciate it.

b. Have pairs of students practice and present conversations based on this model, using different words from the page.

2 Location! Location!
ACTIVITY HANDBOOK PAGES 10–11

If you choose to do Version 1, ask questions such as the following:

> Where are the peeled apples? [They're between the cookie sheet and the pie plate.]
> Where's the wooden spoon? [It's on the floor.]
> Where's the colander? [It's in the sink.]
> Where's the turkey? [It's on the roasting rack, in the roasting pan.]
> Where's the rolling pin? [It's in the woman's hands.]
> Where's the whisk? [It's in the bowl.]
> Where's the strainer? [It's between the ladle and the spatula.]
> Where's the cake pan? [It's in the cabinet.]
> Where's the egg beater? [It's on the wall above the bowl.]
> Where's the grater? [It's in front of the casserole dish.]

If you choose to do Version 2, make statements such as the following:

> It's on the stove in front of the double boiler. [The wok.]

It's between the can opener and the peeler. [The bottle opener.]
It's on the stove on top of the saucepan. [The lid.]
It's in the open drawer. [The ice cream scoop.]
It's on the counter next to the grater. [The garlic press.]
It's between the bowl and the measuring spoon. [The measuring cup.]
It's next to the pie plate. [The kitchen timer.]
It's between the mixing bowl and the cookie sheet. [The cookie cutter.]
It's close to the casserole dish and the roasting pan. [The carving knife.]

3 Chain Game: In My Kitchen
ACTIVITY HANDBOOK PAGES 2–3

Begin the chain as follows: "In my kitchen I have a wok," and have students continue it. For example:

> Teacher: In my kitchen I have a wok.
> Student 1: In my kitchen I have a wok and a saucepan.
> Student 2: In my kitchen I have a wok, a saucepan, and a double boiler.
>   Etc.

4 Movable Categories
ACTIVITY HANDBOOK PAGE 11
ACTIVITY MASTER 74

Call out the following categories and have students go to the appropriate side of the room:

utensils for cutting
utensils for mixing and stirring
utensils for serving food
utensils for measuring
utensils you hold in your hand
utensils for baking
utensils that use water
utensils you use on top of the stove
utensils with handles
utensils you use to open things

5 Category Dictation
ACTIVITY HANDBOOK PAGE 2

Dictate words that fit into the above categories.

6 Drawing Game

ACTIVITY HANDBOOK PAGE 6
ACTIVITY MASTER 74

Have teams compete to identify kitchen utensils and cookware items drawn by one of their team members.

7 Kitchen Utensil and Cookware Associations

ACTIVITY HANDBOOK PAGE 2

Call out kitchen utensil and cookware words and have groups write down as many associations as they can think of. For example:

wok: [vegetables/rice/stir-fry/hot/oil/ quick]
colander: [pasta/boiled vegetables/steam/ rinse/water]
spatula: [pancakes/bacon/flip/frying pan]
roasting rack: [chicken/duck/turkey/beef/oven]
rolling pin: [pies/dough/flour/pastries]

8 What's the Question?

ACTIVITY HANDBOOK PAGE 16

Describe various cookware and kitchen utensils and have students respond by asking: "What's a _____?" or "What are _____s?" For example:

Teacher: You use this to drain vegetables.
Student: What's a colander?

Teacher: You bake cookies on this.
Student: What's a cookie sheet?

Teacher: You open cans with this.
Student: What's a can opener?

Teacher: You bake casseroles in this.
Student: What's a casserole dish?

Teacher: You fry food in this.
Student: What's a skillet?

Teacher: You measure cooking time with this.
Student: What's a kitchen timer?

Teacher: You serve soup with this.
Student: What's a ladle?

Teacher: You serve ice cream with this.
Student: What's an ice cream scoop?

Teacher: You cut food with this.
Student: What's a knife?

Teacher: You cover a pot with this.
Student: What's a lid?

9 It's Something That . . .

ACTIVITY HANDBOOK PAGE 9
ACTIVITY MASTER 74

Have students give definitions of kitchen utensils and cookware words to each other beginning with "It's something that . . . " For example:

It's something that you use to peel vegetables. [A vegetable peeler.]
It's something that you use to cover a pot. [A lid.]
It's something that you use to drain pasta. [A colander.]
It's something that you use to stir food into a hot liquid. [A wooden spoon.]
It's something that you use to cut large pieces of meat. [A carving knife.]

10 Finish the Sentence!

ACTIVITY HANDBOOK PAGE 7

Begin sentences such as the following for students to complete:

I stir-fry vegetables in a . . . *wok.*
I serve soup with a . . . *ladle.*
I mix ingredients for cookies in a . . . *mixing bowl.*
I remove cookies from the cookie sheet with a . . . *spatula.*
I cover a pot with a . . . *lid.*
I cut meat with a . . . *carving knife.*
I saute onions in a . . . *skillet.*
I boil water in a . . . *pot.*
I measure spices with a . . . *measuring spoon.*

11 Connections

ACTIVITY HANDBOOK PAGE 4
ACTIVITY MASTER 74

Have students make connections between two kitchen utensils and cookware items. For example:

cake pan—pie plate
You use both for baking.

can opener—saucepan
A can opener opens the soup, which you heat in a saucepan.

cookie sheet—rolling pin
You use both for baking.

(continued)

12 General-to-Specific Clue Game
ACTIVITY HANDBOOK PAGE 7

Possible clues:

Clue 1: It's made of plastic, metal, or glass.
Clue 2: You use it for cooking.
Clue 3: You use it for baking.
Clue 4: It can fit in a drawer.
Clue 5: It measures liquids and solids.

[Answer: measuring cup]

Clue 1: It fits in your hand.
Clue 2: It has only one use.
Clue 3: It doesn't need to be washed.
Clue 4: It's made of plastic or metal.
Clue 5: You use it when you're thirsty.

[Answer: bottle opener]

Clue 1: You use it while preparing vegetables or fruit.
Clue 2: The important part is made of metal.
Clue 3: It can fit in a drawer.
Clue 4: It can hurt you if you aren't careful.
Clue 5: It cuts food.

[Answer: knife]

Clue 1: It's made of metal or glass.
Clue 2: You use it on the stove.
Clue 3: It cooks food.
Clue 4: It has three pieces, including the lid.
Clue 5: You use it to cook food slowly.

[Answer: double boiler]

13 Ranking
ACTIVITY HANDBOOK PAGE 13

Have students look at the kitchen utensils and cookware items on *Picture Dictionary* page 59. Have them choose five items they use the most. For example:

knife
pot
wooden spoon
spatula
can opener

Variations: Have students choose five items they use the least, or have students choose the ten most essential items in a kitchen.

14 Word Study

a. Have students look at the words on *Picture Dictionary* page 59 and identify all the words that end with *-er*. Have them answer the following questions:

What's the base verb of this word?
Is the word a noun or an adjective?

b. Have students look at the words on *Picture Dictionary* page 59 and identify all the words that end with *-ing*. Have them answer the following questions:

What's the base verb of this word?
Is the word a noun or an adjective?

15 Inventions
ACTIVITY HANDBOOK PAGE 9

In pairs or small groups, have student invent their own kitchen utensil or cookware. Have them give their invention a name and draw a picture of it. Then have them present their ideas to the class.

LESSON OBJECTIVE

Students will learn the names for the most popular fast foods in the United States.

RESOURCES

AUDIO PROGRAM

Words & Dialogs
Cassette 2B
CD 3: Tracks 8, 9

MULTI-LEVEL WORKBOOKS

Literacy Workbook
Beginning & Intermediate Lifeskills Workbooks
Beginning & Intermediate Vocabulary Workbooks

ACTIVITY MASTERS

Reproducibles:
A8, A75

TRANSPARENCY

Overhead: T60

LANGUAGE & CULTURE NOTES

Reproducible: LC60

WORDLINKS

longman.com/wordbyword

VOCABULARY INTRODUCTION

- Preview
- Present
- Practice

MODEL CONVERSATION PRACTICE

There are two model conversations—the first for words 1–17 and the second for words 18–27. Introduce and practice the first model before going on to the second. For each model:

1. Have students look at the model illustration. Set the scene:
   Model 1: "A server is talking to a customer at a fast-food restaurant."
   Model 2: "An employee is talking to his supervisor at a fast-food restaurant."

2. Present the model using words 1 and 6 for the first model and word 18 for the second model.

3. Choral Repetition Practice: Full-Class and Individual.

4. Have pairs practice the model.

5. Have pairs present the model.

6. Call on pairs to present a new conversation using words 2 and 7 for the first model and word 19 for the second model.

7. Have pairs practice new conversations.

8. Have pairs present new conversations.

SPELLING PRACTICE

Say a word, and have students spell it aloud or write it. Or, using the transparency, point to an item and have students write the word.

WRITING AND DISCUSSION

Have students respond to the questions as a class, in pairs, or in small groups. Or have students write their responses, share their writing with other students, and discuss in class.

Making Connections

Resource Materials Bring in, or have students bring in, the following materials for vocabulary practice:

- *Menus from fast-food restaurants listed on the Internet:* Talk about the foods offered on the menu. What foods have students tried? Which foods do they recommend?

- *Magazine pictures of fast foods and fast-food restaurants:* Identify the kinds of foods advertised.

- *Advertisements for fast foods and fast-food restaurants:* Compare prices of different restaurants.

Community Task Have individual students (or groups of students) visit different fast-food restaurants and report about the quality, taste, and value of the food in each restaurant.

Communication Activities

① Clap in Rhythm
ACTIVITY HANDBOOK PAGE 3

Have students name different fast-food words to a clapping rhythm.

② True or False?
ACTIVITY HANDBOOK PAGE 15

Make statements such as the following about fast foods and have students decide whether the statements are true or false. For example:

People put ketchup and mustard on their pizza. [False. People put ketchup and mustard on sandwiches and sometimes on french fries.]
Hamburgers are made with pork. [False. Hamburgers are made with beef.]
French fries are fried potatoes. [True.]
Nachos are potato chips with cheese sauce. [False. Nachos are corn chips with cheese sauce.]
Burritos are usually filled with rice and fish. [False. Burritos are usually filled with rice, beans, and meat.]
Pizza is served cold. [False. Pizza is served hot.]
Frozen yogurt is similar to ice cream. [True.]
A milkshake is a mix of milk and coffee. [False. A milkshake is mix of milk and ice cream.]
Chili is made with meat, onions, peppers, and tomatoes. [True.]
A cheeseburger has no meat, only cheese. [False. A cheeseburger is a sandwich with both meat and cheese.]

③ Ask Me a Question!
ACTIVITY HANDBOOK PAGE 2
ACTIVITY MASTER 75

Have students walk around trying to guess each other's fast-food items by asking yes/no questions. For example:

Is it warm?	[Yes.]
Is it sweet?	[No.]
Is it a sandwich?	[Yes.]
Does it have meat?	[Yes.]
Does it have beef?	[No.]
Is it a chicken sandwich?	[Yes.]

Is it warm?	[No.]
Is it cold?	[Yes.]
Is it sweet?	[Yes.]
Is it ice cream?	[No.]
Is it a milkshake?	[Yes.]

④ Chain Game: I Was So Hungry
ACTIVITY HANDBOOK PAGES 2–3

Begin the chain as follows: "I was so hungry I ate two cheeseburgers," and have students continue it. For example:

Teacher: I was so hungry I ate two cheeseburgers.
Student 1: I was so hungry I ate two cheeseburgers and a hot dog.
Student 2: I was so hungry I ate two cheeseburgers, a hot dog, and a slice of pizza.
Etc.

⑤ Tic Tac Definitions
ACTIVITY HANDBOOK PAGE 15
ACTIVITY MASTER 8

Have students fill in the tic tac grid with any nine fast-food words they wish. Give definitions such as the following, and have students cross out on their grids the words you have defined:

grilled ground beef with bread [hamburger]
grilled ground beef with melted cheese and bread [cheeseburger]
fried fish with lettuce, mayonnaise, and bread [fish sandwich]
fried chicken with lettuce, mayonnaise, and bread [chicken sandwich]
fried potatoes [french fries]
corn chips with cheese and tomato salsa [nachos]
fried beans, rice, and meat wrapped in a flour tortilla [burrito]
bread, tomato, and cheese baked in a hot oven [pizza]
a stew of ground beef, tomato, and spices [chili]
lettuce, tomatoes, cucumbers, and carrots [salad]
ice cream, syrup, and milk blended together [milkshake]

⑥ Movable Categories
ACTIVITY HANDBOOK PAGE 11
ACTIVITY MASTER 75

Call out the following categories and have students go to the appropriate side of the room:

fried foods
foods with meat
foods with dairy
drinks
desserts
foods with vegetables
foods you eat cold
foods you eat warm
condiments
utensils for eating

7 What Are They Doing?

Have students write sentences about what people are doing in the illustration on *Picture Dictionary* page 60. For example:

> A man is putting mustard on his hamburger.
> A woman is putting a straw into her soda.
> A boy is paying for food.

8 Ranking

ACTIVITY HANDBOOK PAGE **13**

Write fast food items on the board, and have students rank them from the healthiest to the least healthy. For example:

> burrito
> fish sandwich
> hamburger
> cheeseburgers
> french fries

Variations: Students can also rank the foods from those they most frequently eat to those they least frequently eat, and from the foods they like the best to the foods they like the least.

9 Survey

Have students conduct a class survey.

a. Have each student choose one question to ask the other students. For example:

> How often do you eat _____?
> Where do you go to get the best _____?
> What's your favorite fast-food restaurant?

b. Have students report their results to the class.

10 Class Discussion: Food and Culture

Discuss the following questions with the class:

> Which of the foods on *Picture Dictionary* page 60 are traditional foods in your country?
> Which of the foods on *Picture Dictionary* page 60 are now popular in your country?
> Are any of these foods not acceptable to eat according to your religion?
> Who eats fast food in your country?
> Why is fast food so popular today?
> Do you like fast food?

11 Funny Fast Foods!

a. Write on the board:

> _____ likes _____ _____s!

b. Ask students to think of a first name, an adjective, and the name of a fast food, all beginning with the same sound. (If possible, have students use their own first names.)

c. Have students create sentences based on the skeletal model on the board. For example:

> Barbara likes *big* burritos!
> Harry likes *hot* hamburgers!
> Charlie likes *cheddar* cheeseburgers!

12 Write the Recipe

a. In pairs, have students choose one fast food and write a recipe explaining how to prepare that food. Encourage students to use all the new vocabulary they have learned from *Picture Dictionary* pages 48–60. For example:

> *Hamburger*
> Fry the ground beef in a skillet.
> Put the cooked meat on a roll.
> Add ketchup and mustard.

b. Have students share their recipes with the class.

Variation: Have students explain their recipes without identifying the food they are preparing. Have the class try to identify the food.

LESSON OBJECTIVE

Students will learn the names for the foods most often served in American coffee shops and sandwich shops.

RESOURCES

AUDIO PROGRAM	MULTI-LEVEL WORKBOOKS	ACTIVITY MASTERS
Words & Dialogs	Literacy Workbook	**Reproducibles:**
Cassette 2B	Beginning & Intermediate Lifeskills Workbooks	A76, A77
CD 3: Tracks 10, 11	Beginning & Intermediate Vocabulary Workbooks	

TRANSPARENCY	LANGUAGE & CULTURE NOTES	WORDLINKS
Overhead: T61	**Reproducible:** LC61	longman.com/wordbyword

VOCABULARY INTRODUCTION

- Preview
- Present
- Practice

MODEL CONVERSATION PRACTICE

There are two model conversations—the first for words 1–21 and the second for words 22–35. Introduce and practice the first model before going on to the second. For each model:

1. Have students look at the model illustration. Set the scene:

   Model 1: "Someone is ordering in a sandwich shop."

   Model 2: "Someone is ordering in a sandwich shop."

2. Present the model using words 1, 8, and 15 for the first model and words 22 and 29 for the second model.

3. Choral Repetition Practice: Full-Class and Individual.

4. Have pairs practice the model.

5. Have pairs present the model.

6. Call on pairs to present a new conversation using words 2, 9, and 16 for the first model and words 23 and 30 for the second model.

7. Have pairs practice new conversations.

8. Have pairs present new conversations.

SPELLING PRACTICE

Say a word, and have students spell it aloud or write it. Or, using the transparency, point to an item and have students write the word.

WRITING AND DISCUSSION

Have students respond to the questions as a class, in pairs, or in small groups. Or have students write their responses, share their writing with other students, and discuss in class.

Making Connections

Resource Materials Bring in, or have students bring in, the following materials for vocabulary practice:

- *Menus from coffee shops:* Talk about the foods on the menu. What foods have students tried? Which foods do they recommend?

Community Task Have individual students (or groups of students) visit different coffee shops and report about the quality and value of the food and service in each coffee shop.

Communication Activities

1 Clap in Rhythm
ACTIVITY HANDBOOK PAGE 3

Have students name different coffee shop and sandwich words to a clapping rhythm.

2 Chain Game: I Was So Hungry
ACTIVITY HANDBOOK PAGES 2–3

Begin the chain as follows: "I was so hungry I ate two bagels," and have students continue it. For example:

Teacher:	I was so hungry I ate two bagels.
Student 1:	I was so hungry I ate two bagels and some bacon.
Student 2:	I was so hungry I ate two bagels, some bacon, and home fries.
Etc.	

3 Ask Me a Question!
ACTIVITY HANDBOOK PAGE 2
ACTIVITY MASTER 76

Have students walk around trying to guess each other's food items by asking yes/no questions. For example:

Do you eat it for lunch?	[No.]
Is it sweet?	[Yes.]
Do you eat it for breakfast?	[Yes.]
Do you heat it?	[No.]
Do you eat it with butter?	[No.]
Is it round?	[Yes.]
Is it a donut?	[Yes.]

Do you eat it for lunch?	[Yes.]
Is it a sandwich?	[Yes.]
Is it a meat sandwich?	[No.]
Is it an egg salad sandwich?	[Yes.]

4 Movable Categories
ACTIVITY HANDBOOK PAGE 11
ACTIVITY MASTER 76

Call out the following categories and have students go to the appropriate side of the room:

sandwiches
drinks
baked goods
breads for sandwiches
foods with meat
drinks with caffeine
cold drinks
hot drinks
sweet foods
salty foods

5 Category Dictation
ACTIVITY HANDBOOK PAGE 2

Dictate words that fit into the following categories:

breakfast foods
lunch foods

6 Concentration
ACTIVITY HANDBOOK PAGE 3
ACTIVITY MASTER 77

Have students shuffle the cards and place them face-down in four rows of 5 each, then attempt to find cards that match.

7 Ranking
ACTIVITY HANDBOOK PAGE 13

Write food items from *Picture Dictionary* page 61 on the board and have students rank them from healthiest to the least healthy. For example:

> tuna fish sandwich
> chicken salad sandwich
> corned beef sandwich
> bacon
> sausage

Variations: Students can also rank the foods from those they most frequently eat to those they least frequently eat, and from the foods they like the best to the foods they like the least.

8 Survey

Have students conduct a class survey.

a. Have each student choose one question to ask the other students. For example:

Do you ever eat _____?
Where do you go to get the best _____?
What's your favorite coffee shop?

b. Have students report their results to the class.

9 Invent a Sandwich!
ACTIVITY HANDBOOK PAGE 9

As a class, in pairs, or in small groups, have students invent a sandwich. They should name it, tell what's in it, tell what kind of bread it's on, and suggest other things that can be added to it.

LESSON OBJECTIVE

Students will learn the names of restaurant occupations, the verbs for restaurant work, and the vocabulary for areas and items in restaurants.

RESOURCES

AUDIO PROGRAM
Words & Dialogs
Cassette 2B
CD 3: Tracks 12–16

MULTI-LEVEL WORKBOOKS

Literacy Workbook
Beginning & Intermediate Lifeskills Workbooks
Beginning & Intermediate Vocabulary Workbooks

ACTIVITY MASTERS
Reproducibles:
A8, A78, A79

TRANSPARENCIES
Overheads: T62, T63

LANGUAGE & CULTURE NOTES
Reproducible: LC62–63

WORDLINKS

longman.com/wordbyword

VOCABULARY INTRODUCTION

- Preview
- Present
- Practice

MODEL CONVERSATION PRACTICE

There are five model conversations—the first for words 4–9, the second for words 10–12, the third for words 1–2 and 13–16, the fourth for words A–H, and the fifth for words 23–37. Introduce and practice each model before going on to the next. For each model:

1. Have students look at the model illustration. Set the scene:

   Model 1: "A hostess is seating customers in a restaurant."
   Model 2: "A waitress is talking to a customer."
   Model 3: "A husband and wife are at the salad bar."
   Model 4: "A restaurant manager is talking to a busperson."
   Model 5: "A busperson is talking to a waitress."

2. Present the model. (When presenting the fourth model, use word A, and for the fifth model, use words 23 and 24.)

3. Choral Repetition Practice: Full-Class and Individual.

4. Have pairs practice the model.

5. Have pairs present the model.

6. Call on students to present a new conversation using any appropriate word they wish.

7. Have pairs practice new conversations.

8. Have pairs present new conversations.

ADDITIONAL CONVERSATION PRACTICE

Before students practice the additional conversations, you may want to have them listen to the examples on the Audio Program.

Conversation 1 Set the scene: "Someone is looking for a job in a restaurant." Have students practice and present conversations with any words they wish.

Conversation 2 Set the scene: "A customer is talking to a server." Have students practice and present conversations with any words they wish.

SPELLING PRACTICE

Say a word, and have students spell it aloud or write it. Or, using the transparency, point to an item and have students write the word.

WRITING AND DISCUSSION

Have students respond to the questions as a class, in pairs, or in small groups. Or have students write their responses, share their writing with other students, and discuss in class.

Resource Materials Bring in, or have students bring in, the following materials for vocabulary practice:

● *Advertisements from the Yellow Pages for various restaurants in the area:* Ask students: Which of these restaurants have you tried? Are they good? How is the service? How is the food? Which restaurant do you most recommend?

● *Newspaper reviews of local restaurants:* Ask students: Does this review recommend the restaurant? What's good about the restaurant? What's not so good about the restaurant? Would you like to go to this restaurant? Why? Why not?

Community Task Have individual students (or groups of students) visit different restaurants and write down all the vocabulary items they see in the restaurant that match the vocabulary on *Picture Dictionary* pages 62 and 63.

Communication Activities

1 Drawing Game
ACTIVITY HANDBOOK PAGE 6
ACTIVITY MASTER 78

Have teams compete to identify restaurant items drawn by one of their team members.

2 Tic Tac Definitions
ACTIVITY HANDBOOK PAGE 15
ACTIVITY MASTER 8

Have students fill in the tic tac grid with any nine of the following restaurant words:

hostess	busperson
host	waitress
high chair	chef
booster seat	tip
menu	check
dining room	kitchen
teaspoon	knife

Give definitions such as the following and have students cross out on their grids the words you have defined:

a woman who greets and seats restaurant customers [hostess]
a man who greets and seats restaurant customers [host]
a seat at the table for a baby [high chair]
a seat at the table for a young child [booster seat]
the list of dishes the restaurant serves [menu]
the area where customers sit to eat [dining room]
the smallest spoon [teaspoon]
the person who clears dishes from the tables [busperson]
the woman who takes the order and serves the food [waitress]

a very well-trained cook [chef]
the money customers leave for the servers [tip]
the bill [check]
the area where the food is prepared [kitchen]
the piece of silverware you use to cut your food [knife]

3 Read, Write, and Draw
ACTIVITY HANDBOOK PAGE 13

Have students write each other letters in which they describe their favorite restaurants.

4 Restaurant Match Game
ACTIVITY HANDBOOK PAGE 11
ACTIVITY MASTER 79

Have students find the person whose card matches theirs.

5 What Goes Where?

Have students look at the illustration of a table setting on *Picture Dictionary* page 63 and tell the part of the place setting you're describing.

Teacher: It goes to the upper right of the dinner plate. What is it?
Student: The water glass.

Teacher: It goes to the left of the dinner fork. What is it?
Student: The salad fork.

Variation 1: Do the activity in pairs or small groups, with students taking turns telling the locations.

Variation 2: Divide the class into teams and do the activity as a game.

(continued)

6 True or False?

ACTIVITY HANDBOOK PAGE 15

Make statements such as the following about the place setting on *Picture Dictionary* page 63. Have students decide whether they're true or false. For example:

The soup spoon goes to the right of the teaspoon. [True.]

The knife goes to the left of the dinner plate. [False. The knife goes to the right of the dinner plate.]

The napkin goes under the two spoons. [False. The napkin goes under the two forks.]

The soup bowl goes on top of the dinner plate. [True.]

The wine glass goes to the left of the water glass. [False. The wine glass goes to the right of the water glass.]

The salad fork goes to the right of the dinner fork. [False. The salad fork goes to the left of the dinner fork.]

The salad plate goes to the left of the bread-and-butter plate. [True.]

The cup goes under the saucer. [False. The cup goes on top of the saucer.]

The bread-and-butter plate goes between the salad plate and the dinner plate. [True.]

The teaspoon goes between the knife and the soup spoon. [True.]

7 Set the Table!

a. Bring in plastic and paper items used in place settings, enough for every pair of students if possible.

b. Have pairs of students give instructions to each other on how to set the table.

Variation: Have students tell you how to set the table. Follow the instructions they give you.

8 What's Wrong?

Set up an incorrect place setting, and have students tell you what's wrong and how to make it right.

9 Discussion: Place Settings in Different Countries

As a class, in pairs, or in small groups, talk about how the table is set in different countries that students are familiar with.

10 Class Discussion: Tipping

Have students discuss the following questions in small groups or as a class:

Do you usually leave a tip?

How much money do you usually leave for a tip? (5% of the check? 10%? 15%? 20%?)

Do you tip in fast-food restaurants? How about in coffee shops? How about in restaurants?

Is it a good idea to leave a big tip? Why? Why not?

Is it a good idea to leave a small tip? Why? Why not?

LESSON OBJECTIVE

Students will learn typical food selections on a menu in a restaurant serving traditional American food.

RESOURCES

AUDIO PROGRAM
Words & Dialogs
Cassette 3A
CD 3: Tracks 17, 18

MULTI-LEVEL WORKBOOKS

Literacy Workbook
Beginning & Intermediate Lifeskills Workbooks
Beginning & Intermediate Vocabulary Workbooks

ACTIVITY MASTER
Reproducible:
A80

TRANSPARENCY
Overhead: T65

LANGUAGE & CULTURE NOTES
Reproducible: LC65

WORDLINKS
longman.com/wordbyword

VOCABULARY INTRODUCTION

- Preview
- Present
- Practice

MODEL CONVERSATION PRACTICE

Words 1–6 are appetizers, words 7–11 are salads, words 12–17 are main courses, words 18–23 are side dishes, and words 24–29 are desserts.

1. Have students look at the model illustration. Set the scene: "A waiter is talking to a customer in a restaurant."
2. Present the model with the first word in each category: words 1, 7, 12, 18, and 24.
3. Choral Repetition Practice: Full-Class and Individual.
4. Have pairs practice the model.
5. Have pairs present the model.
6. Call on students to present a new conversation using different foods in each category.
7. Have pairs practice new conversations.
8. Have pairs present new conversations.

SPELLING PRACTICE

Say a word, and have students spell it aloud or write it. Or, using the transparency, point to an item and have students write the word.

WRITING AND DISCUSSION

Have students respond to the questions as a class, in pairs, or in small groups. Or have students write their responses, share their writing with other students, and discuss in class.

Making Connections

Resource Materials Bring in, or have students bring in, the following materials for vocabulary practice:

○ *Restaurant menus:* Talk about the dishes on the menus. Ask students: Which dishes do you know? Do you like those dishes? Which dishes would you like to try?

Community Task Have individual students (or groups of students) visit different restaurants and give a review of the food and service.

Communication Activities

1 Chain Game
ACTIVITY HANDBOOK PAGES 2–3

Begin the chain as follows: "I went to a restaurant, and I ordered baked chicken," and have students continue it. For example:

> Teacher: I went to a restaurant, and I ordered baked chicken.
> Student 1: I went to a restaurant, and I ordered baked chicken and a spinach salad.
> Student 2: I went to a restaurant, and I ordered baked chicken, a spinach salad, and mashed potatoes.
> Etc.

2 Concentration
ACTIVITY HANDBOOK PAGE 3
ACTIVITY MASTER 80

Have students shuffle the cards and place them face-down in three rows of 6 each, then attempt to find cards that match.

3 True or False?
ACTIVITY HANDBOOK PAGE 15

Make statements such as the following about the dishes on *Picture Dictionary* page 64. Have students decide whether the statements are true or false. For example:

> Tomato juice is an appetizer. [True.]
> French fries are potatoes. [True.]
> Prime rib is a kind of beef. [True.]
> Apple pie is an appetizer. [False. Apple pie is a dessert.]
> Chicken wings are a main course. [False. Chicken wings are an appetizer.]
> Veal cutlet is a kind of chicken. [False. Veal is young beef.]
> Mixed vegetables are served cold. [False. They're served hot.]
> Greek salad has cheese and olives in it. [True.]
> Jello is a side dish. [False. Jello is a dessert.]
> Nachos are corn chips with cheese and salsa. [True.]

4 Category Dictation
ACTIVITY HANDBOOK PAGE 2

Dictate dishes that fit into the following categories:

> appetizers
> salads
> main courses
> side dishes
> desserts

5 Role Play: I'm Sorry, but We Don't Have Any

a. Put the following conversational framework on the board:

> A. What would you like for a/an _____?
> (appetizer/salad/main course/side dish)
> B. I'd like the _____, please.
> A. I'm sorry, but we don't have any today. How about _____?
> B. No, thank you. I really don't like _____. I'll have _____.
> A. Okay. I'll bring it/them right away.

b. Have pairs of students create role plays based on this model and any appropriate vocabulary words they wish, and then present their conversations to the class. For example:

> A. What would you like for an appetizer?
> B. I'd like the nachos, please.
> A. I'm sorry, but we don't have any today. How about potato skins?
> B. No, thank you. I really don't like potato skins. I'll have tomato juice.
> A. Okay. I'll bring it right away.

6 Restaurant Role Plays

In pairs or in small groups, have students create a role play based on any restaurant situation they choose. In order for students to practice as much of the vocabulary as possible, tell them they must use at least four items from the vocabulary list in their role plays. Encourage students to be as creative as they wish. Have students present their role plays to the class.

Variation: After the role-play presentation has begun, give one of the following situation cards to the customer:

> You're in a hurry because you have tickets to see a play.

> You're upset because your food is cold. Ask the waiter or waitress to heat your food or bring you something else.

> The restaurant is out of everything you order.

> There's a fly in your soup! Complain to the manager of the restaurant.

> You didn't get what you ordered. Ask the waiter or waitress to take the food back and give you what you ordered.

7 Make Your Own Menu!

Have pairs of students design a restaurant menu with their favorite foods. Have students share their menus with the class.

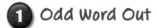
1 Odd Word Out

Read the following lists of words, and have students identify the category and the "odd word out"—the word that doesn't fit the category:

hamburger, hot dog, veal cutlet, relish, meatloaf
[Category: MEATS. Odd word out: relish]

eggs, pancakes, waffles, toast, bacon, spaghetti and meatballs
[Category: BREAKFAST FOODS. Odd word out: spaghetti and meatballs]

shopper, cashier, bagger, clerk, manager
[Category: SUPERMARKET OCCUPATIONS. Odd word out: shopper]

ketchup, mustard, relish, pickles, paper towels
[Category: CONDIMENTS. Odd word out: paper towels]

potato chips, tortilla chips, corned beef, pretzels, popcorn
[Category: SNACK FOODS. Odd word out: corned beef]

milk, soda, cheese, butter, cream cheese
[Category: DAIRY PRODUCTS. Odd word out: soda]

salmon, haddock, flounder, trout, clams
[Category: FISH. Odd word out: clams]

chicken, scallops, mussels, crabs
[Category: SHELLFISH. Odd word out: chicken]

broccoli, apples, spinach, eggplant, carrots
[Category: VEGETABLES. Odd word out: apples]

peaches, grapes, watermelon, formula, tangerines
[Category: FRUIT. Odd word out: formula]

tissues, napkins, paper towels, scanner, toilet paper
[Category: PAPER PRODUCTS. Odd word out: scanner]

host, waitress, chef, bottle opener, dishwasher
[Category: RESTAURANT OCCUPATIONS. Odd word out: bottle opener]

chocolate cake, ice cream, apple pie, pudding, tacos
[Category: DESSERTS. Odd word out: tacos]

pint, cup, tea, quart, gallon
[Category: UNITS OF MEASURE. Odd word out: tea]

soda, coffee, iced tea, lemonade, bagel
[Category: BEVERAGES. Odd word out: bagel]

shopping cart, scale, booth, shopping basket, aisle
[Category: THINGS IN A SUPERMARKET. Odd word out: booth]

Variation: Do the activity as a game with competing teams.

2 Finish the Sentence!

ACTIVITY HANDBOOK PAGE 7

Begin sentences such as the following for students to complete:

A chef is someone who . . .
A bagger is someone who . . .
A hostess is someone who . . .
A cashier is someone who . . .
A busperson is someone who . . .
A diner is someone who . . .
A shopper is someone who . . .
A manager is someone who . . .
A clerk is someone who . . .

3 Category Dictation

ACTIVITY HANDBOOK PAGE 2

Dictate words from *Picture Dictionary* pages 48–64 that fit the following categories:

vegetables
fruits
vegetable dishes
meat dishes
seafood
drinks

4 Likes and Dislikes

a. Have students make two columns on a piece of paper. One column heading is I like, and the other is I dislike.

b. Dictate foods from *Picture Dictionary* pages 48–64 and have students write the items in the appropriate column. For example:

I like	I dislike
tuna fish	spinach salad
mashed potatoes	pineapple

5 Drawing Game

ACTIVITY HANDBOOK PAGE 6
ACTIVITY MASTERS 64, 66, 74, 78

Have teams compete to identify vocabulary items drawn by one of their team members.

6 Miming Game

ACTIVITY HANDBOOK PAGE 11
ACTIVITY MASTER 81

Have students take turns pantomiming food actions. The class tries to guess what the person is doing.

7 Letter Game

ACTIVITY HANDBOOK PAGE 9

Say statements such as the following and have teams compete to identify the items:

I'm thinking of a fruit that starts with *a*.	[apple]
I'm thinking of a snack food that starts with *p*.	[popcorn]
I'm thinking of a poultry item that starts with *t*.	[turkey]
I'm thinking of a vegetable that starts with *b*.	[beet]
I'm thinking of a meat product that starts with *p*.	[pork]
I'm thinking of a dairy product that starts with *b*.	[butter]
I'm thinking of a frozen food that starts with *i*.	[ice cream]
I'm thinking of a kitchen utensil that starts with *g*.	[grater]
I'm thinking of a sandwich that starts with *e*.	[egg salad sandwich]

8 Ask Me a Question!

ACTIVITY HANDBOOK PAGE 2
ACTIVITY MASTERS 64, 66, 67, 68, 69, 70

Have students walk around trying to guess each other's food items by asking yes/no questions. For example:

Is it in the _____ Section?
Is it (color)?
Do you drink it?
Do you cook it?

Variation: Do the activity as a game by dividing the class into two teams. One person comes to the front of the room and thinks of an item. The two teams compete against each other, trying to guess the item by asking yes/no questions.

9 Supermarket Talk!

ACTIVITY HANDBOOK PAGE 17

Have students choose a word from *Picture Dictionary* pages 48–55. Have students think about their word for a few minutes. Call on individual students to speak for one minute about their word.

Variation: The students cannot use the name of the item, and the class must guess what item the student is talking about.

10 Find the Right Person!

ACTIVITY HANDBOOK PAGES 6–7
ACTIVITY MASTER 82

Practice the following questions before having students do the activity:

Do you like french fries/tomato juice/shellfish?
How many cups of coffee do you drink a day?
How often do you eat in a restaurant?
How often do you eat fast food?
What do you eat for breakfast?
Do you leave big tips in restaurants?
Do you eat meat?

11 Where Do They Belong?

a. Brainstorm with students and write on the board possible categories for supermarket items. For example:

sections of a supermarket
fish
shellfish
items you can put in sandwiches
items you slice
items you should cook
items you eat raw
items you buy cold
items that come in a jar
items that come in a can

b. Divide the class into small groups or into teams (if you wish to do the activity as a game) and have students write down as many things as they can think of for each category.

12 Food Combinations

Begin the following phrases and have students complete each with the first food item that comes to mind. (The most typical American responses are given.)

salt and . . .	[pepper]
oil and . . .	[vinegar]
bacon and . . .	[eggs]
macaroni and . . .	[cheese]
cream and . . .	[sugar]
cheese and . . .	[crackers]
hot dogs and . . .	[hamburgers]
lettuce and . . .	[tomatoes]
strawberries and . . .	[cream]
baked potato and . . .	[sour cream]
bagels and . . .	[cream cheese]
cake and . . .	[ice cream]
mustard and . . .	[ketchup]
meat and . . .	[potatoes]
peanut butter and . . .	[jelly]

Variation: You can also do the activity in pairs or in small groups and then compare the results.

UNIT 8 Colors and Clothing

AUDIO PROGRAM

Words & Dialogs
Audio Cassette 3A
Audio CD 3:
   Tracks 19–40

WordSong: *Fashion*
Audio Cassette 7A
Audio CD 8: Tracks 2
   (Vocal) & 3 (Sing-along)
Song Masters S15, S16

WORKBOOKS

For Multi-Level Practice
Literacy Workbook
Beginning Lifeskills Workbook
Beginning Vocabulary Workbook
Intermediate Lifeskills Workbook
Intermediate Vocabulary Workbook

WORDLINKS

Internet Resources through the
***Word by Word* Companion Website**

http://www.longman.com/wordbyword

ACTIVITY MASTERS

Reproducibles for Communication Activities
A8, A83–A98

TRANSPARENCIES

Full-Color Overheads for Class Practice
T65–T73

LANGUAGE & CULTURE NOTES

Information for Teachers &
Intermediate /Advanced Students
LC65–LC73

VOCABULARY GAME CARDS

For Vocabulary Practice,
Activities, & Games
Cards 225–262

LESSON OBJECTIVE

Students will learn the most common color names.

RESOURCES

AUDIO PROGRAM	MULTI-LEVEL WORKBOOKS	ACTIVITY MASTER
Words & Dialogs	Literacy Workbook	**Reproducible**:
Cassette 3A	Beginning & Intermediate Lifeskills Workbooks	A83
CD 3: Tracks 19–21	Beginning & Intermediate Vocabulary Workbooks	
TRANSPARENCY	**LANGUAGE & CULTURE NOTES**	**WORDLINKS**
Overhead: T65	Reproducible: LC65	longman.com/wordbyword

VOCABULARY INTRODUCTION

- Preview
- Present
- Practice

MODEL CONVERSATION PRACTICE

1. Have students look at the model illustration. Set the scene: "A young couple are on a date."
2. Present the model.
3. Choral Repetition Practice: Full-Class and Individual.
4. Have pairs practice the model.
5. Have pairs present the model.
6. Call on pairs to present a new conversation using word 2.
7. Have pairs practice new conversations.
8. Have pairs present new conversations.

ADDITIONAL CONVERSATION PRACTICE

Before students practice the additional conversations, you may want to have them listen to the examples on the Audio Program.

Conversation 1 Have students practice and present conversations with any words they wish.

Conversation 2 Have students practice and present conversations with any words they wish.

SPELLING PRACTICE

Say a word, and have students spell it aloud or write it. Or, using the transparency, point to an item and have students write the word.

WRITING AND DISCUSSION

Have students respond to the questions as a class, in pairs, or in small groups. Or have students write their responses, share their writing with other students, and discuss in class.

Making Connections

Resource Materials Bring in, or have students bring in, the following materials for vocabulary practice:

- *Colorful pictures from magazines:* Have students identify all the colors they see in the pictures.

- *Flags or pictures of flags from different countries:* Have students identify the colors in the flags. Have students explain the symbolic meaning of the flag colors if they know them.

Community Task Have individual students (or groups of students) walk around the school and see how many objects they can find for each color depicted on *Picture Dictionary* page 65. Have students compare lists to see who found the most objects for each color.

Communication Activities

1 Expand the Conversation
ACTIVITY HANDBOOK PAGE 6

Expand the model conversation to include several items of the person's favorite color.

a. Write the following on the board:

A. What's your favorite color?
B. _____. I have a (color) _____, a (color) _____, (color) _____s, and (color) _____s.
A. Boy! You certainly like (color)!

b. Have pairs of students practice and present conversations based on this model, using different words from the page.

2 Clap in Rhythm
ACTIVITY HANDBOOK PAGE 3

Have students name different colors to a clapping rhythm.

3 Try to Remember!

Have pairs of students sit back-to-back and tell the colors of the clothes their partner is wearing. (Don't tell them what they're going to do until after they're seated back-to-back!)

4 Color Associations

Name a color, and have students as a class, in pairs, or in small groups brainstorm all the things they can think of that are that color. If you do it as a paired or group activity, compare the different lists.

5 More Color Associations

a. Divide the class into groups.

b. Have each group decide on a color and make a list of things that are associated with that color. For example:

blue: [the sky/the ocean/a person's eyes/. . .]

c. Each group reads its list without telling the color, and others guess what the color is.

6 The Color Category Game
ACTIVITY MASTER 83

a. Make two copies of Activity Master 91 and cut them up into cards.

b. Divide the class into two teams.

c. Ask one player from each team to come to the front of the room and sit facing his or her team.

d. Give copies of the same card to the two players in the front. (Make sure these players understand all the words on the cards.)

e. The first player announces the category: "Things that are green." That person then gives a clue for the first word. For example:

It grows on the ground in front of houses and in parks.

f. That person's teammates have one try to guess the answer. If they're correct, they get a point and the team member gives a clue for the second word. If they don't guess the first word, the play goes to the other team, and they have a chance to guess the word based on the clue they've just heard.

g. Continue the game with other color category cards. The team with the most points wins the game.

7 Chain Story
ACTIVITY HANDBOOK PAGE 3

Begin the story as follows: "It was a beautiful day. The sky was blue, and the sun was bright yellow."

8 My Favorite Color

a. Have students sit in groups according to their favorite colors.

b. Ask students to discuss in their groups why they like that color better than any other.

c. Regroup the students so that all the different colors are represented in each group.

d. Each student should then try to convince the others why his or her color is better than the others.

9 Guess What I'm Thinking Of!

ACTIVITY HANDBOOK PAGE 8

Have students take turns thinking of an item for others to guess. For example:

Student 1: I'm thinking of something red.
Student 2: Is it in this classroom?
Student 1: No.
Student 3: Is it in the house?
Student 1: No.
Student 4: Is it outside?
Student 1: Yes.
Student 5: Is it a stop sign?
Student 1: Yes.

Student 1: I'm thinking of something that looks white.
Student 2: Is it in this classroom?
Student 1: No.
Student 3: Is it outside?
Student 1: Yes.
Student 4: Is it in the sky?
Student 1: Yes.
Student 5: Is it the moon?
Student 1: Yes.

10 Look at the Picture!

a. Choose any earlier lesson in the *Picture Dictionary* and have students look at it.

b. Have students identify all the colors they see in the illustration.

11 Look Around!

Tell students to look around and describe all the colors they see.

Variation: Have students close their eyes and try to remember the colors of items in the room.

LESSON OBJECTIVE

Students will learn the names of clothing worn by both men and women.

RESOURCES

AUDIO PROGRAM

Words & Dialogs
Cassette 3A
CD 3: Tracks 22–24

WordSong: *Fashion*
Cassette 7A • CD 8: Tracks 2, 3
Song Masters S15, S16

MULTI-LEVEL WORKBOOKS

Literacy Workbook
Beginning & Intermediate Lifeskills Workbooks
Beginning & Intermediate Vocabulary Workbooks

VOCABULARY GAME CARDS

Cards 225–253

ACTIVITY MASTERS

Reproducibles: A84, A85

TRANSPARENCY

Overhead: T66

LANGUAGE & CULTURE NOTES

Reproducible: LC66

WORDLINKS

longman.com/wordbyword

VOCABULARY INTRODUCTION

- Preview
- Present
- Practice

MODEL CONVERSATION PRACTICE

1. Have students look at the model illustration. Set the scene: "A daughter and mother are talking."
2. Present the model.
3. Choral Repetition Practice: Full-Class and Individual.
4. Have pairs practice the model.
5. Have pairs present the model.
6. Call on pairs to present a new conversation using word 2.
7. Have pairs practice new conversations.
8. Have pairs present new conversations.

ADDITIONAL CONVERSATION PRACTICE

Before students practice the additional conversations, you may want to have them listen to the examples on the Audio Program.

Conversation 1 Have students practice and present conversations with any words they wish.

Conversation 2 Have students practice and present conversations with any words they wish.

SPELLING PRACTICE

Say a word, and have students spell it aloud or write it. Or, using the transparency, point to an item and have students write the word.

WRITING AND DISCUSSION

Have students respond to the questions as a class, in pairs, or in small groups. Or have students write their responses, share their writing with other students, and discuss in class.

♫♫ WORDSONG ♫♫

1. Have students listen to the vocal version of *Fashion* one or more times. Then have students listen again as they read the song lyrics on Song Master S15.
2. Have students sing as you play either the vocal or the sing-along version of the song.
3. For fun, have a song competition in which students perform solo or in groups and the class votes for the best performance.
4. For additional practice, students can complete the cloze exercise on Song Master S16.

VOCABULARY GAME CARDS

Have students practice vocabulary, do activities, and play games with Vocabulary Game Cards 225–253. Activities and games are described in the set of cards.

Resource Materials Bring in, or have students bring in, the following materials for vocabulary practice:

● *Magazine pictures of people wearing different kinds of clothing:* Talk about how the people are dressed.

● *Newspaper advertisements for clothing:* Talk about the clothing that is currently fashionable.

Community Task Have individual students (or groups of students) investigate a certain type of clothing (for example, men's suits, evening gowns, sports clothes) by visiting different clothing stores in the area. Have them compare the quality and cost of the clothing these stores sell.

Communication Activities

1 Letter Game
ACTIVITY HANDBOOK PAGE 9

Say statements such as the following and have teams compete to identify the items:

I'm thinking of a piece of clothing that starts with *o*.	[overalls]
I'm thinking of a piece of clothing that starts with *t*.	[tuxedo]
I'm thinking of a piece of clothing that starts with *m*.	[maternity dress]
I'm thinking of a piece of clothing that starts with *s*.	[suit]
I'm thinking of a piece of clothing that starts with *j*.	[jumper]
I'm thinking of a piece of clothing that starts with *l*.	[leggings]

2 Category Dictation
ACTIVITY HANDBOOK PAGE 2

Dictate words that fit into the following categories:

men's clothing
women's clothing
unisex clothing

3 What Should I Wear?

Tell places you might be going, and have students suggest different items to wear. For example:

I'm going to the movies. What should I wear?
I'm going to the office. What should I wear?
I'm going to a play. What should I wear?
I'm going to a party. What should I wear?
I'm going to a wedding. What should I wear?
I'm going to a funeral. What should I wear?

Variation: Do the activity in pairs. One student tells the other his or her plans, and the other suggests what to wear.

4 Try to Remember!

Have pairs of students sit back-to-back and describe the clothes their partner is wearing. (Don't tell them what they're going to do until after they're seated back-to-back!)

5 What Goes with What?

Ask students what they would typically wear with certain pieces of clothing. For example:

What would you wear with overalls?
What would you wear with a flannel shirt?
What would you wear with a skirt?
What would you wear with shorts?

6 Chain Game: I'm Going on a Trip
ACTIVITY HANDBOOK PAGES 2–3

Begin the chain as follows: "I'm going on a trip, and I'm going to pack a vest," and have students continue it. For example:

Teacher: I'm going on a trip, and I'm going to pack a vest.
Student 1: I'm going on a trip, and I'm going to pack a vest and two neckties.
Student 2: I'm going on a trip, and I'm going to pack a vest, two neckties, and a sport coat.
Etc.

7 Describing Pictures

Bring in pictures from magazines, newspapers, or mail order clothing catalogs that depict items presented in this lesson. As a class, in pairs, or in small groups, have students describe what the people in the pictures are wearing.

(continued)

8 What's the Question?

ACTIVITY HANDBOOK PAGE 16

Describe various clothing items and have students respond by asking: "What's a _____?" or "What are _____s?" For example:

Teacher: You wear it around your neck and sometimes it's very colorful.
Student: What's a necktie?

Teacher: It's a one-piece item of clothing that many people wear while they work.
Student: What are overalls?

Teacher: It's a simple top that people wear for warmth over casual clothes.
Student: What's a jacket?

Teacher: It's an elegant dress a woman might wear on a very special occasion.
Student: What's an evening gown?

Teacher: It's a top you wear when you play in the park.
Student: What's a T-shirt?

9 Movable Categories

ACTIVITY HANDBOOK PAGE 11
ACTIVITY MASTER 84

Call out the following categories and have students go to the appropriate side of the room:

casual clothes
formal clothes
women's clothes
unisex clothes
men's clothes
clothes for the office
clothes for school
clothes for a day at the park

10 It's Something That . . .

ACTIVITY HANDBOOK PAGE 9
ACTIVITY MASTER 84

Have students give each other definitions of clothing words beginning with "It's something that . . ." For example:

It's something that people wear over their shirts to keep warm. [sweater]

It's something that men wear to weddings. [tuxedo]

It's something that men wear with their shirts and jackets. [necktie]

It's something that people wear on a hot day. [shorts]

It's something that only women wear. [dress]

11 Guess What I'm Thinking Of!

ACTIVITY HANDBOOK PAGE 8

Have students take turns thinking of clothing items for others to guess. For example:

Student 1: I'm thinking of an item of clothing.
Student 2: Is someone wearing it in this room?
Student 1: Yes.
Student 3: Is a woman wearing it?
Student 1: Yes.
Student 4: Is it only for women to wear?
Student 1: Yes.
Student 5: Is it a dress?
Student 1: Yes.

12 Find the Right Person!

ACTIVITY HANDBOOK PAGES 6–7
ACTIVITY MASTER 85

Practice the following questions before having students do the activity:

Do you wear a suit often?
Do you wear shorts often?
Do you have a bow tie?
Do you like to wear neckties?
Do you like to wear turtlenecks?

13 Everybody Likes a Bargain!

a. Divide the class into pairs or small groups.

b. Have students talk with each other about the best places to buy different types of clothing—i.e., which stores have the best bargains.

c. Have students compare their recommendations.

14 It's My Favorite

Have pairs of students describe to each other their favorite articles of clothing and why they are their favorites. Then have the pairs report back to the class.

15 A Fashion Show

Put on a fashion show! Have students describe each other's clothing as if they were modeling in a fashion show. For example:

This is Henry. He's wearing jeans, a yellow jersey, and a green blazer.

LESSON OBJECTIVE

Students will learn the names of outerwear clothing.

RESOURCES

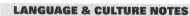

AUDIO PROGRAM		MULTI-LEVEL WORKBOOKS	ACTIVITY MASTER
Words & Dialogs Cassette 3A CD 3: Tracks 25–27	**WordSong:** *Fashion* Cassette 7A • CD 8: Tracks 2, 3 Song Masters S15, S16	Literacy Workbook Beginning & Intermediate Lifeskills Workbooks Beginning & Intermediate Vocabulary Workbooks	**Reproducible:** A86

TRANSPARENCY	LANGUAGE & CULTURE NOTES	WORDLINKS
Overhead: T67	**Reproducible:** LC67	longman.com/wordbyword

VOCABULARY INTRODUCTION

- Preview
- Present
- Practice

MODEL CONVERSATION PRACTICE

1. Have students look at the model illustration. Set the scene: "A wife and husband are talking."
2. Present the model with *cool* and word 1, *cold* and word 5, *raining* and word 12, and *snowing* and word 23.
3. Choral Repetition Practice: Full-Class and Individual.
4. Have pairs practice the model.
5. Have pairs present the model.
6. Call on pairs to present a new conversation using any weather condition and appropriate clothing item they wish.
7. Have pairs practice new conversations.
8. Have pairs present new conversations.

ADDITIONAL CONVERSATION PRACTICE

Before students practice the additional conversations, you may want to have them listen to the examples on the Audio Program.

Conversation 1 Have students practice and present conversations with any words they wish.

Conversation 2 Have students practice and present conversations with any words they wish.

SPELLING PRACTICE

Say a word, and have students spell it aloud or write it. Or, using the transparency, point to an item and have students write the word.

WRITING AND DISCUSSION

Have students respond to the questions as a class, in pairs, or in small groups. Or have students write their responses, share their writing with other students, and discuss in class.

Making Connections

Resource Materials Bring in, or have students bring in, the following materials for vocabulary practice:

- *Magazine pictures of people wearing different kinds of outerwear:* Talk about how the people are dressed.

- *Newspaper advertisements for outerwear:* Talk about the outerwear that is currently fashionable.

Community Task Have individual students (or groups of students) investigate a certain type of outerwear (for example, leather jackets, ski wear, rain gear) by visiting different clothing stores. Have them compare the quality and cost of the clothing these stores sell.

Communication Activities

1 Letter Game
ACTIVITY HANDBOOK PAGE 9

Say statements such as the following and have teams compete to identify the items:

I'm thinking of a piece of clothing that starts with *c*.	[coat]
I'm thinking of a piece of clothing that starts with *o*.	[overcoat]
I'm thinking of a piece of clothing that starts with *h*.	[hat]
I'm thinking of a piece of clothing that starts with *j*.	[jacket]
I'm thinking of a piece of clothing that starts with *w*.	[windbreaker]
I'm thinking of a piece of clothing that starts with *t*.	[trench coat]
I'm thinking of a piece of clothing that starts with *g*.	[gloves]
I'm thinking of a piece of clothing that starts with *m*.	[mittens]
I'm thinking of a piece of clothing that starts with *s*.	[ski jacket]
I'm thinking of a piece of clothing that starts with *p*.	[parka]

2 Category Dictation
ACTIVITY HANDBOOK PAGE 2

Dictate words that fit into the following categories:

coats
outerwear for the head
outerwear for the hands

3 What Should I Wear?

Tell places you might be going, and have students suggest different items to wear. For example:

I'm going skiing. What should I wear?
It's wintertime. I'm going to the office. What should I wear?
It's raining. What should I wear?

4 Miming Game
ACTIVITY HANDBOOK PAGE 11
ACTIVITY MASTER 86

Have students take turns pantomiming putting on outerwear items. The class tries to guess what the person is putting on. For example:

You're putting on sunglasses.
You're putting on tights.

5 Drawing Game
ACTIVITY HANDBOOK PAGE 6
ACTIVITY MASTER 86

Have teams compete to identify outerwear items drawn by one of their team members.

6 Chain Game: I'm Going to Alaska
ACTIVITY HANDBOOK PAGES 2–3

Begin the chain as follows: "I'm going to Alaska, and I'm going to pack a scarf," and have students continue it. For example:

Teacher: I'm going to Alaska, and I'm going to pack a scarf.
Student 1: I'm going to Alaska, and I'm going to pack a scarf and mittens.
Student 2: I'm going to Alaska, and I'm going to pack a scarf, mittens, and a parka.
Etc.

Variation: Begin the chain as follows: "I'm going skiing."

7 Telephone
ACTIVITY HANDBOOK PAGE 14

Begin the activity with the following sentence: "It's cold out! Put on your down vest and parka, ski hat, and mittens. And don't forget your scarf!"

8 Guess What I'm Thinking Of!
ACTIVITY HANDBOOK PAGE 8

Have students take turns thinking of clothing items for others to guess. For example:

Student 1: I'm thinking of a piece of outerwear.
Student 2: Is it for the rain?
Student 1: No.
Student 3: Is it for the cold?
Student 1: Yes.
Student 4: Is it a kind of coat?
Student 1: No.
Student 5: Is it a hat?
Student 1: Yes.

Student 1: I'm thinking of a piece of outerwear.
Student 2: Is it for the rain?
Student 1: Yes.
Student 3: Is it a coat?
Student 1: No.
Student 4: Is it for you feet?
Student 1: Yes.
Student 5: Is it rain boots?
Student 1: Yes.

9 What's the Question?

ACTIVITY HANDBOOK PAGE 16

Describe various outerwear items and have students respond by asking: "What's a _____?" or "What are _____s?" For example:

Teacher: It's knit, and you wear it on your head.
Student: What's a ski hat?

Teacher: It's a light jacket.
Student: What are sunglasses?

Teacher: It covers your whole face.
Student: What's a ski mask?

Teacher: It's a long coat you wear over a suit.
Student: What's an overcoat?

Teacher: It's a hat you wear on sunny days.
Student: What's a baseball cap?

Teacher: It's something to carry on a rainy day.
Student: What's an umbrella?

10 Ask Me a Question!

ACTIVITY HANDBOOK PAGE 2
ACTIVITY MASTER 86

Have students walk around trying to guess each other's outerwear items by asking yes/no questions. For example:

Do you put it on your head?	[No.]
Do you wear it in the rain?	[Yes.]
Do you put it on your feet?	[Yes.]
Is it a pair of rain boots?	[Yes.]
Do you wear it in the rain?	[No.]
Do you wear it in the cold?	[No.]
Do you wear it in the sunshine?	[Yes.]
Do you wear it on your head?	[Yes.]
Is it a baseball cap?	[Yes.]

11 Movable Categories

ACTIVITY HANDBOOK PAGE 11
ACTIVITY MASTER 86

Call out the following categories and have students go to the appropriate side of the room:

outerwear for the head
outerwear for the hands
outerwear for the legs and feet
outerwear for the top half of the body
outerwear for skiing
outerwear for the rain

12 Everybody Likes a Bargain!

a. Divide the class into pairs or small groups.

b. Have students talk with each other about the best places to buy different outerwear.

c. Have students compare their recommendations.

13 Ranking

ACTIVITY HANDBOOK PAGE 13

Have students look at the outerwear items on *Picture Dictionary* page 67 and choose the five most essential outerwear items for their climate. If possible, have students write two lists: one for their home country and one for their current country. For example:

In (my home country)	In (the US)
sunglasses	down vest
raincoat	parka
umbrella	gloves
windbreaker	overcoat
trench coat	scarf

LESSON OBJECTIVE

Students will learn the names of sleepwear and underwear items.

RESOURCES

AUDIO PROGRAM

Words & Dialogs
Cassette 3A
CD 3: Tracks 28, 29

MULTI-LEVEL WORKBOOKS

Literacy Workbook
Beginning & Intermediate Lifeskills Workbooks
Beginning & Intermediate Vocabulary Workbooks

ACTIVITY MASTERS

Reproducibles:
A8, A87

TRANSPARENCY

Overhead: T68

LANGUAGE & CULTURE NOTES

Reproducible: LC68

WORDLINKS

longman.com/wordbyword

VOCABULARY INTRODUCTION

- Preview
- Present
- Practice

MODEL CONVERSATION PRACTICE

1. Have students look at the model illustration. Set the scene: "A husband and wife are talking."
2. Present the model with word 1.
3. Choral Repetition Practice: Full-Class and Individual.
4. Have pairs practice the model.
5. Have pairs present the model.
6. Call on pairs to present a new conversation using word 3.
7. Have pairs practice new conversations.
8. Have pairs present new conversations.

SPELLING PRACTICE

Say a word, and have students spell it aloud or write it. Or, using the transparency, point to an item and have students write the word.

WRITING AND DISCUSSION

Have students respond to the questions as a class, in pairs, or in small groups. Or have students write their responses, share their writing with other students, and discuss in class.

Making Connections

Resource Materials Bring in, or have students bring in, the following materials for vocabulary practice:

- *Magazine pictures of people wearing different kinds of underwear and sleepwear:* Talk about how the people are dressed.

- *Newspaper advertisements for sleepwear and underwear:* Talk about the sleepwear and underwear that is currently fashionable.

Community Task Have individual students (or groups of students) investigate a certain type of underwear or sleepwear (for example, pajamas, women's underwear, men's and women's sock wear) by visiting different clothing stores in the area. Have them compare the quality and cost of the clothing these stores sell.

Communication Activities

1 True or False?
ACTIVITY HANDBOOK PAGE 15

Make statements such as the following about the items on *Picture Dictionary* page 68. Have students decide whether the statements are true or false. For example:

People wear slippers outside the house. [False. People wear slippers only inside the house.]
Men wear bras. [False. Only women wear bras.]
Boxer shorts are looser than briefs. [True.]
Both men and women wear pajamas. [True.]
A full slip goes under a suit. [False. A full slip goes under a dress.]
People wear long underwear to keep warm. [True.]
Men wear camisoles under their shirts. [False. Women wear camisoles under their blouses. Men wear T-shirts.]
Tights are thicker than pantyhose. [True.]
Stockings must be attached to a special belt. [True.]
Panties are smaller than briefs. [True.]

2 Chain Game: I'm Going on a Trip . . .
ACTIVITY HANDBOOK PAGES 2–3

Begin the chain as follows: "I'm going on a trip, and I'm going to pack pajamas," and have students continue it. For example:

Teacher: I'm going on a trip, and I'm going to pack pajamas.
Student 1: I'm going on a trip, and I'm going to pack pajamas and slippers.
Student 2: I'm going on a trip, and I'm going to pack pajamas, slippers, and a bathrobe.
Etc.

3 Category Dictation
ACTIVITY HANDBOOK PAGE 2

Dictate words that fit into the following categories:

men's sleepwear
women's sleepwear
unisex sleepwear
men's underwear
women's underwear
unisex underwear

4 Guess What I'm Thinking Of!
ACTIVITY HANDBOOK PAGE 8

Have students take turns thinking of clothing items for others to guess. For example:

Student 1: I'm thinking of a sleepwear item.
Student 2: Is it two pieces?

Student 1: No.
Student 3: Is it a nightshirt?
Student 1: No.
Student 4: Is it a nightgown?
Student 1: Yes.

Student 1: I'm thinking of an underwear item.
Student 2: Do men wear it?
Student 1: No.
Student 3: Is it for the legs and feet?
Student 1: Yes.
Student 4: Do girls wear it?
Student 1: Yes.
Student 5: Is it a pair of knee highs?
Student 1: Yes.

5 Tic Tac Definitions
ACTIVITY HANDBOOK PAGE 15
ACTIVITY MASTER 8

Have students fill in the tic tac grid with any nine underwear or sleepwear words they wish. Give definitions such as the following and have students cross out on their grids the words you have defined:

Two-piece sleepwear. [pajamas]
One-piece sleepwear for women. [nightgown]
One-piece sleepwear for men and women. [nightshirt]
Shoes for inside the house. [slippers]
One-piece sleepwear for young children. [blanket sleeper]
Men sometimes wear it under their shirts. [undershirt]
Women sometimes wear it under their blouses. [camisole]
Men wear them when it is especially cold outside. [long johns]
Women often wear it under a skirt. [half slip]
Young girls wear them in the winter with their dresses. [tights]

6 Movable Categories
ACTIVITY HANDBOOK PAGE 11
ACTIVITY MASTER 87

Call out the following categories and have students go to the appropriate side of the room:

men's sleepwear
women's sleepwear
men's underwear
women's lingerie
clothing for the feet and legs
clothing for adults only
clothing for children only
clothing for both children and adults

LESSON OBJECTIVE

Students will learn the names of exercise clothing and footwear items.

RESOURCES

AUDIO PROGRAM		MULTI-LEVEL WORKBOOKS	ACTIVITY MASTER
Words & Dialogs Cassette 3A CD 3: Tracks 30, 31	**WordSong:** *Fashion* Cassette 7A • CD 8: Tracks 2, 3 Song Masters S15, S16	Literacy Workbook Beginning & Intermediate Lifeskills Workbooks Beginning & Intermediate Vocabulary Workbooks	**Reproducible:** A88

TRANSPARENCY	LANGUAGE & CULTURE NOTES	WORDLINKS
Overhead: T1	**Reproducible:** LC69	longman.com/wordbyword

VOCABULARY INTRODUCTION

- Preview
- Present
- Practice

MODEL CONVERSATION PRACTICE

There are two model conversations—the first for words 1–12 and the second for words 13–27. Introduce and practice the first model before going on to the second. For each model:

1. Have students look at the model illustration. Set the scene:

    Model 1: "Two people in a laundromat are talking."
    Model 2: "Two co-workers are talking."

2. Present Model 1 with word 1 and Model 2 with word 13.

3. Choral Repetition Practice: Full-Class and Individual.

4. Have pairs practice the model.

5. Have pairs present the model.

6. Call on pairs to present a new conversation using word 2 for the first model and word 14 for the second model.

7. Have pairs practice new conversations.

8. Have pairs present new conversations.

SPELLING PRACTICE

Say a word, and have students spell it aloud or write it. Or, using the transparency, point to an item and have students write the word.

WRITING AND DISCUSSION

Have students respond to the questions as a class, in pairs, or in small groups. Or have students write their responses, share their writing with other students, and discuss in class.

Making Connections

Resource Materials Bring in, or have students bring in, the following materials for vocabulary practice:

- *Magazine pictures of people wearing different kinds of exercise clothing and footwear:* Talk about how the people are dressed.

- *Newspaper advertisements for exercise clothing and footwear:* Talk about the exercise clothing and footwear that is currently fashionable.

Community Task Have individual students (or groups of students) investigate a certain type of exercise clothing or footwear (for example, warm-up suit, running shoes, boots) by visiting different stores in the area. Have them compare the quality and cost of the items these stores sell.

Communication Activities

1 Letter Game
ACTIVITY HANDBOOK PAGE 9

Say statements such as the following and have teams compete to identify the items:

I'm thinking of a kind of footwear that starts with *p*.	[pumps]
I'm thinking of a kind of footwear that starts with *f*.	[flip-flops]
I'm thinking of a kind of footwear that starts with *b*.	[boots]
I'm thinking of a kind of footwear that starts with *t*.	[tennis shoes]
I'm thinking of a kind of footwear that starts with *l*.	[loafers]

2 Category Dictation
ACTIVITY HANDBOOK PAGE 2

Dictate words that fit into the following categories:

shoes for men only
shoes for women only
shoes for both men and women

3 What Goes With It?

Mention different kinds of shoes, and have students suggest different clothing items to wear. For example:

Teacher: What goes with cowboy boots?
Student 1: jeans
Student 2: a jacket

Teacher: What goes with high heels?
Student 1: a dress
Student 2: a skirt
Student 3: an evening gown

4 What Shoes Should I Wear?

Tell things you're going to be doing, and ask students what shoes you should wear. For example:

I'm going to play tennis. What kind of shoes should I wear?
I'm going to walk on the beach. What kind of shoes should I wear?
I'm going to relax and read a book. What kind of shoes should I wear?
I'm going to repair my front steps. What kind of shoes should I wear?
I'm going mountain climbing. What kind of shoes should I wear?
I'm going to a job interview today. What kind of shoes should I wear?

5 Drawing Game
ACTIVITY HANDBOOK PAGE 6
ACTIVITY MASTER 88

Have teams compete to identify exercise clothing or footwear items drawn by one of their team members.

6 True or False?
ACTIVITY HANDBOOK PAGE 15

Make statements such as the following about the items on *Picture Dictionary* page 69. Have students decide whether the statements are true or false. For example:

Pumps have low heels. [True.]
Men often wear cover-ups after swimming. [False. Women often wear cover-ups after swimming.]
A tank top is for cold weather. [False. A tank top is for warm or hot weather.]
High tops are a kind of sneaker. [True.]
Flip-flops are popular beach shoes. [True.]
People wear leotards when they play tennis. [False. People wear leotards for ballet, dance, or gymnastics.]
Lycra shorts are loose fitting. [False. Lycra is very tight fitting material.]
Sandals are winter shoes. [False. Sandals are summer shoes.]

7 Ask Me a Question!
ACTIVITY HANDBOOK PAGE 2
ACTIVITY MASTER 88

Have students walk around trying to guess each other's exercise clothing and footwear items by asking yes/no questions. For example:

Do you put them on your feet?	[Yes.]
Do women wear them?	[Yes.]
Do men wear them?	[Yes.]
Do you wear them at the beach?	[No.]
Do you wear them when you run?	[Yes.]
Are they running shoes?	[Yes.]

8 Ranking
ACTIVITY HANDBOOK PAGE 13

Have students look at the footwear items on *Picture Dictionary* page 69 and choose the four most essential items. For example:

Essential Footwear
pumps
boots
tennis shoes
sandals

LESSON OBJECTIVE

Students will learn the names of jewelry and accessories most commonly worn in the United States.

RESOURCES

AUDIO PROGRAM		MULTI-LEVEL WORKBOOKS	VOCABULARY GAME CARDS
Words & Dialogs Cassette 3A CD 3: Tracks 32–34	WordSong: *Fashion* Cassette 7A • CD 8: Tracks 2, 3 Song Masters S15, S16	Literacy Workbook Beginning & Intermediate Lifeskills Workbooks Beginning & Intermediate Vocabulary Workbooks	Cards 254–262

ACTIVITY MASTERS	TRANSPARENCY	LANGUAGE & CULTURE NOTES	WORDLINKS
Reproducibles: A89, A90	**Overhead**: T70	**Reproducible**: LC70	longman.com/wordbyword

VOCABULARY INTRODUCTION

- Preview
- Present
- Practice

MODEL CONVERSATION PRACTICE

There are two model conversations—the first for singular words and the second for plural words. Introduce and practice the first model before going on to the second. For each model:

1. Have students look at the model illustration. Set the scene:

   Model 1: "A husband and wife are in the yard. The husband is upset because he can't find his ring."

   Model 2: "Two friends are at a health club. One is upset because she can't find her earrings."

2. Present the model.
3. Choral Repetition Practice: Full-Class and Individual.
4. Have pairs practice the model.
5. Have pairs present the model.
6. Call on pairs to present a new conversation, using word 2 for the first model and word 8 for the second model.
7. Have pairs practice new conversations.
8. Have pairs present new conversations.

ADDITIONAL CONVERSATION PRACTICE

Before students practice the additional conversations, you may want to have them listen to the examples on the Audio Program.

Conversation 1 Have students practice and present conversations with any words they wish.

Conversation 2 Have students practice and present conversations with any words they wish.

SPELLING PRACTICE

Say a word, and have students spell it aloud or write it. Or, using the transparency, point to an item and have students write the word.

WRITING AND DISCUSSION

Have students respond to the questions as a class, in pairs, or in small groups. Or have students write their responses, share their writing with other students, and discuss in class.

VOCABULARY GAME CARDS

Have students practice vocabulary, do activities, and play games with Vocabulary Game Cards 254–262. Activities and games are described in the set of cards.

Resource Materials Bring in, or have students bring in, the following materials for vocabulary practice:

- *Fashion magazine advertisements for jewelry and accessories:* Talk about the jewelry and accessories depicted in the ads.

- *Catalogs for jewelry and accessories:* Talk about the items and their prices.

- *The items themselves:* Invite students to show each other their jewelry and accessories. Ask students to explain how they got the item and tell any story that may be related to the item.

Community Task Have individual students (or groups of students) visit different jewelry or department stores in the area and report about the jewelry these stores sell and the prices.

Communication Activities

1 Clap in Rhythm
ACTIVITY HANDBOOK PAGE 3

Have students name different words for jewelry and accessories to a clapping rhythm.

2 Concentration
ACTIVITY HANDBOOK PAGE 3
ACTIVITY MASTER 89

Have students shuffle the cards and place them face-down in three rows of 6 each, then attempt to find cards that match.

3 Category Dictation
ACTIVITY HANDBOOK PAGE 2

Dictate words that fit into the following categories:

> things that carry other things
> jewelry

4 Drawing Game
ACTIVITY HANDBOOK PAGE 6
ACTIVITY MASTER 90

Have teams compete to identify jewelry and accessory items drawn by one of their team members.

5 Classroom List

As a class, have students make a list on the board of all the items from *Picture Dictionary* page 70 that they see people wearing in their classroom, and accessory items such as purses, book bags, and backpacks.

6 Wish List

As a class, in pairs, or in small groups, have students decide what jewelry they would buy if they had $25,000 to spend!

7 My Favorite Piece of Jewelry

As a class, in pairs, or in small groups, have students tell about the favorite piece of jewelry they own:

> Did they buy it?
> Was it a gift? From whom?
> What does it look like?
> Why is it their favorite?

8 What's the Question?
ACTIVITY HANDBOOK PAGE 16

Give the definition of a piece of jewelry or an accessory and have students respond by asking "What's a/an _____?" or "What are _____s?" For example:

> Teacher: You use it to carry coins.
> Student: What's a change purse?

> Teacher: You have them on your shirt sleeves instead of buttons.
> Student: What are cuff links?

This activity can be done as a game with competing teams. It can also be done by having teams come up with the descriptions that they then ask others.

9 Question the Answer!
ACTIVITY HANDBOOK PAGE 13
ACTIVITY MASTER 90

Students pick Jewelry and Accessories Word Cards and think of a question for which that word could be the answer. For example:

> Card: belt
> Student: What holds up your pants?

> Card: change purse
> Student: What do you use to carry coins?

> Card: barrette
> Student: What do you use to hold back your hair?

LESSON OBJECTIVE

Students will learn the names of types of clothing, types of material, patterns on clothing material, and general sizes.

RESOURCES

AUDIO PROGRAM

Words & Dialogs
Cassette 3A
CD 3: Tracks 35, 36

MULTI-LEVEL WORKBOOKS

Literacy Workbook
Beginning & Intermediate Lifeskills Workbooks
Beginning & Intermediate Vocabulary Workbooks

ACTIVITY MASTER

Reproducible:
A91

TRANSPARENCY

Overhead: T71

LANGUAGE & CULTURE NOTES

Reproducible: LC71

WORDLINKS

longman.com/wordbyword

VOCABULARY INTRODUCTION

- Preview
- Present
- Practice

MODEL CONVERSATION PRACTICE

There are three model conversations—the first for words 1–24, the second for words 25–32, and the third for words 33–37. Introduce and practice the first model before going on to the second and third. For each model:

1. Have students look at the model illustration. Set the scene:

   Model 1: "A salesperson is talking to a customer in a store."
   Model 2: "A husband and wife are shopping in a department store."
   Model 3: "A salesperson is talking to a customer in a department store."

2. Present each model. (For Model 2, use words 25 and 26. For Model 3, use word 33.)

3. Choral Repetition Practice: Full-Class and Individual.

4. Have pairs practice the model.

5. Have pairs present the model.

6. Call on pairs to present a new conversation using word 2 for the first model, words 27 and 28 for the second model, and word 34 for the third model.

7. Have pairs practice new conversations.

8. Have pairs present new conversations.

SPELLING PRACTICE

Say a word, and have students spell it aloud or write it. Or, using the transparency, point to an item and have students write the word.

WRITING AND DISCUSSION

Have students respond to the question as a class, in pairs, or in small groups. Or have students write their responses, share their writing with other students, and discuss in class.

Making Connections

Resource Materials Bring in, or have students bring in, the following materials for vocabulary practice:

- *Fashion magazines:* Talk about the types of clothing, the clothing material, and the patterns in the clothing depicted in the magazines.

- *Clothing Mail-Order Catalogs (in print or online):* Have students choose items they like in the catalog. Working in pairs, have students describe the clothing items, their material, patterns, and size range.

Community Task Have individual students (or groups of students) visit different clothing stores in the area and report about the latest fashion trends in colors and types of material and patterns.

Communication Activities

1. True or False?
ACTIVITY HANDBOOK PAGE 15

Make statements about the clothes students are wearing. Have students decide whether the statements are true or false. For example:

> Mario is wearing a long-sleeved shirt and corduroy pants. [False. He's wearing a short-sleeved shirt and cotton pants.]

2. Drawing Game
ACTIVITY HANDBOOK PAGE 6
ACTIVITY MASTER 91

Have teams compete to identify clothing types and patterns drawn by one of their team members.

3. Guess Who!

a. Ask students to write on a piece of paper what they are wearing. Students should not write their names on their papers.

b. Collect the students' descriptions, read them to the class, and have students identify who wrote them.

Variation: Write all the clothing submitted by the students on a sheet of paper and make copies for the class. Have students then identify who everybody is.

4. Category Dictation
ACTIVITY HANDBOOK PAGE 2

Dictate words that fit into the following categories:

> words to describe shirts
> words to describe sweaters
> words to describe socks

5. Chain Story
ACTIVITY HANDBOOK PAGE 3

Begin the story as follows: "Today I saw a woman wearing the craziest clothes. She was wearing a polka-dotted polyester scarf."

6. Draw and Label
ACTIVITY HANDBOOK PAGE 5

Have students draw and label a picture that might be in a fashion magazine.

7. Which One Is It?

a. Tape to the board a variety of similar but different pictures. For example:

> several pictures of neckties, all with different patterns
> shirts with different colored stripes
> skirts with different prints

b. Describe a picture and have students identify which picture you are describing.

c. Have students take turns being the one who describes.

8. Clothing Associations
ACTIVITY HANDBOOK PAGE 2

Call out clothing words and have groups write down as many associations as they can think of. For example:

> denim: [jacket/jeans/shorts/blue/cotton/casual]
> linen: [shirt/pants/skirt/jacket/summer]
> leather: [boots/shoes/purse/pants/belt]
> sweater: [wool/cotton/cardigan/crewneck/V-neck]

9. It's a Puzzle!
ACTIVITY HANDBOOK PAGE 9

Cut out pictures from fashion magazines and create puzzles out of the pictures for students to identify and put together by asking questions. For example:

> Is there a person in your picture with a plaid jacket?
> Is there a child in your picture in a linen dress?
> Is there a person in a striped suit?
> Is there a man in a black tuxedo?

10. Do You Remember?
ACTIVITY HANDBOOK PAGE 5

Briefly show students a picture from a fashion magazine. Have students write down everything they remember about the picture

11. A Fashion Show

Put on a fashion show! Have students describe each other's clothing as if they were modeling in a fashion show. For example:

> Carla is wearing a striped blue blouse with solid red pants and a red and blue plaid belt.

LESSON OBJECTIVE

Students will learn how to describe problems with the fitting or condition of their clothing.

RESOURCES

 AUDIO PROGRAM
Words & Dialogs
Cassette 3A
CD 3: Tracks 37, 38

MULTI-LEVEL WORKBOOKS
Literacy Workbook
Beginning & Intermediate Lifeskills Workbooks
Beginning & Intermediate Vocabulary Workbooks

ACTIVITY MASTERS
Reproducibles:
A92–A94

TRANSPARENCY
Overhead: T72

LANGUAGE & CULTURE NOTES
Reproducible: LC72

WORDLINKS
longman.com/wordbyword

VOCABULARY INTRODUCTION

- Preview
- Present
- Practice

MODEL CONVERSATION PRACTICE

There are three model conversations—the first for words 1–16, the second for phrases 17–20, and the third for phrases 21–25. Introduce and practice the first model before going on to the second and third. For each model:

1. Have students look at the model illustration. Set the scene:
   Model 1: "A husband and wife are shopping in a department store."
   Model 2: "A customer is returning a jacket at a department store."
   Model 3: "A customer and a tailor are talking."
2. Present the model.
3. Choral Repetition Practice: Full-Class and Individual.
4. Have pairs practice the model.
5. Have pairs present the model.
6. Call on pairs to present a new conversation using words 3–4 for the first model, phrase 18 for the second model, and phrase 22 for the third model.
7. Have pairs practice new conversations.
8. Have pairs present new conversations.

SPELLING PRACTICE

Say a word or phrase, and have students spell it aloud or write it. Or, using the transparency, point to an item and have students write the word or phrase.

WRITING AND DISCUSSION

Have students respond to the question as a class, in pairs, or in small groups. Or have students write their responses, share their writing with other students, and discuss in class.

Making Connections

Resource Materials Bring in, or have students bring in, the following materials for vocabulary practice:

- *Newspaper photographs of people:* Talk about the condition and fit of the clothes on the people in the pictures.

Communication Activities

① Clothing Associations
ACTIVITY HANDBOOK PAGE 2

Call out clothing words and have groups write down as many associations as they can think of. For example:

pants:	[long/short/tight/baggy/striped/ checked]
shoes:	[narrow/wide/solid/fancy/plain]
gloves:	[heavy/light/leather]
jacket:	[heavy/light/short/long/large/small]

② Telephone
ACTIVITY HANDBOOK PAGE 14

Begin the activity with the following sentence: "After the long trip, his shirt was stained, he had a missing button on his jacket, and his briefcase had a broken zipper!"

③ Opposites Concentration
ACTIVITY HANDBOOK PAGE 3
ACTIVITY MASTER 92

Have students shuffle the cards and place them face-down in four rows of 4 each, then attempt to find matching opposites.

④ Miming Game
ACTIVITY HANDBOOK PAGE 11
ACTIVITY MASTER 93

Have students take turns pantomiming problems with clothing items. The class tries to guess what the problem is. For example:

The sleeves on your shirt are too long.
Your pants are too baggy.

⑤ Chain Story
ACTIVITY HANDBOOK PAGE 3

Begin the story as follows: "My cousin Alice looked terrible at the wedding. She was wearing a dress that was too big."

Then begin another story as follows: "My cousin Al looked terrible at the wedding. He was wearing a suit that was too baggy."

⑥ Clothing Match Game
ACTIVITY HANDBOOK PAGE 11
ACTIVITY MASTER 94

Have students find the person whose card matches theirs.

⑦ A Clothing Scavenger Hunt

a. Make up a list of various clothing items such as the following:

loose pants
fancy shoes
a dark T-shirt
a long skirt
high heels
a wide tie

b. Give each student a copy of the list.

c. Have students walk around the school to find people who are wearing those items. They should write the person's name (if possible) and a description of the article of clothing.

d. The first person to successfully find all the clothing items is the winner.

LESSON OBJECTIVE

Students will learn how to describe the steps in doing laundry and the names of products people use to do laundry.

RESOURCES

AUDIO PROGRAM

Words & Dialogs
Cassette 3A
CD 3: Tracks 39, 40

MULTI-LEVEL WORKBOOKS

Literacy Workbook
Beginning & Intermediate Lifeskills Workbooks
Beginning & Intermediate Vocabulary Workbooks

ACTIVITY MASTERS

Reproducibles:
A95, A96

TRANSPARENCY

Overhead: T73

LANGUAGE & CULTURE NOTES

Reproducible: LC73

WORDLINKS

longman.com/wordbyword

VOCABULARY INTRODUCTION

- Preview
- Present
- Practice

MODEL CONVERSATION PRACTICE

There are three model conversations—the first for words A–I, the second for words 4–6, 11, 14–17, and 23, and the third for words 7–9, 13 and 20. Introduce and practice the first model before going on to the second and third. For each model:

1. Have students look at the model illustration. Set the scene:

   Model 1: "Two friends are talking."
   Model 2: "A customer is talking to a clerk in a store."
   Model 3: "A customer is talking to a clerk in a store."

2. Present the model with word A for the first model, word 4 for the second model, and word 7 for the third model.

3. Choral Repetition Practice: Full-Class and Individual.

4. Have pairs practice the model.

5. Have pairs present the model.

6. Call on pairs to present a new conversation using word B for the first model, word 5 for the second model, and word 8 for the third model.

7. Have pairs practice new conversations.

8. Have pairs present new conversations.

SPELLING PRACTICE

Say a word, and have students spell it aloud or write it. Or, using the transparency, point to an item and have students write the word.

WRITING AND DISCUSSION

Have students respond to the questions as a class, in pairs, or in small groups. Or have students write their responses, share their writing with other students, and discuss in class.

Making Connections

Resource Materials Bring in, or have students bring in, the following materials for vocabulary practice:

- *Newspaper and magazine advertisements for household cleaning products and laundry items:* Have students talk about which products they use to do their laundry.

Community Task Have individual students (or groups of students) visit a local laundromat. Have them make a list of the laundry products they see and the actions they see people doing there. Have students report back to the class and compare their observations.

Communication Activities

1 Chain Game
ACTIVITY HANDBOOK PAGES 2–3

Begin the chain as follows: "This is how I do laundry. First. . .," and have students continue it. For example:

> Teacher: This is how I do laundry. First . . .
> Student 1: This is how I do laundry. First I sort the laundry.
> Student 2: This is how I do laundry. First I sort the laundry. Then I load the washer.
> Etc.

2 Movable Categories
ACTIVITY HANDBOOK PAGE 11
ACTIVITY MASTER 95

Call out the following categories and have students go to the appropriate side of the room:

> things for washing clothes
> things for drying clothes
> things for ironing clothes
> things for putting clothes away

3 Category Dictation
ACTIVITY HANDBOOK PAGE 2

Dictate words that fit into the above categories.

4 True or False Definitions
ACTIVITY HANDBOOK PAGE 15

Give true and false definitions of laundry words and have students decide which are true and which are false. For example:

> You use a laundry basket to carry dirty clothes to the washer. [True.]
> Fabric softener prevents wrinkles. [True.]
> Starch makes a fabric soft. [False. It makes a fabric stiff.]
> You use a clothespin to hang clothes in a closet. [False. You use a clothespin to hang clothes on a clothesline.]
> You need to iron wrinkled clothing. [True.]
> The lint trap collects excess detergent that gets stuck in the dryer. [False. It collects excess lint—clothing fiber that gets stuck in the dryer.]
> To load the washer means to take out all the wet clothes. [False. To load the washer means to fill the washer with dirty clothes.]
> You use bleach to clean dark clothing. [False. You use bleach to clean light-colored clothing.]

> You add spray starch to the washer when you load the laundry. [False. You use spray starch when you iron clothes.]
> To put things away means to put things on shelves and in drawers, where they belong. [True.]

5 Ask Me a Question!
ACTIVITY HANDBOOK PAGE 2
ACTIVITY MASTER 95

Have students walk around trying to guess each other's laundry items by asking yes/no questions. For example:

> Is it something for holding laundry?   [Yes.]
> Is it a laundry bag?   [No.]
> Is it a laundry basket?   [Yes.]
>
> Is it something for drying laundry?   [Yes.]
> Does it use electricity or gas?   [No.]
> Is it a clothesline?   [No.]
> Is it a clothespin?   [Yes.]

6 Question the Answer!
ACTIVITY HANDBOOK PAGE 13
ACTIVITY MASTER 95

Students pick Laundry Word Cards and think of a question for which that word could be the answer. For example:

> Card: clothesline
> Student: Where do you hang your clothes?
>
> Card: ironing board
> Student: What do you iron your clothes on?
>
> Card: closet
> Student: Where do you hang your shirts?
>
> Card: washer
> Student: What machine washes clothes?

7 Put in Order!
ACTIVITY MASTER 96

a. Make enough copies of Activity Master 104 for half the class and cut it into strips.

b. Give each pair of students a set of the cut-up strips.

c. Have each pair put the strips in the correct order for doing laundry.

(continued)

8 Miming Game

ACTIVITY HANDBOOK PAGE 11
ACTIVITY MASTER 96

Have students take turns pantomiming a laundry action. The class tries to guess what the person is doing. For example:

You're folding the laundry.
You're unloading the washer.

9 What's the Object?

ACTIVITY HANDBOOK PAGE 16

Call out verbs, and have students add appropriate objects. For example:

load . . . *the washer/the dryer*
hang . . . *the clothes/the shirts/the pants*
iron . . . *the wrinkled clothing*
add . . . *detergent/fabric softener/bleach*
fold . . . *the laundry/the clothing*
sort . . . *the laundry/the light clothing/the dark clothing*

10 Group Discussion

Have students in small groups discuss these questions and then report back to the class.

Who does the laundry in your house?
Who irons the clothes in your house?
Why do women usually do the laundry?
Do you have any suggestions on how to do laundry better?
Is it better to dry clothes on a clothesline or in a dryer? Why? Why not?
Is it good to use bleach on clothes? Why? Why not?
Was doing the laundry any different when you were growing up? How was it different?

Unit 8 Communication Activity Review

1 Odd Word Out

Read the following lists of words, and have students identify the category and the "odd word out"—the word that doesn't fit the category:

stockings, boots, tights, pantyhose
[Category: THINGS FOR THE LEGS. Odd word out: boots]

ear muffs, gloves, hat, cap
[Category: OUTERWEAR FOR THE HEAD. Odd word out: gloves]

leather jacket, umbrella, raincoat, rain boots
[Category: RAINWEAR. Odd word out: leather jacket]

pajamas, pants, nightgown, nightshirt
[Category: SLEEPWEAR. Odd word out: pants]

skirt, dress, evening gown, tuxedo
[Category: WOMEN'S CLOTHES. Odd word out: tuxedo]

overalls, tuxedo, evening gown, three-piece suit
[Category: FORMAL CLOTHING. Odd word out: overalls]

ring, necklace, earrings, makeup bag
[Category: JEWELRY. Odd word out: makeup bag]

backpack, suspenders, briefcase, purse
[Category: BAGS. Odd word out: suspenders]

striped, small, plaid, polka dotted, paisley
[Category: PATTERNS. Odd word out: small]

corduroy, denim, flannel, polyester
[Category: MATERIAL MADE FROM COTTON. Odd word out: polyester]

stained, ripped, broken, flowered
[Category: CLOTHING PROBLEMS. Odd word out: flowered]

starch, fabric softener, chain, laundry detergent
[Category: PRODUCTS FOR DOING LAUNDRY. Odd word out: chain]

sandals, boots, flip-flops, thongs
[Category: SUMMER SHOES. Odd word out: boots]

jockstrap, jockey shorts, stockings, long johns
[Category: MEN'S UNDERWEAR. Odd word out: stockings]

ski mask, down vest, T-shirt, parka
[Category: COLD WEATHER CLOTHING: Odd word out: T-shirt]

extra-large, long-sleeved, small, medium
[Category: CLOTHING SIZES: Odd word out: long-sleeved]

straw, V-neck, crewneck, cardigan
[Category: KINDS OF SWEATERS. Odd word out: straw]

silk, cuff links, leather, linen,
[Category: MATERIALS. Odd word out: cuff links]

red, pink, orange, blue
[Category: COLORS WITH RED IN THEM. Odd word out: blue]

green, purple, yellow, orange
[Category: COLORS WITH YELLOW IN THEM. Odd word out: purple]

2 Finish the Sentence!
ACTIVITY HANDBOOK PAGE 7

Begin sentences such as the following for students to complete:

A maternity dress is something that . . .
Suspenders are something that . . .
A uniform is something that . . .
A down vest is something that . . .
Pantyhose are something that . . .
Swimming trunks are something that . . .
Hiking boots are something that . . .
A belt is something that . . .
A string of pearls is something that . . .
Knee-high socks are something that . . .
A lint trap is something that . . .
A locket is something that . . .

3 Category Dictation
ACTIVITY HANDBOOK PAGE 2

Dictate words from *Picture Dictionary* pages 65–73 that fit any three of the following categories:

underwear
outerwear
material
jewelry
colors
work clothes
types of shirts
sleepwear
exercise clothing
footwear
sizes
patterns

(continued)

4 Likes and Dislikes

a. Have students make two columns on a piece of paper. One column heading is I like to wear and the other is I don't like to wear.

b. Dictate clothing from *Picture Dictionary* pages 65–73 and have students write the items in the appropriate column. For example:

I like to wear	I don't like to wear
evening gowns	shorts
turtlenecks	suits
cowboy boots	flip-flops

5 Drawing Game

ACTIVITY HANDBOOK PAGE 6
ACTIVITY MASTERS 84, 86, 87, 88, 90, 95

Have teams compete to identify vocabulary items drawn by one of their team members.

6 Letter Game

ACTIVITY HANDBOOK PAGE 9

Say statements such as the following and have teams compete to identify the items:

I'm thinking of sleepwear that starts with *p*.	[pajamas]
I'm thinking of a color that starts with *g*.	[green]
I'm thinking of a pattern that starts with *ch*.	[checked]
I'm thinking of a material that starts with *c*.	[cotton]
I'm thinking of a color that starts with *o*.	[orange]
I'm thinking of exercise clothing that starts with *t*.	[tank top]
I'm thinking of exercise clothing that starts with *s*.	[sweatpants]
I'm thinking of footwear that starts with *s*.	[sneakers]
I'm thinking of jewelry that starts with *b*.	[bracelet]

7 Ask Me a Question!

ACTIVITY HANDBOOK PAGE 2
ACTIVITY MASTERS 84, 86, 87, 88, 90

Have students walk around trying to guess each other's clothing items by asking yes/no questions. For example:

Do you wear it in warm weather?
Do you wear it when you go out at night?
Do you wear it when you stay home?
Do you wear it on your feet?

Variation: Do the activity as a game by dividing the class into two teams. One person comes to the front of the room and thinks of a clothing item. The two teams compete against each other, trying to guess the item by asking yes/no questions.

8 Find the Right Person!

ACTIVITY HANDBOOK PAGES 6–7
ACTIVITY MASTER 97

Practice the following questions before having students do the activity:

Do you have a missing button?
Do you have a pair of overalls?
Do you like to wear jewelry?
Do you like to wear baggy pants?
Do you carry a briefcase to school or to work?
Do you like paisley patterns?
Do you like the color purple?
Do you ever wear a tie?
Do you iron shirts quickly?
Do you wear sandals?

9 What Shoes Should I Wear?

Tell things you're going to be doing, and ask students what shoes you should wear. For example:

I'm going to play tennis. What kind of shoes should I wear?
I'm going to walk on the beach. What should I wear?
I'm going to stay home and watch TV. What should I wear?
I'm going to work in the office. What should I wear?
I'm going mountain climbing. What should I wear?
I'm going to a wedding. What should I wear?
I'm going to watch a baseball game. What should I wear?

TOPICS	DICTIONARY	TEACHER'S GUIDE
The Department Store	74	186–188
Shopping	75	189–190
Video and Audio Equipment	76	191–192
Telephones and Cameras	77	193–195
Computers	78	196–197
The Toy Store	79	198–200
Unit 9 Communication Activity Review	74–79	201–202

AUDIO PROGRAM

Words & Dialogs
Audio Cassette 3A
Audio Cassette 3B
Audio CD 3:
    Tracks 41–56

WordSong: *Wilson's Department Store*
Audio Cassette 7A
Audio Cassette 7B
Audio CD 8: Tracks 4
    (Vocal) & 5 (Sing-along)
Song Masters S17, S18

WORKBOOKS

For Multi-Level Practice

Literacy Workbook
Beginning Lifeskills Workbook
Beginning Vocabulary Workbook
Intermediate Lifeskills Workbook
Intermediate Vocabulary Workbook

WORDLINKS

**Internet Resources through the
Word by Word Companion Website**

http://www.longman.com/wordbyword

ACTIVITY MASTERS

Reproducibles for Communication Activities
A8, A84, A87, A88, A90, A98–A108

TRANSPARENCIES

Full-Color Overheads for Class Practice
T74–T79

LANGUAGE & CULTURE NOTES

**Information for Teachers &
Intermediate /Advanced Students**
LC74–LC79

LESSON OBJECTIVE

Students will learn vocabulary related to a department store.

RESOURCES

AUDIO PROGRAM		**MULTI-LEVEL WORKBOOKS**	**ACTIVITY MASTERS**
Words & Dialogs Cassette 3A CD 3: Tracks 41, 42	**WordSong:** *Wilson's Department Store* Cassette 7A, 7B • CD 8: Tracks 4, 5 Song Masters S17, S18	Literacy Workbook Beginning & Intermediate Lifeskills Workbooks Beginning & Intermediate Vocabulary Workbooks	**Reproducibles**: A84, A87, A88, A90, A98, A99

TRANSPARENCY	**LANGUAGE & CULTURE NOTES**	**WORDLINKS**
Overhead: T74	**Reproducible:** LC74	longman.com/wordbyword

VOCABULARY INTRODUCTION

- Preview
- Present
- Practice

MODEL CONVERSATION PRACTICE

There are two model conversations. Introduce and practice the first model before going on to the second. For each model:

1. Have students look at the model illustration. Set the scene:

    Model 1: "A customer is talking to a security guard in a department store."
    Model 2: "A customer is talking to a salesperson in a department store."

2. Present the model.
3. Choral Repetition Practice: Full-Class and Individual.
4. Have pairs practice the model.
5. Have pairs present the model.
6. Call on pairs to present a new conversation using words 5 and 6 for the first model and *bracelets* and word 2 for the second model.
7. Have pairs practice new conversations.
8. Have pairs present new conversations.

SPELLING PRACTICE

Say a word, and have students spell it aloud or write it. Or, using the transparency, point to an item and have students write the word.

WRITING AND DISCUSSION

Have students respond to the question as a class, in pairs, or in small groups. Or have students write their responses, share their writing with other students, and discuss in class.

♫♫ WordSong ♫♫

1. Have students listen to the vocal version of *Wilson's Department Store* one or more times. Then have students listen again as they read the song lyrics on Song Master S17.
2. Have students sing as you play either the vocal or the sing-along version of the song.
3. For fun, have a song competition in which students perform solo or in groups and the class votes for the best performance.
4. For additional practice, students can complete the cloze exercise on Song Master S18.

Making Connections

Resource Materials Bring in, or have students bring in, the following materials for vocabulary practice:

- *Newspaper advertisements for different department stores:* Talk about what's on sale at the big department stores in town.
- *Department store catalogs:* Compare styles and prices of clothing sold at two different department stores.

Community Task Have individual students (or groups of students) visit a department store, look at its directory, tour the store, and then draw a map of where each department is located in the store.

Communication Activities

1 Associations
ACTIVITY HANDBOOK PAGE 2

Call out departments of a department store and have groups write down as many associations as they can think of. For example:

Jewelry Department:	[watch/rings/earrings/ necklaces/chains/lockets/ pins/pearls]
Women's Clothing Department:	[blouses/dresses/pants/ skirts/nightgowns/bras/ pantyhose/maternity dresses]
Men's Clothing Department:	[suits/ties/slacks/ jerseys/jeans/shorts/ jackets]

2 Mystery Word Association Game
ACTIVITY HANDBOOK PAGES 11–12

Have students write associations for department store *mystery words* for others to guess. For example:

skirts/dresses/coats/ belts	[Women's Clothing Department]
couch/table/chair/ bookcase	[Furniture Department]
washing machine/ dryer/microwave oven	[Household Appliances Department]
wrapping paper/tape/ ribbon/boxes	[Gift Wrap Counter]

3 Movable Categories
ACTIVITY HANDBOOK PAGE 11
ACTIVITY MASTERS 84, 87, 88, 90

Call out the departments of a department store and have students with items that can be found in those departments go to the appropriate side of the room.

4 Category Dictation
ACTIVITY HANDBOOK PAGE 2

Dictate words that fit into the following categories:

Household Appliance Department
Housewares Department
Men's Clothing Department
Women's Clothing Department

5 Chain Game
ACTIVITY HANDBOOK PAGES 2–3

Begin the chain as follows: "I went to the Jewelry Counter and bought some earrings," and have students continue it. For example:

Teacher: I went to the Jewelry Counter and bought some earrings.
Student 1: I went to the Jewelry Counter and bought some earrings. Then I went to the Housewares Department and bought some plates.
Student 2: I went to the Jewelry Counter and bought some earrings. Then I went to the Housewares Department and bought some plates. Then I went to the snack bar and had a cup of coffee.
Etc.

6 True or False?
ACTIVITY HANDBOOK PAGE 15

Make statements such as the following about the department store depicted on *Picture Dictionary* page 74. Have students decide whether they're true or false. For example:

The store directory is near the entrance. [True]
The Furniture Department is on the first floor. [False. It's on the third floor.]
The Perfume Counter, the Jewelry Counter, and the Women's Clothing Department are all on the same floor. [False. The Perfume Counter and the Jewelry Counter are on the first floor, and the Women's Clothing Department is on the second floor.]
There's a water fountain close to the Customer Service Counter. [True.]
There's an elevator next to the entrance of the store. [False. The elevator is next to the escalator.]
You can buy refrigerators and TVs in the Household Appliances Department. [False. You can't buy TVs in the Household Appliances Department.]
The Men's Clothing Department is on the third floor. [False. The Men's Clothing Department is on the first floor.]
The ladies' room is on the fourth floor. [True.]
The snack bar is next to the Furniture Department. [False. The snack bar is between the Customer Service Counter and the Gift Wrap Counter.]
The customer pickup area is on the third floor. [False. It's on the first floor.]

(continued)

7. Picture This!
ACTIVITY HANDBOOK PAGES 12–13

Describe the layout of a department store, and have students draw what you describe. For example:

> There are five floors in this department store. On the first floor, there's a Jewelry Counter on the left. Next to the Jewelry Counter is the Women's Clothing Department. There's an elevator . . .

8. Listen and Number
ACTIVITY HANDBOOK PAGE 10

In pairs, have one student make up a story using department store words and have the other student number the pictures in their order of occurrence in the story.

9. Finish the Sentence!
ACTIVITY HANDBOOK PAGE 7

Begin sentences such as the following for students to complete:

> You can buy dresses in the . . . *Women's Clothing Department.*
> You can get a drink at the . . . *water fountain.*
> You can get something to eat at the . . . *snack bar.*
> Radios? Look in the . . . *Electronics Department.*
> Nightgowns? Look in the . . . *Women's Clothing Department.*
> You can return that item at the . . . *Customer Assistance Counter.*
> You can pick up your package at the . . . *customer pickup area.*
> You can walk upstairs on the . . . *escalator.*
> You can ride upstairs on the . . . *elevator.*
> You can buy a tuxedo in the . . . *Men's Clothing Department.*

10. Department Store Match Game
ACTIVITY HANDBOOK PAGE 11
ACTIVITY MASTER 98

Have students find the person whose card matches theirs.

11. Department Store Role Plays
ACTIVITY MASTER 99

a. Make copies of Activity Master 99 and cut them up into cards. Place the cards face-down on a desk at the front of the room.

b. Have a pair of students come up to the front of the class. Student A picks up the card and is the shopper with the *problem*. Student B works at the department store and gives advice to Student A. For example:

> A. Excuse me. Where can I find the Men's Clothing Department?
> B. It's on the third floor, next to the Women's Clothing Department.
> A. Did you say the fifth floor?
> B. No. The third floor.
> A. Thank you.
> B. No problem.

12. Stand Up for Housewares!

a. Say the name of a department or section in a department store.

b. Tell students you're going to say four words. If they hear a word that is associated with that department or section, they should stand up. If they hear a word that is not associated with that department, they should sit down. For example:

Home Furnishings:
sofa	[stand]
coffee table	[remain standing]
toaster	[sit]
blouse	[remain sitting]

Gift Wrap Counter:
paper towel	[sit]
ribbon	[stand]
calculator	[sit]
bow	[stand]

Children's Clothing:
evening gown	[sit]
sweater	[stand]
tuxedo	[sit]
T-shirt	[stand]

customer pickup area:
big boxes	[stand]
refrigerators	[remain standing]
water fountain	[sit]
snack bar	[remain sitting]

LESSON OBJECTIVE

Students will learn the vocabulary people use when shopping.

RESOURCES

AUDIO PROGRAM		MULTI-LEVEL WORKBOOKS	ACTIVITY MASTER
Words & Dialogs Cassette 3A CD 3: Tracks 43, 44	**WordSong:** *Wilson's Department Store* Cassette 7A, 7B • CD 8: Tracks 4, 5 Song Masters S17, S18	Literacy Workbook Beginning & Intermediate Lifeskills Workbooks Beginning & Intermediate Vocabulary Workbooks	**Reproducible:** A100

TRANSPARENCY	LANGUAGE & CULTURE NOTES	WORDLINKS
Overhead: T75	**Reproducible:** LC75	longman.com/wordbyword

VOCABULARY INTRODUCTION

- Preview
- Present
- Practice

MODEL CONVERSATION PRACTICE

There are two model conversations—the first for words A–F and the second for words 1–13. Introduce and practice the first model before going on to the second. For each model:

1. Have students look at the model illustration. Set the scene:

   Model 1: "A customer is talking to a salesperson in a department store."

   Model 2: "A husband and wife are shopping in a department store."

2. Present the model with word A for the first model and words 5 and 1 for the second model.

3. Choral Repetition Practice: Full-Class and Individual.

4. Have pairs practice the model.

5. Have pairs present the model.

6. Call on pairs to present a new conversation using word B for the first model and words 6 and 2 for the second model.

7. Have pairs practice new conversations.

8. Have pairs present new conversations.

SPELLING PRACTICE

Say a word or phrase, and have students spell it aloud or write it. Or, using the transparency, point to an item and have students write the word or phrase.

WRITING AND DISCUSSION

Have students respond to the questions as a class, in pairs, or in small groups. Or have students write their responses, share their writing with other students, and discuss in class.

Making Connections

Resource Materials Bring in, or have students bring in, the following materials for vocabulary practice:

○ *Department store sale fliers with advertisements for discounts:* Talk about the regular price and the sale price for various items in the flier. Also talk about the material and the sizes available for various items.

Community Task Have individual students (or groups of students) visit different stores and report about their return and exchange policies.

Communication Activities

1 Shopping Associations
ACTIVITY HANDBOOK PAGE 2

Call out shopping words and have groups write down as many associations as they can think of. For example:

care instructions:	[wash/cold water only/no bleach/cool iron/dry clean only]
receipt:	[price/sale price/sales tax/total price/paper/credit card number]
shopping:	[try on/get some information about/look for something/pay for/buy]
sale sign:	[discount/sale price/today only]
material:	[cotton/polyester/leather/wool/straw]

2 Chain Story
ACTIVITY HANDBOOK PAGE 3

Begin the story as follows: "I went shopping yesterday."

3 Listen and Number
ACTIVITY HANDBOOK PAGE 10

In pairs, have one student make up a story using shopping words and have the other student number the pictures in their order of occurrence in the story.

4 Find the Right Person!
ACTIVITY HANDBOOK PAGES 6–7
ACTIVITY MASTER 100

Practice the following questions before having students do the activity:

How often do you go shopping for clothes?
Do you return things often?
Do you like to shop?
Do you shop only when there are sales?
Do you keep your receipts?
Did you exchange an item recently? When?
Do you try on clothes before buying them?

5 Finish the Sentence!
ACTIVITY HANDBOOK PAGE 7

Begin sentences such as the following for students to complete:

If you buy something and it's broken, you should . . . *return it.*
To find the price of something, you have to look at the . . . *price tag.*

To find out the material of a dress, you look at the . . . *label.*
To find out how you should wash a piece of clothing, look at the . . . *care instructions.*
After you buy something, the cashier will give you a . . . *receipt.*
To find out the size of a pair of pants, you look at the . . . *label.*
Before you pay for shoes, you should . . . *try them on.*
On a receipt there is the price of your items, the sales tax, and finally the . . . *total price.*

6 Tell a Story

a. Divide the class into pairs.

b. Have each pair choose one scene on *Picture Dictionary* page 75 and make up a story about the people in the illustration, what they are doing, and why they are doing it.

c. Have the pairs read their stories aloud to the class and have the class listen and decide which picture on page 75 the story describes.

7 Investigate!

Have small groups of students visit various stores and get information about their return and exchange policies. Brainstorm questions in class such as the following:

What is your return policy?
How many days do I have to return something?
When I return something, do you give money back or store credit?
Can I return something if I lost the receipt?
If I buy this today and then tomorrow it goes on sale can I come back and get the sale price?
If something I buy here doesn't work, can I exchange it?

8 Class Discussion on Sales Tax

Discuss the following questions in small groups or as a class:

What items are taxed where you live? Is food taxed? Are clothes taxed? Are cars taxed?
Are there different taxes for different kinds of purchases? Is there a luxury tax? Is there a restaurant tax? Is there a gasoline tax?
Is the tax included in the price? Is it a separate item on your receipt?
Do you think all purchases should be taxed? Why or why not? Which items should not be taxed?

LESSON OBJECTIVE

Students will learn the names of common video and audio equipment.

RESOURCES

AUDIO PROGRAM
Words & Dialogs
Cassette 3A
CD 3: Tracks 45–47

MULTI-LEVEL WORKBOOKS
Literacy Workbook
Beginning & Intermediate Lifeskills Workbooks
Beginning & Intermediate Vocabulary Workbooks

ACTIVITY MASTERS
Reproducibles:
A101, A102

TRANSPARENCY
Overhead: T76

LANGUAGE & CULTURE NOTES
Reproducible: LC76

WORDLINKS
longman.com/wordbyword

VOCABULARY INTRODUCTION

- Preview
- Present
- Practice

MODEL CONVERSATION PRACTICE

1. Have students look at the model illustration. Set the scene: "A salesperson and a customer are talking in a store."
2. Present the model.
3. Choral Repetition Practice: Full-Class and Individual.
4. Have pairs practice the model.
5. Have pairs present the model.
6. Call on pairs to present a new conversation using word 2.
7. Have pairs practice new conversations.
8. Have pairs present new conversations.

ADDITIONAL CONVERSATION PRACTICE

Before students practice the additional conversations, you may want to have them listen to the examples on the Audio Program.

Conversation 1 Have students practice and present conversations with any words they wish.

Conversation 2 Have students practice and present conversations with any words they wish.

SPELLING PRACTICE

Say a word, and have students spell it aloud or write it. Or, using the transparency, point to an item and have students write the word.

WRITING AND DISCUSSION

Have students respond to the questions as a class, in pairs, or in small groups. Or have students write their responses, share their writing with other students, and discuss in class.

Making Connections

Resource Materials Bring in, or have students bring in, the following materials for vocabulary practice:

- *Newspaper advertisements for video and audio equipment:* Identify the kinds of equipment in the ads.

- *Brochures and catalogs for video and audio equipment:* Identify the kinds of equipment in the brochures and catalogs, and then have students identify which kinds of equipment they use themselves.

Community Task Have individual students (or groups of students) investigate the price of one model of electronic equipment by visiting different electronic stores in the area. Have students report which store offers the best price.

Communication Activities

1 Movable Categories
ACTIVITY HANDBOOK PAGE 11
ACTIVITY MASTER 101

Call out the following categories and have students go to the appropriate side of the room:

thing that show pictures
things that play music
things that record pictures
things that record music
things that are portable
things that are not portable

2 Category Dictation
ACTIVITY HANDBOOK PAGE 2

Dictate words that fit into any of the above categories.

3 Concentration
ACTIVITY HANDBOOK PAGE 3
ACTIVITY MASTER 102

Have students shuffle the cards and place them face-down in three rows of 6 each, then attempt to find cards that match.

4 Cooperative Definitions
ACTIVITY HANDBOOK PAGE 4

Have groups write definitions of video and audio equipment words and then pass their definitions to other groups.

5 It's Something That . . .
ACTIVITY HANDBOOK PAGE 9
ACTIVITY MASTER 101

Have students give definitions of video and audio equipment words to each other beginning with "It's something that . . . " For example:

It's something that can wake you up in the morning. [A clock radio.]
It's something that plays DVDs. [A DVD player.]
It's something that you can carry to hear the news. [A radio.]
It's something that you can wear so that only you can hear the music. [Headphones.]
It's something that produces sound. [Speakers.]

6 Ranking
ACTIVITY HANDBOOK PAGE 13

Have students look at all the video and audio equipment on *Picture Dictionary* page 76 and choose the four most important items. Then have students rank them according to their importance in their daily lives, with 1 being most important and 4 being less important. For example:

1. radio
2. CD player
3. television
4. portable CD player

Variation: You could also have students rank the items according to cost or newness on the market.

7 Create a Commercial!

a. Have students work in pairs or in small groups to develop an advertisement for one kind of video or audio equipment on *Picture Dictionary* page 76.

b. Have students present their commercials to the class.

8 Comparison Shopping

a. Tell students to cut out advertisements for video and audio equipment from newspapers and magazines.

b. As a class, in pairs, or in small groups, have students compare prices and features of the different products. If you wish, you can make a chart of the information on the board.

9 Class Discussion: Technology

Have students discuss these questions in small groups or as a class:

Look at the items on *Picture Dictionary* page 76. Which equipment existed when your parents were young? Which equipment existed when you were young? Which equipment is new?

Have the products in this lesson improved the quality of your life? How? Are there any disadvantages to these products? What are they?

If you could have just one piece of equipment from this lesson, which one would you choose? Why?

LESSON OBJECTIVE

Students will learn the names of the most common telephone and camera equipment.

RESOURCES

AUDIO PROGRAM

Words & Dialogs
Cassette 3B
CD 3: Tracks 48–50

MULTI-LEVEL WORKBOOKS

Literacy Workbook
Beginning & Intermediate Lifeskills Workbooks
Beginning & Intermediate Vocabulary Workbooks

ACTIVITY MASTERS

Reproducibles:
A103, A104

TRANSPARENCY

Overhead: T77

LANGUAGE & CULTURE NOTES

Reproducible: LC77

WORDLINKS

longman.com/wordbyword

VOCABULARY INTRODUCTION

- Preview
- Present
- Practice

MODEL CONVERSATION PRACTICE

1. Have students look at the model illustration. Set the scene: "A salesperson and a customer are talking in a store."
2. Present the model.
3. Choral Repetition Practice: Full-Class and Individual.
4. Have pairs practice the model.
5. Have pairs present the model.
6. Call on pairs to present a new conversation using word 2.
7. Have pairs practice new conversations.
8. Have pairs present new conversations.

ADDITIONAL CONVERSATION PRACTICE

Before students practice the additional conversations, you may want to have them listen to the examples on the Audio Program.

Conversation 1 Have students practice and present conversations with any words they wish.

Conversation 2 Have students practice and present conversations with any words they wish.

SPELLING PRACTICE

Say a word, and have students spell it aloud or write it. Or, using the transparency, point to an item and have students write the word.

WRITING AND DISCUSSION

Have students respond to the questions as a class, in pairs, or in small groups. Or have students write their responses, share their writing with other students, and discuss in class.

Making Connections

Resource Materials Bring in, or have students bring in, the following materials for vocabulary practice:

- *Newspaper and magazine advertisements for telephones and for cameras:* Talk about the products depicted in the advertisements.

- *Brochures and catalogs:* Talk about which items students would want and why.

Community Task Have individual students (or groups of students) investigate the price of one model of camera or phone by visiting different electronic stores. Have students report which store offers the best price.

Communication Activities

1 Movable Categories
ACTIVITY HANDBOOK PAGE 11
ACTIVITY MASTER 103

Call out the following categories and have students go to the appropriate side of the room:

> things related to a telephone
> things related to a camera
> things that plug into an electrical outlet
> things that are battery-operated
> things that are portable

2 Category Dictation
ACTIVITY HANDBOOK PAGE 2

Dictate words that fit into any of the above categories.

3 Concentration
ACTIVITY HANDBOOK PAGE 3
ACTIVITY MASTER 104

Have students shuffle the cards and place them face-down in three rows of 6 each, then attempt to find cards that match.

4 Cooperative Definitions
ACTIVITY HANDBOOK PAGE 4

Have groups write definitions of telephone and camera equipment words and then pass their definitions to other groups.

5 What's the Question?
ACTIVITY HANDBOOK PAGE 16

Describe various telephone and camera equipment and have students respond by asking: "What's a _____?"or "What are _____s?" For example:

Teacher: You show slides and movies on this.
Student: What's a movie screen?

Teacher: You leave messages on this when the person isn't home.
Student: What's an answering machine?

Teacher: It stabilizes electrical energy so a machine is not damaged when you plug it in.
Student: What's a voltage regulator?

Teacher: It records images when it's exposed to light.
Student: What is film?

Teacher: It focuses the camera.
Student: What's a lens?

Teacher: It transmits a copy of any page over the phone line.
Student: What's a fax?

Teacher: It has three legs and holds up a camera.
Student: What's a tripod?

Teacher: It's a phone that you can use anywhere close to your phone line.
Student: What's a cordless phone?

Teacher: It's a phone you can use anywhere you go.
Student: What's a cell phone?

Teacher: It stores energy so that you don't need to use an electrical outlet.
Student: What's a battery?

6 Ask Me a Question!
ACTIVITY HANDBOOK PAGE 2
ACTIVITY MASTER 103

Have students walk around trying to guess each other's telephone and camera items by asking yes/no questions. For example:

Do you answer it?	[No.]
Is it electric?	[No.]
Is it part of something else?	[Yes.]
Is it small?	[Yes.]
Is it part of a camera?	[Yes.]
Is it film?	[Yes.]
Do you use it to speak with someone?	[Yes.]
Is it portable?	[Yes.]
Is it a cordless phone?	[No.]
Is it a cell phone?	[Yes.]

7 Ranking
ACTIVITY HANDBOOK PAGE 13

Have students look at all the telephone and camera equipment on *Picture Dictionary* page 77 and choose the four most important items. Then have students rank them according to their importance in their daily lives, with 1 being most important and 4 being least important. For example:

1. cell phone
2. telephone
3. answering machine
4. digital camera

Variation: You could also have students rank the items according to cost or newness on the market.

8 Word Clues
ACTIVITY HANDBOOK PAGE 17
ACTIVITY MASTER 103

Have students take turns giving one-word clues to team members who try to guess the word. For example:

[The word is *fax machine*.]
Team 1 Player: "telephone"   [Team 1 guesses]
Team 2 Player: "letter"   [Team 2 guesses]
Team 1 Player: "fast"   [Team 1 guesses]

[The word is *digital camera*.]
Team 1 Player: "pictures"   [Team 1 guesses]
Team 2 Player: "fast"   [Team 2 guesses]
Team 1 Player: "computer"   [Team 1 guesses]

9 Got It!
ACTIVITY HANDBOOK PAGE 7

Have groups of students ask yes/no questions in an attempt to identify telephone and camera items. For example:

Is it a type of camera?   [No.]
Is it a part of a camera?   [Yes.]
Do you look through it?   [Yes.]
Is it a lens?   [Yes.]

10 Create a Commercial!

a. Have students work in pairs or in small groups to develop an advertisement for one kind of telephone and camera equipment on *Picture Dictionary* page 77.

b. Have students consider the following questions:

What's the name of your product?
What are the special features of your product?
Who would want to buy your product?
Is your commercial for TV or radio?

c. Have students present their commercials to the class.

11 Comparison Shopping

a. Tell students to cut out advertisements for telephone services, telephone equipment, or camera equipment from newspapers and magazines.

b. As a class, in pairs, or in small groups, have students compare prices and features of the different products. If you wish, you can make a chart of the information on the board.

12 Class Discussion: Technology

Have students discuss these questions in small groups or as a class:

Look at the items on *Picture Dictionary* page 77. Which kind of telephone existed when your parents were young? Which kind of telephone existed when you were young? Which kind of telephone is new?

Has the cell phone improved the quality of your life? How? What are some disadvantages of this technology?

Has the digital camera improved the quality of your life? How? What are some disadvantages of this technology?

If you had to choose only one piece of equipment from *Picture Dictionary* page 77, which one would you choose? Why?

13 What Do They Need?
ACTIVITY MASTER 103

a. Give each student a Telephone and Camera Word Card.

b. Call out an occupation—for example: *photographer*.

c. Tell students if they have a word on their card that a person with this occupation would need, they should go to the right side of the room. All others should go to the left.

d. Continue with *secretary, bookkeeper, accountant.*

LESSON OBJECTIVE

Students will learn the names of common computer equipment.

RESOURCES

AUDIO PROGRAM

Words & Dialogs
Cassette 3B
CD 3: Tracks 51–53

MULTI-LEVEL WORKBOOKS

Literacy Workbook
Beginning & Intermediate Lifeskills Workbooks
Beginning & Intermediate Vocabulary Workbooks

ACTIVITY MASTERS

Reproducibles:
A105, A106

TRANSPARENCY

Overhead: T78

LANGUAGE & CULTURE NOTES

Reproducible: LC78

WORDLINKS

longman.com/wordbyword

VOCABULARY INTRODUCTION

- Preview
- Present
- Practice

MODEL CONVERSATION PRACTICE

1. Have students look at the model illustration. Set the scene: "A salesperson and a customer are talking in a store."
2. Present the model.
3. Choral Repetition Practice: Full-Class and Individual.
4. Have pairs practice the model.
5. Have pairs present the model.
6. Call on pairs to present a new conversation using word 2.
7. Have pairs practice new conversations.
8. Have pairs present new conversations.

ADDITIONAL CONVERSATION PRACTICE

Before students practice the additional conversations, you may want to have them listen to the examples on the Audio Program.

Conversation 1 Have students practice and present conversations with any words they wish.

Conversation 2 Have students practice and present conversations with any words they wish.

SPELLING PRACTICE

Say a word, and have students spell it aloud or write it. Or, using the transparency, point to an item and have students write the word.

WRITING AND DISCUSSION

Have students respond to the questions as a class, in pairs, or in small groups. Or have students write their responses, share their writing with other students, and discuss in class.

Making Connections

Resource Materials Bring in, or have students bring in, the following materials for vocabulary practice:

- *Newspaper and magazine advertisements for computer equipment:* Talk about the products depicted in the advertisements.

- *Brochures and catalogs:* Talk about which items students would want and why.

Community Task Have individual students (or groups of students) investigate the price of one computer model by visiting different computer stores in the area. Have students report which store offers the best price.

Communication Activities

1 Concentration

ACTIVITY HANDBOOK PAGE 3
ACTIVITY MASTER 105

Have students shuffle the cards and place them face-down in three rows of 6 each, then attempt to find cards that match.

2 Cooperative Definitions

ACTIVITY HANDBOOK PAGE 4

Have groups write definitions of computer equipment words and then pass their definitions to other groups.

3 Find the Right Computer Person!

ACTIVITY HANDBOOK PAGES 6–7
ACTIVITY MASTER 106

Practice the following questions before having students do the activity:

How many hours do you spend at a computer every week?
What kind of software do you use?
Do you like to use computers?
Do you use computers in your work?
What kind of computer and computer equipment do you have?
What kind of computer do you like best to use?

4 Create a Commercial!

a. Have students work in pairs or in small groups to develop an advertisement for a piece of computer equipment on *Picture Dictionary* page 78.

b. Have students consider the following questions:

What's the name of your product?
What are the special features of your product?
Who would want to buy your product?
Is your commercial for TV or radio?

c. Have students present their commercials to the class.

5 Comparison Shopping

a. Tell students to cut out advertisements for computer equipment from newspapers and magazines.

b. As a class, in pairs, or in small groups, have students compare prices and features of the different products. If you wish, you can make a chart of the information on the board.

6 Class Discussion: Computers

Have students discuss these questions in small groups or as a class:

Look at the items on *Picture Dictionary* page 78. Which kind of computer existed when your parents were young? Which kind of computer existed when you were young? Which kind of computer is new?

Have computers improved the quality of life? How? What are some disadvantages to using computers?

Have computers reduced or increased the amount of time people work?

LESSON OBJECTIVE

Students will learn the names of the most common toys children use in the United States.

RESOURCES

AUDIO PROGRAM
Words & Dialogs
Cassette 3B
CD 3: Tracks 54–56

MULTI-LEVEL WORKBOOKS
Literacy Workbook
Beginning & Intermediate Lifeskills Workbooks
Beginning & Intermediate Vocabulary Workbooks

ACTIVITY MASTERS
Reproducibles:
A8, A107, A108

TRANSPARENCY
Overhead: T79

LANGUAGE & CULTURE NOTES
Reproducible: LC79

WORDLINKS
longman.com/wordbyword

VOCABULARY INTRODUCTION

- Preview
- Present
- Practice

MODEL CONVERSATION PRACTICE

1. Have students look at the model illustration. Set the scene: "A customer and a clerk are talking in a toy store."
2. Present the model with word 1.
3. Choral Repetition Practice: Full-Class and Individual.
4. Have pairs practice the model.
5. Have pairs present the model.
6. Call on pairs to present a new conversation using word 2.
7. Have pairs practice new conversations.
8. Have pairs present new conversations.

ADDITIONAL CONVERSATION PRACTICE

Before students practice the additional conversations, you may want to have them listen to the examples on the Audio Program.

Conversation 1 Have students practice and present conversations with any words they wish.

Conversation 2 Have students practice and present conversations with any words they wish.

SPELLING PRACTICE

Say a word, and have students spell it aloud or write it. Or, using the transparency, point to an item and have students write the word.

WRITING AND DISCUSSION

Have students respond to the questions as a class, in pairs, or in small groups. Or have students write their responses, share their writing with other students, and discuss in class.

Making Connections

Resource Materials Bring in, or have students bring in, the following materials for vocabulary practice:

- *Toy catalogs:* Identify the toys in the catalog without reading the descriptions in the catalog.

- *The smaller, more portable toys themselves:* Give students an opportunity to look at and touch the toys and imagine all the different ways they can be used. (For example: Colored markers can be used to make signs, draw pictures, and color in pictures.)

Community Task Have individual students (or groups of students) visit different toy stores and report about the toys and their prices that these stores sell.

Communication Activities

1 Chain Game
ACTIVITY HANDBOOK PAGES 2–3

Begin the chain as follows: "I went to the toy store and bought a jump rope," and have students continue it. For example:

    Teacher: I went to the toy store and bought a jump rope.
    Student 1: I went to the toy store and bought a jump rope and construction paper.
    Student 2: I went to the toy store and bought a jump rope, construction paper, and a rubber ball.
    Etc.

2 Letter Game
ACTIVITY HANDBOOK PAGE 9

Say statements such as the following and have teams compete to identify the items:

I'm thinking of a toy that starts with *w*.   [wagon]
I'm thinking of a toy that starts with *t*.   [tricycle]
I'm thinking of a toy that starts with *j*.   [jigsaw puzzle]
I'm thinking of a toy that starts with *d*.   [doll]
I'm thinking of a toy that starts with *c*.   [crayons]
I'm thinking of a toy that starts with *r*.   [rubber ball]
I'm thinking of a toy that starts with *h*.   [hula hoop]
I'm thinking of a toy that starts with *c*.   [construction set]
I'm thinking of a toy that starts with *a*.   [action figure]
I'm thinking of a toy that starts with *t*.   [toy truck]

3 Clap in Rhythm
ACTIVITY HANDBOOK PAGE 3

Have students name different toys to a clapping rhythm.

4 Drawing Game
ACTIVITY HANDBOOK PAGE 6
ACTIVITY MASTER 107

Have teams compete to identify toys drawn by one of their team members.

5 Tic Tac Definitions
ACTIVITY HANDBOOK PAGE 15
ACTIVITY MASTER 8

Have students fill in the tic tac grid with any nine toy words they wish. Give definitions such as the following, and have students cross out on their grids the words you have defined:

thick colored paper [construction paper]
a small toy car that looks like a real car [matchbox car]
two hand pieces that can communicate with each other without wires [walkie-talkie set]
a bicycle with three wheels for small children [tricycle]
a pretend house that children can play inside [play house]
a thick cord for children to jump over [jump rope]
a ball you can inflate [beach ball]
a doll that looks like a comic book or movie hero [action figure]
colorful wax sticks small children use for coloring and drawing [crayons]
a soft cloth toy that looks like an animal [stuffed animal]

6 Movable Categories
ACTIVITY HANDBOOK PAGE 11
ACTIVITY MASTER 107

Call out the following categories and have students go to the appropriate side of the room:

toys for drawing, modeling, and painting
outdoor toys
electronic toys
transportation toys
building toys
toys for doll play
toys for a game or competition
toys for children ages 1-5
toys for children ages 6-10
toys for children ages 11-16
toys that give you exercise

(continued)

Concentration

ACTIVITY HANDBOOK PAGE 3
ACTIVITY MASTER 108

Have students shuffle the cards and place them face-down in three rows of 6 each, then attempt to find cards that match.

 Miming Game

ACTIVITY HANDBOOK PAGE 11
ACTIVITY MASTER 107

Have students take turns pantomiming using various toys. The class tries to guess what toy the person is playing with.

9 Toy Talk!

ACTIVITY HANDBOOK PAGE 17
ACTIVITY MASTER 107

Give students a Toy Store Word Card and have them speak to the class for one minute about that toy. They can talk about anything associated with it—for example, they can describe it, tell how to use it, and tell who it is appropriate for.

 Class Discussion

In pairs or in small groups, have students look at the items depicted on *Picture Dictionary* page 79, discuss the following questions, and then report back to the class:

> In your opinion, what is the best toy? Why?
> What is the worst toy? Why?
> Which toys would you want your children to have? Why?
> Which toys *wouldn't* you want your children to have? Why?
> If you could buy only one toy, which toy would you buy? Why?

Option: Have students conduct a class survey using any or all of the questions above and then tabulate the results.

11 Invent a Toy!

ACTIVITY HANDBOOK PAGE 9

Have students invent a new toy and then present their ideas to the class.

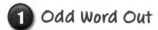

1 Odd Word Out

Read the following lists of words, and have students identify the category and the "odd word out"—the word that doesn't fit the category:

wagon, skateboard, bicycle, disk drive, tricycle
[Category: TOYS WITH WHEELS. Odd word out: disk drive]

computer game, educational software, battery, spreadsheet program, word-processing program
[Category: SOFTWARE. Odd word out: battery]

lens, flash, camera case, hula hoop, film
[Category: CAMERA EQUIPMENT. Odd word out: hula hoop]

keyboard, pager, track ball, mouse, joystick
[Category: COMPUTER EQUIPMENT. Odd word out: pager]

speakers, camcorder, digital camera, scanner, video camera
[Category: EQUIPMENT THAT RECORDS IMAGES. Odd word out: speakers]

boombox, personal cassette player, escalator, hand-held video game, cell phone
[Category: PORTABLE EQUIPMENT. Odd word out: escalator]

return, buy, try on, pay for, calculator
[Category: SHOPPING ACTIONS. Odd word out: calculator]

plasma, headphones, portable, LCD, projection
[Category: TYPES OF TV SCREENS. Odd word out: headphones]

slide projector, tape deck, sound system, radio, turntable
[Category: EQUIPMENT TO LISTEN TO MUSIC. Odd word out: slide projector]

CD-ROM, floppy disk, elevator, film, record
[Category: THINGS THAT HOLD SOUND AND INFORMATION. Odd word out: elevator]

2 Finish the Sentence!
ACTIVITY HANDBOOK PAGE 7

Begin sentences such as the following for students to complete:

A store directory helps customers . . .
A shortwave radio receives many . . .
A tuner is something you use to . . .
A flash attachment is something that . . .
A tripod is something that . . .
An answering machine is something that . . .
A surge protector is something that . . .

You use a modem to . . .
You use a fax machine to . . .
Care instructions tell you how . . .

3 Category Dictation
ACTIVITY HANDBOOK PAGE 2

Dictate words from *Picture Dictionary* pages 74–79 that fit any three of the following categories:

video equipment
audio equipment
telephone equipment
camera equipment
equipment for watching a movie
outdoor toys
toys for young children
departments in a department store
information on a receipt

4 Drawing Game
ACTIVITY HANDBOOK PAGE 6
ACTIVITY MASTERS 101, 103, 107

Have teams compete to identify vocabulary items drawn by one of their team members.

5 Letter Game
ACTIVITY HANDBOOK PAGE 9

Say statements such as the following and have teams compete to identify the items:

I'm thinking of computer equipment that starts with *c*.	[cable]
I'm thinking of a department in a store that starts with *h*.	[housewares]
I'm thinking of audio equipment that starts with *t*.	[turntable]
I'm thinking of a TV that starts with *l*.	[LCD TV]
I'm thinking of kind of lens that starts with *z*.	[zoom lens]
I'm thinking of a kind of computer that starts with *d*.	[desktop]
I'm thinking of a kind of software that starts with *w*.	[word-processing]
I'm thinking of a toy that starts with *j*.	[jigsaw puzzle]
I'm thinking of a kind of radio that starts with *c*.	[clock radio]

(continued)

6 Ask Me a Question!

ACTIVITY HANDBOOK PAGE 2
ACTIVITY MASTERS 101, 103, 107

Have students walk around trying to guess each other's items by asking yes/no questions. For example:

Do you plug it in?
Do you use it with a computer?
Do you use it in a sound system?
Is it video equipment?

7 Guess the Object!

ACTIVITY HANDBOOK PAGES 7–8

Tell what different things are used for and have students guess the item. For example:

You use it to take pictures and keep them in a computer.	[A digital camera.]
You use it to see where each department in the store is.	[The store directory.]
You use it when you're shopping and you're thirsty.	[A water fountain.]
You use it when you return an item to a store.	[A receipt.]
You use it to listen to records.	[A turntable.]
You use them to listen to music without bothering the people around you.	[Headphones.]
You use it to hold up a camera.	[A tripod.]
You use it to collect messages when you aren't home.	[An answering machine.]
You use it when you're taking a picture, and you want to focus on something far away.	[A zoom lens.]

8 What Equipment Should I Use?

Tell things you need to do and ask students what equipment you should use. For example:

I want to take pictures at my sister's wedding. What equipment should I use?

I have to send this application to the office immediately. What equipment should I use?

I'm traveling, and I need to call my family. What equipment should I use?

I want to listen to this new CD. What equipment should I use?

I want to watch this new video. What equipment should I use?

I want to watch this new DVD. What equipment should I use?

I want to see these slides. What equipment should I use?

I want to listen to the world news. What equipment should I use?

I want to talk on the phone while I move around my house. What equipment should I use?

I want to go up to the fourth floor, but I can't walk up stairs. What equipment should I use?

I need to recharge these batteries. What equipment should I use?

UNIT 10 Community Services

TOPICS	DICTIONARY	TEACHER'S GUIDE
The Bank	80	204–206
Finances	81	207–208
The Post Office	82	209–210
The Library	83	211–213
Community Institutions	84	214–216
Crime and Emergencies	85	217–218
Unit 10 Communication Activity Review	80–85	219–220

AUDIO PROGRAM

Words & Dialogs
Audio Cassette 3B
Audio CD 3:
  Tracks 57, 58
Audio CD 4:
  Tracks 2–12

WordSong: *Bills to Pay*
Audio Cassette 7B
Audio CD 8: Tracks 6
  (Vocal) & 7 (Sing-along)
Song Masters S19, S20

WORKBOOKS

For Multi-Level Practice
Literacy Workbook
Beginning Lifeskills Workbook
Beginning Vocabulary Workbook
Intermediate Lifeskills Workbook
Intermediate Vocabulary Workbook

WORDLINKS

Internet Resources through the
***Word by Word* Companion Website**
http://www.longman.com/wordbyword

ACTIVITY MASTERS

Reproducibles for Communication Activities
A8, A109–A114

TRANSPARENCIES

Full-Color Overheads for Class Practice
T80–T85

LANGUAGE & CULTURE NOTES

Information for Teachers &
Intermediate /Advanced Students
LC80–LC85

LESSON OBJECTIVE

Students will learn the titles of bank personnel and the names for common banking activities and transactions.

RESOURCES

AUDIO PROGRAM
Words & Dialogs
Cassette 3B
CD 3: Tracks 57, 58

MULTI-LEVEL WORKBOOKS
Literacy Workbook
Beginning & Intermediate Lifeskills Workbooks
Beginning & Intermediate Vocabulary Workbooks

ACTIVITY MASTER
Reproducible:
A109

TRANSPARENCY
Overhead: T80

LANGUAGE & CULTURE NOTES
Reproducible: LC80

WORDLINKS
longman.com/wordbyword

VOCABULARY INTRODUCTION

- Preview
- Present
- Practice

MODEL CONVERSATION PRACTICE

There are three model conversations—the first for words A–G, the second for words 5–7, and the third for words 8–13. Introduce and practice the first model before going on to the second and third. For each model:

1. Have students look at the model illustration. Set the scene:

    Model 1: "A wife and husband are talking."
    Model 2: "A husband and wife are talking."
    Model 3: "Two bank robbers are planning to rob the State Street Bank."

2. Present the first model with word A, the second model with word 5, and the third model with word 8.

3. Choral Repetition Practice: Full-Class and Individual.

4. Have pairs practice the model.

5. Have pairs present the model.

6. Call on pairs to present a new conversation using word B for the first model, word 6 for the second model, and word 9 for the third model.

7. Have pairs practice new conversations.

8. Have pairs present new conversations.

SPELLING PRACTICE

Say a word or phrase, and have students spell it aloud or write it. Or, using the transparency, point to an item and have students write the word or phrase.

WRITING AND DISCUSSION

Have students respond to the questions as a class, in pairs, or in small groups. Or have students write their responses, share their writing with other students, and discuss in class.

Making Connections

Resource Materials Bring in, or have students bring in, the following materials for vocabulary practice:

- *Bank brochures:* Talk about services and products the banks offer.

- *The banking items themselves:* Have students identify the different items.

Community Task Have individual students (or groups of students) visit different banks and investigate the various kinds of accounts offered by the banks. Have students report back to the class.

Communication Activities

1 What's the Question?
ACTIVITY HANDBOOK PAGE 16

Describe various banking items and have students respond by asking: "What's a _____?" or "What are _____s?" For example:

Teacher: You use this when you don't want to pay for the purchase immediately.
Student: What's a credit card?

Teacher: It's a good idea to take this with you when you go on a trip.
Student: What are traveler's checks?

Teacher: You use this when you put money in your account.
Student: What's a deposit slip?

Teacher: This is the person you speak to when you want to deposit or withdraw money from your account.
Student: What's a teller?

Teacher: This is the person who makes sure everyone in the bank is safe.
Student: What's a security guard?

Teacher: This is the person you speak to when you apply for a loan.
Student: What's a bank officer?

Teacher: You use this when you want to keep something valuable in a safe place.
Student: What's a safe deposit box?

Teacher: This is where people keep money, important documents, and valuable possessions.
Student: What's a bank vault?

Teacher: You use this when you have a savings account.
Student: What's a passbook?

2 What's the Object?
ACTIVITY HANDBOOK PAGE 16

Call out verbs and have students add appropriate objects. For example:

make . . . a deposit/a withdrawal
cash . . . a check/a traveler's check
get . . . traveler's checks/cash/a safe deposit box

3 Chain Story
ACTIVITY HANDBOOK PAGE 3

Begin the story as follows: "Yesterday I went to the bank. First, I opened an account."

4 True or False Definitions
ACTIVITY HANDBOOK PAGE 15

Give true and false definitions of banks words and have students decide which are true and which are false. For example:

You fill out a deposit slip when you take money out of your account. [False. You fill out a deposit slip when you put money *into* your account.]

You fill out a withdrawal slip when you take money out of your account. [True.]

You can replace traveler's checks if you lose them. [True.]

A teller is the person who helps you open an account. [False. A teller is the person who handles the money transactions.]

An ATM machine is open twelve hours a day. [False. An ATM machine is open 24 hours a day.]

A safe deposit box is a good place to keep very valuable items such as jewelry. [True.]

You use a passbook for a checking account. [False. You use a passbook for a savings account.]

A bank officer is the person who helps you apply for a loan. [True.]

To change dollars for yen is to exchange currency. [True.]

5 Same and Different
ACTIVITY HANDBOOK PAGE 13

Write pairs of bank words on the board and have students think of similarities and differences between the pairs. For example:

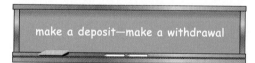
make a deposit—make a withdrawal

Both are transactions.
Both involve a teller or an ATM machine.

To make a deposit is to put money in an account.
To make a withdrawal is to take money out of an account.

open an account—apply for a loan

Both require identification and documentation.
Both involve a bank officer.

To open an account is easy to do.
To apply for a loan is more difficult.

(continued)

Other pairs of word to compare:

check—traveler's check
ATM card—credit card
teller—bank officer
bank vault—safe deposit box

6 Let's Bank On It!

Bring to class examples of blank checks, deposit slips, and withdrawal slips. Have students practice filling them out.

7 What Can You Do in a Bank?

ACTIVITY HANDBOOK PAGES 15–16

Have pairs or groups of students make a list of all the things you can do at a bank. For example:

cash a check
get traveler's checks
apply for a loan
make a deposit
use an ATM card
put things in a safe deposit box
exchange currency

8 Banking Match Game

ACTIVITY HANDBOOK PAGE 11
ACTIVITY MASTER 109

Have students find the person whose card matches theirs.

9 A Trip to the Bank

Have students go to a bank and copy down all the printed words and phrases they see around the bank. Have a class discussion about the words students report back. Examples they might find:

Customer Service
Equal Opportunity Lender
Loan and Credit Rates
Mortgages
Interest Rates
Safe Deposit
Teller Services
Member FDIC (Federal Deposit Insurance Corporation)

10 Class Discussion: Comparing Banking Services

Bring to class bank advertisements from newspapers. As a class, in pairs, or in small groups, compare the services offered by different banks.

Page 81 FINANCES

LESSON OBJECTIVE

Students will learn forms of payments, types of household bills, and vocabulary for managing finances and using an ATM.

RESOURCES

AUDIO PROGRAM		MULTI-LEVEL WORKBOOKS	ACTIVITY MASTER
Words & Dialogs Cassette 3B CD 4: Tracks 2, 3	**WordSong:** *Bills to Pay* Cassette 7B • CD 8: Tracks 6, 7 Song Masters S19, S20	Literacy Workbook Beginning & Intermediate Lifeskills Workbooks Beginning & Intermediate Vocabulary Workbooks	**Reproducible:** A110

TRANSPARENCY	LANGUAGE & CULTURE NOTES	WORDLINKS
Overhead: T81	**Reproducible:** LC81	longman.com/wordbyword

VOCABULARY INTRODUCTION

- Preview
- Present
- Practice

MODEL CONVERSATION PRACTICE

There are three model conversations—the first for words 1–5, the second for words 6–21, and the third for words 22–29. Introduce and practice the first model before going on to the second and third. For each model:

1. Have students look at the model illustration. Set the scene:

   Model 1: "A customer is talking to a salesperson in a store."
   Model 2: "A husband and wife are talking."
   Model 3: "A man is asking his grandson how to use an ATM machine."

2. Present the first model with word 1, the second model with word 6, and the third model with phrase 22.

3. Choral Repetition Practice: Full-Class and Individual.

4. Have pairs practice the model.

5. Have pairs present the model.

6. Call on pairs to present a new conversation using word 3 for the first model, phrase 16 for the second model, and phrase 23 for the third model.

7. Have pairs practice new conversations.

8. Have pairs present new conversations.

SPELLING PRACTICE

Say a word or phrase, and have students spell it aloud or write it. Or, using the transparency, point to an item and have students write the word or phrase.

WRITING AND DISCUSSION

Have students respond to the questions as a class, in pairs, or in small groups. Or have students write their responses, share their writing with other students, and discuss in class.

♪♫ WordSong ♪♫

1. Have students listen to the vocal version of *Bills to Pay* one or more times. Then have students listen again as they read the song lyrics on Song Master S19.

2. Have students sing as you play either the vocal or the sing-along version of the song.

3. For fun, have a song competition in which students perform solo or in groups and the class votes for the best performance.

4. For additional practice, students can complete the cloze exercise on Song Master S20.

PICTURE DICTIONARY PAGE 81   **207**

Resource Materials Bring in, or have students bring in, the following materials for vocabulary practice:

○ *Household bills:* Blank out the personal information on several bills and show to the class. Discuss which utility companies students in the class use.

○ *The forms of payment themselves:* Have students identify cash, a check, a credit card, a checkbook, a money order, and a traveler's check.

Community Task Have individual students (or groups of students) visit different banks and investigate the services offered by the banks. Have students report back to the class and identify which bank offers the most services.

Communication Activities

1 Chain Story
ACTIVITY HANDBOOK PAGE 3

Begin the story as follows: "Yesterday I paid the bills. First I paid the water bill."

2 Ranking
ACTIVITY HANDBOOK PAGE 13

Have students look at the Household Bills on *Picture Dictionary* page 81 and rank them from the most to the least expensive (on a monthly basis).

Then have students look at the Forms of Payment on *Picture Dictionary* page 81 and rank them from the most to the least frequently used.

3 Line Up!
ACTIVITY MASTER 110

a. Copy Activity Master 118, cut it up, and distribute it to seven students

b. Have students memorize their lines and then work together to arrange themselves in a line from the first step to the last.

Variation: Students can work in pairs to read and arrange the cards on a table top.

4 Debate

Have students in pairs, small groups, or as a class debate any of the following statements:

> You should never use a credit card.
> It's less expensive to use money orders than checks.
> You should never carry more than $10 in cash.
> Rent is usually less expensive than a mortgage payment.
> You shouldn't use the Internet to do any financial transactions.
> Traveler's checks are the best way to travel with money.

5 Careful Reading

Bring utility bills to class. Blank out any personal information and make photocopies to distribute to students. Have students answer the following questions:

> What are the dates of service?
> How much is the bill?
> Is there a minimum payment?
> When is the due date?
> Where do you send the bill?
> What number can you call if you have any questions?

LESSON OBJECTIVE

Students will learn the names of the mail products sold and the titles of personnel at a United States post office.

RESOURCES

AUDIO PROGRAM

Words & Dialogs
Cassette 3B
CD 4: Tracks 4, 5

MULTI-LEVEL WORKBOOKS
Literacy Workbook
Beginning & Intermediate Lifeskills Workbooks
Beginning & Intermediate Vocabulary Workbooks

ACTIVITY MASTERS
Reproducibles:
A8, A111

TRANSPARENCY
Overhead: T82

LANGUAGE & CULTURE NOTES
Reproducible: LC82

WORDLINKS
longman.com/wordbyword

VOCABULARY INTRODUCTION

- Preview
- Present
- Practice

MODEL CONVERSATION PRACTICE

There are four model conversations—the first for words 1–4, the second for words 5–9, the third for words 10–17, and the fourth for words 19–22. Introduce and practice the first model before going on to the next. For each model:

1. Have students look at the model illustration. Set the scene:

   Model 1: "Two roommates are talking."
   Model 2: "A clerk and customer are talking at the post office."
   Model 3: "A clerk and customer are talking at the post office."
   Model 4: "Two roommates are talking."

2. Present the first model with word 1, the second model with word 5, the third model with word 10, and the fourth model with word 19.

3. Choral Repetition Practice: Full-Class and Individual.

4. Have pairs practice the model.

5. Have pairs present the model.

6. Call on pairs to present a new conversation using word 2 for the first model, word 6 for the second model, word 11 for the third model, and word 20 for the fourth model.

7. Have pairs practice new conversations.

8. Have pairs present new conversations.

SPELLING PRACTICE

Say a word, and have students spell it aloud or write it. Or, using the transparency, point to an item and have students write the word.

WRITING AND DISCUSSION

Have students respond to the questions as a class, in pairs, or in small groups. Or have students write their responses, share their writing with other students, and discuss in class.

Making Connections

Resource Materials Bring in, or have students bring in, the following materials for vocabulary practice:

- *Various envelopes that have been addressed:* Show the envelopes to the class and ask student comprehension questions—for example, What is the person's last name? What state does the person live in?, etc.

- *Post office brochure describing post office services* (can be downloaded from the USPS website): Talk about the different services and products offered.

- *The post office items themselves:* Have students identify the different forms, types of mail, and other post office items.

Community Task Have individual students (or groups of students) visit a post office in the area and report about the quality of service and the products offered. Also, have them make a list of all the signs they see in the post office and on the mailboxes.

Communication Activities

1 Send Me a Letter!

Give each student a piece of paper the size of an envelope. Dictate the information that goes on an envelope and have students write the information in the appropriate place on the *envelope*.

2 How Much Does It Cost?

As a class, in pairs, or in small groups, have students tell how much it costs and how long it takes to send letters and packages to places where they commonly send things.

3 Post Office Associations

ACTIVITY HANDBOOK PAGE 2

Call out post office words and have groups write down as many associations as they can think of.
For example:

stamp:	[put on/lick]
envelope:	[lick/seal/open/address]
package:	[wrap/tape/address/deliver]
letter:	[mail/send/receive/open/ address/register/deliver]
money order:	[purchase/sign]
scale:	[weigh/letter/send]
change-of-address form:	[fill out/sign/move]

4 What Can You Do?

ACTIVITY HANDBOOK PAGES 15–16

Have students make a list of all the things they do in a post office. For example:

mail a letter
send a package
buy stamps
fill out a change-of-address form
send a registered letter
register for the selective service

5 Post Office Match Game

ACTIVITY HANDBOOK PAGE 11
ACTIVITY MASTER 111

Have students find the person whose card matches theirs.

6 Post Office Chain Game

ACTIVITY HANDBOOK PAGES 2–3

Begin the chain as follows: "I went to the post office and sent a letter first class," and have students continue it. For example:

> Teacher: I went to the post office and sent a letter first class."

> Student 1: I went to the post office, sent a letter first class, and bought a book of stamps.
> Student 2: I went to the post office, sent a letter first class, bought a book of stamps, and got a money order.

> Etc.

7 Tic Tac Definitions

ACTIVITY HANDBOOK PAGE 15
ACTIVITY MASTER 8

Have students fill in the tic tac grid with any nine post office words they wish. Give definitions such as the following, and have students cross out on their grids the words you have defined:

a letter that folds itself into an envelope [air letter]
mail that's guaranteed to arrive the next day [express mail]
mail that moves more slowly, but is less expensive to send [parcel post]
a set of twenty stamps sold in a small package [book of stamps]
the 5-9 digit number that identifies the location of an address [zip code]
a machine that measures weight [scale]
the person who delivers the mail to businesses and homes [mail carrier]
mail delivery that provides proof the mail has been delivered [certified mail]
words printed across the postage that indicate the date and location of the post office of origin [postmark]

8 Linking Words

ACTIVITY HANDBOOK PAGE 10

Begin the linking activity by writing the word *letter* in the upper left corner of the board. Students use that as the starting point for *linking* other post office words. For example:

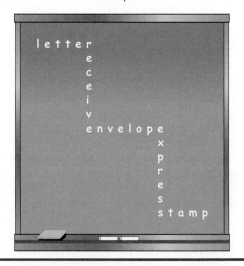

LESSON OBJECTIVE

Students will learn about the sections of a library, names of various materials held by libraries, and the titles of library personnel.

RESOURCES

AUDIO PROGRAM

Words & Dialogs
Cassette 3B
CD 4: Tracks 6–8

MULTI-LEVEL WORKBOOKS

Literacy Workbook
Beginning & Intermediate Lifeskills Workbooks
Beginning & Intermediate Vocabulary Workbooks

ACTIVITY MASTER

Reproducible:
A8

TRANSPARENCY
Overhead: T83

LANGUAGE & CULTURE NOTES
Reproducible: LC83

WORDLINKS
longman.com/wordbyword

VOCABULARY INTRODUCTION

- Preview
- Present
- Practice

MODEL CONVERSATION PRACTICE

There are two model conversations—the first for words 1, 2, and 6–32 and the second for words 8–23 and 26–28. Introduce and practice the first model before going on to the second. For each model:

1. Have students look at the model illustration. Set the scene:

    Model 1: "Someone is asking the library clerk for information."
    Model 2: "Someone is asking the library clerk for information."

2. Present the first model with words 1 and 2, and the second model with words 26 and 23.

3. Choral Repetition Practice: Full-Class and Individual.

4. Have pairs practice the model.

5. Have pairs present the model.

6. Call on pairs to present a new conversation using words 6 and 7 for the first model and words 9 and 8 for the second model.

7. Have pairs practice new conversations.

8. Have pairs present new conversations.

ADDITIONAL CONVERSATION PRACTICE

Before students practice the additional conversations, you may want to have them listen to the examples on the Audio Program.

Conversation 1 Set the scene: "Someone is talking to a library clerk." Have students practice and present conversations with any words they wish.

Conversation 2 Set the scene: "Someone is talking to a library clerk." Have students practice and present conversations with any words they wish.

SPELLING PRACTICE

Say a word, and have students spell it aloud or write it. Or, using the transparency, point to an item and have students write the word.

WRITING AND DISCUSSION

Have students respond to the questions as a class, in pairs, or in small groups. Or have students write their responses, share their writing with other students, and discuss in class.

7 Cooperative Definitions

ACTIVITY HANDBOOK PAGE 4

Have groups write definitions of community institution words and then pass their definitions to other groups.

8 Who Am I?

ACTIVITY HANDBOOK PAGE 17

Tell about different community institution occupations and have students guess who you are talking about. For example:

Teacher: I work in an ambulance. I try to save lives. I take care people in medical emergencies. Who am I?
Student: An EMT.

Teacher: I organize activities for young people at the recreation center. Who am I?
Student: An activities director.

Teacher: I collect garbage. Who am I?
Student: A sanitation worker.

Teacher: I take care of children in a child-care center. Who am I?
Student: A child-care worker.

Teacher: I run the city. Who am I?
Student: The mayor.

Teacher: I take care of senior citizens. Who am I?
Student: A senior care worker.

Teacher: I make sure a neighborhood is safe. I respond to emergencies and arrest people who break the law. Who am I?
Student: A police officer.

Teacher: I put out fires. Who am I?
Student: A firefighter.

9 Ask Me a Question!

ACTIVITY HANDBOOK PAGE 2
ACTIVITY MASTER 112

Have students walk around trying to guess each other's community institution words by asking yes/no questions. For example:

Is it a place in the community?	[No.]
Is it a person who works in the community?	[Yes.]
Does the person work in emergencies?	[Yes.]
Does the person have medical knowledge?	[No.]
Is the person a police officer?	[Yes.]

Is it an emergency vehicle?	[No.]
Is it a person who works in the community?	[No.]
Is it a place in the community?	[Yes.]
Is it a place of worship?	[No.]
Is it a center?	[No.]
Is it a place for emergencies?	[Yes.]
Is it a hospital?	[Yes.]

10 Word Clues

ACTIVITY HANDBOOK PAGE 17
ACTIVITY MASTER 112

Have students take turns giving one-word clues to team members who try to guess the word. For example:

The word is *gym*.

Team 1 Player:	"basketball"	[Team 1 guesses]
Team 2 Player:	"handball"	[Team 2 guesses]
Team 1 Player:	"indoor"	[Team 1 guesses]

The word is *nursery*.

Team 1 Player:	"babies"	[Team 1 guesses]
Team 2 Player:	"cribs"	[Team 2 guesses]
Team 1 Player:	"blankets"	[Team 1 guesses]

11 Community Institutions Match Game

ACTIVITY HANDBOOK PAGE 11
ACTIVITY MASTER 113

Have students find the person whose card matches theirs.

12 Community Investigations

a. Divide the class into pairs or small groups. Have each group choose one community institution to investigate. Have them find out the following information:

Where it is located?
Is there more than one? Name all the addresses.
What hours is it open?
What services does it provide?

b. Have students report their information to the class.

Expansion: Students can compile their information and publish a community services guide for the school.

LESSON OBJECTIVE

Students will learn the names of emergencies and crimes and how to report these to emergency response workers.

RESOURCES

AUDIO PROGRAM

Words & Dialogs
Cassette 3B
CD 4: Tracks 11, 12

MULTI-LEVEL WORKBOOKS

Literacy Workbook
Beginning & Intermediate Lifeskills Workbooks
Beginning & Intermediate Vocabulary Workbooks

TRANSPARENCY
Overhead: T85

LANGUAGE & CULTURE NOTES
Reproducible: LC85

WORDLINKS
longman.com/wordbyword

VOCABULARY INTRODUCTION

- Preview
- Present
- Practice

MODEL CONVERSATION PRACTICE

There are three model conversations—the first for words 1–13, the second for words 14–18, and the third for words 19–22. Introduce and practice the first model before going to the second and third. For each model:

1. Have students look at the model illustration. Set the scene:

    Model 1: "Someone is calling to report an emergency."
    Model 2: "A driver is talking to a police officer."
    Model 3: "Two people are speaking at a town meeting."

2. Present the first model with word 1, the second model with word 14, and the third model with word 19.

3. Choral Repetition Practice: Full-Class and Individual.

4. Have pairs practice the model.

5. Have pairs present the model.

6. Call on pairs to present a new conversation using word 2 for the first model, word 15 for the second model, and word 20 for the third model.

7. Have pairs practice new conversations.

8. Have pairs present new conversations.

SPELLING PRACTICE

Say a word, and have students spell it aloud or write it. Or, using the transparency, point to an item and have students write the word.

WRITING AND DISCUSSION

Have students respond to the questions as a class, in pairs, or in small groups. Or have students write their responses, share their writing with other students, and discuss in class.

Making Connections

Resource Materials Bring in, or have students bring in, the following materials for vocabulary practice:

● *Crime log from a local newspaper:* Have students identify the types of crimes that occur in their neighborhoods.

Community Task Have a police officer visit the school to explain what to do in an emergency. It would be helpful if the officer also addressed concerns immigrants have about reporting crimes.

1 Associations

ACTIVITY HANDBOOK PAGE 2

Call out crime and emergency words and have groups write down as many associations as they can think of. For example:

blackout: [darkness/flashlights/fear/quiet/candles]
fire: [911/firefighters/smoke/ambulances]
drug dealing: [dealers/crime/money/jail]
chemical spill: [oil/explosions/trucks]
gas leak: [smell/explosion/danger]

2 Cooperative Definitions

ACTIVITY HANDBOOK PAGE 4

Have groups write definitions of crimes and emergencies and then pass their definitions to other groups.

3 Tell a Story!

a. Divide the class into small groups.

b. Have each group write a description of one of the scenes depicted on *Picture Dictionary* page 85. They should tell who the people are and what they're doing.

c. Have each group read their description to the class and see if the class can identify the scene.

4 Class Discussion: Emergencies

In small groups, have students discuss the following questions:

Have you ever been in one of the emergencies on *Picture Dictionary* page 85?
What happened? How did you feel? What did you do?

5 Class Discussion: Crimes

Have students discuss the following questions:

Have you ever seen one of the crimes on *Picture Dictionary* page 85? What happened? What did you do?
What crimes occur in your community?
Do you worry about crime? What kind of crime worries you the most?
How can people help prevent crime?

6 Investigation: Emergency Response

a. Write on the board:

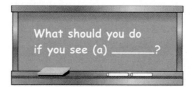

What should you do if you see (a) _____?

b. Have pairs of students choose one situation from *Picture Dictionary* page 85 and investigate the answer. Students can contact their local police station and ask questions or they can do an Internet search.

c. Have students report their answers back to the class.

7 Class Discussion: Preventive Measures

As a class, have students discuss the following questions:

What kinds of crimes and emergencies on *Picture Dictionary* page 85 can you help to prevent? How can you help prevent them?
Which ones can you *not* prevent? Why not?

Unit 10 Communication Activity Review

1 Odd Word Out

Read the following lists of words, and have students identify the category and the "odd word out"—the word that doesn't fit the category:

church, recreation center, synagogue, mosque, temple
[Category: PLACES OF WORSHIP. Odd word out: recreation center]

EMT, reference librarian, police officer, firefighter
[Category: EMERGENCY RESPONSE PEOPLE. Odd word out: reference librarian]

shelves, newspapers, magazines, journals
[Category: PERIODICALS. Odd word out: shelves]

atlas, dictionary, encyclopedia, foreign language books
[Category: REFERENCE BOOKS. Odd word out: foreign language books]

burglary, murder, assault, kidnapping, dump
[Category: CRIMES. Odd word out: dump]

cash, letter, check, credit card, money order
[Category: FORMS OF PAYMENT. Odd word out: letter]

mailbox, return address, zip code, stamp, postmark
[Category: THINGS ON AN ENVELOPE. Odd word out: mailbox]

postal clerk, mail carrier, postal worker, parcel post
[Category: POST OFFICE EMPLOYEES. Odd word out: parcel post]

police car, fire engine, gas leak, ambulance
[Category: EMERGENCY VEHICLES. Odd word out: gas leak]

make a deposit, make a withdrawal, balance the checkbook, apply for a loan, open an account
[Category: THINGS TO DO IN A BANK. Odd word out: balance your checkbook]

2 Finish the Sentence!
ACTIVITY HANDBOOK PAGE 7

Begin sentences such as the following for students to complete:

A bank keeps all its money is in the . . . *bank vault*.
The bank employee who handles money transactions is a . . . *teller*.
To mail a letter, you need a . . . *stamp*.
When I travel, I don't use cash. I use . . . *traveler's checks*.
Every time I write a check, I record the transaction in my . . . *check register*.
I don't have a checking account, so I pay my bills with . . . *money orders*.
I borrowed money when I bought my house. Every month I have to make a . . . *mortgage payment*.
When a boy turns 18 years old in the United States, he must fill out a . . . *selective service registration form*.
When I want a letter to arrive somewhere the next day, I send it . . . *express mail*.
A place of worship for Muslims is a . . . *mosque*.
A place that has activities for elderly people is a . . . *senior center*.
When a person kills another person on purpose, it is called . . . *murder*.

3 Who Am I?
ACTIVITY HANDBOOK PAGE 17

Tell about different occupations and have students guess who you are talking about. For example:

Teacher: I help people find books or information in the library. Who am I?
Student: A librarian.

Teacher: I work in an ambulance. I take care of people in medical emergencies. Who am I?
Student: An EMT.

Teacher: I check out books for people in the library. Who am I?
Student: A library clerk.

(continued)

Teacher: I work in a post office. Who am I?
Student: A postal worker.

Teacher: I organize activities for children at the recreation center. Who am I?
Student: An activities director.

Teacher: I answer the phone when a person calls 911. Who am I?
Student: An emergency operator.

Teacher: I deliver mail to people's homes. Who am I?
Student: A mail carrier.

Teacher: I collect garbage. Who am I?
Student: A sanitation worker.

Teacher: I take care of children in a child-care center. Who am I?
Student: A child-care worker.

Teacher: I deposit money, cash checks, and make withdrawals for bank customers. Who am I?
Student: A teller.

Teacher: I run the city. Who am I?
Student: The mayor.

Teacher: I take care of senior citizens. Who am I?
Student: A senior care worker.

Teacher: I answer customers' questions, I help customers open new bank accounts, and I help customers complete loan applications. Who am I?
Student: A bank officer.

Teacher: I make sure a neighborhood is safe. I respond to emergencies and arrest people who break the law. Who am I?
Student: A police officer.

Teacher: I put out fires. Who am I?
Student: A firefighter.

4 Community Institution Quiz Game
ACTIVITY MASTER 114

a. Divide the class into four teams.

b. Copy and cut up Activity Master 122 into separate cards and place the cards face-down in a pile.

c. Have teams take turns answering your questions. Give each team a time limit to answer each question (30 seconds or 1 minute).

d. The team with the most correct answers wins.

TOPICS	DICTIONARY	TEACHER'S GUIDE
The Body	86–87	222–224
Ailments, Symptoms, and Injuries	88–89	225–226
First Aid	90	227–228
Medical Emergencies and Illnesses	91	229–230
The Medical Exam	92	231–232
Medical and Dental Procedures	93	233–234
Medical Advice	94	235–236
Medicine	95	237–239
Medical Specialists	96	240–242
The Hospital	97	243–245
Personal Hygiene	98–99	246–248
Baby Care	100	249–250
Unit 11 Communication Activity Review	86–100	251–252

AUDIO PROGRAM

Words & Dialogs	WordSong: *Power Up*
Audio Cassette 3B	Audio Cassette 7B
Audio Cassette 4A	Audio CD 8: Tracks 8
Audio CD 4:	(Vocal) & 9 (Sing-along)
Tracks 13–40	Song Masters S21, S22

WORKBOOKS

For Multi-Level Practice

Literacy Workbook
Beginning Lifeskills Workbook
Beginning Vocabulary Workbook
Intermediate Lifeskills Workbook
Intermediate Vocabulary Workbook

WORDLINKS

Internet Resources through the
***Word by Word* Companion Website**

http://www.longman.com/wordbyword

ACTIVITY MASTERS

Reproducibles for Communication Activities
A8, A115–A135

TRANSPARENCIES

Full-Color Overheads for Class Practice
T86–T100

LANGUAGE & CULTURE NOTES

Information for Teachers &
Intermediate /Advanced Students
LC86–87—LC100

LESSON OBJECTIVE

Students will learn the names of the external parts of the body and internal organs and bones of the body.

RESOURCES

AUDIO PROGRAM

Words & Dialogs
Cassette 3B
CD 4: Tracks 13–15

MULTI-LEVEL WORKBOOKS

Literacy Workbook
Beginning & Intermediate Lifeskills Workbooks
Beginning & Intermediate Vocabulary Workbooks

ACTIVITY MASTERS

Reproducibles:
A115, A116

TRANSPARENCIES

Overheads: T86, T87

LANGUAGE & CULTURE NOTES

Reproducible: LC86–87

WORDLINKS

longman.com/wordbyword

VOCABULARY INTRODUCTION

- Preview
- Present
- Practice

MODEL CONVERSATION PRACTICE

1. Have students look at the model illustration. Set the scene: "A patient in a hospital is talking to a friend who came to see him."
2. Present the model.
3. Choral Repetition Practice: Full-Class and Individual.
4. Have pairs practice the model.
5. Have pairs present the model.
6. Call on pairs to present a new conversation using word 3.
7. Have pairs practice new conversations.
8. Have pairs present new conversations.

ADDITIONAL CONVERSATION PRACTICE

Before students practice the additional conversations, you may want to have them listen to the examples on the Audio Program.

Conversation 1 Have students practice and present conversations with the suggested words.

Conversation 2 Have students practice and present conversations with the suggested words.

SPELLING PRACTICE

Say a word, and have students spell it aloud or write it. Or, using the transparency, point to an item and have students write the word.

WRITING AND DISCUSSION

Have students respond to the questions as a class, in pairs, or in small groups. Or have students write their responses, share their writing with other students, and discuss in class.

Making Connections

Resource Materials Bring in, or have students bring in, the following materials for vocabulary practice:

- *Magazine pictures:* Have students identify external body parts.
- *Physiology textbooks:* Have students identify internal body parts.
- *Brochures and pamphlets from doctors' offices:* Have students identify the body parts depicted in the illustrations.

Communication Activities

1 Body Parts

Bring to class a selection of pictures that you have cut so that only a small section of a particular body part is visible. Have students guess what the body part is. For example: a toe, a shoulder, an elbow, a lip, a shin.

2 Chain Game
ACTIVITY HANDBOOK PAGES 2–3

Begin the chain as follows: "The head is connected to the neck," and have students continue it. For example:

> Teacher: The head is connected to the neck . . .
> Student 1: and the neck is connected to the shoulders . . .
> Student 2: and the shoulders are connected to the back . . .
> Etc.

Note: Play the game several times starting from different parts of the body.

3 Clap in Rhythm
ACTIVITY HANDBOOK PAGE 3

Have students name different body parts to a clapping rhythm.

4 Linking Words
ACTIVITY HANDBOOK PAGE 10

Begin the linking activity by writing the word *thigh* in the upper left corner of the board. Students use that as the starting point for *linking* other body words. For example:

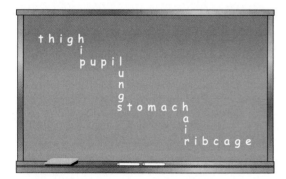

5 Draw and Label
ACTIVITY HANDBOOK PAGE 5

Have students draw a picture of a person and label the external body parts.

6 Simon Says

This game consists of a series of rapid commands, which students follow only when the command is preceded by the words *Simon says*. If the student follows the command when the words *Simon says* are not spoken, that student must sit down. The last student to remain standing wins the game.

a. Have all the students stand up.

b. Say, "Simon says touch your head." (The students touch their heads.)

c. Say, "Simon says touch your knee." (The students touch their knees.)

d. Say, "Touch your elbow." (Any student who touches his or her elbow must sit down and not continue to play.)

Note: The commands should be said quickly to allow as little time as possible to think about *Simon says*.

Variation: Have different students take turns leading the game.

7 Ask Me a Question!
ACTIVITY HANDBOOK PAGE 2
ACTIVITY MASTERS 115, 116

Have students walk around trying to guess each other's body items by asking yes/no questions. For example:

Is it part of your leg?	[No.]
Is it part of your hand?	[No.]
Is it part of your head?	[Yes.]
Is it your nose?	[No.]
Is it smaller than your nose?	[No.]
Is it your ear?	[Yes.]
Is it part of your leg?	[Yes.]
Does it bend?	[Yes.]
Is it your knee?	[Yes.]

(continued)

8 Movable Categories

ACTIVITY HANDBOOK PAGE 11
ACTIVITY MASTERS 115, 116

Call out the following categories and have students
go to the appropriate side of the room:

parts of the arm
parts of the leg
parts of the face
things that come in *twos* (arms, legs, eyes, etc.)
internal organs
bones
parts of the mouth
parts of the eye

9 Category Dictation

ACTIVITY HANDBOOK PAGE 2

Dictate words that fit into the above categories.

10 General-to-Specific Clue Game

ACTIVITY HANDBOOK PAGE 7

Possible clues:

Clue 1: They're organs.
Clue 2: They're inside your body.
Clue 3: There are two of them.
Clue 4: You can live without one of them.
Clue 5: They clean your blood.
   [Answer: kidneys]

Clue 1: You can't live without it.
Clue 2: It works all the time, even when you're
         sleeping.
Clue 3: It's very delicate.
Clue 4: It's the heaviest part of a baby's body.
Clue 5: It's round.
   [Answer: brain]

11 Listen, Remember, and Touch

a. Have students stand or sit in pairs.

b. Partner A names five parts of the body.

c. When Partner A has finished, Partner B must
   point to all the parts of his or her body in the
   order that Partner A named them.

d. Partner A and Partner B then change roles.

12 Body Word Game: E Is for Elbow

a. Divide the class into teams.

b. Name a letter of the alphabet and have the
   teams write down all the parts of the body they
   can think of that begin with that letter.

The team with the most correct answers wins the
game.

13 Body Investigation

a. Have each student choose one organ to study.

b. Have students research the assigned organ and
   find the answers to the following questions:

   Where is it located?
   What is its function?

c. Have students report their findings in class in
   brief, one-minute presentations.

LESSON OBJECTIVE

Students will learn the most common vocabulary for ailments, symptoms, and injuries.

RESOURCES

AUDIO PROGRAM

Words & Dialogs
Cassette 3B
CD 4: Tracks 16–20

MULTI-LEVEL WORKBOOKS

Literacy Workbook
Beginning & Intermediate Lifeskills Workbooks
Beginning & Intermediate Vocabulary Workbooks

ACTIVITY MASTER
Reproducible:
A117

TRANSPARENCIES
Overheads: T88, T89

LANGUAGE & CULTURE NOTES
Reproducible: LC88–89

WORDLINKS
longman.com/wordbyword

VOCABULARY INTRODUCTION

- Preview
- Present
- Practice

MODEL CONVERSATION PRACTICE

There are four model conversations—the first for words 1–19, the second for words 20–26, the third for words 27–38, and the fourth for words 39–50. Introduce and practice the first model before going on to the next. For each model:

1. Have students look at the model illustration. Set the scene:

    Model 1: "One co-worker is concerned about another."
    Model 2: "A wife is concerned about her husband."
    Model 3: "A doctor and patient are talking."
    Model 4: "A doctor is talking to a patient in the emergency room."

2. Present the first model using word 1, the second model using word 20, the third model using word 27, and the fourth model using word 39.

3. Choral Repetition Practice: Full-Class and Individual.

4. Have pairs practice the model.

5. Have pairs present the model.

6. Call on pairs to present a new conversation using word 2 for the first model, word 21 for the second model, word 31 for the third model, and word 40 for the fourth model.

7. Have pairs practice new conversations.

8. Have pairs present new conversations.

ADDITIONAL CONVERSATION PRACTICE

Before students practice the additional conversation, you may want to have them listen to the examples on the Audio Program.

Conversation Have students practice and present conversations with any words they wish.

SPELLING PRACTICE

Say a word, and have students spell it aloud or write it. Or, using the transparency, point to an item and have students write the word.

WRITING AND DISCUSSION

Have students respond to the questions as a class, in pairs, or in small groups. Or have students write their responses, share their writing with other students, and discuss in class.

Resource Materials Bring in, or have students bring in, the following materials for vocabulary practice:

● *Magazine advertisements for medications:* Identify the ailments and symptoms associated with these medications.

● *Brochures and pamphlets for common ailments:* Identify the symptoms for these ailments.

Community Task Have individual students (or groups of students) visit a pharmacy and ask the pharmacist what the best medication is for one common ailment (cough, headache, sore throat, nausea, insect bite, sunburn, etc.). Have students report their findings to the class.

Communication Activities

1 Telephone
ACTIVITY HANDBOOK PAGE **14**

Begin the activity with the following sentence: "I have a headache, a sore throat, and a bad cough."

2 Chain Game: You Think That's Bad?!
ACTIVITY HANDBOOK PAGES **2–3**

Begin the chain as follows: "I have a toothache," and have students continue it. For example:

> Teacher: I have a toothache.
> Student 1: You think that's bad?! I have a toothache and a sunburn.
> Student 2: You think that's bad?! I have a toothache, a sunburn, and an insect bite.
> Etc.

3 What's the Matter with Them?

Use any or all of the following for this activity:

- the illustrations on *Picture Dictionary* pages 88 and 89
- pictures of people with ailments or injuries
- pictures that show people with facial expressions that indicate discomfort of some sort

Ask students what each person in the picture is saying. Have students make up a story about the person: What happened? How does he or she feel?

4 What Do You Do When . . . ?

Have students work in pairs, interviewing each other about what they do when they have various ailments. Have students report back to the class about the person they interviewed.

5 These Are My Symptoms

Divide the class into small groups. Have each group choose an ailment or injury and make a list of symptoms for that ailment or injury. The class then guesses what the *mystery ailment* is. For example:

> I have a runny nose. I'm congested. I have a temperature. I have the chills. I have a cough. And my eyes are watery.
>
> [Answer: cold]
>
> I'm itchy. I have a rash. My arm is swollen. My arm hurts. My arm is hot.
>
> [Answer: insect bite]

6 Symptom and Ailment Match Game
ACTIVITY HANDBOOK PAGE **11**
ACTIVITY MASTER **117**

Have students find the person whose card matches theirs.

7 Home Remedies

As a class, in pairs, or in small groups, have students discuss home remedies for common ailments.

8 Most Common Accidents

In pairs or small groups, have students choose one area to investigate on the Internet and then report back to the class.

Suggestion: Have students go to a search engine and type in one of the following keyword searches:

> most common accidents for babies under six months
> most common accidents for children under five years old
> most common household accidents
> most common workplace accidents
> most common kinds of car accidents

LESSON OBJECTIVE

Students will learn the vocabulary for standard first-aid equipment and the vocabulary for the most important first-aid maneuvers in life threatening emergencies.

RESOURCES

AUDIO PROGRAM

Words & Dialogs
Cassette 4A
CD 4: Tracks 21, 22

MULTI-LEVEL WORKBOOKS

Literacy Workbook
Beginning & Intermediate Lifeskills Workbooks
Beginning & Intermediate Vocabulary Workbooks

ACTIVITY MASTERS

Reproducibles:
A118, A119

TRANSPARENCY

Overhead: T90

LANGUAGE & CULTURE NOTES

Reproducible: LC90

WORDLINKS

longman.com/wordbyword

VOCABULARY INTRODUCTION

- Preview
- Present
- Practice

MODEL CONVERSATION PRACTICE

There are two model conversations—the first for words 3–14 and the second for phrases a–e and words 15–19. Introduce and practice the first model before going on to the second. For each model:

1. Have students look at the model illustration. Set the scene:

   Model 1: "A husband and wife are talking."
   Model 2: "Someone is asking a stranger for help."

2. Present the first model using word 3 and the second model using phrase a and word 15.

3. Choral Repetition Practice: Full-Class and Individual.

4. Have pairs practice the model.

5. Have pairs present the model.

6. Call on pairs to present a new conversation using word 4 for the first model and phrase b and word 16 for the second model.

7. Have pairs practice new conversations.

8. Have pairs present new conversations.

SPELLING PRACTICE

Say a word or phrase, and have students spell it aloud or write it. Or, using the transparency, point to an item and have students write the word or phrase.

WRITING AND DISCUSSION

Have students respond to the questions as a class, in pairs, or in small groups. Or have students write their responses, share their writing with other students, and discuss in class.

Making Connections

Resource Materials Bring in, or have students bring in, the following materials for vocabulary practice:

- *CPR and first-aid instruction booklets:* Identify the first-aid equipment used and the life-saving measures taken.

Community Task Have individual students (or groups of students) find out where a CPR and first-aid course is offered. Have them find out the following about the course: its price, location, and time. Have students compare what they have learned and identify the best course offerings in the area.

Communication Activities

1 Chain Game
ACTIVITY HANDBOOK PAGES 2–3

Begin the chain as follows: "My first-aid kit has a first-aid manual," and have students continue it. For example:

Teacher: My first-aid kit has a first-aid manual.
Student 1: My first-aid kit has a first-aid manual and some Band-Aids™.
Student 2: My first-aid kit has a first-aid manual, some Band-Aids, and some hydrogen peroxide.
Etc.

2 What Do You Do When . . . ?
ACTIVITY MASTER 118

a. Have students work in pairs, interviewing each other about what they should do in the case of an injury.

b. Have students report back to the class about what they learned in their interviews.

3 Medical Advice

a. Tell each student to think of a first-aid emergency.

b. Call on individual students to tell their injury. For example:

I sprained my wrist.

c. Other students then give advice. For example:

You should hold it up so it doesn't swell.
You should wrap it in an Ace™ bandage.
You should put ice on it.
You should take non-aspirin pain reliever.

4 Finish the Sentence!
ACTIVITY HANDBOOK PAGE 7

Begin sentences such as the following for students to complete:

When you go camping, you should always bring a . . . first-aid kit.
When you have a cut, you should cover it with a . . . bandage.
When you need to clean a cut with dirt inside, you should use . . . hydrogen peroxide.
When a person isn't breathing, you should use . . . rescue breathing.
When a person is bleeding severely, you should make a . . . tourniquet.
When a person is choking, you should use . . . the Heimlich maneuver.
When you have swelling around an insect bite, you should use some . . . antihistamine cream.

When a person doesn't have a pulse, you should use . . . CPR.
When a person has broken his or her arm, you should use a . . . splint.

5 It's Something That . . .
ACTIVITY HANDBOOK PAGE 9
ACTIVITY MASTER 119

Have students give definitions of first-aid words to each other beginning with "It's something that . . ." For example:

It's something that you use when you sprain your ankle. [An Ace bandage.]
It's something that you must do if someone is choking. [The Heimlich maneuver.]
It's something that you need to use when you have a cut. [Antibiotic ointment.]
It's something that you take when you have a fever. [Non-aspirin pain reliever.]
It's something that you must do if someone isn't breathing. [Rescue breathing.]

6 Movable Categories
ACTIVITY HANDBOOK PAGE 11
ACTIVITY MASTER 119

Call out the following questions and have students go to the appropriate side of the room:

What do you use to take care of a scrape?
What do you use to take care of a very deep cut?
What do you use to take care of a sprained ankle?
What do you use to take care of a broken finger?
What do you use to take care of a person who isn't breathing?
What do you use to take care of a headache?
What do you use to take care of an insect bite?

7 Make Your Own First-Aid Kit!

Have students go on the Internet and find products that they would need to assemble their own first-aid kit. For example:

antibiotic ointment: Bacitracin
adhesive bandage: Band-Aid
aspirin: Bayer® aspirin

8 First-Aid Investigation

a. Individually or in groups, have students go to the Internet and do a keyword search to investigate one of the following topics: the Heimlich maneuver; CPR; first aid for fainting, a broken bone, an insect bite, a snake bite, a sprained ankle, a cut, a head injury.

b. Have students present their information to the class.

LESSON OBJECTIVE

Students will learn the vocabulary for common medical emergencies and illnesses.

RESOURCES

AUDIO PROGRAM
Words & Dialogs
Cassette 4A
CD 4: Tracks 23, 24

MULTI-LEVEL WORKBOOKS
Literacy Workbook
Beginning & Intermediate Lifeskills Workbooks
Beginning & Intermediate Vocabulary Workbooks

ACTIVITY MASTER
Reproducible:
A8

TRANSPARENCY
Overhead: T91

LANGUAGE & CULTURE NOTES
Reproducible: LC91

WORDLINKS
longman.com/wordbyword

VOCABULARY INTRODUCTION

- Preview
- Present
- Practice

MODEL CONVERSATION PRACTICE

There are two model conversations—the first for words 1–11 and the second for words 12–25. Introduce and practice the first model before going on to the second. For each model:

1. Have students look at the model illustration. Set the scene:

   Model 1: "A 911 emergency operator is talking to someone who has called to report an injury."
   Model 2: "Two co-workers are talking during a break at work."

2. Present the first model using word 1 and the second model using word 12.

3. Choral Repetition Practice: Full-Class and Individual.

4. Have pairs practice the model.

5. Have pairs present the model.

6. Call on pairs to present a new conversation using word 4 for the first model and word 13 for the second model.

7. Have pairs practice new conversations.

8. Have pairs present new conversations.

SPELLING PRACTICE

Say a word or phrase, and have students spell it aloud or write it. Or, using the transparency, point to an item and have students write the word or phrase.

WRITING AND DISCUSSION

Have students respond to the questions as a class, in pairs, or in small groups. Or have students write their responses, share their writing with other students, and discuss in class.

Making Connections

Resource Materials Bring in, or have students bring in, the following materials for vocabulary practice:

- *Medical booklets on vaccines for measles, mumps, and chickenpox:* Identify the symptoms of these diseases.

- *Medical booklets on the treatment of diabetes, heart disease, high blood pressure, and TB:* Identify the symptoms of these illnesses.

Community Task Have pairs of students do an Internet search to find out what the most common medical emergencies are in different situations (airplanes, boats, hiking, etc.). Have students report their findings to the class and compare notes.

Communication Activities

1 Tic Tac Definitions

ACTIVITY HANDBOOK PAGE 14
ACTIVITY MASTER 8

Have students fill in the tic tac grid with any nine medical emergency or illness words they wish. Give definitions such as the following, and have students cross out on their grids the words you have defined:

> not responsive [unconscious]
> a reaction to excessive heat (The symptoms include fever, confusion, hot and dry skin, rapid breathing, weak pulse, and unconsciousness.) [heatstroke]
> when the skin freezes [frostbite]
> when a person takes more of a medication than he or she should [overdose on drugs]
> a virus that causes fever, body aches, and exhaustion (Tens of millions of people in the United States get it each year.) [the flu]
> the most common infection of the throat [strep throat]
> a contagious viral disease that causes the swelling of the salivary glands located between the ear and the jaw [mumps]
> a highly contagious viral illness with symptoms of a fever, cough, red eyes, and rash [measles]
> a virus that causes 250 to 500 small, itchy blisters or red spots on the skin [chicken pox]
> the uncontrolled growth of abnormal cells that have mutated [cancer]

2 Category Dictation

ACTIVITY HANDBOOK PAGE 2

Dictate words that fit into the previous categories.

3 True or False?

ACTIVITY HANDBOOK PAGE 15

Make statements such as the following about the scene on *Picture Dictionary* page 91. Have students decide whether the statements are true or false. For example:

> A person gets heatstroke from too much heat. [True.]
> A person can go into shock after a car accident. [True.]
> Chicken pox is a disease most people get in old age. [False. Chicken pox is a childhood disease.]
> If a person takes too much of a drug at one time, the person has an overdose on drugs. [True.]
> Diabetes is a heart condition. [False. Diabetes is a blood sugar condition.]

> There is only one kind of cancer. [False. There are many kinds of cancer—for example: liver, skin cancer, breast cancer.]
> Frostbite is caused by too much time in the sun. [False. Frostbite is caused by too much time in freezing temperatures.]
> An unconscious person is breathing but cannot respond. [True.]
> Measles are a medical emergency. [False. Measles are a disease.]

4 Illness Investigation

a. Individually or in groups, have students investigate on the Internet one of the illnesses on *Picture Dictionary* page 91. (*Note:* There are many good medical encyclopedias on the Internet, including Medline Plus—a service of the U.S. National Library of Medicine.) Have students find out the following information:

> the definition of the illness
> its symptoms
> its treatment
> its prognosis

b. Have students present their information to the class.

LESSON OBJECTIVE

Students will learn the steps taken in a regular check-up.

RESOURCES

AUDIO PROGRAM	MULTI-LEVEL WORKBOOKS	ACTIVITY MASTERS
Words & Dialogs	Literacy Workbook	
Cassette 4A	Beginning & Intermediate Lifeskills Workbooks	**Reproducibles**:
CD 4: Tracks 25, 26	Beginning & Intermediate Vocabulary Workbooks	A120, A121
TRANSPARENCY	**LANGUAGE & CULTURE NOTES**	**WORDLINKS**
Overhead: T92	**Reproducible:** LC92	longman.com/wordbyword

VOCABULARY INTRODUCTION

- Preview
- Present
- Practice

MODEL CONVERSATION PRACTICE

There are three model conversations—the first and second for phrases A–H, and the third for words 1–3 and 5–9. Introduce and practice the first model before going on to the second and third. For each model:

1. Have students look at the model illustration. Set the scene:

> Model 1: "A nurse is talking to a patient in the doctor's office."
> Model 2: "A wife and husband are talking about his medical exam."
> Model 3: "A doctor is pointing out the new scale to a patient."

2. Present the model.
3. Choral Repetition Practice: Full-Class and Individual.
4. Have pairs practice the model.
5. Have pairs present the model.
6. Call on pairs to present a new conversation using phrase B for the first model, phrase C for the second model, and word 2 for the third model.
7. Have pairs practice new conversations.
8. Have pairs present new conversations.

SPELLING PRACTICE

Say a word or phrase, and have students spell it aloud or write it. Or, using the transparency, point to an item and have students write the word or phrase.

WRITING AND DISCUSSION

Have students respond to the questions as a class, in pairs, or in small groups. Or have students write their responses, share their writing with other students, and discuss in class.

Making Connections

Resource Materials Bring in, or have students bring in, the following materials for vocabulary practice:

- *Medical booklets on routine exams:* Identify the steps of a routine exam.

Community Tasks Have individual students (or pairs of students) investigate the location and services offered by medical clinics in their community. Have students report back to the class.

Communication Activities

1 Concentration
ACTIVITY HANDBOOK PAGE 3
ACTIVITY MASTER 120

Have students shuffle the cards and place them face-down in four rows of 4 each, then attempt to find cards that match.

2 Miming Game
ACTIVITY HANDBOOK PAGE 11
ACTIVITY MASTER 120 (WORDS ONLY)

Have pairs of students take turns pantomiming medical exam actions. The class tries to guess what the *doctor* is doing. For example:

You're checking her blood pressure.
You're drawing some blood.

3 All in Order
ACTIVITY MASTER 120 (WORDS ONLY)

a. Make copies of the words in the concentration card set for half the students in the class. Cut up into cards.

b. In pairs, have students arrange the actions in the most logical order of a medical exam.

c. Have students read aloud their sequencing. Discuss any difference of opinions.

4 Chain Story
ACTIVITY HANDBOOK PAGE 3

Begin the story as follows: "Yesterday I visited my doctor for a medical exam."

5 Ask Me a Question!
ACTIVITY HANDBOOK PAGE 2
ACTIVITY MASTER 121

Have students walk around trying to guess each other's medical exam items by asking yes/no questions. For example:

Is it a machine?	[No.]
Is it an instrument?	[Yes.]
Is it something a doctor uses?	[Yes.]
Is it a stethoscope?	[No.]
Is it a syringe?	[Yes.]
Is it a machine?	[No.]
Is it an instrument?	[Yes.]
Is it something a doctor uses?	[No.]
Is it a scale?	[No.]
Is it a thermometer?	[Yes.]

6 What's the Question?
ACTIVITY HANDBOOK PAGE 16

Describe various medical exam items and have students respond by asking: "What's a _____?" or "What are _____s?" For example:

Teacher: You use this to see if someone has a fever.
Student: What's a thermometer?

Teacher: You use this to listen to the heart.
Student: What's a stethoscope?

Teacher: You use this to measure blood pressure.
Student: What's a blood pressure gauge?

Teacher: You use this to give a person a shot.
Student: What's a syringe?

Teacher: The patient sits and lays on it during the examination.
Student: What's an examination table?

Teacher: You use this to check a patient's eyesight.
Student: What's an eye chart?

Teacher: You use this to see the bones and lungs inside a person's body.
Student: What's an X-ray machine?

Teacher: You use this to measure a person's weight.
Student: What's a scale?

7 Medical Associations
ACTIVITY HANDBOOK PAGE 2

Call out medical exam words and have groups write down as many associations as they can think of. For example:

thermometer:	[fever/temperature/headache/flu]
stethoscope:	[listen/heart/lungs/breathing]
needle:	[syringe/shot/draw blood/tests]
eye chart:	[eyesight/eye glasses/vision/letters]
scale:	[weigh/weight/heavy/pounds/kilos]

8 Dictate and Discuss

a. Dictate one of the following statements:

Everyone needs to visit a doctor once a year for a check-up.
If you have one or two X-rays a year, it's bad for your health.
It's dangerous to use the same syringe for two different patients.

b. In small groups, have students discuss their opinions of the statement.

c. As a class, vote in agreement or disagreement with the statement and then have students discuss their reasons.

LESSON OBJECTIVE

Students will learn the vocabulary for common medical and dental procedures and the names of the equipment used in these procedures.

RESOURCES

AUDIO PROGRAM
Words & Dialogs
Cassette 4A
CD 4: Tracks 27, 28

MULTI-LEVEL WORKBOOKS
Literacy Workbook
Beginning & Intermediate Lifeskills Workbooks
Beginning & Intermediate Vocabulary Workbooks

ACTIVITY MASTERS
Reproducibles:
A8, A122, A123

TRANSPARENCY
Overhead: T93

LANGUAGE & CULTURE NOTES
Reproducible: LC93

WORDLINKS
longman.com/wordbyword

VOCABULARY INTRODUCTION

- Preview
- Present
- Practice

MODEL CONVERSATION PRACTICE

There are two model conversations—the first for phrases A–H and words 14–20 and the second for words 9, 10, 12, 13, 22, 23, and 26. Introduce and practice the first model before going on to the second. For each model:

1. Have students look at the model illustration. Set the scene:

   Model 1: "A doctor and patient are talking."
   Model 2: "A doctor and nurse are talking."

2. Present the first model using phrase A and the second model using word 9.

3. Choral Repetition Practice: Full-Class and Individual.

4. Have pairs practice the model.

5. Have pairs present the model.

6. Call on pairs to present a new conversation using word 14 for the first model and word 10 for the second model.

7. Have pairs practice new conversations.

8. Have pairs present new conversations.

SPELLING PRACTICE

Say a word or phrase, and have students spell it aloud or write it. Or, using the transparency, point to an item and have students write the word or phrase.

WRITING AND DISCUSSION

Have students respond to the question as a class, in pairs, or in small groups. Or have students write their responses, share their writing with other students, and discuss in class.

Making Connections

Resource Materials Bring in, or have students bring in, the following materials for vocabulary practice:

- *Medical history forms:* Read through a medical history form with the class.

- *Medical brochures and pamphlets from doctors' waiting rooms:* Identify the medical procedures students have learned from this lesson.

Communication Activities

1 Tic Tac Definitions
ACTIVITY HANDBOOK PAGE 15
ACTIVITY MASTER 8

Have students fill in the tic tac grid with any nine medical and dental procedure words they wish. Give definitions such as the following, and have students cross out on their grids the words you have defined:

> the place patients wait until the doctor can see them [waiting room]
> the person who greets patients when they come to the doctor's office [receptionist]
> a paper that asks general health questions [medical history form]
> the person who takes care of patients and helps the doctor [nurse]
> a liquid you use to clean cuts [alcohol]
> you make these with needle and thread to close a wound [stitches]

2 Medical Associations
ACTIVITY HANDBOOK PAGE 2

Call out medical exam words and have groups write down as many associations as they can think of. For example:

> stitches: [cut/surgery/doctor/pain]
> cast: [broken leg/crutches/accident]
> injection: [pain/arm/hurt/needle]
> drill: [dentist/noise/pain/cavity/filling]

3 What's the Question?
ACTIVITY HANDBOOK PAGE 16

Describe a medical and dental procedure item and have students respond by asking "What's a/an _____?" or "What are _____s?" For example:

> Teacher: You use this when you clean a wound.
> Student: What's alcohol?
>
> Teacher: You use these to help you walk.
> Student: What are crutches?
>
> Teacher: You use these to close a wound.
> Student: What are stitches?
>
> Teacher: You use this when you break a bone.
> Student: What's a cast?

4 Medical and Dental Procedure Match Game
ACTIVITY HANDBOOK PAGE 11
ACTIVITY MASTER 122

Have students find the person whose card matches theirs.

5 Miming Game
ACTIVITY HANDBOOK PAGE 11
ACTIVITY MASTER 123 (ALL WORDS EXCEPT FOR THE PEOPLE)

Have students take turns pantomiming medical and dental procedure words. The class tries to guess what the person is doing or what the person is using. For example:

> You're cleaning the wound.
> You're using crutches.

6 Before and After

Suggest some situations (*befores*) and have students suggest possible *afters*. For example:

Before:	*After:*
I cut myself with a knife.	I had stitches.
I broke my leg.	The doctor put me in a cast.
The doctor put a cast on my leg.	I had to use crutches.
The dentist drilled the cavity.	The dentist filled the tooth.
My knee was swelling.	The nurse put an ice pack on it.
First the nurse cleaned the wound.	Then she dressed it.

7 Medical and Dental Talk!
ACTIVITY HANDBOOK PAGE 17
ACTIVITY MASTER 123

Give students a Medical and Dental Procedure Word Card and have them speak to the class for one minute about that item.

8 Finish the Sentence!
ACTIVITY HANDBOOK PAGE 7

Begin sentences such as the following for students to complete:

> A nurse cleans the wound with . . . *cotton balls and alcohol.*
> A dentist drills the tooth with a . . . *drill.*
> The receptionist asks the patient for an . . . *insurance card.*
> The dentist examines the patient's . . . *teeth.*
> The doctor closes the wound with . . . *stitches.*
> The dental hygienist uses gloves when he or she . . . *cleans your teeth.*
> When you break a leg, you must wear a . . . *cast.*
> When you sprain your elbow, you must wear a . . . *sling.*

LESSON OBJECTIVE

Students will learn the vocabulary for the most common medical advice doctors give their patients.

RESOURCES

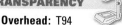**AUDIO PROGRAM**

Words & Dialogs	**WordSong:** *Power Up*
Cassette 4A	Cassette 7B • CD 8: Tracks 8, 9
CD 4: Tracks 29, 30	Song Masters S21, S22

MULTI-LEVEL WORKBOOKS

Literacy Workbook
Beginning & Intermediate Lifeskills Workbooks
Beginning & Intermediate Vocabulary Workbooks

ACTIVITY MASTERS
Reproducibles:
A8, A124–A126

TRANSPARENCY
Overhead: T94

LANGUAGE & CULTURE NOTES
Reproducible: LC94

WORDLINKS
longman.com/wordbyword

VOCABULARY INTRODUCTION

- Preview
- Present
- Practice

MODEL CONVERSATION PRACTICE

There are two model conversations. Introduce and practice the first model before going on to the second. For each model:

1. Have students look at the model illustration. Set the scene:

   Model 1: "A doctor is giving advice to a patient."
   Model 2: "A husband is asking his wife about her medical examination."

2. Present the first model using word 1 and the second model using word 2.

3. Choral Repetition Practice: Full-Class and Individual.

4. Have pairs practice the model.

5. Have pairs present the model.

6. Call on pairs to present a new conversation using word 9 for the first model and word 15 for the second model.

7. Have pairs practice new conversations.

8. Have pairs present new conversations.

SPELLING PRACTICE

Say a word or phrase, and have students spell it aloud or write it. Or, using the transparency, point to an item and have students write the word or phrase.

WRITING AND DISCUSSION

Have students respond to the questions as a class, in pairs, or in small groups. Or have students write their responses, share their writing with other students, and discuss in class.

♫♫ WORDSONG ♫♫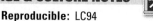

1. Have students listen to the vocal version of *Power Up* one or more times. Then have students listen again as they read the song lyrics on Song Master S21.

2. Have students sing as you play either the vocal or the sing-along version of the song.

3. For fun, have a song competition in which students perform solo or in groups and the class votes for the best performance.

4. For additional practice, students can complete the cloze exercise on Song Master S22.

Making Connections

Resource Materials Bring in, or have students bring in, the following materials for vocabulary practice:

- *Medical brochures and pamphlets from doctors' waiting rooms:* Talk about the medical advice given in the brochures.

Communication Activities

1 Telephone
ACTIVITY HANDBOOK PAGE 14

Begin the activity with the following sentence: "My doctor thinks I should go on a diet, exercise, take vitamins, and get counseling."

2 Medical Associations
ACTIVITY HANDBOOK PAGE 2

Call out medical advice words and have groups write down as many associations as they can think of. For example:

gargle: [sore throat/fever/strep throat]
heating pad: [cramps/stiff neck]
counseling: [depression/family problems/talking]
wheelchair: [broken leg/broken foot/sprained ankle/hospital]
blood work: [syringe/draw blood/diabetes/heart disease/blood tests]

3 Medical Advice Interview
ACTIVITY MASTER 124

a. Have students work in pairs, interviewing each other about what they should do in the case of different ailments, symptoms, injuries, and illnesses (see *Picture Dictionary* pages 88–89 and 91).

b. Have students report back to the class about what they learned in their interviews.

4 Tic Tac Definitions
ACTIVITY HANDBOOK PAGE 15
ACTIVITY MASTER 8

Have students fill in the tic tac grid with any nine medical advice words they wish. Give definitions such as the following, and have students cross out on their grids the words you have defined:

stay in bed several days or weeks to get better [rest in bed]
eat special foods [go on a diet]
a device that you place on a part of the body to relieve pain with heat [heating pad]
a machine that puts water in the air so that dry air won't irritate your throat, nose, or lungs [humidifier]
a machine with a filter that cleans the air of dust and pollen [air purifier]
a stick you use to help you walk [cane]
metal bands on the teeth that push teeth in the right direction [braces]
a device someone who can't walk uses to get around [wheelchair]

an ancient Chinese medical practice [acupuncture]
something a medical specialist does to exercise an injured part of your body [physical therapy]

5 Medical Advice

a. Tell each student to think of an ailment or an injury. Have students look at the vocabulary on *Picture Dictionary* pages 88–89 and 91 for ideas.

b. Call on individual students to tell about a medical problem. For example:

I have a cough.
I hurt my back.

c. Other students then give advice. For example:

You should use a humidifier.
You should use a heating pad.

6 Case Histories

Talk about the people depicted in the illustrations for words 1–7 on *Picture Dictionary* page 94. Have students make up a story about each of them:

Who are they?
What's the matter?
What are they doing for medical treatment?

7 What's the Question?
ACTIVITY HANDBOOK PAGE 16

Describe various medical advice words and have students respond by asking: "What's a _____?" or "What are _____s?" For example:

Teacher: You use this to help you walk.
Student: What's a walker?

Teacher: You use this when you aren't able to walk.
Student: What's a wheelchair?

Teacher: You do this to lose weight.
Student: What's a diet?

Teacher: You use these to make your teeth straight.
Student: What are braces?

8 Medical Advice Match Game
ACTIVITY HANDBOOK PAGE 11
ACTIVITY MASTER 125

Have students find the person whose card matches theirs.

9 Bleep!
ACTIVITY HANDBOOK PAGE 2
ACTIVITY MASTER 126

Have students create conversations based on three Medical Advice Word Cards that they select.

LESSON OBJECTIVE

Students will learn vocabulary related to common, readily available medications and treatments.

RESOURCES

AUDIO PROGRAM		MULTI-LEVEL WORKBOOKS 	ACTIVITY MASTERS
Words & Dialogs	**WordSong:** *Power Up*	Literacy Workbook	**Reproducibles:**
Cassette 4A	Cassette 7B • CD 8: Tracks 8, 9	Beginning & Intermediate Lifeskills Workbooks	A127, A128
CD 4: Tracks 31, 32	Song Masters S21, S22	Beginning & Intermediate Vocabulary Workbooks	

TRANSPARENCY	LANGUAGE & CULTURE NOTES	WORDLINKS
Overhead: T95	**Reproducible:** LC95	longman.com/wordbyword

VOCABULARY INTRODUCTION 🎧

- Preview
- Present
- Practice

MODEL CONVERSATION PRACTICE 🎧

There are two model conversations—the first for words 1–13 and the second for words 14–19. Introduce and practice the first model before going on to the second. For each model:

1. Have students look at the model illustration. Set the scene:

   Model 1: "A husband is asking his wife about her doctor's advice."

   Model 2: "A customer is talking to a pharmacist in a drug store."

2. Present the first model using word 1 and the second model using word 14.

3. Choral Repetition Practice: Full-Class and Individual.

4. Have pairs practice the model.

5. Have pairs present the model.

6. Call on pairs to present a new conversation using word 6 for the first model and word 15 for the second model.

7. Have pairs practice new conversations.

8. Have pairs present new conversations.

SPELLING PRACTICE

Say a word, and have students spell it aloud or write it. Or, using the transparency, point to an item and have students write the word.

WRITING AND DISCUSSION

Have students respond to the questions as a class, in pairs, or in small groups. Or have students write their responses, share their writing with other students, and discuss in class.

Making Connections

Resource Materials Bring in, or have students bring in, the following materials for vocabulary practice:

- *Medicine labels:* Read directions and dosages with the class.

- *Newspaper and magazine advertisements for medicines:* Have students identify the symptoms these medications relieve or the illnesses they cure.

- *Brochures and pamphlets for medicines:* Have students identify the symptoms these medications relieve or the illnesses they cure.

Community Task Have individual students (or pairs of students) visit a pharmacy and ask the pharmacist what the most popular forms of an over-the-counter medication is. Have each student or pairs of students choose a different item to investigate (aspirin, non-aspirin pain reliever, vitamins, cough syrup, antacid tablets, decongestant spray, and eye drops). Have students report their findings to the class.

1. Concentration

ACTIVITY HANDBOOK PAGE 3
ACTIVITY MASTER 127

Have students shuffle the cards and place them face-down in three rows of 6 each, then attempt to find cards that match.

2. What's on the Label?

a. Bring prescription drug bottles with labels to class. Have students read and discuss the information on the labels: the expiration date, the dosage, other instructions, how many refills, etc.

b. Bring over-the-counter drugs with labels to class. Have students read and discuss the information on the labels.

3. Telephone

ACTIVITY HANDBOOK PAGE 14

Begin the activity with the following sentence: "Take two tablets every four hours with food."

4. The Best Medicine

Tell each student to think of an ailment or an injury. Call on individual students to tell what ailment or injury they *have*. Other students should then give advice using one of the medicine words on *Picture Dictionary* page 95. For example:

> You should use nasal spray.
> I recommend cough drops.

5. What's the Question?

ACTIVITY HANDBOOK PAGE 16

Describe an item of medicine and have students respond by asking: "What's a ____?" or "What are ____s?" For example:

Teacher: You use it when your nose is stuffy.
Student: What's nasal spray?

Teacher: You use them when your eyes are itchy.
Student: What are eye drops?

Teacher: You use it when you have a headache and your stomach is sensitive.
Student: What's non-aspirin pain reliever?

Teacher: You take it before you go to sleep when you have a cough.
Student: What is cough syrup?

Teacher: You take them when your stomach is bothering you.
Student: What are antacid tablets?

Teacher: You rub this on your skin.
Student: What's an ointment? *or* What's a cream?

Teacher: You use this when you measure liquid medicine.
Student: What's a teaspoon? *or* What's a tablespoon?

Teacher: You suck on these when your throat is sore.
Student: What are throat lozenges?

Teacher: You take these when you have a cold with many symptoms.
Student: What are cold tablets?

Teacher: You take these when you don't eat enough healthy food.
Student: What are vitamins?

6. Ranking

ACTIVITY HANDBOOK PAGE 13

Write the following medicine items on the board and have students rank them from items they use the most to items they use the least. For example:

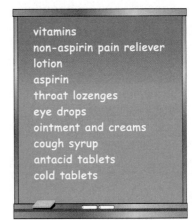

vitamins
non-aspirin pain reliever
lotion
aspirin
throat lozenges
eye drops
ointment and creams
cough syrup
antacid tablets
cold tablets

Variation: Have students rank the medicines from least expensive to the most expensive, or the least advertised to the most advertised.

7 Acting Sick

a. Write different *stage directions* such as the following on small cards and distribute them to students in the class:

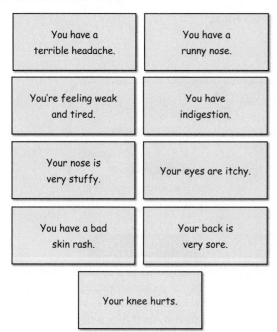

You have a terrible headache.	You have a runny nose.
You're feeling weak and tired.	You have indigestion.
Your nose is very stuffy.	Your eyes are itchy.
You have a bad skin rash.	Your back is very sore.
Your knee hurts.	

b. Have students act out their ailments, and have others make recommendations such as "You need throat lozenges" or "You should put an icepack on your back!"

8 Medicine Match Game

ACTIVITY HANDBOOK PAGE 11
ACTIVITY MASTER 128

Have students find the person whose card matches theirs.

9 Name That Brand!

With the help of the class, make a list of popular name brands for medicines, such as:

aspirin: Bayer®
cough drops: Smith Brothers®
antacid tablets: Alka Seltzer®
eye drops: Murine®

10 Most Doctors Recommend . . .

Cut out advertisements for over-the-counter medicines from magazines, newspapers, and advertising circulars. Discuss the following questions:

What is the problem (symptom, illness)?
How can this medicine help?
Who is the advertisement for?
Does the advertisement make you want to buy the medicine?
Is this a good advertisement? Why or why not?

11 Invent a Medicine!

ACTIVITY HANDBOOK PAGE 9

Divide the class into small groups. Have each group *invent* a medicine. They should name it, give instructions for its use, and tell what it cures. Have the groups then describe their products to the class. If you wish, you can have students create television commercials for their products.

LESSON OBJECTIVE

Students will learn the names of the most common medical specialists.

RESOURCES

AUDIO PROGRAM

Words & Dialogs
Cassette 4A
CD 4: Tracks 33, 34

MULTI-LEVEL WORKBOOKS

Literacy Workbook
Beginning & Intermediate Lifeskills Workbooks
Beginning & Intermediate Vocabulary Workbooks

ACTIVITY MASTERS

Reproducibles:
A8, A129

TRANSPARENCY

Overhead: T96

LANGUAGE & CULTURE NOTES

Reproducible: LC96

WORDLINKS

longman.com/wordbyword

VOCABULARY INTRODUCTION

- Preview
- Present
- Practice

MODEL CONVERSATION PRACTICE

There are two model conversations. Introduce and practice the first model before going on to the second. For each model:

1. Have students look at the model illustration. Set the scene:

   Model 1: "A doctor is talking to a patient."
   Model 2: "A wife and husband are talking."

2. Present the first model using word 1 and the second model using word 2.

3. Choral Repetition Practice: Full-Class and Individual.

4. Have pairs practice the model.

5. Have pairs present the model.

6. Call on pairs to present a new conversation using word 3 for the first model and word 4 for the second model.

7. Have pairs practice new conversations.

8. Have pairs present new conversations.

SPELLING PRACTICE

Say a word, and have students spell it aloud or write it. Or, using the transparency, point to an item and have students write the word.

WRITING AND DISCUSSION

Have students respond to the questions as a class, in pairs, or in small groups. Or have students write their responses, share their writing with other students, and discuss in class.

Making Connections

Resource Materials Bring in, or have students bring in, the following materials for vocabulary practice:

- *Medical Services Directory:* Download a directory of medical services from a hospital website. Have students identify the specialists involved in each service area.

Community Task Have individual students (or groups of students) visit a local medical clinic or medical arts building and find out which specialists practice there. Have students report back to the class.

Communication Activities

1 Who Am I?

ACTIVITY HANDBOOK PAGE 17

Tell about different medical specialists and have students guess who you are talking about.
For example:

Teacher: I practice an ancient form of Chinese medicine. Who am I?
Student: An acupuncturist.

Teacher: I talk with my patients about their problems. Who am I?
Student: A counselor./A psychiatrist.

Teacher: I help my patients get stronger and move better. Who am I?
Student: A physical therapist.

Teacher: I help patients who can't hear well. Who am I?
Student: An audiologist.

Teacher: I'm a children's doctor. Who am I?
Student: A pediatrician.

Teacher: I treat very old people. Who am I?
Student: A gerontologist.

Teacher: I treat people who have broken bones. Who am I?
Student: An orthopedist.

Teacher: I treat people with heart problems. Who am I?
Student: A cardiologist.

Teacher: I treat people who hurt their backs. Who am I?
Student: A chiropractor.

2 Concentration

ACTIVITY HANDBOOK PAGE 3
ACTIVITY MASTER 129

Have students shuffle the cards and place them face-down in three rows of 6 each, then attempt to find cards that match.

3 Mystery Word Association Game

ACTIVITY HANDBOOK PAGE 2

Have students write associations for medical specialist *mystery words* for others to guess.
For example:

itchy eyes/asthma/itchy skin/allergies	[allergist]
heart/breathing/exercise/diet	[cardiologist]
cast/crutches/X-rays/broken bones	[orthopedist]
braces/teenagers/teeth/nice smiles	[orthodontist]

4 Tic Tac Definitions

ACTIVITY HANDBOOK PAGE 15
ACTIVITY MASTER 8

Have students fill in the tic tac grid with any nine medical specialist words they wish. Give definitions such as the following, and have students cross out on their grids the words you have defined. (See the Language & Cultures Notes for definitions of all the medical specialists on *Picture Dictionary* page 96.)

a doctor who specializes in the heart [cardiologist]
a doctor who specializes in women's reproductive health [gynecologist]
a doctor who specializes in the treatment of children [pediatrician]
a doctor who specializes in the treatment of elderly patients [gerontologist]
a doctor who specializes in the treatment of the eyes [ophthalmologist]
a doctor who specializes in the treatment of hearing problems [audiologist]
a medical doctor who specializes in the treatment of mental health patients and can prescribe medications [psychiatrist]
a doctor who specializes in stomach and digestive health [gastroenterologist]
a specialist who manipulates muscles to correct spinal problems [chiropractor]
a dental specialist who corrects the placement of teeth with braces [orthodontist]

(continued)

5 True or False?

ACTIVITY HANDBOOK PAGE 15

Make statements such as the following about medical specialists and have students decide whether they're true or false. For example:

> A person with stomach problems should visit a gastroenterologist. [True.]
> Pediatricians treat teenagers. [True. Pediatricians can treat children until they are adult age.]
> Acupuncturists are medical doctors in the United States. [False. Acupuncturists have training in acupuncture and may also have a medical degree, but a medical degree is not required to practice acupuncture.]
> There is no difference between a counselor and a psychiatrist. [False. A psychiatrist can prescribe medication and a counselor can't.]
> A woman who is pregnant should visit a gynecologist. [True.]
> A person with a broken leg should see an audiologist. [False. A person with a broken leg should see an orthopedist.]
> Gerontologists specialize in Chinese medicine. [False. Gerontologists specialize in treating elderly people.]
> A person with allergies should visit an ophthalmologist. [False. A person with allergies should visit an allergist.]
> A person who gets strep throat many times should visit an ear, nose, and throat specialist. [True.]
> A person who has a heart attack should visit a cardiologist. [True.]

6 Ranking

ACTIVITY HANDBOOK PAGE 13

Have students look at the list of medical specialists on *Picture Dictionary* page 96 and rank the top five according to the ones they see most frequently. For example:

> pediatrician
> orthodontist
> physical therapist
> gynecologist
> gastroenterologist

7 Class Survey: Doctors and Health Care

As a class, in pairs, or in small groups, discuss some or all of the following statements:

> Doctors make too much money.
> The government should pay for health care.
> People should take more responsibility for their own health.
> People go to the doctor too often.
> People trust their doctors too much.
> You usually have to wait too long to see the doctor.
> Male doctors are better than female doctors.

Take a poll of students' opinions and tabulate the results.

8 Class Discussion: Wise Words

Discuss with the class the meaning of the following American proverbs:

> An apple a day keeps the doctor away.
> An ounce of prevention is worth a pound of cure.

LESSON OBJECTIVE

Students will learn the vocabulary of places, people, and things in the hospital.

RESOURCES

AUDIO PROGRAM

Words & Dialogs
Cassette 4A
CD 4: Tracks 35, 36

MULTI-LEVEL WORKBOOKS

Literacy Workbook
Beginning & Intermediate Lifeskills Workbooks
Beginning & Intermediate Vocabulary Workbooks

TRANSPARENCY
Overhead: T97

LANGUAGE & CULTURE NOTES
Reproducible: LC97

WORDLINKS
longman.com/wordbyword

VOCABULARY INTRODUCTION

- Preview
- Present
- Practice

MODEL CONVERSATION PRACTICE

There are three model conversations—the first for words 2–10, the second for words 11–21 and 23–25, and the third for words 11–21, 23–25, and A–H. Introduce and practice the first model before going on to the second and third. For each model:

1. Have students look at the model illustration. Set the scene:
   - Model 1: "A nurse is showing a patient what's in the hospital room."
   - Model 2: "A little boy is talking to someone who works at the hospital."
   - Model 3: "A lab technician is talking to an orderly."

2. Present the first model using word 2, the second model using word 11, and the third model using words 11 and A.

3. Choral Repetition Practice: Full-Class and Individual.

4. Have pairs practice the model.

5. Have pairs present the model.

6. Call on pairs to present a new conversation using word 3 for the first model, word 12 for the second model, and words 15 and C for the third model.

7. Have pairs practice new conversations.

8. Have pairs present new conversations.

SPELLING PRACTICE

Say a word, and have students spell it aloud or write it. Or, using the transparency, point to an item and have students write the word.

WRITING AND DISCUSSION

Have students respond to the question as a class, in pairs, or in small groups. Or have students write their responses, share their writing with other students, and discuss in class.

Making Connections

Resource Materials Bring in, or have students bring in, the following materials for vocabulary practice:

- *Hospital brochure with directory:* Read a directory of a local hospital. Have students locate the different hospital departments from *Picture Dictionary* page 97 and medical specialties from *Picture Dictionary* page 96.

- *Internet pictures from hospital virtual tours:* Take a virtual tour of a local hospital on the Internet. Print the pictures. Have students identify items in the pictures.

Community Task Have students find out how many hospitals there are in the area. Have students report their findings to the class. Compile a complete list and make enough copies for each student in the class.

Communication Activities

1 Who Am I?

ACTIVITY HANDBOOK PAGE **17**

Tell about different hospital personnel and have students guess who you are talking about.
For example:

Teacher: I help women deliver babies naturally. Who am I?
Student: A midwife.
Teacher: I take care of patients and give them their medicine. Who am I?
Student: A nurse.
Teacher: I go to accident scenes in an ambulance and give emergency care. Who am I?
Student: An EMT.
Teacher: I make sure all the hospital patients are eating food that is good for them. Who am I?
Student: A dietician.
Teacher: I study samples of blood and urine to find out what illness a patient has. Who am I?
Student: A lab technician.
Teacher: I help the surgeon in the operating room. Who am I?
Student: A surgical nurse.
Teacher: I give patients medicine so they don't feel pain during surgery. Who am I?
Student: An anesthesiologist.
Teacher: I move patients from one part of the hospital to another part. Who am I?
Student: An orderly.
Teacher: I read X-rays. Who am I?
Student: A radiologist.
Teacher: I take X-rays of patients. Who am I?
Student: An X-ray technician.

2 Association Game

ACTIVITY HANDBOOK PAGE **2**

Call out hospital words A–H and have groups write down as many associations as they can think of. For example:

patient's room: [patient/hospital bed/TV/hospital gown/call button/medical chart]
nurse's station: [nurse/desk/computer/orderly/dietician/charts]
waiting room: [chairs/couches/volunteers/family and friends/TV/nervous]
ER: [EMT/doctor/nurse/accidents/gurney/ambulance/emergencies]
operating room: [surgeon/surgical nurse/stitches/lights/blood/syringe/gloves]

3 Mystery Word Association Game

ACTIVITY HANDBOOK PAGES **11–12**

As an alternative to Activity 2 above, have students write associations for hospital *mystery words* for others to guess. For example:

patient/hospital bed/TV/ hospital gown/call button/ medical chart — [patient's room]

nurse/desk/computer/ orderly/dietician/charts — [nurse's station]

chairs/couches/volunteers/ family and friends/TV/ nervous — [waiting room]

EMT/doctor/nurse/accidents/ gurney/ambulance/ emergencies — [ER]

surgeon/surgical nurse/ stitches/lights/blood/ syringe/gloves — [operating room]

4 Category Dictation

ACTIVITY HANDBOOK PAGE **2**

Dictate words that fit into the following categories:

waiting room
birthing room
radiology
laboratory

5 True or False?

ACTIVITY HANDBOOK PAGE **15**

Make statements about the scenes depicted on *Picture Dictionary* page 97. Have students decide whether they're true or false. For example:

Scene A:
The patient has an I.V. in his arm. [True.]
The doctor is carrying an X-ray. [False. He's carrying a stethoscope.]
The bed pan is on the floor. [False. It's on a table.]
There's a medical chart on the wall. [False. It's on the bed.]

Scene B:
There's a patient in a wheelchair. [True.]
The dietitian is talking to a doctor. [False. She's talking to an orderly.]
There are computers in the nurse station. [True.]

Scene C:
The surgeon is wearing gloves. [True.]
The anesthesiologist has a syringe around her neck. [False. She has a stethoscope around her neck.]
The surgeon is wearing a mask. [True.]

6 Listen and Number

ACTIVITY HANDBOOK PAGE 10

In pairs, have one student make up a story using hospital words and have the other student number the pictures in their order of occurrence in the story.

7 Finish the Sentence!

ACTIVITY HANDBOOK PAGE 7

Begin sentences such as the following for students to complete:

Hospital patients wear . . . *hospital gowns*.
A call button calls a . . . *nurse*.
An obstetrician helps . . . *deliver babies*.
A radiologist looks at . . . *X-rays*.
An EMT travels in an . . . *ambulance*.
An anesthesiologist works in the . . . *operating room / delivery room*.
A patient moves a hospital bed with a . . . *bed control*.
The patient's information is on a . . . *medical chart*.
A dietician makes sure the patients eat the right . . . *food*.

8 Stand Up!

a. Say the name of a part of the hospital—for example, "radiology."

b. Tell students you're going to say four words. If they hear a word that is associated with that part of a hospital, they should stand up. If they hear a word that is *not* associated with that part of a hospital, they should sit down. For example:

radiology:	X-ray	[stand up]
	radiologist	[remain standing]
	crutches	[sit down]
	stitches	[remain sitting]
patient's room:	midwife	[sit down]
	bed pan	[stand up]
	vital signs monitor	[remain standing]
	examination table	[sit down]
laboratory:	blood work	[stand up]
	anesthetic	[sit down]
	lab technician	[stand up]
	I.V.	[sit down]

birthing room:	midwife	[stand up]
	obstetrician	[stand up]
	radiologist	[sit down]
	volunteer	[sit down]

9 What's the Story?

a. In pairs, have students make up a story about one of the scenes on *Picture Dictionary* page 97. Have students answer the following questions:

What are their names?
What are they doing?
Is someone sick? What's the problem?
What happened before this scene? What will happen next?

b. Have students read their stories to the class. Have the class identify which picture they are describing.

10 Take a Virtual Tour

If students have access to the Internet, have them take a virtual tour of a hospital in their area. Have them write a list of all the vocabulary items they can identify in the tour and report back to the class.

LESSON OBJECTIVE

Students will learn verbs and products used for personal hygiene and appearance.

RESOURCES

AUDIO PROGRAM
Words & Dialogs
Cassette 4A
CD 4: Tracks 37, 38

MULTI-LEVEL WORKBOOKS
Literacy Workbook
Beginning & Intermediate Lifeskills Workbooks
Beginning & Intermediate Vocabulary Workbooks

ACTIVITY MASTERS
Reproducibles:
A130–A132

TRANSPARENCIES
Overheads: T98, T99

LANGUAGE & CULTURE NOTES
Reproducible: LC98–99

WORDLINKS
longman.com/wordbyword

VOCABULARY INTRODUCTION

- Preview
- Present
- Practice

MODEL CONVERSATION PRACTICE

There are three model conversations. Introduce and practice the first model before going on to the second and third. For each model:

1. Have students look at the model illustration. Set the scene:

    Model 1: "A mother is talking to her son."

    Model 2: "A customer is talking to a clerk in the store."

    Model 3: "A customer is talking to a clerk in the store."

2. Present the first model using word A, the second model using word 1, and the third model using word 2.

3. Choral Repetition Practice: Full-Class and Individual.

4. Have pairs practice the model.

5. Have pairs present the model.

6. Call on pairs to present a new conversation using word B for the first model, word 8 for the second model, and word 3 for the third model.

7. Have pairs practice new conversations.

8. Have pairs present new conversations.

SPELLING PRACTICE

Say a word or phrase, and have students spell it aloud or write it. Or, using the transparency, point to an item and have students write the word or phrase.

WRITING AND DISCUSSION

Have students respond to the questions as a class, in pairs, or in small groups. Or have students write their responses, share their writing with other students, and discuss in class.

Making Connections

Resource Materials Bring in, or have students bring in, the following materials for vocabulary practice:

- *Newspaper and magazine advertisements for personal hygiene products:* Have students identify the products.

- *Personal hygiene items:* Distribute the items to small groups and have students explain how to use each item.

Community Task Assign students a personal hygiene item to investigate. Have each student go to a store, see how many different brands there are of that product, compare the features of different brands and the prices, and report back to the class.

Communication Activities

1 Chain Game
ACTIVITY HANDBOOK PAGES 2–3

Begin the chain as follows: "I'm going on a trip and I'm going to take a razor," and have students continue it. For example:

> Teacher: "I'm going on a trip and I'm going to take a razor."
>
> Student 1: "I'm going on a trip and I'm going to take a razor and shampoo."
>
> Student 2: "I'm going on a trip and I'm going to take a razor, shampoo, and a hair brush."
>
> Etc.

Variation: Start another story with this sentence: "This morning, after I got up, I took a shower. Then . . ."

2 What's in the Bag? [Variation 1]

a. Collect as many personal hygiene products as there are students in the class and put the items in a large bag.

b. Have each student put his or her hand in the bag, feel the object, and try to guess what it is.

3 What's in the Bag? [Variation 2]

a. Collect a variety of personal hygiene products and put each one in a small brown lunch-size bag. Put all the bags on a desk or table in front of the room.

b. Divide the class into pairs. One member of the pair goes to the desk, takes a bag, and looks inside.

c. The second partner tries to guess what's in the bag by asking questions.

d. When the second partner has guessed the object, he or she returns the bag to the desk and gets another for the first partner to guess.

4 Telephone
ACTIVITY HANDBOOK PAGE 14

Begin the activity with the following sentence: "This morning I took a shower. Then I put on body lotion, deodorant, and powder. Then I brushed my teeth and shaved."

5 Movable Categories
ACTIVITY HANDBOOK PAGE 11
ACTIVITY MASTERS 130, 131

Call out the following categories and have students go to the appropriate side of the room:

> things you use to brush and clean your teeth
> things you use to take a bath
> things you use to take a shower
> things you use to wash your hair
> things you use to style your hair
> things you use to shave
> things you use to do your nails
> things you use to polish your shoes
> makeup
> things you use on your face
> things that have a scent
> things you use on your hands
> things that have a brush
> things that are liquid

6 Category Dictation
ACTIVITY HANDBOOK PAGE 2

Dictate words that fit into the above categories.

7 Drawing Game
ACTIVITY HANDBOOK PAGE 6
ACTIVITY MASTERS 130, 131

Have teams compete to identify personal hygiene products drawn by one of their team members.

8 Miming Game: Guess the Action!
ACTIVITY HANDBOOK PAGE 11
ACTIVITY MASTER 132

Have students take turns pantomiming personal hygiene actions. The class tries to guess what the person is doing. For example:

> You're brushing your teeth.
> You're combing your hair.

9 Miming Game: Guess the Product!
ACTIVITY HANDBOOK PAGE 11
ACTIVITY MASTERS 130, 131

Have students take turns pantomiming personal hygiene products. The class tries to guess what product the person is using. For example:

> You're using deodorant.
> You're using a razor.

(continued)

10 Guess the Object!
ACTIVITY HANDBOOK PAGES 7–8

Tell what different personal hygiene products are used for and have students guess the item. For example:

You use it to clean your hair. [Shampoo.]
You use it to make your eyelashes darker and thicker. [Mascara.]
You use it to cut your nails. [A nail clipper.]
You use it to shave your face with no shaving cream. [An electric shaver.]
You use it to make your leather shoes shiny. [Shoe polish.]
You use it to have good breath. [Mouthwash.]
You use it to clean the food from between your teeth. [Dental floss.]
You use it to dry your hair. [A hair dryer.]
You use it to wash your skin. [Soap.]
You use it to keep your hair dry when you take a shower. [A shower cap.]

11 Ask Me a Question!
ACTIVITY HANDBOOK PAGE 2
ACTIVITY MASTERS 130, 131

Have students walk around trying to guess each other's personal hygiene product items by asking yes/no questions. For example:

Is it makeup?	[No.]
Do both men and women use it?	[Yes.]
Is it liquid?	[Yes.]
Do you use it on your hair?	[No.]
Do you use it in your mouth?	[Yes.]
Is it mouthwash?	[Yes.]

Is it makeup?	[No.]
Do both men and women use it?	[No.]
Is it liquid?	[Yes.]
Is it aftershave?	[Yes.]

12 It's Something That . . .
ACTIVITY HANDBOOK PAGE 9
ACTIVITY MASTERS 130, 131

Have students give definitions of personal hygiene product words to each other beginning with "It's something that . . ." For example:

It's something that people use to shine their shoes. [Shoe polish.]
It's something that women use to curl their hair. [A curling iron.]
It's something that people use to whiten their teeth. [Teeth whitener.]
It's something that people use to shape their nails. [An emery board or nail file.]
It's something that women use to make their cheeks red. [Blush.]

13 Name That Brand!

With the help of the class, make a list of popular name brands for personal hygiene products, such as:

makeup: Maybelline®, L'Oreal®
shampoo: Clairol®
soap: Levers®, Ivory®
razors for men: Gillette®
moisturizer: Vaseline®

14 Things in Common
ACTIVITY HANDBOOK PAGE 14
ACTIVITY MASTERS 130, 131

Have students think of two personal hygiene products that have things in common. For example:

razor blade—nail clipper
Both are small.
Both are sharp.
Both can cut.

aftershave lotion—hand lotion
Both have a pleasant scent.
Both are used to soften the skin.

bubble bath—soap
Both clean the skin.
Both are used with water.

15 Word Clues
ACTIVITY HANDBOOK PAGE 17
ACTIVITY MASTERS 130, 131, 132

Have students take turns giving clues to team members who try to guess the personal hygiene product or action. For example:

The word is *toothpaste*.
Team 1 Player:	"mouth"	[Team 1 guesses]
Team 2 Player:	"clean"	[Team 2 guesses]
Team 1 Player:	"tube"	[Team 1 guesses]

The word is *shampoo*.
Team 1 Player:	"hair"	[Team 1 guesses]
Team 2 Player:	"shower"	[Team 2 guesses]
Team 1 Player:	"clean"	[Team 1 guesses]

The action is *do my nails*.
Team 1 Player:	"nail polish"	[Team 1 guesses]
Team 2 Player:	"emery board"	[Team 2 guesses]
Team 1 Player:	"nail clipper"	[Team 1 guesses]

16 TV Commercials

Have each student choose a personal hygiene product from *Picture Dictionary* page 98 or 99, and prepare a television commercial for that item. Have students present their commercials to the class.

LESSON OBJECTIVE

Students will learn vocabulary related to the care of a baby.

RESOURCES

AUDIO PROGRAM

Words & Dialogs
Cassette 4A
CD 4: Tracks 39, 40

MULTI-LEVEL WORKBOOKS

Literacy Workbook
Beginning & Intermediate Lifeskills Workbooks
Beginning & Intermediate Vocabulary Workbooks

ACTIVITY MASTER

Reproducible:
A133

TRANSPARENCY

Overhead: T100

LANGUAGE & CULTURE NOTES

Reproducible: LC100

WORDLINKS

longman.com/wordbyword

VOCABULARY INTRODUCTION

- Preview
- Present
- Practice

MODEL CONVERSATION PRACTICE

There are two model conversations—the first for words A–I and the second for words 1–18. Introduce and practice the first model before going on to the second. For each model:

1. Have students look at the model illustration. Set the scene:

   Model 1: "A husband and wife are talking."
   Model 2: "A husband is leaving for the store. He wants to know what they need."

2. Present the first model using word A and the second model using word 2.

3. Choral Repetition Practice: Full-Class and Individual.

4. Have pairs practice the model.

5. Have pairs present the model.

6. Call on pairs to present a new conversation using word B for the first model and word 1 for the second model.

7. Have pairs practice new conversations.

8. Have pairs present new conversations.

SPELLING PRACTICE

Say a word, and have students spell it aloud or write it. Or, using the transparency, point to an item and have students write the word.

WRITING AND DISCUSSION

Have students respond to the questions as a class, in pairs, or in small groups. Or have students write their responses, share their writing with other students, and discuss in class.

Making Connections

Resource Materials Bring in, or have students bring in, the following materials for vocabulary practice:

- *Baby magazines:* Have students identify the baby-care products.

- *Newspaper and magazine advertisements for baby items:* Have students identify the baby-care products.

- *Brochures and catalogs of baby products:* Have students identify the baby-care products.

Community Task Assign each student a baby-care item to investigate. Have that student go to a store, see how many different brands there are of that product, compare the features of different brands and the prices, and report back to the class.

1 Chain Game
ACTIVITY HANDBOOK PAGES 2–3

Begin the chain as follows: "A baby needs baby food," and have students continue it. For example:

    Teacher: A baby needs baby food.
    Student 1: A baby needs baby food and vitamins.
    Student 2: A baby needs baby food, vitamins, and diapers.
      Etc.

2 Movable Categories
ACTIVITY HANDBOOK PAGE 11
ACTIVITY MASTER 133

Call out the following categories and have students go to the appropriate side of the room:

    things you use to clean the baby
    things you put on a baby
    things you use to feed a baby
    things that go in a baby's mouth
    things that are in a child-care center

3 Category Dictation
ACTIVITY HANDBOOK PAGE 2

Dictate words that fit into the above categories.

4 Drawing Game
ACTIVITY HANDBOOK PAGE 6
ACTIVITY MASTER 133

Have teams compete to identify baby-care items drawn by one of their team members.

5 Daffy Debate!
ACTIVITY HANDBOOK PAGE 5
ACTIVITY MASTER 133

Have students debate which baby-care items are more important than others.

6 Ranking
ACTIVITY HANDBOOK PAGE 13

Have students review the baby-care items on page 100 and choose:

    the five most essential items for a baby
    the five least essential items for a baby
    the items that people used to take care of babies one hundred years ago
    the items that people used to take care of babies fifty years ago

7 What's the Question?
ACTIVITY HANDBOOK PAGE 16

Describe an item from page 100 of the *Picture Dictionary* and have students respond by asking: "What's _____?" or "What are _____s?" For example:

    Teacher: This is what a baby drinks from a bottle.
    Student: What's formula?

    Teacher: This is what a baby eats.
    Student: What's baby food?

    Teacher: You use these to fasten a cloth diaper.
    Student: What are diaper pins?

    Teacher: You use these when a baby is learning to use a toilet.
    Student: What are training pants?

    Teacher: This cleans a baby's hair.
    Student: What's baby shampoo?

    Teacher: Some doctors say children should have some every day.
    Student: What are liquid vitamins?

8 Finish the Sentence!
ACTIVITY HANDBOOK PAGE 7

Begin sentences such as the following for students to complete:

    You put a cloth diaper on a baby with . . . *diaper pins*.
    You wash a baby's hair with . . . *baby shampoo*.
    You clean a baby's ears with . . . *cotton swabs*.
    You feed a baby with . . . *baby food*.
    To keep the baby's clothes clean while the baby eats, you put on a . . . *bib*.
    A child keeps his or her belongings at school in a . . . *cubby*.

9 Dictate and Discuss

a. Dictate one or more of the following statements to the class:

    It's better to feed a baby formula than breast milk.
    It's better for a baby to go to a child-care center than to stay home with a parent.
    Disposable diapers are better for a baby than cloth diapers.
    Babies are happy when you read to them.

b. In small groups, have students discuss their opinions of the statement.

c. As a class, vote in agreement or disagreement with the statement and then have students discuss their reasons.

Unit 11 Communication Activity Review

1 Odd Word Out

Read the following lists of words, and have students identify the category and the "odd word out"—the word that doesn't fit the category:

broken leg, sore throat, fever, runny nose, cough
[Category: symptoms of a cold. Odd word out: broken leg]

diabetes, heart disease, mumps, blood work, AIDS
[Category: illnesses. Odd word out: blood work]

walker, wheelchair, ointment, crutches, cane
[Category: things that help a person walk or move. Odd word out: ointment]

tablets, ointment, cream, lotion, moisturizer
[Category: things you put on your skin. Odd word out: tablets]

cough drops, throat lozenges, antacid tablets, gurney
[Category: medicine you put in your mouth. Odd word out: gurney]

pediatrician, child-care worker, psychiatrist, cardiologist, orthopedist,
[Category: medical specialists. Odd word out: child-care worker]

orderly, dietician, surgeon, radiologist, patient
[Category: people who work in a hospital. Odd word out: patient]

elbow, nose, knee, ankle, hip
[Category: moving body parts. Odd word out: nose]

disposable diaper, baby shampoo, teeth whitener, bottle, pacifier
[Category: baby-care items. Odd word out: teeth whitener]

mouthwash, Band-Aid, toothpaste, dental floss, toothbrush
[Category: personal hygiene for the mouth. Odd word out: Band-Aid]

face powder, eyeliner, mascara, lipstick, humidifier
[Category: makeup Odd word out: humidifier]

scale, blood pressure gauge, bubble bath, examination table, eye chart
[Category: things in a doctor's office. Odd word out: bubble bath]

lips, shin, calf, knee, thigh,
[Category: parts of the leg. Odd word out: lips]

kidneys, bladder, heart, knuckle, liver
[Category: internal organs. Odd word out: knuckle]

2 Finish the Sentence!
ACTIVITY HANDBOOK PAGE 7

Begin sentences such as the following for students to complete:

If I have a headache, I should take some . . . *aspirin or non-aspirin pain reliever*.

If you have chest pain and shortness of breath, you should visit a . . . *cardiologist*.

If you have cramps and diarrhea often, you should visit a . . . *gastroenterologist*.

If you break a bone, you should see an . . . *orthopedist*.

If you break your arm, you'll need a . . . *cast*.

If you sprain your ankle, you'll need an . . . *elastic bandage*.

If you have depression, you should see a . . . *psychiatrist*.

A doctor listens to your heart with a . . . *stethoscope*.

If you have a very bad wound, the doctor will close it with . . . *stitches*.

If you have the flu, the doctor will tell you to . . . *rest, drink fluids, and take aspirin*.

To clean a wound, you need . . . *hydrogen peroxide and cotton balls*.

If you use sunscreen, you won't get a . . . *sunburn*.

If someone is choking, you should use the . . . *Heimlich maneuver*.

A nurse will draw your blood with a . . . *syringe*.

Air purifiers are helpful for people with . . . *asthma*.

3 Who Am I?
ACTIVITY HANDBOOK PAGE 17

Tell about different occupations and have students guess who you are talking about. For example:

Teacher: I'm a sick person in the hospital. Who am I?
Student: A patient.

Teacher: I help deliver babies at home or in the hospital. Who am I?
Student: A midwife.

Teacher: I take care of people in medical emergencies. Who am I?
Student: An EMT.

Teacher: I read X-rays. Who am I?
Student: A radiologist.

Teacher: I work in a laboratory in a hospital. Who am I?
Student: A lab technician.

Teacher: I help the surgeon. Who am I?
Student: A surgical nurse.

(continued)

Teacher: I make sure patients don't feel pain during surgery. Who am I?
Student: An anesthesiologist.

Teacher: I talk with my patients about their problems. Who am I?
Student: A counselor/psychiatrist.

Teacher: I'm a children's doctor. Who am I?
Student: A pediatrician.

Teacher: I treat very old people. Who am I?
Student: A gerontologist.

Teacher: I treat people who have broken bones. Who am I?
Student: An orthopedist.

Teacher: I treat people with heart problems. Who am I?
Student: A cardiologist.

Teacher: I treat people's teeth. Who am I?
Student: A dentist.

Teacher: I straighten people's teeth. Who am I?
Student: An orthodontist.

Teacher: I clean people's teeth. Who am I?
Student: A dental hygienist.

Teacher: I help out at a hospital, but I don't get paid. Who am I?
Student: A volunteer.

4 Quiz Game
ACTIVITY MASTER 134

a. Divide the class into four teams.

b. Copy and cut up Activity Master 143 and place cards face-down in a pile.

c. Have the teams take turns answering your questions. Give each team a time limit to answer each question (30 seconds or 1 minute).

d. The team with the most correct answers wins.

5 Letter Game
ACTIVITY HANDBOOK PAGE 9

Say statements such as the following and have teams compete to identify the items:

I'm thinking of a medical specialist that begins with *g*.	[gynecologist]
I'm thinking of an illness that that starts with *t*.	[TB]
I'm thinking of a medical emergency that starts with *f*.	[frostbite]

I'm thinking of a baby-care item that starts with *p*.	[pacifier]
I'm thinking of a hair style item that starts with *c*.	[curling iron]
I'm thinking of a kind of medicine that starts with *d*.	[decongestant spray]
I'm thinking of something in a first-aid kit that starts with *t*.	[tweezers]
I'm thinking of a body part that starts with *j*.	[jaw]

6 Category Dictation
ACTIVITY HANDBOOK PAGE 2

Dictate words from *Picture Dictionary* pages 86–100 that fit any three of the following categories:

baby care
illnesses
ailments and symptoms
injuries
equipment in a doctor's office

7 Listen, Remember, and Touch

a. Have students stand or sit in pairs.

b. Partner A names five parts of the body.

c. When Partner A has finished, Partner B must point to all the parts of his or her body in the order that Partner A named them.

d. Partner A and Partner B then change roles.

8 Drawing Game
ACTIVITY HANDBOOK PAGE 6
ACTIVITY MASTERS 121, 123 (things only), 126 (things only), 130, 131

Have teams compete to identify vocabulary items drawn by one of their team members.

9 Specialist Match Game
ACTIVITY HANDBOOK PAGE 11
ACTIVITY MASTER 135

Have students find the person whose card matches theirs.

UNIT 12 · School, Subjects, and Activities

TOPICS	DICTIONARY	TEACHER'S GUIDE
Types of Schools	101	254–256
The School	102	257–259
School Subjects	103	260–261
Extracurricular Activities	104	262–264
Mathematics	105	265–267
Measurements and Geometric Shapes	106	268–269
English Language Arts and Composition	107	270–271
Literature and Writing	108	272–273
Geography	109	274–276
Science	110	277–278
The Universe	111	279–280
Unit 12 Communication Activity Review	101–111	281–282

AUDIO PROGRAM

Words & Dialogs
Audio Cassette 4A
Audio Cassette 4B
Audio CD 4:
  Tracks 41–57
Audio CD 5:
  Tracks 2–15

WordSong: _After School_
Audio Cassette 7B
Audio CD 8: Tracks 10
  (Vocal) & 11 (Sing-along)
Song Masters S23, S24

WORKBOOKS

For Multi-Level Practice
Literacy Workbook
Beginning Lifeskills Workbook
Beginning Vocabulary Workbook
Intermediate Lifeskills Workbook
Intermediate Vocabulary Workbook

WORDLINKS

Internet Resources through the
Word by Word Companion Website
http://www.longman.com/wordbyword

ACTIVITY MASTERS

Reproducibles for Communication Activities
A8, A136–A157

TRANSPARENCIES

Full-Color Overheads for Class Practice
T101–T111

LANGUAGE & CULTURE NOTES

Information for Teachers &
Intermediate /Advanced Students
LC101–LC111

VOCABULARY GAME CARDS

For Vocabulary Practice,
Activities, & Games
Cards 263–298

LESSON OBJECTIVE

Students will learn about the types of schools in the United States.

RESOURCES

AUDIO PROGRAM	MULTI-LEVEL WORKBOOKS	ACTIVITY MASTERS
Words & Dialogs	Literacy Workbook	
Cassette 4A	Beginning & Intermediate Lifeskills Workbooks	**Reproducibles**:
CD 4: Tracks 41–43	Beginning & Intermediate Vocabulary Workbooks	A136, A137
TRANSPARENCY	LANGUAGE & CULTURE NOTES	WORDLINKS
Overhead: T101	**Reproducible**: LC101	longman.com/wordbyword

VOCABULARY INTRODUCTION

- Preview
- Present
- Practice

MODEL CONVERSATION PRACTICE

There are two model conversations. Introduce and practice the first model before going on to the second. For each model:

1. Have students look at the model illustration. Set the scene:

    Model 1: "The manager of a fast-food restaurant is interviewing a teenager for a job."
    Model 2: "Someone is interviewing for a job."

2. Present the first model using word 1 and the second model using word 5.

3. Choral Repetition Practice: Full-Class and Individual.

4. Have pairs practice the model.

5. Have pairs present the model.

6. Call on pairs to present a new conversation using word 2 for the first model and word 6 for the second model.

7. Have pairs practice new conversations.

8. Have pairs present new conversations.

ADDITIONAL CONVERSATION PRACTICE

Before students practice the additional conversations, you may want to have them listen to the examples on the Audio Program.

Conversation 1 Have students practice and present conversations with any words they wish.

Conversation 2 Have students practice and present conversations with any words they wish.

SPELLING PRACTICE

Say a word, and have students spell it aloud or write it. Or, using the transparency, point to an item and have students write the word.

WRITING AND DISCUSSION

Have students respond to the questions as a class, in pairs, or in small groups. Or have students write their responses, share their writing with other students, and discuss in class.

Making Connections

Resource Materials Bring in, or have students bring in, the following materials for vocabulary practice:

- *School newspapers:* Have students read a school newspaper that is published on the Internet.

- *Websites prepared by cities and towns describing their schools:* Print out a website description of local schools. Have students identify how many schools are in the area.

Community Task Have students (or groups of students) investigate schools in the area. Assign a different type of school to each student or group of students (preschool, elementary school, adult school, etc.). They should find the answers to the following questions: How many of this type of school are there in the area? What are their names? Where are they?

Communication Activities

1 Name the Place!
ACTIVITY HANDBOOK PAGE 12

Call out words or phrases associated with a type of school and have students try to name the school. For example:

learn to read/ eight-year-olds/ classrooms:	[elementary school]
twelve-year olds:	[middle school]
teenagers/many different classes:	[high school]
four years/bachelor's degree:	[college]
three-year-olds/sing songs/ playground:	[preschool]
four-year college/master degrees/doctorate degrees:	[university]
teenagers/fixing cars/ cutting hair:	[vocational school]
adults/ESL/basic education:	[adult school]
doctors/many years of study:	[medical school]
two-year college/local/ associate's degree or bachelor's degree:	[community college]

2 True or False?
ACTIVITY HANDBOOK PAGE 15

Make statements such as the following about the types of schools on *Picture Dictionary* page 101. Have students decide whether the statements are true or false. For example:

Preschool students go to college. [False. Preschool is for very young children.]
Elementary school is for ages 10–14. [False. Elementary school is for ages 5–10.]
Middle school grades are usually 6, 7, and 8. [True.]
High school has five grades in it. [False. High school has four grades: 9, 10, 11, 12.]
You have to finish high school to go to adult school. [False. Adult school offers classes for high school diplomas as well as other basic education classes.]
Vocational school is for high school students. [True.]
Community colleges offer two-year and four-year degrees. [True.]
You have to be a high school graduate to go to college. [True.]
Law school is part of a college program. [False. Law school is a program for people who have finished college.]

3 Letter Game
ACTIVITY HANDBOOK PAGE 9

Say statements such as the following and have teams compete to identify the items:

I'm thinking of a type of school that starts with *e*.	[elementary school]
I'm thinking of a type of school that starts with *g*.	[graduate school]
I'm thinking of a type of school that starts with *v*.	[vocational school]
I'm thinking of a type of school that starts with *t*.	[trade school]
I'm thinking of a type of school that starts with *h*.	[high school]
I'm thinking of a type of school that starts with *u*.	[university]
I'm thinking of a type of school that starts with *a*.	[adult school]
I'm thinking of a type of school that starts with *j*.	[junior high school]
I'm thinking of a type of school that starts with *m*.	[middle school]
I'm thinking of a type of school that starts with *p*.	[preschool school]

4 Here's What I'm Thinking Of!
ACTIVITY HANDBOOK PAGE 8

Make statements about types of schools and have students guess what you're thinking of. For example:

A. I'm thinking of a type of school that teaches very young children.
B. Preschool.

A. I'm thinking of a type of school that teaches trades to teenagers.
B. Vocational school.

A. I'm thinking of a type of school that teaches people how to be doctors.
B. Medical school.

A. I'm thinking of a type of school that teaches people how to be lawyers.
B. Law school.

A. I'm thinking of a large school that teaches adults in both colleges and graduate schools.
B. University.

A. I'm thinking of a type of school that teaches children in grades 5–8.
B. Junior high school.

A. I'm thinking of a type of school that prepares teenagers for college.
B. High school.

(continued)

A. I'm thinking of a type of school that prepares adults for work in two-year degree programs.
B. Community college.

A. I'm thinking of a type of school that offers a bachelor's degree program.
B. College.

5 Chain Game
ACTIVITY HANDBOOK PAGES 2–3

Begin the chain as follows: "First I went to preschool," and have students continue it. For example:

Teacher: First I went to preschool.
Student 1: First I went to preschool. Then I went to elementary school.
Student 2: First I went to preschool. Then I went to elementary school. Then I went to middle school.
Etc.

6 Listen and Number
ACTIVITY HANDBOOK PAGE 10

In pairs, have one student make up a story using types of school words and have the other student number the pictures in their order of occurrence in the story.

7 Mystery Word!
ACTIVITY HANDBOOK PAGE 11

Have a student leave the room, return, and ask yes/no questions in an attempt to identify the school mystery word. For example:

Is it a type of school for adults?	[No.]
Is it a type of school for very young children?	[No.]
Is it a type of school for teenagers?	[Yes.]
Do the teenagers study history and literature?	[No.]
Is it a vocational school?	[Yes.]
Is it a type of school for adults?	[Yes.]
Is it a four-year school?	[No.]
Is it a very big school with many degrees?	[Yes.]
Is it a university?	[Yes.]

8 What Can You Do?
ACTIVITY HANDBOOK PAGES 15–16

Have students make a list of all the things students do at each type of school. For example:

Preschool
sing songs
make music
play outside
paint and draw
eat a snack
take a nap

College
study in the library
take exams
live in a dormitory
study very hard

9 Mystery Word Conversations
ACTIVITY HANDBOOK PAGE 12

Have pairs of students create and present dialogs between a teacher and a student. The class then guesses where the conversation is taking place.

10 School Match Game
ACTIVITY HANDBOOK PAGE 11
ACTIVITY MASTER 136

Have students find the person whose card matches theirs.

11 Education Histories
ACTIVITY MASTER 137

a. Have students complete the Educational History Form.

b. In pairs or small groups, have students compare their histories. Have them ask each other the following questions:

Was it a good school?
What did you like about the school? What didn't you like?

Expansion: Use the information gathered from this activity to do a "Find the Right Person!" activity (Activity Handbook Page 6) with the whole class.

Page 102 THE SCHOOL

LESSON OBJECTIVE

Students will learn the vocabulary of a school—the places in a school building as well as the people who work there.

RESOURCES

AUDIO PROGRAM
Words & Dialogs
Cassette 4A
CD 4: Tracks 44, 45

MULTI-LEVEL WORKBOOKS
Literacy Workbook
Beginning & Intermediate Lifeskills Workbooks
Beginning & Intermediate Vocabulary Workbooks

ACTIVITY MASTERS
Reproducibles:
A138, A139

TRANSPARENCY
Overhead: T102

LANGUAGE & CULTURE NOTES
Reproducible: LC102

WORDLINKS
longman.com/wordbyword

VOCABULARY INTRODUCTION

- Preview
- Present
- Practice

MODEL CONVERSATION PRACTICE

There are two model conversations—the first for words A–D and G–M and the second for words 1–14 and A–M. Introduce and practice the first model before going on to the second. For each model:

1. Have students look at the model illustration. Set the scene:
    Model 1: "A teacher is talking to a student in the school hallway."
    Model 2: "A visitor to a school is asking a student a question."

2. Present the first model using word A and the second model using words 1 and A.

3. Choral Repetition Practice: Full-Class and Individual.

4. Have pairs practice the model.

5. Have pairs present the model.

6. Call on pairs to present a new conversation using word B for first model and words 2 and B for the second model.

7. Have pairs practice new conversations.

8. Have pairs present new conversations.

SPELLING PRACTICE

Say a word, and have students spell it aloud or write it. Or, using the transparency, point to an item and have students write the word.

WRITING AND DISCUSSION

Have students respond to the questions as a class, in pairs, or in small groups. Or have students write their responses, share their writing with other students, and discuss in class.

Making Connections

Resource Materials Bring in, or have students bring in, the following materials for vocabulary practice:

- *School newspapers:* Have students read a school newspaper that is published on the Internet.

- *Websites prepared by cities and towns describing their schools:* Print out a website description of a local school. Have students identify the facilities of the school.

Community Task Have individual students (or groups of students) visit websites of local schools and report about the school facilities and personnel. They should answer questions such as the following: Is there a school gym? Is there a library? Is there a full-time nurse? How many teachers are at the school?

Communication Activities

1 Name the Place!

ACTIVITY HANDBOOK PAGE 12

Call out words or phrases associated with places in a school and have students try to name the place. For example:

change clothes/sneakers/gym:	[locker room]
sit/watch a football game:	[bleachers]
applications for college/ counselor:	[guidance office]
experiments/science:	[science lab]
teacher/desks/books/ students/blackboard:	[classroom]
food/tables/lunch monitors:	[cafeteria]
seats/stage/assemblies:	[auditorium]
sick/medicine/call home:	[nurse's office]
play football/play soccer:	[field]
lockers/between classes/ hall passes:	[hallway]

2 Do You Remember?

ACTIVITY HANDBOOK PAGE 5

Have students write down everything they remember about the school scenes depicted on *Picture Dictionary* page 102.

If you do Variation 1, ask questions such as the following:

Is there a clock in the library?
Is the principal talking on the phone?
Are there two cafeteria workers in the cafeteria?
Are there lockers in the hallway?
Are students running on the track?
Are there school buses in front of the school?
Are students eating in the cafeteria?
Is there a field next to the track?
Is there a map in the classroom?
Is there a security guard in front of the school building?

3 True or False?

ACTIVITY HANDBOOK PAGE 15

Make statements such as the following about the scenes on *Picture Dictionary* page 102. Have students decide whether the statements are true or false. For example:

The principal is meeting with a parent. [False. He's is alone working in his office.]
There are two lunchroom monitors in the cafeteria. [False. There's one.]
The custodian is in the gym. [False. The custodian is in the auditorium.]

The students are playing baseball in the gym [False. They're playing basketball.]
The school nurse is taking care of a student. [True.]
The guidance counselor is talking with a student. [True.]
Two security officers are talking in the hallway. [False. One security officer is talking to the assistant principal the hallway.]
There are many students in the auditorium. [False. Only the custodian is in the auditorium.]
There are five students in the library. [False. There are fours students and the school librarian.]
The school secretary is answering the phone. [False. She's talking to a student.]

4 Listen and Number

ACTIVITY HANDBOOK PAGE 10

In pairs, have one student make up a story using school words and have the other student number the pictures in their order of occurrence in the story.

5 What Can You Do?

ACTIVITY HANDBOOK PAGES 15–16

Have students make a list of all the things they do at school. For example:

sit in class
take notes
eat lunch
play basketball in the gym
watch a football game in the bleachers
talk about colleges with a counselor

6 Who Am I?

ACTIVITY HANDBOOK PAGE 17

Tell about different school personnel and have students guess who you are talking about. For example:

Teacher: I help students choose their courses. Who am I?
Student: The guidance counselor.

Teacher: I teach science. Who am I?
Student: The science teacher.

Teacher: I teach gym class. Who am I?
Student: The P.E. teacher.

Teacher: I help students find books and information. Who am I?
Student: The school librarian.

Teacher: I manage the whole school. Who am I?
Student: The principal.

Teacher: I help the principal manage the school. Who am I?
Student: The assistant principal.

Teacher: I make sure the students eat their lunches. Who am I?
Student: The lunchroom monitor.

Teacher: I serve students their food. Who am I?
Student: The cafeteria worker.

Teacher: I make sure the students and teachers are safe. Who am I?
Student: The security officer.

Teacher: I take care of students when they are sick or need their medicine. Who am I?
Student: The school nurse.

7 Mystery Word!
ACTIVITY HANDBOOK PAGE 11

Have a student leave the room, return, and ask yes/no questions in an attempt to identify the school mystery word. For example:

Is it a person?	[No.]
Is it a place?	[Yes.]
Do students go there when they aren't feeling well?	[No.]
Do they eat there?	[No.]
Do they study there?	[Yes.]
Is it the library?	[Yes.]
Is it a person?	[Yes.]
Is it a teacher?	[No.]
Is it a professional?	[Yes.]
Is it the school nurse?	[Yes.]

8 Bleep!
ACTIVITY HANDBOOK PAGE 2
ACTIVITY MASTER 138

Have students create conversations based on three School Places Word Cards that they select.

9 Mystery Word Conversations
ACTIVITY HANDBOOK PAGE 12

Have pairs of students create and present dialogs between a student and one of the school personnel. The class then guesses where the conversation is taking place.

10 School Match Game
ACTIVITY HANDBOOK PAGE 11
ACTIVITY MASTER 139

Have students find the person whose card matches theirs.

11 Chain Game
ACTIVITY HANDBOOK PAGES 2–3

Begin the chain as follows: "I went to the cafeteria to get a snack," and have students continue it. For example:

Teacher: I went to the cafeteria to get a snack.
Student 1: I went to the cafeteria to get a snack, and then I went to the gym to exercise.
Student 2: I went to the cafeteria to get a snack. Then I went to the gym to exercise, and then I went to the library to get a book.
Etc.

12 Who Is Speaking?

a. Divide the class into small groups.

b. Have each group choose one of the people who works at a school and think of something that person might say. For example:

"We're going to have a big test tomorrow." [a teacher]
"Put your tray down and sit down!" [a lunchroom monitor]
"I think you sprained your ankle!" [the school nurse]
"Would you like to study Chinese or Spanish?" [the guidance counselor]

c. Have the groups present their *quotes* for the others to guess who it is.

13 A Special Person

a. In small groups, have students answer the following questions:

In all your years in school, who was your favorite teacher? Why?
In all your years in school, who was the worst teacher you ever had? Why?
Did you have a coach, counselor, or teacher who changed the way that you think about the world? Who was that? How did the person influence you?

b. Have students then individually write about one person who had a special impact on their education and life.

LESSON OBJECTIVE

Students will learn the vocabulary of subjects that high school students in the United States commonly study.

RESOURCES

AUDIO PROGRAM

Words & Dialogs
Cassette 4A
CD 4: Tracks 46, 47

MULTI-LEVEL WORKBOOKS

Literacy Workbook
Beginning & Intermediate Lifeskills Workbooks
Beginning & Intermediate Vocabulary Workbooks

VOCABULARY GAME CARDS

Cards 263–282

ACTIVITY MASTERS

Reproducibles:
A140, A141

TRANSPARENCY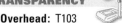

Overhead: T103

LANGUAGE & CULTURE NOTES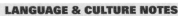

Reproducible: LC103

WORDLINKS

longman.com/wordbyword

VOCABULARY INTRODUCTION

- Preview
- Present
- Practice

MODEL CONVERSATION PRACTICE

1. Have students look at the model illustration. Set the scene: "Two students are talking."
2. Present the model.
3. Choral Repetition Practice: Full-Class and Individual.
4. Have pairs practice the model.
5. Have pairs present the model.
6. Call on pairs to present a new conversation using words 3 and 4.
7. Have pairs practice new conversations.
8. Have pairs present new conversations.

SPELLING PRACTICE

Say a word, and have students spell it aloud or write it. Or, using the transparency, point to an item and have students write the word.

WRITING AND DISCUSSION

Have students respond to the questions as a class, in pairs, or in small groups. Or have students write their responses, share their writing with other students, and discuss in class.

VOCABULARY GAME CARDS

Have students practice vocabulary, do activities, and play games with Vocabulary Game Cards 263–282. Activities and games are described in the set of cards.

Making Connections

Resource Materials Bring in, or have students bring in, the following materials for vocabulary practice:

- *Download a course catalog from a high school website:* Talk about the different offerings students have at the high school. If possible, get course catalogs from two different schools and compare the offerings.

Community Task Have the class tour the local high school.

Communication Activities

① Clap in Rhythm
ACTIVITY HANDBOOK PAGE 3

Have students name different school subjects to a clapping rhythm.

② Chain Game
ACTIVITY HANDBOOK PAGES 2–3

Begin the chain as follows: "I take English," and have students continue it. For example:

    Teacher: I take English.
    Student 1: I take English and math.
    Student 2: I take English, math, and history.
      Etc.

③ School Subject Associations
ACTIVITY HANDBOOK PAGE 2

Call out school subjects and have groups write down as many associations as they can think of. For example:

geography:	[maps/rivers/mountains/seas/oceans/continents/cities]
art:	[draw/paint/paper/clay/pottery/Picasso]
history:	[the French Revolution/The Civil War/World War II/Queen Elizabeth]
music:	[songs/notes/drums/singing/orchestra/Mozart]
government:	[citizen/vote/election/Senate/Congress]

④ Name That Subject!

a. Divide the class into two teams.

b. Bring to class books in different subject areas.

c. For each book, name a topic from the table of contents and have a student on Team 1 try to guess the subject. If he or she guesses correctly, that team gets 1 point. If the student doesn't take a guess or guesses incorrectly, a student on the other team has a chance to guess.

d. Continue naming topics until the subject is guessed. Then go on to the next book.

e. The team that guesses the most subjects wins the game.

⑤ Pair Interviews: School Days

Divide the class into pairs. Have students interview each other about the classes they took or are taking in school. Have the pairs then report back to the class about their interviews. Sample interview questions:

    What is/was your favorite subject? Why?
    What is/was your least favorite subject? Why?
    What is/was your easiest class? Why?
    What is/was your most difficult class? Why?
    What is/was your most unusual class? Why?

⑥ School Talk!
ACTIVITY HANDBOOK PAGE 17
ACTIVITY MASTER 140

Give students a School Subject Card and have them speak to the class for one minute about that school subject.

⑦ Daffy Debate!
ACTIVITY HANDBOOK PAGE 5
ACTIVITY MASTER 140

Have students debate which school subjects are more important than others.

⑧ Ranking
ACTIVITY HANDBOOK PAGE 13

Have students look at the school subjects and choose the five most important subjects everyone should study in high school. In small groups, have students explain their reasons for their selections.

⑨ Find the Right Person!
ACTIVITY HANDBOOK PAGES 6–7
ACTIVITY MASTER 141

Practice the following questions before having students do the activity:

    Do you like math/history?
    Did you like music class/art class best?
    Do you speak French/Spanish?
    Did you study computer science/chemistry/business education/driver's education?

LESSON OBJECTIVE

Students will learn about the extracurricular activities that high schools in the United States commonly offer.

RESOURCES

AUDIO PROGRAM		MULTI-LEVEL WORKBOOKS	VOCABULARY GAME CARDS
Words & Dialogs Cassette 4A CD 4: Tracks 48, 49	**WordSong:** *After School* Cassette 7B • CD 8: Tracks 10 (Vocal) & 11 (Sing-along) Song Masters S23, S24	Literacy Workbook Beginning & Intermediate Lifeskills Workbooks Beginning & Intermediate Vocabulary Workbooks	Cards 283–298

ACTIVITY MASTERS	TRANSPARENCY	LANGUAGE & CULTURE NOTES	WORDLINKS
Reproducibles: A142, A143	**Overhead**: T104	**Reproducible**: LC104	longman.com/wordbyword

VOCABULARY INTRODUCTION

- Preview
- Present
- Practice

MODEL CONVERSATION PRACTICE

1. Have students look at the model illustration. Set the scene: "Two students are talking."
2. Present the model using words 1 and 7.
3. Choral Repetition Practice: Full-Class and Individual.
4. Have pairs practice the model.
5. Have pairs present the model.
6. Call on pairs to present a new conversation using words 2 and 8.
7. Have pairs practice new conversations.
8. Have pairs present new conversations.

SPELLING PRACTICE

Say a word, and have students spell it aloud or write it. Or, using the transparency, point to an item and have students write the word.

WRITING AND DISCUSSION

Have students respond to the questions as a class, in pairs, or in small groups. Or have students write their responses, share their writing with other students, and discuss in class.

♫♫ WordSong ♫♫

1. Have students listen to the vocal version of *After School* one or more times. Then have students listen again as they read the song lyrics on Song Master S23.
2. Have students sing as you play either the vocal or the sing-along version of the song.
3. For fun, have a song competition in which students perform solo or in groups and the class votes for the best performance.
4. For additional practice, students can complete the cloze exercise on Song Master S24.

VOCABULARY GAME CARDS

Have students practice vocabulary, do activities, and play games with Vocabulary Game Cards 283–298. Activities and games are described in the set of cards.

Page 105 MATHEMATICS

LESSON OBJECTIVE

Students will learn the vocabulary of mathematics.

RESOURCES

AUDIO PROGRAM
Words & Dialogs
Cassette 4B
CD 4: Tracks 50–57

MULTI-LEVEL WORKBOOKS
Literacy Workbook
Beginning & Intermediate Lifeskills Workbooks
Beginning & Intermediate Vocabulary Workbooks

ACTIVITY MASTER
Reproducible:
A8

TRANSPARENCY
Overhead: T105

LANGUAGE & CULTURE NOTES
Reproducible: LC105

WORDLINKS
longman.com/wordbyword

ARITHMETIC VOCABULARY INTRODUCTION

- Preview
- Present
- Practice

MODEL CONVERSATION PRACTICE

The first model conversation in this lesson practices arithmetic.

1. Have students look at the model illustration. Set the scene: "A teacher is asking a student a question."
2. Present the model.
3. Choral Repetition Practice: Full-Class and Individual.
4. Have pairs practice the model.
5. Have pairs present the model.
6. Call on pairs to present a new conversation using a subtraction problem.
7. Have pairs practice new conversations.
8. Have pairs present new conversations.

FRACTIONS VOCABULARY INTRODUCTION

- Preview
- Present
- Practice

MODEL CONVERSATION PRACTICE

The second and third model conversations in this lesson practice fractions. Follow the steps above for introducing and practicing the models.

Model 2: "A customer is asking a salesperson a question."

Model 3: "A wife and husband are talking in the car."

PERCENTS VOCABULARY INTRODUCTION

- Preview
- Present
- Practice

MODEL CONVERSATION PRACTICE

The fourth and fifth conversations in this lesson practice percents. Follow the steps above for introducing and practicing the models.

Model 4: "Two students are talking."
Model 5: "A newscaster and weather forecaster are talking."

TYPES OF MATH VOCABULARY INTRODUCTION

- Preview
- Present
- Practice

MODEL CONVERSATION PRACTICE

The sixth conversation in this lesson practices types of math. Follow the steps above for introducing and practicing the models.

1. Have students look at the model illustration. Set the scene: "Two students are talking."
2. Present the model using *algebra*.
3. Choral Repetition Practice: Full-Class and Individual.
4. Have pairs practice the model.
5. Have pairs present the model.
6. Call on pairs to present a new conversation using *geometry*.
7. Have pairs practice new conversations.
8. Have pairs present new conversations.

SPELLING PRACTICE

Say a mathematics word, and have students spell it aloud or write it. Or, using the transparency, point to an item and have students write the word.

WRITING AND DISCUSSION

Have students respond to the questions as a class, in pairs, or in small groups. Or have students write their responses, share their writing with other students, and discuss in class.

Making Connections

Resource Materials Bring in, or have students bring in, the following materials for vocabulary practice:

● *Math books:* Have students read the equations aloud.

● *Advertisements for sales with fractions and percents off the original price:* Have students read the prices aloud.

Community Task Have individual students look for and cut out numbers mentioned in the newspaper: in articles, advertisements, or the weather report. Have students read their pieces from the newspaper to the class and explain the context of those numbers.

Communication Activities

1 Addition Game

a. Call out a number and have students write it down.

b. Student A then calls out another number that everybody writes down and adds to the first number. Student B then calls out a third number that is added to the total of the first two numbers. Continue around the class, with each student calling out a number that is added to the previous total. For example:

		Students write . . .
Teacher:	3	3
Student A:	4	7
Student B:	12	19
Student C:	4	23
Student D:	7	30
Etc.		

c. See if everybody agrees with the final total.

Variation: Do the above activity with subtraction.

2 Tic Tac Arithmetic

ACTIVITY HANDBOOK PAGE **15**
ACTIVITY MASTER **8**

Have students fill in the tic tac grid with any nine numbers from 1 to 40. Make up simple arithmetic problems, and have students cross out the answer if it is one of the numbers they have written down.

3 Number Puzzle

Give the following instructions to your students:

1. Choose any number.	(3)
2. Multiply by 2.	(6)
3. Add 4.	(10)
4. Divide the result in half.	(5)
5. Subtract 2.	(3)

The resulting number in step 5 should be the number the student started with.

Variation: Students can do this exercise in pairs after they practice a few times with the teacher.

4 Class Survey

a. Divide the class into pairs.

b. Have each pair decide on a question they would like to ask the whole class. For example:

What's your favorite flavor of ice cream?
Who is your favorite movie star?
What's the most difficult language?

c. Have each pair interview all the members of the class for an answer to their survey question.

d. Each pair should then tabulate the answers and give the results in percentages.

5 What Can You Do?

ACTIVITY HANDBOOK PAGES 15–16

Have students make a list of all the things they do with mathematics. For example:

Arithmetic
balance a checkbook
calculate a sale price
calculate how much pizza to buy
estimate a grocery bill
calculate a tip

6 True or False?

ACTIVITY HANDBOOK PAGE 15

Make statements such as the following and have students decide whether the statements are true or false. For example:

Three plus four equals eight. [False.]
Eleven minus two is nine. [True.]
Ten times three is thirty-three. [False.]
Fifty divided by five is ten. [True.]
One quarter equals two halves. [False.]
Two sixths equal one third. [True.]
Fifty percent of fifteen dollars is eight dollars.
  [False.]
100 percent of seventeen is seventeen. [True.]

7 A Story About Fractions

Note: This activity is for more advanced students.

Tell the following story and have students write the fractions they hear:

A math teacher was trying to teach his class about fractions. He decided to bring a cake into class to illustrate how something is divided into portions.

"If I cut this cake into two pieces, what will I have?" the teacher asked. *"One half,"* said one student. "Good," said the teacher. "Now if I divide it again in half, what will I get?" *"One quarter,"* replied another student. "And what happens if I cut it again?" "You get *one eighth*." "Right again," said the teacher. "I'm going to cut it again. Now what do I have?" *"One sixteenth,"* was the reply. "Yes," said the teacher. "That's wonderful! Now I'm going to cut it once more. What's the result this time?" The students all thought for a moment and one of them answered, *"One thirty second."* "That's fantastic!" the teacher said excitedly. "You're really catching on! Now I'm going to cut it once more. What do we have this time?" And the whole class responded, "CRUMBS!" And they were right.

LESSON OBJECTIVE

Students will learn the vocabulary of measurements, lines, geometric shapes, and solid figures.

RESOURCES

AUDIO PROGRAM	MULTI-LEVEL WORKBOOKS	ACTIVITY MASTERS
Words & Dialogs Cassette 4B CD 5: Tracks 2, 3	Literacy Workbook Beginning & Intermediate Lifeskills Workbooks Beginning & Intermediate Vocabulary Workbooks	**Reproducibles**: A8, A144, A145
TRANSPARENCY Overhead: T106	**LANGUAGE & CULTURE NOTES** Reproducible: LC106	**WORDLINKS** longman.com/wordbyword

VOCABULARY INTRODUCTION

- Preview
- Present
- Practice

MODEL CONVERSATION PRACTICE

There are five model conversations—the first for words 1–9, the second for words 11–12, the third for words 17–22, the fourth for words 23–27, and the fifth for words 13–27. Introduce and practice the first model before going to the others. For each model:

1. Have students look at the model illustration. Set the scene:

   Model 1: "A wife and husband are talking."
   Model 2: "A son and father are talking."
   Model 3: "A teacher and student are talking."
   Model 4: "A teacher and student are talking."
   Model 5: "A husband and wife are looking at a modern painting in the museum."

2. Present the first model using words 1 and 5, the second model using word 11, the third model using word 17, the fourth model using word 23, and the fifth model using words 13 and 14.

3. Choral Repetition Practice: Full-Class and Individual.

4. Have pairs practice the model.

5. Have pairs present the model.

6. Call on pairs to present a new conversation using words 2 and 6 for the first model, word 12 for the second model, word 18 for the third model, word 24 for the fourth model, and words 15 and 16 for the fifth model.

7. Have pairs practice new conversations.

8. Have pairs present new conversations.

SPELLING PRACTICE

Say a word, and have students spell it aloud or write it. Or, using the transparency, point to an item and have students write the word.

Making Connections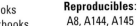

Resource Materials Bring in, or have students bring in, the following materials for vocabulary practice:

- *A measuring tape:* Measure students' height and arm spread and the size of the classroom and its furniture.

- *Photographs of modern art paintings:* Identify the lines, shapes, and figures in the artwork.

- *Any real objects that are examples of geometric shapes or solid figures:* Identify the shapes and figures of the items.

Community Task Have individual students find an object at home that represents a solid figure and bring it to class for the class to identify.

Communication Activities

1 Listen and Draw

a. Describe a series of geometric shapes and have students draw what you describe. For example:

> Draw a square.
> Draw a circle around the outside of the square.
> Draw a triangle inside the square.
> Draw another triangle inside that triangle.

b. Have students compare their drawings.

Variation: As a class, in pairs, or in small groups, have students describe shapes for others to draw.

2 Finish the Sentence!
ACTIVITY HANDBOOK PAGE 7

Begin sentences such as the following for students to complete:

> There are twelve inches in a . . . *foot.*
> There are three feet in a . . . *yard.*
> A geometric shape with four equal sides is a . . . *square.*
> The distance around a circle is its . . . *circumference.*
> Two lines that intersect at a right angle are . . . *perpendicular lines.*
> The highest point of a triangle is the . . . *apex.*
> An angle larger than 90 degrees is an . . . *obtuse angle.*
> An angle less than 90 degrees is an . . . *acute angle.*
> A solid figure with six sides that are equal squares is a . . . *cube.*
> A thousand meters is a . . . *kilometer.*

3 Geometric Pantomime
ACTIVITY HANDBOOK PAGE 11
ACTIVITY MASTER 144

Have students take turns pantomiming the measurement, shape, or figure on the card. Other students then guess what measurement or shape the person is depicting.

4 Tic Tac Shapes
ACTIVITY HANDBOOK PAGE 15
ACTIVITY MASTER 8

Have students fill in the tic tac grid with any nine vocabulary words they wish from *Picture Dictionary* page 106. Draw shapes and figures on the board, and tell students to cross out any word they have written on their grids that you have drawn.

5 Concentration
ACTIVITY HANDBOOK PAGE 3
ACTIVITY MASTER 145

Have students shuffle the cards and place them face-down in three rows of 6 each, then attempt to find cards that match.

6 What Am I?
ACTIVITY HANDBOOK PAGE 15
ACTIVITY MASTER 144

Pin word cards on students' backs and have them ask yes/no questions to identify which measurement or shape they *are.* For example:

Am I a measurement?	[No.]
Am I a solid figure?	[No.]
Am I a shape?	[Yes.]
Do I have curved lines?	[No.]
Do I have straight lines?	[Yes.]
Do I have four sides?	[Yes.]
Are my sides equal length?	[No.]
Am I a rectangle?	[Yes.]
Am I a measurement?	[Yes.]
Am I an English measurement?	[Yes.]
Am I long?	[No.]
Am I an inch?	[No.]
Am I a foot?	[Yes.]

7 Find It!
ACTIVITY MASTER 144 (without measurements)

a. Give every student a word card. Tell students they have three minutes to find something in the classroom that represents the line, shape, or figure on their card.

b. Have students show the class what they have found.

8 Measure It!

a. In pairs, have students measure the height, width, depth, and length of an object in the classroom and write down the measurements.

b. Have pairs take turns reading their measurements to the class as the class tries to identify the object in the classroom.

Note: If students are not accustomed to the customary measurement system of inches, feet, and yards, this activity can help them develop a sense for those measurement units.

LESSON OBJECTIVE

Students will learn the vocabulary of English grammar and the writing process.

RESOURCES

AUDIO PROGRAM	MULTI-LEVEL WORKBOOKS	ACTIVITY MASTER
Words & Dialogs Cassette 4B CD 5: Tracks 4–7	Literacy Workbook Beginning & Intermediate Lifeskills Workbooks Beginning & Intermediate Vocabulary Workbooks	**Reproducible**: A146
TRANSPARENCY	**LANGUAGE & CULTURE NOTES**	**WORDLINKS**
Overhead: T107	**Reproducible:** LC107	longman.com/wordbyword

TYPES OF SENTENCES & PARTS OF SPEECH VOCABULARY INTRODUCTION

- Preview
- Present
- Practice

MODEL CONVERSATION PRACTICE

The first two models practice types of sentences (words A–D) and parts of speech (words 1–7). Introduce and practice the first model before going on to the second. For each model:

1. Have students look at the model illustration. Set the scene:

   Model 1: "A teacher and student are talking."
   Model 2: "A teacher and student are talking."

2. Present the first model using word A and the second model using word 1.

3. Choral Repetition Practice: Full-Class and Individual.

4. Have pairs practice the model.

5. Have pairs present the model.

6. Call on pairs to present a new conversation using word B for the first model and word 2 for the second model.

7. Have pairs practice new conversations.

8. Have pairs present new conversations.

PUNCTUATION MARKS & THE WRITING PROCESS VOCABULARY INTRODUCTION

- Preview
- Present
- Practice

MODEL CONVERSATION PRACTICE

The third and fourth models practice punctuation marks (words 8–15) and the writing process (words 16–21). Introduce and practice the third model before going on to the fourth. For each model:

1. Have students look at the model illustration. Set the scene:

   Model 3: "Two students are discussing a composition that one of them wrote."
   Model 4: "A teacher and student are talking."

2. Present the third model using word 8 and the fourth model using word 16.

3. Choral Repetition Practice: Full-Class and Individual.

4. Have pairs practice the model.

5. Have pairs present the model.

6. Call on pairs to present a new conversation using word 9 for the third model and word 17 for the fourth model.

7. Have pairs practice new conversations.

8. Have pairs present new conversations.

SPELLING PRACTICE

Say a word, and have students spell it aloud or write it. Or, using the transparency, point to an item and have students write the word.

Resource Materials Bring in, or have students bring in, the following materials for vocabulary practice:

- *An English grammar book:* Have students do punctuation exercises from a grammar book.

- *Paragraphs from stories or articles:* Have students identify the parts of speech of the words.

Community Task Have individual students find a sentence or paragraph from an advertisement and bring it to class. Since advertising language is sometimes ungrammatical, have students work together in groups or as a class to edit the language to make it grammatically correct.

Communication Activities

1 Drawing Game
ACTIVITY HANDBOOK PAGE **6**
ACTIVITY MASTER **146**

Have teams compete to identify language items written by one of their team members.

2 Finish the Sentence!
ACTIVITY HANDBOOK PAGE **7**

Begin sentences such as the following for students to complete:

> At the end of a declarative sentence put a . . . *period.*
> At the end of an interrogative sentence put a . . . *question mark.*
> At the end of an imperative sentence put a . . . *period.*
> At the end of an exclamatory sentence put an . . . *exclamation point.*
> To indicate possession use an s with an . . . *apostrophe.*
> A person, place, or thing is a . . . *noun.*
> A word that expresses action is a . . . *verb.*
> A word that substitutes for a noun is a . . . *pronoun.*
> A word that describes a noun is an . . . *adjective.*
> A word that describes a verb is an . . . *adverb.*

3 Find It!
ACTIVITY MASTER **146**

a. Give every student an English Language Arts Word Card.

b. Tell students they have three minutes to find an example of printed English text that uses that item. They can look in books, textbooks, classroom signs, etc.

c. Have students read to the class the text that uses their item.

4 Correct It!

a. Choose a passage of English that is familiar to students, perhaps from a story they are reading. Write the passage on the board, but do not include any punctuation.

b. Have students take turns reading portions of the text and adding the punctuation.

c. Have the class compare their corrected version with the original printed text.

5 Edit It!

a. Bring to class multiple advertisements with incomplete or incorrect grammar.

b. In pairs, have students choose one advertisement and develop a grammatically correct way to express what the advertisement expresses.

c. Have students present their grammatically correct advertisements to the class.

LESSON OBJECTIVE

Students will learn the vocabulary of types of literature and writing.

RESOURCES

AUDIO PROGRAM

Words & Dialogs
Cassette 4B
CD 5: Tracks 8, 9

MULTI-LEVEL WORKBOOKS

Literacy Workbook
Beginning & Intermediate Lifeskills Workbooks
Beginning & Intermediate Vocabulary Workbooks

ACTIVITY MASTER

Reproducible:
A147

TRANSPARENCY
Overhead: T108

LANGUAGE & CULTURE NOTES
Reproducible: LC108

WORDLINKS
longman.com/wordbyword

VOCABULARY INTRODUCTION

- Preview
- Present
- Practice

MODEL CONVERSATION PRACTICE

1. Have students look at the model illustration. Set the scene: "A husband and wife are talking."
2. Present the model using word 1.
3. Choral Repetition Practice: Full-Class and Individual.
4. Have pairs practice the model.
5. Have pairs present the model.
6. Call on pairs to present a new conversation using word 2.
7. Have pairs practice new conversations.
8. Have pairs present new conversations.

SPELLING PRACTICE

Say a word, and have students spell it aloud or write it. Or, using the transparency, point to an item and have students write the word.

WRITING AND DISCUSSION

Have students respond to the questions as a class, in pairs, or in small groups. Or have students write their responses, share their writing with other students, and discuss in class.

Making Connections

Resource Materials Bring in, or have students bring in, the following materials for vocabulary practice:

- *Books and periodicals:* Have students identify the genre of each item.

Community Task Have the class visit a book store and draw a map of the store's floor plan, identifying the locations of its different genres.

Communication Activities

① Finish the Sentence!
ACTIVITY HANDBOOK PAGE **7**

Begin sentences such as the following for students to complete:

> A book-length story about imaginary people and events is a . . . *novel.*
> A written account of another person's life is a . . . *biography.*
> A written account of someone's own life is an . . . *autobiography.*
> An article that expresses an opinion about an issue in the news is an . . . *editorial.*
> A non-fiction composition that presents research on a subject is a . . . *report.*
> A short piece of fiction is a . . . *short story.*
> A piece of writing for internal communication in a business is a . . . *memo.*
> The abbreviation of electronic mail is . . . *e-mail.*
> A short letter that expresses thanks for a gift is a . . . *thank-you note.*
> A communication in real time via the Internet with other Internet users is an . . . *instant message.*

② Ranking
ACTIVITY HANDBOOK PAGE **13**

Write items 1–12 on the board and have students rank the four items they most like to read and the four they least like to read. For example:

Most Like to Read	Least Like to Read
non-fiction	biographies
essays	autobiographies
magazine articles	poetry
editorials	short stories

③ Recommended Reading

a. In small groups, have students write the titles of pieces they have read that they recommend for each genre.

b. Have the groups report to the class. Write a master list on the board of recommended readings.

④ Bestseller List

Bring to class copies of the newspaper's list of the week's bestsellers. Ask students the following questions:

> Have you heard about any of these books?
> What genre is each book? (novel, short story, poetry, biography, autobiography, essay)
> Which book would you most like to read? Why?

⑤ Find the Right Person!
ACTIVITY HANDBOOK PAGES **6–7**
ACTIVITY MASTER **147**

Practice the following questions before having students do the activity:

> How often do you write e-mails?
> How often do you write instant messages?
> How often do you write letters?
> How often do you read a newspaper?
> Did you receive a thank-you note this year?
> Do you like to read magazines more than newspapers?
> How many novels do you read a year?
> How many non-fiction books do you read a year?
> Do you like poetry?
> Do you like biographies?

⑥ Dictate and Discuss

a. Dictate one of the following statements to the class:

> Letters are more personal than e-mails.
> People don't write thank-you notes enough.
> A newspaper shouldn't have editorials, only news reports.
> Teenagers shouldn't write instant messages.
> E-mail is a great way to stay in touch with friends.

b. In small groups, have students discuss their opinions of the statement.

c. As a class, vote in agreement or disagreement with the statement and then have students discuss their reasons.

LESSON OBJECTIVE

Students will learn vocabulary related to topographical features of the earth.

RESOURCES

AUDIO PROGRAM

Words & Dialogs
Cassette 4B
CD 5: Tracks 10, 11

MULTI-LEVEL WORKBOOKS

Literacy Workbook
Beginning & Intermediate Lifeskills Workbooks
Beginning & Intermediate Vocabulary Workbooks

TRANSPARENCY
Overhead: T109

LANGUAGE & CULTURE NOTES
Reproducible: LC109

WORDLINKS
longman.com/wordbyword

VOCABULARY INTRODUCTION

- Preview
- Present
- Practice

MODEL CONVERSATION PRACTICE

1. Have students look at the model illustration. Set the scene: "Two hikers are talking."
2. Present the model using *forest,* then present it using *woods.*
3. Choral Repetition Practice: Full-Class and Individual.
4. Have pairs practice the model.
5. Have pairs present the model.
6. Call on pairs to present a new conversation using word 2.
7. Have pairs practice new conversations.
8. Have pairs present new conversations.

SPELLING PRACTICE

Say a word, and have students spell it aloud or write it. Or, using the transparency, point to an item and have students write the word.

WRITING AND DISCUSSION

Have students respond to the questions as a class, in pairs, or in small groups. Or have students write their responses, share their writing with other students, and discuss in class.

Making Connections

Resource Materials Bring in, or have students bring in, the following materials for vocabulary practice:

○ *National Geographic magazine:* Have students identify the geography in the pictures.

Community Task Have individual students visit an area close to the community and report about the geographical features they see.

Communication Activities

1 Picture This!
ACTIVITY HANDBOOK PAGES 12–13

Describe a landscape and have students draw what you describe. For example:

> There are several tall mountains in the background. The mountain on the right has a waterfall that leads to rapids. In the center there's a lake, and to the left of the lake there's . . .

2 Secret Word Associations
ACTIVITY HANDBOOK PAGE 14

Have students choose a geographical item, brainstorm associations with and examples of that word, and see if the class can guess the word. For example:

dark/green/wet/lots of animals/the Amazon:	[rainforest]
dry/sand/hot/lonely/the Sahara:	[desert]
tall/rocky/cold/Sierra Nevada:	[mountain range]
salt water/quiet/boats/port:	[bay]

3 Where Am I?

Describe a scene using words from *Picture Dictionary* page 109 and have students guess where you are. For example:

> Teacher: I see lots of trees all around me, several small animals, and some small streams.
> Student: You're in the woods.
> Teacher: Everywhere I look I see just sky and water.
> Student: You're on the ocean.

Variation: Do the activity in pairs or small groups, where students describe scenes and others guess where they are.

4 Geography Crossword
ACTIVITY HANDBOOK PAGES 4–5

Have students connect geography words to create a crossword. For example:

5 Listen and Number
ACTIVITY HANDBOOK PAGE 10

In pairs, have one student tell a story using geography words and have the other student number the pictures in their order of occurrence in the story.

6 What Can You Do?
ACTIVITY HANDBOOK PAGES 15–16

Have students make a list of all the things they do at different geographical sites. For example:

Forest
go camping
hike
fish
hunt

Lake
sail
swim
sunbathe
fish

(continued)

7 Ranking
ACTIVITY HANDBOOK PAGE 13

Have students review the geographical features on *Picture Dictionary* page 109 and choose their three favorite geographical features and then their three least favorite. For example:

Favorite	Least Favorite
mountain range	desert
meadow	rainforest
stream	jungle

8 Describe the Pictures

a. Bring to class pictures of landscapes from magazines or the Internet.

b. Have pairs of students choose one picture to describe in a written paragraph.

c. Have students read their descriptions aloud and have the class listen and identify the picture of the landscape

9 Survey

a. Give each student or pair of students one of the following questions:

Have you ever been in a rainforest? Where?
Have you ever been on a mountain peak? Where?
Have you ever swum in a lake? Where?
Have you ever seen an ocean? Where?
Have you ever been to a desert? Where?
Have you ever been in a canyon? Where?
Have you ever been on an island? Where?
Have you ever seen a waterfall? Where?
Have you ever been on a peninsula? Where?

b. Have students circulate around the class and survey all their classmates.

c. When students are finished, have them tally their results and present them to the class.

10 Investigate!

a. Brainstorm names of places around the world (countries/regions/states) and write a list on the board.

b. Have students choose one place to investigate.

c. Have students research the geography of the land and give a brief five-minute report to the class. Students can supplement their talk with images downloaded from the Internet.

LESSON OBJECTIVE

Students will learn the vocabulary of materials and procedures used in scientific experiments in school.

RESOURCES

AUDIO PROGRAM
Words & Dialogs
Cassette 4B
CD 5: Tracks 12, 13

MULTI-LEVEL WORKBOOKS
Literacy Workbook
Beginning & Intermediate Lifeskills Workbooks
Beginning & Intermediate Vocabulary Workbooks

ACTIVITY MASTERS
Reproducibles:
A148–A150

TRANSPARENCY
Overhead: T110

LANGUAGE & CULTURE NOTES
Reproducible: LC110

WORDLINKS
longman.com/wordbyword

VOCABULARY INTRODUCTION

- Preview
- Present
- Practice

MODEL CONVERSATION PRACTICE

There are two model conversations—the first for words 1–18 and the second for phrases A–F. Introduce and practice the first model before going on to the second. For each model:

1. Have students look at the model illustration. Set the scene:

   Model 1: "Two students are talking."
   Model 2: "A teacher and student are talking."

2. Present the first model using word 1 and the second model using phrase A.

3. Choral Repetition Practice: Full-Class and Individual.

4. Have pairs practice the model.

5. Have pairs present the model.

6. Call on pairs to present a new conversation using word 2 for the first model and phrase B for the second model.

7. Have pairs practice new conversations.

8. Have pairs present new conversations.

SPELLING PRACTICE

Say a word or phrase, and have students spell it aloud or write it. Or, using the transparency, point to an item and have students write the word or phrase.

WRITING AND DISCUSSION

Have students respond to the questions as a class, in pairs, or in small groups. Or have students write their responses, share their writing with other students, and discuss in class.

Making Connections

Resource Materials Bring in, or have students bring in, the following materials for vocabulary practice:

- *Science experiment materials:* Have students identify the different items and explain how to use them.

- *Science fair project winners from the Internet:* Download a few samples of students' award-winning experiments and read with the class. Have students identify the problem, hypothesis, procedure, observations, and conclusions of the experiment.

Community Tasks If your school has a science room, have the class take a tour with the science teacher.

Have your class take a tour of a science laboratory in the area. Universities usually have some laboratories open to the public.

Communication Activities

1 Chain Game
ACTIVITY HANDBOOK PAGES 2–3

Begin the chain as follows: "In my science class I use a test tube," and have students continue it. For example:

> Teacher: In my science class I use a test tube.
> Student 1: In my science class I use a test tube and a beaker.
> Student 2: In my science class I use a test tube, a beaker, and a Bunsen burner.
> Etc.

2 Concentration
ACTIVITY HANDBOOK PAGE 3
ACTIVITY MASTER 148

Have students shuffle the cards and place them face-down in three rows of 6 each, then attempt to find cards that match.

3 Movable Categories
ACTIVITY HANDBOOK PAGE 11
ACTIVITY MASTER 149

Call out the following categories and have students go to the appropriate side of the room:

> things made of glass
> things you use for measuring
> things you use with liquids
> things you use with solids
> things you use with heat

4 Category Dictation
ACTIVITY HANDBOOK PAGE 2

Dictate words that fit into the above categories.

5 Drawing Game
ACTIVITY HANDBOOK PAGE 6
ACTIVITY MASTER 149

Have teams compete to identify science items drawn by one of their team members.

6 Line Up!
ACTIVITY MASTER 150

a. Make a copy of Activity Master 161, cut it up, and distribute it to six students

b. Have students memorize their lines and then work together to arrange themselves in a line from the first step to the last.

Variation: Students can work in pairs to read and arrange the cards on a table top.

7 Design an Experiment

Science experiments are not limited to beakers and Bunsen burners. Have your students design an experiment on how to learn English better using the Scientific Method.

a. In pairs, have students state a problem, form a hypothesis, and plan an experiment. Some possible problems could be:

> how to memorize English words better
> how to develop better listening comprehension of English
> how to pronounce English better

b. Have students write their hypotheses and experiment plans on poster board. Host a *Science Fair* so all the students can read each others' experiment plans.

LESSON OBJECTIVE

Students will learn vocabulary of the physical features of the universe and of equipment used in space exploration and the study of astronomy.

RESOURCES

AUDIO PROGRAM

Words & Dialogs
Cassette 4B
CD 5: Tracks 14, 15

MULTI-LEVEL WORKBOOKS

Literacy Workbook
Beginning & Intermediate Lifeskills Workbooks
Beginning & Intermediate Vocabulary Workbooks

TRANSPARENCY
Overhead: T111

LANGUAGE & CULTURE NOTES
Reproducible: LC111

WORDLINKS
longman.com/wordbyword

VOCABULARY INTRODUCTION

- Preview
- Present
- Practice

MODEL CONVERSATION PRACTICE

There are two model conversations—the first for words 1–24 and the second for words 28–30. Introduce and practice the first model before going on to the second. For each model:

1. Have students look at the model illustration. Set the scene:

   Model 1: "A father and daughter are talking."
   Model 2: "A reporter is asking a question at a press conference."

2. Present the first model using word 1 and the second model using word 28.

3. Choral Repetition Practice: Full-Class and Individual.

4. Have pairs practice the model.

5. Have pairs present the model.

6. Call on pairs to present a new conversation using word 2 for the first model and word 29 for the second model.

7. Have pairs practice new conversations.

8. Have pairs present new conversations.

SPELLING PRACTICE

Say a word, and have students spell it aloud or write it. Or, using the transparency, point to an item and have students write the word.

WRITING AND DISCUSSION

Have students respond to the questions as a class, in pairs, or in small groups. Or have students write their responses, share their writing with other students, and discuss in class.

Making Connections

Resource Materials Bring in, or have students bring in, the following materials for vocabulary practice:

- *Pictures from an astronomy textbook:* Have students identify items in the pictures.

- *Pictures from an observatory website:* Have students identify items in the pictures.

- *Reports from an Internet UFO report center:* Find places close by that have reported sightings of UFOs.

Community Task Have the class visit the local science museum and see the exhibit on the solar system, or if possible, visit a planetarium show.

Communication Activities

1 **Clap in Rhythm**
ACTIVITY HANDBOOK PAGE **3**

Have students name different universe words to a clapping rhythm.

2 **Chain Game: On My Trip to Outer Space . . .**
ACTIVITY HANDBOOK PAGES **2–3**

Begin the chain as follows: "On my trip to outer space, I saw Venus," and have students continue it. For example:

Teacher: "On my trip to outer space, I saw Venus."
Student 1: "On my trip to outer space, I saw Venus and a space station."
Student 2: "On my trip to outer space, I saw Venus, a space station, and Mars."
Etc.

3 **Finish the Sentence!**
ACTIVITY HANDBOOK PAGE **7**

Begin sentences such as the following for students to complete:

A galaxy is a collection of . . . *stars.*
A famous constellation is The Little . . . *Dipper.*
A solar eclipse is when the moon passes between Earth and the . . . *sun.*
A lunar eclipse is when Earth passes between the sun and the . . . *moon.*
The planet closest to the sun is . . . *Mercury.*
The planet farthest from the sun is . . . *Pluto.*
A chunk of rock or metal that is flying through space is a . . . *meteor.*
When we can only see half the moon we call it a . . . *quarter moon.*
When we can see all the moon we call it a . . . *full moon.*
A person who studies the stars is called an . . . *astronomer.*
A person who travels in spacecraft is called an . . . *astronaut.*

4 **Category Dictation**
ACTIVITY HANDBOOK PAGE **2**

Dictate words that fit into the above categories.

5 **Ranking**
ACTIVITY HANDBOOK PAGE **13**

Have students rank the planets according to the following criteria: smallest to largest, closest to the sun to farthest from the sun, with the most moons to with the least. For example:

Smallest	Closest to the Sun	Most Moons
Pluto	Mercury	Jupiter (60)
Mercury	Venus	Saturn (31)
Mars	Earth	Uranus (27)
Venus	Mars	Neptune (13)
Earth	Jupiter	Mars (2)
Neptune	Saturn	Pluto (1)
Uranus	Uranus	Earth (1)
Saturn	Neptune	Venus (0)
Jupiter	Pluto	Mercury (0)

6 **Information Search**

a. Tell each student to choose one universe item he or she would like to learn more about.

b. Have students do research on what they have chosen and report their findings back to the class.

c. Compile the information students bring to class into a *Universe and Space Exploration* notebook.

7 **Role Play: A UFO Has Landed!**

Have groups of students create a role play in which a UFO has landed and its inhabitants encounter a group of *earthlings*. Have each group present its role play and let the class vote on the most original!

1 Odd Word Out

Read the following lists of words, and have students identify the category and the "odd word out"—the word that doesn't fit the category:

classroom, library, track, gym, football
[Category: PLACES IN SCHOOL. Odd word out: football]

school nurse, astronomer, coach, teacher, principal
[Category: SCHOOL PERSONNEL. Odd word out: astronomer]

math, English, history, science, centimeter
[Category: SCHOOL SUBJECTS. Odd word out: centimeter]

height, width, yearbook, depth, length
[Category: MEASUREMENTS. Odd word out: yearbook]

band, hallway, debate club, choir, community service
[Category: EXTRACURRICULAR ACTIVITIES. Odd word out: hallway]

cube, geometry, trigonometry, statistics, calculus
[Category: TYPES OF MATH. Odd word out: cube]

cylinder, sphere, cone, pyramid, triangle
[Category: SOLID FIGURES. Odd word out: triangle]

adjective, adverb, period, noun, preposition
[Category: PARTS OF SPEECH. Odd word out: period]

yard, brainstorm, organize ideas, write a first draft, revise
[Category: WRITING PROCESS. Odd word out: yard]

comma, fiction, semi-colon, colon, quotation marks
[Category: PUNCTUATION. Odd word out: fiction]

poetry, short stories, novels, river
[Category: FICTION. Odd word out: river]

pond, lake, note, ocean, river
[Category: BODIES OF WATER. Odd word out: note]

memo, letter, short story, note, instant message
[Category: KINDS OF LETTERS. Odd word out: short story]

Mercury, satellite, Jupiter, Saturn, Earth
[Category: PLANETS. Odd word out: satellite]

2 Who Am I?
ACTIVITY HANDBOOK PAGE 17

Tell about different occupations and have students guess who you are talking about. For example:

Teacher: I take care of sick students at school. Who am I?
Student: The school nurse.

Teacher: I manage the school. Who am I?
Student: The principal.

Teacher: I travel in a spacecraft. Who am I?
Student: An astronaut.

Teacher: I study the stars. Who am I?
Student: An astronomer

Teacher: I serve food to students in school. Who am I?
Student: A cafeteria worker.

Teacher: I teach gym class. Who am I?
Student: The P.E. teacher.

Teacher: I manage and teach the football team. Who am I?
Student: The coach.

Teacher: I help the principal manage the school. Who am I?
Student: The assistant principal.

Teacher: I make sure the students eat their lunches. Who am I?
Student: A lunchroom monitor.

3 School Quiz Game
ACTIVITY MASTER 151

a. Divide the class into four teams.

b. Make a copy of Activity Master 163, cut it up in to cards, and place the cards face-down in a pile on a table in front of the room.

c. Pick cards from the pile and have the teams take turns answering your questions. Give each team a time limit to answer each question (30 seconds or 1 minute)

d. The team with the most correct answers wins.

(continued)

4 Letter Game

ACTIVITY HANDBOOK PAGE 9

Say statements such as the following and have teams compete to identify the items:

I'm thinking of a type of school that starts with *p*.	[preschool]
I'm thinking of a type of school that starts with *m*.	[medical school]
I'm thinking of a person who works in a school that starts with *c*.	[custodian]
I'm thinking of a school subject that starts with *p*.	[physics]
I'm thinking of an extracurricular subject that that starts with *c*.	[chess club]
I'm thinking of a type of math that starts with *t*.	[trigonometry]
I'm thinking of a metric measurement that starts with *c*.	[centimeter]
I'm thinking of a type of sentence that starts with *e*.	[exclamatory]
I'm thinking of a punctuation mark that starts with *q*.	[quotation marks]
I'm thinking of a kind of non-fiction that starts with *a*.	[autobiography]
I'm thinking of a kind a geographical word that starts with *c*.	[canyon]
I'm thinking of a science classroom item that starts with *t*.	[test tube]
I'm thinking of something in the universe that starts with *g*.	[galaxy]

5 Drawing Game

ACTIVITY HANDBOOK PAGE 6
ACTIVITY MASTERS 138, 144, 148

Have teams compete to identify vocabulary items drawn by one of their team members.

6 School Studies

Have students individually make lists of all the subjects they studied in their school careers. In pairs, have students compare their lists.

7 Who Said It?

a. Give each student a piece of paper and ask everyone to write the answers to the following questions:

What is your favorite subject to study? Why?
What is your favorite place in the world? Why?

b. Collect the papers, read each one, and see if the class can match the answers with the students who wrote them.

UNIT 13 Work

TOPICS	DICTIONARY	TEACHER'S GUIDE
Occupations I	112–113	284–285
Occupations II	114–115	286–289
Job Skills and Activities	116–117	290–291
Job Search	118	292–293
The Workplace	119	294–296
Office Supplies and Equipment	120	297–299
The Factory	121	300–302
The Construction Site	122	303–305
Job Safety	123	306–307
Unit 13 Communication Activity Review	112–123	308–309

AUDIO PROGRAM

Words & Dialogs	WordSong: *Working*
Audio Cassette 4B	Audio Cassette 7B
Audio Cassette 5A	Audio CD 8: Tracks 12
Audio CD 5:	(Vocal) & 13 (Sing-along)
Tracks 16–36	Song Masters S25, S26

WORKBOOKS

For Multi-Level Practice

Literacy Workbook
Beginning Lifeskills Workbook
Beginning Vocabulary Workbook
Intermediate Lifeskills Workbook
Intermediate Vocabulary Workbook

WORDLINKS

Internet Resources through the
***Word by Word* Companion Website**

http://www.longman.com/wordbyword

ACTIVITY MASTERS

Reproducibles for Communication Activities
A8, A152–A175

TRANSPARENCIES

Full-Color Overheads for Class Practice
T112–T113—T123

LANGUAGE & CULTURE NOTES

Information for Teachers &
Intermediate /Advanced Students
LC112–113—LC123

VOCABULARY GAME CARDS

For Vocabulary Practice,
Activities, & Games
Cards 299–374

LESSON OBJECTIVE

Students will learn the names of common occupations.

RESOURCES

AUDIO PROGRAM

Words & Dialogs
Cassette 4B
CD 5: Tracks 16–18

WordSong: *Working*
Cassette 7B • CD 8: Tracks 12, 13
Song Masters S25, S26

MULTI-LEVEL WORKBOOKS

Literacy Workbook
Beginning & Intermediate Lifeskills Workbooks
Beginning & Intermediate Vocabulary Workbooks

VOCABULARY GAME CARDS

Cards 299–336

ACTIVITY MASTERS

Reproducibles: A152, A153, A156, A157, A160

TRANSPARENCIES

Overheads:
T112–T113

LANGUAGE & CULTURE NOTES

Reproducible: LC112–113

WORDLINKS

longman.com/wordbyword

VOCABULARY INTRODUCTION

- Preview
- Present
- Practice

MODEL CONVERSATION PRACTICE

1. Have students look at the model illustration. Set the scene: "Two people at a health club are making conversation while they are exercising."
2. Present the model.
3. Choral Repetition Practice: Full-Class and Individual.
4. Have pairs practice the model.
5. Have pairs present the model.
6. Call on pairs to present a new conversation using word 2.
7. Have pairs practice new conversations.
8. Have pairs present new conversations.

ADDITIONAL CONVERSATION PRACTICE

Before students practice the additional conversations, you may want to have them listen to the examples on the Audio Program.

Conversation 1 Have students practice and present conversations with any words they wish.

Conversation 2 Have students practice and present conversations with any words they wish.

SPELLING PRACTICE

Say a word, and have students spell it aloud or write it. Or, using the transparency, point to an item and have students write the word.

WRITING AND DISCUSSION

Have students respond to the questions as a class, in pairs, or in small groups. Or have students write their responses, share their writing with other students, and discuss in class.

♪♪ WORDSONG ♪♪

1. Have students listen to the vocal version of *Working* one or more times. Then have students listen again as they read the song lyrics on Song Master S25.
2. Have students sing as you play either the vocal or the sing-along version of the song.
3. For fun, have a song competition in which students perform solo or in groups and the class votes for the best performance.
4. For additional practice, students can complete the cloze exercise on Song Master S26.

VOCABULARY GAME CARDS

Have students practice vocabulary, do activities, and play games with Vocabulary Game Cards 299–336. Activities and games are described in the set of cards.

Resource Materials Bring in, or have students bring in, the following materials for vocabulary practice:

- *Want ads from the newspaper for a variety of occupations:* Identify the occupations listed in the want ads.

- *Career counseling materials that describe different occupations:* Identify the training or schooling required for the occupations.

Community Tasks If available within the school system, invite the career counselor to speak with students about career opportunities.

Have individual students do an online search for *career fairs*. Have each student research a different occupation and find out the opportunities, requirements, and salary for that occupation and then report back to the class.

Have pairs of students interview a person about his or her occupation and then report back to the class.

Communication Activities

See the Communication Activities on pages 371–374 for *Occupations II*.

LESSON OBJECTIVE

Students will learn the names of common occupations.

RESOURCES

AUDIO PROGRAM		MULTI-LEVEL WORKBOOKS	VOCABULARY GAME CARDS
Words & Dialogs Cassette 4B CD 5: Tracks 19–21	**WordSong:** *Working* Cassette 7B • CD 8: Tracks 12, 13 Song Masters S25, S26	Literacy Workbook Beginning & Intermediate Lifeskills Workbooks Beginning & Intermediate Vocabulary Workbooks	Cards 299–374

ACTIVITY MASTERS	TRANSPARENCIES	LANGUAGE & CULTURE NOTES	WORDLINKS
Reproducibles: A154, A155, A158, A159, A161	**Overheads:** T114–T115	**Reproducible:** LC114–115	longman.com/wordbyword

VOCABULARY INTRODUCTION

- Preview
- Present
- Practice

MODEL CONVERSATION PRACTICE

1. Have students look at the model illustration. Set the scene: "A bank officer is talking to someone who is applying for a loan."
2. Present the model.
3. Choral Repetition Practice: Full-Class and Individual.
4. Have pairs practice the model.
5. Have pairs present the model.
6. Call on pairs to present a new conversation using word 2.
7. Have pairs practice new conversations.
8. Have pairs present new conversations.

ADDITIONAL CONVERSATION PRACTICE

Before students practice the additional conversations, you may want to have them listen to the examples on the Audio Program.

Conversation 1 Have students practice and present conversations with any words they wish.

Conversation 2 Have students practice and present conversations with any words they wish.

SPELLING PRACTICE

Say a word, and have students spell it aloud or write it. Or, using the transparency, point to an item and have students write the word.

WRITING AND DISCUSSION

Have students respond to the questions as a class, in pairs, or in small groups. Or have students write their responses, share their writing with other students, and discuss in class.

VOCABULARY GAME CARDS

Have students practice vocabulary, do activities, and play games with Vocabulary Game Cards 299–374. Activities and games are described in the set of cards.

Resource Materials Bring in, or have students bring in, the following materials for vocabulary practice:

- *Want ads from the newspaper for a variety of occupations:* Identify the occupations listed in the want ads.

- *Career counseling materials that describe different occupations:* Identify the training or schooling required for the occupations.

Community Tasks If available within the school system, invite the career counselor to speak with students about career opportunities.

Have individual students do an online search for *career fairs*. Have each student research a different occupation and find out the opportunities, requirements, and salary for that occupation and then report back to the class.

Have pairs of students interview a person about his or her occupation and then report back to the class.

Communication Activities

The following activities are appropriate for both *Occupations* I and *Occupations* II. You can do the activities separately for each lesson or together for both lessons.

1 Concentration
ACTIVITY HANDBOOK PAGE 3
ACTIVITY MASTERS **152, 153** (for *Occupations* I) and **154, 155** (for *Occupations* II)

Have students shuffle the cards and place them face-down in three rows of 6 each, then attempt to find cards that match.

2 Who Am I?
ACTIVITY HANDBOOK PAGE 17

Tell about different occupations and have students guess who you are talking about. For example:

Occupations I
Teacher: I build walls with stones. Who am I?
Student: A bricklayer.

Teacher: I answer customer questions about products. Who am I?
Student: A customer service representative.

Teacher: I supervise work in a factory. Who am I?
Student: A foreman.

Teacher: I visit sick patients in their home and take care of them. Who am I?
Student: A home health aide.

Teacher: I stay home with the children and manage the house. Who am I?
Student: A homemaker.

Occupations II
Teacher: I write newspaper articles. Who am I?
Student: A journalist.

Teacher: I take care of a woman's fingernails and toenails. Who am I?
Student: A manicurist.

Teacher: I take pictures. Who am I?
Student: A photographer.

Teacher: I call people in their homes and try to sell them products. Who am I?
Student: A telemarketer.

Teacher: I build things with metal. Who am I?
Student: A welder.

3 Ask Me a Question!
ACTIVITY HANDBOOK PAGE 2
ACTIVITY MASTERS **156, 157** (for *Occupations* I) and **158, 159** (for *Occupations* II)

Have students walk around trying to guess each other's occupations by asking yes/no questions. For example:

Occupations I

Do you work outside?	[No.]
Do you work in an office?	[Yes.]
Do you manage people?	[No.]
Do you design things?	[Yes.]
Do you design houses?	[Yes.]
Are you an architect?	[Yes.]

Occupations II

Do you work outside?	[No.]
Do you work in an office?	[No.]
Do you work in a store?	[No.]
Do you repair things?	[No.]
Do you build things?	[No.]
Do you design things?	[No.]
Do you work in a restaurant?	[Yes.]
Are you a waitress?	[Yes.]

4 It's Someone Who . . .

ACTIVITY HANDBOOK PAGE 9
ACTIVITY MASTERS 156, 157 (for *Occupations I*) and 158, 159 (for *Occupations II*)

Have students give definitions of occupations to each other beginning with "It's someone who . . ." For example:

Occupations I
It's someone who performs in plays and movies. [An actor.]
It's someone who builds things. [A carpenter.]
It's someone who keys information in a computer. [A data entry clerk.]
It's someone who catches fish. [A fisher.]
It's someone who sews clothing. [A garment worker.]

Occupations II
It's someone who works in a post office. [A postal worker.]
It's someone who paints houses. [A painter.]
It's someone who collects garbage. [A sanitation worker.]
It's someone who serves food in a restaurant. [A waiter/waitress.]
It's someone who puts products on the shelves of a store. [A stock clerk.]

5 Cooperative Definitions

ACTIVITY HANDBOOK PAGE 4

Have groups write definitions of occupations and then pass their definitions to other groups.

6 What Do They Use?

a. Divide the class into small groups.

b. Call out one of the occupations and have each group write down as many words as they can think of that a person in that occupation would need or use.

c. Have the groups call out their words and make a common list on the board.

d. Tell students they can question a word, in which case the student who suggested it must explain the reason for including it.

7 What's Happening?

Have each student choose one of the people depicted in the *Picture Dictionary* and say a few sentences about what he or she is doing.

8 Occupation Crossword

ACTIVITY HANDBOOK PAGES 4–5

Have students connect occupation words to create a crossword. For example:

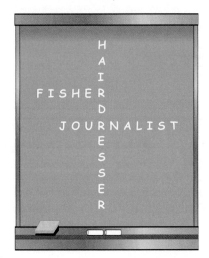

9 Occupation Match Game

ACTIVITY HANDBOOK PAGE 11
ACTIVITY MASTERS 160 (for *Occupations I*), 161 (for *Occupations II*)

Have students find the person whose card matches theirs.

10 Things in Common

ACTIVITY HANDBOOK PAGE 14

Have students think of two occupations that have things in common. For example:

barber—assembler
Both use their hands.
Both work indoors.
Both stand while they work.

truck driver—delivery person
Both use vehicles.
Both go to different places around town.
Both transport things.

secretary—journalist
Both use computers.
Both use the phone a lot.
Both spend a lot of time writing.

11 Occupation Talk!

ACTIVITY HANDBOOK PAGE 17
ACTIVITY MASTERS 156, 157 (for *Occupations I*) and 158, 159 (for *Occupations II*)

Give students an Occupation Word Card, and have them speak to the class for one minute about that occupation.

12 Movable Categories

ACTIVITY HANDBOOK PAGE 11
ACTIVITY MASTERS 156, 157 (for *Occupations I*) and 158, 159 (for *Occupations II*)

Call out the following categories and have students go to the appropriate side of the room:

people who work outside
people who use computers in their work
people who work in stores
people who prepare and serve food
people who take care of other people
people who use vehicles
people who wear a uniform
people who use machines (other than computers)
people who carry heavy loads
people who build things
people who are good at math
people who entertain others

13 Ranking

ACTIVITY HANDBOOK PAGE 13

Have students look at the occupations listed on *Picture Dictionary* page 112 and rank the three best paying and three worst paying jobs. For example:

Best Paying
businessman/businesswoman
computer software engineer
accountant

Worst Paying
child day-care worker
artist
babysitter

Variation: Students can also rank the jobs according to the amount of education they require and the level of interest they hold (interesting/boring).

14 Interesting Occupations

In pairs, have students look at each one of the occupations pages on *Picture Dictionary* pages 112–115 and answer the following questions:

On this page, which occupation would you most like to have? Why?
What education or training do you need for this occupation?
Do you know someone who has this occupation?

15 Take a Walk!

Have students form small groups and walk down a street in a business area near your school. Have them write down all the occupations they see and then report their findings back to the class.

16 Word Clues

ACTIVITY HANDBOOK PAGE 17
ACTIVITY MASTERS 156, 157 (for *Occupations I*) and 158, 159 (for *Occupations II*)

Have students take turns giving one-word clues to team members who try to guess the occupation. For example:

[The word is *mechanic*.]
Team 1 Player:	"garage"	[Team 1 guesses]
Team 2 Player:	"car"	[Team 2 guesses]
Team 1 Player:	"fix"	[Team 1 guesses]

[The word is *receptionist*.]
Team 1 Player:	"office"	[Team 1 guesses]
Team 2 Player:	"telephone"	[Team 2 guesses]
Team 1 Player:	"smile"	[Team 1 guesses]

[The word is *serviceman/servicewoman*.]
Team 1 Player:	"armed forces"	[Team 1 guesses]
Team 2 Player:	"military"	[Team 2 guesses]
Team 1 Player:	"soldier"	[Team 1 guesses]

17 What's the Story?

Have each student choose a person depicted in the *Picture Dictionary* and tell a story about that person. Possible questions to answer are:

Who is he/she?
What is his/her occupation?
Where does he/she work?
What does he/she do at work every day?
Is it interesting? Why or why not?
Where does he/she live?

Encourage students to be as creative as they wish.

18 Pair Interviews

Have students interview each other about their occupations and report back to the class about their partner's job. If students wish, they can choose an occupation other than their own, perhaps an occupation they would like to have.

19 Read the Classified Ads

Bring to class the classified section of a newspaper. In pairs, have students choose a job and role play an applicant calling an employer for more information about that job.

LESSON OBJECTIVE

Students will learn the names of skills and activities associated with various occupations and work sites.

RESOURCES

AUDIO PROGRAM 	MULTI-LEVEL WORKBOOKS 	ACTIVITY MASTERS
Words & Dialogs Cassette 4B CD 5: Tracks 22–24	**WordSong:** *Working* Cassette 7B • CD 8: Tracks 12, 13 Song Masters S25, S26	Literacy Workbook Beginning & Intermediate Lifeskills Workbooks Beginning & Intermediate Vocabulary Workbooks	**Reproducibles:** A162, A163

TRANSPARENCIES	LANGUAGE & CULTURE NOTES	WORDLINKS
Overheads: T116, T117	**Reproducible:** LC116–117	longman.com/wordbyword

VOCABULARY INTRODUCTION

- Preview
- Present
- Practice

MODEL CONVERSATION PRACTICE

1. Have students look at the model illustration. Set the scene: "An agent is talking to an actress."
2. Present the model.
3. Choral Repetition Practice: Full-Class and Individual.
4. Have pairs practice the model.
5. Have pairs present the model.
6. Call on pairs to present a new conversation using word 2.
7. Have pairs practice new conversations.
8. Have pairs present new conversations.

ADDITIONAL CONVERSATION PRACTICE

Before students practice the additional conversations, you may want to have them listen to the examples on the Audio Program.

Conversation 1 Have students practice and present conversations with any words they wish.

Conversation 2 Have students practice and present conversations with any words they wish.

SPELLING PRACTICE

Say a word, and have students spell it aloud or write it. Or, using the transparency, point to an item and have students write the word.

WRITING AND DISCUSSION

Have students respond to the question as a class, in pairs, or in small groups. Or have students write their responses, share their writing with other students, and discuss in class.

Making Connections

Resource Materials Bring in, or have students bring in, the following materials for vocabulary practice:

- *Want ads from the newspaper for a variety of occupations:* Identify the skills required for each occupation.
- *Career counseling materials that describe different occupations:* Identify the activities of each occupation.

Community Tasks If available within the school system, invite the career counselor to speak with students about different careers.

Have pairs of students interview a person about his or her occupation and then report back to the class.

Communication Activities

1 This Is Your Life [Variation 1]

Have students choose a scene on *Picture Dictionary* pages 116–117 and tell a few sentences about the person and what he or she is doing.

2 This Is Your Life [Variation 2]

Have students select a scene on *Picture Dictionary* pages 116–117 and make up a story about the person in the scene. Possible questions to answer are:

Who is he/she?
What's his/her occupation?
Where does he/she work?
Is his/her work interesting? Why or why not?
Where does he/she live?
Does this person have a family?

Encourage students to be as creative as they wish.

3 Miming Game
ACTIVITY HANDBOOK PAGE 11
ACTIVITY MASTER 162

Have students take turns pantomiming job activities. The class tries to guess what the person is doing. For example:

You're singing.
You're filing papers.

4 What's the Object?
ACTIVITY HANDBOOK PAGE 16

Call out job activities and have students add appropriate objects. For example:

assemble . . . *components/computers/toys/cars*
prepare . . . *vegetables/sandwiches/dinner*
paint . . . *houses/walls/ceilings/fences/pictures*
sew . . . *dresses/shirts/skirts/pants/coats*
clean . . . *houses/offices/buildings/refrigerators*

5 What Do They Do?

a. Divide the class into small groups.

b. Give each group the name of an occupation and have them write down all the work activities they can think of that are associated with that occupation.

c. Have the groups report back to the class and see if the class can add other activities.

6 Mystery Word Association Game
ACTIVITY HANDBOOK PAGES 11–12

Have students write work activities for occupation *mystery words* for others to guess. For example:

take care of children/ clean/cook/manage the house	[homemaker]
speak many languages/ type/write	[translator]
cook/serve/prepare food	[food service worker]
write/type/interview/ travel	[journalist]
type/file/speak	[secretary]

7 Movable Categories
ACTIVITY HANDBOOK PAGE 11
ACTIVITY MASTER 162

Call out the following categories and have students go to the appropriate side of the room:

things you can do with a vehicle
things you can do with words
things you can do with your voice
things you can do outside
things you can do with food
things you can do with buildings
things you can do with your hands
things you can do with equipment

8 Category Dictation
ACTIVITY HANDBOOK PAGE 2

Dictate words that fit into the above categories.

9 Job Skill and Activity Match Game
ACTIVITY HANDBOOK PAGE 11
ACTIVITY MASTER 163

Have students find the person whose card matches theirs.

10 Who Is It?

a. On a piece of paper have students write down a list of their job skills.

b. Collect the papers and redistribute them.

c. Have students read the list of skills aloud and guess who that person is.

LESSON OBJECTIVE

Students will learn the vocabulary related to looking for and applying for a job in the United States.

RESOURCES

AUDIO PROGRAM		MULTI-LEVEL WORKBOOKS 	ACTIVITY MASTER
Words & Dialogs Cassette 4B CD 5: Tracks 25, 26	**WordSong:** *Working* Cassette 7B ● CD 8: Tracks 12, 13 Song Masters S25, S26	Literacy Workbook Beginning & Intermediate Lifeskills Workbooks Beginning & Intermediate Vocabulary Workbooks	**Reproducible:** A164

TRANSPARENCY	LANGUAGE & CULTURE NOTES	WORDLINKS
Overhead: T118	**Reproducible:** LC118	longman.com/wordbyword

VOCABULARY INTRODUCTION

● Preview
● Present
● Practice

MODEL CONVERSATION PRACTICE

There are two model conversations—the first for words 1–3 and the second for phrases D–F and H–M. Introduce and practice the first model before going on to the second. For each model:

1. Have students look at the model illustration. Set the scene:

    Model 1: "Two friends are talking."

    Model 2: "A mother is asking her son about his job interview."

2. Present the first model using word 1 and the second model using phrase D.

3. Choral Repetition Practice: Full-Class and Individual.

4. Have pairs practice the model.

5. Have pairs present the model.

6. Call on pairs to present a new conversation using word 2 for the first model and phrase E for the second model.

7. Have pairs practice new conversations.

8. Have pairs present new conversations.

SPELLING PRACTICE

Say a word or phrase, and have students spell it aloud or write it. Or, using the transparency, point to an item and have students write the word or phase.

WRITING AND DISCUSSION

Have students respond to the questions as a class, in pairs, or in small groups. Or have students write their responses, share their writing with other students, and discuss in class.

Making Connections

Resource Materials Bring in, or have students bring in, the following materials for vocabulary practice:

○ *Classified ads from the newspaper or employment websites:* Have pairs of students look for a certain kind of job opening (teacher, assembler, etc.) and then explain what jobs are available and how to apply.

○ *A sample resume (downloaded from career counseling websites):* Identify the person's skills, qualifications, and experience. Identify what kind of job this person would want to apply for.

Community Tasks If possible, invite a job counselor to come to class to talk about the application process and how to write a resume.

Invite the school director to talk about the job application process for teachers at your school.

Communication Activities

1 Chain Story

ACTIVITY HANDBOOK PAGE 3

Begin the story as follows: "Bob needed to get a new job, so he read want ads in the newspaper."

2 What's the Story?

a. In pairs, have students look at the scenes on *Picture Dictionary* page 118 and write a story about the person looking for a job. Make sure they answer the following questions:

What's his name?
What kind of work is he looking for?
What's his job experience?
What are his skills and qualifications?

b. Have students tell their stories to the class.

3 Survey: How to Find a Job

a. Have students interview other students in the school about how they found their jobs. Possible survey questions:

What job do you have now?
How did you find out about the job you have now?
Did you fill out an application?
Did you send a resume?
Did you have an interview?

b. Have students report their results and then discuss the following questions:

What jobs do students have?
What was the most common way to find out about a job?
How many people sent in resumes?
How many people filled out applications?
Which kinds of jobs required applications?
Which kinds of jobs required resumes?

4 Find the Right Person!

ACTIVITY HANDBOOK PAGES 6–7
ACTIVITY MASTER 164

Practice the following questions before having students do the activity:

Do you have a resume?
Did you ever fill out a job application?
Did you ever have a job interview?
Did you ever find a job through a want ad in the newspaper?

Do you work part-time?
Do you work full-time?
Do you get good benefits?
Are you looking for a job right now?
How often do you read the classified ads?
What days do you work?

5 Dictate and Discuss

a. Dictate one of the following statements to the class:

A well-written resume will get you a good job.
It doesn't matter what you wear at a job interview.
The only way to get a job is with family connections to the business.
Never ask about the salary during an interview.

b. In small groups, have students discuss their opinions of the statement.

c. As a class, vote in agreement or disagreement with the statement and then have students discuss their reasons.

6 The Job Interview

a. Divide the class into two teams.

b. Have Team 1 write a list of questions an employer might ask at an interview. For example:

What's your experience?
What are your skills?
Do you have references?
When are you ready to work?

c. Have Team 2 write a list of questions an applicant might ask at an interview. For example:

What are the job responsibilities?
How much is the pay?
What are the hours?
What benefits do you offer?

d. Match pairs of students from Teams 1 and 2 and have them interview each other.

e. Have the pairs present their interviews to the class.

7 Job Interview Role Play

Call on several pairs of students to present a role play of the interview between the interviewer and job applicant on *Picture Dictionary* page 118.

LESSON OBJECTIVE

Students will learn vocabulary for the office workplace.

RESOURCES

AUDIO PROGRAM	MULTI-LEVEL WORKBOOKS 	ACTIVITY MASTERS 
Words & Dialogs Cassette 4B CD 5: Tracks 27, 28	**WordSong:** *Working* Cassette 7B • CD 8: Tracks 12, 13 Song Masters S25, S26	Literacy Workbook Beginning & Intermediate Lifeskills Workbooks Beginning & Intermediate Vocabulary Workbooks	**Reproducibles:** A165, A166

TRANSPARENCY	LANGUAGE & CULTURE NOTES	WORDLINKS
Overhead: T119	**Reproducible:** LC119	longman.com/wordbyword

VOCABULARY INTRODUCTION

- Preview
- Present
- Practice

MODEL CONVERSATION PRACTICE

There are three model conversations—the first for words A–H, the second for words 1–29, and the third for phrases a–f. Introduce and practice the first model before going on to the second and third. For each model:

1. Have students look at the model illustration. Set the scene:

   Model 1: "Two co-workers are talking."
   Model 2: "Two co-workers are talking in the employee lounge."
   Model 3: "Two co-workers are talking."

2. Present the first model using word A and any name you wish, the second model using word 1, and the third model using phrase a and any name you wish.

3. Choral Repetition Practice: Full-Class and Individual.

4. Have pairs practice the model.

5. Have pairs present the model.

6. Call on pairs to present a new conversation using word B for the first model, word 2 for the second model, and phrase b for the third model.

7. Have pairs practice new conversations.

8. Have pairs present new conversations.

SPELLING PRACTICE

Say a word, and have students spell it aloud or write it. Or, using the transparency, point to an item and have students write the word.

WRITING AND DISCUSSION

Have students respond to the question as a class, in pairs, or in small groups. Or have students write their responses, share their writing with other students, and discuss in class.

Making Connections

Resource Materials Bring in, or have students bring in, the following materials for vocabulary practice:

- *Office supply catalogs:* Have students identify items they have learned in this lesson.

Community Task Visit the school office. Have the students take a tour and identify all the objects, areas, and personnel they see.

Communication Activities

1 True or False?
ACTIVITY HANDBOOK PAGE 15

Make statements such as the following about the scene on *Picture Dictionary* page 119. Have students decide whether the statements are true or false. For example:

> The boss is in the office. [True.]
> The receptionist is taking a message. [True.]
> The supply room is between the mailroom and the storage room. [False. It's next to the storage room.]
> There is no one in the conference room. [False. There are five people in the conference room.]
> The vending machine is in the work area. [False. The vending machine is in the employee lounge.]
> The copier is in the supply cabinet. [False. The copier is in the work area.]
> The computer workstation is in a cubicle. [False. The computer workstation is in the work area.]
> The file clerk is sorting the mail. [False. The file clerk is filing.]
> The message board is in the employee lounge. [True.]
> There's a presentation board in the conference room. [True.]

2 Do You Remember?
ACTIVITY HANDBOOK PAGE 5

Have students write down everything they remember about the workplace depicted in the *Picture Dictionary*.

If you do Variation 1, ask questions such as the following:

> Where's the conference room? [Between the reception area and the mailroom.]
> Where's the office assistant? [In the mailroom.]
> How many people are in the employee lounge? [Five.]
> Where's the boss? [In her office.]
> Where is the typewriter? [In a cubicle.]
> Where is the copier? [In the work area.]
> Where is the paper shredder? [Next to the copy machine.]
> Where is the water cooler? [In the employee lounge.]
> Where is the coat rack? [In the reception area.]
> How many people are in the conference room? [Five.]

3 Workplace Associations
ACTIVITY HANDBOOK PAGE 2

Call out workplace words and have groups write down as many associations as they can think of. For example:

> swivel chair: [desk/comfortable/leather/sitting]
> adding machine: [numbers/accountant/bills]
> postal scale: [letters/packages/weight/ stamps]
> coffee machine: [coffee/cream/hot/sugar/coins]
> typewriter: [noise/letters/envelopes/typist]

4 What Can You Do?
ACTIVITY HANDBOOK PAGES 15–16

Have students make a list of all the things they do in different areas of the workplace. For example:

> mailroom
> weigh letters
> weigh packages
> sort the mail
>
> conference room
> have a meeting
> give a presentation
> take notes
> listen
> speak

5 Picture This!
ACTIVITY HANDBOOK PAGES 12–13

Describe a workplace scene and have students draw what you describe. For example:

> In this office, there's a reception area in the right corner when you enter the building. To the left of the reception area is a large office with six computer workstations. On the back wall, there's . . .

6 Read, Write, and Draw
ACTIVITY HANDBOOK PAGE 13

For students who work in an office or are familiar with an office, have them write letters to each other in which they describe their offices. Students then exchange letters and draw pictures to illustrate what they read in the letters.

(continued)

7 Ask Me a Question!
ACTIVITY HANDBOOK PAGE 2
ACTIVITY MASTER 165

Have students walk around trying to guess each other's workplace items by asking yes/no questions. For example:

Are you a room in an office?	[No.]
Are you an item in an office?	[Yes.]
Are you related to work?	[No.]
Are you related to leisure?	[Yes.]
Can I put something on you?	[No.]
Can I put something in you?	[Yes.]
Do you take money?	[Yes.]
Are you a vending machine?	[Yes.]
Are you an item in an office?	[No.]
Are you a room in an office?	[Yes.]
Do many people stay in you?	[No.]
Are you the storage room?	[No.]
Are you the supply room?	[Yes.]

8 Movable Categories
ACTIVITY HANDBOOK PAGE 11
ACTIVITY MASTER 165

Call out the following categories and have students go to the appropriate side of the room:

    things that use electricity
    things that make noise
    places in a workplace
    places with doors
    pieces of furniture
    things that cut

9 Category Dictation
ACTIVITY HANDBOOK PAGE 2

Dictate words that fit into the above categories and the following two additional categories:

    office occupations
    things you do in an office

10 Office Talk!
ACTIVITY HANDBOOK PAGE 17
ACTIVITY MASTER 165

Give students a Workplace Word Card and have them speak to the class for one minute about that workplace word.

11 Ranking
ACTIVITY HANDBOOK PAGE 13

Have students look at the items in an office workplace and decide what the three most essential things are to a functioning office (not including people) and rank these from 1–3. For example:

    1. computer workstation
    2. copier
    3. supply cabinet

12 Workplace Match Game
ACTIVITY HANDBOOK PAGE 11
ACTIVITY MASTER 166

Have students find the person whose card matches theirs.

Note: The questions and answers on Activity Master 178 refer to the workplace depicted on *Picture Dictionary* page 119.

13 A Visit to an Office

Have students visit an office and write down all the things from the vocabulary list on *Picture Dictionary* page 119 as well as any other things they see. Have students report back to the class and talk about the new words.

LESSON OBJECTIVE

Students will learn the names of common supplies and equipment in an office.

RESOURCES

AUDIO PROGRAM
Words & Dialogs
Cassette 5A
CD 5: Tracks 29, 30

MULTI-LEVEL WORKBOOKS
Literacy Workbook
Beginning & Intermediate Lifeskills Workbooks
Beginning & Intermediate Vocabulary Workbooks

ACTIVITY MASTERS
Reproducibles: A167, A168

TRANSPARENCY
Overhead: T120

LANGUAGE & CULTURE NOTES
Reproducible: LC120

WORDLINKS
longman.com/wordbyword

VOCABULARY INTRODUCTION

- Preview
- Present
- Practice

MODEL CONVERSATION PRACTICE

There are two model conversations—the first for words 2–12 and the second for words 13–34. Introduce and practice the first model before going on to the second. For each model:

1. Have students look at the model illustration. Set the scene:

    Model 1: "Two co-workers are talking."
    Model 2: "The office manager is talking to an office assistant."

2. Present the first model using word 2 and the second model using word 13.

3. Choral Repetition Practice: Full-Class and Individual.

4. Have pairs practice the model.

5. Have pairs present the model.

6. Call on pairs to present a new conversation using word 3 for the first model and word 14 for the second model.

7. Have pairs practice new conversations.

8. Have pairs present new conversations.

SPELLING PRACTICE

Say a word, and have students spell it aloud or write it. Or, using the transparency, point to an item and have students write the word.

WRITING AND DISCUSSION

Have students respond to the questions as a class, in pairs, or in small groups. Or have students write their responses, share their writing with other students, and discuss in class.

Making Connections

Resource Materials Bring in, or have students bring in, the following materials for vocabulary practice:

- *Office supply catalogs or the office supply items themselves:* Have students identify items they have learned in this lesson.

Community Task Have individual students (or groups of students) visit office supply stores in the area and investigate the price of one or two items and then report back to the class.

Communication Activities

1 ## Clap in Rhythm
ACTIVITY HANDBOOK PAGE **3**

Have students name different office supplies and
equipment to a clapping rhythm.

2 ## Letter Game
ACTIVITY HANDBOOK PAGE **9**

Say statements such as the following and have teams
compete to identify the items:

I'm thinking of an office supply that starts with *s*.	[stapler]
I'm thinking of an office supply that starts with *p*.	[pushpin]
I'm thinking of an office supply that starts with *r*.	[rubber band]
I'm thinking of an office supply that starts with *e*.	[envelope]
I'm thinking of an office supply that starts with *f*.	[file folder]
I'm thinking of an office supply that starts with *l*.	[legal pad]
I'm thinking of an office supply that starts with *c*.	[clipboard]
I'm thinking of an office supply that starts with *p*.	[Post-It note pad]
I'm thinking of an office supply that starts with *a*.	[appointment book]
I'm thinking of an office supply that starts with *t*	[typewriter cartridge]

3 ## Chain Game
ACTIVITY HANDBOOK PAGES **2–3**

Begin the chain as follows: "I went to the office
supply store and I bought some paper clips," and have
students continue it. For example:

Teacher: I went to the office supply store and I
bought some paper clips.
Student 1: I went to the office supply store and I
bought some paper clips and staples.
Student 2: I went to the office supply store and I
bought some paper clips, staples, and a
stapler.

Etc.

4 ## What's in the Bag? [Variation 1]

a. Collect as many small office supplies as there are
students in the class and put the items in a large
bag.

b. Have each student put his or her hand in the bag,
feel an object, and try to guess what it is.

5 ## What's in the Bag? [Variation 2]

a. Collect a variety of small office supplies and put
each one in a small, brown lunch-size bag. Put all
the bags on a desk or table in front of the room.

b. Divide the class into pairs. One member of the
pair goes to the desk, takes a bag, and looks
inside.

c. The second partner tries to guess what is in the
bag by asking questions.

d. When the second partner has guessed the object,
he or she returns the bag to the desk and gets
another one for the first partner to guess.

6 ## Concentration
ACTIVITY HANDBOOK PAGE **3**
ACTIVITY MASTER **167**

Have students shuffle the cards and place them
face-down in three rows of 6 each, then attempt to
find cards that match.

7 ## Category Dictation
ACTIVITY HANDBOOK PAGE **2**

Dictate words that fit into the following categories:

things for scheduling
things that stick
things that you use for mail
things made of paper
kinds of ink

8 Ask Me a Question!

ACTIVITY HANDBOOK PAGE 2
ACTIVITY MASTER 168

Have students walk around trying to guess each other's office supply items by asking yes/no questions. For example:

Can you write on it?	[Yes.]
Does it stick on?	[Yes.]
Is it a Post-It note?	[No.]
Is it a mailing label?	[Yes.]
Can you write on it?	[No.]
Does it hold papers together?	[Yes.]
Is it a paper clip?	[No.]
Is it a stapler?	[Yes.]

9 What Do I Need?

Call out the following situations and have students offer suggestions on what you need.

I made a terrible typing error! What do I need?

I want to put this announcement on the bulletin board. What do I need?

I want to write letter to another company. What do I need?

I want to hold these papers together temporarily. What do I need?

I need to mail this package. What do I need?

My pencil is broken, and it won't write! What do I need?

10 Same and Different

ACTIVITY HANDBOOK PAGE 13

Write pairs of office supply words on the board and have students think of similarities and differences between the pairs. For example:

envelope—mailer

You use both to mail things.
Both take stamps.
An envelope is smaller than a mailer.
A mailer is thicker than an envelope.

glue—rubber cement

Both are a kind of glue.
You use both to make paper stick to other paper.
Rubber cement is clear.
Glue is thinner and opaque.

11 Daffy Debate!

ACTIVITY HANDBOOK PAGE 5
ACTIVITY MASTER 168

Have students debate which office supply items are more important than others.

Page 121 THE FACTORY

LESSON OBJECTIVE

Students will learn the names of personnel, objects, and departments of a factory.

RESOURCES

AUDIO PROGRAM
Words & Dialogs
Cassette 5A
CD 5: Tracks 31, 32

MULTI-LEVEL WORKBOOKS
Literacy Workbook
Beginning & Intermediate Lifeskills Workbooks
Beginning & Intermediate Vocabulary Workbooks

ACTIVITY MASTERS
Reproducibles:
A8, A169

TRANSPARENCY
Overhead: T121

LANGUAGE & CULTURE NOTES
Reproducible: LC121

WORDLINKS
longman.com/wordbyword

VOCABULARY INTRODUCTION

- Preview
- Present
- Practice

MODEL CONVERSATION PRACTICE

There are two model conversations. Introduce and practice the first model before going on to the second. For each model:

1. Have students look at the model illustration. Set the scene:

   Model 1: "Two factory workers are talking."
   Model 2: "Two factory workers are talking."

2. Present the first model using word 1 and the second model using word 3.

3. Choral Repetition Practice: Full-Class and Individual.

4. Have pairs practice the model.

5. Have pairs present the model.

6. Call on pairs to present a new conversation using word 2 for the first model and word 4 for the second model.

7. Have pairs practice new conversations.

8. Have pairs present new conversations.

SPELLING PRACTICE

Say a word, and have students spell it aloud or write it. Or, using the transparency, point to an item and have students write the word.

WRITING AND DISCUSSION

Have students respond to the questions as a class, in pairs, or in small groups. Or have students write their responses, share their writing with other students, and discuss in class.

Making Connections

Resource Materials Bring in, or have students bring in, the following materials for vocabulary practice:

- *Brochures, pamphlets, and other information about local factories:* Have students identify the vocabulary they learned from this lesson.

Community Tasks Have students find out what factories are located in the community and report back to the class.

As a class, take a tour of a local factory.

1 True or False?
ACTIVITY HANDBOOK PAGE 15

Make statements such as the following about the scene on *Picture Dictionary* page 121. Have students decide whether the statements are true or false. For example:

> The forklift is in the warehouse. [True.]
> The hand truck is empty. [False. There are boxes on the hand truck.]
> Someone is having an interview for a job at the factory. [True.]
> Today is payday at the factory. [True.]
> This factory makes cars. [False. It makes stuffed animals.]
> The packer assembles the product. [False. The packer puts the product in boxes.]
> The union notices are in the employee lounge. [True.]
> There are three people on the loading dock. [False. There are two people.]
> The forklift fits into the freight elevator. [True.]
> There is only one work station in the factory. [False. There are many work stations.]

2 Picture This!
ACTIVITY HANDBOOK PAGES 12–13

Describe a factory scene and have students draw what you describe. For example:

> In this factory there's an assembly line with five work stations on the bottom floor. To the right of the work station there's . . .

3 Read, Write, and Draw
ACTIVITY HANDBOOK PAGE 13

If any of your students work in a factory or are familiar with one, have them write each other letters in which they describe the factories. Have students exchange letters and draw pictures to illustrate what they read in their letters.

4 Tic Tac Definitions
ACTIVITY HANDBOOK PAGE 15
ACTIVITY MASTER 8

Have students fill in the tic tac grid with any nine factory words they wish. Give definitions such as the following, and have students cross out on their grids the words you have defined:

> the area where the factory stores manufactured merchandise [warehouse]

> a small motor-driven vehicle that moves merchandise from one area to another [forklift]
> the worker who packs the product for shipment [packer]
> a large elevator that transports merchandise from one floor to another [freight elevator]
> the department that ships merchandise to stores [shipping department]
> a cart on wheels that you use to load and unload merchandise [hand truck/dolly]
> the area where delivery trucks make deliveries and receive merchandise [loading dock]
> the office that hires new employees and handles other employee issues [personnel office]
> workers write their opinions on workplace issues and place their comments here [suggestion box]

5 Do You Remember?
ACTIVITY HANDBOOK PAGE 5

Have students write down everything they remember about the factory depicted in the *Picture Dictionary*.

If you do Variation 1, ask questions such as the following:

> Where are the time cards?
> Is the quality control supervisor a man or a woman?
> What's between the loading dock and the personnel office?
> Are there any workers on break?
> How many boxed products on are the assembly line?
> Is someone opening a locker in the picture?
> Is the forklift operator a man or a woman?
> How many boxes are on the dolly on the loading dock?
> Is there a line of people outside the personnel office?
> How many packers are there in this scene?

6 A Typical Day at the Factory

Have each student make up a story about a typical day at the factory, using at least 12 of the vocabulary words. Have students tell their stories to the class.

7 Chain Story
ACTIVITY HANDBOOK PAGE 3

Begin the story as follows: "Alice had a good day at work today. She punched the time clock at 8:00."

(continued)

8 Factory Match Game
ACTIVITY HANDBOOK PAGE 11
ACTIVITY MASTER 169

Have students find the person whose card matches theirs.

9 Factory Crossword
ACTIVITY HANDBOOK PAGES 4–5

Have students connect factory words to create a crossword. For example:

10 Hot Spot!
ACTIVITY HANDBOOK PAGE 8

Have students from competing teams sit in the *hot spot* in front of the class, listen to clues given by their team members about factory items, and attempt to identify the words.

11 Listen and Number
ACTIVITY HANDBOOK PAGE 10

In pairs, have one student make up a story using factory words and have the other student number the pictures in their order of occurrence in the story.

LESSON OBJECTIVE

Students will learn vocabulary related to the machinery and other heavy equipment, tools, and materials found at a construction site.

RESOURCES

AUDIO PROGRAM 	MULTI-LEVEL WORKBOOKS	ACTIVITY MASTERS
Words & Dialogs Cassette 5A CD 5: Tracks 33, 34	Literacy Workbook Beginning & Intermediate Lifeskills Workbooks Beginning & Intermediate Vocabulary Workbooks	**Reproducibles**: A170, A171
TRANSPARENCY Overhead: T122	**LANGUAGE & CULTURE NOTES** Reproducible: LC122	**WORDLINKS** longman.com/wordbyword

VOCABULARY INTRODUCTION

- Preview
- Present
- Practice

MODEL CONVERSATION PRACTICE

There are three model conversations—the first for words 1–10, the second for words 11–21, and the third for words 22–30. Introduce and practice the first model before going on to the second and third. For each model:

1. Have students look at the model illustration. Set the scene:

   Model 1: "Two construction workers are talking."
   Model 2: "Two construction workers are talking."
   Model 3: "Two construction workers are talking."

2. Present the first model using word 1, the second model using word 11, and the third model using word 22.

3. Choral Repetition Practice: Full-Class and Individual.

4. Have pairs practice the model.

5. Have pairs present the model.

6. Call on pairs to present a new conversation using word 2 for the first model, word 12 for the second model, and word 27 for the third model.

7. Have pairs practice new conversations.

8. Have pairs present new conversations.

SPELLING PRACTICE

Say a word, and have students spell it aloud or write it. Or, using the transparency, point to an item and have students write the word.

WRITING AND DISCUSSION

Have students respond to the questions as a class, in pairs, or in small groups. Or have students write their responses, share their writing with other students, and discuss in class.

Making Connections

Resource Materials Bring in, or have students bring in, the following materials for vocabulary practice:

- *Brochures and catalogs from building supply stores:* Have students identify the vocabulary from this lesson.

- *Images of heavy construction machinery (downloaded from manufacturers' websites such as Caterpillar):* Have students identify vocabulary from this lesson.

Community Task Have individual students (or groups of students) visit a construction site and write a list of all the equipment they can identify and then report back to class.

Communication Activities

1 Chain Game
ACTIVITY HANDBOOK PAGES 2–3

Begin the chain as follows: "I went to a construction site, and I saw a wheelbarrow," and have students continue it. For example:

> Teacher: I went to a construction site, and I saw a wheelbarrow.
> Student 1: I went to a construction site, and I saw a wheelbarrow and scaffolding.
> Student 2: I went to a construction site, and I saw a wheelbarrow, scaffolding, and a backhoe.
> Etc.

2 Movable Categories
ACTIVITY HANDBOOK PAGE 11
ACTIVITY MASTER 170

Call out the following categories and have students go to the appropriate side of the room:

> heavy equipment
> construction materials
> hand-held equipment
> things you drive
> small tools
> equipment you use to tear things down
> things that you operate manually
> things that you operate mechanically

3 Category Dictation
ACTIVITY HANDBOOK PAGE 2

Dictate words that fit into the above categories.

4 Miming Game
ACTIVITY HANDBOOK PAGE 11
ACTIVITY MASTER 170

Have students think of a construction site object and pantomime using it. See if others can guess what the object is.

5 It's Something That . . .
ACTIVITY HANDBOOK PAGE 9
ACTIVITY MASTER 170

Have students give definitions of construction words to each other beginning with "It's something that . . ." For example:

> It's something that carries tools around your waist. [A toolbelt.]
> It's something that builds a wall. [Drywall.]
> It's something that can break up hard rock in the ground. [A jackhammer.]
> It's something that makes it possible for workers to work on upper stories of a building. [Scaffolding.]
> It's something that carries electrical currents. [Wire.]

6 True or False?
ACTIVITY HANDBOOK PAGE 15

Make statements such as the following about the scene on *Picture Dictionary* page 122. Have students decide whether the statements are true or false. For example:

> There's one trailer at the construction site. [True.]
> All the construction workers are men. [False. Three are women.]
> The person in the cherry picker is building a roof. [False. The person in the cherry picker is fixing a street light.]
> The crane is carrying a girder. [True.]
> There's lumber in the pickup truck. [True.]
> The cement mixer is larger than the concrete mixer. [False. The cement mixer is smaller than the concrete mixer.]
> A construction worker is using a shovel to lay the bricks. [False. She's using a trowel.]
> The front-end loader is loading a pickup truck. [False. It's loading a dump truck.]
> The sledgehammer is next to the pickax. [True.]

What's the Question?
ACTIVITY HANDBOOK PAGE 16

Describe various construction items and have students respond by asking: "What's a _____?" or "What are _____s?" For example:

Teacher: It a very big, heavy hammer.
Student: What's a sledgehammer?

Teacher: These are the drawings or plans for a building.
Student: What are blueprints?

Teacher: It's a small truck that carries small loads.
Student: What's a pickup truck?

Teacher: It's a large truck that carries large loads.
Student: What's a dump truck?

Teacher: It's a flexible metal strip you use to make measurements.
Student: What's a tape measure?

Teacher: It carries small loads around the construction site.
Student: What's a wheelbarrow?

Teacher: It's a tool that spreads or smoothes the mortar between bricks.
Student: What's a trowel?

Teacher: It's a vehicle that pushes dirt.
Student: What's a bulldozer?

Teacher: It's material that goes in the walls and ceilings of buildings so heat doesn't escape from the building.
Student: What's insulation?

Teacher: It's a place on the construction site that serves as an office or rest area for the workers.
Student: What's a trailer?

Teacher: It's something construction workers wear that holds their tools.
Student: What's a toolbelt?

Teacher: It's a piece of heavy machinery that scoops up dirt, carries it from one spot to another, and loads it in a dump truck.
Student: What's a front-end loader?

 A Visit to a Construction Site

If possible, have students visit a construction site and find the answers to the following questions:

> How many items on *Picture Dictionary* page 122 can you find?
> What other equipment do you see that isn't in the *Picture Dictionary*?
> What occupations do people have at the construction site? (For example: electricians, heavy equipment operators, plumbers, bricklayers, carpenters.)

Have students report their findings back to the class.

 Construction Site Match Game
ACTIVITY HANDBOOK PAGE 11
ACTIVITY MASTER 171

Have students find the person whose card matches theirs.

10 What's the Story?

Have each student choose a person depicted in the scene on *Picture Dictionary* page 122 and tell a story about that person. Possible questions to answer are:

> Who is he/she?
> What is his/her occupation?
> Where does he/she work?
> What does he/she do at work every day?
> Is it interesting? Why or why not?

Encourage students to be as creative as they wish.

LESSON OBJECTIVE

Students will learn the names of safety equipment used on the job.

RESOURCES

AUDIO PROGRAM	MULTI-LEVEL WORKBOOKS	ACTIVITY MASTERS

AUDIO PROGRAM
Words & Dialogs
Cassette 5A
CD 5: Tracks 35, 36

MULTI-LEVEL WORKBOOKS
Literacy Workbook
Beginning & Intermediate Lifeskills Workbooks
Beginning & Intermediate Vocabulary Workbooks

ACTIVITY MASTERS
Reproducibles:
A8, A172–A174

TRANSPARENCY
Overhead: T123

LANGUAGE & CULTURE NOTES
Reproducible: LC123

WORDLINKS
longman.com/wordbyword

VOCABULARY INTRODUCTION

- Preview
- Present
- Practice

MODEL CONVERSATION PRACTICE

There are three model conversations—the first for words 1–13, the second for words 14–21, and the third for words 22–25. Introduce and practice the first model before going on to the second and third. For each model:

1. Have students look at the model illustration. Set the scene:

   Model 1: "One co-worker is warning another."
   Model 2: "One co-worker is warning another."
   Model 3: "Two co-workers are talking."

2. Present the first model using word 1, the second model using word 14, and the third model using word 22.

3. Choral Repetition Practice: Full-Class and Individual.

4. Have pairs practice the model.

5. Have pairs present the model.

6. Call on pairs to present a new conversation using word 2 for the first model, word 15 for the second model, and word 23 for the third model.

7. Have pairs practice new conversations.

8. Have pairs present new conversations.

SPELLING PRACTICE

Say a word, and have students spell it aloud or write it. Or, using the transparency, point to an item and have students write the word.

WRITING AND DISCUSSION

Have students respond to the questions as a class, in pairs, or in small groups. Or have students write their responses, share their writing with other students, and discuss in class.

Making Connections

Resource Materials Bring in, or have students bring in, the following materials for vocabulary practice:

- *Images of people at work (downloaded from search engines with keywords* People at Work *or* Job Safety*):* Have students identify the safety equipment they see workers in the pictures wearing. For pictures of workers doing dangerous work without safety equipment, have students recommend what the workers should wear.

- *Catalogs for working gear (downloaded from store websites):* Have students cut out examples of safety equipment, label the items, and make a collage.

Community Task Invite a person from OSHA (Occupational Safety and Health Administration) to speak with the class about basic safety precautions in fields of work in which students are interested.

Communication Activities

1 Clap in Rhythm
ACTIVITY HANDBOOK PAGE 3

Have students name different pieces of job safety equipment to a clapping rhythm.

2 Job Safety Associations
ACTIVITY HANDBOOK PAGE 2

Call out an occupation and have groups write down as much job safety equipment associated with that occupation as they can think of. For example:

construction worker:	[helmet/goggles/toe guard]
welder:	[helmet/safety glasses/gloves]
assembler:	[goggles/back support]
doctor:	[latex gloves/mask]

3 Concentration
ACTIVITY HANDBOOK PAGE 3
ACTIVITY MASTER 172

Have students shuffle the cards and place them face-down in three rows of 6 each, then attempt to find cards that match.

4 Tic Tac Definitions
ACTIVITY HANDBOOK PAGE 15
ACTIVITY MASTER 8

Have students fill in the tic tac grid with any nine job safety words they wish. Give definitions such as the following, and have students cross out on their grids the words you have defined:

You wear this to protect your head from falling objects. [hard hat/helmet]
You wear these to protect your ears from loud noises. [earplugs]
You wear these to protect your eyes from flying objects. [goggles]
You wear this to protect your chest from sudden impact. [safety vest]
You wear these to protect your lower legs, ankles, and feet from impact. [safety boots]
You wear this to protect your feet from falling objects. [toe guard]
You wear these to protect your ears from loud noises as well as to keep them warm. [safety earmuffs]
You wear this to prevent contamination from your breath. [mask]
You wear these to protect your hands from hazardous materials such as chemicals or blood. [latex gloves]
You wear this to protect your lungs while you work with hazardous material (such as asbestos) or gases (such as smoke). [respirator]

You use this piece of medical equipment to shock the heart into beating if it has stopped. You use this as a last resort to save a person's life. [defibrillator]

5 Drawing Game
ACTIVITY HANDBOOK PAGE 6
ACTIVITY MASTER 173

Have teams compete to identify job safety equipment drawn by one of their team members.

6 Find the Right Person!
ACTIVITY HANDBOOK PAGES 6–7
ACTIVITY MASTER 174

This activity is appropriate if your students work in occupations that require the use of safety equipment.

Practice the following questions before having students do the activity:

What safety equipment do you wear at work?
Do you ever wear back support?
Do you ever wear earplugs?
Where are the emergency exits of this school?
Do you have a first-aid kit at work?
Where is a fire extinguisher at your workplace?
Did you ever see an accident at your workplace?

7 What's Happening?

Have each student choose one of the people depicted on *Picture Dictionary* page 123 and say one sentence about what he or she is doing.

8 What's the Story?

Have each student choose a person depicted on *Picture Dictionary* page 123 and tell a story about that person. Possible questions to answer are:

Who is he/she?
What's his/her occupation?
Where does he/she work?
What does he/she do at work every day?
Is it interesting? Why or why not?
Where does he/she live?

Encourage students to be as creative as they wish.

9 Job Safety Talk!
ACTIVITY HANDBOOK PAGE 17
ACTIVITY MASTERS 172 (words only) or 173

Give students a Job Safety Word Card and have them speak to the class for one minute about the importance of that item.

Unit 13 Communication Activity Review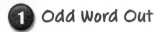

1 Odd Word Out

Read the following lists of words, and have students identify the category and the "odd word out"—the word that doesn't fit the category:

bricklayer, carpenter, construction worker, lawyer
[Category: OCCUPATIONS RELATED TO CONSTRUCTION. Odd word out: lawyer]

waiter, truck driver, server, food-service worker, cook
[Category: RESTAURANT OCCUPATIONS. Odd word out: truck driver]

dockworker, pharmacist, medical assistant, home attendant, health-care aide
[Category: HEALTH OCCUPATIONS. Odd word out: dockworker]

receptionist, secretary, office assistant, businesswoman, child day-care worker
[Category: OFFICE OCCUPATIONS. Odd word out: child day-care worker]

foreman, telemarketer, line supervisor, boss, manager,
[Category: SUPERVISORY OCCUPATIONS. Odd word out: telemarketer]

respond to an ad, request information, fill out an application, go to an interview, make copies
[Category: STEPS TO A JOB SEARCH. Odd word out: make copies]

index card, stationery, stapler, legal pad, memo pad
[Category: PAPER PRODUCTS. Odd word out: stapler]

copier, file cabinet, electric pencil sharpener, computer, shredder
[Category: OFFICE MACHINES THAT USE ELECTRICITY. Odd word out: file cabinet]

conference room, mailroom, office, supply room, loading dock
[Category: PLACES IN AN OFFICE. Odd word out: loading dock]

travel agent, factory worker, line supervisor, packer, shipping clerk
[Category: FACTORY OCCUPATIONS. Odd word out: travel agent]

clean, cook, draw, mailbox, grow
[Category: VERBS. Odd word out: mailbox]

dump truck, copier, bulldozer, crane, cherry picker
[Category: CONSTRUCTION VEHICLES. Odd word out: copier]

brick, lumber, time clock, drywall, plywood
[Category: BUILDING MATERIALS. Odd word out: time clock]

poisonous, firefighter, flammable, hazardous, electrical hazard
[Category: HAZARDS. Odd word out: firefighter]

2 Who Am I?

ACTIVITY HANDBOOK PAGE 17

Tell about different occupations and have students guess who you are talking about. For example:

Teacher: I file papers at the office. Who am I?
Student: A file clerk.

Teacher: I greet people when they walk in and I answer the phone. Who am I?
Student: A receptionist.

Teacher: I write correspondence, schedule appointments, file papers, and answer the phone. Who am I?
Student: A secretary.

Teacher: I serve food in a cafeteria. Who am I?
Student: A food-service worker.

Teacher: I mow lawns. Who am I?
Student: A landscaper.

Teacher: I make sure the products don't have any problems before they leave the factory. Who am I?
Student: A quality control supervisor.

Teacher: I work in the military. Who am I?
Student: A serviceman/servicewoman.

Teacher: I sell things on the phone. Who am I?
Student: A telemarketer.

Teacher: I collect trash. Who am I?
Student: A sanitation worker.

3 Quiz Game

ACTIVITY MASTER 175

a. Divide the class into four teams.

b. Copy and cut up Activity Master 187 and place cards face-down in a pile.

c. Have the teams take turns answering your questions. Give each team a time limit to answer each question (30 seconds or 1 minute).

d. The team with the most correct answers wins.

4 Mystery Word Conversations

ACTIVITY HANDBOOK PAGE 12

Have groups create mystery conversations about any of the occupations from Unit 13 without naming the occupation. The class tries to guess what the occupation is. For example:

A. How was work today?
B. It was a long day. We flew from San Francisco to Chicago to San Antonio and back.
[Answer: pilot]

5 Miming Game

ACTIVITY HANDBOOK PAGE 11
ACTIVITY MASTERS 168, 173

Have students take turns pantomiming using job safety equipment or office supplies and equipment. The class tries to guess what object the person is using.

6 Who Said It?

a. Give each student a piece of paper and ask them to write answers to the following questions:

What occupation did you want to have when you were a child?
If you work now, what's your occupation?
What occupation would you like to have?

b. Collect the papers, read each one, and see if the class can match the answers with the students who wrote them.

UNIT 14 Transportation and Travel

AUDIO PROGRAM

Words & Dialogs
Audio Cassette 5A
Audio CD 5:
   Tracks 37–55

WordSong: *Great Big World*
Audio Cassette 7B
Audio CD 8: Tracks 14
   (Vocal) & 15 (Sing-along)
Song Masters S27, S28

WORKBOOKS

For Multi-Level Practice
Literacy Workbook
Beginning Lifeskills Workbook
Beginning Vocabulary Workbook
Intermediate Lifeskills Workbook
Intermediate Vocabulary Workbook

WORDLINKS

Internet Resources through the
***Word by Word* Companion Website**
http://www.longman.com/wordbyword

ACTIVITY MASTERS

Reproducibles for Communication Activities
A8, A176–A193

TRANSPARENCIES

Full-Color Overheads for Class Practice
T125–T133

LANGUAGE & CULTURE NOTES

Information for Teachers &
Intermediate /Advanced Students
LC124–LC133

LESSON OBJECTIVE

Students will learn the vocabulary of public transportation — specifically trains, buses, subways, and taxis.

RESOURCES

AUDIO PROGRAM		MULTI-LEVEL WORKBOOKS	ACTIVITY MASTERS
Words & Dialogs Cassette 5A CD 5: Tracks 37, 38	**WordSong:** *Great Big World* Cassette 7B • CD 8: Tracks 14, 15 Song Masters S27, S28	Literacy Workbook Beginning & Intermediate Lifeskills Workbooks Beginning & Intermediate Vocabulary Workbooks	**Reproducibles**: A176–A178

TRANSPARENCY	LANGUAGE & CULTURE NOTES	WORDLINKS
Overhead: T124	**Reproducible:** LC124	longman.com/wordbyword

VOCABULARY INTRODUCTION

- Preview
- Present
- Practice

MODEL CONVERSATION PRACTICE

There are two model conversations—the first for words A–E and the second for words 1, 7, 8, 10–19, 21, and 23–25. Introduce and practice the first model before going on to the second. For each model:

1. Have students look at the model illustration. Set the scene:

   Model 1: "Two co-workers are talking."
   Model 2: "Two strangers are talking on the street."

2. Present the first model using word A and the second model using word 1.

3. Choral Repetition Practice: Full-Class and Individual.

4. Have pairs practice the model.

5. Have pairs present the model.

6. Call on pairs to present a new conversation using word B for the first model and word 7 for the second model.

7. Have pairs practice new conversations.

8. Have pairs present new conversations.

SPELLING PRACTICE

Say a word, and have students spell it aloud or write it. Or, using the transparency, point to an item and have students write the word.

WRITING AND DISCUSSION

Have students respond to the questions as a class, in pairs, or in small groups. Or have students write their responses, share their writing with other students, and discuss in class.

♪♪ WORDSONG ♪♪

1. Have students listen to the vocal version of *Great Big World* one or more times. Then have students listen again as they read the song lyrics on Song Master S27.

2. Have students sing as you play either the vocal or the sing-along version of the song.

3. For fun, have a song competition in which students perform solo or in groups and the class votes for the best performance.

4. For additional practice, students can complete the cloze exercise on Song Master S28.

Resource Materials Bring in, or have students bring in, the following materials for vocabulary practice:

● *Train, bus, and subway schedules:* Identify which transportation has more frequent service.

● *Subway and bus maps:* Identify which public transportation serves the area of the school.

Community Task Have students call the local public transportation system authority to get information about public transportation service to the school's area. Have each student call to find out a different piece of information: the schedule of the subway, the route of a bus, etc. Have students report back to class and make a comprehensive public transportation bulletin board with all the information students need to get to class without a car.

Communication Activities

❶ Concentration
ACTIVITY HANDBOOK PAGE 3
ACTIVITY MASTER 176

Have students shuffle the cards and place them face-down in three rows of 6 each, then attempt to find cards that match.

❷ Finish the Sentence!
ACTIVITY HANDBOOK PAGE 7

Begin sentences such as the following for students to complete:

You buy a train ticket at the . . . *ticket window.*
To find out when a train leaves, look at the . . . *arrival and departure board.*
To change from one bus to another you ask for a . . . *transfer.*
To get to the subway, you walk through a . . . *turnstile.*
You pay for the subway with a . . . *token* (or *fare card*).
You can find taxis waiting for passengers at a . . . *taxi stand.*
On a bus, you put luggage in the . . . *luggage compartment.*
To find out where the bus comes from and where it goes, you ask about the . . . *bus route.*
If you want to catch a city bus, wait at a . . . *bus stop.*
The person who manages the train and asks passengers for tickets is the . . . *conductor.*

❸ Cooperative Definitions
ACTIVITY HANDBOOK PAGE 4

Have groups write definitions of public transportation items and then pass their definitions to other groups.

❹ Got It!
ACTIVITY HANDBOOK PAGE 7

Have groups of students ask yes/no questions in an attempt to identify public transportation items. For example:

Is it a person?	[No.]
Is it in a train station?	[No.]
Is it in a subway?	[No.]
Is it on a bus?	[Yes.]
Is it the baggage compartment?	[Yes.]
Is it a person?	[Yes.]
Is it in a taxi?	[Yes.]
Is it a taxi driver?	[No.]
Is it a passenger?	[Yes.]

❺ Public Transportation Crossword
ACTIVITY HANDBOOK PAGES 4–5

Have students connect public transportation words to create a crossword. For example:

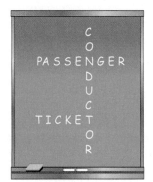

6 Question the Answer!

ACTIVITY HANDBOOK PAGE 13
ACTIVITY MASTER 177

Students pick Public Transportation Word Cards and think of a question for which that word could be the answer. For example:

Card: conductor
Student: Who collects the train tickets?

Card: fare
Student: What's the amount of money you pay the taxi driver?

Card: platform
Student: Where do you go to get on a train?

Card: token
Student: What coin do you use to pay for the subway?

7 Word Clues

ACTIVITY HANDBOOK PAGE 17
ACTIVITY MASTER 177

Have students take turns giving one-word clues to team members who try to guess the word. For example:

[The word is *bus stop*.]
Team 1 Player: "wait"   [Team 1 guesses]
Team 2 Player: "corner"   [Team 2 guesses]
Team 1 Player: "get on"   [Team 1 guesses]

[The word is *ferry*.]
Team 1 Player: "boat"   [Team 1 guesses]
Team 2 Player: "commute"   [Team 2 guesses]
Team 1 Player: "harbor"   [Team 1 guesses]

8 Public Transportation Match Game

ACTIVITY HANDBOOK PAGE 11
ACTIVITY MASTER 178

Have students find the person whose card matches theirs.

9 General-to-Specific Clue Game

ACTIVITY HANDBOOK PAGE 7

Possible clues:

Clue 1: Most people use this.
Clue 2: It can be big or small.
Clue 3: Sometimes you keep it, sometimes you don't.
Clue 4: You use it for short or long trips.
Clue 5: Sometimes you carry it, sometimes you don't.
Clue 6: It has a handle or a strap.

[Answer: luggage]

10 What's the Story?

Have each student choose a person depicted on *Picture Dictionary* page 124 and tell a story about that person. Possible questions to answer are:

Who is he/she?
What's his/her occupation?
Where does he/she work?
Where does he/she live?
Where is he/she coming from?
Where is he/she going?

Encourage students to be as creative as they wish.

11 Chain Story

ACTIVITY HANDBOOK PAGE 3

Begin the story as follows: "You won't believe what happened to me yesterday when I tried to take the train to New York!"

12 Mystery Word Conversations

ACTIVITY HANDBOOK PAGE 12

Have groups create and present mystery conversations about public transportation without naming the place. The class tries to guess where the conversation is taking place. For example:

A. Hurry! I can hear it coming!
B. But I can't get in! I put the token in, but the turnstile isn't turning!

[Answer: subway station]

13 Ranking

ACTIVITY HANDBOOK PAGE 13

Write the following public transportation items on the board and have students rank them from public transportation they use the most to the one they use the least.

bus
subway
taxi
ferry

Other possible rankings: from the most expensive to the least expensive, the most convenient to the least convenient, the most polluting to the least polluting.

LESSON OBJECTIVE

Students will learn the names of the most popular types of vehicles.

RESOURCES

AUDIO PROGRAM		MULTI-LEVEL WORKBOOKS	ACTIVITY MASTERS
Words & Dialogs Cassette 5A CD 5: Tracks 39–41	**WordSong:** *Great Big World* Cassette 7B • CD 8: Tracks 14, 15 Song Masters S27, S28	Literacy Workbook Beginning & Intermediate Lifeskills Workbooks Beginning & Intermediate Vocabulary Workbooks	**Reproducibles:** A8, A179, A180

TRANSPARENCY	LANGUAGE & CULTURE NOTES	WORDLINKS 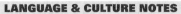
Overhead: T125	**Reproducible:** LC125	longman.com/wordbyword

VOCABULARY INTRODUCTION

- Preview
- Present
- Practice

MODEL CONVERSATION PRACTICE

1. Have students look at the model illustration. Set the scene: "A car salesperson is talking to a customer."
2. Present the model.
3. Choral Repetition Practice: Full-Class and Individual.
4. Have pairs practice the model.
5. Have pairs present the model.
6. Call on pairs to present a new conversation using word 2.
7. Have pairs practice new conversations.
8. Have pairs present new conversations.

ADDITIONAL CONVERSATION PRACTICE

Before students practice the additional conversations, you may want to have them listen to the examples on the Audio Program.

Conversation 1 Have students practice and present conversations with any words they wish.

Conversation 2 Have students practice and present conversations with any words they wish.

SPELLING PRACTICE

Say a word, and have students spell it aloud or write it. Or, using the transparency, point to an item and have students write the word.

WRITING AND DISCUSSION

Have students respond to the questions as a class, in pairs, or in small groups. Or have students write their responses, share their writing with other students, and discuss in class.

Making Connections

Resource Materials Bring in, or have students bring in, the following materials for vocabulary practice:

- *Vehicle advertisements from newspapers and magazines:* Have students identify the vehicle types in the advertisements.

- *Images of vehicles (downloaded from the Internet):* Have students identify the vehicle types.

Community Tasks Have students take a walk around the school neighborhood and identify the vehicle types they see. Have students return to class and compare notes.

Have groups of students do Internet research to find out what the best-selling vehicles were in the United States this past year and in recent years. Have students compare their reports and try to identify any trends in the kinds of vehicles U.S. residents most like to drive.

1 Concentration
ACTIVITY HANDBOOK PAGE 3
ACTIVITY MASTER 179

Have students shuffle the cards and place them face-down in three rows of 6 each, then attempt to find cards that match.

2 Clap in Rhythm
ACTIVITY HANDBOOK PAGE 3

Have students name different vehicle types to a clapping rhythm.

3 Movable Categories
ACTIVITY HANDBOOK PAGE 11
ACTIVITY MASTER 180

Call out the following categories and have students go to the appropriate side of the room:

  cars
  trucks
  bikes
  vehicles that fit only two passengers
  vehicles that fit three passengers
  vehicles that fit five passengers
  vehicles that fit seven passengers
  vehicles for carrying loads

4 Category Dictation
ACTIVITY HANDBOOK PAGE 2

Dictate words that fit into the above categories.

5 Got It!
ACTIVITY HANDBOOK PAGE 7

Have groups of students ask yes/no questions in an attempt to identify vehicle types. For example:

Is it a car?	[No.]
Is it a truck?	[No.]
Does it have a motor?	[No.]
Is it a bicycle?	[Yes.]
Is it a truck?	[No.]
Is it a car?	[Yes.]
Does it carry a lot of passengers?	[No.]
Is it small?	[Yes.]
Is it a sports car?	[Yes.]

6 Cooperative Definitions
ACTIVITY HANDBOOK PAGE 4

Have groups write definitions of types of vehicles and then pass their definitions to other groups.

7 Vehicle Crossword
ACTIVITY HANDBOOK PAGES 4–5

Have students connect vehicle words to create a crossword. For example:

8 Question the Answer!
ACTIVITY HANDBOOK PAGE 13
ACTIVITY MASTER 180

Students pick Vehicle Word Cards and think of a question for which that word could be the answer. For example:

    Card: convertible
    Student: What kind of car has a top that can come
             down?

    Card: sports car
    Student: What's the fastest kind of vehicle?

    Card: moped
    Student: What is a motorized bicycle?

    Card: minivan
    Student: What vehicle can fit a family of six?

(continued)

9 Tic Tac Definitions

ACTIVITY HANDBOOK PAGE 15
ACTIVITY MASTER 8

Have students fill in the tic tac grid with any nine vehicle words they wish. Give definitions such as the following, and have students cross out on their grids the words you have defined:

a car with either two or four doors and a lockable, enclosed trunk compartment for storage in the rear [sedan]

a car with a roof that goes down [convertible]

a car with a very fast engine and race-car styling [sports car]

a car that uses both electricity and gas for power [hybrid]

a blend of a *car* and a *jeep* [S.U.V.]

a small van that can carry up to seven passengers [minivan]

a small truck with an open rear storage area [pickup truck]

an elongated car that can carry many passengers comfortably [limousine]

a special vehicle that can take a disabled vehicle to a garage for repairs [tow truck]

a truck that carries furniture [moving van]

10 Word Clues

ACTIVITY HANDBOOK PAGE 17
ACTIVITY MASTER 180

Have students take turns giving one- or two-word clues to team members who try to guess the word. For example:

[The word is *tractor trailer*.]
Team 1 Player: "big"   [Team 1 guesses]
Team 2 Player: "big loads"   [Team 2 guesses]
Team 1 Player: "long distance" [Team 1 guesses]

[The word is *hatchback*.]
Team 1 Player: "small"   [Team 1 guesses]
Team 2 Player: "convenient"   [Team 2 guesses]
Team 1 Player: "extra door"   [Team 1 guesses]

[The word is *limousine*.]
Team 1 Player: "long"   [Team 1 guesses]
Team 2 Player: "weddings"   [Team 2 guesses]
Team 1 Player: "many   [Team 1 guesses]
              passengers"

11 Mystery Word Conversations

ACTIVITY HANDBOOK PAGE 12

Have groups create and present mystery conversations about vehicle types without naming the vehicle. The class tries to guess what the conversation is about. For example:

A. Oh! I like that one!
B. It would be fun to drive in the summer! We could put the top down and enjoy the sunshine.
A. But it would be so windy!
B. Who cares?!
   [Answer: convertible]

12 Ranking

ACTIVITY HANDBOOK PAGE 13

Have students look at the vehicles on *Picture Dictionary* page 125 and choose the five:

most expensive cars
least expensive vehicles
vehicles that can carry the most passengers
cars that use the most gasoline
healthiest vehicles to use

13 Advantages and Disadvantages

a. On the board draw two columns with <u>Advantages</u> as the heading for one and <u>Disadvantages</u> as the heading for the other.

b. Name a type of vehicle (for example—*sports car*) and have students think about the advantages and disadvantages of the vehicle. For example:

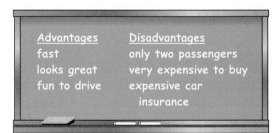

14 Who Said It?

a. Give each student a piece of paper and ask them to write the answers to the questions: Which type of vehicle would you most like to have? Why?

b. Collect the papers, read each one, and see if the class can match the answers with the students who wrote them.

LESSON OBJECTIVE

Students will learn the vocabulary for the parts of a car.

RESOURCES

AUDIO PROGRAM		MULTI-LEVEL WORKBOOKS	ACTIVITY MASTERS 
Words & Dialogs Cassette 5A CD 5: Tracks 42, 43	**WordSong:** *Great Big World* Cassette 7B • CD 8: Tracks 14, 15 Song Masters S27, S28	Literacy Workbook Beginning & Intermediate Lifeskills Workbooks Beginning & Intermediate Vocabulary Workbooks	**Reproducibles:** A8, A181–A184

TRANSPARENCIES	LANGUAGE & CULTURE NOTES	WORDLINKS
Overheads: T126, T127	**Reproducible:** LC126–127	longman.com/wordbyword

VOCABULARY INTRODUCTION

- Preview
- Present
- Practice

MODEL CONVERSATION PRACTICE

There are three model conversations. Introduce and practice the first model before going on to the second and third. For each model:

1. Have students look at the model illustration. Set the scene:

   Model 1: "A car mechanic is talking to a customer."

   Model 2: "A gas station attendant is talking to a customer."

   Model 3: "A husband and wife are talking."

2. Present the first model using word 2, the second model using word 45, and the third model using word 1.

3. Choral Repetition Practice: Full-Class and Individual.

4. Have pairs practice the model.

5. Have pairs present the model.

6. Call on pairs to present a new conversation using word 3 for the first model, word 46 for the second model, and word 4 for the third model.

7. Have pairs practice new conversations.

8. Have pairs present new conversations.

SPELLING PRACTICE

Say a word, and have students spell it aloud or write it. Or, using the transparency, point to an item and have students write the word.

WRITING AND DISCUSSION

Have students respond to the questions as a class, in pairs, or in small groups. Or have students write their responses, share their writing with other students, and discuss in class.

Making Connections

Resource Materials Bring in, or have students bring in, the following materials for vocabulary practice:

- *Automobile owners' manuals:* Talk about the car parts featured in the manual and about standard maintenance of the vehicle.

- *Model car kits:* Have students identify the car parts on a model car. If it is an older model, have students compare the car parts to contemporary ones and identify which ones have changed.

- *Brochures for new cars:* Have students identify special features using vocabulary they learned in this lesson.

Community Task Individually, in pairs, or in small groups, have students take a careful look at their own car, their family's car, or a car belonging to a friend and identify as many parts of the car as they can.

Communication Activities

1 **Clap in Rhythm**
ACTIVITY HANDBOOK PAGE 3

Have students name different car part words to a clapping rhythm.

2 **Letter Game**
ACTIVITY HANDBOOK PAGE 9

Say statements such as the following and have teams compete to identify the items:

I'm thinking of a car part that starts with *a*.	[antenna]
I'm thinking of a car part that starts with *f*.	[fender]
I'm thinking of a car part that starts with *c*.	[clutch]
I'm thinking of a car part that starts with *g*.	[glove compartment]
I'm thinking of a car part that starts with *v*.	[visor]
I'm thinking of a car part that starts with *s*.	[speedometer]
I'm thinking of a car part that starts with *h*.	[hubcap]
I'm thinking of a car part that starts with *b*.	[bumper]
I'm thinking of a car part that starts with *t*.	[tailpipe]
I'm thinking of a car part that starts with *l*.	[license plate]

3 **Tic Tac Definitions**
ACTIVITY HANDBOOK PAGE 15
ACTIVITY MASTER 8

Have students fill in the tic tac grid with any nine car parts they wish. Give definitions such as the following, and have students cross out on their grids the words you have defined:

the part of the fender that can touch another car without causing too much damage [bumper]
the part of the car that protrudes on the front and back [fender]
a movable section of the roof of a car [sunroof]
something that reduces the noise of the engine [muffler]
the system of gears that transmits the engine power to the wheels [transmission]
a device you use to lift the car to change a tire [jack]
something you light to warn oncoming vehicles of an accident or that your car has stopped on the side of the road [flare]
the lid to the gas tank [gas cap]
the flap that you lower to block the sun from your eyes while you're driving [visor]

the gauge that indicates how fast the car is moving [speedometer]
the gauge that indicates the number of miles a car has gone [odometer]

4 **Concentration**
ACTIVITY HANDBOOK PAGE 3
ACTIVITY MASTER 181

Have students shuffle the cards and place them face-down in three rows of 4 each, then attempt to find cards that match.

5 **Finish the Sentence!**
ACTIVITY HANDBOOK PAGE 7

Begin sentences such as the following for students to complete:

To see the car behind you, look through the . . . *rearview mirror*.
To look at the engine, you have to lift up the . . . *hood*.
To start a dead battery, you need . . . *jumper cables*.
To stop a car, you step on the . . . *brake pedal*.
You can tell how fast you're going by looking at the . . . *speedometer*.
To park safely on a hill, you use the . . . *emergency brake*.
When you put gas in the car, you first have to take off the . . . *gas cap*.
When you want to warn the cars around you, you press the . . . *horn*.
When it rains, you turn on the . . . *windshield wipers*.

6 **It's Something That . . .**
ACTIVITY HANDBOOK PAGE 9
ACTIVITY MASTERS 182, 183

Have students give definitions of car parts to each other beginning with "It's something that . . ." For example:

It's something that indicates which way the driver is turning. [The turn signal.]
It's something that protects the driver from getting hurt if there is a car accident. [An air bag.]
It's something that puts gas in the car. [A gas pump.]
It's something that you keep in case you get a flat tire. [A spare tire.]
It's something that you turn on when you're driving at night. [Headlights.]

7 What's the Question?

ACTIVITY HANDBOOK PAGE 16

Describe various car parts and have students respond by asking: "What's a _____?" or "What are _____s?" For example:

Teacher: It melts the ice on your windshield.
Student: What's a defroster?

Teacher: They tell you when there's a problem with your car.
Student: What are warning lights?

8 General-to-Specific Clue Game

ACTIVITY HANDBOOK PAGE 7

Possible clues:

Clue 1: Every car should have one.
Clue 2: Some cars don't have one.
Clue 3: You only use it when you have to.
Clue 4: You use it for emergencies.
Clue 5: You keep it in a special place in the trunk.
Clue 6: It requires special tools to put it on.
Clue 7: A car has four regular ones.

[Answer: spare tire]

Possible clues:

Clue 1: Every car must have two.
Clue 2: You don't need them every time you drive.
Clue 3: They're on the outside of the car.
Clue 4: You can replace them easily.
Clue 5: It's dangerous to drive in the rain without them.
Clue 6: They move back and forth.

[Answer: windshield wipers]

9 Question the Answer!

ACTIVITY HANDBOOK PAGE 13
ACTIVITY MASTERS 182, 183

Students pick Car Part Word Cards and think of a question for which that word could be the answer. For example:

Card: license plate
Student: What's something that legally identifies your car?

Card: trunk
Student: Where do you carry your luggage?

Card: radiator
Student: What cools the car engine?

Card: gas
Student: What is the most common car fuel?

10 Word Clues

ACTIVITY HANDBOOK PAGE 17
ACTIVITY MASTERS 182, 183

Have students take turns giving one-word clues to team members who try to guess the car part. For example:

[The word is *windshield wiper*.]
Team 1 Player: "rain"   [Team 1 guesses]
Team 2 Player: "clean"   [Team 2 guesses]
Team 1 Player: "glass"   [Team 1 guesses]

[The word is *brake pedal*.]
Team 1 Player: "slow"   [Team 1 guesses]
Team 2 Player: "stop"   [Team 2 guesses]
Team 1 Player: "press"   [Team 1 guesses]

[The word is *muffler*.]
Team 1 Player: "exhaust"   [Team 1 guesses]
Team 2 Player: "quiet"   [Team 2 guesses]
Team 1 Player: "metal"   [Team 1 guesses]

11 Movable Categories

ACTIVITY HANDBOOK PAGE 11
ACTIVITY MASTERS 182 or 183 (use one set at a time)

Call out the following categories and have students go to the appropriate side of the room:

engine parts
parts on the outside of a car
part of the dashboard
luxury items

12 Category Dictation

ACTIVITY HANDBOOK PAGE 2

Dictate words that fit into the above categories.

13 Car Parts and Maintenance Match Game

ACTIVITY HANDBOOK PAGE 11
ACTIVITY MASTER 184

Have students find the person whose card matches theirs.

14 Car Talk!

ACTIVITY HANDBOOK PAGE 17
ACTIVITY MASTERS 182, 183

Give students a Car Parts Word Card, and have them speak to the class for one minute about that item.

LESSON OBJECTIVE

Students will learn the vocabulary of highways and streets.

RESOURCES

AUDIO PROGRAM	
Words & Dialogs Cassette 5A CD 5: Tracks 44, 45	**WordSong:** *Great Big World* Cassette 7B • CD 8: Tracks 14, 15 Song Masters S27, S28

MULTI-LEVEL WORKBOOKS

Literacy Workbook
Beginning & Intermediate Lifeskills Workbooks
Beginning & Intermediate Vocabulary Workbooks

ACTIVITY MASTER

Reproducible:
A8

TRANSPARENCY
Overhead: T128

LANGUAGE & CULTURE NOTES
Reproducible: LC128

WORDLINKS
longman.com/wordbyword

VOCABULARY INTRODUCTION

- Preview
- Present
- Practice

MODEL CONVERSATION PRACTICE

1. Have students look at the model illustration. Set the scene: "A radio station's helicopter is talking to the announcer about the location of an accident."
2. Present the model using word 1.
3. Choral Repetition Practice: Full-Class and Individual.
4. Have pairs practice the model.
5. Have pairs present the model.
6. Call on pairs to present a new conversation using word 2.
7. Have pairs practice new conversations.
8. Have pairs present new conversations.

SPELLING PRACTICE

Say a word, and have students spell it aloud or write it. Or, using the transparency, point to an item and have students write the word.

WRITING AND DISCUSSION

Have students respond to the questions as a class, in pairs, or in small groups. Or have students write their responses, share their writing with other students, and discuss in class.

Making Connections

Resource Materials Bring in, or have students bring in, the following materials for vocabulary practice:

- *Interstate highway maps:* Look at regional maps and identify the highways, tunnels, and bridges.
- *City maps:* Look at local maps and identify the streets, intersections, one-way streets, and blocks.
- *Local traffic reports from the radio or Internet:* Have students listen to or read the local report and identify the trouble spots on a local map.

Community Task Have individual students draw a street map of their route to school. Have them draw in as much detail as possible, including traffic lights, one-way streets, tunnels, and bridges.

1 Chain Game

ACTIVITY HANDBOOK PAGES 2–3

Begin the chain as follows: "While traveling down the highway, I saw a tollbooth," and have students continue it. For example:

> Teacher: While traveling down the highway, I saw a tollbooth.
> Student 1: While traveling down the highway, I saw a tollbooth and an overpass.
> Student 2: While traveling down the highway, I saw a tollbooth, an overpass, and an underpass.
> Etc.

2 True or False?

ACTIVITY HANDBOOK PAGE 15

Make statements such as the following about the scene on *Picture Dictionary* page 128. Have students decide whether the statements are true or false. For example:

> A truck is going into the tunnel. [True.]
> A car has stopped at the tollbooth. [True.]
> A truck is going onto the bridge. [False. It's an S.U.V.]
> There are two overpasses over the highway. [False. There's one overpass.]
> A truck is coming out of the tollbooth. [True.]
> There are three lanes in each direction on the highway. [True.]
> There are three crosswalks in the scene. [False. There are four crosswalks.]
> The overpass has four lanes in each direction. [False. The overpass has two lanes.]
> One car is on the entrance ramp to the highway. [False. Two cars are on the entrance ramp.]
> One car is on the exit ramp of the highway. [True.]

3 What's the Question?

ACTIVITY HANDBOOK PAGE 16

Describe various highway and street words and have students respond by asking: "What's a _____?" or "What are _____s?" For example:

> Teacher: This is where drivers stop and pay money on a highway.
> Student: What's a tollbooth?
>
> Teacher: This is where pedestrians cross the street.
> Student: What's a crosswalk?
>
> Teacher: This is where two streets cross each other.
> Student: What's an intersection?

> Teacher: This is a big road that goes from state to state.
> Student: What's an interstate?
>
> Teacher: This divides the highway into lanes.
> Student: What's a broken line?
>
> Teacher: This indicates no one can pass.
> Student: What's a solid line?
>
> Teacher: This is a structure that goes over water.
> Student: What's a bridge?
>
> Teacher: This is a structure that goes underground.
> Student: What's a tunnel?
>
> Teacher: This is the thin strip of land that separates the two directions of an interstate highway.
> Student: What's a median?
>
> Teacher: This sign indicates where to get off a highway.
> Student: What's an exit sign?

This activity can also be done as a game with competing teams. It can also be done by having teams come up with the descriptions that they then ask others.

4 Tic Tac Definitions

ACTIVITY HANDBOOK PAGE 15
ACTIVITY MASTER 8

Have students fill in the tic tac grid with any nine highway and street words they wish. Give definitions such as the following, and have students cross out on their grids the words you have defined:

> a concrete block that separates lanes going in opposite directions [divider/barrier]
> the side of a road [shoulder]
> a line that indicates that passing is permitted [broken line]
> a line that indicates that passing is not permitted [solid line]
> the exit road from an interstate highway [exit/exit ramp]
> the term for roads in cities [street]
> this indicates an area where passing is not permitted; it also indicates that it's not possible to turn [double yellow line]
> the area for pedestrians to cross a road [crosswalk]
> the place where two roads cross [intersection]
> a light at an intersection that tells which cars can go and which cars must stop [traffic light/traffic signal]

(continued)

5 Picture This!

a. Give each student a copy of a simple map showing a few intersecting streets. For example:

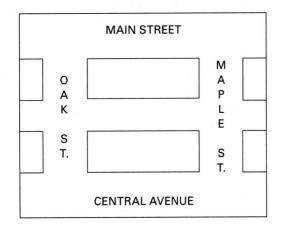

b. Describe the streets and have students draw what you describe. For example:

> There's a broken line in the middle of Maple Street.
> There's a double yellow line in the middle of Main Street.
> There are four lanes on Central Avenue. There's a car in the middle lane.
> Oak Street is a one-way street.

Variation 1: Do the activity in pairs, with students taking turns describing and drawing.

Variation 2: One student comes to the board and the rest of the class gives instructions for that student to draw streets on the board.

6 Neighborhood Watch

Have groups of students write a description of the streets and their markings in the neighborhood around the school. (Assign a different one- or two-block area to each group.) Have the groups report back to the class. For example:

> There are three lanes on Grant Avenue.
> There's a broken line between each lane.
> There's a one-way street sign on Franklin Street and a traffic light at the corner.

7 Role Play: I'm Going to Have to Give You a Ticket!

a. Have pairs of students create role plays between a police officer and a person who has been stopped for a violation either on a highway or a city street. Tell students they must use at least five of the vocabulary words from *Picture Dictionary* page 128 in their role plays.

b. Have students present their role plays to the class, and have the *witnesses* decide whether the driver in each role play deserved a ticket.

8 Dangerous Roads!

Every community has an especially dangerous road or intersection where accidents are more likely to happen.

a. In small groups, have students draw and describe a particularly dangerous road or intersection where driving safely is difficult.

b. Have groups report to the class. Is there one especially dangerous area that everyone mentioned?

Page 129 PREPOSITIONS OF MOTION

LESSON OBJECTIVE

Students will learn the prepositions to describe motion using much of the vocabulary from the previous lesson.

RESOURCES

AUDIO PROGRAM
Words & Dialogs
Cassette 5A
CD 5: Tracks 46, 47

MULTI-LEVEL WORKBOOKS
Literacy Workbook
Beginning & Intermediate Lifeskills Workbooks
Beginning & Intermediate Vocabulary Workbooks

TRANSPARENCY
Overhead: T129

LANGUAGE & CULTURE NOTES
Reproducible: LC129

WORDLINKS
longman.com/wordbyword

VOCABULARY INTRODUCTION

- Preview
- Present
- Practice

MODEL CONVERSATION PRACTICE

There are two model conversations—the first for words 1–8 and the second for words 9–13. Introduce and practice the first model before going on to the second. For each model:

1. Have students look at the model illustration. Set the scene:
   - Model 1: "A wife is giving directions to her husband."
   - Model 2: "A husband and wife are talking on their cell phones."
2. Present the model.
3. Choral Repetition Practice: Full-Class and Individual.
4. Have pairs practice the model.
5. Have pairs present the model.
6. Call on pairs to present a new conversation using word 2 for the first model and word 10 for the second model.
7. Have pairs practice new conversations.
8. Have pairs present new conversations.

SPELLING PRACTICE

Say a word, and have students spell it aloud or write it. Or, using the transparency, point to an item and have students write the word.

WRITING AND DISCUSSION

Have students respond to the questions as a class, in pairs, or in small groups. Or have students write their responses, share their writing with other students, and discuss in class.

Making Connections

Resource Materials Bring in, or have students bring in, the following materials for vocabulary practice:

- *Images of cars or people in motion from magazines, newspapers, and the Internet:* Have students describe the motions.

Community Task Have the class take a walk around the block of the school and write a list of the motions they observe—for example: a car is driving down the street, a person is walking up some stairs. Come back to class and compare notes.

Communication Activities

1 Chain Game

ACTIVITY HANDBOOK PAGES 2–3

Begin the chain as follows: "On my way to work today, I walked over a bridge," and have students continue it. For example:

> Teacher: On my way to work today, I walked over a bridge.
> Student 1: On my way to work today, I walked over a bridge and down some stairs.
> Student 2: On my way to work today, I walked over a bridge, down some stairs, and across a street.
> Etc.

2 Telephone

ACTIVITY HANDBOOK PAGE 14

Begin the activity with the following sentence: "Yesterday I had a busy day around town. I got on a bus and went downtown. I got off at Broadway and walked down to 42nd Street. I walked around the neighborhood and looked at the lights."

3 On My Way to School

a. Have students write a description of how they come to school, paying special attention to the prepositions of motion.

b. Have pairs of students share their writing and answer the following questions:

> Who has a longer commute to school?
> Who has a more interesting commute to school?

4 What's the Object?

ACTIVITY HANDBOOK PAGE 16

Call out prepositions and have students add appropriate street and highway objects. For example:

> over . . . a bridge/an overpass
> under . . . a bridge/an overpass
> through . . . a tunnel/a tollbooth

5 "In Motion" Around Town

Note: Before doing the following activity, review with the class ways to express frequency. For example, *once a day, twice a week, three times a month*, etc.

a. Choose any of the questions below that are relevant to your community and write them on the board, filled in with names of real locations.

> How often do you go over the _____ bridge?
> How often do you walk around the _____ neighborhood?
> How often do you go through the _____ tunnel?
> How often do you get on the _____ train?
> How often do you get into a taxicab?
> How often do you go under the _____ (bridge/overpass)?
> How often do you walk across _____ Avenue?
> How often do you drive past the _____ (monument)?
> How often do you get onto the _____ (interstate highway)?

b. Divide the class into pairs and have students ask each other the questions

c. Call on students to report back to the class and see which student does each of these motion activities most often.

6 Mystery Destinations

a. Brainstorm interesting places to go in the community. Write the ideas on the board.

b. Divide the class into small groups.

c. Have each group choose a destination from the board and create detailed directions explaining how to get there from the school. Tell students they can't say what the destination is.

d. Call on the groups to present their directions and have the class try to guess what the *mystery destination* is.

LESSON OBJECTIVE

Students will learn the meaning of common traffic signs and the vocabulary for directions.

RESOURCES

AUDIO PROGRAM
Words & Dialogs
Cassette 5A
CD 5: Tracks 48, 49

MULTI-LEVEL WORKBOOKS
Literacy Workbook
Beginning & Intermediate Lifeskills Workbooks
Beginning & Intermediate Vocabulary Workbooks

ACTIVITY MASTER
Reproducible: A185

TRANSPARENCY
Overhead: T130

LANGUAGE & CULTURE NOTES
Reproducible: LC130

WORDLINKS
longman.com/wordbyword

VOCABULARY INTRODUCTION

- Preview
- Present
- Practice

MODEL CONVERSATION PRACTICE

There are three model conversations—the first for words 1–16, the second for words 17–20, and the third for words 21–26. Introduce and practice the first model before going on to the second and third. For each model:

1. Have students look at the model illustration. Set the scene:

   Model 1: "A wife is warning her husband about a traffic sign."

   Model 2: "A husband and wife are driving. She's asking him for directions."

   Model 3: "A teenage boy is taking a driving test. The examiner is giving him instructions."

2. Present the first model using word 1, the second model using word 17, and the third model using word 21.

3. Choral Repetition Practice: Full-Class and Individual.

4. Have pairs practice the model.

5. Have pairs present the model.

6. Call on pairs to present a new conversation using word 2 for the first model, word 18 for the second model, and word 22 for the third model.

7. Have pairs practice new conversations.

8. Have pairs present new conversations.

SPELLING PRACTICE

Say a word, and have students spell it aloud or write it. Or, using the transparency, point to an item and have students write the word.

WRITING AND DISCUSSION

Have students respond to the questions as a class, in pairs, or in small groups. Or have students write their responses, share their writing with other students, and discuss in class.

Making Connections

Resource Materials Bring in, or have students bring in, the following materials for vocabulary practice:

- *Driver's education chapter on signs:* Have students identify the signs.

- *Images of signs downloaded from the Internet:* Have students identify the signs.

- *Local, regional, or national maps:* Have students identify what towns, cities, or states are in the north, south, east, or west.

Community Task Have groups of students take a walk around the block of the school and write a list of the signs they see. Come back to class and compare notes.

Communication Activities

❶ Chain Game
ACTIVITY HANDBOOK PAGES 2–3

Begin the chain as follows: "While driving through town, I saw a stop sign," and have students continue it. For example:

Teacher: While driving through town, I saw a stop sign.

Student 1: While driving through town, I saw a stop sign and a yield sign.

Student 2: While driving through town, I saw a stop sign, a yield sign, and a merging traffic sign.

Etc.

❷ True or False?
ACTIVITY HANDBOOK PAGE 15

While pointing to signs on *Picture Dictionary* page 130, make statements such as the following and have students decide whether the statements are true or false. For example:

Number 9: This sign means there's a crosswalk. [True.]

Number 2: This sign means there's no right turn. [False. It means there's no left turn.]

Number 11: This sign means there's a school crossing nearby. [True.]

Number 12: This sign means the traffic is merging together. [True.]

Number 4: This sign means there's no right turn. [False. It means there's no U-turn.]

Number 10: This sign means there's a rest stop nearby for tired travelers. [False. This sign means there's a railroad crossing.]

Number 15: This sign means that the road has a lot of curves. [False. This sign means that the road gets slippery when it rains.]

Number 3: This sign means right turn only. [False. It means no right turn.]

Number 14: This sign means right turn only. [False. It means turn here to follow an alternate route because the street is under construction.]

Number 6: This sign means you aren't allowed to drive in here. [True.]

❸ Concentration
ACTIVITY HANDBOOK PAGE 3
ACTIVITY MASTER 185

Have students shuffle the cards and place them face-down in three rows of 6 each, then attempt to find cards that match.

❹ Telephone
ACTIVITY HANDBOOK PAGE 14

Begin the activity with the following sentence: "Today I drove to Bloomington, Indiana. I drove north on 65 to route 128. I turned left on 128 and went east for two miles."

❺ Which Direction?

a. Bring to class a large map of the region or the nation.

b. In groups, have students study the map.

c. Say the first letter of a town, city, or state and its direction in relation to your community and have students give the answer. For example:

I'm thinking of a town south of us that starts with *A*.   [Abington]

I'm thinking of a state north of us that starts with *M*.   [Minnesota]

I'm thinking of a city east of us that starts with *N*.   [New York City]

Variation: Do the activity as a game with competing teams. The team with the most number of correct answers wins.

❻ Listen and Number
ACTIVITY HANDBOOK PAGE 10

In pairs, have one student make up a story using traffic signs and direction words and have the other student number the pictures in their order of occurrence in the story.

❼ What Should a Driver Do?

Name a sign and point to it on *Picture Dictionary* page 130. Ask students: "What should a driver do when he or she sees the sign?" For example:

Teacher *[pointing to #1]*: Stop.
Student 1: Come to a full stop and look both ways.

Teacher *[pointing to #9]*: Pedestrian Crossing.
Student 2: Slow down to look for pedestrians.
Student 3: If a pedestrian is crossing the street, you must stop.

Page 131 THE AIRPORT

LESSON OBJECTIVE

Students will learn the vocabulary for the five major areas of an airport—Check-In, Security, The Gate, Baggage Claim, and Customs and Immigration.

RESOURCES

AUDIO PROGRAM		MULTI-LEVEL WORKBOOKS	ACTIVITY MASTERS
Words & Dialogs Cassette 5A CD 5: Tracks 50, 51	**WordSong:** *Great Big World* Cassette 7B • CD 8: Tracks 14, 15 Song Masters S27, S28	Literacy Workbook Beginning & Intermediate Lifeskills Workbooks Beginning & Intermediate Vocabulary Workbooks	**Reproducibles:** A186, A187

TRANSPARENCY	LANGUAGE & CULTURE NOTES	WORDLINKS
Overhead: T131	**Reproducible:** LC131	longman.com/wordbyword

VOCABULARY INTRODUCTION

- Preview
- Present
- Practice

MODEL CONVERSATION PRACTICE

There are two model conversations. Introduce and practice the first model before going on to the second. For each model:

1. Have students look at the model illustration. Set the scene:

    Model 1: "An airplane passenger is asking someone for information."

    Model 2: "A husband and wife are in an airport, and the husband is very upset."

2. Present the first model using word 2 and the second model using word 1.

3. Choral Repetition Practice: Full-Class and Individual.

4. Have pairs practice the model.

5. Have pairs present the model.

6. Call on pairs to present a new conversation using word 3 for the first model and word 4 for the second model.

7. Have pairs practice new conversations.

8. Have pairs present new conversations.

SPELLING PRACTICE

Say a word, and have students spell it aloud or write it. Or, using the transparency, point to an item and have students write the word.

WRITING AND DISCUSSION

Have students respond to the questions as a class, in pairs, or in small groups. Or have students write their responses, share their writing with other students, and discuss in class.

Making Connections

Resource Materials Bring in, or have students bring in, the following materials for vocabulary practice:

- *An airport map (can be downloaded from the Internet):* Have students identify the areas on the map.

- *A customs declaration form (can be downloaded from the Internet):* Have students practice completing the form.

Community Task Have the class visit the airport and identify the different areas and personnel.

Communication Activities

1 True or False?
ACTIVITY HANDBOOK PAGE 15

Make statements such as the following about the scene on *Picture Dictionary* page 131. Have students decide whether the statements are true or false. For example:

> The passenger in the check-in area is carrying two suitcases. [False. He's carrying one suitcase.]
> The ticket agent is a woman. [True.]
> The person going through the metal detector is bringing a carry-on bag. [True.]
> There's a long line at the check-in counter. [False. There is only one passenger there.]
> A passenger at the check-in counter is getting his boarding pass. [True.]
> In the baggage claim area, a woman is carrying a garment bag. [False. A man is carrying a garment bag.]
> There's a customs officer in the baggage claim area. [False. There are only passengers in the baggage claim area.]
> At customs, the passenger is showing her passport to the customs officer. [False. She's showing him her customs declaration form.]
> At the immigration desk, the immigration officer is holding the passenger's passport. [True.]

2 Do You Remember?
ACTIVITY HANDBOOK PAGE 5

Have students write down everything they remember about the airport depicted on *Picture Dictionary* page 131.

If you do Variation 1, ask questions such as the following:

> Is the ticket agent a man or a woman?
> How many passengers are in the boarding area?
> What is the woman with the baggage cart doing?
> What is the customs officer holding?
> What is the passenger at the check-in counter holding?
> What is the passenger in customs doing?
> How many people are in the baggage claim area?
> Where is the baggage claim check attached on a suitcase?
> How many luggage carts are there in the baggage claim area?
> How many bags do you see in the security area?

3 Concentration
ACTIVITY HANDBOOK PAGE 3
ACTIVITY MASTER 186

Have students shuffle the cards and place them face-down in three rows of 6 each, then attempt to find cards that match.

4 It's Something That . . .
ACTIVITY HANDBOOK PAGE 9
ACTIVITY MASTER 187

Have students give definitions of airport words to each other beginning with "It's something that . . ." For example:

> It's something that you must walk through at the security checkpoint. [A metal detector.]
> It's something that you carry with you on the airplane. [A carry-on bag.]
> It's something that you must show the immigration officer. [A passport.]
> It's something that helps you move your baggage from one area of the airport to another. [A baggage cart.]
> It's something that shows you when the airplanes are arriving and leaving. [An arrival and departure monitor.]

5 Finish the Sentence!
ACTIVITY HANDBOOK PAGE 7

Begin sentences such as the following for students to complete:

> You buy your ticket at the . . . *ticket counter*.
> In order to get onto the airplane, you need to show your . . . *boarding pass*.
> When you go through customs, you have to fill out a . . . *customs declaration form*.
> The person who looks at your passport is an . . . *immigration officer*.
> The person who gives you your airplane ticket is a . . . *ticket agent*.
> The person who looks at your luggage when you arrive in a new country is a . . . *customs officer*.
> The place you wait to get on the plane is the . . . *boarding area*.
> The machine your carry-on bag passes through is an . . . *X-ray machine*.
> The document that says you are allowed to stay in a foreign country is a . . . *visa*.
> The bag you use to carry suits and dresses is a . . . *garment bag*.

6 Ask Me a Question!

ACTIVITY HANDBOOK PAGE 2
ACTIVITY MASTER 187

Have students walk around trying to guess each other's airport word items by asking yes/no questions. For example:

Is it a part of the check-in area?	[No.]
Is it a person?	[No.]
Is it something you carry?	[Yes.]
Is it a suitcase?	[No.]
Is it a document?	[Yes.]
Is it a passport?	[Yes.]

Is it a part of the baggage claim area?	[No.]
Is it a person?	[No.]
Is it something you carry?	[No.]
Is something to help you with the baggage?	[Yes.]
Is it a luggage carrier?	[No.]
Is it a baggage cart?	[Yes.]

7 Chain Story

ACTIVITY HANDBOOK PAGE 3

Begin the story as follows: "I had a terrible day at the airport yesterday. First I went to the check-in counter and I couldn't find my ticket."

8 Connections

ACTIVITY HANDBOOK PAGE 4
ACTIVITY MASTER 187

Have students make connections between two airport items. For example:

garment bag—check-in counter
You don't check in your garment bag at the check-in counter.

suitcase—passport
You shouldn't carry your passport in your suitcase.

9 Bleep!

ACTIVITY HANDBOOK PAGE 2
ACTIVITY MASTER 187

Have students create conversations based on three Airport Word Cards that they select.

10 Stand Up

a. Say the name of an airport area.

b. Tell students you're going to say four airport items. If they hear something that is associated with that area, they should stand up. If they hear a word that is not associated with that area, they should sit down. For example:

Check-In:

ticket	[stand up]
suitcase	[remain standing]
customs	[sit down]
visa	[remain sitting]

Security:

gate	[sit down]
X-ray machine	[stand up]
immigration	[sit down]
metal detector	[stand up]

The Gate:

boarding area	[stand up]
boarding pass	[remain standing]
customs	[sit down]
arrival and departure monitor	[remain sitting]

Baggage Claim:

boarding pass	[sit down]
luggage carrier	[stand up]
ticket	[sit down]
baggage claim check	[stand up]

11 Listen and Number

ACTIVITY HANDBOOK PAGE 10

In pairs, have one student make up a story using airport words and have the other student number the pictures in their order of occurrence in the story.

LESSON OBJECTIVE

Students will learn the vocabulary of the features of an airplane and the steps in airplane travel.

RESOURCES

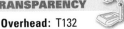

AUDIO PROGRAM

Words & Dialogs
Cassette 5A
CD 5: Tracks 52, 53

WordSong: *Great Big World*
Cassette 7B • CD 8: Tracks 14, 15
Song Masters S27, S28

MULTI-LEVEL WORKBOOKS
Literacy Workbook
Beginning & Intermediate Lifeskills Workbooks
Beginning & Intermediate Vocabulary Workbooks

ACTIVITY MASTERS
Reproducibles:
A188–A190

TRANSPARENCY
Overhead: T132

LANGUAGE & CULTURE NOTES
Reproducible: LC132

WORDLINKS
longman.com/wordbyword

VOCABULARY INTRODUCTION

● Preview
● Present
● Practice

MODEL CONVERSATION PRACTICE

There are two model conversations—the first for words 1–23 and the second for actions A–K. Introduce and practice the first model before going on to the second. For each model:

1. Have students look at the model illustration. Set the scene:

   Model 1: "A little boy is asking his father about the airplane."

   Model 2: "A security officer is giving instructions to a passenger."

2. Present the first model using word 1 and the second model using phrase A.

3. Choral Repetition Practice: Full-Class and Individual.

4. Have pairs practice the model.

5. Have pairs present the model.

6. Call on pairs to present a new conversation using word 2 for the first model and phrase B for the second model.

7. Have pairs practice new conversations.

8. Have pairs present new conversations.

SPELLING PRACTICE

Say a word or phrase, and have students spell it aloud or write it. Or, using the transparency, point to an item and have students write the word or phrase.

WRITING AND DISCUSSION

Have students respond to the questions as a class, in pairs, or in small groups. Or have students write their responses, share their writing with other students, and discuss in class.

Making Connections

Resource Materials Bring in, or have students bring in, the following materials for vocabulary practice:

● *Airline brochures and pamphlets that describe the features of different airplanes (can be downloaded from the Internet):* Talk about the features of the airplane.

Community Task Have individual students (or groups of students) interview frequent travelers to get good airplane travel advice.

Communication Activities

1 Drawing Game
ACTIVITY HANDBOOK PAGE 6
ACTIVITY MASTER 188

Have teams compete to identify airplane travel items drawn by one of their team members.

2 Miming Game I
ACTIVITY HANDBOOK PAGE 11
ACTIVITY MASTER 188 (*Note:* Omit *terminal* and *airplane.*)

Have students take turns pantomiming airplane travel items. The class tries to guess what object the person is using or where the person is.

3 Miming Game II
ACTIVITY HANDBOOK PAGE 11
ACTIVITY MASTER 189

Have students take turns pantomiming airplane travel actions. The class tries to guess what the person is doing. For example:

> You're putting your computer in a tray at the security checkpoint.
> You're walking through the metal detector.

4 Put In Order!
ACTIVITY MASTER 189

a. Divide the class into pairs.

b. Make copies of Activity Master 202 for half the class.

c. Cut it up into separate cards and give each pair a set.

d. Have the pairs put the actions in the correct order.

e. Call on students to read their cards aloud to make sure their order is correct.

5 Here's What I'm Thinking Of!
ACTIVITY HANDBOOK PAGE 8

Make statements about airplane travel words and have students guess what you're thinking of. For example:

> Teacher: I'm thinking of the place where you put your carry-on bags.
> Student: An overhead compartment.

> Teacher: I'm thinking of what you put on if the plane lands in the water.
> Student: A life vest.

> Teacher: I'm thinking of the place the plane takes off and lands.
> Student: The runway.

> Teacher: I'm thinking of the person who takes care of the passengers.
> Student: The flight attendant.

> Teacher: I'm thinking of the person who helps the pilot fly the plane.
> Student: The co-pilot.

> Teacher: I'm thinking of the place everyone must go if they need to leave the airplane in an emergency.
> Student: An emergency exit.

> Teacher: I'm thinking of the place where they make sure planes don't crash when they take off and land.
> Student: The control tower.

> Teacher: I'm thinking of the place a passenger can sit to look out a window.
> Student: A window seat.

> Teacher: I'm thinking of what the passenger eats a meal on.
> Student: The tray table.

> Teacher: I'm thinking of the thing that a passenger presses if he or she needs a flight attendant.
> Student: The call button.

6 Question the Answer!
ACTIVITY HANDBOOK PAGE 13
ACTIVITY MASTER 188

Students pick Airplane Travel Word Cards and think of a question for which that word could be the answer. For example:

> Card: control tower
> Student: What's the place that gives instructions to pilots?

> Card: seat belt
> Student: What do you have to buckle when you take off?

> Card: call button
> Student: What do you press if you need a flight attendant?

> Card: overhead compartment
> Student: Where do you stow your carry-on bag?

(continued)

What Am I?

ACTIVITY HANDBOOK PAGE 15
ACTIVITY MASTER 188

Pin word cards on students' backs and have them ask yes/no questions to identify which airplane travel word they *are*. For example:

Am I something a passenger uses?	[No.]
Am I part of the airplane?	[Yes.]
Am I the cockpit?	[No.]
Am I the lavatory?	[No.]
Am I the aisle?	[Yes.]

Am I something a passenger uses?	[Yes.]
Am I something that gives instructions?	[Yes.]
Am I a sign?	[No.]
Am I emergency equipment?	[Yes.]
Am I an emergency instruction card?	[Yes.]

 ## Connections

ACTIVITY HANDBOOK PAGE 4
ACTIVITY MASTER 188

Have students make connections between two airplane travel items. For example:

cockpit—passenger
A passenger is not allowed in the cockpit.

tray—runway
The tray can't be down when the plane is traveling along the runway.

carry-on bag—aisle
You can't put your carry-on bag in the aisle.

 ## Word Clues

ACTIVITY HANDBOOK PAGE 17
ACTIVITY MASTER 188

Have students take turns giving one- and two- word clues to team members who try to guess the word. For example:

[The word is *overhead compartment*.]
Team 1 Player: "stow"	[Team 1 guesses]
Team 2 Player: "luggage"	[Team 2 guesses]
Team 1 Player: "above"	[Team 1 guesses]

[The word is *emergency exit*.]
Team 1 Player: "door"	[Team 1 guesses]
Team 2 Player: "no children"	[Team 2 guesses]
Team 1 Player: "open"	[Team 1 guesses]

[The word is *aisle*.]
Team 1 Player: "walk"	[Team 1 guesses]
Team 2 Player: "no bags"	[Team 2 guesses]
Team 1 Player: "flight attendant"	[Team 1 guesses]

 ## Mystery Word Conversations

ACTIVITY HANDBOOK PAGE 12

Have groups create and present mystery conversations about airplane travel items without naming the item. The class tries to guess where the conversation is taking place. For example:

A. Here's your snack.
B. Just a minute. As soon as I open this, I can take the snack. Oh dear! It won't open.
A. Try pulling on it.
   [Answer: tray table]

 ## Airplane Travel Crossword

ACTIVITY HANDBOOK PAGES 4–5

Have students connect airplane travel words to create a crossword. For example:

 ## Find the Right Person!

ACTIVITY HANDBOOK PAGES 6–7
ACTIVITY MASTER 190

Practice the following questions before having students do the activity:

What seat do you like on an airplane?
Were you ever in the cockpit of an airplane?
Do you always take a carry-on bag?
Do you like to travel in airplanes?
How often do you travel in airplanes?
Do you always look for the emergency exits on an airplane?

LESSON OBJECTIVE

Students will learn the vocabulary for the areas and personnel of a hotel.

RESOURCES

AUDIO PROGRAM

Words & Dialogs
Cassette 5A
CD 5: Tracks 54, 55

WordSong: *Great Big World*
Cassette 7B • CD 8: Tracks 14, 15
Song Masters S27, S28

MULTI-LEVEL WORKBOOKS
Literacy Workbook
Beginning & Intermediate Lifeskills Workbooks
Beginning & Intermediate Vocabulary Workbooks

ACTIVITY MASTERS
Reproducibles:
A191, A192

TRANSPARENCY
Overhead: T133

LANGUAGE & CULTURE NOTES
Reproducible: LC133

WORDLINKS
longman.com/wordbyword

VOCABULARY INTRODUCTION

- Preview
- Present
- Practice

MODEL CONVERSATION PRACTICE

There are two model conversations. Introduce and practice the first model before going on to the second. For each model:

1. Have students look at the model illustration. Set the scene:

   Model 1: "These two people are making conversation at a party."
   Model 2: "A hotel guest is asking a hotel employee for information."

2. Present the first model using word 1 and the second model using word 2.

3. Choral Repetition Practice: Full-Class and Individual.

4. Have pairs practice the model.

5. Have pairs present the model.

6. Call on pairs to present a new conversation using word 3 for the first model and word 4 for the second model.

7. Have pairs practice new conversations.

8. Have pairs present new conversations.

SPELLING PRACTICE

Say a word, and have students spell it aloud or write it. Or, using the transparency, point to an item and have students write the word.

WRITING AND DISCUSSION

Have students respond to the questions as a class, in pairs, or in small groups. Or have students write their responses, share their writing with other students, and discuss in class.

Making Connections

Resource Materials Bring in, or have students bring in, the following materials for vocabulary practice:

- *Hotel brochures (can be downloaded from the Internet):* Have students identify the hotel's features and services. Have students compare several hotels and then decide where they would like to stay.

Community Task Have individual students (or groups of students) visit different hotels in the area and identify their features, services, and rates. Have students report back to the class and decide which hotels provide the best services for their rates.

Communication Activities

1 True or False?
ACTIVITY HANDBOOK PAGE 15

Make statements such as the following about the scene on *Picture Dictionary* page 133. Have students decide whether the statements are true or false. For example:

> The hotel guest is opening his room with a key. [True.]
>
> A housekeeper is walking down the hall with her housekeeping cart. [False. She's entering a guest room.]
>
> The ice machine is in the lobby. [False. The ice machine is next to the elevator on a floor with guest rooms.]
>
> The exercise room is next to the restaurant. [False. It's next to the pool.]
>
> The guest arrived in a taxicab. [False. The guest arrived in a car.]
>
> The bellhop is talking to the bell captain. [False. He's putting luggage on the luggage cart.]
>
> The concierge is located in the lobby. [True.]
>
> There are two guests at the front desk. [False. There's one guest.]
>
> The doorman is opening the front door for a guest who is leaving the hotel. [False. The guest is entering the hotel.]
>
> The customers in the restaurant are receiving room service. [False. A guest in a room is receiving room service.]
>
> A bellhop is waiting in the lobby. [False. There are no bellhops in the lobby.]
>
> Someone is giving a presentation in the meeting room. [True.]

2 Do You Remember?
ACTIVITY HANDBOOK PAGE 5

Have students write down everything they remember about the hotel depicted on *Picture Dictionary* page 133.

If you do Variation 1, ask questions such as the following:

> Is the desk clerk a man or a woman?
> How many chairs are there in the lobby?
> Where is the housekeeper?
> What is the bellhop holding?
> What is the doorman holding?
> How many people are swimming in the pool?
> Where is the ice machine?
> How many waiters are there in the restaurant?
> How many suitcases does the man who arrived in the car have?

3 Concentration
ACTIVITY HANDBOOK PAGE 3
ACTIVITY MASTER 191

Have students shuffle the cards and place them face-down in three rows of 6 each, then attempt to find cards that match.

4 Category Dictation
ACTIVITY HANDBOOK PAGE 2

Dictate words that fit into the following categories:

> hotel employees
> places in a hotel
> hotel services

5 Who Am I?
ACTIVITY HANDBOOK PAGE 17

Tell about different hotel personnel occupations and have students guess who you are talking about. For example:

> Teacher: I carry bags for the hotel guests. Who am I?
> Student: A bellhop.
>
> Teacher: I park cars for the hotel guests. Who am I?
> Student: A parking attendant.
>
> Teacher: I supervise the bellhops. Who am I?
> Student: A bellhop captain.
>
> Teacher: I check in hotel guests. Who am I?
> Student: A desk clerk.
>
> Teacher: I get reservations and tickets for hotel guests. Who am I?
> Student: A concierge.
>
> Teacher: I clean the guest rooms. Who am I?
> Student: A housekeeper.
>
> Teacher: I stay at a hotel when I'm traveling. Who am I?
> Student: A guest.
>
> Teacher: I open the door for hotel guests. Who am I?
> Student: A doorman.

6 Finish the Sentence!

ACTIVITY HANDBOOK PAGE 7

Begin sentences such as the following for students to complete:

You check in at the . . . *front desk.*
You swim in the . . . *pool.*
You get ice from the . . . *ice machine.*
You give a presentation in the . . . *meeting room.*
The housekeeper cleans the . . . *guest rooms.*
You open the guest room with a . . . *room key.*
The bellhop carries your bags on a . . . *luggage cart.*
You order room service from your . . . *guest room.*
Guests can buy small items at the . . . *gift shop.*
People go to different floors of the hotel in
  an . . . *elevator.*

7 Ask Me a Question!

ACTIVITY HANDBOOK PAGE 2
ACTIVITY MASTER 192

Have students walk around trying to guess each other's hotel words by asking yes/no questions. For example:

Is it a person?	[No.]
Is it a place in the hotel?	[Yes.]
Is it downstairs?	[Yes.]
Is it the lobby?	[No.]
Is it the restaurant?	[Yes.]
Is it a person?	[Yes.]
Is it a hotel employee?	[Yes.]
Is it an employee who works outside	[No.]
Is it an employee who talks with the guests?	[Yes.]
Is it the desk clerk?	[No.]
Is it the concierge?	[Yes.]

8 Connections

ACTIVITY HANDBOOK PAGE 4
ACTIVITY MASTER 192

Have students make connections between two hotel items. For example:

concierge—restaurant
The concierge gets restaurant reservations for guests.

doorman—front desk
The doorman doesn't work at the front desk.

9 Chain Story

ACTIVITY HANDBOOK PAGE 3

Begin the story as follows: "I stayed at a very nice hotel."

10 Bleep!

ACTIVITY HANDBOOK PAGE 2
ACTIVITY MASTER 192

Have students create conversations based on three Hotel Word Cards that they select.

11 Listen and Number

ACTIVITY HANDBOOK PAGE 10

In pairs, have one student make up a story using hotel words and have the other student number the pictures in their order of occurrence in the story.

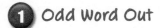

1 Odd Word Out

Read the following lists of words, and have students identify the category and the "odd word out"—the word that doesn't fit the category:

bus, train, sedan, subway, ferry, taxicab
[Category: PUBLIC TRANSPORTATION. Odd word out: sedan]

bus driver, pilot, co-pilot, cab driver, bellhop, conductor
[Category: TRANSPORTATION OCCUPATIONS. Odd word out: bellhop]

doorman, desk clerk, housekeeper, concierge, parking attendant, visor
[Category: HOTEL OCCUPATIONS. Odd word out: visor]

radiator, fan belt, roof rack, dipstick, air filter, alternator
[Category: CAR ENGINE PARTS. Odd word out: roof rack]

minivan, odometer, gas gauge, warning lights, speedometer, power outlet
[Category: PARTS OF A DASHBOARD. Odd word out: minivan]

sports car, sedan, bicycle, station wagon, hatchback
[Category: TYPES OF CARS. Odd word out: bicycle]

tow truck, moving van, moped, tractor trailer, pickup truck
[Category: TYPES OF TRUCKS. Odd word out: moped]

yield, left lane, right lane, shoulder, middle lane
[Category: PARTS OF A HIGHWAY. Odd word out: yield]

north, detour, south, east, west
[Category: DIRECTIONS. Odd word out: detour]

terminal, baggage claim, pool, security checkpoint, gate
[Category: PLACES IN AN AIRPORT. Odd word out: pool]

ticket agent, pilot, flight attendant, security officer, limousine, immigration officer
[Category: AIRPLANE TRAVEL OCCUPATIONS. Odd word out: limousine]

horn, highway, road, street, avenue
[Category: TYPES OF ROADS. Odd word out: horn]

over, under, into, out of, off, air, down
[Category: PREPOSITIONS OF MOTION. Odd word out: air]

check in at the gate, get a boarding pass, parallel park, board the plane, stow your carry-on bag
[Category: ACTIONS IN AIRPLANE TRAVEL. Odd word out: parallel park]

2 Do You Remember?
ACTIVITY HANDBOOK PAGE 5

Have students look at any of the scenes on *Picture Dictionary* pages 125–133. Have them write down everything they remember about the scenes.

3 Who Am I?
ACTIVITY HANDBOOK PAGE 17

Tell about different occupations and have students guess who you are talking about. For example:

Teacher: I check in passengers. Who am I?
Student: A ticket agent.

Teacher: I check in hotel guests. Who am I?
Student: A desk clerk.

Teacher: I make sure the passengers don't bring weapons on the plane. Who am I?
Student: A security officer.

Teacher: I examine what travelers are bringing into this country. Who am I?
Student: A customs officer.

Teacher: I make sure all people entering the United States have legal documentation. Who am I?
Student: An immigration officer.

Teacher: I run a train. Who am I?
Student: A conductor.

Teacher: I drive a bus. Who am I?
Student: A bus driver.

Teacher: I open the door for people. Who am I?
Student: A doorman.

Teacher: I take care of passengers on the plane. Who am I?
Student: A flight attendant.

Teacher: I help the pilot fly the airplane. Who am I?
Student: A co-pilot.

4 Mystery Word Association Game
ACTIVITY HANDBOOK PAGES 11–12

Have students write associations for any of the following *mystery words* for others to guess: airport, train station, bus, car engine, truck, airplane, passenger car, hotel, street signs, taxicab. For example:

terminals/baggage claim/check in/immigration and customs/ security checkpoint/gate/ control tower   [airport]

conductor/ticket/ticket window/ track/platform/arrival and departure board   [train station]

5 Transportation Quiz Game
ACTIVITY MASTER 193

a. Divide the class into four teams.

b. Copy and cut up Activity Master 206 and place cards face-down in a pile.

c. Have the teams take turns answering your questions. Give each team a time limit to answer each question (30 seconds or 1 minute).

d. The team with the most correct answers wins.

6 Category Dictation
ACTIVITY HANDBOOK PAGE 2

Dictate words from *Picture Dictionary* pages 124–133 that fit into the following categories:

occupations
places you go to take different kinds of transportation
vehicles that use gas for fuel

7 Who Said It?

a. Give each student a piece of paper and ask them to write answers to the following questions:

How do you come to school?
What's your favorite form of public transportation?
What's your favorite kind of car?
Do you like airplane travel? Why or why not?

b. Collect the papers, read each one, and see if the class can match the answers with the students who wrote them.

8 Plan a Trip!

a. In small groups, have students plan a weeklong trip anywhere in the world. To plan the trip, they must go online or call travel agents to determine the price and schedule for the transportation and hotels.

b. Have the groups present their trip plans to the class. Have the class vote on the following:

What is the most luxurious trip?
What is the most economic trip?
What is the most romantic trip?
What is the most interesting and informative trip?

UNIT 15 Recreation and Entertainment

TOPICS	DICTIONARY	TEACHER'S GUIDE
Hobbies, Crafts, and Games	134–135	339–341
Places to Go	136	342–344
The Park and the Playground	137	345–347
The Beach	138	348–350
Outdoor Recreation	139	351–352
Individual Sports and Recreation	140–141	353–355
Team Sports	142	356–357
Team Sports Equipment	143	358–360
Winter Sports and Recreation	144	361–362
Water Sports and Recreation	145	363–365
Sport and Exercise Actions	146	366–368
Entertainment	147	369–371
Types of Entertainment	148–149	372–374
Musical Instruments	150	375–377
Unit 15 Communication Activity Review	134–150	378–379

AUDIO PROGRAM

Words & Dialogs
Audio Cassette 5B
Audio Cassette 6A
Audio CD 6:
　Tracks 2–33

WordSong: *Going to the Beach*
Audio Cassette 7B
Audio CD 8: Tracks 16 (Vocal) & 17 (Sing-along)
Song Masters S29, S30

WORKBOOKS
For Multi-Level Practice
Literacy Workbook
Beginning Lifeskills Workbook
Beginning Vocabulary Workbook
Intermediate Lifeskills Workbook
Intermediate Vocabulary Workbook

WORDLINKS
Internet Resources through the *Word by Word* Companion Website
http://www.longman.com/wordbyword

ACTIVITY MASTERS
Reproducibles for Communication Activities
A8, A194–A216

TRANSPARENCIES
Full-Color Overheads for Class Practice
T134–135—T150

LANGUAGE & CULTURE NOTES
Information for Teachers & Intermediate /Advanced Students
LC134–135—LC150

LESSON OBJECTIVE

Students will learn vocabulary of craft activities and popular hobbies, games, and indoor activities.

RESOURCES

AUDIO PROGRAM

Words & Dialogs
Cassette 5B
CD 6: Tracks 2, 3

MULTI-LEVEL WORKBOOKS

Literacy Workbook
Beginning & Intermediate Lifeskills Workbooks
Beginning & Intermediate Vocabulary Workbooks

ACTIVITY MASTERS

Reproducibles:
A8, A194–A196

TRANSPARENCIES

Overheads: T134, T135

LANGUAGE & CULTURE NOTES

Reproducible: LC134–135

WORDLINKS

longman.com/wordbyword

VOCABULARY INTRODUCTION

- Preview
- Present
- Practice

MODEL CONVERSATION PRACTICE

There are three model conversations. Introduce and practice the first model before going on to the second and third. For each model:

1. Have students look at the model illustration. Set the scene:

    Model 1: "Two co-workers are talking during a break at work."

    Model 2: "A salesperson and a customer are talking."

    Model 3: "A brother and sister are trying to decide what to do."

2. Present the first model using word A, the second model using word 1, and the third model using word 35.

3. Choral Repetition Practice: Full-Class and Individual.

4. Have pairs practice the model.

5. Have pairs present the model.

6. Call on pairs to present a new conversation using word B for the first model, word 2 for the second model, and word 36 for the third model.

7. Have pairs practice new conversations.

8. Have pairs present new conversations.

SPELLING PRACTICE

Say a word or phrase, and have students spell it aloud or write it. Or, using the transparency, point to an item and have students write the word or phrase.

WRITING AND DISCUSSION

Have students respond to the questions as a class, in pairs, or in small groups. Or have students write their responses, share their writing with other students, and discuss in class.

Resource Materials Bring in, or have students bring in, the following materials for vocabulary practice:

- *Catalogs and brochures from knitting and crafts stores:* Have students identify vocabulary they have learned in this lesson. Have students also identify which craft activities they would be most interested in doing.

- *Photography magazines:* Have students identify some of the equipment that hobby photographers use.

- *Origami paper and book of instructions:* Have the class learn how to make a classic origami form such as the crane.

- *Board games, including instructions for their use:* Have small groups of students play the games they know but use English vocabulary for the pieces (see *Language and Culture Notes*). Or introduce the whole class to a new game and have pairs or groups of students play.

Community Task Have each student chose an item on *Picture Dictionary* pages 134–135 to find in a local craft or game store. Have students report on the cost of the item and where one can buy it.

Communication Activities

1 Clap in Rhythm
ACTIVITY HANDBOOK PAGE 3

Have students name different hobbies, crafts, and games to a clapping rhythm.

2 Tic Tac Definitions
ACTIVITY HANDBOOK PAGE 15
ACTIVITY MASTER 8

Have students fill in the tic tac grid with any nine hobby, craft, and game words they wish.Give definitions such as the following, and have students cross out on their grids the words you have defined:

- something that holds the framed canvas or paper someone is painting [easel]
- a thick cotton material that stretches over a wooden frame [canvas]
- a pad of medium weight paper for drawing [sketch book]
- a woodworking project in a box with all the necessary supplies to complete the work [woodworking kit]
- thin colored paper that you fold [origami paper]
- a box with everything a person needs to build a small replicas of objects, such as an airplane, train, or car [model kit]
- a book that describes all the species of bird in a certain region [field guide]
- a black suit in an English deck of cards [clubs]
- another black suit in an English deck of cards [spades]
- a red suit in an English deck of cards [diamonds]
- another red suit in an English deck of cards [hearts]
- a game you play on a board with rows of alternating black and white squares (The object is to capture your opponent's king.) [chess]

- a game you play on a board with rows of alternating red and black squares (The object is jump over your opponent's disks in order to capture them.) [checkers]
- a board game in which you buy properties and houses [Monopoly]
- a board game that has a board with letter pieces [Scrabble]
- software program you use to search on the Internet [web browser]

3 Hobby, Craft, and Game Associations
ACTIVITY HANDBOOK PAGE 2

Call out hobby, craft, and game words and have groups write down as many associations as they can think of. For example:

sew:	[sewing machine/needle/thread/thimble/safety pin]
make pottery:	[clay/potter's wheel/pots/cups/bowls]
play board games:	[chess/win/lose/checkers/dice/Scrabble]

4 What's the Object?
ACTIVITY HANDBOOK PAGE 16

Call out verbs and have students add appropriate objects. For example:

sew . . . *a skirt/a dress/fabric/curtains*
draw . . . *a picture/a sketch/a portrait*
crochet . . . *a blanket/a tablecloth/a bedspread*
knit . . . *a hat/gloves/a scarf*

5 Name the Hobby!
ACTIVITY HANDBOOK PAGE 12

Call out words associated with hobbies and have students try to name the hobby. For example:

Teacher: yarn
Student: knit

Teacher: binoculars
Student: go bird-watching

Teacher: clay
Student: make pottery

Teacher: needle
Student: sew

Teacher: sketch book
Student: draw

6 Beanbag Toss!

Have students toss a beanbag back and forth. As a student tosses the beanbag, he or she calls out a word associated with a hobby, craft, or game. The person who catches the beanbag must immediately name the hobby or handicraft associated with that item.

7 Ask Me a Question!
ACTIVITY HANDBOOK PAGE 2
ACTIVITY MASTER 194

Have students walk around trying to guess each other's hobbies by asking yes/no questions. For example:

Is it a game?	[No.]
Is it a craft?	[Yes.]
Do you use paint?	[No.]
Do you use clay?	[Yes.]
Is it pottery?	[Yes.]
Is it a game?	[No.]
Is it a craft?	[No.]
Is it a hobby?	[Yes.]
Do you do it outside?	[No.]
Is it a collection?	[Yes.]
Is it a coin collection?	[Yes.]

8 Movable Categories
ACTIVITY HANDBOOK PAGE 11
ACTIVITY MASTER 195

Call out the following categories and have students go to the appropriate side of the room:

collections	going online
models	photography
bird-watching	astronomy
board games	cards

9 Mystery Word Conversations
ACTIVITY HANDBOOK PAGE 12

Have groups create mystery conversations about hobbies, crafts, or games without naming the item. The class tries to guess what they are doing. For example:

A. Oh! Look at that one!
B. Where? I can't see it!
A. Up there in the tree. Here, use my binoculars.
B. Now I see it! It's beautiful! Is it a cardinal?
[Answer: go bird-watching]

10 Word Clues
ACTIVITY HANDBOOK PAGE 17
ACTIVITY MASTER 194

Have students take turns giving one- or two-word clues to team members who try to guess the hobby, craft, or game. For example:

[The word is *sew*.]
Team 1 Player: "needle"	[Team 1 guesses]
Team 2 Player: "thread	[Team 2 guesses]
Team 1 Player: "sewing machine"	[Team 1 guesses]

[The word is *do woodworking*.]
Team 1 Player: "kit"	[Team 1 guesses]
Team 2 Player: "wood"	[Team 2 guesses]
Team 1 Player: "hammer"	[Team 1 guesses]

11 Demonstration Time!

Have students talk about and demonstrate their handicrafts and hobbies.

12 Game Day!

Have a *game day* on which everybody brings in games for the class to play!

13 Find the Right Person!
ACTIVITY HANDBOOK PAGES 6–7
ACTIVITY MASTER 196

Practice the following questions before having students do the activity:

What hobbies do you have?
Do you like to sew? paint with watercolor? collect things? go online? play chess?
Do you know how to knit? draw a good picture of an animal? do origami?
Do you like to play Monopoly?
Do you have a collection?
Do you know how to play Scrabble?

LESSON OBJECTIVE

Students will learn the vocabulary for places to go in one's free time.

RESOURCES

AUDIO PROGRAM

Words & Dialogs
Cassette 5B
CD 6: Tracks 4, 5

MULTI-LEVEL WORKBOOKS

Literacy Workbook
Beginning & Intermediate Lifeskills Workbooks
Beginning & Intermediate Vocabulary Workbooks

ACTIVITY MASTERS

Reproducibles:
A197, A198

TRANSPARENCY

Overhead: T136

LANGUAGE & CULTURE NOTES

Reproducible: LC136

WORDLINKS

longman.com/wordbyword

VOCABULARY INTRODUCTION

- Preview
- Present
- Practice

MODEL CONVERSATION PRACTICE

There are three model conversations. Introduce and practice the first model before going on to the second and third. For each model:

1. Have students look at the model illustration. Set the scene:

    Model 1: "A wife and a husband are making plans for the day."

    Model 2: "Two co-workers are talking during a break at work."

    Model 3: "Two co-workers are talking during a break at work."

2. Present the first model using word 1, the second model using word 2, and the third model using word 3.

3. Choral Repetition Practice: Full-Class and Individual.

4. Have pairs practice the model.

5. Have pairs present the model.

6. Call on pairs to present a new conversation using word 10 for the first model, word 11 for the second model, and word 13 for the third model.

7. Have pairs practice new conversations.

8. Have pairs present new conversations.

SPELLING PRACTICE

Say a word, and have students spell it aloud or write it. Or, using the transparency, point to an item and have students write the word.

WRITING AND DISCUSSION

Have students respond to the questions as a class, in pairs, or in small groups. Or have students write their responses, share their writing with other students, and discuss in class.

Making Connections

Resource Materials Bring in, or have students bring in, the following materials for vocabulary practice:

- *Tourist book about your community:* Have students identify places to go in their community.

- *Newspaper section on "Arts and Leisure":* Have students identify places to go in their community.

Community Task Have each student chose a place from *Picture Dictionary* page 136 and find out where one is in your community or region. Have students find out the cost (if any) and hours. Have students report back to the class.

Communication Activities

1. Clap in Rhythm
ACTIVITY HANDBOOK PAGE 3

Have students name different places to go to a clapping rhythm.

2. Places to Go Associations
ACTIVITY HANDBOOK PAGE 2

Call out places to go and have groups write down as many associations as they can think of. For example:

museum:	[art/dinosaurs/admission/exhibits]
zoo:	[elephants/lions/monkeys/birds/ camels]
carnival:	[rides/candy/food/games/sideshows]
planetarium:	[stars/planets/lasers/dark]

3. Mystery Word Associations
ACTIVITY HANDBOOK PAGES 11–12

Have students write associations for places to go *mystery words* for others to guess. For example:

Brad Pitt/adventure/popcorn/ romance	[movies]
used toys/old clothes/old furniture/ low prices	[yard sale]
actor/actress/Shakespeare/acts	[play]
fish/turtles/tropical fish/water/ penguins	[aquarium]

4. Name the Place to Go!
ACTIVITY HANDBOOK PAGE 12

Call out words associated with places to go and have students try to name the place. For example:

Teacher: playground
Student: park

Teacher: revolutionary war
Student: historic site

Teacher: pottery
Student: craft fair

Teacher: flowers
Student: botanical garden

Teacher: music
Student: concert

Teacher: Shakespeare
Student: theater

Teacher: Grand Canyon
Student: national park

Teacher: rides
Student: amusement park

Teacher: peaks
Student: mountains

Teacher: swimming
Student: beach

5. Movable Categories
ACTIVITY HANDBOOK PAGE 11
ACTIVITY MASTER 197

Call out the following categories and have students go to the appropriate side of the room:

places to go outdoors
places to go indoors
public places to go
private places to go
places to go for young children
places to go close to our school
places that charge admission

6. Mystery Word Conversations
ACTIVITY HANDBOOK PAGE 12

Have groups create mystery conversations *in a place to go* without naming where they are. The class tries to guess where the conversation is taking place. For example:

A. That's interesting! But I can't figure out what it is.
B. It doesn't matter. Just look at the colors and shapes.
A. Hmm. It would look great in our dining room. How much is it?
[Answer: art gallery]

7. Word Clues
ACTIVITY HANDBOOK PAGE 17
ACTIVITY MASTER 197

Have students take turns giving one-word clues to team members who try to guess the place to go. For example:

[The word is *craft fair*.]
Team 1 Player: "pottery"   [Team 1 guesses]
Team 2 Player: "needlepoint" [Team 2 guesses]
Team 1 Player: "painting"   [Team 1 guesses]

[The word is *national park*.]
Team 1 Player: "mountains"   [Team 1 guesses]
Team 2 Player: "rivers"   [Team 2 guesses]
Team 1 Player: "Yosemite"   [Team 1 guesses]

[The word is *historic site*.]
Team 1 Player: "monument"   [Team 1 guesses]
Team 2 Player: "history"   [Team 2 guesses]
Team 1 Player: "Gettsyburg"   [Team 1 guesses]

(continued)

8 Ranking

ACTIVITY HANDBOOK PAGE 13

Have students look at the places to go on *Picture Dictionary* page 136 and rank them according to the following criteria:

the five most interesting places to go
  on the weekend
the five most expensive places to go
the five most affordable places to go
the five places you most frequently go
the three places you have never been to
the three most educational places to go

9 Find the Right Person!

ACTIVITY HANDBOOK PAGES 6–7
ACTIVITY MASTER 198

Practice the following questions before having students do the activity:

Did you go to a museum recently? an art gallery?
  a concert? an amusement park?
  a national park in the US? an aquarium?
  a planetarium? When did you go?
Did you ever buy anything at a yard sale?
Did you go to the movies recently? When did you go?

10 Our Best Choices!

a. In small groups, have students recommend places to go in the community.

b. Have students report their ideas to class. Write a master list on the board.

c. Have students vote on the best places to go in their community. Each student can vote three times. Tally the votes.

d. Write a final list reflecting which places were the most popular choices. Post the list on a student bulletin board for other students in the school to read.

LESSON OBJECTIVE

Students will learn vocabulary for the features of a park with a playground.

RESOURCES

AUDIO PROGRAM
Words & Dialogs
Cassette 5B
CD 6: Tracks 6, 7

MULTI-LEVEL WORKBOOKS
Literacy Workbook
Beginning & Intermediate Lifeskills Workbooks
Beginning & Intermediate Vocabulary Workbooks

ACTIVITY MASTER
Reproducible:
A199

TRANSPARENCY
Overhead: T137

LANGUAGE & CULTURE NOTES
Reproducible: LC137

WORDLINKS
longman.com/wordbyword

VOCABULARY INTRODUCTION

- Preview
- Present
- Practice

MODEL CONVERSATION PRACTICE

There are two model conversations—the first for words 1–22 and the second for words 17–23. Introduce and practice the first model before going on to the second. For each model:

1. Have students look at the model illustration. Set the scene:

   Model 1: "A young boy is asking someone about what's in the park."
   Model 2: "A father is talking to his daughter."

2. Present the first model using word 1 and the second model using word 17.

3. Choral Repetition Practice: Full-Class and Individual.

4. Have pairs practice the model.

5. Have pairs present the model.

6. Call on pairs to present a new conversation using word 2 for the first model and word 18 for the second model.

7. Have pairs practice new conversations.

8. Have pairs present new conversations.

SPELLING PRACTICE

Say a word, and have students spell it aloud or write it. Or, using the transparency, point to an item and have students write the word.

WRITING AND DISCUSSION

Have students respond to the question as a class, in pairs, or in small groups. Or have students write their responses, share their writing with other students, and discuss in class.

Making Connections

Resource Materials Bring in, or have students bring in, the following materials for vocabulary practice:

- *Brochures and pamphlets from recreation departments:* Have students identify the features of local parks.

- *A city or town map showing the locations of parks:* Have students identify the names and locations of local parks.

Community Task Have individual students (or groups of students) visit local parks and write down what features they have, and then report back to the class about cleanliness, safety, beauty, and convenience of each park.

Communication Activities

1 True or False?
ACTIVITY HANDBOOK PAGE 15

Make statements such as the following about the scene on *Picture Dictionary* page 137. Have students decide whether the statements are true or false. For example:

> There are three children in the sandbox. [False. There are two children in the sandbox.]
> There are two seesaws in the playground. [True.]
> A man is sitting on the bench and feeding the birds. [False. A woman is sitting on the bench and feeding the birds.]
> One child is going down the slide. [True.]
> The fountain is near the skateboard ramp. [True.]
> The picnic area has several trash cans. [False. There's one trash can.]
> The sandbox is next to the duck pond. [False. The sandbox is in the playground.]
> People are playing baseball in the ballfield. [True.]
> Two people are having a picnic together. [True.]
> There's a line at the water fountain. [False. Only one child is drinking from the water fountain.]
> A father and daughter are riding on the bicycle path. [False. A mother and son are riding on the bicycle path.]

2 Picture This!
ACTIVITY HANDBOOK PAGES 12–13

Describe a park scene and have students draw what you describe. For example:

> In this park there's a pond in the middle with six benches around it. On the left side there's a playground with . . .

3 Read, Write, and Draw
ACTIVITY HANDBOOK PAGE 13

Have students write each other letters in which they describe a park they know well.

4 What Can You Do?
ACTIVITY HANDBOOK PAGES 15–16

Have students make a list of all the things they do in a park. For example:

> sit and read
> play in the sandbox
> jog
> feed the ducks
> have a picnic
> take a walk

5 What's the Story?

Have each student choose a person depicted on *Picture Dictionary* page 137 and tell a story about that person. Possible questions to answer are:

> Who is he/she?
> What is he/she doing?
> Who is he/she with?
> How does he/she feel?
> Does he/she come here often?

Encourage students to be as creative as they wish.

6 A Trip to the Park

Have students go individually or in small groups to a park. Ask them to write down all the things they see happening in the park and report their findings back to the class.

7 Park Talk!
ACTIVITY HANDBOOK PAGE 17
ACTIVITY MASTER 199

Give students a Park and Playground Word Card, and have them speak to the class for one minute about that item.

8 What's the Question?
ACTIVITY HANDBOOK PAGE 16

Describe various park and playground items, and have students respond by asking: "What's a _____?" or "What are _____s?" For example:

> Teacher: I can cook my hamburgers on it.
> Student: What's a grill?
>
> Teacher: Children climb on it.
> Student: What's a climbing wall?
>
> Teacher: People play baseball there.
> Student: What's a ballfield?
>
> Teacher: It's a place to park a bike.
> Student: What's a bike rack?
>
> Teacher: It's an area for skateboarders.
> Student: What's a skateboard ramp?
>
> Teacher: It's a place when people can run.
> Student: What's a jogging path?
>
> Teacher: It's an area for young children to play.
> Student: What's a playground?
>
> Teacher: It's an amusement ride for young children.
> Student: What's a carousel?

Teacher: It's where people play tennis.
Student: What's a tennis court?

Teacher: People drink from it.
Student: What's a water fountain?

9 Ask Me a Question!

ACTIVITY HANDBOOK PAGE 2
ACTIVITY MASTER 199

Have students walk around trying to guess each other's park and playground words by asking yes/no questions. For example:

Do you walk on it?	[No.]
Do you ride your bicycle on it?	[No.]
Do you sit on it?	[Yes.]
Is it a bench?	[No.]
Is it in the playground?	[Yes.]
Is it a swing?	[Yes.]
Do you sit on it?	[No.]
Do you walk on it?	[No.]
Do you ride your bicycle on it?	[Yes.]
Is it a bike path?	[Yes.]

10 Do You Remember?

ACTIVITY HANDBOOK PAGE 5

Have students write down everything they remember about the park depicted on *Picture Dictionary* page 137.

If you do Variation 1, ask questions such as the following:

How many people are on the swings?
Where's the water fountain?
How many people are jogging?
How many children are riding bikes?
Is there anyone swimming in the duck pond?
How many people are looking at the fountain?
How many bikes are in the bike rack?
How many trees do you see in the park?
Is anyone playing soccer?
Is anyone playing tennis?

11 Park and Playground Crossword

ACTIVITY HANDBOOK PAGES 4-5

Have students connect park and playground words to create a crossword. For example:

12 Interviews!

a. In pairs, have students ask each other the following questions:

Do you go to the park often?
What parks do you like to go to? Why?
What do you do in the park?

b. Have students write reports explaining their partner's responses.

13 Parks in History

a. In small groups, have students discuss the following questions:

What was your favorite park when you were a child?
What was in that park?
How are parks different now from when you were a child?
Do you think parks today are better than when you were a child?

b. Have students report their ideas to the class.

LESSON OBJECTIVE

Students will learn the natural features of a beach and the recreational activities and equipment people use at the beach. See *Picture Dictionary* page 145 for related vocabulary.

RESOURCES

AUDIO PROGRAM		MULTI-LEVEL WORKBOOKS	ACTIVITY MASTERS
Words & Dialogs	**WordSong:** *Going to the Beach*	Literacy Workbook	**Reproducibles:**
Cassette 5B	Cassette 7B • CD 8: Tracks 16, 17	Beginning & Intermediate Lifeskills Workbooks	A8, A200, A201
CD 6: Tracks 8, 9	Song Masters S29, S30	Beginning & Intermediate Vocabulary Workbooks	

TRANSPARENCY	LANGUAGE & CULTURE NOTES	WORDLINKS
Overhead: T138	**Reproducible:** LC138	longman.com/wordbyword

VOCABULARY INTRODUCTION

- Preview
- Present
- Practice

MODEL CONVERSATION PRACTICE

There are two model conversations—the first for words 1–26 and the second for words 9–11, 13, 15–18, and 21. Introduce and practice the first model before going to the second. For each model:

1. Have students look at the model illustration. Set the scene:

   Model 1: "Two friends are just arriving at the beach."

   Model 2: "A wife and husband are leaving for the beach."

2. Present the first model using word 1 and the second model using word 13.

3. Choral Repetition Practice: Full-Class and Individual.

4. Have pairs practice the model.

5. Have pairs present the model.

6. Call on pairs to present a new conversation using word 2 for the first model and word 15 for the second model.

7. Have pairs practice new conversations.

8. Have pairs present new conversations.

SPELLING PRACTICE

Say a word, and have students spell it aloud or write it. Or, using the transparency, point to an item and have students write the word.

WRITING AND DISCUSSION

Have students respond to the questions as a class, in pairs, or in small groups. Or have students write their responses, share their writing with other students, and discuss in class.

♫♫ WORDSONG ♫♫

1. Have students listen to the vocal version of *Going to the Beach* one or more times. Then have students listen again as they read the song lyrics on Song Master S29.

2. Have students sing as you play either the vocal or the sing-along version of the song.

3. For fun, have a song competition in which students perform solo or in groups and the class votes for the best performance.

4. For additional practice, students can complete the cloze exercise on Song Master S30.

Resource Materials Bring in, or have students bring in, the following materials for vocabulary practice:

- *Magazine pictures or images downloaded from the Internet of beach scenes:* Have students identify what they see in the beach scene.

- *Brochures and catalogs from sporting goods stores depicting beach-related items:* Talk about the advertised items and what they are used for.

Community Task Have individual students (or groups of students) investigate beaches in the region and report back to the class about the beach's location, admission cost, services, and lifeguard presence.

Communication Activities

1 Do You Remember?
ACTIVITY HANDBOOK PAGE 5

Have students write down everything they remember about the beach scene depicted on *Picture Dictionary* page 138.

If you do Variation 1, ask questions such as the following:

> What's the lifeguard doing?
> How many children are playing with the sand?
> What is the mother putting on her son?
> Is a man or a woman surfing on a wave?
> Is the child with the surfboard entering or leaving the water?
> Is anyone sitting under the umbrella?
> How many vendors are on the beach?
> Is there a line at the snack bar?
> Is the lifeguard wearing sunglasses?
> Is a boy or a girl flying a kite?
> Is a boy or a girl building a sand castle?

2 Chain Story
ACTIVITY HANDBOOK PAGE 3

Begin the story as follows: "I'm going to the beach today. I'm taking a beach umbrella."

3 Movable Categories
ACTIVITY HANDBOOK PAGE 11
ACTIVITY MASTER 200

Call out the following categories and have students go to the appropriate side of the room:

> things to use in the sand
> things to use in the water
> things for protection from the sun
> things to lie or sit on
> people on the beach
> activities you do at the beach
> things you carry to the beach

4 Category Dictation
ACTIVITY HANDBOOK PAGE 2

Dictate words that fit into the above categories.

5 Tic Tac Definitions
ACTIVITY HANDBOOK PAGE 15
ACTIVITY MASTER 8

Have students fill in the tic tac grid with any nine beach words they wish. Give definitions such as the following, and have students cross out on their grids the words you have defined:

> a seat at the top of a ladder to give a good view of the water [lifeguard stand]
> a floating device that you throw to a swimmer in danger [life preserver]
> a place that sells fast foods such as hot dogs, french fries, soda, and ice cream [snack bar/refreshment stand]
> someone who rides the waves on a board [surfer]
> a person who walks around the beach to sell drinks, snack foods, and other beach items [vendor]
> a collapsible chair that people often take to the beach to sit on [beach chair]
> a piece of cotton fabric you use to dry off the body [beach towel]
> a small wide board you use to ride waves and play in the surf [boogie board]
> glasses that shade the eyes in strong sunlight [sunglasses]

6 What Can You Do?
ACTIVITY HANDBOOK PAGES 15–16

Have students make a list of all the things they do at the beach. For example:

> sit on a beach chair   read a book
> fly a kite   sunbathe
> build a sand castle   swim

(continued)

7 It's Something That . . .

ACTIVITY HANDBOOK PAGE 9
ACTIVITY MASTER 200

Have students give definitions of beach words
to each other beginning with "It's something that . . ."
For example:

It's something that you put on your skin to protect
you from the sun. [Sunscreen.]
It's something that you collect seashells in or fill with
sand. [A bucket/pail.]
It's something that you use to dig into the sand.
[A shovel.]
It's something that you sit on at the beach.
[A beach chair.]
It's something that protects your face and neck from
the sun. [A sun hat.]

8 Got It!

ACTIVITY HANDBOOK PAGE 7

Have groups of students ask yes/no questions in an
attempt to identify beach items. For example:

Do you use it in the water?	[No.]
Is it something you take to the beach?	[Yes.]
Do you use it in the sand?	[No.]
Does it protect you from the sun?	[Yes.]
Is it suntan lotion?	[Yes.]

9 Beach Associations

ACTIVITY HANDBOOK PAGE 2

Call out beach words and have groups write down as
many associations as they can think of. For example:

lifeguard:	[lifeguard stand/whistle/sit/watch]
kite:	[fly/sky/string/colorful/wind/clouds]
vendor:	[ice cream/hot dogs/soda/thirsty]
sunbather:	[beach blanket/sun/suntan lotion/radio]
surfboard:	[wave/fun/Hawaii/danger]

10 Secret Word Associations

ACTIVITY HANDBOOK PAGE 14

Have students choose a beach item, brainstorm
associations with that word, and see if the class can
guess the word. For example:

juice/water/drink/cold:	[cooler]
food/drinks/ice cream/building:	[snack bar]
sand/pail/dig/build/play:	[shovel]
eyes/sun/dark/see:	[sunglasses]

11 General-to-Specific Clue Game

ACTIVITY HANDBOOK PAGE 7

Possible clues:

Clue 1: You carry it to the beach.
Clue 2: You use it on the beach.
Clue 3: It can be very colorful.
Clue 4: You use it for protection from the sun.
Clue 5: You can sit under it.
   [Answer: beach umbrella]

Clue 1: You carry it to the beach.
Clue 2: You use it on the beach.
Clue 3: It's light until it's full.
Clue 4: You use it to make sand castles.
   [Answer: bucket]

12 Beach Talk!

ACTIVITY HANDBOOK PAGE 17
ACTIVITY MASTER 200

Give students a Beach Word Card, and have them
speak to the class for one minute about that item.

13 What's the Story?

Have each student choose a person depicted on
Picture Dictionary page 138 and tell a story about
that person. Possible questions to answer are:

Who is he/she?
What is he/she doing at the beach?
Why did he/she come to the beach today?
Does he/she come to the beach very often?
Is he/she having a good time?

Encourage students to be as creative as they wish.

14 Find the Right Person!

ACTIVITY HANDBOOK PAGES 6–7
ACTIVITY MASTER 201

Practice the following questions before having
students do the activity:

Do you like to go to the beach? sunbathe? build sand
castles? walk on the beach?
fly kites?
Do you wear sunscreen on the beach?
Do you like to collect shells or rocks?
Do you know how to surf?
When was the last time you went to the beach?
Do you wear a sun hat when you go to the beach?

LESSON OBJECTIVE

Students will learn the vocabulary for outdoor recreation in the woods and mountains.

RESOURCES

AUDIO PROGRAM
Words & Dialogs
Cassette 5B
CD 6: Tracks 10, 11

MULTI-LEVEL WORKBOOKS
Literacy Workbook
Beginning & Intermediate Lifeskills Workbooks
Beginning & Intermediate Vocabulary Workbooks

ACTIVITY MASTERS
Reproducibles:
A202, A203

TRANSPARENCY
Overhead: T139

LANGUAGE & CULTURE NOTES
Reproducible: LC139

WORDLINKS
longman.com/wordbyword

VOCABULARY INTRODUCTION

- Preview
- Present
- Practice

MODEL CONVERSATION PRACTICE

There are two model conversations—the first for words A–E and the second for words 1–22. Introduce and practice the first model before going on to the second. For each model:

1. Have students look at the model illustration. Set the scene:

   Model 1: "A husband and wife are making plans for the weekend."

   Model 2: "This couple just arrived at a camping site."

2. Present the first model using word A and the second model using word 1.

3. Choral Repetition Practice: Full-Class and Individual.

4. Have pairs practice the model.

5. Have pairs present the model.

6. Call on pairs to present a new conversation using word B for the first model and word 2 for the second model.

7. Have pairs practice new conversations.

8. Have pairs present new conversations.

SPELLING PRACTICE

Say a word, and have students spell it aloud or write it. Or, using the transparency, point to an item and have students write the word.

WRITING AND DISCUSSION

Have students respond to the questions as a class, in pairs, or in small groups. Or have students write their responses, share their writing with other students, and discuss in class.

Making Connections

Resource Materials Bring in, or have students bring in, the following materials for vocabulary practice:

- *Brochures and catalogs featuring camping supplies:* Have students identify the outdoor recreation items from this lesson.

- *Trail maps:* Show students how to read a trail map with elevations. Show them several trails and have them judge if those trails are strenuous or easy.

- *Brochures from state and national parks:* Have students identify what outdoor recreation possibilities are in the region.

Community Task Have groups of students investigate the facilities available at a different local, state, or national park in the region. Have each group report back to the class.

Communication Activities

1 Outdoor Associations
ACTIVITY HANDBOOK PAGE 2

Call out outdoor recreation words and have groups write down as many associations as they can think of. For example:

thermos: [cold/hot/coffee/water/juice/pour]
camping stove: [light/match/cook/pan/fuel/burner]

2 Drawing Game
ACTIVITY HANDBOOK PAGE 6
ACTIVITY MASTER 202

Have teams compete to identify outdoor recreation items drawn by one of their team members.

3 What's the Story?

Have pairs of students choose a scene depicted on *Picture Dictionary* page 139 and tell a story about it. Possible questions to answer are:

What are their names?
What are they doing?
Are they on vacation?
Who else is with them?
Are they enjoying themselves?
What's going to happen next?

Encourage students to be as creative as they wish.

4 Personal Experiences

Have a student who is familiar with any of the activities depicted tell about his or her experiences in more detail. Write any new vocabulary on the board.

5 Movable Categories
ACTIVITY HANDBOOK PAGE 11
ACTIVITY MASTER 202

Call out the following categories and have students go to the appropriate side of the room:

hiking
picnicking
camping
rock climbing
mountain biking

6 Category Dictation
ACTIVITY HANDBOOK PAGE 2

Dictate words that fit into the above categories.

7 Chain Game
ACTIVITY HANDBOOK PAGES 2-3

Begin the chain as follows: "I went on a picnic and I took a picnic basket." Have students repeat and then tell about *another* type of outdoor recreation activity. For example:

Teacher: I went on a picnic and I took a picnic basket.
Student 1: I went on a picnic and I took a picnic basket. I went camping and I took a tent.
Student 2: I went on a picnic and I took a picnic basket. I went camping and I took a tent. I went rock climbing and I took rope.
Etc.

8 What Should We Bring?

a. Brainstorm with students and write on the board all the items you might take on a camping or hiking trip. Include the items on *Picture Dictionary* page 139 as well as others.

b. Tell students they can bring only five of these items on the trip. Have each student make a list of the five items he or she would bring, beginning with the most important.

c. Have students sit in small groups, comparing and discussing their lists. Have each group decide on a list of five items the whole group can agree on.

d. Compare the groups' decisions.

9 Outdoor Recreation Match Game: The Nervous Camper!
ACTIVITY HANDBOOK PAGE 11
ACTIVITY MASTER 203

a. Set the scene: "Two people are going camping. One of them is very nervous. He or she is afraid of all the things that might happen. The other is a more experienced camper and isn't worried at all."

b. Have students find the person whose card matches theirs.

LESSON OBJECTIVE

Students will learn the vocabulary of individual sports and sporting equipment as well as individual recreational activities and equipment. See *Picture Dictionary* page 69 for related vocabulary.

RESOURCES

AUDIO PROGRAM

Words & Dialogs
Cassette 5B
CD 6: Tracks 12, 13

MULTI-LEVEL WORKBOOKS
Literacy Workbook
Beginning & Intermediate Lifeskills Workbooks
Beginning & Intermediate Vocabulary Workbooks

ACTIVITY MASTERS
Reproducibles:
A204–A206

TRANSPARENCIES
Overheads: T140, T141

LANGUAGE & CULTURE NOTES
Reproducible: LC140–141

WORDLINKS
longman.com/wordbyword

VOCABULARY INTRODUCTION

- Preview
- Present
- Practice

MODEL CONVERSATION PRACTICE

There are two model conversations—the first for words A–V and the second for words 1–52. Introduce and practice the first model before going on to the second. For each model:

1. Have students look at the model illustration. Set the scene:

   Model 1: "Two co-workers are talking during a break at work."

   Model 2: "A husband and wife are talking."

2. Present the first model using word A and the second model using word 1.

3. Choral Repetition Practice: Full-Class and Individual.

4. Have pairs practice the model.

5. Have pairs present the model.

6. Call on pairs to present a new conversation using word I for the first model and word 2 for the second model.

7. Have pairs practice new conversations.

8. Have pairs present new conversations.

SPELLING PRACTICE

Say a word, and have students spell it aloud or write it. Or, using the transparency, point to an item and have students write the word.

WRITING AND DISCUSSION

Have students respond to the questions as a class, in pairs, or in small groups. Or have students write their responses, share their writing with other students, and discuss in class.

Making Connections

Resource Materials Bring in, or have students bring in, the following materials for vocabulary practice:

- *Brochures and catalogs from sporting goods stores:* Have students identify the sports and the sports equipment from this lesson.

- *Informational literature from national sports associations:* Have students find out if there is a chapter of this sports organization in their area.

Community Task Have individual students (or groups of students) each investigate a different kind of sport and find out where it's possible to learn and play that sport in the local community. Have students report back to the class.

Communication Activities

1 Name the Sport!
ACTIVITY HANDBOOK PAGE 12

Call out words associated with individual sports and have students try to name the sport. For example:

Teacher: knee pads
Student: inline skating

Teacher: bike
Student: cycling

Teacher: safety goggles
Student: racquetball

Teacher: paddle
Student: ping pong

Teacher: birdie
Student: badminton

Teacher: flying disc
Student: Frisbee

Teacher: pool stick
Student: billiards

Teacher: trampoline
Student: gymnastics

Teacher: rowing machine
Student: work out

Teacher: black belt
Student: martial arts

2 Movable Categories I
ACTIVITY HANDBOOK PAGE 11
ACTIVITY MASTER 204

Call out the following categories and have students go to the appropriate side of the room:

sports that require special footwear
sports that require a net
sports that require a ball
sports that require a special place to do it or play it
sports that you can do almost anywhere
sports you play outdoors
sports you play indoors
sports that require protection for a part of the body
sports that require throwing
sports you can play alone
sports that require two or more people

3 Movable Categories II
ACTIVITY HANDBOOK PAGE 11
ACTIVITY MASTERS 205, 206

Call out the following categories and have students go to the appropriate side of the room:

balls
safety equipment
footwear
rackets
indoor equipment
outdoor equipment
things that are metal

4 Category Dictation
ACTIVITY HANDBOOK PAGE 2

Dictate words that fit into the categories of either of the above activities.

5 Stand Up for Sports!

a. Say the name of an individual sport.

b. Tell students you're going to say four words. If they hear a word that is associated with that sport, they should stand up. If they hear a word that is not associated with that sport, they should sit down. For example:

Billiards:
pool table	[stand up]
pool stick	[remain standing]
treadmill	[sit down]
golf ball	[remain sitting]

Racquetball:
paddle	[sit down]
safety goggles	[stand up]
bike	[sit down]
racquet	[stand up]

Horseback riding:
skateboard	[sit down]
saddle	[stand up]
knee pads	[sit down]
reins	[stand up]

Archery:
bow and arrow	[stand up]
target	[remain standing]
Frisbee	[sit down]
jogging suit	[remain sitting]

6 Listen and Number
ACTIVITY HANDBOOK PAGE 10

In pairs, have one student make up a story using individual sport words and have the other student number the pictures in their order of occurrence in the story.

7 It's a Puzzle!
ACTIVITY HANDBOOK PAGE 9

Cut out pictures of individual sports and create puzzles out of the pictures for students to identify and put together by asking questions. For example:

Is someone rollerblading in your picture?
I have a ping pong table in my picture.
My picture has people doing gymnastics.
There's someone working out on a treadmill in my picture.

8 Sports Associations
ACTIVITY HANDBOOK PAGE 2

Call out individual sport words and have groups write down as many associations as they can think of. For example:

jogging:	[jogging suit/jogging shoes/morning/park/exercise]
work out:	[treadmill/gym/video/rowing machine/exercise bike]
golf:	[outdoors/relaxing/golf balls/golf clubs/walking]
ping pong:	[paddle/Chinese/net/ping pong ball/indoor]
horseback riding:	[saddle/horse/reins/stirrups/western saddle/rodeo]

9 Secret Word Associations
ACTIVITY HANDBOOK PAGE 14

Have students choose an individual sport item, brainstorm associations with that word, and see if the class can guess the word. For example:

shorts/shoes/healthy/park/exercise:	[jogging]
saddle/reins/stirrups/trails/animal:	[horseback riding]
paddle/table/net/ball/fast:	[ping pong]
gym/weights/strong/barbells/heavy:	[weightlifting]

10 Miming Game
ACTIVITY HANDBOOK PAGE 11
ACTIVITY MASTER 204

Have students take turns pantomiming individual sports. The class tries to guess what sport the person is doing. For example:

You're boxing.
You're playing ping pong.

11 Sports Talk!
ACTIVITY HANDBOOK PAGE 17
ACTIVITY MASTER 204

Give students an Individual Sport and Recreation Word Card, and have them speak to the class for one minute about that sport or activity.

12 Things in Common
ACTIVITY HANDBOOK PAGE 14

Have students think of two individual sports or sports equipment items that have things in common. For example:

tennis—ping pong
Both use a piece of equipment you hold in your hand to move the ball.
Both have two or four players.
Both use balls.
In both sports, the ball bounces off a surface.
In both, the ball moves fast.
In both, the players take turns hitting the ball.

skateboard—inline skating
Both use wheels.
Both require balance.
Both can be dangerous.
Both are fast sports.

13 Ranking
ACTIVITY HANDBOOK PAGE 13

Have students look at the individual sports listed on Picture Dictionary pages 140 and 141 and rank them 1-5 (with 1 being the most) according to the following criteria:

the five that require the most skill
the five that are the most dangerous
the five that are the most interesting to watch
the five that are the most expensive
the five that give the most health benefits
the five that you most want to try
the five that you never want to try

LESSON OBJECTIVE

Students will learn the vocabulary of several popular American team sports. See *Picture Dictionary* page 143 for further depictions of each of these sports.

RESOURCES

AUDIO PROGRAM
Words & Dialogs
Cassette 5B
CD 6: Tracks 14–16

MULTI-LEVEL WORKBOOKS
Literacy Workbook
Beginning & Intermediate Lifeskills Workbooks
Beginning & Intermediate Vocabulary Workbooks

ACTIVITY MASTERS
Reproducibles:
A207, A208

TRANSPARENCY
Overhead: T142

LANGUAGE & CULTURE NOTES
Reproducible: LC142

WORDLINKS
longman.com/wordbyword

VOCABULARY INTRODUCTION

- Preview
- Present
- Practice

MODEL CONVERSATION PRACTICE

1. Have students look at the model illustration. Set the scene: "Two people on a date are talking."
2. Present the model.
3. Choral Repetition Practice: Full-Class and Individual.
4. Have pairs practice the model.
5. Have pairs present the model.
6. Call on pairs to present a new conversation using word B.
7. Have pairs practice new conversations.
8. Have pairs present new conversations.

ADDITIONAL CONVERSATION PRACTICE

Before students practice the additional conversations, you may want to have them listen to the examples on the Audio Program.

Conversation 1 Have students practice and present conversations with any words they wish.

Conversation 2 Set the scene: "A coach is talking to players on the team." Have students practice and present conversations with any words they wish.

SPELLING PRACTICE

Say a word, and have students spell it aloud or write it. Or, using the transparency, point to an item and have students write the word.

WRITING AND DISCUSSION

Have students respond to the questions as a class, in pairs, or in small groups. Or have students write their responses, share their writing with other students, and discuss in class.

Making Connections

Resource Materials Bring in, or have students bring in, the following materials for vocabulary practice:

- *Sports magazines:* Show students pictures in the magazine and have students identify the sport.

- *Articles from the sports section of the newspaper:* Have students identify the sport of each professional or school team mentioned in the paper and where they play.

Community Tasks Have individual students (or groups of students) each choose a different sport to investigate. Have them find out where people (non-professionals) play these sports and what intramural leagues are in the area for people of their age to play. Have them report back to the class.

Have individual students (or groups of students) each choose a different professional sport to investigate. Have them find out where professional teams play these sports in the region and what the sport seasons are. Have them report back to the class.

Communication Activities

1 Miming Game
ACTIVITY HANDBOOK PAGE 11
ACTIVITY MASTER 207

Have students take turns pantomiming team sports. The class tries to guess what sport the person is doing. For example:

> You're playing baseball.
> You're playing soccer.

2 It's a Puzzle!
ACTIVITY HANDBOOK PAGE 9

Cut out pictures of team sports and create puzzles out of the pictures for students to identify and put together by asking questions. For example:

> Are people playing baseball in your picture?
> I have a hockey rink in my picture.
> I have several lacrosse players in my picture.
> There's a volleyball court in my picture.

3 Movable Categories
ACTIVITY HANDBOOK PAGE 11
ACTIVITY MASTER 207

Call out the following categories and have students go to the appropriate side of the room:

> sports that require special footwear
> sports that require a net
> sports you play outdoors
> sports you play indoors
> sports that require throwing
> sports that require kicking
> sports you play in warm weather
> sports you play in cold weather
> sports you can play anytime
> sports that require protection for a part of the body

4 Category Dictation
ACTIVITY HANDBOOK PAGE 2

Dictate words that fit into the above categories.

5 Verb Associations
ACTIVITY HANDBOOK PAGE 2

a. Divide the class into small groups.

b. For each of the sports on *Picture Dictionary* page 142, have the groups write down as many verb associations as they can think of. For example:

> baseball: [hit/swing/throw/catch/run]
> football: [throw/run/tackle/catch/kick]
> basketball: [throw/run/dribble/bounce/turn]
> soccer: [run/kick/pass]

6 Sports Talk!
ACTIVITY HANDBOOK PAGE 17
ACTIVITY MASTER 207

Give students a Team Sport Word Card, and have them speak to the class for one minute about that sport.

7 Find the Right Person!
ACTIVITY HANDBOOK PAGES 6–7
ACTIVITY MASTER 208

Practice the following questions before having students do the activity:

> Do you like to watch baseball? football?
>   ice hockey? basketball?
> Do you like to play volleyball? softball? soccer?
> Do you know the rules of baseball? football?
>   lacrosse?

8 Survey

a. Give each student or a pair of students one of the following questions:

> What is your favorite professional team sport to watch?
> What is your favorite team? (*soccer/baseball/etc.*)
> Do you think professional players make too much money?
> What is your favorite team sport to play?

b. Have students survey other students in the school.

c. When students are finished, have them tally their results and present them to the class in a bar graph.

9 Find the Answer!
ACTIVITY HANDBOOK PAGE 6

Possible questions students might want to have answered:

> What is the leading baseball/football/ice hockey/basketball/soccer team in the country?
> What are the names of the major professional baseball/football/ice hockey/basketball/soccer leagues?
> What are the names of the minor professional baseball/football/ice hockey/basketball/soccer leagues?
> What are the sport seasons for baseball/softball/football/lacrosse/ice hockey/volleyball/basketball/soccer?

LESSON OBJECTIVE

Students will learn the vocabulary of equipment used in the team sports presented on *Picture Dictionary* page 142.

RESOURCES

AUDIO PROGRAM
Words & Dialogs
Cassette 5B
CD 6: Tracks 17–19

MULTI-LEVEL WORKBOOKS
Literacy Workbook
Beginning & Intermediate Lifeskills Workbooks
Beginning & Intermediate Vocabulary Workbooks

ACTIVITY MASTER
Reproducible:
A209

TRANSPARENCY
Overhead: T143

LANGUAGE & CULTURE NOTES
Reproducible: LC143

WORDLINKS
longman.com/wordbyword

VOCABULARY INTRODUCTION

- Preview
- Present
- Practice

MODEL CONVERSATION PRACTICE

1. Have students look at the model illustration. Set the scene: "A daughter and father are talking."
2. Present the model.
3. Choral Repetition Practice: Full-Class and Individual.
4. Have pairs practice the model.
5. Have pairs present the model.
6. Call on pairs to present a new conversation using word 2.
7. Have pairs practice new conversations.
8. Have pairs present new conversations.

ADDITIONAL CONVERSATION PRACTICE

Before students practice the additional conversations, you may want to have them listen to the examples on the Audio Program.

Conversation 1 Have students practice and present conversations with any words they wish.

Conversation 2 Have students practice and present conversations with any words they wish.

SPELLING PRACTICE

Say a word, and have students spell it aloud or write it. Or, using the transparency, point to an item and have students write the word.

WRITING AND DISCUSSION

Have students respond to the questions as a class, in pairs, or in small groups. Or have students write their responses, share their writing with other students, and discuss in class.

Making Connections

Resource Materials Bring in, or have students bring in, the following materials for vocabulary practice:

- *Sports magazines:* Show students pictures in the magazine and have them identify the sports equipment.

- *Brochures and catalogs from sporting goods stores:* Have students identify the sports and the sports equipment they have learned in this lesson.

Community Task Have individual students (or groups of students) each choose a different type of team sports equipment to investigate. Have them find out where they can buy the equipment and about how much the piece would cost. Have students report back to class.

Communication Activities

1 Name the Sport!
ACTIVITY HANDBOOK PAGE 12

Call out words associated with team sports equipment and have students try to name the sport. For example:

Teacher: face guard
Student: lacrosse

Teacher: catcher's mitt
Student: baseball

Teacher: bat
Student: baseball

Teacher: shinguards
Student: soccer

Teacher: puck
Student: hockey

Teacher: shoulder pads
Student: football

Teacher: backboard
Student: basketball

Teacher: hoop
Student: basketball

Teacher: glove
Student: baseball

Teacher: batting helmet
Student: baseball

2 Finish the Sentence!
ACTIVITY HANDBOOK PAGE 7

Begin sentences such as the following for students to complete:

In baseball, you hit the ball with a . . . *bat*.
In basketball, you try to shoot the ball into the . . . *hoop*.
In volleyball, you try to hit the ball over the . . . *net*.
In hockey, you try to hit the . . . *puck*.
When you play soccer, to protect your legs, you wear . . . *shinguards*.
When you play football, to protect your head, you wear a . . . *helmet*.
When you play hockey, to protect your face, you wear a . . . *hockey mask*.
When you play hockey, to protect your hands, you wear . . . *hockey gloves*.
When you play lacrosse, to protect your face you wear a . . . *face guard*.
The catcher in baseball wears a . . . *mask*.
In soccer, you can't use your hands to move the . . . *ball*.

3 Drawing Game
ACTIVITY HANDBOOK PAGE 6
ACTIVITY MASTER 209

Have teams compete to identify team sports equipment drawn by one of their team members.

4 Movable Categories
ACTIVITY HANDBOOK PAGE 11
ACTIVITY MASTER 209

Call out the following categories and have students go to the appropriate side of the room:

sports that use gloves
sports that use helmets
sports that use balls
sports that use nets
sports that use sticks
sports that require face protection

5 Category Dictation
ACTIVITY HANDBOOK PAGE 2

Dictate words that fit into the above categories.

6 It's Something That . . .
ACTIVITY HANDBOOK PAGE 9
ACTIVITY MASTER 209

Have students give definitions of team sports equipment to each other beginning with "It's something that. . . ." For example:

It's something that a hockey player uses to hit the puck. [A hockey stick.]
It's something that protects a football player's head. [A helmet.]
It's something that a baseball catcher uses to catch the ball. [A catcher's mitt.]
It's something that identifies which players are on which team. [A uniform.]
It's something that a lacrosse player uses to throw the ball. [A lacrosse stick.]

(continued)

Ask Me a Question!

ACTIVITY HANDBOOK PAGE 2
ACTIVITY MASTER 209

Have students walk around trying to guess each other's team sports equipment items by asking yes/no questions. For example:

Do you wear it?	[Yes.]
Do you wear it on your hand?	[No.]
Do you wear it on your head?	[Yes.]
Do you use it in hockey?	[No.]
Do you use it in baseball?	[Yes.]
Is it a batting helmet?	[Yes.]

Do you wear it?	[No.]
Do you carry it?	[No.]
Is it part of the field?	[Yes.]
Is it for basketball?	[No.]
Is it for volleyball?	[Yes.]
Is it a volleyball net?	[Yes.]

8 Question the Answer!

ACTIVITY HANDBOOK PAGE 13
ACTIVITY MASTER 209

Students pick Team Sports Equipment Word Cards and think of a question for which that word could be the answer. For example:

Card: backboard
Student: What's behind the basketball hoop?

Card: shoulder pads
Student: What does a football player wear to protect his shoulders?

Card: bat
Student: What does a baseball player use to hit a ball?

Card: face guard
Student: What does a lacrosse player wear to protect his face?

9 Stand Up for Sports!

a. Say the name of a team sport.

b. Tell students you're going to say four words. If they hear a word that is associated with that sport, they should stand up. If they hear a word that is not associated with that sport, they should sit down. For example:

Soccer:
shinguards	[stand up]
soccer ball	[remain standing]
hoop	[sit down]
face guard	[remain sitting]

Lacrosse:
skates	[sit down]
stick	[stand up]
mitt	[sit down]
lacrosse ball	[stand up]

Baseball:
shoulder pads	[sit down]
bat	[stand up]
catcher's mask	[remain standing]
net	[sit down]

Volleyball:
net	[stand up]
ball	[remain standing]
backboard	[sit down]
helmet	[remain sitting]

10 Sports Associations

ACTIVITY HANDBOOK PAGE 2

Call out team sport words and have groups write down as many associations as they can think of. For example:

soccer:	[goal/World Cup/ball/shinguards/field/mud]
football:	[touchdown/helmet/shoulder pads/football/field]
ice hockey:	[cold/ice/hockey sticks/puck/goal/net/hockey gloves/hockey mask]
softball:	[ball/field/bases/girls/bat/catcher's mitt]
basketball:	[sneakers/hoop/shorts/basketball/backboard]

11 Secret Word Associations

ACTIVITY HANDBOOK PAGE 14

Have students choose a team sports equipment item, brainstorm associations with that word, and see if the class can guess the word. For example:

stick/puck/mask/glove/ice:	[hockey]
glove/mitt/World Series/umpire:	[baseball]
helmet/shoulder pads/field/pass:	[football]
jump/hoop/net/tall/dribble:	[basketball]

LESSON OBJECTIVE

Students will learn the vocabulary of winter sports and recreational activities.

RESOURCES

AUDIO PROGRAM
Words & Dialogs
Cassette 5B
CD 6: Tracks 20–22

MULTI-LEVEL WORKBOOKS
Literacy Workbook
Beginning & Intermediate Lifeskills Workbooks
Beginning & Intermediate Vocabulary Workbooks

ACTIVITY MASTER
Reproducible:
A210

TRANSPARENCY
Overhead: T144

LANGUAGE & CULTURE NOTES
Reproducible: LC144

WORDLINKS
longman.com/wordbyword

VOCABULARY INTRODUCTION

- Preview
- Present
- Practice

MODEL CONVERSATION PRACTICE

1. Have students look at the model illustration. Set the scene: "Two friends are talking in front of a sporting goods store."
2. Present the model.
3. Choral Repetition Practice: Full-Class and Individual.
4. Have pairs practice the model.
5. Have pairs present the model.
6. Call on pairs to present a new conversation using word B.
7. Have pairs practice new conversations.
8. Have pairs present new conversations.

ADDITIONAL CONVERSATION PRACTICE

Before students practice the additional conversations, you may want to have them listen to the examples on the Audio Program.

Conversation 1 Have students practice and present conversations with any words they wish.

Conversation 2 Have students practice and present conversations with any words they wish.

SPELLING PRACTICE

Say a word, and have students spell it aloud or write it. Or, using the transparency, point to an item and have students write the word.

WRITING AND DISCUSSION

Have students respond to the questions as a class, in pairs, or in small groups. Or have students write their responses, share their writing with other students, and discuss in class.

Making Connections

Resource Materials Bring in, or have students bring in, the following materials for vocabulary practice:

- *Brochures and catalogs from sporting goods stores:* Have students identify the sports and the sports equipment from this lesson.

- *Sports magazines on skiing, cross-country skiing, skating, and snowmobiling:* Show students pictures in the magazine and have them identify the sports equipment.

Community Task Have individual students (or groups of students) each choose a different type of winter sports equipment to investigate. Have them find out where they can buy the equipment and about how much the piece would cost. Have students report back to class.

Communication Activities

1 True or False?
ACTIVITY HANDBOOK PAGE 15

Make statements such as the following about the scene on *Picture Dictionary* page 144. Have students decide whether the statements are true or false. For example:

> The person downhill skiing is a woman. [False. It's a man.]
> There are three people in the bobsled. [False. There are four people in the bobsled.]
> The person figure skating is a woman. [True.]
> The person cross-country skiing is wearing goggles. [False. She isn't wearing goggles.]
> Two children are sledding on the saucer. [False. Only one child is sledding on the saucer.]
> The ice-skater is covering his blades with skate guards. [True.]
> Snowmobiles have bindings. [False. Skies and snowboards have bindings.]

2 Do You Remember?
ACTIVITY HANDBOOK PAGE 5

Have students write down everything they remember about the winter sports scenes depicted on *Picture Dictionary* page 144.

If you do Variation 1, ask questions such as the following:

> Which sports are in the top row?
> Which sports are in the bottom row?
> How many people are bobsledding?
> How many people are sledding?
> How many people are skiing?
> How many people are skating?
> How many people are wearing hats?
> How many people are wearing helmets?
> How many people are wearing scarves?
> How many ski poles does the downhill skier have?

3 Ask Me a Question!
ACTIVITY HANDBOOK PAGE 2
ACTIVITY MASTER 210

Have students walk around trying to guess each other's winter sports equipment items by asking yes/no questions. For example:

> Do you use it on ice?   [No.]
> Do you use it on snow?   [Yes.]
> Do you sit on it?   [Yes.]
> Is it a sledding dish?   [Yes.]
>
> Do you use it on snow?   [No.]
> Do you use it on ice?   [Yes.]
> Do you wear it?   [Yes.]
> Is it ice skates?   [Yes.]

4 Sports Associations
ACTIVITY HANDBOOK PAGE 2

Call out winter sport words and have groups write down as many associations as they can think of. For example:

> downhill skiing: [skis/ski boots/bindings/poles]
> figure skating: [ice/ice skates/ballet/Olympics]
> bobsledding: [cold/fast/dangerous/Olympics]
> snowboarding: [snow/cold/snowboard/bindings]
> snowmobiling: [machine/fast/noisy/gasoline]

5 Sports Talk!
ACTIVITY HANDBOOK PAGE 17
ACTIVITY MASTER 210

Give students a Winter Sports and Recreation Word Card, and have them speak to the class for one minute about that item.

6 Ranking
ACTIVITY HANDBOOK PAGE 13

Have students look at the winter sports listed on *Picture Dictionary* page 144 and rank them 1–3 (with 1 being the most) according to the following criteria:

> the three that require the most training
> the three that are the most dangerous
> the three that are the most interesting to watch
> the three that are the most expensive
> the three that give the most health benefits
> the three that you most want to try
> the three that you never want to try

7 Find the Answer!
ACTIVITY HANDBOOK PAGE 6

Possible questions students might want to have answered:

> Where in our area can I downhill ski? cross-country ski? ice skate? figure skate? snowboard? sled? bobsled? snowmobile?
> Are there downhill skiing/figure skating/bobsledding competitions in our area?

LESSON OBJECTIVE

Students will learn the vocabulary of water sports and recreational activities.

RESOURCES

AUDIO PROGRAM

Words & Dialogs
Cassette 5B
CD 6: Tracks 23–25

WordSong: *Going to the Beach*
Cassette 7B • CD 8: Tracks 16, 17
Song Masters S29, S30

MULTI-LEVEL WORKBOOKS

Literacy Workbook
Beginning & Intermediate Lifeskills Workbooks
Beginning & Intermediate Vocabulary Workbooks

ACTIVITY MASTERS

Reproducibles:
A211, A212

TRANSPARENCY
Overhead: T145

LANGUAGE & CULTURE NOTES
Reproducible: LC145

WORDLINKS
longman.com/wordbyword

VOCABULARY INTRODUCTION

- Preview
- Present
- Practice

MODEL CONVERSATION PRACTICE

1. Have students look at the model illustration. Set the scene: "Two friends are talking."
2. Present the model.
3. Choral Repetition Practice: Full-Class and Individual.
4. Have pairs practice the model.
5. Have pairs present the model.
6. Call on pairs to present a new conversation using word B.
7. Have pairs practice new conversations.
8. Have pairs present new conversations.

ADDITIONAL CONVERSATION PRACTICE

Before students practice the additional conversations, you may want to have them listen to the examples on the Audio Program.

Conversation 1 Have students practice and present conversations with any words they wish.

Conversation 2 Have students practice and present conversations with any words they wish.

SPELLING PRACTICE

Say a word, and have students spell it aloud or write it. Or, using the transparency, point to an item and have students write the word.

WRITING AND DISCUSSION

Have students respond to the questions as a class, in pairs, or in small groups. Or have students write their responses, share their writing with other students, and discuss in class.

Making Connections

Resource Materials Bring in, or have students bring in, the following materials for vocabulary practice:

- *Brochures and catalogs from sporting goods stores:* Have students identify the sports and sports equipment from this lesson.

- *Sports magazines for sailing, surfing, and fishing:* Show students pictures in the magazine and have them identify the sports equipment.

- *Brochures from resorts and other facilities offering summer waterfront activities:* Have students identify the sports offered by each facility.

Community Task Have individual students (or groups of students) each investigate a different kind of water sport and find out where one can learn and do that sport in the local community. Have students report back to the class.

Communication Activities

1 Chain Game
ACTIVITY HANDBOOK PAGES 2-3

Begin the chain as follows: "I had a wonderful vacation in the Caribbean," and have students continue it. For example:

Teacher: I had a wonderful vacation in the Caribbean.
Student 1: I had a wonderful vacation in the Caribbean. I went sailing.
Student 2: I had a wonderful vacation in the Caribbean. I went sailing and scuba diving.
Etc.

2 Name the Sport!
ACTIVITY HANDBOOK PAGE 12

Call out words associated with water sports and have students try to name the sport. For example:

Teacher: oars
Student: rowing

Teacher: paddle
Student: canoeing or kayaking

Teacher: goggles
Student: swimming

Teacher: bathing cap
Student: swimming

Teacher: mask
Student: snorkeling

Teacher: fins
Student: snorkeling

Teacher: wet suit
Student: scuba diving

Teacher: air tank
Student: scuba diving

Teacher: tow rope
Student: waterskiing

Teacher: reel
Student: fishing

3 Sports Associations
ACTIVITY HANDBOOK PAGE 2

Call out water sports and recreation words and have groups write down as many associations as they can think of. For example:

surfing: [surfboard/waves/falling/balance]
swimming: [goggles/bathing cap/water/kick/dive]
scuba diving: [wet suit/air tank/diving mask/coral reefs]
fishing: [fish/fishing rod/net/bait]
sailing: [sailboat/life vest/wind/race/speed]

4 Movable Categories I
ACTIVITY HANDBOOK PAGE 11
ACTIVITY MASTER 211

Call out the following categories and have students go to the appropriate side of the room:

sports you do *on* the water
sports you do *in* the water
sports you do underwater
sports for which you use mostly your arms
sports for which you use mostly your legs
sports for which you use both arms and legs

5 Movable Categories II
ACTIVITY HANDBOOK PAGE 11
ACTIVITY MASTER 212

Call out the following categories and have students go to the appropriate side of the room:

boats   things to wear
boat equipment   things made of ropes
safety equipment

6 Category Dictation
ACTIVITY HANDBOOK PAGE 2

Dictate words that fit into the categories of either of the above activities.

7 What's the Question?
ACTIVITY HANDBOOK PAGE 16

Describe various water sport items on *Picture Dictionary* page 145, and have students respond by asking: "What's a/an _____?" or "What are _____?" For example:

Teacher: You hold on to this when you ski behind a boat.
Student: What's a towrope?

Teacher: You use these to make a rowboat move.
Student: What are oars?

Teacher: This is your oxygen supply when you're underwater.
Student: What's an air tank?

Teacher: You wear this when you go swimming at the beach.
Student: What's a swimsuit?

Teacher: You wear these to protect your eyes when you swim.
Student: What are goggles?

Teacher: You wear this to help you in case you have a boating accident.
Student: What's a life vest?

8 Ranking
ACTIVITY HANDBOOK PAGE 13

Have students look at the water sports listedon *Picture Dictionary* page 145 and rank them 1-3 (with 1 being the most) according to the following criteria:

the three that require the most skill
the three that are the most dangerous
the three that are the most interesting to watch
the three that are the most expensive
the three that give the most health benefits
the three that you would most like to try
the three that you would never want to try

9 Water Sports Experiences

Have students who have done any of the water sports activities on *Picture Dictionary* page 145 tell about their experiences.

10 Things in Common
ACTIVITY HANDBOOK PAGE 14

Have students think of two water sports or sports equipment items that have things in common. For example:

kayaking—canoeing
Both use paddles.
Both can be individual sports.
Both use long, light, and narrow boats.

windsurfing—surfing
To do both, you stand on a board.
Both require balance.
Both can be dangerous.
Both are fast sports.

goggles—diving mask
Both help a swimmer see underwater.
You wear both on the head.
Both are for swimming.

11 Survey

a. Give each student or a pair of students one of the following questions:

Do you like to go sailing?
Do you like to go canoeing?
Do you like to go rowing?
Do you like to go kayaking in the ocean?
Do you like to go kayaking in a lake?
Do you like to go white-water rafting?
Do you like to go snorkeling?
Do you like to go scuba diving?
Do you like to go surfing?
Do you like to go windsurfing?
Do you like to go waterskiing?
Do you like to go fishing?
Do you like to swim?

b. Have students circulate around the class and survey their classmates.

c. When students are finished, have them tally their results and present them to the class in a bar graph.

d. Discuss the following questions:

What are the most popular water sports in the class?
What are the least popular water sports in the class?

12 Water Sports Crossword
ACTIVITY HANDBOOK PAGES 4-5

Have students connect water sports words to create a crossword. For example:

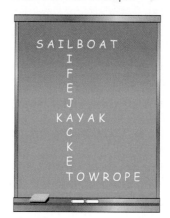

LESSON OBJECTIVE

Students will learn the vocabulary of actions used in sports and exercise.

RESOURCES

AUDIO PROGRAM

Words & Dialogs
Cassette 5B
CD 6: Tracks 26, 27

MULTI-LEVEL WORKBOOKS

Literacy Workbook
Beginning & Intermediate Lifeskills Workbooks
Beginning & Intermediate Vocabulary Workbooks

ACTIVITY MASTER

Reproducible:
A213

TRANSPARENCY

Overhead: T146

LANGUAGE & CULTURE NOTES

Reproducible: LC146

WORDLINKS

longman.com/wordbyword

VOCABULARY INTRODUCTION

- Preview
- Present
- Practice

MODEL CONVERSATION PRACTICE

There are three model conversations—the first for words 1–10, the second for words 11–23, and the third for words 24–30. Introduce and practice the first model before going on to the second and third. For each model:

1. Have students look at the model illustration. Set the scene:

    Model 1: "A baseball coach is talking to one of his players."

    Model 2: "An exercise instructor is leading an exercise class."

    Model 3: "A gym teacher is giving instructions to the class."

2. Present the first model using word 1, the second model using word 11, and the third model using word 24.

3. Choral Repetition Practice: Full-Class and Individual.

4. Have pairs practice the model.

5. Have pairs present the model.

6. Call on pairs to present a new conversation using word 2 for the first model, word 12 for the second model, and word 25 for the third model.

7. Have pairs practice new conversations.

8. Have pairs present new conversations.

SPELLING PRACTICE

Say a word, and have students spell it aloud or write it. Or, using the transparency, point to an item and have students write the word.

WRITING AND DISCUSSION

Have students respond to the questions as a class, in pairs, or in small groups. Or have students write their responses, share their writing with other students, and discuss in class.

Making Connections

Resource Materials Bring in, or have students bring in, the following materials for vocabulary practice:

- *Sports and health and fitness magazines:* Have students describe what they see people doing in the photographs.

- *Tapes of sporting events (baseball/football/tennis/basketball):* Have students describe what they see people doing in the games.

Community Tasks Have individual students (or groups of students) visit a park or gym and write a list of what actions they see people doing.

Have individual students watch a very short segment of a professional game on TV and describe what actions the players are doing.

Communication Activities

1 Simon Says

This game consists of a series of rapid commands that students follow only when the command is preceded by the words *Simon says*. If the student follows the command when the words *Simon says* are not spoken, that student must sit down. The last student to remain standing wins the game.

a. Have all the students stand up.

b. Say "Simon says stretch." (The students stretch.)

c. Say "Simon says bend." (The students bend.)

d. Say "Hop!" (Any students who hop must sit down and not continue to play.)

Note: The commands should be said in rapid order to allow as little time as possible to think about "Simon says."

Variation: Have different students take turns leading the game.

2 What's the Object?
ACTIVITY HANDBOOK PAGE 16

Call out verbs and have students add appropriate objects. For example:

hit . . . *a baseball/a volleyball/a birdie*
lift . . . *weights/a skating partner*
shoot . . . *an arrow/a basketball*
dribble . . . *a basketball/a soccer ball*
pass . . . *a basketball/a soccer ball/a hockey puck*

3 Miming Game
ACTIVITY HANDBOOK PAGE 11
ACTIVITY MASTER 213

Have students take turns pantomiming sport and exercise actions. The class tries to guess what the person is doing. For example:

You're pitching a ball.
You're lifting weights.

4 Beanbag Toss!

Have students toss a beanbag back and forth. As a student tosses the beanbag, he or she calls out a sport or exercise action. The person who catches the beanbag must immediately name the sport or exercise associated with that action.

5 Mime Chain

This activity works like a typical chain game, except that it's done through pantomiming the sport and exercise actions depicted on *Picture Dictionary* page 146.

a. Begin the game by bending.

b. Student 1 bends and then pantomimes another activity. For example: Student 1 bends and then stretches.

c. Continue around the room in this fashion with each student miming what the previous students did and adding another action.

d. Play the game again, beginning and ending with different students.

If the class is large, you can divide students into groups to give each student more *sport and exercise action* practice.

6 Action Categories

a. Write the following on the board:

baseball	tennis	weightlifting
football	swimming	calisthenics
basketball	golf	aerobics

b. Have groups of students decide which actions depicted on *Picture Dictionary* page 146 are associated with each of the categories on the board.

c. Have the groups compare their answers.

Answer Key:
baseball: [hit/pitch/throw/catch]
football: [pass/kick]
tennis: [serve]
basketball: [bounce/dribble/shoot]
swimming: [swim/dive]
weightlifting: [pull/lift]
aerobics: [stretch/bend/walk/run/hop/skip/
               jump/deep knee bend/sit/lie down/
               reach/swing/push]
calisthenics: [push-up/sit-up/leg lift/jumping
               jack/deep knee bend/somersault/
               cartwheel/handstand]
golf: [bend/swing/hit/reach/stretch]

(continued)

7 Stand Up for Sports!

a. Say the name of a sport.

b. Tell students you're going to say four words. If they hear a word that is associated with that sport, they should stand up. If they hear a word that is not associated with that sport, they should sit down. For example:

Martial arts:
jump	[stand up]
kick	[remain standing]
dribble	[sit down]
shoot	[remain sitting]

Frisbee:
bounce	[sit down]
throw	[stand up]
swim	[sit down]
pass	[stand up]

Archery:
cartwheel	[sit down]
shoot	[stand up]
dive	[sit down]
stretch	[stand up]

Volleyball:
serve	[stand up]
hit	[remain standing]
somersault	[sit down]
dribble	[remain sitting]

8 Whisk!

ACTIVITY HANDBOOK PAGES 16–17

Have the class try to guess a sport or exercise action a student is thinking of by asking questions with the word *whisk*. For example:

Do you *whisk* when you play baseball?
Do you *whisk* outdoors?
Do you *whisk* in a gym?
Do you *whisk* to a teammate?

9 Chain Response: "So You Want to Play?"

a. Have students sit in a circle. You begin by saying to Student 1, "So you want to ____?" (For example, "So you want to play basketball?")

b. Student 1 responds by saying, "Yes. I can ____ very well." (For example, "Yes. I can dribble very well.")

c. Student 1 turns to Student 2 and says, "So you want to ____?" (For example, "So you want to do aerobics?")

d. Student 2 responds by saying, "Yes. I can ____ very well." (For example, "Yes. I can stretch very well.")

e. Continue in this fashion around the circle, with each student responding to a question and asking the next student a question.

10 Design a Two-Minute Workout

a. In pairs, have students design a two-minute workout, using vocabulary from this lesson.

b. Have students take turns instructing the class on how to do the workout and have the class follow their instructions.

11 Survey

a. Give each student or a pair of students one of the following questions:

Can you do a handstand?
Can you do a cartwheel?
Can you do a somersault?
Can you swim?
Can you reach your toes?
Can you jump and touch this?
Can you dive?
Can you do twenty sit-ups?
Can you do twenty jumping jacks?
Can you do ten deep knee bends?
Can you lift me?

b. Have students circulate around the class and survey their classmates. Where appropriate they can challenge the student to see if he or she really can do it.

c. When students are finished, have them tally their results and present them to the class in a bar graph.

d. Discuss the following questions:

Do these results surprise you?
Is this class physically fit?

LESSON OBJECTIVE

Students will learn vocabulary related to the most popular forms of entertainment and performing arts. See *Picture Dictionary* pages 148 and 149 for related vocabulary.

RESOURCES

AUDIO PROGRAM	MULTI-LEVEL WORKBOOKS	ACTIVITY MASTERS
Words & Dialogs	Literacy Workbook	**Reproducibles**:
Cassette 5B	Beginning & Intermediate Lifeskills Workbooks	A8, A214
CD 6: Tracks 28, 29	Beginning & Intermediate Vocabulary Workbooks	

TRANSPARENCY	LANGUAGE & CULTURE NOTES	WORDLINKS
Overhead: T147	**Reproducible:** LC147	longman.com/wordbyword

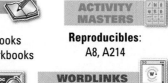

VOCABULARY INTRODUCTION

- Preview
- Present
- Practice

MODEL CONVERSATION PRACTICE

There are two model conversations—the first for words A–G and the second for words 1–17. Introduce and practice the first model before going on to the second. For each model:

1. Have students look at the model illustration. Set the scene:
   - Model 1: "Two co-workers are talking at the end of the work day."
   - Model 2: "This couple is attending a play."

2. Present the first model using word A and the second model using word 1.

3. Choral Repetition Practice: Full-Class and Individual.

4. Have pairs practice the model.

5. Have pairs present the model.

6. Call on pairs to present a new conversation using word B for the first model and word 2 for the second model.

7. Have pairs practice new conversations.

8. Have pairs present new conversations.

SPELLING PRACTICE

Say a word, and have students spell it aloud or write it. Or, using the transparency, point to an item and have students write the word.

WRITING AND DISCUSSION

Have students respond to the questions as a class, in pairs, or in small groups. Or have students write their responses, share their writing with other students, and discuss in class.

Making Connections

Resource Materials Bring in, or have students bring in, the following materials for vocabulary practice:

○ *Newspaper advertisements for movies, plays, concerts, operas, and ballets:* Have students identify what is happening (a play, a movie), who is performing (name of actor, comedian, musician), and where it is being performed (theater, concert hall, comedy club).

○ *Programs from theater, opera, ballet, and concert performances:* Have students bring in programs from performances they have recently attended. Have students explain briefly what they saw and how they liked it.

Community Task Have individual students (or pairs of students) choose a kind of entertainment and find out what's playing and where in your community. Have students report back to the class.

Communication Activities

1 Tic Tac Definitions
ACTIVITY HANDBOOK PAGE 15
ACTIVITY MASTER 8

Have students fill in the tic tac grid with any nine entertainment words they wish. Give definitions such as the following, and have students cross out on their grids the words you have defined:

a theatrical work [play]
the traditional term for a male stage and movie
  performer [actor]
the traditional term for a female stage and movie
  performer [actress]
a musical performance [concert]
a large theater where orchestras perform concerts
  [concert hall]
a person who plays a musical instrument [musician]
the person who leads a symphony [conductor]
a group of musicians who play music together [band]
a play set to music in which performers sing and act
  their lines [opera]
a female ballet performer [ballerina]
the place where audiences see comedians perform
  [comedy club]
a stage performer who tells funny jokes and stories
  [comedian]

2 Movable Categories
ACTIVITY HANDBOOK PAGE 11
ACTIVITY MASTER 214

Call out the following categories and have students go to the appropriate side of the room:

people
types of entertainment
performers
places

3 Category Dictation
ACTIVITY HANDBOOK PAGE 2

Dictate words that fit into the above categories.

4 Got It!
ACTIVITY HANDBOOK PAGE 7

Have groups of students ask yes/no questions in an attempt to identify entertainment items. For example:

Is it a place?   [No.]
Is it a person?   [Yes.]
Is it a performer?   [Yes.]
Is it a female?   [Yes.]
Is it an actress?   [Yes.]

5 Word Clues
ACTIVITY HANDBOOK PAGE 17
ACTIVITY MASTER 214

Have students take turns giving one-word clues to team members who try to guess the word.
For example:

[The word is orchestra.]
Team 1 Player: "group"   [Team 1 guesses]
Team 2 Player: "music"   [Team 2 guesses]
Team 1 Player: "conductor"   [Team 1 guesses]

6 Bleep!
ACTIVITY HANDBOOK PAGE 2
ACTIVITY MASTER 214

Have students create conversations based on three Entertainment Word Cards that they select.

7 Chain Story
ACTIVITY HANDBOOK PAGE 3

Begin the story as follows: "I was walking past the theater last week, and I noticed that they were performing one of my favorite plays. I decided to buy a ticket."

8 Personal Experiences

As a class, in pairs, or in small groups, have students tell about a time they went to the theater, symphony, opera, ballet, or a movie.

9 Entertainment Crossword
ACTIVITY HANDBOOK PAGES 4-5

Have students connect entertainment words to create a crossword. For example:

10 Survey

a. Give each student or a pair of students one of the following questions:

> Who is your favorite actor?
> Who is your favorite actress?
> Who is your favorite musician?
> What is your favorite orchestra?
> Who is your favorite comedian?
> Who is your favorite opera singer?
> Who is your favorite ballet dancer?
> Who is your favorite singer?
> What is your favorite band?
> What is your favorite play?
> What is your favorite opera?
> What is your favorite ballet?
> What is your favorite movie?
> What is your favorite kind of entertainment?

b. Have students circulate around the class and survey their classmates.

c. When students are finished, have them tally their results and present them to the class in a bar graph.

d. Discuss the following questions:

> Do these results surprise you?
> Who are the most popular entertainers?
> What are the most popular forms of entertainment?

11 Ranking
ACTIVITY HANDBOOK PAGE 13

Have students look at the kinds of entertainment on *Picture Dictionary* page 147 and rank the three kinds of entertainment they most prefer and the three kinds of entertainment they least often attend. For example:

> My Favorite Entertainment
> 1. movies
> 2. plays
> 3. concerts
>
> I Least Often Attend
> 1. operas
> 2. comedy clubs
> 3. ballets

12 Find the Answer!
ACTIVITY HANDBOOK PAGE 6

Possible questions students might want to have answered:

> What opera is playing in our city?
> How many concert halls are there?
> How many comedy clubs are there?
> How many movie theaters are there?
> Who performs ballet here?
> What bands are playing this weekend?
> Does our town have a symphony orchestra? Where does it play?
> How can I get inexpensive tickets to a play?
> How can I get inexpensive tickets to a concert?
> How can I get inexpensive tickets to an opera?

LESSON OBJECTIVE

Students will learn the vocabulary of performing arts entertainment—music, plays, movies, and television programs. See *Picture Dictionary* page 147 for related vocabulary.

RESOURCES

AUDIO PROGRAM

Words & Dialogs
Cassette 6A
CD 6: Tracks 30, 31

MULTI-LEVEL WORKBOOKS

Literacy Workbook
Beginning & Intermediate Lifeskills Workbooks
Beginning & Intermediate Vocabulary Workbooks

TRANSPARENCIES

Overheads: T148, T149

LANGUAGE & CULTURE NOTES

Reproducible: LC148–149

WORDLINKS

longman.com/wordbyword

VOCABULARY INTRODUCTION

- Preview
- Present
- Practice

MODEL CONVERSATION PRACTICE

1. Have students look at the model illustration. Set the scene: "Two college roommates are talking."

2. Present the model using words A and 1.

3. Choral Repetition Practice: Full-Class and Individual.

4. Have pairs practice the model.

5. Have pairs present the model.

6. Call on pairs to present a new conversation using words B and 2.

7. Have pairs practice new conversations.

8. Have pairs present new conversations.

SPELLING PRACTICE

Say a word, and have students spell it aloud or write it. Or, using the transparency, point to an item and have students write the word.

WRITING AND DISCUSSION

Have students respond to the questions as a class, in pairs, or in small groups. Or have students write their responses, share their writing with other students, and discuss in class.

Making Connections

Resource Materials Bring in, or have students bring in, the following materials for vocabulary practice:

- *Music CDs and their cases:* Have students guess the kind of music first by looking at the image of the musicians on the case and then by listening to the music.

- *TV listings from the newspaper and/or special television magazines:* Have students identify the types of programs in the listings for today or tonight.

- *Newspaper advertisements for movies and plays:* Have students guess the kind of movies and plays they are by looking at their advertisements.

- *Tapes of movies or TV shows:* Show students short clips of movies and shows and have them identify the genre.

Communication Activities

1 Music! Music! Music!

Bring in tapes of different kinds of music and have students identify what type of music it is. Ask students:

How does this music make you feel?
What does the music make you think about?

If any students in the class have any particular talent for singing or playing an instrument, have them demonstrate the different types of music.

2 Clap in Rhythm
ACTIVITY HANDBOOK PAGE 3

Have students name different kinds of music (or movies, or TV programs) to a clapping rhythm.

3 Stop the Music!

For this game, you will need samples of different kinds of music, as in Activity 1.

a. Divide the class into two teams.

b. Have a member of each team come to the front of the class.

c. Start to play some music, and when a player thinks he or she knows what kind of music it is, that person shouts out, "Stop the music!" That person then guesses. If he or she is correct, that team gets a point.

d. Continue with other contestants and other types of music. The team with the most correctly guessed musical answers wins the game.

4 Letter Game
ACTIVITY HANDBOOK PAGE 9

Say statements such as the following and have teams compete to identify the items:

I'm thinking of a kind of music   [folk]
   that starts with *f*.
I'm thinking of a kind of music   [popular]
   that starts with *p*.
I'm thinking of a kind of music   [gospel]
   that starts with *g*.
I'm thinking of a kind of music   [jazz]
   that starts with *j*.
I'm thinking of a kind of music   [hip hop]
   that starts with *h*.
I'm thinking of a kind of music   [reggae]
   that starts with *r*.

5 Here's an Example

a. Divide the class into small groups.

b. Call out a type of entertainment from the vocabulary list and have the groups write down as many examples as they can think of. For example:

classical music: [Brahms/Mahler/Beethoven]
a musical: [Cats/The Lion King/Oklahoma/A Chorus Line/Rent]
a TV game show: [Wheel of Fortune/Who Wants to Be a Millionaire?]
a news program: [60 minutes/Lehrer News Hour/ Nightline]
a western: [The Good, the Bad, and the Ugly/High Noon]

c. Have the groups call out their examples. The group with the longest list wins.

d. Tell students they can question an example, in which case the student who suggested the association must explain the reason for that association.

6 Class Music Survey

a. Divide the class into pairs and have them talk about the following:

What kind of music makes you feel happy?
What kind of music makes you feel sad or sentimental?
What kind of music makes you feel nostalgic?
What's the most romantic kind of music?
What's the best kind of music to dance to?
What's the best kind of music to sing along to?
What's the best kind of music to hear at a concert?

b. Have the pairs report back to the class and compare students' ideas. If you wish, you can make a chart of the results on the board.

7 Ranking
ACTIVITY HANDBOOK PAGE 13

Have students look at the kinds of music on *Picture Dictionary* page 148 and rank the three kinds they like most and the three they like least. For example:

I Like the Most	I Like the Least
classical	country
popular	rock
folk	rap

(continued)

8 Recommended Entertainment

a. In small groups, have students share the names of good plays, movies, and TV programs they have seen that they recommend.

b. Have the groups report to the class. Write master lists on the board of recommended plays, recommended movies, and recommended TV programs.

9 Entertainment Guessing Game

Have pairs or groups of students prepare a brief movie or television scene and present it to the class. The class must decide what kind of movie or TV program it is (for example, talk show, sitcom, war movie, etc.). Have the class vote on the best presentation.

10 Entertainment Associations
ACTIVITY HANDBOOK PAGE 2

Call out entertainment words and have groups write down as many associations as they can think of. For example:

game show:	[questions/answers/guess/money/prizes]
classical music:	[orchestra/concert/conductor/Beethoven/Mozart]
nature program:	[TV/animals/habitats/educational]
war movie:	[bombs/actors/noise/fear/heroes]
folk music:	[guitars/singers/traditional]

11 Dictate and Discuss

a. Dictate one of the following statements to the class:

Classical music makes you smart.
Theater is a dying art.
Children under eight years old should not go to the movies.
Reality shows are educational.
There's too much violence on TV.

b. In small groups, have students discuss their opinions of the statements.

c. As a class, vote in agreement or disagreement with the statement and then have students discuss their reasons.

12 Game Show: That's Entertainment!

Create a television game show called *That's Entertainment!*

a. Divide the class into two teams.

b. Choose a student to be the host or hostess of the program.

c. Have the class design a set for the program and create commercials that they can present before and after the program and during the commercial breaks.

d. The object of the game is for contestants to identify the type of television program or movie based on a quote that the host or hostess reads to them. Let the class decide what the prizes are and what the rules of the game are.

Possible quotes:
"I cried when I saw that play." [drama]
"That show really makes me laugh. I watch it every week." [sitcom]
"I have to know what's going to happen next. I can't miss it!" [soap opera]
"My children love to watch those silly characters every Saturday morning." [cartoon]
"I wish I could understand it without the subtitles." [foreign film]
"Did you see the one where people from Pluto invaded New York City?" [science fiction movie]
"I liked the part where they had to survive in the jungle with only a little food and no other supplies!" [adventure movie]
"I don't like them. There's too much violence!" [war movie]
"Most of them don't give an accurate picture of the Native Americans." [western]
"I can't believe the subjects they talk about!" [talk show]
"I'm sure I'd be very nervous and not be able to answer any questions correctly!" [game show]

13 Find the Answer!
ACTIVITY HANDBOOK PAGE 6

Possible questions students might want to have answered:

What are the top ten songs in popular music this week?
What movie made the most money last weekend?
What music concerts are here this weekend?
What's the longest running TV show on TV today?
What's the most popular prime-time show?
What movies are playing this weekend?
What channels have home shopping?
What channels have children's programs on Saturday morning?

LESSON OBJECTIVE

Students will learn the names of the most common musical instruments. See *Picture Dictionary* pages 148 and 149 for related vocabulary and general background information.

RESOURCES

AUDIO PROGRAM
Words & Dialogs
Cassette 6A
CD 6: Tracks 32, 33

MULTI-LEVEL WORKBOOKS
Literacy Workbook
Beginning & Intermediate Lifeskills Workbooks
Beginning & Intermediate Vocabulary Workbooks

ACTIVITY MASTER
Reproducible:
A215

TRANSPARENCY
Overhead: T150

LANGUAGE & CULTURE NOTES
Reproducible: LC150

WORDLINKS
longman.com/wordbyword

VOCABULARY INTRODUCTION

- Preview
- Present
- Practice

MODEL CONVERSATION PRACTICE

There are three model conversations. Introduce and practice the first model before going on to the second and third. For each model:

1. Have students look at the model illustration. Set the scene:
   - Model 1: "A father is talking to his daughter's date."
   - Model 2: "Two students in the school band are talking."
   - Model 3: "One friend is visiting another and is wondering about a loud noise that she hears."
2. Present the model.
3. Choral Repetition Practice: Full-Class and Individual.
4. Have pairs practice the model.
5. Have pairs present the model.
6. Call on pairs to present a new conversation using word 2 for the first model, word 17 for the second model, and word 21 for the third model.
7. Have pairs practice new conversations.
8. Have pairs present new conversations.

SPELLING PRACTICE

Say a word, and have students spell it aloud or write it. Or, using the transparency, point to an item and have students write the word.

WRITING AND DISCUSSION

Have students respond to the questions as a class, in pairs, or in small groups. Or have students write their responses, share their writing with other students, and discuss in class.

Making Connections

Resource Materials Bring in, or have students bring in, the following materials for vocabulary practice:

- *Recordings of different instruments:* Have students listen and try to identify the instruments that they hear.
- *Pictures of an orchestra:* Have students identify the instruments that they see.
- *Internet websites on instrument sounds:* Have students visit websites that give examples of the different sounds of instruments.

Community Task Have the class attend an orchestral concert (often high school orchestras and music schools have inexpensive or free concerts). Have each student watch and listen to a different musician and then report how much that musician played in each of the musical pieces.

Communication Activities

1 Clap in Rhythm
ACTIVITY HANDBOOK PAGE 3

Have students name different musical instrument words to a clapping rhythm.

2 Chain Game: My Uncle Harry
ACTIVITY HANDBOOK PAGES 2-3

Begin the chain as follows: "My Uncle Harry plays the oboe," and have students continue it. For example:

Teacher: My Uncle Harry plays the oboe.
Student 1: Well, my Uncle Harry plays the oboe and the violin.
Student 2: Well, my Uncle Harry plays the oboe, the violin, and the tuba.
Etc.

3 True or False Definitions
ACTIVITY HANDBOOK PAGE 15

Give true and false definitions of musical instruments and have students decide which are true and which are false. For example:

A piccolo is smaller than a flute. [True.]
A harmonica is larger than a recorder. [False. A harmonica is smaller than a recorder.]
A piano is a keyboard instrument. [True.]
A harp is the largest string instrument. [True.]
A viola has a higher pitch than a violin. [False. It has a lower pitch.]
A bassoon has a lower pitch than an oboe. [True.]
A xylophone is a keyboard instrument. [False. It's a percussion instrument.]
The banjo is a common instrument in orchestras. [False. The banjo is a common instrument in country and folk music.]
A tuba has a higher pitch than a trumpet. [False. It has a lower pitch.]
The French horn is a common instrument in reggae. [False. It's a common instrument in classical music.]

4 Movable Categories
ACTIVITY HANDBOOK PAGE 11
ACTIVITY MASTER 215

Call out the following categories and have students go to the appropriate side of the room:

instruments that have strings
instruments that have keys
instruments you blow into
instruments you strike
instruments you can carry
woodwinds
brass instruments
percussion instruments
keyboard instruments
instruments that use electricity
instruments that rest on the floor

5 Category Dictation
ACTIVITY HANDBOOK PAGE 2

Dictate words that fit into the above categories.

6 What's That Sound?

Bring in recordings of different instruments or go on an instrument sound website and see if students can identify the sound each instrument makes.

Variation: Do the above as a game with competing teams.

7 Drawing Game
ACTIVITY HANDBOOK PAGE 6
ACTIVITY MASTER 215

Have teams compete to identify musical instruments drawn by one of their team members.

8 Ask Me a Question!

ACTIVITY HANDBOOK PAGE 2
ACTIVITY MASTER 215

Have students walk around trying to guess each other's musical instruments by asking yes/no questions. For example:

Is it small?	[Yes.]
Does it have keys?	[No.]
Is it a woodwind?	[Yes.]
Is it a piccolo?	[Yes.]
Is it small?	[No.]
Does it have keys?	[No.]
Is it a percussion instrument?	[No.]
Is it a string instrument?	[Yes.]
Is it a harp?	[Yes.]

9 What Kind of Music?

Before doing this activity, review the different types of music depicted on *Picture Dictionary* page 148.

a. Name an instrument and have students say what type of music they associate that instrument with. For example:

Teacher: French horn
Student: classical music

Teacher: organ
Student: gospel music

b. Name a type of music and have students say what instrument they associate it with. For example:

Teacher: rock music
Student: electric guitar

Teacher: country music
Student: banjo

10 Center Stage!

If any students in the class know how to play musical instruments, have them bring them into class and play them.

11 Ranking

ACTIVITY HANDBOOK PAGE 13

Have students look at the musical instruments on *Picture Dictionary* page 150 and rank the three they like to listen to most.

Variations: Students can also choose the three instruments they least like to listen to and the three instruments they would most like to play.

12 Daffy Debate!

ACTIVITY HANDBOOK PAGE 5
ACTIVITY MASTER 215

Have students debate which musical instruments are more important than others.

13 Musical Instrument Talk!

ACTIVITY HANDBOOK PAGE 17
ACTIVITY MASTER 215

Give students a Musical Instrument Word Card and have them speak to the class for one minute about that instrument.

1 Odd Word Out

Read the following lists of words, and have students identify the category and the "odd word out"—the word that doesn't fit the category:

thread, needle, treadmill, pin cushion, thimble, sewing machine
[Category: sewing equipment. Odd word out: treadmill]

chess, checkers, Monopoly, Scrabble, backgammon, telescope
[Category: games. Odd word out: telescope]

planetarium, handstand, zoo, fair, art gallery, amusement park
[Category: places to go. Odd word out: handstand]

easel, ballfield, tennis court, playground, picnic area, duck pond
[Category: areas in a park. Odd word out: easel]

lifeguard, sailboard, surfer, sunbather, swimmer, vendor
[Category: people at the beach. Odd word out: sailboard]

hat, sunglasses, trampoline, beach umbrella, sunscreen
[Category: protective gear from the sun. Odd word out: trampoline]

tent, snorkel, sleeping bag, hatchet, camping stove, Swiss army knife
[Category: camping equipment. Odd word out: snorkel]

running, inline skating, bowling, badminton, museum
[Category: individual sports. Odd word out: museum]

baseball, clay, softball, lacrosse, soccer, volleyball
[Category: team sports. Odd word out: clay]

classical, folk, rap, nature program, hip hop, reggae
[Category: types of music. Odd word out: nature program]

tuba, documentary, drama, western, horror, comedy
[Category: types of movies. Odd word out: tuba]

sports program, children's program, grill, cartoons, reality show, soap opera
[Category: types of tv programs. Odd word out: grill]

violin, banjo, harp, electric guitar, tambourine
[Category: string instruments. Odd word out: tambourine]

flute, piccolo, recorder, saxophone, bassoon, xylophone
[Category: woodwinds. Odd word out: xylophone]

2 Quiz Game
ACTIVITY MASTER 216

a. Divide the class into four teams.

b. Copy and cut up Activity Master 230 and place cards face-down in a pile.

c. Pick cards from the pile and have the teams take turns answering your questions. Give each team a time limit to answer each question (30 seconds or 1 minute).

d. The team with the most correct answers wins.

3 Drawing Game
ACTIVITY HANDBOOK PAGE 6
ACTIVITY MASTERS 195, 200, 202, 205, 206, 212, 215

Have teams compete to identify the items drawn by one of their team members.

4 Clap in Rhythm
ACTIVITY HANDBOOK PAGE 3

To a clapping rhythm, have students name different words in the following categories:

hobbies
places to go
sports
types of entertainment

5 Dialogs

a. Divide the class into pairs.

b. Have each pair create dialogs that include the following questions:

> What do you like to do in your free time?
> What kind of _____ do you like?
> Do you like to play _____?
> What's your favorite _____?
> Who's your favorite _____?

c. Call on pairs to act out their conversations for the class.

6 Ranking
ACTIVITY HANDBOOK PAGE 13

Have students review the sports on pages 140–142 and 144–145 and rank the seven most popular sports to play, the seven least popular sports to play, the five most popular professional sports to watch, and the five most popular Olympic sports to watch.

7 Do You Remember?
ACTIVITY HANDBOOK PAGE 5

Have students look at any one of the scenes on *Picture Dictionary* pages 134–150. Have them write down everything they remember about the scene.

8 Category Dictation
ACTIVITY HANDBOOK PAGE 2

Dictate words from *Picture Dictionary* pages 134–150 that fit into the following categories:

> sports
> places to go
> things to do indoors
> things to do outdoors
> types of movies
> types of music

9 Who Said It?

a. Give each student a piece of paper and ask them to write answers to the following questions:

> What's your favorite thing to do on the weekend?
> What's your favorite sport to play?
> What's your favorite sport to watch on TV?
> Do you do any crafts? If you do, which ones?
> What's your favorite board game to play?
> What are your favorite places to go?
> What is your favorite kind of music to listen to?
> What is your favorite kind of movie?
> What is your favorite kind of TV program?

b. Collect the papers, read each one, and see if the class can match the answers with the students who wrote them.

10 Plan a Weekend!

a. In small groups, have students plan a weekend of recreational activities. To plan the weekend, they must figure out the price and schedule for the recreation and entertainment by reading the newspaper and looking at online listings.

b. Have the groups present their trip plans to the class. Have the class vote:

> What is the most economical weekend plan?
> What is the most expensive weekend plan?
> What is the most romantic weekend plan?
> What is the most educational weekend plan?
> What is the most athletic weekend plan?

UNIT 16 Nature

AUDIO PROGRAM

Words & Dialogs	WordSong: *Word by Word Theme*
Audio Cassette 6A	Audio Cassette 7B
Audio CD 6: Tracks 34–47	Audio CD 8: Tracks 18 (Vocal) & 19 (Sing-along) Song Masters S31, S32

WORKBOOKS

For Multi-Level Practice

Literacy Workbook
Beginning Lifeskills Workbook
Beginning Vocabulary Workbook
Intermediate Lifeskills Workbook
Intermediate Vocabulary Workbook

WORDLINKS

Internet Resources through the *Word by Word* Companion Website

http://www.longman.com/wordbyword

ACTIVITY MASTERS

Reproducibles for Communication Activities
A8, A217–A229

TRANSPARENCIES

Full-Color Overheads for Class Practice
T151–T159

LANGUAGE & CULTURE NOTES

Information for Teachers & Intermediate /Advanced Students
LC151–LC159

LESSON OBJECTIVE

Students will learn vocabulary related to the structures, equipment, and animals found on a farm.

RESOURCES

AUDIO PROGRAM
Words & Dialogs
Cassette 6A
CD 6: Tracks 34, 35

MULTI-LEVEL WORKBOOKS
Literacy Workbook
Beginning & Intermediate Lifeskills Workbooks
Beginning & Intermediate Vocabulary Workbooks

ACTIVITY MASTER
Reproducible:
A217

TRANSPARENCY
Overhead: T151

LANGUAGE & CULTURE NOTES
Reproducible: LC151

WORDLINKS
longman.com/wordbyword

VOCABULARY INTRODUCTION

- Preview
- Present
- Practice

MODEL CONVERSATION PRACTICE

There are three model conversations. Introduce and practice the first model before going on to the second and third. For each model:

1. Have students look at the model illustration. Set the scene:

   Model 1: "A new hired hand is asking about the farm."

   Model 2: "A young boy is telling his mother about some loose animals on the farm."

   Model 3: "A TV reporter is interviewing a husband and wife who own a farm."

2. Present the first model with word 1, the second model with words 9 and 3, and the third model with word 31.

3. Choral Repetition Practice: Full-Class and Individual.

4. Have pairs practice the model.

5. Have pairs present the model.

6. Call on pairs to present a new conversation using word 2 for the first model, words 11 and 7 for the second model, and word 32 for the third model.

7. Have pairs practice new conversations.

8. Have pairs present new conversations.

SPELLING PRACTICE

Say a word, and have students spell it aloud or write it. Or, using the transparency, point to an item and have students write the word.

WRITING AND DISCUSSION

Have students respond to the question as a class, in pairs, or in small groups. Or have students write their responses, share their writing with other students, and discuss in class.

Making Connections

Resource Materials Bring in, or have students bring in, the following materials for vocabulary practice:

- *Images of farms from magazines or downloaded from the Internet:* Have students identify the farming vocabulary from this lesson.

Community Tasks If possible, take the class on a farm tour. Many communities have farms that are open to the public certain days of the week for educational tours. These farms may be historic living museums, cooperative farms, or privately owned farms that run a retail business on the farm (usually selling farm produce in a farm store).

If it isn't possible for the class to visit a farm together, then have groups of students investigate farms in the community that can be visited after school hours. Have students report back to class.

Communication Activities

1 Movable Categories
ACTIVITY HANDBOOK PAGE 11
ACTIVITY MASTER 217

Call out the following categories and have students go to the appropriate side of the room:

> people
> animals
> equipment
> buildings or structures
> areas where things grow

2 Category Dictation
ACTIVITY HANDBOOK PAGE 2

Dictate words that fit into the above categories.

3 Finish the Sentence!
ACTIVITY HANDBOOK PAGE 7

Begin sentences such as the following for students to complete:

> The farmer's family lives in the . . . *farmhouse.*
> The hens are in the . . . *hen house.*
> We plant onions and tomatoes in our . . . *garden.*
> We have a lot of fruit trees in our . . . *orchard.*
> When it's cold, the horses stay in the . . . *stable.*
> Chickens stay in the . . . *chicken coop.*
> A male chicken is a . . . *rooster.*
> Pigs stay in a . . . *pig pen.*
> Horses and cows eat . . . *hay.*

4 What's the Question?
ACTIVITY HANDBOOK PAGE 16

Describe various farm items and have students respond by asking: "What's a _____?" or "What are _____s?" For example:

> Teacher: This is an animal that gives milk.
> Student: What's a cow?

> Teacher: This provides water to our crops.
> Student: What's an irrigation system?

> Teacher: This is what horses and cows eat.
> Student: What's hay?

> Teacher: This is where horses sleep when it's cold.
> Student: What's a stable?

> Teacher: These animals are raised for their wool.
> Student: What are sheep?

> Teacher: These animals produce eggs.
> Student: What are hens?

> Teacher: This is where cows are free to walk around and eat grass.
> Student: What's a pasture?

> Teacher: These are the people who help the farmer with the farm work.
> Student: Who are hired hands and farm workers?

> Teacher: Farmers put this in the garden and in fields to scare away birds.
> Student: What's a scarecrow?

> Teacher: This is where you find hay on a farm.
> Student: What's a barn?

5 Question the Answer!
ACTIVITY HANDBOOK PAGE 13
ACTIVITY MASTER 217

Students pick farm word cards and think of a question for which that word could be the answer. For example:

> Card: pigpen
> Student: What's the place where pigs live?

> Card: turkey
> Student: What's the bird many Americans eat on Thanksgiving?

> Card: orchard
> Student: Where do apple and pears grow?

> Card: rice
> Student: What grass plant feeds most of the world?

6 What Am I?

ACTIVITY HANDBOOK PAGE 15
ACTIVITY MASTER 217

Pin word cards on students' backs and have them ask yes/no questions to identify which farm item they *are*. For example:

Am I an animal?	[No.]
Am I piece of farm equipment?	[No.]
Am I a building?	[Yes.]
Am I am farmhouse?	[No.]
Am I a barn?	[Yes.]
Am I a piece of farm equipment?	[No.]
Am I a building?	[No.]
Am I an animal?	[Yes.]
Do I make food?	[No.]
Am I a sheep?	[Yes.]

7 Word Clues

ACTIVITY HANDBOOK PAGE 17
ACTIVITY MASTER 217

Have students take turns giving one-word clues to team members who try to guess the word. For example:

[The word is *corn*.]
Team 1 Player:	"food"	[Team 1 guesses]
Team 2 Player:	"yellow"	[Team 2 guesses]
Team 1 Player:	"white"	[Team 1 guesses]

[The word is *rooster*.]
Team 1 Player:	"chicken"	[Team 1 guesses]
Team 2 Player:	"male"	[Team 2 guesses]
Team 1 Player:	"noisy"	[Team 1 guesses]

8 A Sheep Says "Baa-a-a!"

Have students imitate the noises of various animals in their native language and have others guess which animal it is. Compare how different languages represent different animal sounds.

Variation: Students can go on the Internet and use the keywords *animal sounds* to find many websites that produce the natural animal sounds or compare how different languages imitate animal sounds.

9 Farm Crossword

ACTIVITY HANDBOOK PAGES 3–4

Have students connect farm words to create a crossword. For example:

LESSON OBJECTIVE

Students will learn the names of common animals and pets.

RESOURCES

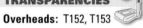

AUDIO PROGRAM		MULTI-LEVEL WORKBOOKS	ACTIVITY MASTERS
Words & Dialogs	**WordSong:** *Word by Word Theme*	Literacy Workbook	**Reproducibles:**
Cassette 6A	Cassette 7B • CD 8: Tracks 18, 19	Beginning & Intermediate Lifeskills Workbooks	A218, A219
CD 6: Tracks 36, 37	Song Masters S31, S32	Beginning & Intermediate Vocabulary Workbooks	

TRANSPARENCIES	LANGUAGE & CULTURE NOTES	WORDLINKS
Overheads: T152, T153	**Reproducible:** LC152–153	longman.com/wordbyword

VOCABULARY INTRODUCTION

- Preview
- Present
- Practice

MODEL CONVERSATION PRACTICE

There are two model conversations. Introduce and practice the first model before going on to the second. For each model:

1. Have students look at the model illustration. Set the scene:

    Model 1: "Two friends are at the zoo."
    Model 2: "Two people on a date are talking."

2. Present the first model with word 1 and the second model with word 34.

3. Choral Repetition Practice: Full-Class and Individual.

4. Have pairs practice the model.

5. Have pairs present the model.

6. Call on pairs to present a new conversation using word 2 for the first model and word 35 for the second model.

7. Have pairs practice new conversations.

8. Have pairs present new conversations.

SPELLING PRACTICE

Say a word, and have students spell it aloud or write it. Or, using the transparency, point to an item and have students write the word.

WRITING AND DISCUSSION

Have students respond to the questions as a class, in pairs, or in small groups. Or have students write their responses, share their writing with other students, and discuss in class.

♫♪ WordSong ♫♪

1. Have students listen to the vocal version of the *Word by Word Theme* one or more times. Then have students listen again as they read the song lyrics on Song Master S31.

2. Have students sing as you play either the vocal or the sing-along version of the song.

3. For fun, have a song competition in which students perform solo or in groups and the class votes for the best performance.

4. For additional practice, students can complete the cloze exercise on Song Master S32.

Resource Materials Bring in, or have students bring in, the following materials for vocabulary practice:

- *Images of animals downloaded from the Internet:* Have students identify the animals from this lesson.
- *Brochures and pamphlets from animal protection organizations:* Discuss with the class which animals are endangered.

- *Aesop's Fables:* These fables feature many different animals. Find the fables online. Read a fable to the class.

Community Task Have the class take a field trip to a local zoo or petting farm. Have students write the names of all the animals they see there.

Communication Activities

1 Clap in Rhythm
ACTIVITY HANDBOOK PAGE 3

Have students name different animals to a clapping rhythm.

2 Picture Match-Ups
ACTIVITY HANDBOOK PAGE 12

Find pictures of animals, make double copies of them, distribute them, and have students attempt to match the pictures by describing them to each other. For example:

I have an animal with black stripes.
I have a small gray animal with a bushy tail.
I have a large animal with no hair and short legs.
There's a small rodent in my picture.

3 Movable Categories
ACTIVITY HANDBOOK PAGE 11
ACTIVITY MASTERS 218 OR 219

Call out the following categories and have students go to the appropriate side of the room:

animals in a circus
animals in a zoo
animals in a house
animals in a hole in the ground
animals in a jungle
animals in a tree
animals in a large open space

4 Category Dictation
ACTIVITY HANDBOOK PAGE 2

Dictate words that fit into the following categories:

animals with tails
animals with hooves
animals with spots
animals with tusks

5 Animal Associations
ACTIVITY HANDBOOK PAGE 2

Call out names of animals and have groups write down as many associations as they can think of. For example:

porcupine: [brown/fat/sharp needles]
bat: [night/fly/wings/scary]
tiger: [stripes/paws/hungry]
giraffe: [tall/spots/gentle]
donkey: [noisy/stubborn/strong]

6 Here's What I'm Thinking Of!
ACTIVITY HANDBOOK PAGE 8

Make statements such as the following and have students guess the animal you're thinking of. For example:

A. I'm thinking of an animal that can make everything smell bad.
B. A skunk.

A. I'm thinking of an animal that has quills instead of soft fur.
B. A porcupine.

A. I'm thinking of an animal that almost disappeared in 1900 because people hunted it for its fur coat.
B. A buffalo.

A. I'm thinking of a rodent that is a popular pet with sharp teeth and a small tail.
B. A hamster.

A. I'm thinking of a cat that has a large mane.
B. A lion.

A. I'm thinking of a young dog.
B. A puppy.

A. I'm thinking of a young cat.
B. A kitten.

A. I'm thinking of a small kind of horse.
B. A pony.

(continued)

7 What Am I?
ACTIVITY HANDBOOK PAGE 15
ACTIVITY MASTERS 218 OR 219

Pin word cards on students' backs and have them ask yes/no questions to identify which animal they *are*. For example:

Do I live in the woods?	[No.]
Do I like water?	[Yes.]
Am I small?	[No.]
Am I dangerous?	[No.]
Do I live with others?	[Yes.]
Am I a hippopotamus?	[Yes.]
Do I live in the woods?	[Yes.]
Am I small?	[No.]
Am I dangerous?	[Yes.]
Do I live with others?	[No.]
Am I a leopard?	[Yes.]

8 Word Clues
ACTIVITY HANDBOOK PAGE 17
ACTIVITY MASTERS 218 OR 219

Have students take turns giving word clues to team members who try to guess the word. For example:

[The word is *rabbit*.]
Team 1 Player: "small"	[Team 1 guesses]
Team 2 Player: "fur"	[Team 2 guesses]
Team 1 Player: "ears"	[Team 1 guesses]
Team 2 Player: "carrots"	[Team 2 guesses]

[The word is *orangutan*.]
Team 1 Player: "large"	[Team 1 guesses]
Team 2 Player: "orange"	[Team 2 guesses]
Team 1 Player: "ape"	[Team 1 guesses]
Team 2 Player: "gentle"	[Team 2 guesses]

[The word is *giraffe*.]
Team 1 Player: "tall"	[Team 1 guesses]
Team 2 Player: "herbivore"	[Team 2 guesses]
Team 1 Player: "gentle"	[Team 1 guesses]
Team 2 Player: "spots"	[Team 2 guesses]

9 Connections
ACTIVITY HANDBOOK PAGE 4
ACTIVITY MASTERS 218 OR 219

Have students make connections between two animals. For example:

panther—monkey
They both live in the forest.

moose—elephant
A moose has antlers and an elephant has tusks.

koala bear—deer
Both are gentle animals.

10 Amazing Animals!

Have students associate the name of an animal with an adjective having the same initial letter. For example:

a *g*igantic *g*iraffe
a *h*ilarious *h*yena
a *s*melly *s*kunk

Have students draw pictures of their *amazing animals*.

11 It's a Puzzle!
ACTIVITY HANDBOOK PAGE 9

Cut out pictures of animals and create puzzles out of the pictures for students to identify and put together by asking questions. For example:

My picture has an animal with a hump and one with quills.
I see an animal with large ears.
Do you have water in your picture?
There's a cat and a kitten in my picture.

12 Daffy Debate!
ACTIVITY HANDBOOK PAGE 5
ACTIVITY MASTERS 218 OR 219

Have students debate which animals are more important to humankind than others.

13 Darwin's Dilemma!

a. Divide the class into pairs or small groups.

b. Have students create imaginary animals, using body parts from different existing animals. Students should name the animal (using syllables from the names of animals they used), draw a picture of the animal, create the sound that animal would make, and give information about where the animal lives and what it eats.

c. Have students then present their animals to the class.

14 Find the Answer!
ACTIVITY HANDBOOK PAGE 6

Possible questions students might want to have answered:

Which of the animals (on page 152 or 153) are endangered?
Why does the leopard have spots?
Why does an elephant have tusks?
Why does a horse have a tail?
Are wolves dangerous?
How intelligent are chimpanzees?

LESSON OBJECTIVE

Students will learn common species of birds and insects.

RESOURCES

AUDIO PROGRAM
Words & Dialogs
Cassette 6A
CD 6: Tracks 38, 39

 MULTI-LEVEL WORKBOOKS
Literacy Workbook
Beginning & Intermediate Lifeskills Workbooks
Beginning & Intermediate Vocabulary Workbooks

ACTIVITY MASTERS
Reproducibles:
A220, A221

TRANSPARENCY
Overhead: T154

 LANGUAGE & CULTURE NOTES
Reproducible: LC154

 WORDLINKS
longman.com/wordbyword

VOCABULARY INTRODUCTION

- Preview
- Present
- Practice

MODEL CONVERSATION PRACTICE

There are two model conversations—the first for words 1–41 and the second for words 24–41. Introduce and practice the first model before going to the second. For each model:

1. Have students look at the model illustration. Set the scene:

    Model 1: "A husband and wife are bird-watching."

    Model 2: "A wife is warning her husband about an insect that's on his shirt."

2. Present the first model with words 1 and 2 and the second model with word 24.

3. Choral Repetition Practice: Full-Class and Individual.

4. Have pairs practice the model.

5. Have pairs present the model.

6. Call on pairs to present a new conversation using words 3 and 4 for the first model and word 25 for the second model.

7. Have pairs practice new conversations.

8. Have pairs present new conversations.

SPELLING PRACTICE

Say a word, and have students spell it aloud or write it. Or, using the transparency, point to an item and have students write the word.

WRITING AND DISCUSSION

Have students respond to the questions as a class, in pairs, or in small groups. Or have students write their responses, share their writing with other students, and discuss in class.

Making Connections

Resource Materials Bring in, or have students bring in, the following materials for vocabulary practice:

- *Bird-watching guides:* Have students find the birds in the lesson in the guide.

- *Images of birds and insects downloaded from the Internet:* Have students identify the birds and insects in this lesson.

- *Aesop's Fables:* Read the story of *The Ant and the Grasshopper* to the class.

- *Nursery rhymes:* Read or sing the following rhyme:

    The itsy bitsy spider went up the water spout.
    Down came the rain and washed the spider out.
    Up came the sun and dried up all the rain.
    So the itsy bitsy spider went up the spout again.

Community Task Have students write a log of all the birds and insects they see for three days. Have students report their findings to the class.

Communication Activities

1 Clap in Rhythm
ACTIVITY HANDBOOK PAGE 3

Have students name different birds and insects to a clapping rhythm.

2 Chain Game
ACTIVITY HANDBOOK PAGES 2–3

Begin the chain as follows: "I went for a walk and saw a sparrow," and have students continue it. For example:

Teacher: I went for a walk and saw a sparrow.
Student 1: I went for a walk and saw a sparrow and a blue jay.
Student 2: I went for a walk and saw a sparrow, a blue jay, and a seagull.
Etc.

3 Concentration
ACTIVITY HANDBOOK PAGE 3
ACTIVITY MASTER 220

Have students shuffle the cards and place them face-down in three rows of 6 each, then attempt to find cards that match.

4 Picture Match-Ups
ACTIVITY HANDBOOK PAGE 12

Find pictures of birds and insects, make double copies of them, distribute them, and have students attempt to match the pictures by describing them to each other. For example:

I have a large brown bird with big yellow eyes sitting in a tree.
I have a pink bird with long legs standing in the water.

5 Question the Answer!
ACTIVITY HANDBOOK PAGE 13
ACTIVITY MASTER 221

Students pick Bird and Insect Word Cards and think of a question for which that word could be the answer. For example:

Card: spider
Student: What's an insect with eight legs that catches insects in a web?

Card: firefly
Student: What's a small insect that sends off short flashes of light?

Card: pigeon
Student: What's a bird that lives in cities?

6 Guess What I'm Thinking Of!
ACTIVITY HANDBOOK PAGE 8

Have students take turns thinking of birds and insects for others to guess. For example:

A. I'm thinking of a bird that's very colorful and can talk.
B. A parrot.
A. I'm thinking of an insect that crawls when it's born and then changes into a flying insect.
B. A butterfly.

7 Bird and Insect Associations
ACTIVITY HANDBOOK PAGE 2

Call out names of birds and insects and have groups write down as many associations as they can think of. For example:

owl: [eyes/big/brown/tree/night/wise]
mosquito: [buzz/itchy/bite/small]
scorpion: [danger/poison/hairy/spider]
hummingbird: [humming/small/strong]
cardinal: [red/singer/winter bird/flying]

8 What Am I?
ACTIVITY HANDBOOK PAGE 15
ACTIVITY MASTER 221

Pin word cards on students' backs and have them ask yes/no questions to identify which bird or insect they *are*. For example:

Am I a bird? [No.]
Am I an insect? [Yes.]
Do I fly? [Yes.]
Do I bite? [Yes.]
Am I a mosquito? [Yes.]

Am I an insect? [No.]
Am I a bird? [Yes.]
Do I fly? [No.]
Do I swim? [Yes.]
Am I a penguin? [Yes.]

9 Find the Answer!
ACTIVITY HANDBOOK PAGE 6

Possible questions students might want to have answered:

Which of the birds on *Picture Dictionary* page 154 are endangered?
Which birds can't fly?
What is the migration pattern of a (hummingbird/goose)?
Do bees die after they sting someone?
How many legs does a centipede have?

LESSON OBJECTIVE

Students will learn the names of fish and sea animals found throughout the world's oceans, as well as various amphibians and reptiles.

RESOURCES

AUDIO PROGRAM

Words & Dialogs
Cassette 6A
CD 6: Tracks 40, 41

MULTI-LEVEL WORKBOOKS

Literacy Workbook
Beginning & Intermediate Lifeskills Workbooks
Beginning & Intermediate Vocabulary Workbooks

TRANSPARENCY

Overhead: T155

LANGUAGE & CULTURE NOTES

Reproducible: LC155

WORDLINKS

longman.com/wordbyword

VOCABULARY INTRODUCTION

- Preview
- Present
- Practice

MODEL CONVERSATION PRACTICE

There are two model conversations—the first for words 1–39 and the second for words 26–39. Introduce and practice the first model before going to the second. For each model:

1. Have students look at the model illustration. Set the scene:

    Model 1: "A husband and wife are looking at fish in the aquarium."
    Model 2: "A wife and husband are setting up their camp site."

2. Present the first model with words 1 and 2 and the second model with words 26 and 27.

3. Choral Repetition Practice: Full-Class and Individual.

4. Have pairs practice the model.

5. Have pairs present the model.

6. Call on pairs to present a new conversation using words 3 and 4 for the first model and words 28 and 29 for the second model.

7. Have pairs practice new conversations.

8. Have pairs present new conversations.

SPELLING PRACTICE

Say a word, and have students spell it aloud or write it. Or, using the transparency, point to an item and have students write the word.

WRITING AND DISCUSSION

Have students respond to the questions as a class, in pairs, or in small groups. Or have students write their responses, share their writing with other students, and discuss in class.

Making Connections

Resource Materials Bring in, or have students bring in, the following materials for vocabulary practice:

- *Images downloaded from the Internet:* Have students identify the fish, sea animals, and reptiles in the images.

- *Virtual tours of aquariums:* On the Internet have students take a virtual tour of an aquarium.

Community Tasks If possible, take the class on a field trip to an aquarium in the area.

If students live by a large body of water, have students find out what fish and sea animals live there. Have students report to the class.

Communication Activities

1 Clap in Rhythm

ACTIVITY HANDBOOK PAGE 3

Have students name different fish, sea animals, and reptiles to a clapping rhythm.

2 Fantastic Fish!

Have students associate the name of a fish, sea animal, or reptile with an adjective having the same initial letter. For example:

a *terrific tortoise*
a *bashful boa* constrictor
a *lazy lizard*

Have students draw pictures of their *fantastic fish!*

3 Chain Game

ACTIVITY HANDBOOK PAGES 2–3

Begin the chain as follows: "Down by the water, I saw a swordfish," and have students continue it. For example:

Teacher: Down by the water, I saw a swordfish.
Student 1: Down by the water, I saw a swordfish and a starfish.
Student 2: Down by the water, I saw a swordfish, a starfish, and a dolphin.
Etc.

4 Fishy Associations

ACTIVITY HANDBOOK PAGE 2

Call out fish, sea animals, and reptiles and have groups write down as many associations as they can think of. For example:

octopus:	[large/tentacles/squeeze]
turtle:	[shell/slow/hide/quiet]
rattlesnake:	[reptile/large/deadly/noisy]
shark:	[large/fish/deadly]
otter:	[cute/busy/social/hardworking]

5 Category Dictation

ACTIVITY HANDBOOK PAGE 2

Dictate words that fit into the following categories:

fish
mammals
sea animals
amphibians
reptiles

6 Guess What I'm Thinking Of!

ACTIVITY HANDBOOK PAGE 8

Have students take turns thinking of fish, sea animals, or reptiles for others to guess. For example:

A. I'm thinking of a large fish that lives in cold water and is a popular food.
B. A cod.
A. I'm thinking of an animal that moves very slowly and has a spiral-shaped shell.
B. A snail.

7 Fish Talk!

As a class, in pairs, or in small groups, have students tell what fish, sea animal, or reptile they would like to be, and why.

8 Darwin's Dilemma!

Have pairs or groups of students create imaginary fish, sea animals, or reptiles using body parts from different existing ones. Students should name the creature (using syllables from the names of those they used), draw a picture of it, and give information about where it lives and what it eats. Have students then present their creations to the class.

9 Find the Answer!

ACTIVITY HANDBOOK PAGE 6

Possible questions students might want to have answered:

What's the difference between a sea lion and a seal? a newt and a salamander? a toad and a frog?
What country in the world hunts the most tuna?
Are whales endangered?
Where can I see dolphins?
What kinds of reptiles live in our region?

LESSON OBJECTIVE

Students will learn the vocabulary of the physical features of a tree and of a flower, along with several common species of trees, flowers, and plants.

RESOURCES

AUDIO PROGRAM
Words & Dialogs
Cassette 6A
CD 6: Tracks 42, 43

MULTI-LEVEL WORKBOOKS
Literacy Workbook
Beginning & Intermediate Lifeskills Workbooks
Beginning & Intermediate Vocabulary Workbooks

ACTIVITY MASTERS
Reproducibles:
A222–A224

TRANSPARENCIES
Overheads: T156, T157

LANGUAGE & CULTURE NOTES
Reproducible: LC156–157

WORDLINKS
longman.com/wordbyword

VOCABULARY INTRODUCTION

- Preview
- Present
- Practice

MODEL CONVERSATION PRACTICE

There are three model conversations—the first for words 11–22, the second for words 31–33, and the third for words 40–57. Introduce and practice the first model before going on to the second and third. For each model:

1. Have students look at the model illustration. Set the scene:

    Model 1: "A wife and husband are taking a walk and noticing trees."
    Model 2: "One friend is warning the other about some poison ivy."
    Model 3: "A wife and husband are admiring flowers in the window of a flower shop."

2. Present the first model with word 11, the second model with word 31, and the third model with word 40.

3. Choral Repetition Practice: Full-Class and Individual.

4. Have pairs practice the model.

5. Have pairs present the model.

6. Call on pairs to present a new conversation using word 12 for the first model, word 32 for the second model, and word 41 for the third model.

7. Have pairs practice new conversations.

8. Have pairs present new conversations.

SPELLING PRACTICE

Say a word, and have students spell it aloud or write it. Or, using the transparency, point to an item and have students write the word.

WRITING AND DISCUSSION

Have students respond to the questions as a class, in pairs, or in small groups. Or have students write their responses, share their writing with other students, and discuss in class.

Making Connections

Resource Materials Bring in, or have students bring in, the following materials for vocabulary practice:

- *Gardening magazines:* Have students identify the plants and trees with the vocabulary from this lesson.

Community Task Have students write a log of all the trees, plants, and flowers they see for three days. Have students report their findings to the class.

Communication Activities

1 Chain Game: While Walking Down the Street . . .
ACTIVITY HANDBOOK PAGES **2–3**

Begin the chain as follows: "While walking down the street, I saw a cherry tree," and have students continue it. For example:

Teacher: While walking down the street, I saw a cherry tree.
Student 1: While walking down the street, I saw a cherry tree and a birch tree.
Student 2: While walking down the street, I saw a cherry tree, a birch tree, and a gardenia.
Etc.

2 Concentration
ACTIVITY HANDBOOK PAGE **3**
ACTIVITY MASTER **222**

Have students shuffle the cards and place them face-down in three rows of 6 each, then attempt to find cards that match.

3 Movable Categories I
ACTIVITY HANDBOOK PAGE **11**
ACTIVITY MASTER **223**

Call out the following categories and have students go to the appropriate side of the room:

parts of a tree
tall trees
trees that lose their leaves in the winter
flowering trees
vines
plants and trees that are poisonous
trees that produce food

4 Movable Categories II
ACTIVITY HANDBOOK PAGE **11**
ACTIVITY MASTER **224**

Call out the following categories and have students go to the appropriate side of the room:

tropical flowers
red flowers
white flowers
parts of a flower
fragrant flowers

5 Tree, Flower, and Plant Associations
ACTIVITY HANDBOOK PAGE **2**

Call out trees, flowers, or plants and have groups write down as many associations as they can think of. For example:

jasmine: [tea/medicine/night/India]
rose: [pink/red/white/petal/stem/thorn]
crocus: [early spring/purple/small/bulb]

6 Mystery Word Association Game
ACTIVITY HANDBOOK PAGES **11–12**

Have students write associations for plant, flower, or tree *mystery words* for others to guess. For example:

cut flower/pink/long-lasting: [carnation]
green and red/Christmas plant: [poinsettia]
beaches/deserts/dates/tall: [palm trees]

7 Question the Answer!
ACTIVITY HANDBOOK PAGE **13**
ACTIVITY MASTERS **223, 224**

Students pick Tree, Plant, and Flower Word Cards and think of a question for which that word could be the answer. For example:

Card: petal
Student: What's the colored part of a flower?

Card: stem
Student: What supports the leaves and flowers?

Card: bark
Student: What's the skin of a tree?

Card: cactus
Student: What plant grows in the desert?

8 Here's What I'm Thinking Of!
ACTIVITY HANDBOOK PAGE **8**
ACTIVITY MASTERS **223, 224**

Make statements about words in the lesson and have students guess what you're thinking of. For example:

A. I'm thinking of something that grows on a pine tree and has seeds on it.
B. A pine cone.

A. I'm thinking of a tree that grows very tall.
B. A redwood.

A. I'm thinking of a vine with groups of three leaves that has a poisonous oil.
B. Poison ivy.

LESSON OBJECTIVE

Students will learn vocabulary related to energy resources, conservation efforts, and environmental issues.

RESOURCES

AUDIO PROGRAM		MULTI-LEVEL WORKBOOKS	ACTIVITY MASTERS
Words & Dialogs	**WordSong:** *Word by Word Theme*	Literacy Workbook	**Reproducibles:** A225, A226
Cassette 6A	Cassette 7B • CD 8: Tracks 18, 19	Beginning & Intermediate Lifeskills Workbooks	
CD 6: Tracks 44, 45	Song Masters S31, S32	Beginning & Intermediate Vocabulary Workbooks	

TRANSPARENCY	LANGUAGE & CULTURE NOTES	WORDLINKS
Overhead: T158	**Reproducible:** LC158	longman.com/wordbyword

VOCABULARY INTRODUCTION

- Preview
- Present
- Practice

MODEL CONVERSATION PRACTICE

There are three model conversations—the first for words 1–8, the second for words 9–12, and the third for words 13–18. Introduce and practice the first model before going on to the second and third. For each model:

1. Have students look at the model illustration. Set the scene:
   - Model 1: "College students are having a discussion about sources of energy."
   - Model 2: "Two friends are talking about energy conservation."
   - Model 3: "Someone is going around a neighborhood asking people to sign a petition about the environment."

2. Present the first model with word 1, the second model with word 9, and the third model with word 13.

3. Choral Repetition Practice: Full-Class and Individual.

4. Have pairs practice the model.

5. Have pairs present the model.

6. Call on pairs to present a new conversation using word 2 for the first model, word 10 for the second model, and word 14 for the third model.

7. Have pairs practice new conversations.

8. Have pairs present new conversations.

SPELLING PRACTICE

Say a word or phrase, and have students spell it aloud or write it. Or, using the transparency, point to an item and have students write the word or phrase.

WRITING AND DISCUSSION

Have students respond to the questions as a class, in pairs, or in small groups. Or have students write their responses, share their writing with other students, and discuss in class.

Making Connections

Resource Materials Bring in, or have students bring in, the following materials for vocabulary practice:

- *Images of types of pollution and types of energy downloaded from the Internet:* Have students identify the energy sources and the environmental problems in the images.

- *Pamphlets (downloaded from the Internet) on how to conserve energy and water:* Have students read the pamphlets and determine what they already do to conserve energy and water and what they can change to conserve *more* energy and water.

Community Task Have individual students find out about recycling services in their town or community and then report to the class.

Communication Activities

1 Concentration

ACTIVITY HANDBOOK PAGE 3
ACTIVITY MASTER 225

Have students shuffle the cards and place them face-down in three rows of 6 each, then attempt to find cards that match

2 Environment and Energy Associations

ACTIVITY HANDBOOK PAGE 2

Call out energy, conservation, and environmental problem words and have groups write down as many associations as they can think of. For example:

nuclear energy: [Three Mile Island/Chernobyl/ efficient/dangerous]

wind energy: [wind farms/mountains/beaches/ efficient]

acid rain: [corrosion/black monuments]

global warming: [greenhouse gases/cars/trucks/oil/ climate change]

3 Secret Word Associations

ACTIVITY HANDBOOK PAGE 14

Have students choose an energy, conservation, or environment item, brainstorm associations with that word, and see if the class can guess the word. For example:

commute/work/share/driving: [carpool]
cans/glass/newspapers/bins: [recycle]
cars/homes/heat/Middle East: [oil]

4 Word Clues

ACTIVITY HANDBOOK PAGE 17
ACTIVITY MASTER 226

Have students take turns giving clues to team members who try to guess the word. For example:

[The word is *radiation*.]
Team 1 Player: "nuclear"   [Team 1 guesses]
Team 2 Player: "cancer"   [Team 2 guesses]
Team 1 Player: "birth defects" [Team 1 guesses]

[The word is *carpool*.]
Team 1 Player: "conserve"   [Team 1 guesses]
Team 2 Player: "passengers"   [Team 2 guesses]
Team 1 Player: "save money"   [Team 1 guesses]

[The word is *hydroelectric power*.]
Team 1 Player: "river"   [Team 1 guesses]
Team 2 Player: "dams"   [Team 2 guesses]
Team 1 Player: "waterfalls"   [Team 1 guesses]

5 Ask Me a Question!

ACTIVITY HANDBOOK PAGE 2
ACTIVITY MASTER 226

Have students walk around trying to guess each other's energy, conservation, and environment items by asking yes/no questions. For example:

Am I a kind of conservation?   [No.]
Am I a type of energy?   [Yes.]
Do I use water?   [No.]
Do I use wind?   [No.]
Do I use the sun?   [Yes.]
Am I solar energy?   [Yes.]

Am I a type of energy?   [No.]
Am I a kind of conservation?   [No.]
Am I a kind of environmental problem?   [Yes.]
Am I water pollution?   [No.]
Do cars make me happen?   [Yes.]
Am I air pollution?   [Yes.]

6 Survey

a. Give each student or pair of students a card with one of the following questions:

> Do you recycle newspapers?

> Do you recycle glass?

> Do you recycle cans?

> Do you recycle plastics?

> Do you carpool?

> Do you drive a car more than a half hour a day?

> How many gallons of gas do you use a week?

> How many minutes long are your showers?

Do you run the water when you brush your teeth?

Do you let the water run when you wash the dishes?

Do you water plants outdoors?

How much is your average electric bill?

Do you use efficient light bulbs?

Do you have air conditioning in your home?

b. Have students circulate around the class and survey their classmates.

c. When students are finished, have them tally their results and present them to the class in a bar graph.

d. Discuss the following questions:

Do your classmate have good conservation habits?
How can your classmates improve how they use energy and water?

7 Category Dictation
ACTIVITY HANDBOOK PAGE 2

Dictate words that fit into the following categories:

renewable energy sources (no limit to the energy source)
non-renewable energy sources (limited amount of the energy source)

For example:

Renewable Energy Sources	Non-Renewable Energy Sources
solar energy	oil
hydroelectric power	natural gas
wind	coal
geothermal	nuclear energy

8 Advantages and Disadvantages

As a class, brainstorm the advantages and disadvantages of each energy source. Decide which energy sources people should use more.

9 Dictate and Discuss

a. Dictate the following statements and have students discuss them in small groups.

Wind farms should not be located in beautiful places.
Everyone should carpool.
Nuclear energy is too dangerous to use.
Oil prices are too high.
There is no such thing as global warming.

b. Have the groups then report back to the class.

10 Find the Answer!
ACTIVITY HANDBOOK PAGE 6

Possible questions students might want to have answered:

What are the top three environmental problems in our community?
What is acid rain?
What causes air pollution?
What is global warming?
What causes water pollution?
How can we conserve water?
How can we conserve more energy?

11 Energy, Conservation, and the Environment Crossword
ACTIVITY HANDBOOK PAGES 4–5

Have students connect energy, conservation, and environment words to create a crossword.
For example:

LESSON OBJECTIVE

Students will learn the names of natural disasters.

RESOURCES

AUDIO PROGRAM

Words & Dialogs
Cassette 6A
CD 6: Tracks 46, 47

 MULTI-LEVEL WORKBOOKS

Literacy Workbook
Beginning & Intermediate Lifeskills Workbooks
Beginning & Intermediate Vocabulary Workbooks

 ACTIVITY MASTERS

Reproducibles:
A8, A227, A228

TRANSPARENCY
Overhead: T159

LANGUAGE & CULTURE NOTES
Reproducible: LC159

WORDLINKS
longman.com/wordbyword

VOCABULARY INTRODUCTION

- Preview
- Present
- Practice

MODEL CONVERSATION PRACTICE

1. Have students look at the model illustration. Set the scene: "Two co-workers are talking during a break at work."
2. Present the model with word 1.
3. Choral Repetition Practice: Full-Class and Individual.
4. Have pairs practice the model.
5. Have pairs present the model.
6. Call on pairs to present a new conversation using word 2.
7. Have pairs practice new conversations.
8. Have pairs present new conversations.

SPELLING PRACTICE

Say a word, and have students spell it aloud or write it. Or, using the transparency, point to an item and have students write the word.

WRITING AND DISCUSSION

Have students respond to the questions as a class, in pairs, or in small groups. Or have students write their responses, share their writing with other students, and discuss in class.

Making Connections

Resource Materials Bring in, or have students bring in, the following materials for vocabulary practice:

- *Images of natural disasters downloaded from the Internet:* Have students identify the type of natural disaster and, if possible, recall the place and time of the event in the picture.

Community Task Identify the natural disasters most common in your area. Have each group of students choose a different type of natural disaster to research. Have groups find out how local authorities (police, firefighters, and other first-response workers) are prepared in the event of the natural disaster.

Communication Activities

1 Concentration
ACTIVITY HANDBOOK PAGE 3
ACTIVITY MASTER 227

Have students shuffle the cards and place them face-down in three rows of 6 each, then attempt to find cards that match.

2 Natural Disaster Associations
ACTIVITY HANDBOOK PAGE 2

Call out natural disasters and have groups write down as many associations as they can think of.
For example:

tsunami:	[water/destruction/waves/sea]
earthquake:	[falling objects/shaking/tremors]
forest fire:	[fire/heat/drought/destruction]
flood:	[river/water/mud/waves]
avalanche:	[snow/mountains/buried/skiing]

3 Word Clues
ACTIVITY HANDBOOK PAGE 17
ACTIVITY MASTER 228

Have students take turns giving one-word clues to team members who try to guess the word.
For example:

[The word is *mudslide*.]
Team 1 Player:	"rain"	[Team 1 guesses]
Team 2 Player:	"hill"	[Team 2 guesses]
Team 1 Player:	"fall"	[Team 1 guesses]

[The term is *volcanic eruption*.]
Team 1 Player:	"lava"	[Team 1 guesses]
Team 2 Player:	"ash"	[Team 2 guesses]
Team 1 Player:	"smoke"	[Team 1 guesses]

[The word is *hurricane*.]
Team 1 Player:	"wind"	[Team 1 guesses]
Team 2 Player:	"rain"	[Team 2 guesses]
Team 1 Player:	"Carribean"	[Team 1 guesses]

4 Tic Tac Definitions
ACTIVITY HANDBOOK PAGE 15
ACTIVITY MASTER 8

Have students fill in the tic tac grid with any nine natural disasters they wish. Give definitions such as the following, and have students cross out on their grids the words you have defined:

a shaking of the earth from a sudden movement of rock beneath the Earth's surface [earthquake]

the name for a tropical cyclone with sustained winds of 74 miles per hour or greater in the North Atlantic Ocean, Caribbean Sea, and Gulf of Mexico [hurricane]

the name for a tropical cyclone with sustained winds of 74 miles per hour or greater in the western North Pacific Ocean [typhoon]

a winter snowstorm with high winds [blizzard]

a violently rotating column of air that touches the ground [tornado]

when bodies of water overflow onto dry land [flood]

a giant ocean wave [tsunami]

an extended period of abnormally dry weather [drought]

an unplanned fire that is out of control in a wooded area [forest fire]

loose rocks or earth that slide down a slope or hillside [landslide]

a slide of large amounts of snow and ice down a mountain [avalanche]

5 Category Dictation
ACTIVITY HANDBOOK PAGE 2

Dictate natural disasters that fit into the following categories:

wind	fire
earth	water

(continued)

6 Guess the Word!

ACTIVITY HANDBOOK PAGE 8

Write blank letters on the board for natural disaster words, give clues to their meanings, and have teams compete to guess the words. For example:

clue: a giant wave

clue: a very dry period

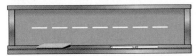

clue: a funnel of air that destroys whatever it touches

clue: a winter snowstorm with high winds

7 Dictate and Discuss

a. Dictate the following statements and have student discuss them in small groups.

> Most mudslides can be prevented.
> Forest fires are natural and we shouldn't try to stop them.
> People shouldn't live close to rivers that flood.

b. Have the groups then report back to the class.

8 Natural Disaster Talk!

ACTIVITY HANDBOOK PAGE 17
ACTIVITY MASTER 228

Give students a Natural Disaster Word Card, and have them speak to the class for one minute about that natural disaster.

9 Find the Answer!

ACTIVITY HANDBOOK PAGE 6

Possible questions students might want to have answered:

> What is the most active volcano on Earth today?
> What was the biggest volcanic eruption?
> Has our community ever had a blizzard? When?
> Has there ever been a forest fire close by? Where? When? What happened?
> Has there ever been a flood nearby? Where? When? What happened?

Unit 16 Communication Activity Review

1 Odd Word Out

Read the following lists of words, and have students identify the category and the "odd word out"—the word that doesn't fit the category:

cow, horse, pig, chicken, lamb, tiger
[Category: FARM ANIMALS. Odd word out: tiger]

alfalfa, corn, rooster, cotton, soybeans, wheat
[Category: FARM CROPS. Odd word out: rooster]

raccoon, gerbil, guinea pig, goldfish, dog, cat
[Category: PETS. Odd word out: raccoon]

bison, moose, porcupine, coyote, grizzly bear, camel
[Category: ANIMALS OF NORTH AMERICA. Odd word out: camel]

lion, polar bear, zebra, gorilla, hyena, giraffe
[Category: ANIMALS OF AFRICA. Odd word out: polar bear]

robin, cricket, blue jay, cardinal, hummingbird, crow, pigeon
[Category: BIRDS. Odd word out: cricket]

fly, mosquito, ladybug, tick, parrot, scorpion
[Category: INSECTS. Odd word out: parrot]

trout, bass, shark, cobra, sea horse, tuna, flounder
[Category: FISH. Odd word out: cobra]

alligator, lizard, crab, crocodile, iguana
[Category: REPTILES. Odd word out: crab]

toad, frog, squid, salamander, newt
[Category: AMPHIBIANS. Odd word out: squid]

whales, antler, porpoise, sea lion, jellyfish, starfish
[Category: SEA ANIMALS. Odd word out: antler]

hoof, tail, whiskers, horn, koala, paw
[Category: PARTS OF AN ANIMAL. Odd word out: koala]

elm, cherry, birch, hibiscus, pine, oak
[Category: KINDS OF TREES. Odd word out: hibiscus]

daisy, marigold, iris, jasmine, coal, violet
[Category: FLOWERS. Odd word out: coal]

acid rain, thorn, water pollution, air pollution, global warming, radiation
[Category: ENVIRONMENTAL PROBLEMS. Odd word out: thorn]

pasture, tornado, earthquake, drought, tsunami
[Category: NATURAL DISASTERS. Odd word out: pasture]

2 Drawing Game
ACTIVITY HANDBOOK PAGE 6
ACTIVITY MASTERS 217, 218, 219, 228

Have teams compete to identify the items drawn by one of their team members.

3 Nature Quiz Game
ACTIVITY MASTER 229

a. Divide the class into four teams.

b. Copy and cut up Activity Master 245 and place cards face-down in a pile.

c. Have the teams take turns answering your questions. Give each team a time limit to answer each question (30 seconds or 1 minute).

d. The team with the most correct answers wins.

4 Clap in Rhythm
ACTIVITY HANDBOOK PAGE 3

To a clapping rhythm, have students name different words in the following categories:

farm animals	sea animals
wild animals	amphibians and reptiles
pets	trees
birds	flowers
insects	natural disasters
fish	

5 Do You Remember?
ACTIVITY HANDBOOK PAGE 5

Have students look at any one of the pictures on pages 151–159. Tell them to close their books and write down everything they remember about the picture.

6 Category Dictation
ACTIVITY HANDBOOK PAGE 2

Dictate words from *Picture Dictionary* pages 151–159 that fit into any of the following categories:

farm animals	sea animals
wild animals	amphibians and reptiles
pets	trees
birds	flowers
insects	natural disasters
fish	

UNIT 17 U.S. Civics

AUDIO PROGRAM

Words & Dialogs
Audio Cassette 6B
Audio CD 7:
   Tracks 2–15

WordSong: *A Better Life*
Audio Cassette 7B
Audio CD 8: Tracks 20
   (Vocal) & 21 (Sing-along)
Song Masters S33, S34

WORKBOOKS

For Multi-Level Practice
Literacy Workbook
Beginning Lifeskills Workbook
Beginning Vocabulary Workbook
Intermediate Lifeskills Workbook
Intermediate Vocabulary Workbook

WORDLINKS

Internet Resources through the
***Word by Word* Companion Website**
http://www.longman.com/wordbyword

ACTIVITY MASTERS

Reproducibles for Communication Activities
A8, A230–A237

TRANSPARENCIES

Full-Color Overheads for Class Practice
T160–T166

LANGUAGE & CULTURE NOTES

**Information for Teachers &
Intermediate /Advanced Students**
LC160–166

LESSON OBJECTIVE

Students will learn the most common forms of identification that are used in the United States.

RESOURCES

AUDIO PROGRAM

Words & Dialogs
Cassette 6B
CD 7: Tracks 2, 3

MULTI-LEVEL WORKBOOKS

Literacy Workbook
Beginning & Intermediate Lifeskills Workbooks
Beginning & Intermediate Vocabulary Workbooks

ACTIVITY MASTERS

Reproducibles:
A8, A230, A231

TRANSPARENCY
Overhead: T160

LANGUAGE & CULTURE NOTES
Reproducible: LC160

WORDLINKS
longman.com/wordbyword

VOCABULARY INTRODUCTION

- Preview
- Present
- Practice

MODEL CONVERSATION PRACTICE

There are two model conversations. Introduce and practice the first model before going on to the second. For each model:

1. Have students look at the model illustration. Set the scene:

   Model 1: "Someone wants to cash a check at a bank. The bank cashier needs to see some identification."

   Model 2: "A husband and wife are talking. The husband is upset. He lost something important."

2. Present the first model with word 1 and the second model with word 2.

3. Choral Repetition Practice: Full-Class and Individual.

4. Have pairs practice the model.

5. Have pairs present the model.

6. Call on pairs to present a new conversation using word 3 for the first model and word 4 for the second model.

7. Have pairs practice new conversations.

8. Have pairs present new conversations.

SPELLING PRACTICE

Say a word, and have students spell it aloud or write it. Or, using the transparency, point to an item and have students write the word.

WRITING AND DISCUSSION

Have students respond to the questions as a class, in pairs, or in small groups. Or have students write their responses, share their writing with other students, and discuss in class.

Making Connections

Resource Materials Bring in, or have students bring in, the following materials for vocabulary practice:

- *Images of identification cards and driver's licenses downloaded from the Internet:* Have students identify the forms of identification in the images.

Community Task Brainstorm types of permits or memberships that require identification (a public library card, membership to a video rental store, car registration, a parking permit, cash checking at a bank, a bank account, a driver's license, etc). Have individual students (or groups of students) choose one and find out what forms of identification are required. Have students report to the class.

Communication Activities

① Clap in Rhythm
ACTIVITY HANDBOOK PAGE 3

Have students name different forms of identification to a clapping rhythm.

② Concentration
ACTIVITY HANDBOOK PAGE 3
ACTIVITY MASTER 230

Have students shuffle the cards and place them face-down in three rows of 6 each, then attempt to find cards that match.

③ Telephone
ACTIVITY HANDBOOK PAGE 14

Begin the activity with the following sentence: "Yesterday I went to apply for a passport. I showed my birth certificate and my driver's license."

④ Guess What I'm Thinking Of!
ACTIVITY HANDBOOK PAGE 8

Have students take turns thinking of forms of identification for others to guess. For example:

A. I'm thinking of a form of identification that you need to drive a car.
B. A driver's license.

A. I'm thinking of a form of identification that you need if you want to travel internationally.
B. A passport.

⑤ Question the Answer!
ACTIVITY HANDBOOK PAGE 13
ACTIVITY MASTER 231

Students pick word cards and think of a question for which that word could be the answer. For example:

Card: work permit
Student: What does a temporary foreign resident need in order to work in the United States?

Card: visa
Student: What is a permit you need to visit, live, or work in a foreign country?

Card: birth certificate
Student: What does each child born in the United States receive?

Card: social security card
Student: What is the form of identification required for applications related to money such as bank loans and credit card applications?

⑥ Letter Game
ACTIVITY HANDBOOK PAGE 9

Say statements such as the following and have teams compete to identify the items:

I'm thinking of a form of identification that starts with *d*.	[driver's license]
I'm thinking of a form of identification that starts with *e*.	[employee I.D. badge]
I'm thinking of a form of identification that starts with *b*.	[birth certificate]
I'm thinking of a form of identification that starts with *v*.	[visa]

⑦ Tic Tac Definitions
ACTIVITY HANDBOOK PAGE 15
ACTIVITY MASTER 8

Have students fill in the tic tac grid with any nine forms of identification they wish. Give definitions such as the following, and have students cross out on their grids the words you have defined:

a permit to drive a car [driver's license]
a form of identification with nine numbers that is necessary for all important money transactions [social security card]
a form of school identification [student I.D. card]
a form of identification at the place where you work [employee I.D. badge]
a card that allows foreign residents to live and work in the United States indefinitely [permanent resident card]
an internationally recognized document that identifies the holder's nationality, name, birth date, and other personal information [passport]
a permit to visit, live, or work in a foreign country [visa]
a document that allows a foreign temporary resident to work legally in the United States [work permit]
a document that identifies the place and time of a child's birth and the names of the child's parents [birth certificate]

⑧ Find the Answer!
ACTIVITY HANDBOOK PAGE 6

Possible questions students might want to have answered:

What forms of identification do you need to get a driver's license? a social security card? a gym membership? a bank account?
What are four examples of proof of residence?

Page 161 U.S. GOVERNMENT

LESSON OBJECTIVE

Students will learn about the three branches of the United States government.

RESOURCES

AUDIO PROGRAM	MULTI-LEVEL WORKBOOKS	ACTIVITY MASTER
Words & Dialogs Cassette 6B CD 7: Tracks 4, 5	Literacy Workbook Beginning & Intermediate Lifeskills Workbooks Beginning & Intermediate Vocabulary Workbooks	**Reproducible**: A232

TRANSPARENCY	LANGUAGE & CULTURE NOTES	WORDLINKS
Overhead: T161	**Reproducible:** LC161	longman.com/wordbyword

VOCABULARY INTRODUCTION

- Preview
- Present
- Practice

MODEL CONVERSATION PRACTICE

There are four model conversations. Introduce and practice each before going on to the next. For each model:

1. Have students look at the model illustration. Set the scene:

> Model 1: "A high school teacher is asking a student a question."
> Model 2: "A teacher in an adult citizenship class is asking a student a question."
> Model 3: "An examiner is asking an applicant a question at her citizenship examination."
> Model 4: "A quiz show host is asking a contestant this question."

2. Present the first model with words 1 and A, the second model with words A and 2, the third model with words 2 and 6, and the fourth model with words 3 and A.

3. Choral Repetition Practice: Full-Class and Individual.

4. Have pairs practice the model.

5. Have pairs present the model.

6. Call on pairs to present a new conversation using words 7 and B for the first model, words A and 4 for the second model, words 4 and 6 for the third model, and words 5 and A for the fourth model.

7. Have pairs practice new conversations.

8. Have pairs present new conversations.

SPELLING PRACTICE

Say a word, and have students spell it aloud or write it. Or, using the transparency, point to an item and have students write the word.

WRITING AND DISCUSSION

Have students respond to the questions as a class, in pairs, or in small groups. Or have students write their responses, share their writing with other students, and discuss in class.

Making Connections

Resource Materials Bring in, or have students bring in, the following materials for vocabulary practice:

- *Newspapers:* Read headlines about people and events in politics, government, and courts and have students identify which branch of government is involved.

Community Task If possible, have the class take a tour of the state house or of state supreme court to learn how these branches of government work.

Communication Activities

1 Government Associations

ACTIVITY HANDBOOK PAGE 2

Call out government words and have groups write
down as many associations as they can think of.
For example:

legislative branch: [representatives/congressmen
and congresswomen/laws]

executive branch: [the cabinet/the president/the
vice-president/the White House]

judicial branch: [Supreme Court/chief justice/
explain laws/Constitution]

the White House: [Washington, D.C./the president/
the Rose Garden/the Oval Office]

cabinet: [Secretary of State/advisors/
Department of Defense/
Secretary of Labor]

2 Here's What I'm Thinking Of!

ACTIVITY HANDBOOK PAGE 8

Make statements such as the following and have
students guess the branch of government you're
thinking of. For example:

A. I'm thinking of a branch of government that
makes the laws.
B. The legislative branch.

A. I'm thinking of a branch of government that
explains the laws.
B. The judicial branch.

A. I'm thinking of a branch of government that
enforces the laws.
B. The executive branch.

A. I'm thinking of the place where the president of
the United States lives and works.
B. The White House.

A. I'm thinking of the group of people who advise and
help the president.
B. The cabinet.

A. I'm thinking of the head of the Supreme Court.
B. The chief justice.

A. I'm thinking of a politician who travels to
Washington, D.C. to represent his or her entire
state.
B. A senator.

A. I'm thinking of the group of people who make laws.
B. The house of representatives.

A. I'm thinking of the place where U.S. senators and
representatives meet to make laws.
B. The Capitol Building.

A. I'm thinking of the place where the Supreme
Court justices meet to explain laws.
B. The Supreme Court Building.

3 What Am I?

ACTIVITY HANDBOOK PAGE 15
ACTIVITY MASTER 232 (except for the three
verb phrases)

Pin word cards on students' backs and have them
ask yes/no questions to identify which part of
government they *are*. For example:

Am I part of the legislative branch? [No.]
Am I part of the executive branch? [No.]
Am I part of the judicial branch? [Yes.]
Am I a person? [No.]
Am I a building? [Yes.]
Am I the Supreme Court Building? [Yes.]

Am I part of the legislative branch? [No.]
Am I part of the executive branch? [Yes.]
Am I a person? [Yes.]
Am I the vice-president? [No.]
Am I the president? [Yes.]

4 Movable Categories

ACTIVITY HANDBOOK PAGE 11
ACTIVITY MASTER 232

Call out the following categories and have students
go to the appropriate side of the room:

legislative branch
executive branch
judicial branch
people who work in government
a group of people who work together
government places
what government does

5 Category Dictation
ACTIVITY HANDBOOK PAGE 2

Dictate words that fit into the above categories:

6 Who Am I?
ACTIVITY HANDBOOK PAGE 17

Tell about different people in government and have students guess who you are talking about. For example:

Teacher: I'm the head of the executive branch. Who am I?
Student: The president.

Teacher: I'm the head of the Supreme Court. Who am I?
Student: The chief justice.

Teacher: I represent a district in my state in the Capitol Building. Who am I?
Student: A representative.

Teacher: I represent my whole state in the Capitol Building. Who am I?
Student: A senator.

Teacher: I'm second to the president. Who am I?
Student: The vice-president.

Teacher: We advise and help the president. Who are we?
Student: The cabinet.

Teacher: We discuss cases and explain the laws. Who are we?
Student: The Supreme Court justices.

Teacher: I live in the White House. Who am I?
Student: The president.

7 U.S. Government Talk!
ACTIVITY HANDBOOK PAGE 17
ACTIVITY MASTER 232 (except for the three verb phrases)

Give students a Government Word Card, and have them speak to the class for one minute about that part of government.

8 Stand Up for Government!

a. Say the name of a branch of government.

b. Tell students you're going to say four words. If they hear a word that is associated with that branch of government, they should stand up. If they hear a word that is not associated with that branch of government, they should sit down. For example:

Executive branch:
president	[stand up]
White House	[remain standing]
senator	[sit down]
Supreme Court justice	[remain sitting]

Judicial branch:
vice-president	[sit down]
Supreme Court	[stand up]
representative	[sit down]
chief justice	[stand up]

Legislative branch:
cabinet	[sit down]
house of representatives	[stand up]
explains the laws	[sit down]
Capitol Building	[stand up]

9 Cooperative Definitions
ACTIVITY HANDBOOK PAGE 4

Have groups write definitions of U.S. government words and then pass their definitions to other groups

10 Find the Answer!
ACTIVITY HANDBOOK PAGE 6

Possible questions students might want to have answered:

How many people work in the White House?
Do senators spend more time in their home districts or in the capitol city?
What important decisions has the Supreme Court made in the last two years?
Who is in the president's cabinet?
Who are the Supreme Court justices?

LESSON OBJECTIVE

Students will learn about the United States Constitution and its Bill of Rights.

RESOURCES

AUDIO PROGRAM

Words & Dialogs
Cassette 6B
CD 7: Tracks 6, 7

WordSong: *A Better Life*
Cassette 7B • CD 8: Tracks 20, 21
Song Masters S33, S34

MULTI-LEVEL WORKBOOKS

Literacy Workbook
Beginning & Intermediate Lifeskills Workbooks
Beginning & Intermediate Vocabulary Workbooks

TRANSPARENCY
Overhead: T162

LANGUAGE & CULTURE NOTES
Reproducible: LC162

WORDLINKS
longman.com/wordbyword

VOCABULARY INTRODUCTION

- Preview
- Present
- Practice

MODEL CONVERSATION PRACTICE

There are four model conversations. Introduce and practice each before going on to the next. For each model:

1. Have students look at the model illustration. Set the scene: "This person is taking the citizenship examination."
2. For the two models in the left column, present the first with phrases A and 1 and the second with phrase 4. For the two models in the right column, present both with phrase 8.
3. Choral Repetition Practice: Full-Class and Individual.
4. Have pairs practice the model.
5. Have pairs present the model.
6. Call on pairs to present a new conversation using phrases B and 3 for the first model, phrase 5 for the second model, and phrase 9 for the third and fourth models.
7. Have pairs practice new conversations.
8. Have pairs present new conversations.

SPELLING PRACTICE

Say a phrase, and have students spell it aloud or write it. Or, using the transparency, point to an item and have students write the phrase.

WRITING AND DISCUSSION

Have students respond to the questions as a class, in pairs, or in small groups. Or have students write their responses, share their writing with other students, and discuss in class.

♪♫ WordSong ♫♪

1. Have students listen to the vocal version of *A Better Life* one or more times. Then have students listen again as they read the song lyrics on Song Master S33.
2. Have students sing as you play either the vocal or the sing-along version of the song.
3. For fun, have a song competition in which students perform solo or in groups and the class votes for the best performance.
4. For additional practice, students can complete the cloze exercise on Song Master S34.

Resource Materials Bring in, or have students bring in, the following materials for vocabulary practice:

● *The Constitution:* Download a copy of the Constitution from the Internet. Ask students to look through it and answer these questions: How many articles are there? How many sections are there under Article three? How many people signed the Constitution? When did they sign it?

● *Newspaper:* Read headlines in the newspaper and ask students which headlines are related to the First Amendment. (For example, the following are related to the First Amendment: a political demonstration, a religious event, a question about prayer in public schools, the newspaper itself, anti-loitering (gang) laws, hate speech.)

Community Task Have students find out when their native countries passed their current constitution. Have students compare their dates in class.

Communication Activities

① True or False?
ACTIVITY HANDBOOK PAGE 15

Make statements such as the following about the U.S. Constitution. Have students decide whether the statements are true or false.

> The Bill of Rights is the "supreme law of the land." [False. The Constitution is the "supreme law of the land."]
> The Preamble is the beginning of the Constitution. [True.]
> The Bill of Rights is the first five amendments to the Constitution. [False. The Bill of Rights is the first ten amendments to the Constitution.]
> The First Amendment protects freedom of speech. [True.]
> The First Amendment protects freedom of religion. [True.]
> The First Amendment protects freedom of transportation. [False. There is no freedom of transportation amendment.]
> One amendment gave women the right to vote. [True.]
> Freedom of assembly means that people can meet together in public places. [True.]
> Freedom of the press means that politicians can say what they want. [False. Freedom of the press means that newspapers and magazines can say what they want. Freedom of speech means people can say what they want.]
> An amendment ended slavery many years ago. [True.]

② Quiz Game

Divide the class into two groups. Have the groups take turns answer the following questions:

> What is the "supreme law of the land"?
> What is the Preamble?
> What is the Bill of Rights?
> Can U.S. residents practice any religion they want?
> Did the original Constitution give African Americans the right to vote?
> Did the original Constitution give women the right to vote?
> Which amendment gave 18-year-old citizens the right to vote?
> Which amendment established income taxes?
> Which amendment ended slavery?
> What does freedom of assembly mean?
> What does freedom of the press mean?
> What does freedom of religion mean?
> What does freedom of speech mean?

③ Constitution Talk!
ACTIVITY HANDBOOK PAGE 17

a. Put the following on index cards:

the Preamble	the Bill of Rights
freedom of speech	freedom of the press
freedom of religion	freedom of assembly

b. Have pairs of students pick a card and then speak together to the class for one minute about that part of the Constitution.

④ Find the Answer!
ACTIVITY HANDBOOK PAGE 6

Possible questions students might want to have answered:

> Who wrote the Constitution?
> Where?
> When did they sign it?
> How many amendments are there?
> Where is the original Constitution now?
> What issue in the news now is about the First Amendment?

LESSON OBJECTIVE

Students will learn about the most important events in United States history.

RESOURCES

AUDIO PROGRAM

Words & Dialogs
Cassette 6B
CD 7: Tracks 8, 9

MULTI-LEVEL WORKBOOKS

Literacy Workbook
Beginning & Intermediate Lifeskills Workbooks
Beginning & Intermediate Vocabulary Workbooks

ACTIVITY MASTERS

Reproducibles:
A8, A233

TRANSPARENCY

Overhead: T163

LANGUAGE & CULTURE NOTES

Reproducible: LC163

WORDLINKS

longman.com/wordbyword

VOCABULARY INTRODUCTION

- Preview
- Present
- Practice

MODEL CONVERSATION PRACTICE

There are two model conversations. Introduce and practice the first model before going on to the second. For each model:

1. Have students look at the model illustration. Set the scene: "A middle-school social studies teacher is asking a student questions."

2. Present the first model with the year 1607 and the second model with the event in 1620.

3. Choral Repetition Practice: Full-Class and Individual.

4. Have pairs practice the model.

5. Have pairs present the model.

6. Call on pairs to present a new conversation using the year 1775 for the first model and the event in 1776 for the second model.

7. Have pairs practice new conversations.

8. Have pairs present new conversations.

WRITING AND DISCUSSION

Have students respond to the questions as a class, in pairs, or in small groups. Or have students write their responses, share their writing with other students, and discuss in class.

Making Connections

Resource Materials Bring in, or have students bring in, the following materials for vocabulary practice:

- *U.S. history textbooks:* Have students look at the table of contents and identify the events they learned in this lesson.

Community Task Have students find out about a historical monument in their community and then add it to the timeline.

Communication Activities

1 History Associations
ACTIVITY HANDBOOK PAGE 2

Call out events in U.S. history and have groups write down as many associations as they can think of. For example:

The Great Depression:	[poor/hungry/unemployment/ stock market crash]
World War II:	[Hitler/Europe/airplanes/ bombs]
Landing on the moon:	[Apollo 11/television/ astronauts/space]
Civil War:	[President Lincoln/north/ south/slavery]
Thomas Edison:	[lightbulb/inventions/ intelligent/electricity]

2 True or False?
ACTIVITY HANDBOOK PAGE 15

Make statements such as the following about events in United States history. Have students decide whether the statements are true or false. Students will need to refer to the timeline as they answer the questions. For example:

Colonists first came to Washington. [False. Colonists first came to Jamestown, Virginia.]

The Revolutionary War lasted for five years. [False. It lasted for eight years.]

George Washington was the first president of the United States. [True.]

The Civil War lasted four years. [True.]

The United States fought in five international wars in the 1900's. [True.]

Representatives wrote the Constitution in 1887. [False. They wrote it in 1787.]

President Washington signed the Emancipation Proclamation. [False. President Lincoln signed the Emancipation Proclamation.]

Neil Armstrong was President of the United States. [False. Neil Armstrong was an astronaut.]

The telephone and the lightbulb were invented in the United States. [True.]

3 Category Dictation
ACTIVITY HANDBOOK PAGE 2

Dictate events that fit into the following categories:

1700s
1800s
1900s

4 Who Am I?
ACTIVITY HANDBOOK PAGE 17

Tell about different people in United States history and have students guess who you are talking about. For example:

Teacher: I was the first president of the United States. Who am I?
Student: George Washington.

Teacher: I invented the lightbulb. Who am I?
Student: Thomas Edison.

Teacher: I invented the telephone. Who am I?
Student: Alexander Graham Bell.

Teacher: I signed the Emancipation Proclamation. Who am I?
Student: President Lincoln.

Teacher: We came to live in Plymouth, Massachusetts. Who are we?
Student: Pilgrims.

Teacher: I landed on the moon. Who am I?
Student: Neil Armstrong.

Teacher: We wrote the Constitution of the United States. Who are we?
Student: Representatives.

Teacher: We came to Jamestown, Virginia in 1607. Who are we?
Student: Colonists.

Teacher: We won the right to vote in 1920. Who are we?
Student: Women.

5 Put In Order!
ACTIVITY MASTER 233

a. Make multiple copies of the Historical Event Strips and cut them into cards.

b. Distribute sets of cards to pairs of students.

c. Have students put the strips in the correct order.

d. Have students compare their answers with the class.

(continued)

6 Stand Up for History!

a. Say the name of a century—for example: 19th century, 1800's.

b. Tell students you're going to tell four events. If they hear an event that occurred in that century, they should stand up. If they hear an event that did not occur in that century, they should sit down. For example:

1600s

Colonists came to Jamestown Virginia.	[stand up]
Pilgrims came to Plymouth colony.	[remain standing]
The Civil War began.	[sit down]
The stock market crashed.	[remain sitting]

1700s

The Korean War began.	[sit down]
The colonies declared their independence.	[stand up]
The civil rights movement began.	[sit down]
Representatives wrote the U.S. Constitution.	[stand up]

1800s

The Revolutionary War ended.	[sit down]
Thomas Edison invented the lightbulb.	[stand up]
The Vietnam War began.	[sit down]
Alexander Graham Bell invented the telephone.	[stand up]

1900s

The March on Washington took place.	[stand up]
The Persian Gulf War began.	[remain standing]
The United States was attacked by terrorists.	[sit down]
Washington became the first president.	[remain sitting]

7 Tic Tac Dates

ACTIVITY HANDBOOK PAGE **15**
ACTIVITY MASTER **8**

Have students fill in the tic tac grid with any nine event dates they wish. Name events in U.S. history and have students cross out on their grids the dates that correspond to events you mention.

8 U.S. History Talk!

ACTIVITY HANDBOOK PAGE **17**

Have students choose an event in U.S. history and have them speak to the class for one minute about that event.

9 Daffy Debate!

ACTIVITY HANDBOOK PAGE **5**

Since there aren't any word cards for this activity, to determine which events will be debated, have students close their eyes and point to events on the timeline. Then have students debate which event in U.S. history was more important.

10 Find the Answer!

ACTIVITY HANDBOOK PAGE **6**

Possible questions students might want to have answered:

What else did Edison invent?
What else did Alexander Graham Bell invent?
What happened in the United States during the Great Depression?
Why did the south and the north fight in the Civil War?
What was life like in the Plymouth Colony?

LESSON OBJECTIVE

Students will learn about the most commonly celebrated holidays in the United States.

RESOURCES

AUDIO PROGRAM
Words & Dialogs
Cassette 6B
CD 7: Tracks 10, 11

MULTI-LEVEL WORKBOOKS
Literacy Workbook
Beginning & Intermediate Lifeskills Workbooks
Beginning & Intermediate Vocabulary Workbooks

ACTIVITY MASTER
Reproducible:
A8

TRANSPARENCY
Overhead: T164

LANGUAGE & CULTURE NOTES
Reproducible: LC164

WORDLINKS
longman.com/wordbyword

VOCABULARY INTRODUCTION

- Preview
- Present
- Practice

MODEL CONVERSATION PRACTICE

There are three model conversations. Introduce and practice the first model before going on to the second and third. For each model:

1. Have students look at the model illustration. Set the scene: "Two students are talking."
2. Present the first model with holiday 1, the second model with holiday 2, and the third model with holiday 10.
3. Choral Repetition Practice: Full-Class and Individual.
4. Have pairs practice the model.
5. Have pairs present the model.
6. Call on pairs to present a new conversation using holiday 3 for the first model, holiday 4 for the second model, and holiday 11 for the third model.
7. Have pairs practice new conversations.
8. Have pairs present new conversations.

SPELLING PRACTICE

Say a holiday, and have students spell it aloud or write it. Or, using the transparency, point to an item and have students write the holiday.

WRITING AND DISCUSSION

Have students respond to the questions as a class, in pairs, or in small groups. Or have students write their responses, share their writing with other students, and discuss in class.

Making Connections

Resource Materials Bring in, or have students bring in, the following materials for vocabulary practice:

- *Items they use to celebrate any of these holidays:* Have students present the items and explain how they use them in the holiday celebrations.

- *Student pictures of their holiday celebrations:* Have students show the pictures and explain what they are doing.

- *Images downloaded from the Internet:* Have students identify the holiday celebrations in the images.

- *A calendar:* Have students identify all the holidays they know about in an American calendar.

Community Task Have individual students (or groups of students) find out about how their community celebrates one of the holidays on page 164. Have students report to the class.

Communication Activities

1 Clap in Rhythm
ACTIVITY HANDBOOK PAGE 3

Have students name different holidays to a clapping rhythm.

2 Letter Game
ACTIVITY HANDBOOK PAGE 9

Say statements such as the following and have teams compete to identify the items:

I'm thinking of a holiday that starts with *N*. [New Year's Day]

I'm thinking of a holiday that starts with *V*. [Valentine's Day]

I'm thinking of a holiday that starts with *I*. [Independence Day]

I'm thinking of a holiday that starts with *H*. [Halloween]

I'm thinking of a holiday that starts with *T*. [Thanksgiving]

I'm thinking of a holiday that starts with *C*. [Christmas]

I'm thinking of a holiday that starts with *R*. [Ramadan]

I'm thinking of a holiday that starts with *K*. [Kwanzaa]

3 Tic Tac Holidays
ACTIVITY HANDBOOK PAGE 15
ACTIVITY MASTER 8

Have students fill in the tic tac grid with any nine holidays they wish. Give definitions such as the following and have students cross out on their grids the holidays you have defined:

a national celebration of the first day of the year [New Year's Day]

a national celebration of an important African-American leader [Martin Luther King, Jr. Day]

a cultural holiday celebrating love [Valentine's Day]

a national holiday that remembers all the nation's military people who died in a war [Memorial Day]

a national holiday that celebrates a new nation [Independence Day]

a night when children dress up in costumes and ask for candy from their neighbors [Halloween]

a national holiday for all the people who served in the military [Veterans Day]

a holiday families celebrate around the dinner table [Thanksgiving]

a Christian holiday that celebrates the birth of Jesus [Christmas]

a Muslim month-long holiday of fasting [Ramadan]

an African holiday that celebrates African traditions and family [Kwanzaa]

the Jewish festival of lights [Hanukkah]

4 Ranking
ACTIVITY HANDBOOK PAGE 13

Have students look at the holidays on *Picture Dictionary* page 164 and rank the three they like most. For example:

I Like the Most
Thanksgiving
Valentine's Day
Independence Day

Then call on students to give their reasons.

5 Holiday Recommendations

a. In small groups, have students make recommendations of fun things to do on each holiday.

b. Have the groups report to the class. Then write a master list of *recommended things to do on holidays*.

6 Secret Word Associations
ACTIVITY HANDBOOK PAGE 14

In pairs or in small groups, have students choose a *secret holiday* from the vocabulary list on *Picture Dictionary* page 164, brainstorm several associations, tell the associated words to the class, and see if students can guess the holiday.

7 Holiday Associations

ACTIVITY HANDBOOK PAGE 2

Call out holidays and have groups write down as many associations as they can think of. For example:

Fourth of July: [parades/red, white, and blue/ fireworks/barbecues]

Ramadan: [month/fasting/Muslim/Islam/ feast]

Thanksgiving: [pilgrims/Native Americans/turkey/ food/family]

Valentine's day: [roses/red and pink/love/romance/ chocolate]

Halloween: [candy/jack-o'-lanterns/night/trick or treat]

8 Dictate and Discuss

a. Dictate one of the following statements to the class:

There are too many military holidays in the United States.

Christmas is the most important Christian holiday of the year.

Hanukkah is the most important Jewish holiday of the year.

People should observe Memorial Day and not go on vacation.

Valentine's Day is only for romantic couples.

Halloween is a dangerous holiday for children.

b. In small groups, have students discuss their opinions of the statements.

c. As a class, vote in agreement or disagreement with the statement and then have students discuss their reasons.

9 Find the Answer!

ACTIVITY HANDBOOK PAGE 6

Possible questions students might want to have answered:

What celebrations take place in our community for New Year's Eve?

What is the song everyone sings on New Year's Eve?

What is the meaning of the hearts and arrows on Valentine's Day?

What does the president of the United States do on Memorial Day?

What is the meaning of the jack-o'-lantern on Halloween?

Why do people eat turkey on Thanksgiving?

Where did that first Thanksgiving meal take place?

Do children under twelve fast during Ramadan?

What are the traditional foods for the feast at the end of Ramadan?

What do the symbols of Kwanzaa mean?

LESSON OBJECTIVE

Students will learn about the legal system, and specifically about the criminal justice system, in the United States.

RESOURCES

AUDIO PROGRAM
Words & Dialogs
Cassette 6B
  Audio CD 7: Tracks 12,13

MULTI-LEVEL WORKBOOKS
Literacy Workbook
Beginning & Intermediate Lifeskills Workbooks
Beginning & Intermediate Vocabulary Workbooks

ACTIVITY MASTERS
Reproducibles:
  A8, A234

TRANSPARENCY
Overhead: T165

LANGUAGE & CULTURE NOTES
Reproducible: LC165

WORDLINKS
longman.com/wordbyword

VOCABULARY INTRODUCTION

- Preview
- Present
- Practice

MODEL CONVERSATION PRACTICE

There are three model conversations. Introduce and practice the first model before going on to the second and third. For each model:

1. Have students look at the model illustration. Set the scene:
   - Model 1: "Two co-workers are talking during a break at work."
   - Model 2: "A husband and wife are watching a crime program on TV."
   - Model 3: "A young boy sitting outside a courtroom wants to know who this person is."

2. Present the first model with any name you wish and phrase A, the second model with phrase B, and the third model with words 1 and 2.

3. Choral Repetition Practice: Full-Class and Individual.

4. Have pairs practice the model.

5. Have pairs present the model.

6. Call on pairs to present a new conversation using phrase C for the first model, phrase D for the second model, and words 7 and 2 for the third model.

7. Have pairs practice new conversations.

8. Have pairs present new conversations.

SPELLING PRACTICE

Say a word, and have students spell it aloud or write it. Or, using the transparency, point to an item and have students write the word.

WRITING AND DISCUSSION

Have students respond to the questions as a class, in pairs, or in small groups. Or have students write their responses, share their writing with other students, and discuss in class.

Making Connections

Resource Materials Bring in, or have students bring in, the following materials for vocabulary practice:

- *Downloaded information from lawyer websites explaining the criminal justice system:* Have students identify the words from this lesson.

Community Task Take a tour of your county court and learn about the local criminal justice system.

Communication Activities

1 Do You Remember?
ACTIVITY HANDBOOK PAGE 5

Have students write down everything they remember about one of the legal system scenes depicted on *Picture Dictionary* page 165.

2 Tic Tac Definitions
ACTIVITY HANDBOOK PAGE 15
ACTIVITY MASTER 8

Have students fill in the tic tac grid with any nine legal system words (1-25) they wish. Give definitions such as the following and have students cross out on their grids the words you have defined:

> the person accused of a crime [suspect]
> the person who arrests the suspect [police officer]
> metal bracelets that hold the suspect's hands behind the back [handcuffs]
> the legal rights every arrested person has [Miranda rights]
> the public official who decides questions that come before a court of justice [judge]
> the money deposit the suspect pays in order to be temporarily released from custody until the trial [bail]
> the place where a trial takes place [courtroom]
> the lawyer who tries to prove the defendant is guilty [prosecuting attorney]
> a person the defense or prosecution calls who saw the crime or has some information about the crime [witness]
> the person who records everything that people say in the trial [court reporter]
> the lawyer who tries to prove the defendant is not guilty [defense attorney]

3 Put in Order!
ACTIVITY MASTER 234

a. Divide the class into pairs or small groups.

b. Make copies of the Legal System Action Strips, cut them into separate strips, and distribute a set to each pair or small group.

c. Have students put the strips in the correct order.

Variation: Distribute one strip per student. Have students memorize their sentences and then arrange themselves in the correct order.

4 Legal System Role Play
ACTIVITY MASTER 234

a. Divide the class into pairs or small groups.

b. Copy the Legal System Action Strips and distribute a set to each pair or small group.

c. Have students choose an event on one of the strips and create a brief role play of what is happening in that strip.

d. Have students perform their role plays and have the class guess what is happening.

5 What's the Question?
ACTIVITY HANDBOOK PAGE 16

Describe various legal system items and have students respond by asking: "What's a _____?" or "What are _____s?" For example:

Teacher: These are metal bracelets the police officer puts on a suspect when the suspect is arrested.
Student: What are handcuffs?

Teacher: These are the arrested person's legal rights.
Student: What are the Miranda rights?

Teacher: These are different for each person in the world.
Student: What are fingerprints?

Teacher: This is the picture the police take of the suspect.
Student: What's a mug shot?

Teacher: This is the money the suspect deposits in order to leave jail until the trial.
Student: What's bail?

Teacher: This is the place where the trial takes place.
Student: What's a courtroom?

Teacher: This is the amount of time a convict must spend in prison.
Student: What's a sentence?

Teacher: This is the place where inmates serve their sentences.
Student: What's a prison?

Teacher: This is the money a convicted person must pay.
Student: What's a fine?

Teacher: This is what the defendant hopes the jury will say at the end of the trial.
Student: What's innocent?

(continued)

6 Chain Story
ACTIVITY HANDBOOK PAGE 3

Begin the story as follows: "This is a story of mistaken identity. Last week, as I was walking, a police officer stopped me."

7 Who Am I?
ACTIVITY HANDBOOK PAGE 17

Tell about different people in the criminal justice system and have students guess who you are talking about. For example:

Teacher: I work inside the prison. Who am I?
Student: A prison guard.

Teacher: I'm the lawyer who tries to prove the defendant is innocent. Who am I?
Student: The defense attorney.

Teacher: I'm the lawyer who tries to prove the suspect is guilty. Who am I?
Student: The prosecuting attorney.

Teacher: I'm the person who lives in a prison as I serve my sentence. Who am I?
Student: A convict/prisoner/inmate.

Teacher: We're the people who watch and listen to the trial and make a final decision whether the defendant is guilty or innocent. Who are we?
Student: The jury.

Teacher: I'm the person who is arrested. Who am I?
Student: The suspect.

Teacher: I'm the person who arrests the suspect. Who am I?
Student: A police officer.

Teacher: I'm the person who supervises the trial. Who am I?
Student: The judge.

Teacher: I'm the person who stands trial. Who am I?
Student: The defendant.

Teacher: I'm the person who records everything people say during the trial. Who am I?
Student: The court reporter.

Teacher: I'm the police officer who brings the defendant into the court and keeps the court in order during the trial. Who am I?
Student: The bailiff.

8 True or False Definitions
ACTIVITY HANDBOOK PAGE 15

Give true and false definitions of legal system words and have students decide which are true and which are false. For example:

When a person is arrested, the police officer reads him or her the Miranda rights. [True.]

When a suspect is booked, the police take the suspect to court. [False. They take the suspect to the police station.]

The prosecuting attorney tries to prove the defendant is guilty. [True.]

The defense attorney tries to prove the suspect is innocent. [True.]

If the suspect doesn't want to appear in court, he or she can pay the bail. [False. The bail releases the suspect from jail until the hearing and trial. The suspect MUST appear in court.]

The defendant has to go to jail if he or she is acquitted. [False. The defendant has to go to jail if he or she is *convicted*.]

When a suspect is booked, the police take his or her picture and fingerprints. [True.]

The verdict is the decision whether the defendant is guilty or innocent. [True.]

The bailiff is the officer who arrests the suspect. [False. The bailiff is the person who makes sure there is order in the court.]

Lawyer and attorney mean the same thing. [True.]

9 Dictate and Discuss

a. Dictate one of the following statements to the class:

The jury system is good because a decision by a group is better than a decision by one judge.
Prisons turn good people into criminals.
Most sentences are too short.
It can be dangerous to be a witness in a trial.
There should be a death penalty.

b. In small groups, have students discuss their opinions of the statements.

c. As a class, vote in agreement or disagreement with the statement and then have students discuss their reasons.

10 Find the Answer!
ACTIVITY HANDBOOK PAGE 6

Possible questions students might want to have answered:

Where is the county courthouse?
How do people get selected for a jury?
What happens during a sentence hearing?
What is the story of Ernesto Miranda and the Miranda rights?
What are the most common crimes in the United States?
How much does an attorney charge for his or her services?

LESSON OBJECTIVE

Students will learn about the path to citizenship and the rights and responsibilities of being a citizen in the United States.

RESOURCES

AUDIO PROGRAM

Words & Dialogs
Cassette 6B
CD 7: Tracks 14, 15

WordSong: *A Better Life*
Cassette 7B • CD 8: Tracks 20, 21
Song Masters S33, S34

MULTI-LEVEL WORKBOOKS

Literacy Workbook
Beginning & Intermediate Lifeskills Workbooks
Beginning & Intermediate Vocabulary Workbooks

ACTIVITY MASTERS

Reproducibles:
A235, A236

TRANSPARENCY

Overhead: T166

LANGUAGE & CULTURE NOTES

Reproducible: LC166

WORDLINKS

longman.com/wordbyword

VOCABULARY INTRODUCTION

- Preview
- Present
- Practice

MODEL CONVERSATION PRACTICE

There are two model conversations. Introduce and practice the first model before going on to the second. For each model:

1. Have students look at the model illustration. Set the scene:

   Model 1: "An examiner is asking an applicant a question at his citizenship examination."

   Model 2: "Two co-workers are talking during a break at work."

2. Present the first model with word 1 and the second model with phrases 8 and 9.

3. Choral Repetition Practice: Full-Class and Individual.

4. Have pairs practice the model.

5. Have pairs present the model.

6. Call on pairs to present a new conversation using phrase 2 for the first model and phrases 9 and 10 for the second model.

7. Have pairs practice new conversations.

8. Have pairs present new conversations.

SPELLING PRACTICE

Say a phrase, and have students spell it aloud or write it. Or, using the transparency, point to an item and have students write the phrase.

WRITING AND DISCUSSION

Have students respond to the questions as a class, in pairs, or in small groups. Or have students write their responses, share their writing with other students, and discuss in class.

Making Connections

Resource Materials Bring in, or have students bring in, the following materials for vocabulary practice:

○ *Downloaded information on U.S. Citizenship and Immigration Services:* Have students identify the words and phrases from this lesson.

Community Task Have individual students (or groups of students) find out where U.S. citizenship classes are offered. Have students find out the times of the classes and the fees. Have students report back to the class.

Communication Activities

1 Concentration

ACTIVITY HANDBOOK PAGE 3
ACTIVITY MASTER 235

Have students shuffle the cards and place them face-down in rows, then attempt to find cards that match.

2 Put in Order!

ACTIVITY MASTER 236

a. Divide the class into pairs or small groups.

b. Copy the Citizenship Action Strips, cut them into separate strips, and distribute a set to each pair or small group.

c. Have students put the strips in the correct order.

Variation: Divide the class into groups of six. Distribute one strip per student. Have students memorize their sentences and then arrange themselves in the correct order.

3 Path to Citizenship Role Play

ACTIVITY MASTER 236

a. Divide the class into pairs or small groups.

b. Copy the Citizenship Action Strips and distribute a set to each pair or small group.

c. Have students choose a step to citizenship on one of the strips and create a brief role play of what is happening in that strip.

d. Have students perform their role plays and have the class guess what is happening.

4 Category Dictation

ACTIVITY HANDBOOK PAGE 2

Dictate words that fit into the following categories:

rights
responsibilities
path to citizenship

5 Chain Story

ACTIVITY HANDBOOK PAGE 3

Begin the story as follows: "I just became a citizen. It took a long time to do."

6 True or False?

ACTIVITY HANDBOOK PAGE 15

Make statements about citizens' rights and responsibilities and the path to citizenship. Have students decide whether they're true or false. For example:

You must be a citizen to serve on a jury. [True.]
The Selective Service System requires all 21-year-old men and women to register. [False. The Selective Service System requires all men 18–26 to register.]
It's a citizen's right to follow the news. [False. It's a citizen's responsibility to follow the news.]
To get citizenship, the applicant must have a naturalization interview. [True.]
The citizenship test is about U.S. government and history. [True.]
Only citizens must obey laws. [False. Everyone, residents and citizens, must obey laws.]
All citizen's have the right to vote. [False. Citizens over the age of 18 years old have the right to vote.]
Attending school board meetings is one way to be a part of community life. [True.]
Many people attend the naturalization ceremony. [True.]
The Oath of Allegiance is the same as the Pledge of Allegiance that some children say in schools. [False. The Oath of Allegiance is a specific oath for people who are becoming citizens.]
Only citizens pay taxes. [False. U.S. residents also pay taxes.]

7 Find the Answer!

ACTIVITY HANDBOOK PAGE 6

Possible questions students might want to have answered:

Where can you find applications for citizenship?
What are ways to be part of community life?
How long is a naturalization interview?
How often does a person serve on a jury?
What questions do they ask in a naturalization interview?
What questions do they ask in a citizenship test?
Where does a citizen vote?
When are election days?

Unit 17 Communication Activity Review

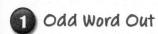

1 Odd Word Out

Read the following lists of words, and have students identify the category and the "odd word out"—the word that doesn't fit the category:

bailiff, driver's license, social security card, student I.D. card, passport
[Category: FORMS OF IDENTIFICATION. Odd word out: bailiff]

legislative, executive, judicial, innocent
[Category: BRANCHES OF GOVERNMENT. Odd word out: innocent]

house of representatives, senate, Supreme Court, Capitol Building, congressmen
[Category: LEGISLATIVE BRANCH. Odd word out: Supreme Court]

president, visa, cabinet, vice-president, White House
[Category: EXECUTIVE BRANCH. Odd word out: visa]

the Preamble, the Bill of Rights, Amendments, Oath of Allegiance
[Category: PARTS OF THE U.S. CONSTITUTION. Odd word out: Oath of Allegiance]

Memorial Day, Supreme Court Building, Valentine's Day, Thanksgiving, Halloween
[Category: HOLIDAYS. Odd word out: Supreme Court Building.]

Ramadan, Independence Day, Hanukkah, Christmas
[Category: RELIGIOUS HOLIDAYS. Odd word out: Independence Day]

bailiff, senator, court reporter, lawyer, judge
[Category: PEOPLE WHO WORK IN THE COURTROOM. Odd word out: senator]

apply for citizenship, take a citizenship test, serve on a jury, have a naturalization interview, attend a naturalization ceremony
[Category: THE PATH TO CITIZENSHIP. Odd word out: serve on a jury]

the Korean War, the Civil War, the Vietnam War, the Persian Gulf War, World War I
[Category: WARS IN THE 20TH CENTURY (OR) FOREIGN WARS. Odd word out: Civil War]

obey laws, serve on a jury, pay taxes, be part of community life, stand trial
[Category: RESPONSIBILITIES AND RIGHTS OF A CITIZEN. Odd word out: stand trial]

suspect, lawyer, defendant, convict, inmate
[Category: THE PERSON STANDING A TRIAL AND VERDICT. Odd word out: lawyer]

2 Finish the Sentence!
ACTIVITY HANDBOOK PAGE 7

Begin sentences such as the following for students to complete:

Some businesses give their workers . . . *employee I.D. badges.*
In order to have a job, a foreign resident must have a . . . *work permit.*
The branch of government that makes the laws is the . . . *legislative branch.*
The branch of government that enforces the laws is the . . . *executive branch.*
The branch of government that explains the laws is the . . . *judicial branch.*
The First Amendment protects the following four freedoms: . . . *freedom of speech, freedom of press, freedom of religion, and freedom of assembly.*
The first president of the United States was . . . *George Washington.*
The US was attacked by terrorists in . . . *2001.*
The American colonies declared their independence in . . . *1776.*
The first day of the calendar year is . . . *New Year's Day.*

3 Category Dictation
ACTIVITY HANDBOOK PAGE 2

Dictate words from *Picture Dictionary* pages 160–166 that fit any three of the following categories:

people
places

(continued)

4 Who Am I?

ACTIVITY HANDBOOK PAGE 17

Tell about different people in government and the legal system and have students guess who you are talking about. For example:

Teacher: I'm the head of the executive branch of government. Who am I?
Student: The president.

Teacher: I'm the head of the Supreme Court. Who am I?
Student: The chief justice.

Teacher: People elect me to work in the house of representatives. Who am I?
Student: A representative, congressman, or congresswoman.

Teacher: I landed on the moon in 1969. Who am I?
Student: Neil Armstrong.

Teacher: I invented the lightbulb. Who am I?
Student: Thomas Edison.

Teacher: I'm in charge of a trial. Who am I?
Student: A judge.

Teacher: I tell the court and jury what I saw. Who am I?
Student: A witness.

Teacher: I live in a prison. Who am I?
Student: A prisoner/A convict/An inmate.

Teacher: If the president dies, I become the head of the executive branch. Who am I?
Student: The vice-president.

Teacher: I'm a judge on the Supreme Court. Who am I?
Student: A Supreme Court justice.

5 U.S. Civics Quiz Game

ACTIVITY MASTER 237

a. Divide the class into four teams.

b. Copy and cut up Activity Master 237 and place cards face-down in a pile.

c. Have the teams take turns answering your questions. Give each team a time limit to answer each question (30 seconds or 1 minute).

d. The team with the most correct answers wins.

6 100 Questions for U.S. Citizenship

a. Print out from the United States Citizenship and Immigration Services website a list of 100 typical questions for the citizenship examination. (http://www.uscis.gov/graphics/services/natz/100q.pdf)

b. Have teams take turns answering the questions. Give each team a time limit to answer each question (30 seconds or 1 minute).

WORD BY WORD ACTIVITY MASTERS

ACTIVITY HANDBOOK

Communicative Strategies for Vocabulary Development

ACTIVITY HANDBOOK

1. Ask Me a Question!

a. Make a copy of the Word Cards Activity Master for the lesson, cut it up, and give a card to each student.

b. Without showing the items on their cards, have students walk around trying to guess each other's item by asking yes/no questions. For example:

[THE LIVING ROOM]

Do you sit on it?	[No.]
Do you put things in it?	[No.]
Do you hang it on the wall?	[Yes.]
Is it a painting?	[Yes.]

[THE BATHROOM]

Is it electric?	[No.]
Do you use it in the shower?	[No.]
Do you use it after a shower?	[Yes.]
Is it a towel?	[Yes.]

Variation: Do the activity as a game by dividing the class into teams. One person comes to the front of the room and thinks of an item. The teams compete against each other, trying to guess the item by asking yes/no questions.

2. Associations

a. Divide the class into small groups.

b. Call out a word or expression from the vocabulary list, and have the groups write down as many associations as they can think of. For example:

[HOUSEHOLD PROBLEMS AND REPAIRS]

plumber: [repair/sink/water/faucet]
carpenter: [build/measure/saw/drill/wood]

[THE CITY]

bus: [bus driver/change/seat/bus stop/
    passengers]
intersection: [crosswalk/pedestrian/traffic/
    traffic light]

[EVERYDAY ACTIVITIES]

wash my face: [water/washcloth/soap/
    towel/clean]
brush my teeth: [toothpaste/morning/
    toothbrush]

c. Have the groups call out their words and make a common list on the board.

d. Tell students they can question a word, in which case the student who suggested the association must explain the reason for that association.

3. Bleep!

a. Make a copy of the Word Cards Activity Master for the lesson, cut it up, mix up the cards, and put them face-down in a pile on a table or desk in front of the room.

b. Divide the class into pairs.

c. Have each pair come to the front of the room, pick three cards from the pile, return to their seats, and create a conversation in which they use those three words.

d. Call on the pairs to present their conversations to the class. But, instead of saying the three words when they come up in the conversations, the pairs say *bleep* instead.

e. Other students then try to guess the *bleeped* words.

4. Category Dictation

Note: This activity is a follow-up to the *Movable Categories* activity (see page 11) in which words from the lesson are grouped into various categories.

a. Have students make four columns on a piece of paper.

b. Dictate any four of the categories from the previous *Movable Categories* activity, and have students write them at the top of the four columns.

c. Dictate words from the lesson, and have students write the items in the appropriate column.

d. As a class, in pairs, or in small groups, have students check their work.

5. Chain Game

a. Begin the game by saying a sentence with one of the words or expressions from the lesson.

b. Student 1 repeats what you said and adds another item.

c. Continue around the room in this fashion, with each student repeating what the previous said and adding another item. For example:

[THE CLASSROOM]

Teacher: In our classroom, there's a globe.
Student 1: In our classroom, there's a globe and some chalk.
Student 2: In our classroom, there's a globe, some chalk, and a computer.
Etc.

[EVERYDAY ACTIVITIES]

Teacher: I got up this morning and took a shower.
Student 1: I got up this morning, took a shower, and brushed my teeth.
Student 2: I got up this morning, took a shower, brushed my teeth, and combed my hair.
Etc.

d. Play the game again, beginning and ending with different students.

If the class is large, you can divide students into groups to give each student more practice.

6. Chain Story

a. Begin a story based on the theme of the lesson. For example:

[THE BEACH]

It was a beautiful sunny day at the beach.

[PUBLIC TRANSPORTATION]

You won't believe what happened to me yesterday when I tried to take the train to New York!

b. Have each student in turn add to the story, using at least one of the vocabulary words from the lesson. Encourage students to be creative.

7. Clap in Rhythm

Object: Once a clapping rhythm is established, the students must continue naming different words from the lesson.

a. Have students sit in a circle.

b. Establish a steady, even beat: one-two-three-four, one-two-three-four, etc., by having students clap their hands to their laps twice and then clap their hands together twice. Repeat throughout the game, maintaining the same rhythm.

c. The object is for each student in turn to name a different word *each time the hands are clapped together.* Nothing is said when students clap their hands on their laps.

Note: The beat never stops! If a student misses a beat, he or she can either wait for the next beat or pass to the next student.

8. Clues

a. Have one student leave the room for a few minutes.

b. Tell the rest of the students to think of ways they use different items in the lesson. Students can either say or write their answers. For example:

[PERSONAL HYGIENE]

I use this to clean my hair.
I use this because I want to smell good.
I use this so my nails will be beautiful.

[JEWELRY AND ACCESSORIES]

I wear this on my wrist.
I wear this around my neck.
I carry my money in this.

c. The student then returns to the classroom, listens as others read or say their clues, and tries to guess the items.

9. Concentration

For this activity, divide the class into groups of four. Make a copy of the Concentration Cards Activity Master for each group and cut it up into cards.

a. Divide each group of four into two teams—Team A and Team B.

b. Give each group a set of Concentration Cards.

c. Have the groups shuffle the cards and place them face-down in rows.

d. Tell students that the object of the game is to find cards that match.

e. A student from Team A turns over two cards, and if they match that team keeps the cards. If the cards don't match, the student turns them face-down and a member of Team B takes a turn.

The play continues until all the cards have been matched. The team with the most correct *matches* wins the game.

10. Connections

a. Make a copy of the Word Cards Activity Master for the lesson, cut it up, and put the cards in two piles on a table or desk in front of the room.

b. Have students take turns picking one card from each pile and trying to make a connection between the two items. The connection may be a similarity, a difference, or some relationship between the two. For example:

> [THE KITCHEN]
>
> *placemat—cutting board*
> [You put dishes on a placemat. You put things on a cutting board before you cut them.]
>
> *refrigerator—burner*
> [A refrigerator is cold. A burner is hot.]
>
> [THE CITY]
>
> *bus—taxi*
> [They both carry passengers. A bus is much larger than a taxi.]
>
> *curb—intersection*
> [You step over the curb before you cross an intersection.]
>
> [THE AIRPORT]
>
> *garment bag—check-in counter*
> [You don't check in your garment bag at the check-in counter.]
>
> *suitcase—passport*
> [You shouldn't carry your passport in your suitcase.]

Variation: Do the activity as a game with two competing teams.

11. Cooperative Definitions

a. Divide the class into small groups of three or four. Give each group a letter designation (i.e., Group A, Group B, . . .) and a piece of paper.

b. Ask each group to write definitions of five vocabulary items from the lesson.

c. When all the groups are ready, have them pass their papers with the definitions to the group on the right. Group A thus passes its definitions to Group B, who passes its definitions to Group C, etc.

d. Each group then reads the definitions it has received, and on a separate piece of paper writes their group letter designation and what item they think is being defined.

e. Continue until each group has seen all the other groups' definitions.

f. Compare the results and see which group has the most correct guesses.

Note: To make sure there is a variety of vocabulary items, you might wish to assign five different words to each group for them to define.

12. Crosswords

a. Ask Student 1 to write a word from the lesson in the middle of the board.

b. Then have Student 1 think of another word that can be linked vertically through a shared letter with the word on the board. The student gives a clue or definition of that word and tells the number of letters in the word and its first letter.

c. Student 2 comes to the board and writes the word so that it crosses the first word vertically, using the shared letter.

d. Student 2 then thinks of a word that can be linked horizontally through a shared letter with the second word and gives clues for that word.

e. Student 3 comes to the board and writes the word so that it crosses the second word horizontally, using the shared letter.

f. The activity continues, with students alternating vertical and horizontal linking words. For example:

> [OCCUPATIONS]
>
> a. Student 1 writes FARMER on the board (see page 5).
> b. Student 1 thinks of the word *hairdresser* and says: "Someone who cuts men's and women's hair. 11 letters. The first letter is H."
> c. Student 2 comes to the board and writes HAIRDRESSER so that it crosses FARMER vertically at the shared letter R.
> d. Student 2 thinks of the word *journalist* and says: "Someone who writes for a newspaper. 10 letters. The first letter is J."

e. Student 3 comes to the board and writes JOURNALIST so that it crosses HAIRDRESSER horizontally at the shared letter R.

13. Daffy Debate!

a. Make a copy of the Word Cards Activity Master for the lesson, cut it up, and put the cards face-down on a table or desk in front of the room.

b. Two students come to the front of the room, and each takes a card.

c. The two must then have a one-minute debate on which item is more important.

d. After the debate, have the class vote on which person's reasons were more convincing.

e. Continue with other students and other *daffy debates.*

14. Disappearing Dialog

a. Write a conversation on the board.

b. Ask for two student volunteers to read the conversation.

c. Erase a few of the words from the dialog. Have two different students read the conversation.

d. Erase more words and call on two more students to read the conversation.

e. Continue erasing words and calling on pairs of students until the dialog has *disappeared.*

15. Do You Remember?

a. Tell students to spend three minutes looking carefully at the scene in the *Picture Dictionary.*

b. Have students close their books and write down everything they remember about the picture—the people, the objects, and their locations.

c. Have students compare notes with a partner and then look at the picture in the *Picture Dictionary* to see how well they remembered the scene.

Variation 1: Instead of students writing descriptions, ask them questions about the scene to see how much they remember. For example:

[THE LIVING ROOM]

What's next to the fireplace?
Where's the plant?
How many table lamps are there?

[THE LIBRARY]

How many people are at the checkout desk?
Where is the card catalog?
Whose library card is it?

Variation 2: Do the above activity in pairs, with each person taking turns asking the other about the picture.

Variation 3: Divide the class into several teams and do the activity as a game, where team members help each other to remember. The team with the most correct answers wins the game.

16. Draw and Label

This activity is appropriate for lessons in which a scene is depicted.

a. Have students draw a scene based on the theme of the lesson, depicting as many items as possible from the vocabulary list. Tell students to label all of the items included in their scenes.

b. As a class, in pairs, or in small groups, have students describe their scenes.

17. Drawing Game

You will need either an hourglass or a watch with a second hand for timing the following game.

a. Make two copies of the Word Cards Activity Master for the lesson, cut them up, and place the two sets of cards in two piles on a table or desk in front of the room. Also, have a pad of paper and pencil next to each team's set of cards.

b. Divide the class into two teams. Have each team sit together in a different part of the room.

c. When you say "Go!," a person from each team comes to the front of the room, picks a card from the pile, and draws the object. The rest of the team then guesses what the object is.

d. When a team correctly guesses the object, another team member picks a card and draws the object written on that card.

e. Continue until each team has guessed all of the objects in their pile.

The team that guesses the objects in the shortest time wins the game.

18. Expand the Conversation

a. Create a dialog that expands upon a conversation from the lesson—either the model conversation or one of the additional conversations at the bottom of the page.

b. Have pairs of students practice and present conversations based on this model, using different words from the lesson.

19. Find the Answer!

a. Have each student select something from the vocabulary list of the lesson that he or she would like to learn more about.

b. Students should then write out a list of questions they would like to have answered about that vocabulary item. For example:

> [PLACES AROUND TOWN]
>
> (*Thinking of a Department Store*)
>
> What do they sell there?
> What hours are they open?
> What are the prices of some of the products?
> Are the prices expensive or inexpensive?
> Are the salespeople friendly?

c. Students should then research answers to their questions by speaking with others, looking at appropriate print sources, or by checking a relevant website on the Internet.

d. When students have collected any pertinent information and/or interviewed as many people as necessary, have them report their findings to the class.

20. Find the Right Person!

The purpose of this activity is for students to walk around the classroom asking questions until they find someone to answer *yes* to one of the questions on the Activity Master.

a. Duplicate the Questionnaire Activity Master for the lesson and give a copy to each student.

b. Practice questions of the type on the questionnaire. For example:

> [EVERYDAY ACTIVITIES—QUESTIONS WITH "DO"]
>
> Do you get up before 5:00 A.M. every day?
> Do you take a shower in the morning?
>
> [TIME—QUESTIONS WITH "DO" AND "ARE"]
>
> Do you go to bed after midnight?
> Are you usually late for English class?

c. Have students walk around the classroom interviewing other students. When a student gets a *yes* answer to the first question, that student writes in the other person's name and then continues interviewing others until getting a *yes* answer to the second question . . . and so on. When a student gets a *yes* answer to a question, have that student ask for more information. For example:

> [EVERYDAY ACTIVITIES]
>
> A. Do you get up before 5:00 A.M. every day?
> B. Yes, I do.
> A. When do you get up?
> B. I usually get up at 4:30.
>
> [TIME]
>
> A. Do you usually go to bed after midnight?
> B. Yes, I do.
> A. Oh. When do you go to bed?
> A. I usually go to bed at 12:30.
>
> A. Are you always on time for appointments?
> B. No, I'm not.
> A. How often are you late?
> B. I'm often late because I don't wear a watch.

d. The first student to fill in names for all the questions wins the game. Have that student then report back to the class about all the people he or she interviewed.

21. Finish the Sentence!

a. Divide the class into two teams.

b. Begin sentences and have students from each team take turns finishing them with appropriate words from the lesson. For example:

> [THE CLASSROOM]
>
> Every student sits on a . . . *chair*.
> You tell the time by looking at the . . . *clock*.
> The person who helps the teacher is the . . . *teacher's aide*.
> You write on the whiteboard with . . . *markers*.
>
> [PLACES AROUND TOWN]
>
> You deposit money in a . . . *bank*.
> You get your clothes cleaned at the . . . *cleaners*.
> You buy tools at the . . . *hardware store*.
> You buy watches and rings at the . . . *jewelry store*.

The team with the most correctly completed sentences wins the game.

22. General-to-Specific Clue Game

a. Divide the class into two teams.

b. Make up clues to describe one of the words in the lesson. The clues should begin with general statements and gradually become more specific. For example:

> [VEGETABLES]
>
> Clue 1: You eat it raw.
> Clue 2: You buy it by the pound or by the individual vegetable.
> Clue 3: You peel it.
> Clue 4: You usually eat it in a salad.
> Clue 5: It's long.
> Clue 6: It's green.
>
> [Answer: a cucumber]
>
> [THE LIBRARY]
>
> Clue 1: It's a book.
> Clue 2: It's non-fiction.
> Clue 3: People can find important information in it.
> Clue 4: You find it in the reference section.
> Clue 5: It has pictures.
> Clue 6: It has maps.
>
> [Answer: an atlas]

c. Give a clue to Team 1. The students on that team have one chance to guess the word. If they don't guess correctly, ask Team 2. The play goes back and forth between the teams, with each team getting one more clue and one more chance to guess each time. The first team to guess the word wins a point.

d. Continue the game with more words and more clues.

The team with the most points wins the game.

23. Got It!

a. Divide the class into groups of four or five.

b. Have each group think of a word from the lesson that they want to make the other students guess.

c. When all the groups are ready, one member of each group goes and sits with the next group on the right.

d. The group members ask the visiting representative yes/no questions about the word until they guess it. For example:

> [TYPES OF ENTERTAINMENT]
>
> Is it part of the theater? [No.]
> Is it a person? [Yes.]
> Is it someone who works in a theater? [Yes.]
> Is it a performer? [Yes.]
>
> [THE BABY'S ROOM]
>
> Is it a toy? [No.]
> Is it a piece of furniture? [Yes.]
> Does it have wheels? [Yes.]

e. When they guess the word, they call out "Got It!" That group gets a point for guessing correctly.

f. The representatives stay with the new group, another word is selected, a new representative is chosen, and the play continues as above.

24. Guess the Object!

Tell what an object is used for and have students identify the object. For example:

> [PERSONAL HYGIENE]
>
> Teacher: You use it to clean your hair.
> Student: Shampoo.
>
> Teacher: You use it to make your eyelashes darker and thicker.
> Student: Mascara.

[GARDENING TOOLS AND ACTIONS]

Teacher: You use it to cut the grass.
Student: A lawnmower.

Teacher: You use it to dig a small hole to plant flowers.
Student: A trowel.

You can also do this activity in pairs, in small groups, or as a game with competing teams.

25. Guess the Word!

a. Divide the class into two teams.

b. Choose a vocabulary word from the lesson, and write on the board a blank for each letter in the word. For example: (*pencil*)

c. Give students a clue about the word. For example: "You use this to write with."

d. The team that guesses the word gets a point. The team with the most points wins the guessing game.

26. Guess What I'm Thinking Of!

a. Tell each student to think of an item from the lesson.

b. Have a student come to the front of the room and tell the class that he or she is thinking of one of the words on that page.

c. The other students in the class try to guess the item by asking yes/no questions. For example:

[THE DINING ROOM]

Student: I'm thinking of something in the dining room.
Class: Can you put things on it? [Yes.]
Do you use it to serve things? [No.]
Is it made of wood? [Yes.]

[CLOTHING]

Student: I'm thinking of an item of clothing.
Class: Is someone in this room wearing it? [Yes.]
Is it for men? [No.]
Is a female wearing it? [Yes.]
Is it blue? [No.]

This activity can also be done in pairs or in small groups.

27. Here's What I'm Thinking Of!

Make statements about words in the lesson, and have students guess the word you're thinking of. For example:

[DAIRY PRODUCTS, JUICES, AND BEVERAGES]

A. I'm thinking of a dairy product that people put on bread.
B. Butter.

A. I'm thinking of a dairy product that people often eat with crackers.
B. Cheese.

[ANIMALS AND PETS]

A. I'm thinking of an animal that has a bushy tail and a white stripe along its back.
B. A skunk.

A. I'm thinking of an animal whose body is covered with sharp quills.
B. A porcupine.

[BIRDS AND INSECTS]

A. I'm thinking of a bird that is very colorful and can talk.
B. A parrot.

A. I'm thinking of an insect that doesn't have any wings and likes to bite humans and small animals.
B. A flea.

Variation: As a class, in pairs, in small groups, or as a game with competing teams, have individual students make the statements and others then guess the word.

28. Hot Spot

a. Divide the class into two teams.

b. Have one member from each team come to the front of the room and sit facing his or her teammates in the *hot spot*.

c. Write one of the vocabulary words from the lesson on a card and show it to Team 1 without showing it to the person sitting in the front of the room.

d. The team members then give clues to their teammate, who tries to guess the word.

e. Repeat with Team 2.

f. Continue until each team member has had a chance to sit in the *hot spot* and guess a word.

Scoring: Give each team a point for each clue given before the word is guessed. *Low score* wins the game.

29. Inventions

a. In pairs or in small groups, have students invent a new item. Have them draw a picture of it, name it, and describe what it's used for.

b. Call on students to describe their creations, and then have the class vote on the most original and *inventive* invention!

Option: Have students create a television commercial for their invention and present it to the class.

30. It's a Puzzle!

a. Cut out from magazines several pictures related to the theme of the lesson. Paste each picture on a piece of cardboard or other heavy paper and cut the picture into four or more pieces.

b. Give each student a piece from one of the puzzles, and tell students to walk around the room and find other pieces to make a complete picture.

The object is not to show each other the puzzle pieces, but to offer information and gather information from others. For example:

[THE LIVING ROOM]

My picture has a green couch next to a fireplace.
I have a wall unit with a television and DVD.
Do you have a bookcase in your picture?

[THE WEATHER]

My picture has lightning.
Is it sunny in your picture?
It's windy in my picture.

c. Continue the activity until all the puzzle pieces are matched. The group of students who match their puzzle first *wins*.

31. It's Something That . . .

a. For this activity, divide the class into small groups. Make a copy of the Word Cards Activity Master for the lesson for each group and cut it up into cards.

b. Have students sit in groups of three or four, and give each group a set of cards. Place the cards face-down in the center of each group.

c. The first player takes the top card and, without showing it to the other players, gives a definition of that word, beginning with "It's something that . . . ." For example:

[THE KITCHEN]

It's something that you use to cook food very quickly.

[PERSONAL HYGIENE]

It's something that people use to shine their shoes.

[CLOTHING]

It's something that people wear over their shirts to keep them warm.

[THE CAR]

It's something you insert the key into to start the car.

d. The person to guess the word keeps the card. If nobody guesses correctly, the person who is holding the card keeps it and the next person takes a turn.

The player who has collected the most cards at the end of the game is the winner.

Variation: Play *It's Someone Who . . .* with lessons depicting people. For example:

[OCCUPATIONS]

It's someone who fixes sinks.

[MEDICAL SPECIALISTS]

It's someone who examines your eyes.

32. Letter Game

a. Divide the class into teams.

b. Say, "I'm thinking of a _____ that starts with _____." For example:

I'm thinking of a vegetable that starts with *a*.
I'm thinking of an item of clothing that starts with *o*.
I'm thinking of an occupation that starts with *p*.

c. The first person to raise his or her hand and guess correctly wins a point for that team.

d. Continue with other letters of the alphabet.

The team that gets the most correct answers is the winner of the game.

33. Linking Words

a. Print one of the vocabulary words from the lesson in the upper left corner of the board.

b. Have the first student think of another vocabulary word that begins with the last letter of the word on the board and *link* that word onto the word on the board in stair fashion.

Note: A student may also link a word associated with the word on the board, not necessarily one from the dictionary lesson.

c. Proceed this way, with each student linking a word onto the end of the previous word. For example:

[THE POST OFFICE]

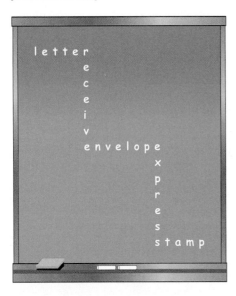

34. Listen and Number

a. Divide the class into pairs.

b. Both Partner A and Partner B should look at the pictures in the dictionary lesson.

c. Partner A chooses six of the objects, actions, or places depicted and makes up a story about them.

d. Partner B listens to the story and numbers the pictures in the order he or she hears them in Partner A's story.

e. Reverse roles.

35. Location! Location!

Version 1:

Have students look at the transparency or the illustration in the *Picture Dictionary* and answer questions about the location of people, places, or objects in the scene. For example:

[THE LIVING ROOM]

A. Where's the floor lamp?
B. It's next to the armchair.

A. Where's the plant?
B. It's on the table behind the sofa.

[THE CITY]

A. Where's the jail?
B. It's behind the police station.

A. Where's the taxi?
B. It's on the street in front of the courthouse.

Variation: Do the activity in pairs or in small groups, with students asking as well as answering the questions. You can also do this as a game with competing teams.

Version 2:

Do the activity as a listening exercise in which you give the location and students tell what you're describing. For example:

[THE LIVING ROOM]

A. It's above the fireplace.
B. The painting.

A. It's in front of the loveseat.
B. The coffee table.

[THE CITY]

A. It's on the street across from the police station.
B. The garbage truck.

A. It's on the sidewalk, in front of the police station.
B. The mailbox.

Variation: Do the activity in pairs or in small groups, with students taking turns telling the locations. You can also do this as a game with competing teams.

Version 3:

a. Divide the class into teams.

b. Have each team prepare ten questions about the location of items on the page.

c. Each team takes a turn asking the other team a question.

The team with the most correct answers wins the game.

36. Match Game

a. Make a copy of the Match Game Cards Activity Master for the lesson and cut it up into cards.

b. Distribute the cards randomly to students.

c. Have students memorize their lines and leave their cards on their desks.

d. Students should then walk around saying their lines until they find their match.

e. When all the pairs have been matched, have them say their lines for the whole class.

f. More advanced students can expand their lines into short dialogs that they perform for the class.

37. Miming Game

a. Make a copy of the Word Cards Activity Master for the lesson, cut it up into cards, and place the cards on a desk or table in front of the room.

b. Have students take turns coming to the front of the room, picking a card, and pantomiming the action on the card (or if it's an object, what someone might do with that item). The class tries to guess the action or object.

Variation: Do the activity as a game with two teams. Make sure you have a watch or clock to time the activity. A member of each team comes to the front and pantomimes. Time how long it takes for the team to guess the correct answer. The winning team is the one that has used the fewest seconds or minutes for the game.

38. Movable Categories

For lessons in which this activity is suggested, you will be provided with a list of the categories for grouping words in the lesson. For example:

[EVERYDAY ACTIVITIES]

things you do in the morning
things you do in the evening
things you do to your body
things you do in the kitchen
things you do to stay clean

[THE CLASSROOM]

things you look at
things you listen to
things you use to write
furniture
things that use electricity

a. Make a copy of the Word Cards Activity Master for the lesson, cut it up, and give each student a card.

b. Call out one of the suggested categories.

c. All the students whose words are appropriate for that category go to the right side of the room. All other students go to the left side.

d. Those who are in the *right group* call out their words for the class to verify.

Variation: For more advanced students, don't give any categories, and have students group themselves any way they wish. Once groups are formed, they can either identify their categories or have others try to guess the category based on the words composing it.

39. Mystery Word!

a. Ask one student to leave the room.

b. Have the class choose a vocabulary word from the lesson.

c. Ask the student to come back into the room and ask yes/no questions in order to determine the *mystery word* the class is thinking of. For example:

[THE SCHOOL]

Is it a person?	[No.]
Is it a place?	[Yes.]
Do people go there when they aren't feeling well?	[No.]
Do they eat there?	[Yes.]

40. Mystery Word Association Game

a. Make copies of a list of all the students in the class, and give the class list to each student.

b. Have each student choose a *mystery word* from the vocabulary list and on another sheet of paper write several words they associate with that word. The words can be verbs, adjectives, ideas, memories, or feelings. For example:

[JOB SKILLS AND ACTIVITIES]

cook/serve/prepare food	[food service worker]
type/file/speak	[secretary]

[THE BEACH]

whistle/sit/watch/save/ drown	[lifeguard]
ice cream/hot dogs/soda/ thirsty/hungry	[vendor]

The student should write his or her name on the paper, but NOT the mystery word from the list.

c. Have students then pass their list of words to the student on their right. That student reads the list of words and writes down next to his or her name the word from the lesson he or she thinks is being referred to.

d. Continue passing the papers around the room to the right until all the students have seen all the papers.

e. Call on each student to identify his or her mystery word, and have the rest of the class check their class list to see if they had guessed correctly. The person with the most correct guesses is the winner.

41. Mystery Word Conversations

a. Divide the class into small groups.

b. Have each group choose an item from the lesson and create a conversation about that item. Tell students they *can't* use the word they chose in their conversations!

c. Call on the groups to present their conversations, and have the class guess what the *mystery word* is.

42. Name It!

Call out in rapid succession words associated with vocabulary items in the lesson. Have students try to *name* the vocabulary words. For example:

[TEAM SPORTS EQUIPMENT]

Teacher: face guard
Student: lacrosse

Teacher: catcher's mitt
Student: baseball

[HOBBIES, CRAFTS, AND GAMES]

Teacher: loom
Student: weaving

Teacher: binoculars
Student: bird-watching

Variation: Do the activity as a game with competing teams.

43. Picture Match-Ups

a. Find in magazines and other sources pictures of items from the *Picture Dictionary* lesson. Make two copies of each picture and paste them on different cards.

b. Give each student a card, which he or she must look at carefully but not show to other students.

c. Students then walk around trying to find their match NOT by naming the item, but by describing it. For example:

[TREES, PLANTS, AND FLOWERS]

I have a purple flower with a yellow center.
I have a tree with branches that touch the ground.

[BIRDS AND INSECTS]

I have a large brown bird with big yellow eyes who is sitting in a tree.
I have a pink bird with long legs standing in the water.

44. Picture This!

Describe a scene, and have students draw what you describe. You can either invent a scene or describe a picture you have taken from a magazine or catalog. For example:

[THE DINING ROOM]

In this dining room, there's a buffet against the side wall. There's a round table in the middle of the room with six dining room chairs. On the table there's . . .

[THE DEPARTMENT STORE]

There are five floors in this department store. On the first floor, there's a Jewelry Department on the left. Next to the Jewelry Department is the Women's Clothing Department. There's an elevator . . .

Variation 1: Do the activity in pairs, with students taking turns describing a scene for the other to draw.

Variation 2: One student comes to the board, and the rest of the class gives instructions for that student to draw the scene on the board.

45. Question the Answer!

a. Make a copy of the Word Cards Activity Master for the lesson and cut it up into cards. Put the cards face-down on a table or desk in front of the room.

b. Divide the class into two teams.

c. A person from Team 1 comes to the front of the room, picks up a card, and reads the word. This is the answer.

d. That person must then think of a question for which that word could be the answer. For example:

[THE KITCHEN]

Card: cookbook
Student: Where do you find recipes?

Card: dish towel
Student: What do you use to dry dishes?

[JEWELRY AND ACCESSORIES]

Card: belt
Student: What holds up your pants?

Card: change purse
Student: What do you use to carry coins?

[PUBLIC TRANSPORTATION]

Card: conductor
Student: Who collects the train tickets?

Card: fare
Student: What do you pay the taxi driver?

If the team member *questions the answer* correctly, that team gets one point. If the person doesn't question the answer correctly, a member from the other team has a chance to do it. The team with the most points wins the game.

46. Ranking

Have students look at the words listed in the lesson, choose five items, and rank them. Depending upon the topic, the ranking might be:

[personal hygiene] items they use the most
[food] foods they eat the most
[outside the home] items they repair the most
[places around town] places they visit the most
[school subjects] most difficult to least difficult
[sports] most popular to least popular
[household bills] largest to smallest

47. Read, Write, and Draw

Have students write each other letters in which they describe a scene based on the theme of the lesson in the *Picture Dictionary*. Students exchange letters and draw pictures to illustrate what they read in the letters. In their illustrations, have students label the items from the *Picture Dictionary* lesson.

48. Same and Different

a. Divide the class into small groups.

b. Write pairs of vocabulary words from the lesson on the board.

c. Have the groups think of similarities and differences between each pair. For example:

[CLOTHING]

shirt—blouse

You wear both above the waist.
Both may have sleeves and a collar.

Blouses are for women.
Shirts are for both men and women.

[THE BANK]

make a deposit—make a withdrawal

Both are transactions.
Both involve a teller or an ATM machine.

To make a deposit is to put money in an account.
To make a withdrawal is to take money out of an account.

49. Secret Word Associations

In pairs or small groups, have students choose one of the vocabulary items from the lesson as a *secret word,* brainstorm several associations, tell the associated words to the class, and see if students can guess the word. For example:

[HOUSEHOLD PROBLEMS AND REPAIRS]

lights/lamps/broken:	[electrician]
flowers/plants/trees:	[gardener]
refrigerators/stoves/ washing machines:	[appliance repairperson]

[THE DEPARTMENT STORE]

dresses/blouses/ skirts/hats:	[Women's Clothing Department]
earrings/necklaces/ bracelets:	[Jewelry Department]
TVs/CD players/ DVD players:	[Electronics Department]

50. Small Talk

a. Explain that *small talk* is a conversation between two people who do not know each other well. The most common subjects of small talk are the weather and people's daily activities and hobbies. The conversation is not personal and does not cover personal information (age, marital status, telephone numbers, addresses, etc.) or money.

b. Divide the class into pairs.

c. Duplicate and cut up the Small Talk Activity Master and give a card to each pair of students.

d. Allow students five minutes to prepare their role plays. Then have students perform their role plays for the class. After each performance, follow up with questions about the characters and the situation.

51. Stand in Order

a. Make a copy of the Word Cards Activity Master for the lesson, cut it up, and give each student a card.

b. Have students then arrange themselves in a line alphabetically according to the word they have.

52. Telephone

a. Have students sit in a circle or semicircle.

b. Make up a sentence using at least two of the words from the lesson and whisper it to the first student. For example:

[OUTSIDE THE HOME]

The lawn chair is in the tool shed between the grill and the lawnmower.

[CONTAINERS AND QUANTITIES]

I need to get a bag of pretzels, two liters of diet soda, and a quart of chocolate chip ice cream.

[AILMENTS, SYMPTOMS, AND INJURIES]

I have a headache, a sore throat, and a bad cough.

c. The first student whispers what he or she heard to the second student, who whispers it to the third student, and so forth. When the message gets back to the last student, that person says it aloud. Is it the same message you started with?

Give each student in the class a chance to start his or her own message.

53. Things in Common

a. Divide the class into several teams.

b. Tell each team to think of two items from the lesson that have some things in common and write down what those similarities are. For example:

[PERSONAL HYGIENE]

razor blade—nail clipper
Both are small.
Both are sharp.
Both can cut.

[OCCUPATIONS]

barber—assembler
Both use their hands.
Both work indoors.
Both stand while they work.

c. Each team reads the similarities *without naming the items,* and the other teams try to guess what the two items are. The team that guesses the most items wins the game.

54. Tic Tac Definitions

a. Duplicate the *Tic Tac Grid* (Activity Master 8) and give a copy to each student. Have students fill in the grid with any nine vocabulary words from the lesson they wish.

b. Give definitions of words from the lesson (see the *Language and Culture Notes* as a resource), and tell students to cross out any word they have written on their grids for which you give the definition.

c. The first person to cross out three words in a straight line—either vertically, horizontally, or diagonally—wins the game.

d. Have the winner call out the words to check accuracy.

55. True or False?

Make statements about the scene depicted in the lesson, and have students decide whether they're true or false. If a statement is false, have students correct it. For example:

[THE BEDROOM]

There's one pillow on the bed.
  [True.]
The mirror is above the chest.
  [False. It's above the dresser.]

[TOOLS AND HARDWARE]

There are two screwdrivers.
  [True.]
The vise is on the wall.
  [False. It's on the workbench.]

Variation: Do the activity as a game with competing teams.

56. True or False Definitions

a. Say a word from the lesson and give a definition of that word. The definition may be true or false. For example:

[OUTSIDE THE HOME]

Front porch: A front porch is a place where people sit to relax and talk.
Lawnmower: You use a lawnmower to clear snow from the driveway.

[OCCUPATIONS]

Butcher: A butcher is a person who cuts meat.
Housekeeper: A housekeeper is a person who buys houses.

b. Students have to decide if the definition is true or false.

Variation: Do the activity as a game with competing teams.

57. What Am I?

a. Make a copy of the Word Cards Activity Master for the lesson and cut it up into cards.

b. Pin a card on each student's back so that the student doesn't see what item he or she *is*.

c. The student must discover his or her identity by asking yes/no questions. For example:

[THE CLASSROOM]

Do you write with me?	[No.]
Do you look at me?	[Yes.]
Am I on the wall?	[Yes.]
Can you find countries on me?	[Yes.]
Am I a map?	[Yes.]

[FRUITS]

Do I have a pit?	[No.]
Am I round?	[Yes.]
Am I blue?	[No.]
Am I red?	[Yes.]
Do I have seeds?	[Yes.]
Am I a tomato?	[Yes.]

Variation: This can be done as a class, in pairs, or in small groups.

58. What Can You Do?

This activity is appropriate for lessons in which places are depicted.

a. Divide the class into pairs or small groups.

b. Have the pairs or groups make a list of all the things they can do in the place depicted in the *Picture Dictionary*. For example:

[THE LIVING ROOM]

What can you do in the living room?
  relax
  watch TV
  read
  listen to the radio
  talk with guests
  play a game

[THE BANK]

What can you do in the bank?
   cash a check
   get traveler's checks
   apply for a loan
   make a deposit
   use an ATM machine
   put things in a safe deposit box

c. Compare students' lists and make a master list on the board.

59. What's the Object?

This activity is appropriate for lessons in which verbs are depicted.

Call out a verb from the vocabulary list and call on students to add an appropriate object. For example:

[EVERYDAY ACTIVITIES]

take . . . *a bath/a shower*
make . . . *breakfast/lunch/dinner/the bed*
get . . . *dressed/undressed*
brush . . . *your hair/your teeth*

[AILMENTS, SYMPTOMS, AND INJURIES]

break . . . *your arm/your leg/your wrist*
scrape . . . *your knee/your elbow/your arm*
cut . . . *your finger/your hand/your leg*
dislocate . . . *your shoulder/your knee/your ankle*

Variation: Do the activity as a game with competing teams.

60. What's the Place?

This activity is appropriate for lessons in which a variety of places are depicted.

Describe a reason for going to or being at places depicted in the lesson, and have students guess which place you're talking about. For example:

[PLACES AROUND TOWN]

You go there to see a play.	[theater]
You go there to see the animals.	[zoo]
You go there when you're sick.	[clinic/hospital]

[THE SCHOOL]

You keep your athletic clothes there.	[lockers]
You watch a football game there.	[bleachers]
You have lunch there.	[cafeteria]

Variation 1: Have students do the activity in pairs, taking turns asking and guessing.

Variation 2: Divide the class into teams and do the activity as a game.

Variation 3: Write the reasons on cards. Have individual students or team members pick a card and name the place described.

61. What's the Question?

Describe vocabulary items from the lesson, and have students respond by asking "What's a/an _____?" or "What are _____s?" For example:

[FRUITS]

Teacher: It's a red fruit people pick in autumn.
Student: What's an apple?

Teacher: It's a yellow fruit you peel before you eat it.
Student: What's a banana?

[MEDICINE]

Teacher: You use it when your nose is stuffy.
Student: What's nasal spray?

Teacher: You use them when your eyes are itchy.
Student: What are eye drops?

Variation: This activity can be done as a game with competing teams. It can also be done by having students give the descriptions that they then ask others.

62. Whisk!

This activity is appropriate for lessons in which actions are depicted.

a. Have a student come to the front of the room and think of one of the activities in the lesson.

b. The class tries to guess the activity by asking yes/no questions in which they substitute the word *whisk* for the activity. For example:

[EVERYDAY ACTIVITIES]

Do you *whisk* in the morning?
Do you *whisk* at mealtime?
Do both men and women *whisk*?
Do you use water when you *whisk*?

[SPORT AND EXERCISE ACTIONS]

Do you *whisk* outdoors?
Do you *whisk* in a gym?
Do you *whisk* when you play basketball?

Variation: Do the activity as a game with two competing teams.

63. Who Am I?

This activity is appropriate for lessons in which people are depicted.

Tell about one of the people depicted in the lesson, and have students guess who it is. For example:

[MEDICAL SPECIALISTS]

Teacher: I treat people with heart problems. Who am I?
Student: A cardiologist.

Teacher: I'm a children's doctor. Who am I?
Student: A pediatrician.

[THE SCHOOL]

Teacher: I help students choose their courses. Who am I?
Student: The guidance counselor.

Teacher: I help students find books and other information. Who am I?
Student: The school librarian.

Variation: Do the activity in pairs, in small groups, or as a game with two competing teams.

64. Word Clues

a. Make a copy of the Word Cards Activity Master for the lesson, cut it up into cards and choose ten of them for the activity.

b. Divide the class into two teams.

c. Have a member of each team come to the front of the room and sit facing his or her team.

d. Show one of the Word Cards to the two players *without showing it to the rest of the class*.

e. The two players take turns giving one-word clues to their teams so that they can guess the word. For example:

[FRUITS]

[The word is *banana*.]
Team 1 Player: "yellow"   [Team 1 guesses]
Team 2 Player: "long"   [Team 2 guesses]
Team 1 Player: "peel"   [Team 1 guesses]

[WORK ACTIVITIES]

[The word is *construct*.]
Team 1 Player: "bridge"   [Team 1 guesses]
Team 2 Player: "building" [Team 2 guesses]
Team 1 Player: "house"   [Team 1 guesses]

Tell each team to listen carefully to the opposing team's clues.

f. Do the same for the other vocabulary words. The team that guesses the most words wins the game.

65. Word Talk!

a. Give each student a Word Card from the Activity Master for the lessons, or have students choose a word from the list in the *Picture Dictionary*.

b. Have students think about their word for a few minutes.

c. Call on individual students to speak for one minute about their word.